## Map

**Key**
- ⬛ gravestone & base
- ⬜ gravestone only
- ▪ base only
- ⬭ no marker
- ▭ iron fence
- ▭ brick or stone enclosure
- 🌳 pepper tree
- 🌲 cypress tree

**D**     **E**     **F**

STEPS

Map grave markers (by number): 35, 36, 37, 68, 70, 69, 71, 115, 105, 72, 104, 103, 101, 102, 67, 66, 34, 33, 32, 38, 65, 64, 73, 39, 60, 59, 61, 95, 94, 93, 63, 74, 75, 96, 100, 99, 97, 91, 92, 76, 98, 107, 106, 53, 58, 77, 54, 52, 51, 78, 79, 108, 109, 55, 90, 89, 80, 110, 50, 56, 81, 88, 82, 49, 57, 87, 114, 85, 86, 111, 83, 84

N    0 — 40 feet

## Burial List

| Name | Plot |
|---|---|
| Jones, Hugh R. | 89 |
| Jones, Isabella | 84 |
| Jones, Jennie | 117 |
| Jones, John B. | 59 |
| Jones, Lewis James | 117 |
| Jones, Martha | 22 |
| Jones, Mary E. | 79 |
| Jones, Thomas | 113 |
| Jones, Thomas M. | 70 |
| Jones, Thomas S. | 69 |
| Leam, Margaret | 91 |
| Leam, May | 91 |
| Love, John | 30 |
| Markley, Andrew J. | 67 |
| Markley, David | 67 |
| Markley, Eliza Jane | 67 |
| Mills, Charles W. | 11 |
| Minett, William C. | 66 |
| Morgan, David | 92 |
| Morris, Alexander | 38 |
| Mortimore, Alvin | 21 |
| Mortimore, Harriet | 21 |
| Mortimore, Richard | 21 |
| Native Sons & Native Daughters of the Golden West monument | 1 |
| Norton, Sarah | 6 |
| Oliver, Jane | 95 |
| Ott, Georg Adam | 76 |
| Piercy, Julia Etta | 85 |
| Pohl, Dora | 110 |
| Pohl, Millie | 110 |
| Powell, Mary | 42 |
| Prosser, Mary | 78 |
| Rees, Elizabeth Ann | 19 |
| Richards, Daniel | 15 |
| Richards, John | 64 |
| Richards, William Timothy | 64 |
| Richmond, Anne | 80 |
| Richmond, Elizabeth | 81 |
| Richmond, Thomas | 80 |
| Ritchards (Richards), Mary | 14 |
| Smith, Evan | 48 |
| Spowart, Annie | 68 |
| Thomas, Elvira | 56 |
| Thomas, Frederick Elias | 5 |
| Thomas, John | 5 |
| Thomas, Rees G. | 56 |
| Tully, Mary | 18 |
| Vaughn family | 33 |
| Waters, Edna Isabella | 116 |
| Waters, John R. | 116 |
| Waters, William | 116 |
| Watts, David | 50 |
| Watts, Theophilus | 50 |
| Williams, Annie | 55 |
| Williams, David R. | 58 |
| Williams, Edward F. | 74 |
| Williams, Watkin | 51 |
| Williams, William L. | 52 |
| Wingate, Robert | 37 |
| Witherow, Barbara L. | 32 |
| Unknown (adult) | 99 |
| Unknown "Infant Babe" | 79 |
| Unknown infants (2) | 69 |

Other Unknown Gravesites
13, 20, 29, 34, 36, 40, 41, 44, 45, 61, 62, 63, 65, 77, 86, 87, 96, 97, 98, 114

# ROSE HILL

## A Comprehensive History of a Pioneer Cemetery in the Mount Diablo Coal Field

## Contra Costa County, California

Traci A. Parent
Black Diamond Mines Regional Preserve

East Bay
Regional Park District

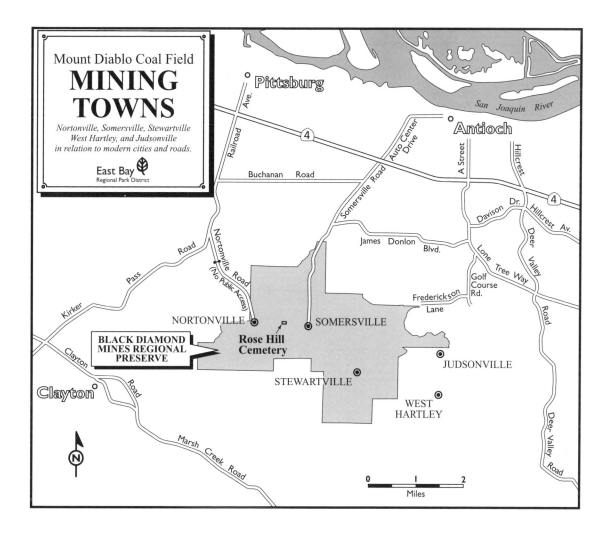

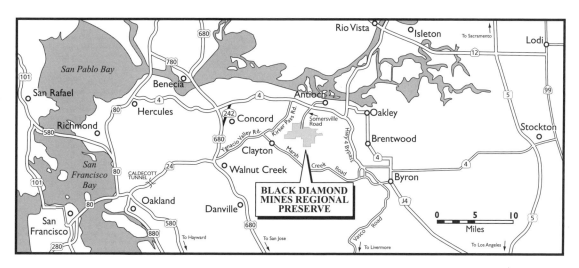

The upper map shows the location of the Mount Diablo Coal Field mining towns and Rose Hill Cemetery in relation to modern cities and roads. The lower map pinpoints the location of Black Diamond Mines Regional Preserve, just south of Antioch and Pittsburg, in the eastern portion of the San Francisco Bay Area.

Researched and Compiled by

# Traci A. Parent

Traci A. Parent, Supervising Naturalist
Black Diamond Mines Regional Preserve
East Bay Regional Park District
5175 Somersville Road
Antioch, CA 94509


bdvisit@ebparks.org

*This publication has been produced by
the Interpretive and Recreation Services Division
of the East Bay Regional Park District.*

ISBN: 978-0-615-36885-6

Library of Congress Control Number: 2010929302

Cover illustration by Lew Crutcher, former Chief of Planning and Design, EBRPD

**East Bay**
**Regional Park District**
2950 Peralta Oaks Court
Oakland, CA 94605-0381
www.ebparks.org

Rose Hill Cemetery, *circa* 1913.

This book is dedicated to the many former residents, descendants, and historians who have so graciously shared information and photographs, helping to preserve the history of the Mount Diablo Coal Field for future generations.

The publication of this book would not have been possible without the generous support and donations received from:

Alice Gibbons, in memory of Russell Gibbons
and the
Pittsburg Women's Community League (PWCL)

East Bay Regional Park District

Rose Hill Cemetery looking south east towards Somersville town site in 1951 (above) and in September 2009 (below). Photograph below by Traci (Gibbons) Parent.

# CONTENTS

# ABOUT THE AUTHOR

Photograph by Edward Willis, EBRPD

Traci (Gibbons) Parent began her career with the East Bay Regional Park District in June 1977 as an intern at the newly-created (1976) Black Diamond Mines Regional Preserve. Her first assignment was to create both a photographic record and documentation of the gravestones and gravesites in historic Rose Hill Cemetery located in the Preserve.

In September 1977, Parent was hired as an Interpretive Student Aide at Black Diamond Mines, becoming a permanent Naturalist in 1979. After serving as Lead Naturalist for several years, she was promoted to her present position as Supervising Naturalist.

In 1979, Parent earned a B.S. degree in Recreation and Park Administration from California State University, Sacramento. She is a charter member of the California Historic Cemetery Alliance, and has been a member of the Association for Gravestone Studies (an international organization) for over twenty-five years. She has attended numerous conferences and workshops relating to cemetery study, documentation, and preservation, and has organized and conducted many workshops for amateur and professional historians, and for educators interested in learning how to use cemeteries to teach local history. In addition, she is a life member and past president of the Contra Costa County Historical Society, and a member of its Board of Directors.

In June 2008, Parent received the Scholastic/ Authorship Award from the Conference of California Historical Societies for this significant historical project focusing on Rose Hill Cemetery. More recently, she co-authored a book, *Black Diamond Mines Regional Preserve* as part of the *Images of America* series with Arcadia Publishing.

Traci Parent continues to search for information relating to pioneer Californians who lived and died in the now-vanished Mount Diablo Coal Field. She searches for elusive primary source materials including family correspondence and papers. She delights in locating descendants who might provide new information and photographs to add to the Preserve's extensive archive of pioneers buried in Rose Hill Cemetery.

# PREFACE

The East Bay Regional Park District has been documenting and repairing gravestones and gravesites in historic Rose Hill Cemetery since 1974, when Black Diamond Mines Regional Preserve became part of the Park District. The information in this record comes from many sources including:

- Cemetery lists compiled in 1922, 1934, 1936, 1953, and 1954 by various individuals
- A plot plan compiled by the Park District in 1974
- Historic photographs
- Oral history accounts with former residents and descendants
- Census records
- Probate records
- Death records
- Assessment lists (property tax)
- Voting registers
- Family histories
- Newspaper articles
- Books
- Business Directories
- Files compiled by University of California at Berkeley archaeology students
- The gravestones themselves

As is typical with historical records, when comparing one source to another, discrepancies appear, including the spelling of names, death ages, death dates, places of birth, and places of death. While an attempt was made to incorporate as much information as possible, and be as accurate as possible, no doubt after the printing of this document, new information will be discovered. If you have information to share regarding Rose Hill Cemetery or information in general about the Mount Diablo Coal Field, please contact us.

Black Diamond Mines Regional Preserve
5175 Somersville Road
Antioch, California 94509
510-544-2750
bdvisit@ebparks.org

# PURPOSE

This document was complied to record the extensive amount of information collected over the years about the gravestones, gravesites, and individuals buried in Rose Hill Cemetery. The cemetery was originally owned by Alvinza Hayward, the chief stockholder of the Black Diamond Coal Mining Company of Nortonville. The company headquarters was located in San Francisco. No original cemetery records have been located and according to some oral accounts, the original records were destroyed during the 1906 San Francisco earthquake and fire. While many burial lists for Rose Hill Cemetery were compiled throughout the years, most are incomplete and many contain inaccurate information. This record was compiled to be as complete and accurate as possible using a variety of sources to verify information. In compiling this document, research was conducted on each individual interred. Many resources were utilized, including:

- Alhambra Cemetery, Martinez, California
- Antioch Family History Center, Antioch, California
- Arroyo Grande Cemetery, Arroyo Grande, California
- Black Diamond Cemetery, Black Diamond, Washington
- Black Diamond Library, Black Diamond, Washington
- The California State Library, Sacramento, California
- The California State Library - Sutro, San Francisco, California
- Clayton Historical Society, Clayton, California
- Community Presbyterian Church, Pittsburg, California
- Contra Costa County Hall of Records, Martinez, California
- Contra Costa County Historical Society History Center, Martinez, California
- Contra Costa County Libraries, Antioch and Pleasant Hill, California
- Coos County Historical Society, North Bend, Oregon
- Doe Library, University of California at Berkeley, Berkeley, California
- Foresthill Protestant Cemetery, Placer County, California
- Hearst Museum, University of California at Berkeley, Berkeley, California
- Holy Cross Cemetery, Antioch, California
- Live Oak Cemetery, Concord, California
- Oakland Regional Family History Center, Oakland, California
- Merced County Historical Society Archives, Merced, California
- Mount Diablo Coal Field residents and descendants
- Oak View Memorial Park Cemetery, Antioch, California
- Oregon State Library, Salem, Oregon
- Pittsburg Historical Society and Museum, Pittsburg, California
- San Francisco Public Library, San Francisco, California
- Santa Clara City Library, Santa Clara, California
- Seattle Public Library, Seattle, Washington
- Sourisseau Academy for State & Local History, San Jose State University, San Jose, California
- Southwestern Oregon Community College Library, Coos Bay, Oregon
- The Bancroft Library, University of California at Berkeley, Berkeley, California

# ACKNOWLEDGEMENTS

Many thanks are due to the individuals who assisted with this enormous project.

Gene Prince and Kathryn Crabtree, with their vast database of gravestone epitaphs of the west, provided some missing phrases for epitaphs in Rose Hill Cemetery.

Idris Evans, of the Welsh American Society of Northern California, translated the Welsh epitaphs on the gravestones, provided assistance with Welsh spellings, and proofread the material.

David Fischer, president of the Southport Land and Commercial Company (formerly the Black Diamond Coal Mining Company of Nortonville), contributed information regarding Alvinza Hayward and Emma (Hayward) Rose, the former property owners.

Mary Hanel, Local History Librarian, Santa Clara City Library, Santa Clara County, California supplied information about gravestone carver Frederick Field.

Sherill and Ed Hecock, of the Pittsburg Historical Society and Museum, Pittsburg, California, contributed information and photographs from their archives.

Cheryl Heller of Walla Walla, Washington, located and photographed the marker for gravestone carver, John W. Combs.

Mary-Ellen Jones, another gravestone enthusiast, edited the manuscript and has provided significant information about gravestone carvers over the years.

Virginia Kysh, of the Antioch Family History Center, Contra Costa County, California, gave assistance in deciphering written records. Additionally she reviewed this manuscript before printing.

Betty Maffei, Executive Director (now retired) of the Contra Costa County Historical Society History Center and the History Center volunteers in Martinez, California supplied photographs and documents from their extensive archives.

Charmetta Mann, of the Live Oak Cemetery Association, Concord, Contra Costa County, California, imparted information about Mount Diablo Coal Field families.

Dan Moiser, Tesla Coal Mines historian, Alameda County, California conveyed information regarding coal mining families.

Peggy Perazzo, with her extensive research of California quarries and stone carvers, shared valuable information regarding gravestone carvers.

Susan Snyder, of The Bancroft Library, University of California, Berkeley, supplied photographs from their impressive archives.

Karen Terhune, Black Diamond volunteer, photo documented each Rose Hill gravestone and gravesite and assisted with the formatting of the historic photographs used in this book.

Kitty Yarborough, long-time Black Diamond volunteer, assisted with copy and newspaper microfilm work.

With grateful acknowledgement to Eleanor Coburn, Joan Dougherty, Mary-Ellen Jones, Virginia Kysh, Ned MacKay, Janet Nadol, Bill Plummer, and Rick Yarborough who volunteered many hours of their time to proofread this document.

With appreciation to the Black Diamond staff and other Park District staff for their assistance and support, especially: Monique Looney, Kevin Damstra, Allison Meador and Edward Willis for proofreading the manuscript; Bob Kanagaki and Exhibit Design Supervisor, Nick Cavagnaro, for their help in compiling the burial maps; and Lane Powell of Public Affairs for his assistance in updating the park location map.

Many thanks to Nancy Kaiser, Interpretive Services Manager for the East Bay Regional Park District, for her support and assistance with bringing this project to conclusion.

My grateful appreciation to Beverly Lane, historian, author, and East Bay Regional Park District Director, for her encouragement and support of this project.

With gratitude to Jessi Brandt and Diane Presler of *Yes i Consult* for their diligence in formatting this manuscript and seeing this project through to completion.

With special thanks to Alice Gibbons, Black Diamond volunteer (and my mother), for the many hours she spent helping to proofread and edit every segment of this manuscript and later edited the completed document. I am eternally grateful for her unending support and encouragement of this project.

To my husband, Randy Parent, I thank you for your patience, understanding, and support of this important endeavor.

This project could not have been completed without the outpouring of photographs, information, and materials received over the years from coal field residents and descendants. Their generous contributions to this worthwhile venture added prized resources to our park archives and helped broaden our knowledge of coal field residents.

Unless otherwise noted, images in this publication come from the extensive collection of Black Diamond Mines Regional Preserve. Others were acquired from:

- California State Library, California History Section, Sacramento

- Contra Costa County Historical Society (CCCHS), Martinez, California

- Merced County Historical Society Archives, Merced, California

- Pittsburg Historical Society (PHS), Pittsburg, California;

- Sourisseau Academy, San Jose State University, San Jose, California

- The Bancroft Library, University of California, Berkeley

With grateful acknowledgment for images contributed by donors, many of whom are former residents or descendants of the Mount Diablo Coal Field:

Father Abeloe

Charity Emrose Alker

Mrs. Thomas Bell

Brem Bessac/Contra Costa County
  Historical Society

Sherilynn Blevins

Pearl Bloom

Charles Bohakel

Bill Boone

Katherine B. Branstetter

Carolyn Christopher

Mary Evans Collyer

Mrs. Reed A. Dawson

Jean DeJong

Norma (Bloching) Dempsey

Madison Devlin

Tony Dunleavy

Ruth Combs Edvalson

Engler Family

Errol Frew

Edna Gibbel

Glenice Gustin

Beverly Hanson

Cheryl Heller

Allen Hermann

Lynn G. Hodge

Andy Husari

Gayle Oberti Jenkins

Mary-Ellen Jones

Elmer (Jack) Lougher

Betty Maffei/Amelia (Ginochio) Peel

Isabel J. Marchio

Ed McInerney

Helen S. Moore

Florence (Lougher) Noia

Todd Norrish

Kenneth and Ron Peck

Linda Robbins

Phillip Rohrbough and  Mary Lape

Margaret Santana

Kay Serrao

G. F. Spencer/Mount Diablo State Park

Louis Stein

David Stogner

Brian Suen

Ray Sullivan

Elizabeth Thomas

Wayne, Tina, and William Rees Thomas

George Vivian

Mrs. A. M. Wade

Agnes I. Wall

Rich Weidenbach

Alice Wildes

Dr. Guy Wingate and Pam Landry

Rick Yarborough

Bill Yost

# Chapter 1

# ROSE HILL CEMETERY
# A BRIEF HISTORY

# ROSE HILL CEMETERY
## A BRIEF HISTORY

Courtesy of The Bancroft Library, University of California, Berkeley

Rose Hill Cemetery, *circa* 1930.

Established *circa* 1865, Rose Hill Cemetery served as a Protestant burial ground for nearly 250 individuals and was the only cemetery located in the Mount Diablo Coal Field. Five communities existed in the coal field. From the west to the east, the towns were: Nortonville, Somersville, Stewartville, West Hartley and Judsonville.

The land encompassing the cemetery was owned by Alvinza Hayward, the president and chief stockholder of the Black Diamond Coal Mining Company of Nortonville. After Hayward died, his entire fortune went to his daughter, Emma Rose and her husband, Andrew Rose. Emma

Rose eventually deeded the land to Contra Costa County in the 1940s. In 1973, transfer of the 2.7-acre historic cemetery to the East Bay Regional Park District was approved by the Contra Costa County Board of Supervisors. The cemetery became part of Black Diamond Mines Regional Preserve, the District's first historic preserve. Over the years, the cemetery has been referred to by a variety of names including Nortonville Cemetery, Somersville Cemetery or the Old Welsh Cemetery. Historical newspaper accounts from the 1800s refer to it as the Somersville Cemetery. Today however, it is called Rose Hill Cemetery, named for Emma Rose.

East Bay Regional Park District

Alvinza Hayward (left) and daughter Emma (Hayward) Rose.

The location of the cemetery is actually closer to Somersville than Nortonville, existing in the same basin area as Somersville. The cemetery sits high on a hill between Nortonville and Somersville town sites, once the two largest coal mining towns in the Mount Diablo Coal Field. Most individuals interred in the cemetery lived in one of these two towns, although some of the individuals interred were residents of Stewartville, West Hartley and Judsonville.

## Other Contra Costa County Cemeteries Serving the Mount Diablo Coal Field

Although the predominate nationality of the coal field was Welsh, other nationalities included Irish, Italian, German, Scottish, Mexican, South American, Canadian, Australian, Chinese and English. The Protestant Welsh are the most common nationality interred in Rose Hill Cemetery. Many of the Catholics, who were generally of Irish or Italian descent, were buried in the Holy Cross Cemetery in nearby Antioch. Other individuals who died in the Mount Diablo Coal Field were buried in a variety of locations in Contra Costa County, including: Oak View Memorial Park in Antioch, Live Oak Cemetery in Concord and the Brentwood, Byron, Knightsen Union Cemetery in Brentwood. Prior to the establishment of Rose Hill and other local cemeteries in the 1860s, some coal field residents were interred in Alhambra Cemetery in Martinez, Contra Costa County, California. Alhambra Cemetery is the oldest cemetery in the county, with graves dating to the early 1850s.

## A Variety of Individuals Were Interred

Children predominate in burials in the cemetery due to the many diseases that swept through the area such as scarlet fever, smallpox, and diphtheria. According to Mr. Ellis Griffiths, former coal field resident who recorded his memories:

> The first small pox [sic] victim was laid to rest about three blocks from the cemetery on another hill because people were very superstitious about the disease.

Whether this individual was a child or adult is not known. There are also a number of men interred who died from mining and other accidents and illnesses. Women died from childbirth and a variety of accidents and illnesses. According to

*The Move of Coal Miners From Nortonville, California to Black Diamond, Washington Territory, 1885*, a Senior Honors Thesis written by Jacqueline Byer Dial in June 1980, a description of a funeral by an acquaintance whose family had lived in Somersville stated:

> ...those who died of contagious diseases were often buried separately or at night as the people thought the disease he died from would not be carried by the night air. Usually the necessary grave was dug by the family or friends then often the same friends and neighbors acted as pall bearers...My aunt remembered seeing funeral processions at nightfall and watching the men carrying the casket while those accompanying them carried flares. This was prior to the days of kerosene lanterns. She was born in Somersville on January 9, 1870, so her recollections went back to her early childhood.

One of the youngest known individuals interred in the cemetery is the day-old Jenkins infant who died April 15, 1880. This unnamed infant was the daughter of Thomas H. and Elizabeth Jenkins. At one time a large marble tablet gravestone was placed in the cemetery in memory of the infant and her father, who died March 24, 1882. The gravestone is missing from the cemetery today, having disappeared before the area became part of the East Bay Regional Park District. A fragment of the gravestone (in storage), the gravestone base at the gravesite, and a photograph are all that document its existence. In 2004, a brass plaque was placed at the site to mark the burial location.

The oldest known person buried in the cemetery is Ruth French, who died at 81 years of age on September 11, 1874. Her marble tablet gravestone can still be seen today in the lower northeast corner of the cemetery. The most notable person buried in the cemetery is Mrs. Sarah Norton. Widow of town founder, Noah Norton, Sarah served as a midwife. According to the *Daily Alta California* newspaper, October 6, 1879, she assisted in delivering over 600 babies.

In addition to miners and mine superintendents, individuals interred in Rose Hill Cemetery represented a variety of occupations including a Contra Costa County clerk, stagecoach driver, shoe maker, farmer, stock raiser, laborer, clerk, constable, midwife, and hotel proprietor.

**Gravesites and Gravestones**

Out of the nearly 250 burials, about 80 gravestones remain today. Not all individuals buried in the cemetery had their own gravestone. Because gravestones were expensive, family members, and sometimes friends, shared stones. Some individuals had no marker at all. Markers or fences made of wood were either destroyed by fire, vandals, or simply deteriorated over time.

The majority of gravestones in the cemetery are marble, the predominate stone used until the 1890s, due to its accessibility and ease of carving with hand tools. However marble weathers easily compared with more durable granite. The invention of the pneumatic drill in the 1890s made granite the material of choice.

As is typical with many cemeteries of the time, gravestones in Rose Hill Cemetery face east, towards the rising sun. With the belief that the deceased are awaiting Resurrection day, individuals were interred in one direction, so that when Resurrection day comes, sitting or standing, they will face Christ and the rising sun.

**Cemetery Vegetation**

The predominant vegetation in the cemetery today is a variety of intentionally-introduced species, the most imposing being the Italian Cypress trees (*Cupressus sempervirens*). The older ones were planted about 100 years ago. Historic photographs, contemporary newspaper accounts, and statements by former residents reveal that other trees such as pine, California pepper (*Schinus molle*), and eucalyptus (*Eucalyptus spp.*) flourished during the period of mining activities as did the bird of paradise bush (*Caesalpinia gilliesii*), the rose, and the iris. Today the area supports Italian cypress, pepper and Eucalyptus trees, daffodils, and bird of paradise shrubs. Replacement trees have been planted by park staff as old growth die. Unfortunately, the non-native and extremely invasive yellow star thistle is spreading quickly throughout the cemetery. This aggressive pest plant has pushed its way into many open-space areas throughout the state and is very difficult to control or eradicate.

## 1934 Native Sons and Native Daughters of the Golden West Monument

In 1934, a monument was erected in Rose Hill Cemetery to commemorate the pioneers of Nortonville and Somersville. This ten-foot high concrete monument, a gift of the Native Sons and Native Daughters of the Golden West, contains a brass memorial plaque donated by the Columbia Steel Company of Pittsburg, Contra Costa County, California. Richard Rains Veale, sheriff of Contra Costa County, spoke at the dedication ceremony in Rose Hill on October 7, 1934. According to an article in the *Antioch Ledger* newspaper on October 8, as Veale concluded his address, he:

> pointed to one of the marble monuments which had fallen to the ground and broken into several pieces. Then he pointed to another one, which though lying flat on the ground, had been pieced together.
>
> Here is something we should look after, he said. We should rehabilitate these monuments. We should find a way to raise the money, either take up a collection or get all interested in making this cemetery a beautiful place to contribute so the work can be done.

## Site Description

Photographic records exist which document destruction of gravestones and other property in Rose Hill Cemetery as early as the 1920s. Newspaper accounts and statements by former residents indicate that some gravestones were broken by cattle using them as scratching posts. In 1953/1954, S. B. Vorenkamp (listed as cemetery reference list 6 on page 993) examined the cemetery in detail, creating the most thorough list of individuals interred in the cemetery. He noted that "there were approximately two wooden 'markers' whose condition were so poor I could not read them."

A former resident described the wooden picket fence that once surrounded the cemetery, and which probably was destroyed by one of the many fires that occurred in the area. In the 1950s, a barbed wire fence was installed to keep cattle out. Later a cyclone fence was built around the cemetery to help reduce vandalism. However, vandals continued to knock gravestones from their bases, often breaking them in half or shattering them into many pieces. Some stones were rolled from one end of the cemetery to the other, making original locations impossible to determine. Other stones were removed from the cemetery and remain missing. Over the years, prison crews were sent to do "clean up."

Additionally the lack of vegetation in the cemetery caused erosion gullies to form during winter rains. Numerous gravestones and bases became buried as the eroding soil washed downhill.

During periods of vandalism, stones were repaired by well-meaning individuals. Pieces of gravestones were put together like a jigsaw puzzle, and then concreted flat on the ground. Often, some of the concrete intended for the back of the stone fell on the face of the stone, obscuring names, dates, and other valuable data. In addition, placing stones flat on the ground made them more vulnerable to weathering. Although this type of preservation had a negative effect on some stones, it is quite possible that fewer stones would have survived if no preservation efforts had been made. Unfortunately, burial sites of many pioneers will never be known. It is impossible to determine how many sites included a footstone (marker placed at the foot of the grave) because they were small and easily lost or stolen.

The photograph above, taken in December 1973, shows erosion gullies that formed
due to winter rains and the lack of vegetation.

## Cemetery Stabilization

Once the cemetery became part of Black
Diamond Mines Regional Preserve, park staff
instituted a program to stabilize the burial ground
by restoring eroded ground and repairing broken
gravestones and fences, and reinstalling them in
the cemetery. The gravesite stabilization effort
is ongoing and utilizes conservation guidelines
established by the Association for Gravestone
Studies and the National Center for Preservation
Technology and Training. Brass plaques have
been placed at some burial locations where
gravestones are missing.

Gravestones to be restored are individually
evaluated to determine the best repair method.
Three basic methods are used to repair the
gravestones in Rose Hill Cemetery: drill and pin,
lamination, and encasement. Examples of these
repair methods are shown on the following pages.

<u>Drill and Pin</u>: The drill and pin method is used
on gravestones that are 2 ½ to 3 inches thick.
Holes are drilled into the broken pieces and brass
or fiberglass rods, secured with epoxy, are used to
pin the pieces back together.

<u>Lamination</u>: This method is only used on
gravestones with a single break. A slab of
approximately 2 inch thick new marble is cut to
the exact shape of the stone and epoxied to the
back of the gravestone.

<u>Encasement</u>: This repair technique is used
for gravestones with multiple breaks, severely
damaged stones, or gravestones with missing
pieces. A slab of new marble is cut 1 ½ inches
larger around the outline of the gravestone. The
exact shape and size of the gravestone is then
carved out of the slab to create a recess for the

East Bay Regional Park District

gravestone to fit into. The gravestone is epoxied into the recess and when complete has a 1 ½ inch border of new marble surrounding the original stone. The approximately ⅛ inch gap that is left between the side edges of the gravestone and the new marble is sealed with Jahn Mortar Mix.

New marble slabs for repairing gravestones, as well as new granite, sandstone, and marble used to reconstruct gravestone bases, have been supplied by V. Fontana and Company of Colma, California. All work performed in the cemetery and on the gravestones is carefully documented with both written and photographic records.

Anyone with information or photographs pertaining to the cemetery is encouraged to contact park staff. The return of gravestones, footstones, and iron fences is welcomed, no questions asked.

Black Diamond Mines Regional Preserve
5175 Somersville Road
Antioch, California 94509
510-544-2750
bdvisit@ebparks.org

Reference 280.1

Rose Hill Cemetery looking west, *circa* 1950s, showing vandalized gravestones.

Reference 379.2

**Drill and pin method.** This method was used to repair the Julia Etta Piercy gravestone. Brass rods were inserted into drill holes in the gravestone. Photograph by Monique Looney.

Reference 292.144

**Repaired Julia Etta Piercy gravestone.** The two pieces of the gravestone have been pinned back together and the gravestone now stands back in Rose Hill Cemetery on a new marble middle base. Photograph by Karen Terhune.

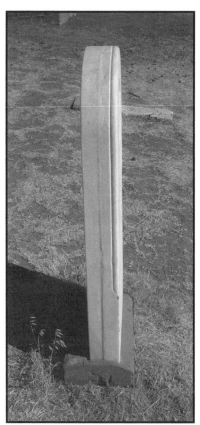

Reference 379.3

**Lamination method.** The Mary Tully gravestone, shown above and below, was repaired with the lamination method. Photographs by Traci (Gibbons) Parent.

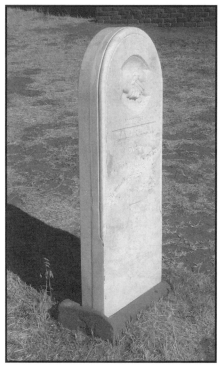

Reference 379.4

Reference 379.5

Reference 379.6

**Encasement method.** This method was used to repair the Austin Jones gravestone. The exact shape and size of the stone was marked and then carved in the new marble slab (above left) to create a recess for the gravestone. Photograph by Doug Fowler.

(Photograph top right)
The gravestone was then epoxied into the recess. An approximately 1 ½ inch border of new marble surrounds the original stone. The gap between the gravestone and marble slab is sealed with Jahn Mortar Mix. Photograph by Traci (Gibbons) Parent.

(Photograph bottom right)
The gravestone now stands back in Rose Hill Cemetery. Photograph by Karen Terhune.

Reference 292.43

Rose Hill Cemetery, 2004.
Photograph by Roger Epperson, EBRPD.

**The Importance of Rose Hill Cemetery Today**

Although at least four burials have occurred in Rose Hill Cemetery after 1900 (Abel Vaughn in 1901, Howell Thomas in 1915, Handel Thomas in 1924, and William T. Davis in 1954), the cemetery has not been active since the close of the coal mines in the early 1900s.

Today the cemetery serves many purposes. It is one of the most popular destinations for park visitors who explore the Preserve. Thousands of school children visit the cemetery annually using the site as a teaching tool while studying a variety of subjects that meet state school curriculum  standards.

The cemetery is also a place where coal field descendants from around the world can learn more about their ancestors by accessing the information available to them on site. The cemetery serves as a special place for people of Welsh ancestry to gather and remember the many Welsh who once lived in the coal field. Members of the Welsh American Society of Northern California have made visits to the cemetery in early spring to see daffodils, the Welsh national flower, blooming there.

Although the individuals interred in Rose Hill Cemetery represent only a small percentage of coal field inhabitants, those who are interred there serve as a permanent reminder of the individuals who once lived and died in the coal mining communities in the Mount Diablo Coal Field.

Reference 379.8

Repaired gravestones in Rose Hill Cemetery, September 2009.
Photograph by Traci (Gibbons) Parent.

# Chapter 2

# INDIVIDUALS INTERRED

# INDIVIDUALS INTERRED

| NAME | DATE OF DEATH | ADULT OR CHILD | AGE AT DEATH | BURIAL LOCATION: SECTION, PLOT # |
|------|------|------|------|------|
| ABRAHAM, Rebecca | 1878, Nov. 1 | A | 18 yrs., 4 mos. | S-D, 55 |
| AITKEN, Katie | 1879, Dec. 24 | C | 8 yrs., 4 mos., 12 dys. | S-C, 17 |
| ANDERSON, Robert | 1900, Oct. 17 | C | 4 yrs., 10 mos. 7 dys. | S-B, 24 |
| BANKS, Albert | 1871, Aug. 21 or 22 | A | 35 – 38 yrs. | unknown |
| BANKS, Ann C. | 1892, Sept. 8 | A | 64 yrs., 3 mos. | unknown |
| BANKS, Joseph | 1883, Aug. 29 | A | 65 yrs., 2 mos., 24, dys. | N-A, 3 |
| BASSETT, (child) | Unknown | C | 5 yrs. | unknown |
| BLACKBURN, Charles W. | 1865, Feb. 20 | C | 9 yrs., 7 mos. | unknown |
| BOWMAN, Charles H. | 1874, Apr. 5 | C | 1 yr., 11 mos. | N-E, 75 |
| BOWMAN, David G. Jr. | 1871, Feb. 3 | C | 1 mo., 14 dys. | N-E, 75 |
| BOWMAN, Violette I. | 1870, Jun. 29 | C | 1 yr., 3 mos. | N-E, 75 |
| BRADSHAW, John | 1881, Oct. 25 | A | 55 yrs., 4 mos., 20 dys. | S-C, 16 |
| BRYANT, Elizabeth Ann | 1877, May 21 | C | 10 yrs., 7 mos., 21 dys. | S-D, 57 |
| BRYANT, Eva Sitera | 1895, Oct. 18 | A | 21 yrs., 11 mos., 21 dys. | unknown |
| BRYANT, Ida Mary | 1863, Jan. 16 | unknown | unknown | unknown |
| BRYANT, Margaret | 1900, Nov. 28 | A | 62 yrs. | unknown |
| BUSSEY, Joseph | 1893 | C | infant | unknown |
| BUXTON, Alfred W. | 1878, Sept. 25 | C | 8 yrs., 8 mos., 8 dys. | N-D, 60 |
| BUXTON, Lulu | 1874, Dec. 15 | C | 1 yr., 2 mos., 18 dys. | N-D, 60 |
| BUXTON, Maggie | 1890, Oct. 22 | A | 40 yrs., 2 mos., 27 dys. | S-B, 25 |
| BUXTON, Thomas | unknown | unknown | unknown | unknown |
| CAIN, Elizabeth O. | 1881, Oct. 27 | A | 47 yrs., 7 mos., 23 dys. | N-A, 2 |
| CLARE, Walter E. | 1883, May 4 | C | 8 yrs., 2 mos., 27 dys. | N-B, 112 |
| CLEMENT, Ann | 1875, Feb. 13 | A | 40 yrs., 10 mos., 17 dys. | S-F, 100 |
| CLEMENT, William H. | 1892, Feb. 29 | A | 66 yrs., 7 mos., 5 dys. | S-F, 100 |
| CONNER, John T. | 1877, Nov. 4 | C | 9 mos., 3 dys. | unknown |

| NAME | DATE OF DEATH | ADULT OR CHILD | AGE AT DEATH | BURIAL LOCATION: SECTION /PLOT # |
|---|---|---|---|---|
| COOPER, George | 1884, Nov. 9 | A | 40 yrs. | S-B, 25 |
| COOPER, John L. | unknown | unknown | unknown | unknown |
| CROWHURST, Elizabeth | 1882 | C | 3 yrs. | unknown |
| DALEY, James | 1873, Dec. 16 | A | approximately 33 yrs. | unknown |
| DAVIES, Evan | 1876, Dec. 23 | A | 30 yrs., 4 mos., 29 days | S-D, 53 |
| DAVIS, Anna | 1869, Aug. 9 | A | 25 yrs. | S-E, 90 |
| DAVIS, David | 1878, July 3 | C | 7 yrs., 8 mos., 29 dys. | N-F, 102 or 103 |
| DAVIS, David B. | 1907, March 25 | A | 79 yrs. | unknown |
| DAVIS, Ellen | 1878, July 16 | A | 33 yrs., 28 days | N-F, 101 |
| DAVIS, Margaret | 1878 | C | approximately 17 yrs. | unknown |
| DAVIS, Morgan | 1874, Aug. 30 | C | 9 yrs., 11 mos., 26 dys. | N-F, 102 or 103 |
| DAVIS, Peter | 1872, Mar. 14 | A | 52 yrs. | S-F, 111 |
| DAVIS, Thomas. J. | 1883, April 9 | A | 39 yrs. | S-D, 59 |
| DAVIS, William T. | 1954, May 26 | A | 79 yrs., 4 mos., 24 days | N-F, 104 |
| DAWSON, Mary A. | 1879, Oct. 7 | C | 4 mos., 7 dys. | S-F, 106 |
| DENNIS, John | unknown | C | approximately 10 yrs. | unknown |
| DODSWORTH, George W. | 1890s | A | unknown | unknown |
| DOULTON, George | 1884 | A | 54 yrs. | unknown |
| DUMAS, Theophile | 1876, July 25 | A | 28 or 38 yrs. | S-C, 47 |
| DUNTON, Clyde C. | unknown | C | infant | unknown |
| DUNTON, Lulu B. | unknown | C | infant | unknown |
| EASTON, Mary | 1886, Nov. | A | approximately 32 yrs. | unknown |
| EDWARDS, Catherine | 1876, Nov. 25 | A | 25 yrs., 5 mos., 13 dys. | N-C, 31 |
| EDWARDS, Clara | 1865, Aug. | C | 1yr., 3 mos. | unknown |
| EDWARDS, Emma | 1865, Feb. 24 | A | 23 yrs. | unknown |
| EDWARDS, John | 1870, Sept. | A | 41 yrs. | unknown |
| EDWARDS, Joseph M. | 1889, Sept. 4 | A | 46 yrs. | N-B, 7a |
| ENGLER, Annie Henrietta | 1877, Sept. 15 | C | 2 yrs., 4 mos. | unknown |
| ENGLER, Charles | 1874, Oct. 6 | C | 1 yr., 4 mos. | unknown |

| NAME | DATE OF DEATH | ADULT OR CHILD | AGE AT DEATH | BURIAL LOCATION: SECTION/PLOT # |
|---|---|---|---|---|
| ENGLER, John | 1875, Sept. 4 | A | 42 yrs., 9 mos., 9 dys. | unknown |
| ENO, Susan J. | 1880, Feb. 3 | C | 6 yrs., 7 mos., 28 dys. | N-F, 71 |
| EVANS, Elizabeth | unknown | C | 6 yrs. | unknown |
| EVANS, John | 1877, Jan. 22 | C | 8 yrs. | S-E, 94 |
| EVANS, John R. | 1877, Feb. 3 | A | 45 yrs. | S-E, 94 |
| EVANS, Rebecca | 1886, Mar. 24 | A | 33 yrs., 1 mo., 23 dys. | S-B, 27 |
| EVANS, William | 1877, Feb. 18 | C | 2 yrs., 4 mos., 6 dys. | S-E, 94 |
| EVANS, William Rodrick | 1870, Feb. 8 | C | 8 yrs., 17 dys. | S-E, 93 |
| FRENCH, Ruth | 1874, Sept. 11 | A | 81 yrs. | N-F, 115 |
| GETHING (GETHIN), William | 1876, July 24 | A | 36 yrs. | S-C, 46 |
| GOULDING, Fanny Sarah | 1865, April 30 | C | 5 yrs., 9 mos., 28 dys. | unknown |
| GOULDING, Joseph J. | 1871, Oct. 6 | A | 19 yrs. | N-F, 72 |
| GOULDING, Thomas J. | 1875, Aug. 15 | C | 13 yrs. | N-F, 72 |
| GOULDING, Thomas Pratten | 1865, Jan. 27 or 31 | C | 7 yrs., 7 mos., 17 dys. | unknown |
| GREEN, Martha J. | 1879, Dec. 8 | C | 7 mos., 19 dys. | S-F, 107 |
| GRIFFITH, (infant) | 1893, Dec. 13 | C | infant | unknown |
| GRIFFITH, David E. | 1900, May 20 | A | 76 yrs. | N-B, 7b |
| GRIFFITH, Emma | unknown | A | unknown | unknown |
| GRIFFITH, Jack | unknown | A | unknown | unknown |
| GRIFFITHS, David W. | 1876, July 25 | A | 42 yrs. | S-D, 49 |
| HABENICHT, Wilhelm C. | 1882, Feb. 25 | A | 18 yrs., 10 mos., 27 dys. | N-A, 4 |
| HAVARD, Elias | 1875, Aug. 27 | C | 4 yrs., 10 mos., 17 dys. | N-D, 39 |
| HAY, John | 1873, Dec. 16 | A | approximately 40 yrs. | unknown |
| HEYCOCK, Richard | 1877, Nov. 14 | C | 8 yrs., 11 mos., 10 dys. | N-D, 35 |
| HOLT, Walter L. | 1882, Jan. 1 | C | 8 yrs., 9 mos. | N-B, 10 |
| HOOK, Alice J. | 1875, Feb. 20 | C | 3 mos., 4 dys. | S-F, 108 |
| HOOK, George B. | 1880, Dec. 16 | A | 31 yrs. | S-F, 109 |
| HOWELL, Sarah | 1870, Oct. 9 | C | 4 yrs., 9 mos. | N-C, 8 |
| HOWELL, Thomas M. | 1870, Sept. 2 | C | 10 yrs., 1 mo., 12 dys. | N-C, 8 |
| HOWELLS, Isaac | 187? | A | 53 yrs. | N-F, 73 |

| NAME | DATE OF DEATH | ADULT OR CHILD | AGE AT DEATH | BURIAL LOCATION: SECTION / PLOT # |
|---|---|---|---|---|
| HUGHES, David M. | 1888, Mar. 12 | A | 37 yrs. | S-B, 12 |
| HUGHES, Margaret | 1876, May 11 | A | 37 yrs., 11 mos., 5 dys. | S-D, 54 |
| HUMPHREYS, Gwelym (Gwylym) | 1877 | C | 6 yrs. | S-C, 43 |
| JAMES, Mary Ann | 1877, Oct. 1 | A | 20 yrs., 6 mos. | N-C, 28 |
| JAMES, Morgan E. | 1890, Sept. 3 | A | approximately 43 years | unknown |
| JAMES, Thomas D. | 1876, July 24 | A | 29 yrs. | S-D, 50 |
| JENKINS, Ebenezer H. | 1874, June 23 | C | 7 yrs., 6 mos., 19 dys. | S-D, 88 |
| JENKINS, Elizabeth Ann | 1870, Sept. 22 | C | 1 mo., 20 dys. | S-D, 88 |
| JENKINS, (infant daughter) | 1880, April 15 | C | 1 dy. | N-B, 9 |
| JENKINS, Thomas H. | 1882, Mar. 24 | A | 52 yrs., 1 mo., 19 dys. | N-B, 9 |
| JENKINS, Thomas Joseph | 1870, Aug. 5 | C | 1 yr., 5 mos., 3 dys. | S-D, 88 |
| JENKINS, Thomas Joseph | 1877, Sept. 5 | C | 5 yrs., 1 mo., 6 dys. | S-D, 88 |
| JEWETT, Emeline F. | 1883, Jan. 14 | A | 57 yrs., 4 mos., 3 dys. | unknown |
| JEWETT, Milton | 1874, Aug. 20 | C | 16 yrs. | N-F, 105 |
| JEWETT, Walter S. | 1869, April 21 | A | 19 yrs. | N-F, 105 |
| JONES, Austin | 1880, Nov. 20 | A | 46 yrs. | S-C, 23 |
| JONES, Benjamin A. | 1911, Jan. 22 | A | 71 yrs. | unknown |
| JONES, Catherine | 1867, May 27 | A | 34 yrs. | S-E, 82 |
| JONES, David Thomas . | 1874, July 10 | C | 2 yrs., 5 mos., 21 dys. | unknown |
| JONES, Davied R. | 1875, Oct. 29 | C | 6 mos., 28 dys. | S-E, 83 |
| JONES, Elizabeth | 1876, Mar. 10 | A | 25 yrs. | S-E, 83 |
| JONES, Elizabeth | 1881, Sept. 17 | A | 43 yrs. | unknown |
| JONES, Ellen | 1890, Aug. 15 | A | 69 yrs. | S-E, 89 |
| JONES, George T. | 1876, Mar. 21 | C | 4 yrs., 7 mos., 9 dys. | Near N-E, 70 |
| JONES, Henry | 1870, Aug. 27 | C | 2 mos., 20 dys. | Near N-E, 70 |
| JONES, Hugh R. | 1869, Nov. | A | 44 yrs. | S-E, 89 |
| JONES, Isabella | 1872, Feb. 5 | C | 3 yrs., 10 mos. | S-E, 84 |
| JONES, Jennie | unknown | C | infant | near S-C, 117 |
| JONES, John | 1869, July 14 | C | 1 dy. | Near N-E, 70 |
| JONES, John B. | 1879, Feb. 9 | A | 38 yrs., 9 mos. | S-D, 59 |

| NAME | DATE OF DEATH | ADULT OR CHILD | AGE AT DEATH | BURIAL LOCATION: SECTION /PLOT # |
|---|---|---|---|---|
| JONES, Lewis James | 1875, Feb. 6 | C | 3 mos., 11 dys. | near S-C, 117 |
| JONES, Martha | 1886, Oct. 27 | A | 18 yrs., 7 mos., 13 dys. | S-C, 22 |
| JONES, Mary E. | 1865, Aug. 21 | C | 3 mos. | S-E, 79 |
| JONES, Thomas | 1878, Nov. 10 | C | 16 mos. | S-C, 113 |
| JONES, Thomas M. | 1896, Mar. 19 | A | 58 yrs., 1 mo., 2 dys. | N-E, 70 |
| JONES, Thomas S. | 1875, Jan. 5 | A | 45 yrs. | N-E, 69 |
| LEAM, Margaret | 1884, Oct. 3 | A | 47 yrs., 9 mos., 8 dys. | S-E, 91 |
| LEAM, May | 1870, Sept. 7 | C | 10 yrs., 4 mos., 4 dys. | S-E, 91 |
| LEAM, Robert | 1900, Feb. 27 | A | 64 yrs. | Near S-E, 91 |
| LEWIS, David John | circa 1881 | C | 4 yrs. | unknown |
| LEWIS, Meredith | 1876, July 24 | A | 38 yrs. | unknown |
| LEWIS, Seth John | unknown | C | infant | unknown |
| LOVE, John | 1877, Mar. 3 | A | 41 yrs., 6 mos., 17 dys. | N-C, 30 |
| MACLEOD, John | circa 1874 | C | 6 mos. | unknown |
| MADDIN, Ella | 1880, July 28 | C | 2 yrs., 6 mos., 10 dys. | unknown |
| MALPASS, Percival Sidney | 1897, circa June | C | 1 yr., 8 mos. | unknown |
| MARKLEY, A. J. | 1870, May 2 | A | 40 yrs. | N-E, 67 |
| MARKLEY, David | 1869, April 19 | C | 4 mos., 11 dys. | N-E, 67 |
| MARKLEY, Eliza Jane | 1869, Mar. 26 | C | 13 yrs., 3 mos., 23 dys. | N-E, 67 |
| MILLS, Charles W. | 1881, Nov. 3 | C | 2 yrs., 1 mo. | N-B, 11 |
| MINETT, William C. | 1866, May 27 | A | 25 yrs. | N-E, 66 |
| MORGAN, Ann | 1873, Sept. 19 | A | 26 yrs. | unknown |
| MORGAN, David | 1882, May 16 | A | 35 yrs., 7 mos., 19 dys. | S-E, 92 |
| MORRIS, Alexander | 1875, April 19 | C | 8 yrs., 20 dys. | N-D, 38 |
| MORTIMORE, Alvin | 1893, Aug. 3 | C | 1 yr., 1 mo. | S-C, 21 |
| MORTIMORE, Harriet | 1885, Jan. 15 | C | 8 yrs., 1 mo., 7 dys. | S-C, 21 |
| MORTIMORE, Richard | 1895, Sept. 4 | A | 52 yrs., 5 mo. 29 dys. | S-C, 21 |
| MUIR, Jane Russel | 1865, Jan. 4 | C | 4 yrs., 9 mos. | unknown |
| NORTON, Sarah | 1879, Oct. 5 | A | 68 yrs. | N-B, 6 |
| OLIVER, Jane | 1880, Mar. 17 | A | 39 yrs., 6 mos. | S-D, 95 |

| NAME | DATE OF DEATH | ADULT OR CHILD | AGE AT DEATH | BURIAL LOCATION: SECTION /PLOT # |
|---|---|---|---|---|
| OLIVER, Thomas J. | 1885, Dec. 10 | A | approximately 45 yrs. | near S-D, 95 |
| OTT, Georg Adam | 1873, Nov. 7 | C | 3 mos. | S-E, 76 |
| PARSONS, Jeanette | 1878 | C | infant | unknown |
| PIERCY, Julia Etta | 1870, Dec. 7 | C | 2 yrs., 11 mos., 8 dys. | S-F, 85 |
| POHL, Dora | 1874, July 14 | C | 6 mos. | S-F, 110 |
| POHL, Millie | 1875, Jan. 16 | C | 3 yrs., 4 dys. | S-F, 110 |
| POWELL, Mary | 1878, April 7 | A | 60 yrs. | S-C, 42 |
| PRICE, Hazel | unknown | unknown | unknown | unknown |
| PRITCHARD, Lupyester | circa 1880 | C | infant - 3 mos. | unknown |
| PROSSER, Mary | 1876, Sept. 24 | A | 52 yrs. | S-E, 78 |
| RAMSAY, (child) | unknown | C | unknown | unknown |
| REES, Elizabeth Ann | 1877, April 6 | C | 6 yrs., 8 mos., 15 dys. | S-C, 19 |
| REES, Margaret | 1875, Oct. 22 | C | 1 yr., 3 mos., 15 dys. | unknown |
| REYNOLDS, George M. | 1876, July 24 | A | 29 yrs. | unknown |
| RICHARDS, Daniel | 1890, Sept. 11 | A | 69 yrs., 1 mo., 22 dys. | S-C, 15 |
| RICHARDS, John | 1874, Aug. 4 | A | 30 yrs. | N-E, 64 |
| RICHARDS, William Timothy | 1874, June 2 | C | 17 mos. | N-E, 64 |
| RICHMOND, Anne | 1882, May 31 | A | 56 yrs., 4 mos., 21 dys. | S-E, 80 |
| RICHMOND, Elizabeth | 1865, Feb. 17 | C | 8 yrs., 5 mos., 11 dys. | S-E, 81 |
| RICHMOND, Thomas | 1882, April 7 | A | 57 yrs., 8 mos., 22 dys. | S-E, 80 |
| RIDDOCK, Mary Jane | 1865, March 2 | C | 7 yrs. | unknown |
| RIDDOCK, Robert | 1865, Feb. 27 | C | 1 yr., 10 mos. | unknown |
| RIDDOCK, Robert | 1867 | C | Infant – 3 weeks | unknown |
| RIDDOCK, William | 1865 | C | 4 yrs. | unknown |
| RITCHARDS (RICHARDS), Mary | 1888, Dec. 13 | A | 63 yrs. | S-C, 14 |
| ROGERS (RODGERS), Elizabeth | 1884 | A | 28 yrs. | unknown |
| SADDLER, (male child) | unknown | C | 2-3 yrs. | unknown |
| SADDLER, Harriet A. | 1884, March 6 | A | 60 yrs., 5 mos., 4 dys. | unknown |
| SCHWARTZ, (infant #1) | circa 1870s | C | infant | unknown |
| SCHWARTZ, (infant #2) | circa 1870s | C | infant | unknown |

| NAME | DATE OF DEATH | ADULT OR CHILD | AGE AT DEATH | BURIAL LOCATION: SECTION / PLOT # |
|------|---------------|----------------|--------------|-----------------------------------|
| SHAW, Hazel Beatrice | 1892, Mar. 17 | C | 4 mos., 24 dys. | unknown |
| SMITH, Evan | 1876, July 30 | A | 27 yrs. | S-C, 48 |
| SPOWART, Annie | 1872, June 7 | C | 11 yrs., 6 mos. | N-D, 68 |
| SPOWART, Eliza | 1872, *circa* June 11 | C | approximately 9 yrs. | unknown |
| SPRATT, William Gladstone | 1891, Jan. 18 | C | 6 mos. | unknown |
| STINE, Catherine | 1882 | C | approximately 17 yrs. | unknown |
| THOMAS, Charles Morgan | 1877, Aug. 12 | C | 5 yrs., 10 mos., 25 dys. | unknown |
| THOMAS, Elizabeth Ann | 1876, June 27 | C | 1 yr., 10 dys. | unknown |
| THOMAS, Elvira | 1870, July 18 | C | 1 yr., 5 mos., 11 dys. | S-D, 56 |
| THOMAS, Frederick Elias | yr.?, Oct. 9 | C | 2 mos. | N-B, 5 |
| THOMAS, Handel | 1924, April 10 | A | 49 yrs., 29 dys. | unknown |
| THOMAS, Howell | 1915, May 14 | A | 78 yrs. | unknown |
| THOMAS, John | 1876, Sept. 29 | A | 23 yrs. | N-B, 5 |
| THOMAS, John D. | 1876, Aug. 3 | C | 3 yrs. | unknown |
| THOMAS, John H. | 1877, Aug. 16 | C | 3 yrs., 2 mos., 20 dys. | unknown |
| THOMAS, Joseph | 1870, Aug. 2 | C | 2 yrs., 11 mos., 6 dys. | unknown |
| THOMAS, Joseph | 1871, Oct. 6 | C | 10 yrs. | unknown |
| THOMAS, Peter Benjamin | 1877, Aug. 12 | C | 8 yrs., 11 mos., 4 dys. | unknown |
| THOMAS, Rees G. | 1875, Dec. 6 | A | 48 yrs., 3 mos., 6 dys. | S-D, 56 |
| TIERNEY, John | unknown | C | approximately 4 yrs. | unknown |
| TOLAN, (child #1) | 1870 | C | unknown | unknown |
| TOLAN, (child #2) | 1870 | C | unknown | unknown |
| TONKINS, John | 1864, Dec. 29 | C | 16 yrs., 3 mos. | unknown |
| TREGELLAS, Annie | 1865, Feb. 19 | C | 7 yrs., 7 mos. | unknown |
| TREGELLAS, James | 1864, Dec. 28 | C | 2 yrs., 21 dys. | unknown |
| TREGELLAS, Joseph | 1865, Feb. 18 | C | 5 yrs., 1 mo. | unknown |
| TULLY, Mary | 1879, Nov. 10 | A | 52 yrs., 10 mos., 15 dys. | S-C, 18 |
| UNKNOWN | unknown | unknown | unknown | S-E, 87 |
| UNKNOWN (adult) | 1875, Feb. 13 | A | 42 yrs. | S-F, 99 |
| UNKNOWN (infant #1) | unknown | C | infant | N-E, 69 |

| NAME | DATE OF DEATH | ADULT OR CHILD | AGE AT DEATH | BURIAL LOCATION: SECTION/PLOT # |
|------|---------------|----------------|--------------|--------------------------------|
| UNKNOWN (infant #2) | unknown | C | infant | N-E, 69 |
| UNKNOWN ("infant babe") | unknown | C | 3 dys. | S-E, 79 |
| VAN AMRINGE, Ellen | 1872, April 2 | A | 22 yrs., 7 mos., 20 dys. | unknown |
| VAUGHN, Abel Sr. | 1901, April 11 | A | 61 yrs. | N-D, 33 |
| VAUGHN, Abel | 1876, Dec. 30 | C | 3 mos. | N-D, 33 |
| VAUGHN, Hannah (Mrs.) | 1881, July 18 | A | 39 yrs. | N-D, 33 |
| VAUGHN, Hannah | 1888, April 18 | A | 19 yrs., 11 mos., 29 dys. | N-D, 33 |
| VAUGHN, Mary | 1880, Sept. 20 | C | 8 yrs. | N-D, 33 |
| VESTNYS, Lorenda A. | 1870, April 1 | C | 1 yr. | unknown |
| WATERS, Edna Isabella (Bella) | 1892, Nov. 18 | C | 3 yrs., 2 mos., 18 dys. | S-B, 116 |
| WATERS, John Robert | 1892, Dec. 2 | C | 5 yrs., 6 mos., 22 dys. | S-B, 116 |
| WATERS, William (Willie) | 1882, April 6 | C | 9 dys. | S-B, 116 |
| WATTS, David | 1876, July 25 | A | adult | S-D, 50 |
| WATTS, Theophilus | 1876, July 24 | A | 27 yrs. | S-D, 50 |
| WILLIAMS, Annie | 1876, Dec. 4 | C | 1 yr., 6 mos., 21 dys. | S-D, 55/S-E, 83 |
| WILLIAMS, David R. | 1873, July 8 | A | 23 yrs. | S-D, 58 |
| WILLIAMS, Edward F. | 1874, May 12 | A | 52 yrs., 8 mos. | N-E, 74 |
| WILLIAMS, Howell M. | 1871, July 6 | C | 2 yrs., 23 dys. | unknown |
| WILLIAMS, Mary M. | 1875, April 22 | C | 2 yrs., 11 mos. | unknown |
| WILLIAMS, Sara Elizabeth | 1870s | C | approximately 2 yrs. | unknown |
| WILLIAMS, Watkin | 1881, Oct. 22 | A | 53 yrs., 6 mos., 27 dys. | S-D, 51 |
| WILLIAMS, William L. | 1876, July 24 | A | 18 yrs., 4 mos. | S-D, 52 |
| WILLIS, Mary Blanche | 1877, April 9 | C | 12 yrs., 7 mos., 6 dys. | unknown |
| WINGATE, Robert | 1875, Feb. 22 | C | 13 mos., 8 dys. | N-D, 37 |
| WITHEROW, Barbara L. | 1876, Aug. 7 | A | 18 yrs., 2 mos., 10 dys. | N-D, 32 |
| WRIGHT, Bertie | 1870, June 26 | C | 3 yrs. | unknown |
| WRIGHT, John Edmund | 1864, Dec. 28 | C | 9 yrs., 10 mos. | unknown |
| WRIGHT, Mary Elizabeth | 1864, Dec. 25 | C | 1 yr., 6 mos. | unknown |
| WRIGHT, Minnie | 1870, June 26 | C | 9 yrs. | unknown |
| WRIGHT, (child) | circa 1865 | C | unknown | unknown |

# Chapter 3

# DESCRIPTIONS FOR PERSONAL AND GRAVESITE INFORMATION

# DESCRIPTIONS FOR PERSONAL
# AND GRAVESITE INFORMATION

Rose Hill Cemetery, *circa* 1920s.
Photograph by La Perla Studio, 205 E. 4th Street, Pittsburg, California.

## PERSONAL INFORMATION:

Since many gravestones are missing and few photographs exist of the these stones, some of the information recorded in this burial record about the individuals interred was acquired from sources other than the gravestone. These sources generally include early cemetery lists, contemporary newspaper articles or obituaries, death records, books, World War I draft registration cards, former residents and/or descendants.

The **sex** of some individuals, such as infants, was not often indicated. If the sex is not known, it is recorded as *unknown*.

For consistency, the month for the **date of birth** and **date of death** is spelled out, followed by the day and year. For some, the date of birth or death was calculated by www.timeanddate.com, based on the age of the individual and the birth or death date. If these dates were calculated, a notation was made on the backside of the individual sheet under *Additional Personal Information*.

If known, the **place of birth** and **place of death** is recorded with the city, county, state and/or country. Most gravestones in Rose Hill Cemetery do not list a place of death.

East Bay Regional Park District

For consistency, if the **age at death** of the individual is known, the words *years, months and days* are spelled out rather than abbreviated as they were on some of the gravestones. Days, months and years were abbreviated different ways on the stones. To see the various abbreviations, refer to the gravestone photographs in this document on pages 1010–1049. For some, the age at death was calculated by www.timeanddate.com, based on the known birth and death date. If it was calculated, a notation was made on the backside of the individual sheet under *Additional Personal Information.*

The **cause of death** was not generally listed on the gravestone. If the cause of death was obtained it is noted.

**Spouse or parents** names were often abbreviated with only the first and middle initials and last name on the gravestone. If known, the full name of the spouse or parents is recorded. If the first name is not known, a blank line is placed before the last name (i.e \_\_\_\_\_ and Eunice Dodsworth).

## GRAVESITE INFORMATION:

If known, the location of gravesite is referenced by section letters and plot numbers.

**Section Letters** – The map is divided into a series of twelve sections, each identified by two letters. The first designation is either letter N, for north section, or S, for south section. This denotes whether the section falls on the north side or the south side of the cemetery. The second letter (A-F) denotes the particular section where the gravesite location is found.

**Plot Numbers** – Each known burial location in the cemetery has been assigned a plot number. The original plot numbers were designated when a cemetery map was compiled by the East Bay Regional Park District in 1973. The map was updated in 2009 to indicate additional gravesites discovered.

**Gravestone** – Indicates whether the gravestone exists or is missing.

**Type of Gravestone** – Refers to the composition of the gravestone. In Rose Hill, they are generally granite or marble, although bronze and concrete markers exist as well.

**Shape of Gravestone** – The shape of the stone is noted. The gravestones are recorded as tablet (a flat marble slab), obelisk (a tall four-sided marble or granite gravestone with a tapering shaft and pyramidal point), or block (a rectangular piece, usually made of granite).

**Inscription** – Includes information written on the stone other than the name, birth and death dates, age and epitaph. Examples of this include: *Children of; Daughter of; Wife of; In Memory of; Father and Mother.*

**Epitaph** – A statement written on the stone in memory of the deceased. Epitaphs often have origins from poems, the *Bible* or church hymns.

**Motif** – Indicates whether the gravestone has a motif(s). Many different motifs appear on the gravestones. The motifs reflect fraternal organizations the men belonged to, feelings about grief, religious beliefs, hope and life after death. Some gravestones have no motif; others may have more than one. Examples of motifs include doves, anchors, lilies, the *Bible*, hands pointing toward Heaven, clasped hands, Odd Fellows and Masonic symbols.

**Carver** – Indicates the carver who produced the stone. The carvers sometimes engraved the name and location of the marble company at the base of the stone. At least nine different gravestone carvers or companies are represented in Rose Hill Cemetery, however most of the gravestones are not signed by the carver.

**Base** – Indicates whether a base or bases for the gravestone exists at the site. A base is the foundation for a gravestone. Some gravestones have three bases known as the bottom (rests on the ground), middle (sits on the bottom base and supports the top base), and top base (supports the gravestone).

**Type of Base** – Indicates the composition of the base. Bases in Rose Hill Cemetery were made of sandstone, marble, granite, or concrete.

**Enclosure** – Indicates if an enclosure exists or is missing at the gravesite. Typically brick or sandstone walls, and/or walls with fences, surround the gravesite. Enclosure refers only to the wall and not the fence that may have existed with the wall. Some gravesites had no enclosure.

**Type of Enclosure** – Indicates the type of material used to surround the gravesite. Types of enclosures include brick wall, sandstone rock wall, and brick enclosure faced with cement/stucco mortar.

**Fence** – Indicates if a fence exists, or is missing, or if one ever existed at all. Not all gravesites had fences.

**Types of Fence** – The fences in Rose Hill were constructed of either wood, wood and wire mesh, or iron. Very few iron fences remain today. Just like gravestones, the fences were often either broken or taken by vandals. In many cases, all that exists at gravesites are fragments of the fence. Evidence, in the form of granite or sandstone cornerstone blocks, which once held the iron fences, exist at some sites to serve as testimony that fences were present. Anything made of wood disappeared before the area became an East Bay Regional Park. Historic photographs, and oral history accounts with former residents often serve as the only documentation that wood, or wood and wire mesh fences, existed at certain sites. Fences were erected to protect the gravesites and/or show a grouping of family graves.

**Fence Motif** – It was common for iron fences of the time to have some type of motif. Motifs often reflected the same symbols as the gravestones. Iron fence motifs included lambs and willow trees, urns, shells, stars, and fleurs-de-lis.

**Additional Personal Information** – Any additional information known about the deceased or their family is recorded.

**Additional Gravesite Information** – Any additional information known about the gravesite is recorded.

**References** – The information on the burial sheet comes from a variety of sources including previous cemetery lists, death records, newspapers, books, photographs, demographic records, probate of will, court and tax assessment records, and the gravestones. All information recorded has been documented in one of these sources. See page 1004 for a list of references used.

Reference 2.18

Rose Hill Cemetery looking east toward Somersville town site in the 1930s. The abandoned Somersville hotel is barely visible in the basin below. The wooden picket fence surrounding the Richard Mortimore and Austin Jones family plots can be seen on the right. In the center of the photograph is the wood and wire fence for the Waters (Edna Isabella, John Robert, and William) children gravesite.

# Chapter 4

# INFORMATION FOR
# INDIVIDUALS INTERRED

# INFORMATION FOR INDIVIDUALS INTERRED

The following section records the names of the individuals interred in Rose Hill Cemetery and provides detailed information regarding their burial site and family history.

For the majority of the individuals listed, their burial and/or burial location in the cemetery has been documented from one or more sources. In addition, descendants provided names of family members for this document with the belief that their ancestors are buried in Rose Hill. Other individuals, presumed to be buried in the cemetery, were added to this record based upon information obtained in newspaper accounts.

Reference 379.9

A rare snowfall, at Black Diamond Mines Regional Preserve, blankets Rose Hill Cemetery on December 7, 2009. Somersville town site can be seen in the basin below the cemetery.
Photograph by Edward Willis, EBRPD.

Reference 363.2

Mount Diablo Coal Field descendants pose for photographs on an old Eucalyptus tree stump in Rose Hill Cemetery in November 1936. Pictured above, left to right, are cousins Milton Gordon, Harriet Mortimore, Alice Mortimore, and George Alvin Gordon. Peggy Gordon is pictured second from the right in the photograph below. Note the iron fences still standing at several of the gravesites.

Reference 363.1

# ABRAHAM,
## Rebecca

**PERSONAL INFORMATION:**

| | |
|---|---|
| SEX: | Female |
| DATE OF BIRTH: | August 1, 1860 |
| DATE OF DEATH: | November 1, 1878 |
| PLACE OF DEATH: | Nortonville, Contra Costa County, California |
| AGE AT DEATH: | 18 years, 4 months |
| CAUSE OF DEATH: | Burned in fire |
| BIRTHPLACE: | |
| SPOUSE: | Daniel R. Abraham |
| PARENTS: | Mr. and Mrs. Hughes |

**GRAVESITE INFORMATION:**

| | |
|---|---|
| LOCATION OF GRAVESITE: | Section S-D, Plot #55 |
| GRAVESTONE: | Missing |
| TYPE OF GRAVESTONE: | Marble |
| SHAPE OF GRAVESTONE: | Tablet (?) |
| INSCRIPTION: | *In memory of* |
| EPITAPH: | *Gone but not forgotten* |
| MOTIF: | |
| CARVER: | |
| BASE: | Exists |
| TYPE OF BASE: | Sandstone with middle marble base |
| ENCLOSURE: | Exists |
| TYPE OF ENCLOSURE: | Brick with granite cornerstones |
| FENCE: | Missing |
| TYPE OF FENCE: | Iron |
| FENCE MOTIF: | Stars |

East Bay Regional Park District

# ABRAHAM, Rebecca

**ADDITIONAL PERSONAL INFORMATION:**
Rebecca Hughes, age 17, of Somersville, Contra Costa County, California, and Daniel R. Abraham, age 21, of Nortonville, Contra Costa County, California, applied for a marriage license on January 22, 1878. The information was recorded in the *Applications for Marriage Licenses, Contra Costa County, 1873-1887*, page 130, located at the Contra Costa County Historical Society History Center in Martinez, California. According to the *Index of Marriage Certificates* obtained from the Contra Costa County Hall of Records in Martinez, Rebecca Hughes and Daniel R. Abraham were married on January 29, 1878 by Rev. John J. Powell; their marriage was recorded in Volume 2, page 215. Their marriage announcement appeared in the *Contra Costa Gazette* newspaper on February 2, 1878 (see page 44). The newspaper article lists their marriage date as January 24th.

After the death of his wife, Rebecca, Daniel R. Abraham remarried and moved to the coal mining area of Black Diamond, King County, Washington. Maggie Lewis, age 20, of Nortonville, Contra Costa County, California, and D. R. Abraham, age 26, also of Nortonville, were issued a marriage license on May 12, 1883. The information was recorded in the *Applications for Marriage Licenses, Contra Costa County, 1873-1887*, page 306.

Listed in the *Black Diamond Cemetery* record, page 9, for Black Diamond, Washington is Meredith L., son of D. R. and Maggie Abraham. Meredith was born March 22, 1884, and died July 18, 1891. Perhaps Meredith's father is the same D. R. Abraham from Nortonville.

Rebecca's age at death comes from Zelma Myrick, who recorded information in a notebook in the 1930s during a visit to Rose Hill Cemetery. According to the *Contra Costa Gazette* newspaper, November 9, 1878, Rebecca died at age 18 years and 6 months.

**ADDITIONAL GRAVESITE INFORMATION:**
The inscription and epitaph also come from Zelma Myrick who recorded the information in a notebook in the 1930s.

The gravestone for Annie Williams sits at the site today. Rebecca's stone was missing prior to acquisition of the cemetery by the East Bay Regional Park District. Rebecca's gravesite appears in a book by Sunset titled *Beautiful California*, Lane Book Company, Menlo Park, CA, 1963, pages 82 and 83.

The brick wall enclosure was rebuilt by the East Bay Regional Park District in 1988. An iron star, a piece of the original fence that once surrounded the gravesite, was found by Black Diamond Rangers at the burial site in July 2009.

**REFERENCES:** 1, 2, 3, 4, 6, 8 (Nov. 9, 1878), 11 (P610.113.6, P610.139.2, P610.147.18, P610.260.25, P610.268.3, P610.285.7, P610.312.4, and P610.362.5), 12, *Black Diamond Cemetery* records, Black Diamond, King County, Washington, see newspaper appendix page 679

Rebecca Abraham gravesite, March 1955.

Rebecca Abraham gravesite, March 1969. Photograph by David Stogner.

---

## MARRIED.

LASSELL—WIGHT—At the residence of the bride's parents, in New York Valley, Jan 23d, by Rev. G. M. Dexter, Mr. Loron M. Lassel, of Nortonville, and Miss Sarah E. Wight, daughter of R. H. Wight, Esq., of New York Valley.

ABRAHAM—HUGHES—Is Nortonville, January 24th, by Rev. J. J. Powell, Daniel R. Abraham of Nortonville, and Rebecca Hughes of Somersville.

---

The second entry listed in this *Contra Costa Gazette* newspaper article from February 2, 1878, announces the marriage of Rebecca Hughes of Somersville and Daniel R. Abraham of Nortonville.

# AITKEN,
## Katie

**PERSONAL INFORMATION:**

| | |
|---|---|
| SEX: | Female |
| DATE OF BIRTH: | August 12, 1871 |
| DATE OF DEATH: | December 24, 1879 |
| PLACE OF DEATH: | |
| AGE AT DEATH: | 8 years, 4 months, 12 days |
| CAUSE OF DEATH: | |
| BIRTHPLACE: | |
| SPOUSE: | None |
| PARENTS: | James and Barbra Aitken |

**GRAVESITE INFORMATION:**

| | |
|---|---|
| LOCATION OF GRAVESITE: | Section S-C, Plot #17 |
| GRAVESTONE: | Exists |
| TYPE OF GRAVESTONE: | Marble |
| SHAPE OF GRAVESTONE: | Tablet |
| INSCRIPTION: | *Dau. of* |
| EPITAPH: | *Weep not Father and Mother for me* |
| | *For I am waiting in glory for thee.* |
| MOTIF: | Nipped rosebud |
| CARVER: | |
| BASE: | Exists |
| TYPE OF BASE: | Sandstone |
| ENCLOSURE: | |
| TYPE OF ENCLOSURE: | |
| FENCE: | |
| TYPE OF FENCE: | |
| FENCE MOTIF: | |

# AITKEN, Katie

**ADDITIONAL PERSONAL INFORMATION:**
The *1880 Census for Somersville Precinct, Contra Costa County, California*, lists James Aitken, age 39, as a miner and native of Scotland. Also listed are his wife, Borbra [sic], age 35, a native of Scotland and their children: David, age 15, a native of Scotland; Jessie, age 7, a native of Indiana; Marian, age 4, a native of California; and William, age 1, a native of California.

James Aitken was listed as a Senior Deacon of the Contra Costa Masonic Lodge No. 227 in Somersville in 1882.

*The Great Register of Contra Costa County, State of California, 1894*, page 1, lists James Aitken as a miner, age 51, 5' 5 ½" tall, fair complexion, light blue eyes, and sandy colored hair. He is listed as a native of Great Britain and a resident of Somersville. He was naturalized on November 4, 1876 in Contra Costa County.

**ADDITIONAL GRAVESITE INFORMATION:**
Zelma Myrick, who recorded information in a notebook in the 1930s during a visit to Rose Hill Cemetery, reported "Stone down."

The gravestone is cracked into three pieces with a small bottom piece of the stone missing. The stone was concreted flat to the ground prior to acquisition by the East Bay Regional Park District.

**REFERENCES:** 1, 2, 3, 4, 6, 11 (P610.31.175 and P610.168.17), 12, 14

Reference 31.175

The vandalized Katie Aitken gravestone is shown pieced together and concreted to the ground. Photograph by Traci (Gibbons) Parent, July 1977.

# ANDERSON,
## Robert

**PERSONAL INFORMATION:**

| | |
|---|---|
| SEX: | Male |
| DATE OF BIRTH: | December 10, 1895 |
| DATE OF DEATH: | October 17, 1900 |
| PLACE OF DEATH: | Somersville, Contra Costa County, California |
| AGE AT DEATH: | 4 years, 10 months, 7 days |
| CAUSE OF DEATH: | Kicked by horse |
| BIRTHPLACE: | Somersville, Contra Costa County, California |
| SPOUSE: | None |
| PARENTS: | Richard and Cora (Butalph) Anderson |

**GRAVESITE INFORMATION:**

| | |
|---|---|
| LOCATION OF GRAVESITE: | Section S-B, Plot #24 |
| GRAVESTONE: | Exists |
| TYPE OF GRAVESTONE: | Bronze plaque |
| SHAPE OF GRAVESTONE: | |
| INSCRIPTION: | |
| EPITAPH: | |
| MOTIF: | |
| CARVER: | |
| BASE: | |
| TYPE OF BASE: | |
| ENCLOSURE: | Exists |
| TYPE OF ENCLOSURE: | Brick with mortar covering |
| FENCE: | |
| TYPE OF FENCE: | |
| FENCE MOTIF: | |

# ANDERSON, Robert

## ADDITIONAL PERSONAL INFORMATION:

Robert's father, Richard, was born in 1854 in Belfast, Ireland. Robert's grandparents (Richard's parents) were Richard and Mary (Carmichael) Anderson. Robert's mother, Cora (Butalph) Anderson, was born in 1866 in Monticello, Iowa.

*The Great Register of the County of Contra Costa in the State of California 1898*, page 79, lists Richard Anderson as a blacksmith age 44, 5' 8 ½" tall with fair complexion, brown hair and eyes. His country of nativity is Ireland and place of residence is Somersville. He was naturalized on August 1, 1896 in Contra Costa County.

*The 1900 Contra Costa County Voting Register for Somersville Precinct* lists Richard Anderson, age 44, as a blacksmith. *The Index of Voters, Somersville Precinct 1900*, lists Richard Anderson age 48, as a resident of Somersville. The *Index of Voters Somersville Precinct, Contra Costa County 1902*, lists Richard Anderson, age 52, of Somersville.

According to the *Contra Costa Times* newspaper, January 17, 1989, Robert's father opened the first blacksmith shop in Pittsburg, California.

The *1900 Census for Somersville, Contra Costa County, California* lists Richard Anderson, age 45, born August 1854, occupation blacksmith and a native of Ireland. His year of immigration to the United States is recorded as 1861 and he has been living in the United States for 39 years. Also listed are his wife Cora, age 34, and their children, all natives of California: Gertrude, age 14; Mary A., age 12; Elizabeth, age 9; Richard, age 6; Robert, age 4; and Thomas, age 1.

According to Anderson family descendants the children were:

- Gertrude, born 1885
- Mary, born 1888
- Elizabeth, born 1890
- Richard, born 1894
- Robert, born 1895
- Thomas, born 1898
- William, born 1901
- Corabelle, born 1904

Richard and Cora Anderson and various family members are listed in the following census records for Contra Costa County, California: *1910 Census for Township 6, 1920 Census for Pittsburg*, and the *1930 Census for Pittsburg*.

## ADDITIONAL GRAVESITE INFORMATION:

The gravesite contains a concrete grave enclosure constructed of brick and covered with concrete with a bronze marker. The bronze marker is 21 ¾" wide by 8 ½" high. A photograph of the gravesite appears in *Contra Costa Living* (a supplement to the *Contra Costa Sunday Times* newspaper), April 11, 1971, page 8.

REFERENCES: 1, 2, 3, 4, 6, 9 (Feb. 23, 1901 and April 5, 1973), 11 (P610.31.190, P610.43.4, P610.47.1, and P610.305.1), 12, 14, *Oakland Tribune* newspaper (Aug. 30, 1964), *Interview with Gertrude (Anderson) Young, Former Somersville Resident*, Feb. 5, 1979, by Traci Gibbons and John Waters, EBRPD, see newspaper appendix page 680

Reference 305.1

Pictured are the children of Richard and Cora Anderson of Somersville, California. Left to right: Mary, Richard, Gertrude, and Elizabeth (seated on right), *circa* 1894. Robert was born approximately one year after this photograph was taken. Gertrude (Anderson) Young, the oldest child in the Anderson family, had the following information to share about her brother during an oral history interview in February 1979:

> ...you know he was...nicest little kid and uh one time they had a...he only had one horse and buggy. This old horse was as gentle as a lamb. ...Robert went up to get the horse and he was hanging onto the horse by its tail. The horse just put his foot out and kicked him [Robert]. Kicked him. And that's the way it went. ...And he was just showin' off.

According to coal field descendants:

> The sad story that has been told to all generations is that of the five year old Robert Anderson who was sent by one of the women of Somersville to get her horse (an old nag) for her. This was without permission of Robert's parents. Robert did as he was told, and according to the story, the horse would not come with him, so like any five year old boy, he went to the back of the horse and pulled on its tail. The horse reared and kicked Robert in the head and he was fatally wounded.

Above: Richard Anderson, blacksmith and former Somersville resident in Pittsburg, Contra Costa County, California. Mr. Anderson worked as a blacksmith on Clayton Road (Clayton, California, just southwest of Somersville) before moving to Somersville. It is believed the family moved to Somersville sometime in the 1890s, and lived there until 1903. When the mines closed, the Andersons moved to Black Diamond (now Pittsburg), Contra Costa County, California. Below: Cora (Butalph) Anderson, wife of Richard Anderson.

# BANKS,
## Albert

## PERSONAL INFORMATION:

SEX:      Male

DATE OF BIRTH:      *Circa* 1836

DATE OF DEATH:      August 21 or 22, 1871

PLACE OF DEATH:      Nortonville, Contra Costa County, California

AGE AT DEATH:      35 - 38 years

CAUSE OF DEATH:

BIRTHPLACE:      Pennsylvania

SPOUSE:

PARENTS:

## GRAVESITE INFORMATION:

LOCATION OF GRAVESITE:      Unknown

GRAVESTONE:      Missing  or never placed

TYPE OF GRAVESTONE:

SHAPE OF GRAVESTONE:

INSCRIPTION:

EPITAPH:

MOTIF:

CARVER:

BASE:

TYPE OF BASE:

ENCLOSURE:

TYPE OF ENCLOSURE:

FENCE:

TYPE OF FENCE:

FENCE MOTIF:

# BANKS, Albert

**ADDITIONAL PERSONAL INFORMATION:**
The *Antioch Ledger* newspaper, August 26, 1871 states that A. Banks died August 22, 1871, aged 38 years. The *Contra Costa Gazette* newspaper, August 26, 1871 states he died August 21, 1871, aged 35 years.

The *1860 Census for San Francisco District 3, San Francisco County, California* lists Albert Banks born *circa* 1837, age 23, as a merchant and native of Pennsylvania.

In April 1869, Albert Banks served as Senior Vice-Commander of Post No. 28, Grand Army of the Republic in Somersville, Contra Costa County, California.

The *1870 Census for Township 3, Contra Costa County, California* lists Albert Banks, born *circa* 1837, age 33, as a clerk in Store and native of Pennsylvania.

**ADDITIONAL GRAVESITE INFORMATION:**
Albert Banks is not listed on any previous cemetery lists. The only reference to his interment in Rose Hill Cemetery comes from the *Contra Costa Gazette* newspaper, August 26, 1871.

**REFERENCES:** 8 (Aug. 26, 1871), 9 (Aug. 26, 1871 – two articles), 10 (page 477), 12, see newspaper appendix page 681

## DIED.

At Nortonville, on Monday last, the 21st inst., ALBERT BANKS, a native of Pennsylvania, aged 35 years.

The deceased was interred at Somersville, and the funeral was conducted under the direction of his comrades of the Grand Army of the Republic connected with the Post at that place.

The obituary above is from the *Contra Costa Gazette* newspaper, August 26, 1871.
The obituary below is from the *Antioch Ledger* newspaper, August 26, 1871.
Note the different death dates and ages listed.

## DIED.

At Nortonville, August 22d, A. Banks, aged 38 years.

## PERSONAL INFORMATION:

| | |
|---|---|
| SEX: | Female |
| DATE OF BIRTH: | June 1828 |
| DATE OF DEATH: | September 8, 1892 |
| PLACE OF DEATH: | Somersville, Contra Costa County, California |
| AGE AT DEATH: | 64 years, 3 months |
| CAUSE OF DEATH: | Kidney problems |
| BIRTHPLACE: | Merthyr Tydfil, South Wales |
| SPOUSE: | Joseph Banks |
| PARENTS: | |

## GRAVESITE INFORMATION:

| | |
|---|---|
| LOCATION OF GRAVESITE: | Unknown |
| GRAVESTONE: | Missing or never placed |
| TYPE OF GRAVESTONE: | |
| SHAPE OF GRAVESTONE: | |
| INSCRIPTION: | |
| EPITAPH: | |
| MOTIF: | |
| CARVER: | |
| BASE: | |
| TYPE OF BASE: | |
| ENCLOSURE: | |
| TYPE OF ENCLOSURE: | |
| FENCE: | |
| TYPE OF FENCE: | |
| FENCE MOTIF: | |

# BANKS, Ann C.

**ADDITIONAL PERSONAL INFORMATION:**
The *Contra Costa Gazette* newspaper, September 14, 1892, lists Ann's age at death as 67 years, 2 months and 28 days. The *Antioch Ledger* newspaper and the *Contra Costa County, California Registers of Death* list her age at death as 64 years. The birth date was calculated by www.timeanddate.com, using the age reported in the *Contra Costa County, California Registers of Death*.

The *1860 Census for Township Six, Placer County, California* lists Ann's year of birth as about 1824. The *1870 Census for Township Six*, Placer County, California lists her year of birth as about 1826.

According to *Contra Costa County, California Register of Deaths*, Ann Banks was a housewife in Somersville. She had problems with her kidneys, which eventually caused her death. Her doctor was W. S. George of Antioch, Contra Costa County, California.

Mrs. Ann Banks is listed in the records of the New York Congregational Church (located in the area now known as Pittsburg, Contra Costa County, California) from 1883. She was removed from the church congregation on April 5, 1892. Manner of removal was death. This may not be the same person since Ann died September 1892.

See Joseph Banks.

**ADDITIONAL GRAVESITE INFORMATION:**
No sources document Ann Banks' burial in Rose Hill Cemetery. According to the County Hall of Records in Martinez, Contra Costa County, California, Ann was living in Somersville at the time of her death. However, her name has not been recorded on any previous Rose Hill Cemetery lists. Since her husband, Joseph Banks, is buried in Rose Hill Cemetery it is most likely that Ann is buried there as well.

**REFERENCES:** 7, 8 (Sept. 14, 1892), 9 (Sept. 10, 1892), 12, see newspaper appendix page 682

Reference 8.22

This photograph, taken in 1971, shows the vandalized gravestone of Joseph Banks (Ann's husband) prior to East Bay Regional Park District acquisition. Although no gravestone has been located for Ann Banks, it is presumed that she may be buried in the cemetery since her husband is interred there and she died in 1892 while living in Somersville. Photograph by Brian Suen.

This photo of the west side of Somersville, Contra Costa County, California was taken in 1878. Rose Hill Cemetery can be seen in the upper right portion of the photograph. Ann C. Banks was listed as a housewife living in Somersville at the time of her death in September 1892.

East Bay Regional Park District

### Cleaning Up.

The Board of Town Trustees has appointed Dr. W. S. George, health officer, Messrs. N. A. Tyler, M. H. Boothby and D. M. Pitts sanitary commissioners. The commissioners are now engaged in making a house to house canvass of the sanitary condition of the town, and are abating nuisances as rapidly as possible. We are glad to learn that the residents of the town are seconding the efforts of the commissioners and promptly abate nuisances when pointed out. Antioch is the easiest town in the State to keep clean and there is no reason why it should be filthy.

The articles above come from the *Antioch Ledger* newspaper, Saturday, September 24, 1892. The "Professional Cards" on the left show the listings for coal field doctors Frank Rattan and W. S. George. Dr. George served as the doctor for Ann C. Banks. These doctors lived in nearby Antioch and often traveled to the coal field to assist those in need.

## PERSONAL INFORMATION:

| | |
|---|---|
| SEX: | Male |
| DATE OF BIRTH: | June 5, 1818 |
| DATE OF DEATH: | August 29, 1883 |
| PLACE OF DEATH: | |
| AGE AT DEATH: | 65 years, 2 months, 24 days |
| CAUSE OF DEATH: | |
| BIRTHPLACE: | England |
| SPOUSE: | Ann C. Banks |
| PARENTS: | |

## GRAVESITE INFORMATION:

| | |
|---|---|
| LOCATION OF GRAVESITE: | Section N-A, Plot # 3 |
| GRAVESTONE: | Exists (partial) |
| TYPE OF GRAVESTONE: | Marble |
| SHAPE OF GRAVESTONE: | Tablet |
| INSCRIPTION: | *In Memory of/the Beloved Husband of* |
| EPITAPH: | *Green be the turf above thee,* |
| | *Companion of my happier days,* |
| | *None knew thee but to love thee,* |
| | *Nor named thee but to praise.* |
| | *Tears fell when thou wert dying* |
| | *From eyes unused to weep,* |
| | *And long where thou art lying,* |
| | *Will tears the cold turf steep.* |
| MOTIF: | Independent Order of Odd Fellows (I.O.O.F.) |
| CARVER: | |
| BASE: | Exists |
| TYPE OF BASE: | Granite |
| ENCLOSURE: | Exists |
| TYPE OF ENCLOSURE: | Sandstone rock wall (partial) |
| FENCE: | Missing |
| TYPE OF FENCE: | Wooden picket |
| FENCE MOTIF: | |

# BANKS, Joseph

**ADDITIONAL PERSONAL INFORMATION:**
The *1860 Census for Township 6, Placer County, California* lists Joseph Banks, age 42, as a miner and native of England. Also listed is his wife, Ann Banks, age 36, a native of Wales. Edward Bradford, age 27, a miner and native of Massachusetts is listed with them.

The *1870 Census for Township Six, Placer County, California* lists Joseph Banks, age 52, as a miner and native of England. Also listed is his wife, Ann C. Banks, born *circa* 1826, age 44, and a native of Wales.

The *1876 Contra Costa County Voting Register* records Joseph's age as 49 years. Based on this information, he would have been born in 1827. However, his gravestone states he was born June 5, 1818. The 1870 census (see above) and the 1880 census (see below) also confirms the birth year of 1818.

Joseph was a native of England and a miner in Nortonville, Contra Costa County, California. He was a member of the Independent Order of Odd Fellows (I.O.O.F.). Since he was employed as a miner in Nortonville, perhaps he belonged to Social Encampment #50, the I.O.O.F. lodge in Nortonville. However another I.O.O.F. Lodge (Mount Diablo #128) also existed in Somersville, Contra Costa County, California.

The *1880 Census for the Nortonville Precinct, Contra Costa County, California* lists Joseph Banks, age 62, as a miner and native of England. He is also listed as having a "liver complaint." His wife, Ann, age 54, is listed as a native of Wales. See Ann C. Banks.

**ADDITIONAL GRAVESITE INFORMATION:**
Zelma Myrick, who recorded information in a notebook in the 1930s during a visit to Rose Hill Cemetery, reported the stone "broken in five pieces." The gravestone is broken and missing pieces.

The rock wall existed prior to acquisition by the East Bay Regional Park District and is most likely not original to the site. Repair work on the rock wall was done by Black Diamond Rangers and volunteers in 1979.

Two Italian cypress trees were originally planted at this site. Only one original tree remains; the north cypress tree fell in 1996. A replacement Cypress tree was planted by the Welsh American Society of Northern California in April 1997.

A 1957 photograph of the Joseph Banks gravesite appears on the front cover and on page 9, of the book *Ansel Adams Singular Images*, Text by Edwin Land, David H. McAlpin, Jon Homes, and Ansel Adams, New York Graphic Society, Boston, MA, 1974. A photograph of the gravesite also appears in *Contra Costa Living* (Supplement to the *Contra Costa Sunday Times* newspaper), April 11, 1971, page 1.

The gravestone was repaired and placed upright in the cemetery by Black Diamond Rangers in 2009.

**REFERENCES:** 1, 2, 3, 4, 6, 11 (P610.19.2, P610.27.1, P610.31.198, and P610.119.3), 12, 14, *Pittsburg Post Dispatch* newspaper (Wednesday, June 15, 1955, page 9)

# BASSETT,
## (child)

## PERSONAL INFORMATION:

SEX:                Male (?)

DATE OF BIRTH:

DATE OF DEATH:

PLACE OF DEATH:

AGE AT DEATH:        5 years

CAUSE OF DEATH:     Yellow jaundice

BIRTHPLACE:

SPOUSE:           None

PARENTS:          Possibly Richard and Sarah Ann (Williams) Bassett

## GRAVESITE INFORMATION:

LOCATION OF GRAVESITE:    Unknown

GRAVESTONE:          Missing or never placed

TYPE OF GRAVESTONE:

SHAPE OF GRAVESTONE:

INSCRIPTION:

EPITAPH:

MOTIF:

CARVER:

BASE:

TYPE OF BASE:

ENCLOSURE:

TYPE OF ENCLOSURE:

FENCE:

TYPE OF FENCE:

FENCE MOTIF:

# BASSETT, (child)

## ADDITIONAL PERSONAL INFORMATION:

Former resident, George Vivian, provided the information about the Bassett child to park staff in the late 1970s. According to descendants and information obtained from www.ancestry.com, Sarah Ann Williams, born January 13, 1864 in Wales, married Richard Bassett, born *circa* 1850, in Llanilid, Glamorganshire, Wales. Richard and Sarah Ann (Williams) Bassett are most likely the parents of the Bassett child buried in Rose Hill Cemetery. Nortonville residents, Richard Bassett, age 34, and Sarah Ann Williams, age 19, applied for a marriage liscense on May 21, 1882. This information was recorded in *Applications for Marriage Licenses, Contra Costa County, 1873-1887*, page 269. According to descendants, a Bassett boy and his father were killed *circa* 1892 when the wagon they were riding in tipped over and fell into a creek. Since former coal field resident, George Vivian, reported that the child died of yellow jaundice, this may not be the same child. Sarah and Richard Bassett may have had at least four, perhaps five children:

- Winifred, born September 23, 1883; died June 24, 1972, Martinez, Contra Costa County, California (married Leroy Beede)
- Charles William, born December 29, 1887, Butte City, Silver Bow County, Montana; died July 12, 1972, Walnut Creek, Contra Costa County, California (married Kitty Adele Juett)
- John, born *circa* 1893; died Feb. 12, 1924, San Francisco, San Francisco County, California
- Male child, died *circa* 1892 (killed in wagon accident)
- Male child (died of yellow jaundice)

After the death of her first husband, Sarah Bassett married John F. Evans. The *1900 Census for Somersville, Contra Costa County, California* lists Sarah A. Evans, age 35, born June 1864 in Wales. The census states that she married in 1897 and has been married for three years. Also listed are her husband, John Evans, age 35, born September 1864 in Wales; and their children John (Bassett) Evans, age 15, born January 1885, in California; and Charley, age 12, born December 1887, in Montana. The *1910 Census for Township 8, Contra Costa County, California* lists Sarah A. Evens [sic], age 45, born *circa* 1865 in Wales, her husband John F. Evens [sic], age 45, born *circa* 1865 in Wales; and their children: John Bassett, age 25, born *circa* 1885 in California; Charles Bassett, age 22, born *circa* 1888 in Montana; and Eunice Bassett, age 7, born *circa* 1903 in California. [Note: Sarah and John Evans married in 1897; Eunice probably would have been born as Evans and not Bassett.] The *1920 Census for Antioch, Contra Costa County, California* lists Sarah Evans, age 54, born *circa* 1866 in Wales. Also listed are her husband, John F. Evans, age 55, born *circa* 1865 in Wales; and their daughter Eunice M. Evans, age 17, born *circa* 1903 in California. The *1930 Census for Antioch, Contra Costa County, California* lists Sarah A. Evans, age 66, born *circa* 1864. Also listed are her husband, John R. Evans, age 65, born *circa* 1865 in Wales; their daughter, Eunice E. Suhr, age 27, born *circa* 1903 in California; son-in-law, Sunnie M. Suhr, age 33, born *circa* 1897; and their daughter, Sally Suhr, age 2, born *circa* 1928. Sarah Ann Bassett Evans died August 15, 1961 in Brentwood, Contra Costa County, California.

## ADDITIONAL GRAVESITE INFORMATION:

A descendant of the Bassett family remembers visiting Rose Hill Cemetery numerous times as a child with her grandmother, Winifred Bassett and Winifred's daughter, Winifred (Bassett) Beede. The descendant believes there may be a member of the Bassett family buried in Rose Hill Cemetery due to the visits made to the cemetery by family members over the years.

## REFERENCES: 12

Somersville school group *circa* 1890s. Winifred Bassett, daughter of Sarah Ann (Williams) and Richard Bassett, is pictured in the back row, the fourth student and first girl from the right. Winifred's hand is resting on the shoulder of the girl next to her. Classmate, Margaret Alice McLay, is posed in the window on the far left. The others in the photograph are unidentified.

Reference 4.2

Group near Somersville Hotel, 1897. The second woman seated on the right with the young boy lying in front of her, is believed to be Sarah Ann (Williams/ Bassett) Evans. Others identified in the photograph are front row, left to right: Annie (Daley) Frank, Nellie (Hollywood) Daley (sometimes spelled "Daly"), Abe Rhine (of Clayton – behind dog), Bob Brown (cook, in white apron with arm around dog), Michael Newman, Florence Lougher (young girl) and her mother, Sarah (Hollywood) Lougher, Sarah (Bassett) Evans, Boxill boy, Boxill girl, and Catherine Boxill. The men sitting in chairs are believed to be: ? McBryde, Peter Burns, Jim Mulhern, and "Paddy" McNamee. The men standing in the back row are believed to be: Jerry Mellyn, Bob Easton, Luke Dickinson, Dave Harris, and Abe Leam.

East Bay Regional Park District

Charles Bassett, age 23, sits beside one of the remaining buildings in Somersville, Contra Costa County, California, *circa* 1910. Charles, the son of Sarah Ann (Williams) Bassett and Richard Bassett, was born December 29, 1887 in Butte City, Montana. When the coal mines closed around 1902, many families, including Charles Bassett, his mother, stepfather, and siblings, left the coal mining area and moved to nearby communities. In 1910, Charles is listed as age 22, single, and his occupation as salesman in a store in the *Census for Township Eight* [Antioch], Contra Costa County, California.

## WOULD CHANGE NAME
## OF BLACK DIAMOND.

A move has been started in Black Diamond to change the name of the town to one which will give the world a better idea of what the place really is. "Black diamond" is a common name for coal and the town received its name many years ago when the coal mines were in operation in and around Nortonville and Somersville. Now the mines have been closed down and there are no more "black diamonds" in this county so the people of that hustling community are casting about for another name for their town. A strong point which is being urged is that neither the Santa Fe or Southern Pacific Railroad have stations by the name of Black Diamond.

The closing of the coal mines had an effect on nearby towns as well, as evidenced in this newspaper article from the *Contra Costa Gazette*, January 28, 1911, regarding the community of Black Diamond (known today as Pittsburg).

# BLACKBURN,
## Charles W.

## PERSONAL INFORMATION:

| | |
|---|---|
| SEX: | Male |
| DATE OF BIRTH: | July 1855 |
| DATE OF DEATH: | February 20, 1865 |
| PLACE OF DEATH: | Somersville, Contra Costa County, California |
| AGE AT DEATH: | 9 years, 7 months |
| CAUSE OF DEATH: | Scarlatina Maligna |
| BIRTHPLACE: | |
| SPOUSE: | None |
| PARENTS: | Mr. and Mrs. Blackburn |

## GRAVESITE INFORMATION:

| | |
|---|---|
| LOCATION OF GRAVESITE: | Unknown |
| GRAVESTONE: | Missing or never placed |
| TYPE OF GRAVESTONE: | |
| SHAPE OF GRAVESTONE: | |
| INSCRIPTION: | |
| EPITAPH: | |
| MOTIF: | |
| CARVER: | |
| BASE: | |
| TYPE OF BASE: | |
| ENCLOSURE: | |
| TYPE OF ENCLOSURE: | |
| FENCE: | |
| TYPE OF FENCE: | |
| FENCE MOTIF: | |

# BLACKBURN, Charles W.

**ADDITIONAL PERSONAL INFORMATION:**
Charles was one of many children who died in Somersville in 1865 from scarlatina maligna (scarlet fever). The other children buried in, or believed to be buried in, Rose Hill Cemetery who died from this disease during the same time period include:

- Thomas Pratten Goulding, died January 31, 1865, age 7 years, 7 months, 17 days

- Jane Russel Muir, died January 4, 1865, age 4 years, 3 (?) months

- Elizabeth Richmond, died February 17, 1865, age 8 years, 5 months, 11 days

- John Tonkins, died December 29, 1865, age 16 years, 3 months

- Annie Tregellas, died February 19, 1865, age 7 years, 7 months

- James Tregellas, died December 28, 1865, age 2 years, 21 days

- Joseph Tregellas, died February 18, 1865, age 5 years, 1 month

- John Edmund Wright, died December 28, 1865, age 9 years, 10 months

- Mary Elizabeth Wright, died December 25, 1865, age 1 year, 6 months

Charles' date of birth was calculated by www.timeanddate.com, based on the date of death and age of death reported in the *Contra Costa Gazette* newspaper, February 25, 1865.

Thomas A. Blackburn was listed in the *1865 Tax Book for Contra Costa County, California* for $25 of improvements in Somersville. Thomas A. Blackburn may have been the father of Charles W. Blackburn.

**ADDITIONAL GRAVESITE INFORMATION:**
The *Contra Costa Gazette* newspaper, February 25, 1865, is the only source that records the death of Charles W. Blackburn in Somersville. It is likely that this child is buried in Rose Hill Cemetery although his name has not been documented as being interred there.

**REFERENCES:** 8 (Feb. 25, 1865), 12, see newspaper appendix (Elizabeth Richmond) page 749

# BOWMAN,
## Charles H.

## PERSONAL INFORMATION:

| | |
|---|---|
| SEX: | Male |
| DATE OF BIRTH: | May 5, 1872 |
| DATE OF DEATH: | April 5, 1874 |
| PLACE OF DEATH: | |
| AGE AT DEATH: | 1 year, 11 months |
| CAUSE OF DEATH | |
| BIRTHPLACE: | |
| SPOUSE: | None |
| PARENTS: | David and Lizzie (Davis) Bowman |

## GRAVESITE INFORMATION:

| | |
|---|---|
| LOCATION OF GRAVESITE: | Section N-E, Plot #75 |
| GRAVESTONE: | Exists |
| TYPE OF GRAVESTONE: | Marble |
| SHAPE OF GRAVESTONE: | Tablet |
| INSCRIPTION: | *Erected by David & Lizzie Bowman to the memory of their children* |
| EPITAPH: | *Tis hard to part with those we love,* |
| | *To God thy meek smiles are gone;* |
| | *Assured a brighter home than ours,* |
| | *In Heaven is now thine own.* |
| MOTIF: | |
| CARVER: | |
| BASE: | Exists |
| TYPE OF BASE: | Sandstone |
| ENCLOSURE: | |
| TYPE OF ENCLOSURE: | |
| FENCE: | |
| TYPE OF FENCE: | |
| FENCE MOTIF: | |

# BOWMAN, Charles H.

**ADDITIONAL PERSONAL INFORMATION:**
The *Assessment List for Contra Costa County, 1872-1873*, states that Charles' father, David Bowman, owned a house in Somersville, Contra Costa County, California valued at $150 and furniture valued at $25.

The *1876 Contra Costa County Voting Register* lists David Goodwin Bowman, 37 years of age, as a native of Maine and stable keeper in Nortonville, Contra Costa County, California.

According to information from the MacPhee Family tree compiled by a descendent, Charles' mother, Elizabeth (Davis) Bowman, was born at Bridgeport, Nova Scotia, Canada, on January 14, 1839, and died in 1892 at the age of 53 years. David and Elizabeth Bowman had at least seven children. In addition to Charles H., there were Will, George, Frank, Stella, Violetta (Violette I.), and David G.

The birth date for Charles was calculated by www.timeanddate.com, using the date of death and age of death found on the gravestone. See David G. and Violette I. Bowman.

**ADDITIONAL GRAVESITE INFORMATION:**
Zelma Myrick, who recorded information in a notebook in the 1930s during a visit to Rose Hill Cemetery, reported the stone "on ground but not broken."

The gravestone was broken in three pieces and concreted flat to the ground prior to acquisition by the East Bay Regional Park District. Charles shares the stone with his siblings, David G. and Violette I. Bowman.

**REFERENCES:** 1, 2, 3, 4, 6, 11 (P610.31.144, P610.119.42, and P610.211.5), 12, 13, 14

Reference 20.1

Somersville town site, looking east, *circa* 1930s. Abandoned buildings, such as the Somersville Hotel seen in the center of the photograph, waste rock piles from the Pittsburg Coal Mine, and exotic trees are all that remain of this once flourishing town.

**PERSONAL INFORMATION:**

| | |
|---|---|
| SEX: | Male |
| DATE OF BIRTH: | December 20, 1870 |
| DATE OF DEATH: | February 3, 1871 |
| PLACE OF DEATH: | |
| AGE AT DEATH: | 1 month, 14 days |
| CAUSE OF DEATH: | |
| BIRTHPLACE: | |
| SPOUSE: | None |
| PARENTS: | David and Lizzie (Davis) Bowman |

**GRAVESITE INFORMATION:**

| | |
|---|---|
| LOCATION OF GRAVESITE: | Section N-E, Plot #75 |
| GRAVESTONE: | Exists |
| TYPE OF GRAVESTONE: | Marble |
| SHAPE OF GRAVESTONE: | Tablet |
| INSCRIPTION: | *Erected by David & Lizzie Bowman to the memory of their children* |
| EPITAPH: | *Tis hard to part with those we love,* |
| | *To God thy meek smiles are gone;* |
| | *Assured a brighter home than ours,* |
| | *In Heaven is now thine own.* |
| MOTIF: | |
| CARVER: | |
| BASE: | Exists |
| TYPE OF BASE: | Sandstone |
| ENCLOSURE: | |
| TYPE OF ENCLOSURE: | |
| FENCE: | |
| TYPE OF FENCE: | |
| FENCE MOTIF: | |

# BOWMAN, David G., Jr.

**ADDITIONAL PERSONAL INFORMATION:**
See Charles H. and Violette I. Bowman.

**ADDITIONAL GRAVESITE INFORMATION:**
The gravestone was broken in three pieces and concreted flat to ground prior to acquisition by the East Bay Regional Park District. David shares the gravestone with siblings, Charles H. and Violette I. Bowman.

**REFERENCES:** 1, 2, 3, 4, 6, 11 (P610.31.144, P610.119.42, and P610.211.5), 12, 14

Reference 18.1

Somersville Hotel and other abandoned buildings stand in Somersville town site, *circa* 1930s. At the time this photograph was taken, the old hotel (pictured on the right) was used by Louis Ginochio, son of Giovanni and Angelina Ginochio of Nortonville, as a sheep barn. The livestock ramp into the converted sheep barn is visible (center). According to the *Assessment List for Contra Costa County, 1872-1873*, David's father, David Bowman, owned a house in Somersville.

## PERSONAL INFORMATION:

| | |
|---|---|
| SEX: | Female |
| DATE OF BIRTH: | March 29, 1869 |
| DATE OF DEATH: | June 29, 1870 |
| PLACE OF DEATH: | Somersville, Contra Costa County, California |
| AGE AT DEATH: | 1 year, 3 months |
| CAUSE OF DEATH: | Scarlet fever |
| BIRTHPLACE: | |
| SPOUSE: | None |
| PARENTS: | David and Lizzie (Davis) Bowman |

## GRAVESITE INFORMATION:

| | |
|---|---|
| LOCATION OF GRAVESITE: | Section N-E, Plot #75 |
| GRAVESTONE: | Exists |
| TYPE OF GRAVESTONE: | Marble |
| SHAPE OF GRAVESTONE: | Tablet |
| INSCRIPTION: | *Erected by David & Lizzie Bowman to the memory of their children* |
| EPITAPH: | *Tis hard to part with those we love,* |
| | *To God thy meek smiles are gone;* |
| | *Assured a brighter home than ours,* |
| | *In Heaven is now thine own.* |
| MOTIF: | |
| CARVER: | |
| BASE: | Exists |
| TYPE OF BASE: | Sandstone |
| ENCLOSURE: | |
| TYPE OF ENCLOSURE: | |
| FENCE: | |
| TYPE OF FENCE: | |
| FENCE MOTIF: | |

# BOWMAN, Violette I.

**ADDITIONAL PERSONAL INFORMATION:**
According to the *Antioch Ledger* newspaper, July 2, 1870, Violette died June 22, 1870 at age 18 months (see page 665). See Charles H. and David G. Bowman.

Violette's birth date was calculated by www.timeanddate.com, using the date of death and age of death found on the gravestone.

**ADDITIONAL GRAVESITE INFORMATION:**
The gravestone was broken in three pieces and concreted flat to ground prior to East Bay Regional Park District acquisition. Violette shares the gravestone with brothers, Charles H. and David G. Bowman Jr.

**REFERENCES:** 1, 2, 3, 4, 6, 8 (July 9, 1870), 9 (July 2, 1870), 11 (P610.31.144, P610.119.42, and P610.211.5), 12, 14, see newspaper appendix page 683

Reference 31.144

The vandalized Bowman family gravestone that has been pieced together and concreted flat to the ground. Photograph taken July 1977 by Traci (Gibbons) Parent.

# BRADSHAW,
## John

## PERSONAL INFORMATION:

| | |
|---|---|
| SEX: | Male |
| DATE OF BIRTH: | June 5, 1826 |
| DATE OF DEATH: | October 25, 1881 |
| PLACE OF DEATH: | Nortonville, Contra Costa County, California |
| AGE AT DEATH: | 55 years, 4 months, 20 days |
| CAUSE OF DEATH: | |
| BIRTHPLACE: | Monmouthshire, Wales |
| SPOUSE: | Mary Bradshaw |
| PARENTS: | John and Ann Bradshaw |

## GRAVESITE INFORMATION:

| | |
|---|---|
| LOCATION OF GRAVESITE: | Section S-C, Plot #16 |
| GRAVESTONE: | Exists (top piece only) |
| TYPE OF GRAVESTONE: | Marble |
| SHAPE OF GRAVESTONE: | Tablet |
| INSCRIPTION: | *In Memory of* |
| EPITAPH: | *Weep not for me as you stand by* |
| | *As I was once as you are now* |
| | *Prepare for death and follow me.* |
| MOTIF: | Independent Order of Odd Fellows (I.O.O.F.) emblem and dove with olive branch |
| CARVER: | |
| BASE: | Exists |
| TYPE OF BASE: | Granite |
| ENCLOSURE: | Exists |
| TYPE OF ENCLOSURE: | Brick with granite blocks |
| FENCE: | Exists |
| TYPE OF FENCE: | Iron/wire/pot metal |
| FENCE MOTIF: | Woven wire with fleurs-de-lis |

# BRADSHAW, John

**ADDITIONAL PERSONAL INFORMATION:**
The age at death for John was calculated by www. timeanddate.com, using the birth date and death date found on the gravestone.

The *1841 Wales Census* lists John Bradshaw, born *circa* 1826, age 15. Also listed are his parents, John, age 50, and Ann, age 40; and siblings Jane, age 10, Elizabeth, age 8 and Benjamin, age 5. All are natives of Monmouthshire, Wales.

A dues receipt dated September 13, 1879 indicates John was a member of Morris Run, Pennsylvania Lodge, No. 698, Independent Order of Odd Fellows (I.O.O.F.). He also belonged to Social Encampment #50 (I.O.O.F.) in Nortonville.

According to information recorded in the family *Bible*, John and Mary Bradshaw had at least 15 children. They were:

- Elizabeth, born 1844; died Dec. 6, 1922
- Benjman [sic], born Dec. 29, 1848; died Feb. 12, 1868
- David, born July 31, 1850
- Elizabeth Ann, born Aug. 25, 1853
- Jane, born June 2, 1855
- Margaret, born Feb. 26, 1857
- Fredrick, born April 15, 1859
- John, born Oct. 25, 1860
- Rozina (Ruth?), born May 2, 1862; died May 28, 1902
- Naomi, born 1863; died Oct. 21, 1903
- Henry Timothy, born June 2, 1864
- Mary, born Sept. 16, 1866; died Feb. 16, 1869
- Yweny, born Jan. 20, 1874
- Thomas, born May 8, 1875; died Dec. 19, 1941
- Benjman [sic], born April 20, 1877; died 1955

**ADDITIONAL GRAVESITE INFORMATION:**
A gravestone rubbing is available. This gravestone was present in 1963 because it was listed on a student term paper by Jim Rotelli.

Three Italian Cypress trees standing within a brick and iron fence enclosure grow at this site. The iron fence and brick enclosure were repaired by park staff in June 1981. The gate to the iron fence is missing. Nine granite blocks hold the iron posts for the fence.

A photograph taken in March 1969 by David Stogner (photograph P610.285.13), shows the top portion of the Bradshaw gravestone broken off and missing. A photograph of the Bradshaw gravesite appears in *Contra Costa Living* (a supplement of the *Contra Costa Sunday Times* newspaper), April 11, 1971, page 8. The photograph shows the top piece of the gravestone broken off and sitting next to the rest of the stone.

The top piece of the stone containing the motif was returned to Black Diamond in April 2009 after missing from the cemetery for approximately 37 years. The piece was left on rental property in Lafayette, Contra Costa County, California in the 1970s and was later retrieved by the property owner.

In April 2007, photographs and a notebook from the Zelma Myrick collection were donated by her descendant, Tony Dunleavy. Zelma Myrick was married to Thomas Bradshaw, son of John Bradshaw. After Thomas died, Zelma married Thomas' brother, Ben. Myrick photographed numerous gravestones in Rose Hill Cemetery and documented the gravesites in a notebook in the 1930s. This valuable information from her notebook along with many of her rare photographs has been included in this document.

**REFERENCES:** 1, 2, 3, 4, 6, 8 (Oct. 29, 1881), 11 (P610.2.9, P610.31.132, P610.31.187, P610.143.4, P610.145.1, P610.153.10, P610.190.1, P610.232.2, P610.232.7, P610.232.8, P610.268.14, P610.285.13, and P610.317.1), 12, *East Contra Costa County Times* newspaper (May 25, 2007, page A3), *Bible* (accession 610.55.5), see newspaper appendix page 684

The John Bradshaw gravesite, *circa* 1939, as photographed by Zelma Myrick. John's gravestone states he is a native of Monmouthshire, England. The obituary from the *Contra Costa Gazette* newspaper, October 29, 1881, states that John was a native of Wales. Monmouthshire is a border county between England and Wales.

Reference 190.1

John and Mary Bradshaw, date unknown.

# BRYANT,
## Elizabeth Ann

**PERSONAL INFORMATION:**

| | |
|---|---|
| SEX: | Female |
| DATE OF BIRTH: | September 30, 1866 |
| DATE OF DEATH: | May 21, 1877 |
| PLACE OF DEATH: | |
| AGE AT DEATH: | 10 years, 7 months, 21 days |
| CAUSE OF DEATH: | |
| BIRTHPLACE: | California |
| SPOUSE: | None |
| PARENTS: | James and Margaret Ann (Bennett) Bryant |

**GRAVESITE INFORMATION:**

| | |
|---|---|
| LOCATION OF GRAVESITE: | Section S-D, Plot #57 |
| GRAVESTONE: | Partial |
| TYPE OF GRAVESTONE: | Marble |
| SHAPE OF GRAVESTONE: | Tablet |
| INSCRIPTION: | *Dau. of* |
| EPITAPH: | *Though lost to sight, to memory dear.* |
| MOTIF: | Hand plucking rosebud/rope with tassels |
| CARVER: | Excelsior Marble Works, San Jose, California |
| BASE: | Exists |
| TYPE OF BASE: | Sandstone with middle marble base |
| ENCLOSURE: | Exists (partial) |
| TYPE OF ENCLOSURE: | Sandstone |
| FENCE: | |
| TYPE OF FENCE: | |
| FENCE MOTIF: | |

# BRYANT, Elizabeth Ann

**ADDITIONAL PERSONAL INFORMATION:**
Elizabeth's birth date was calculated by www.timeanddate.com, based on her age at death and date of death listed on her gravestone. Elizabeth's mother, Margaret Bryant, and sisters, Ida Mary (died Jan. 16, 1863), and Eva Sitera (died Oct.18, 1895), are also believed to be buried in Rose Hill Cemetery. See Eva Sitera Bryant, Ida Mary Bryant, and Margaret Bryant.

The *1900 Census for Somersville, Contra Costa County, California* states that there were seven children in the Bryant family and that only four were living at the time the census was taken.

There were probably eight children in the family. All are believed to have been born in California. They were:

- Ida Mary, birth date unknown and died January 16, 1863; believed to be buried in Rose Hill Cemetery

- Frederick, born *circa* 1864

- John, born *circa* 1865

- Elizabeth Ann, born September 30, 1866 and died May 21, 1877; buried in Rose Hill Cemetery

- James, born *circa* 1869

- Lincoln, born December 1870

- Charles, born *circa* 1871

- Eva Sitera, born *circa* 1874 and died October 18, 1895; believed to be buried in Rose Hill Cemetery

The names and death dates for Ida Mary, Elizabeth Ann, Eva Sitera, and Margaret Bryant come from former coal field resident, Laura (Bryant) Franks, daughter of Eva Sitera Bryant.

According to former coal field resident, Amelia (Ginochio) Peel, Elizabeth Ann's brother, Lincoln Bryant, was employed by Giovanni Ginochio of Nortonville to haul coal in wagons from the Peacock Mine near Nortonville to New York Landing (now present-day Pittsburg) and Rodeo in Contra Costa County. Giovanni operated a boarding house and saloon in Nortonville after the Black Diamond Coal Mining Company had departed the area to mine coal in Washington Territory.

**ADDITIONAL GRAVESITE INFORMATION:**
Less than half of Elizabeth Ann's gravestone exists today. The remains of a sandstone wall enclosure are visible at this site.

A middle marble base once held the gravestone and sat on top of the exiting sandstone base. The gravestone was broken in two pieces and concreted to the ground prior to East Bay Regional Park District acquisition. The small piece of the gravestone that remains today was placed in storage for safekeeping.

**REFERENCES:** 1, 2, 3, 6, 8 (Nov. 14, 1908), 9 (Dec. 1, 1900 and Jan. 5, 1901), 11 (P610.2.8, P610.31.151, P610.98.15, and P610.249.1), 12, 14, *Pittsburg Post Dispatch* newspaper (Wed. June 15, 1955, page 9), *History of Contra Costa County California with Biographical Sketches*, Historic Record Company, Los Angeles, CA, 1926, page 214

The Elizabeth Ann Bryant gravestone, with the top portion leaning against base, and the bottom portion sitting in base. A portion of the Elizabeth Ann Thomas and John D. Thomas gravestone is lying on the ground. Photograph by Madison Devlin, 1962.

The Elizabeth Ann Bryant gravestone, *circa* 1960s.
This stone was one of many that were concreted to the
ground prior to acquisition by the East Bay Regional Park District.

# BRYANT,
## Eva Sitera

## PERSONAL INFORMATION:

| | |
|---|---|
| Sex: | Female |
| Date of Birth: | October 27, 1873 |
| Date of Death: | October 18, 1895 |
| Place of Death: | Nortonville, Contra Costa County, California |
| Age at Death: | 21 years, 11 months, 21 days |
| Cause of Death: | Complications from childbirth (?) |
| Birthplace: | Nortonville, Contra Costa County, California |
| Spouse: | None |
| Parents: | James and Margaret Ann (Bennett) Bryant |

## GRAVESITE INFORMATION:

| | |
|---|---|
| Location of Gravesite: | Unknown |
| Gravestone: | Missing or never placed |
| Type of Gravestone: | |
| Shape of Gravestone: | |
| Inscription: | |
| Epitaph: | |
| Motif: | |
| Carver: | |
| Base: | |
| Type of Base: | |
| Enclosure: | |
| Type of Enclosure: | |
| Fence: | |
| Type of Fence: | |
| Fence Motif: | |

# BRYANT, Eva Sitera

**ADDITIONAL PERSONAL INFORMATION:**
According to former Nortonville resident, Amelia (Ginochio) Peel, Eva was not able to get out of bed after giving birth to her daughter Laura Bryant. Eva died four months after Laura was born. Eva's date of birth comes from her memorial card that was created by her brother Lincoln.

Eva Sitera's mother, Margaret Bryant (died Nov. 28, 1900), and sister, Ida Mary (died Jan. 16, 1863), are also believed to be buried in Rose Hill Cemetery. Another sister, Elizabeth Ann (died May 21, 1877), is known to be buried in Rose Hill. A gravestone once existed at Elizabeth Ann's burial site and her burial in Rose Hill was documented by at least four different sources. See Elizabeth Ann Bryant, Ida Mary Bryant, and Margaret Bryant.

**ADDITIONAL GRAVESITE INFORMATION:**
The names and death dates for Eva Sitera Bryant, Ida Mary Bryant, and Margaret Bryant were provided by former coal field resident Laura (Bryant) Franks, daughter of Eva Sitera Bryant. This is the only source that documents the burial of these individuals in Rose Hill.

**REFERENCES:** 12

## Nortonville Mail Service.

NORTONVILLE, May 17th, 1874.

EDS. GAZETTE: Infallibility of sentiment committed to writing and transferred for publication to the press, may be termed the proverbial characteristic of civilized man. In this communication I am resolved to abstain from falsehood and adhere to reliable and indisputable facts of daily experience in Nortonville. This town contains a population larger than any other in the county and has a legally established post office; but it is the custom of the mail carrier to pass by this office and neither receive letters from, or deliver unto, — neither morning nor evening — but, like a fiery meteor, he goes through to or from the metropolis Somersville. I have no censure for the employe who conveys the mail, as I am assured he is acting in obedience to his superior's command — personally he is much esteemed for his integrity and punctuality to his duties. Whether the orders emanate from the mail contractor or district subordinates, such conduct is odious to Nortonville citizens. Communications via Pacheco requiring an immediate reply, are forwarded to another post office and are frequently detained there unnecessarily. The GAZETTE, which arrives here on Saturday is carried through and is seldom seen in Nortonville until the following Monday. Numerous readers, anxious to devote a leisure hour on Sunday in perusing its columns, are debarred from that privilege on which account they omit it of a working day, and are, therefore, ignorant of county events that transpired through the week previous. If such conduct is continued it would be advisable for Nortonville residents to investigate its source, and if not rectified by local authorities complain of it to the Postmaster General, at Washington.

RHOMBUS.

The Bryant family lived in Nortonville when this article, complaining about the mail service, appeared in the *Contra Costa Gazette* newspaper, June 27, 1874. A rebuttal to this article can be found on page 84.

Laura Bryant, *circa* 1913, daughter of Eva Sitera Bryant.
Laura was born in 1895 in Nortonville, Contra Costa County, California.

# PASSING OF A PIONEER

**Funeral of James Bryant, One of the Early Settlers of Contra Costa County.**

The funeral Thursday of James Bryant marked the passing of one of the pioneers of Contra Costa county, who although comparatively unknown outside of his immediate environment still had much to do with promoting and advancing the interests and growth of the county. James Bryant was born in England over eighty-six years ago, and came to California when a young man, landing from a sailing vessel which had come around the Horn in 112 days from New York to San Francisco. He first went to the mines in Placer county and from there to Marin county, engaging in the wood business in the latter county. After gathering a supply of wood, a fire visited the locality and his year's work went up in smoke. He came to Contra Costa county in 1862 and settled at Nortonville, where he was engaged in mining until about five years ago, when he removed to Martinez and has resided here since. While in Marin county he was married to Margaret M. Bennett, whose death occurred about eight years ago at Nortonville. Seven children blessed their union, four of whom are now living—Fred Bryant of Forest Hill, Placer county, John Bryant of Oleum, James Bryant of San Francisco and Lincoln Bryant of Livermore. These with a granddaughter, Laura Bryant, are the only living relatives.

The funeral services were held at the residence and were conducted by Rev. Mr. Owens of the Congregational Church. A choir composed of Mrs. T. A. McMahon, Mrs. O. L. Marsh, A. J. Soto and George Meese rendered "Lead, Kindly Light," "It is Well With My Soul," and "Nearer My God to Thee." The remains were followed to their last resting place in Alhambra Cemetery by many friends of the family under the guidance of Undertaker Henry J. Curry. The pall-bearers were J. C. Hinrichsen, Manuel Venegas, John Lucas, Wm. Jones, James Daley and F. W. Bryant. The "Gazette" joins with community in extending sympathy to the relatives in this hour of their bereavement.

The *Contra Costa Gazette* newspaper, November 14, 1908 published this obituary for James Bryant, husband of Margaret (Bennett) Bryant. James and Margaret (Bennett) Bryant were the parents of Elizabeth Ann, Eva Sitera, and Ida Mary Bryant.

# BRYANT,
## Ida Mary

## PERSONAL INFORMATION:

SEX:                    Female
DATE OF BIRTH:
DATE OF DEATH:          January 16, 1863
PLACE OF DEATH:
AGE AT DEATH:
CAUSE OF DEATH:
BIRTHPLACE:             California
SPOUSE:                 None
PARENTS:                James and Margaret Ann (Bennett) Bryant

## GRAVESITE INFORMATION:

LOCATION OF GRAVESITE:  Unknown
GRAVESTONE:             Missing or never placed
TYPE OF GRAVESTONE:
SHAPE OF GRAVESTONE:
INSCRIPTION:
EPITAPH:
MOTIF:
CARVER:
BASE:
TYPE OF BASE:
ENCLOSURE:
TYPE OF ENCLOSURE:
FENCE:
TYPE OF FENCE:
FENCE MOTIF:

# BRYANT, Ida Mary

**ADDITIONAL PERSONAL INFORMATION:**
Ida Mary's mother, Margaret Bryant (died Nov. 28, 1900), and sister, Eva Sitera (died Oct. 18, 1895), are also believed to be buried in Rose Hill Cemetery. Another sister, Elizabeth Ann (died May 21, 1877), is known to be buried in Rose Hill. A gravestone once existed at her burial site and her burial in Rose Hill was documented by at least four different sources. See Elizabeth Ann Bryant, Eva Sitera Bryant, and Margaret Bryant.

**ADDITIONAL GRAVESITE INFORMATION:**
The names and death dates for Eva Sitera Bryant, Ida Mary Bryant, and Margaret Bryant were provided by former coal field resident Laura (Bryant) Franks, daughter of Eva Sitera Bryant. This is the only source that documents the burial of these individuals in Rose Hill.

**REFERENCES:** 12

THE NORTONVILLE MAIL COMPLAINT.—Frank Pitts, the obliging and popular Coal Mine and Martinez stage driver, feels a little aggrieved by the complaint of the Nortonville mail service, made in last week's publication by a correspondent, and explains that, it is impossible from its situation to drive the stage to the postoffice door there, as the railroad track is between the road and the building, and it would be highly dangerous, as well as contrary to orders, to leave his team while taking the mail back and forth. Consequently, when there is no one at hand to take or give the mail he is obliged to pass without delivering or receiving. We think our correspondent exonerated the driver from all blame in the matter complained of, and that he is personally over sensitive respecting the complaint; but, as he explains the difficulty it would appear that the postoffice is not on the post road, where it is practicable to deliver and receive the mail as the law is presumed to contemplate ; and this is a matter that the residents of Nortonville, the most populous village in the county, should seek to have remedied in some way.

The Bryant family lived in Nortonville when this article appeared in the *Contra Costa Gazette* newspaper, July 4, 1874. The article complaining about the Nortonville mail service can be found on page 80.

# BRYANT,
## Margaret

## PERSONAL INFORMATION:

| | |
|---|---|
| SEX: | Female |
| DATE OF BIRTH: | *Circa* 1838 |
| DATE OF DEATH: | November 28, 1900 |
| PLACE OF DEATH: | Nortonville, Contra Costa County, California |
| AGE AT DEATH: | 62 years |
| CAUSE OF DEATH: | |
| BIRTHPLACE: | England/Wales |
| SPOUSE: | James Bryant |
| PARENTS: | Mr. and Mrs. Bennett |

## GRAVESITE INFORMATION:

| | |
|---|---|
| LOCATION OF GRAVESITE: | Unknown |
| GRAVESTONE: | Missing or never placed |
| TYPE OF GRAVESTONE: | |
| SHAPE OF GRAVESTONE: | |
| INSCRIPTION: | |
| EPITAPH: | |
| MOTIF: | |
| CARVER: | |
| BASE: | |
| TYPE OF BASE: | |
| ENCLOSURE: | |
| TYPE OF ENCLOSURE: | |
| FENCE: | |
| TYPE OF FENCE: | |
| FENCE MOTIF: | |

# BRYANT, Margaret

## ADDITIONAL PERSONAL INFORMATION:

The *1870 Census for Township Three, Contra Costa County, California* lists Margurete [sic], age 36, a native of England. Also listed is her husband, James Bryant, age 46, a native of England and occupation miner; and their four children: Frederick R., age 6; John, age 5; Elizabeth, age 3; and James, age 1. All are natives of California.

The *1876 Contra Costa County Voting Register* indicates that Margaret's husband, James Bryant, was 52 years of age when he registered to vote on August 21, 1875. He was born in England in 1824 and worked as a miner in Nortonville, Contra Costa County, California.

The *1880 Nortonville Precinct Census, Contra Costa County, California*, lists Margaretann [sic], age 47, as a native of England. Also recorded is her husband, James Bryant, age 58, a native of England and a miner; and their children: Fridrick [sic], age 16, a laborer; John, age 14; James, age 11; Charles, age 9; and Eva, age 6. All are natives of California.

The *1890 Great Register of Voters in Contra Costa County, California*, records James Bryant, age 52, as a miner, a native of England, and resident of Nortonville. *The Great Register of Contra Costa County, California, 1894* lists James Bryant as age 69, 5' 7" tall, light complexion with gray eyes and gray hair. He was a native of Great Britain and a miner living in Nortonville. He was naturalized August 21, 1875 in Contra Costa County. James Bryant was listed as residing in Somersville, Contra Costa County, California, in the July 8, *1896 Contra Costa County Voting Register*. The *1898 Great Register*, page 79, lists James Bryant as a miner, age 73, and living in Somersville. He was 5' 7" tall with gray hair and gray eyes.

The *1900 Census for Somersville Precinct* lists James Bryant, age 77, as immigrating to the United States in 1851 and his wife, Margaret A., age 67, immigrating in 1861. Also listed is a son, Lincoln, age 29, a coal miner and native of England, and Laura, a granddaughter, age 5, and native of California. The census states that Margaret is the mother of 7 and that 4 are living at the time the census was taken. The *1900 Index of Voters, Somersville Precinct, Contra Costa County*, lists James Bryant, age 77, as a resident of Somersville. The *1902 Index of Voters, Somersville Precinct, Contra Costa County* lists James Bryant, age 78, as a resident of Nortonville. According to the *Contra Costa Gazette* newspaper, November 14, 1908, James came to Contra Costa County in 1862 and settled in Nortonville, where he engaged in mining. In approximately 1903, he moved to Martinez, Contra Costa County, California where he died November 8, 1908, at the age of 86, and was interred in Alhambra Cemetery. According to *History of Contra Costa County California with Biographical Sketches*:

> James Bryant, a native of England, died in Martinez November 8, 1908, over eighty-six years of age. He came to California via the Horn, being 112 days on the voyage, and came to this county in 1862. He mined in Nortonville, and five years prior to his death he came to Martinez to live.

See Elizabeth Ann, Eva Sitera, and Ida Mary Bryant.

## ADDITIONAL GRAVESITE INFORMATION:

It is believed that Margaret Bryant is buried in Rose Hill Cemetery since she died in Nortonville and her daughter, Elizabeth Ann Bryant, is buried there. Her name was not recorded on any previous cemetery lists and no newspaper has mentioned her burial in the cemetery. It is also believed that in addition to Elizabeth Ann, two other daughters (Ida Mary, died Jan. 16, 1863, and Eva Sitera, died Oct. 18, 1895) are buried in Rose Hill Cemetery as well.

REFERENCES: 8 (Nov. 14, 1908), 9 (Dec. 1, 1900, Jan. 5, 1901), 12, *History of Contra Costa County California with Biographical Sketches*, Historic Record Company, Los Angeles, CA, 1926, page 214, see newspaper appendix page 684

## PERSONAL INFORMATION:

| | |
|---|---|
| SEX: | Male |
| DATE OF BIRTH: | 1892 |
| DATE OF DEATH: | 1893 |
| PLACE OF DEATH: | Somersville, Contra Costa County, California |
| AGE AT DEATH: | Infant |
| CAUSE OF DEATH: | |
| BIRTHPLACE: | Somersville, Contra Costa County, California |
| SPOUSE: | None |
| PARENTS: | Francis William and Emma Harriet (Parsons) Bussey |

## GRAVESITE INFORMATION:

| | |
|---|---|
| LOCATION OF GRAVESITE: | Unknown |
| GRAVESTONE: | Missing |
| TYPE OF GRAVESTONE: | Marble |
| SHAPE OF GRAVESTONE: | |
| INSCRIPTION: | |
| EPITAPH: | |
| MOTIF: | Lamb |
| CARVER: | |
| BASE: | |
| TYPE OF BASE: | |
| ENCLOSURE: | |
| TYPE OF ENCLOSURE: | |
| FENCE: | Missing |
| TYPE OF FENCE: | Iron |
| FENCE MOTIF: | |

# BUSSEY, Joseph

**ADDITIONAL PERSONAL INFORMATION:**
According to information obtained from descendants, Joseph's father, Francis William Bussey Jr., was born August 12, 1857 or 1858 in Springfield, Sangamon County, Illinois and died December 22, 1920 in Black Diamond, King County, Washington in a mine cave-in. Joseph's mother, Emma Harriett Parsons, was born March 12, 1871 in Nortonville, Contra Costa County, California and died November 4, 1914 in Black Diamond, King County, Washington.

Emma's parents were Emma Henrietta Saddler and Walter Parsons. Emma and Walter married in Martinez, Contra Costa County, California in 1870. Emma Henrietta Saddler Parsons divorced Walter Parsons and married Joseph Fowler Bussey on August 30, 1885. Joseph Fowler Bussey was the brother of Francis William Bussey Jr. (the father of Joseph Bussey buried in Rose Hill Cemetery).

The *1880 Census for Judsonville, Contra Costa County, California* lists Frank Bussey, age 21, born *circa* 1859 in England. He was listed as single and a miner. At the time of the census he was living with: William Berniett, age 24; Mike Glenn, age 28; James Campbell, age 30; and Martin Coughlin, age 29.

The *1890 Great Register of Voters in Contra Costa County, California* records Francis William Bussey as age 27, a native of Illinois, resident of Stewartville and occupation as miner. His date of registration was listed as September 17, 1884.

*The Great Register of Contra Costa County, California, 1894* lists Francis W. Bussey as 33 years and 5 months old, 5 ½ feet tall with fair complexion, blue eyes and auburn hair. He was a miner and native of Illinois living in Stewartville. His date of registration was October 11, 1892.

The *1900 Census for Black Diamond, King County, Washington* lists Frank Bussey, age 42, a native of Illinois and born in August 1857. His occupation is listed as coal miner. Also listed are his wife, Emma, age 29, born March 1871 in California; and children, Alice, age 10; Elsa [sic-Elsie], age 6; Florance [sic-Florence], age 4; and, Leroy, age 2. They had another son George, who was born in Roslyn, Kittitas County, Washington and died there as an infant.

The *1910 Census for Black Diamond, King County, Washington* lists Frank W. Bussey, age 52, as a native of Illinois and born *circa* 1858. His occupation was listed as a miner in a coal mine. Also recorded are: his wife, Emma, age 39, born in California *circa* 1871; and children, Elsa [sic], age 16; Florence, age 14; and Lerow [sic], age 12.

The *1920 Census for Black Diamond, King County, Washington* lists Frank Bussey, age 62 years, a widow, and born in Illinois *circa* 1858. He was living with his daughter Alice (Bussey) Hoag [sic-Haag] and son-in-law Andrew Hoag [sic] and their children, Evelyn, Dorothy, Alice, Ruth, and Clyde.

See Saddler (male) child pages 505 and 506, and Harriet A. Saddler pages 507-510.

**ADDITIONAL GRAVESITE INFORMATION:**
According to a letter received in 2001 from a coal field descendant: Alice Bussey Haag and her sister visited the gravesite of their brother, Joseph Bussey, in the 1950s. Alice Bussey Haag was fours years old when her brother Joseph died. "She [Alice (Bussey) Haag] said she remembered the funeral and that his grave would have an iron fence and a little lamb on his headstone." At the time of their visit nothing was left at the gravesite.

**REFERENCES: 12**

Reference 352.2

Francis William Bussey Jr. (left) and Emma Harriet (Parsons) Bussey, parents of Joseph Bussey. Emma was the daughter of Emma Henrietta (Saddler) Parsons and Walter Parsons. Both mother and daughter married into the Bussey family. Their spouses were brothers to one another. This photograph may possibly be their wedding portrait.

Francis William Bussey Jr. married Emma Harriett Parsons on March 21, 1887 in San Francisco, California. Emma was at least 13 years younger than her husband. They had six children. In addition to Joseph they were: George, born 1887 or 1878, in Roslyn, WA; Alice Maude, born July 8, 1889, in Somersville, CA; Elsie, born April 24, 1894, in Black Diamond, WA; Florence, born 1896, in Black Diamond, WA; and Leroy Frank, born November 18, 1898, in Black Diamond, WA.

Pictured are members of the Bussey and Parsons families. On the far left is Alice Maud (Evans) Tamblyn. Alice's parents were Harriet "Hattie" Louise (Saddler) Evans and David R. Evans. Alice's mother was sister to Emma H. (Saddler) Parsons Bussey. Also pictured are, Emma H. (Saddler) Parsons Bussey (second from right) and her two sons, Wilbert (Bert) A. Parsons (left), and George Walter Parsons (right, wearing a hat). The young girl is Maybelle Bussey, daughter of Francis and Emma H. (Parsons) Bussey and stepsister to Wilbert and George Parsons.

Picnic group at Stewart Grove, Stewartville, no date. Pictured are top row, left to right: 1 George Parsons; 2 Mary Ellen Cooper/Cowper; 3 Maybelle Bussey; 4 Anne Powell; 5 Jonathan (John) Cooper/Cowper (kneeling with dog). Bottom row, left to right: 1 Bess Singlewood; 2 Doc the dog; 3 Della Meehan; 4 Alex Riddock; 5 H. or Dilly Andrews.

# BUXTON,
## Alfred W.

## PERSONAL INFORMATION:

| | |
|---|---|
| SEX: | Male |
| DATE OF BIRTH: | January 17, 1870 |
| DATE OF DEATH: | September 25, 1878 |
| PLACE OF DEATH: | |
| AGE AT DEATH: | 8 years, 8 months, 8 days |
| CAUSE OF DEATH: | |
| BIRTHPLACE: | |
| SPOUSE: | None |
| PARENTS: | Wm. T. and Mary Buxton |

## GRAVESITE INFORMATION:

| | |
|---|---|
| LOCATION OF GRAVESITE: | Section N-D, Plot #60 |
| GRAVESTONE: | Exists |
| TYPE OF GRAVESTONE: | Marble |
| SHAPE OF GRAVESTONE: | Tablet |
| INSCRIPTION: | *Our Children/Children of Wm. T. & Mary Buxton* |
| EPITAPH: | *Our sweet little children have gone* |
| | *To mansions above yonder sky,* |
| | *To gaze on the beautiful throne,* |
| | *Of Him who is seated on high.* |
| MOTIF: | Two lambs/ivy |
| CARVER: | |
| BASE: | Exists |
| TYPE OF BASE: | Granite |
| ENCLOSURE: | Exists |
| TYPE OF ENCLOSURE: | Brick with granite cornerstones |
| FENCE: | Exists |
| TYPE OF FENCE: | Iron |
| FENCE MOTIF: | |

# BUXTON, Alfred W.

**ADDITIONAL PERSONAL INFORMATION:**
The *Assessment List, Contra Costa County, for 1872-1873*, page 12, taken on May 16, 1872, lists William T. Buxton as owning a house in Somersville valued at $125.00. Other "solvent debts" are listed as $50, and furniture at $20.

The *1880 Census for Sommersville* [sic] *Precinct, Contra Costa County, California* lists William Buxton, age 33, as a miner and native of England. Also listed are his wife, Mary, age 32, a native of England and their children: Thomas, age 8; Dela, age 4; and, Alfred, age 6 months; all are natives of California. Two of the children listed in the census, Dela and Alfred, are not the same children buried in Rose Hill Cemetery. Lulu and Alfred Buxton, were interred in the cemetery in the 1870s, prior to the 1880 census. See Lulu Buxton.

The *1890 Great Register of Voters in Contra Costa County, California*, records William Thomas Buxton, age 33, as a native of England and resident of Somersville. His occupation is listed as clerk. His registration date was August 25, 1875. The register also states that he was naturalized on August 24, 1875 in Contra Costa County.

*The Great Register of Contra Costa County, California, 1894*, page 5, lists William Thomas Buxton, age 50, as 5' 10" tall, with light complexion, gray hair, and gray eyes; a miner and native of England. He resided in Stewartville and was naturalized August 21, 1875 in Contra Costa County.

See Lulu Buxton.

**ADDITIONAL GRAVESITE INFORMATION:**
Alfred shares a gravestone with sister, Lulu Buxton, and shares the gravesite with J. B. (John B.) Jones and Thomas J. Davis. The original iron fence stands around this gravesite. The gravestone is broken into three pieces and was concreted to the ground prior to East Bay Regional Park District acquistion. A small piece of the bottom right side of the gravestone sits in the granite base.

A photograph of the gravesite appears in *Contra Costa Living* (a supplement of the *Contra Costa Sunday Times* newspaper - April 11, 1971, page 9). See John B. Jones and Thomas J. Davis.

**REFERENCES:** 1, 2, 3, 4, 6, 11 (P610.31.123, P610.31.138, P610.146.2, and P610.153.11), 12, 14

Lulu and Alfred W. Buxton gravestone, *circa* 1958.

The coal mining community of Stewartville, looking west, June 9, 1896.
William Thomas Buxton (Thomas Buxton), father of Alfred W. and Lulu Buxton,
was listed as residing here in 1894.

# BUXTON,
## Lulu

**PERSONAL INFORMATION:**

| | |
|---|---|
| SEX: | Female |
| DATE OF BIRTH: | September 27, 1873 |
| DATE OF DEATH: | December 15, 1874 |
| PLACE OF DEATH: | |
| AGE AT DEATH: | 1 year, 2 months, 18 days |
| CAUSE OF DEATH: | |
| BIRTHPLACE: | California |
| SPOUSE: | None |
| PARENTS: | Wm. T. and Mary Buxton |

**GRAVESITE INFORMATION:**

| | |
|---|---|
| LOCATION OF GRAVESITE: | Section N-D, Plot #60 |
| GRAVESTONE: | Exists |
| TYPE OF GRAVESTONE: | Marble |
| SHAPE OF GRAVESTONE: | Tablet |
| INSCRIPTION: | *Our Children/Children of Wm. T. & Mary Buxton* |
| EPITAPH: | *Our sweet little children have gone* |
| | *To mansions above yonder sky,* |
| | *To gaze on the beautiful throne,* |
| | *of Him who is seated on high.* |
| MOTIF: | Two lambs/ivy |
| CARVER: | |
| BASE: | Exists |
| TYPE OF BASE: | Granite |
| ENCLOSURE: | Exists |
| TYPE OF ENCLOSURE: | Brick with granite cornerstones |
| FENCE: | Exists |
| TYPE OF FENCE: | Iron |
| FENCE MOTIF: | |

# BUXTON, Lulu

**ADDITIONAL PERSONAL INFORMATION:**
Lulu's date of birth was calculated by www.timeanddate.com, based on her date of death and age at death listed on her gravestone. See Alfred W. Buxton.

**ADDITIONAL GRAVESITE INFORMATION:**
Lulu shares a gravestone with her brother, Alfred W. Buxton, and shares the gravesite with J. B. (John B.) Jones and Thomas J. Davis. The original iron fence stands around this gravesite. The gravestone is broken into three pieces. A small piece of gravestone from the bottom right side sits in the granite base. See J. B. (John B.) Jones and Thomas J. Davis.

**REFERENCES:** 1, 2, 3, 4, 6, 11 (P610.31.123, P610.31.138, P610.146.2, and P610.153.11), 12, 14

Reference 358.1

The vandalized gravestone of Lulu and her brother, Alfred Buxton, sits within the iron fence (foreground) in Rose Hill Cemetery in March 1972. The gravestone sitting within the right-hand-side of the iron fence marks the burial location for J. B. (John B.) Jones and Thomas J. Davis. This view, showing the cyclone fence surrounding the cemetery, looks southeast toward Somersville town site. Photograph by Ray Sullivan.

# BUXTON,
## Maggie

**PERSONAL INFORMATION:**

| | |
|---|---|
| SEX: | Female |
| DATE OF BIRTH: | July 25, 1850 |
| DATE OF DEATH: | October 22, 1890 |
| PLACE OF DEATH: | Stewartville, Contra Costa County, California |
| AGE AT DEATH: | 40 years, 2 months, 27 days |
| CAUSE OF DEATH: | Confinement (childbirth) |
| BIRTHPLACE: | Pennsylvania |
| SPOUSE: | George Cooper (1st husband) |
| | William Thomas Buxton (2nd husband) |
| PARENTS: | John and Catherine Jones |

**GRAVESITE INFORMATION:**

| | |
|---|---|
| LOCATION OF GRAVESITE: | Section S-B, Plot #25 |
| GRAVESTONE: | Exists |
| TYPE OF GRAVESTONE: | Marble |
| SHAPE OF GRAVESTONE: | Obelisk |
| INSCRIPTION: | *Erected by her Parents* |
| EPITAPH: | *Two precious ones from us has gone, Two voices we loved are stilled; A place is vacant in our home, Which never can be filled.* |
| MOTIF: | Basket with lilies/ivy |
| CARVER: | |
| BASE: | Exists |
| TYPE OF BASE: | Granite with middle marble base |
| ENCLOSURE: | Exists |
| TYPE OF ENCLOSURE: | Brick |
| FENCE: | Missing |
| TYPE OF FENCE: | Wood and wire mesh |
| FENCE MOTIF: | |

# BUXTON, Maggie

**ADDITIONAL PERSONAL INFORMATION:**
Maggie's birth date was calculated by www. timeanddate.com, using her date of death and age at death listed on the gravestone. Margaret Cowper [sic], age 36, of Nortonville, Contra Costa County, California, and William T. Buxton, age 44, of Stewartville, Contra Costa County, California, applied for a marriage license *circa* May 1886. Margaret's father's name is listed as John A. Jones on the marriage application record. The information was recorded in *Applications for Marriage Licenses, Contra Costa County, 1873-1887*, page 417, located at the Contra Costa County Historical Society History Center in Martinez, California. Margaret Cooper (Cowper), a widow, married William Thomas Buxton, in San Francisco, California on May 17, 1886. Witnesses were: Benjamin Jones, Lizzie D. Jones, Wm. N. Jones, and Catherine Jones. Information obtained from the *Index to Marriage Certificates*, Contra Costa County Hall of Records, Martinez, California states that Margaret Cowper [sic] married William T. Buxton on May 19, 1886. They were married by Rev. David Hughes and the information is recorded in Volume 3, page 264. A William T. Buxton was married to Mary Buxton and their two children (Lulu and Alfred) are buried in Rose Hill Cemetery. Mary Buxton may have been William's first wife. Lulu and Alfred Buxton died before William married Maggie Buxton. Thomas H. Buxton, who may be the son of William T. Buxton, is also buried in Rose Hill Cemetery. In the document *Trip of Louis Stein and D. F. Myrick to Stewartville, June 24, 1967*, located in the Black Diamond archives, it states:

> W. T. Buxton, owned his own house and that used by Cowper (pronounced Cooper), both in Stewartville. He married Mrs. Cowper, a widow. Son is Thomas H. Buxton.

According to the *Contra Costa County, California Registers of Death*, Maggie died October 21, 1889, at age 40 years, 2 months, and 26 days. She was a native of Pennsylvania and resident of Somersville. Her cause of death was confinement (childbirth) and her doctors were Dewitt and Rattan. *The Great Register of Contra Costa County, California, 1894*, page 5, lists William Thomas Buxton, age 50, as 5' 10" tall, light complexion, gray eyes and gray hair, a miner living in Stewartsville [sic]. He was a native of England and naturalized August 21, 1875 in Contra Costa County. The *Index of Voters, Somersville Precinct, Contra Costa County for 1900*, lists William T. Buxton, age 60, as a resident of Stewartsville [sic]. See George Cooper and Thomas Buxton.

**ADDITIONAL GRAVESITE INFORMATION:**
Maggie Buxton shares a gravestone and gravesite with her first husband, George Cooper. Maggie's gravestone inscription faces west; George Cooper's faces east. The basket of lilies motif appears on the north and east sides. A single lily appears with the epitaph. The gravestone ornamentation (finial) from the top of the stone is missing.

Two marble footstones inscribed with the initials "G. C." and "M. B." exist at the site, but are broken and were concreted flat to the ground prior to Park District acquisition. This marble obelisk sits on a middle marble base. The middle base contains an ivy motif. The gravestone and middle base sit on a granite base. A brick enclosure surrounds the gravesite. The brick work was done prior to East Bay Regional Park District acquisition and after the coal mining days. See George Cooper, Alfred W. Buxton, Lulu Buxton, and Thomas H. Buxton.

**REFERENCES:** 2, 3, 4 , 6, 7, 8 (Oct. 29, 1890 – two articles, July 26, 1884), 9 (Oct. 25, 1890), 11 (P610.31.188, P610.31.189, P610.145.1, and P610.168.25), 12 (Parsons and Buxton), 14, *Pittsburg Post Dispatch* newspaper (Wednesday, June 15, 1955, page 12), *Trip of Louis Stein and D. F. Myrick to Stewartville [sic], June 24, 1967 accompanied by Mrs. James Parsons and her daughter, Mrs. Gibbel*, page 4, see newspaper appendix page 685

Stewartville, Contra Costa County, California, *circa* 1885. An Empire Railroad car sits on the track next to the general store, the second building from left. Stewartville also had a saloon (center) and a meeting hall (right). Maggie Buxton's husband, William T. Buxton, lived in Stewartville prior to their marriage and again after Maggie's death.

Singlewood Hotel, Stewartville, June 9, 1896. Among those pictured are members of the McFadden Brown, Waters, Griffiths, Rodda, and Singlewood families.

## PERSONAL INFORMATION:

SEX:          Male

DATE OF BIRTH:

DATE OF DEATH:

PLACE OF DEATH:

AGE AT DEATH:

CAUSE OF DEATH:

BIRTHPLACE:

SPOUSE:

PARENTS:

## GRAVESITE INFORMATION:

LOCATION OF GRAVESITE:     Unknown

GRAVESTONE:     Missing

TYPE OF GRAVESTONE:

SHAPE OF GRAVESTONE:

INSCRIPTION:

EPITAPH:

MOTIF:

CARVER:

BASE:

TYPE OF BASE:

ENCLOSURE:

TYPE OF ENCLOSURE:

FENCE:

TYPE OF FENCE:

FENCE MOTIF:

# BUXTON, Thomas

**ADDITIONAL PERSONAL INFORMATION:**
Thomas Buxton may have been an adult. Unfortunately the one source that references him lists his name only.

In the oral history *Interview with Lottie Ramirez*, July 26, 1979 with Karana Hattersley-Drayton, pages 27 and 28, former coal field resident, Lottie Ramirez, discusses Mr. Buxton:

> ...Mr. Buxton would be ready at nine o'clock, everybody, or eight o'clock whatever, and they'd go to Mr. Buxton's house where his body was laid out, or was in the casket and his body was laid out....All I remember is Mr. Buxton, and he was buried in Stewartsville [sic]. And he's in the middle of the cemetary [sic] up there where those trees are. Where those tall pine trees are?...And he had a little wire fence around, he did have, I don't know whether he still has or not, I don't know what that grave looked like after I went up there and seen it was such a mess.

**ADDITIONAL GRAVESITE INFORMATION:**
The gravesite for Thomas Buxton was documented only in 1935 (source 3 used for this document; see page 1004). No other source records his burial.

See Maggie Buxton.

**REFERENCES:** 3, 12, *Trip of Louis Stein and D. F. Myrick to Stewartsville [sic], June 24, 1967 accompanied by Mrs. James Parsons and her daughter, Mrs. Gibbel*, page 4- see Maggie Buxton; *Interview with Lottie Ramirez* by Karana Hattersley-Drayton, July 26, 1979

# CAIN,
## Elizabeth O.

**PERSONAL INFORMATION:**

| | |
|---|---|
| SEX: | Female |
| DATE OF BIRTH: | March 4, 1834 |
| DATE OF DEATH: | October 27, 1881 |
| PLACE OF DEATH: | |
| AGE AT DEATH: | 47 years, 7 months, 23 days |
| CAUSE OF DEATH | |
| BIRTHPLACE: | Edinburgh, Scotland |
| SPOUSE: | James Cain |
| PARENTS: | Mr. and Mrs. Gavin |

**GRAVESITE INFORMATION:**

| | |
|---|---|
| LOCATION OF GRAVESITE: | Section N-A, Plot #2 |
| GRAVESTONE: | Exists   (Partial – in storage) |
| TYPE OF GRAVESTONE: | Marble |
| SHAPE OF GRAVESTONE: | Tablet |
| INSCRIPTION: | *Wife of/Native of Scotland* |
| EPITAPH: | *Dear Mother we miss thee.* |
| MOTIF: | Flowers |
| CARVER: | |
| BASE: | Exists |
| TYPE OF BASE: | Granite with middle marble base |
| ENCLOSURE: | Exists |
| TYPE OF ENCLOSURE: | Brick |
| FENCE: | |
| TYPE OF FENCE: | |
| FENCE MOTIF: | |

# CAIN, Elizabeth O.

**ADDITIONAL PERSONAL INFORMATION:**
According to a descendant, the Cain family arrived in the United States before the Civil War and settled in Missouri where they became farmers. While in Missouri, a daughter, Mary, died and three more children (Peter G., Sarah Elizabeth, and James H.) were born. Another child, Marion J., was born in Illinois.

James, Elizabeth, and daughter, Marion Cain, traveled from Missouri to California *circa* 1874 or 1875 via train. They settled in Nortonville, Contra Costa County, California, where James worked as a saloon keeper. Soon after arriving in Nortonville they sent for their other children to join them. Their son, John, sold all the family belongings to buy train tickets and a sack of flour. The flour was their source of food while traveling on the train. The train passengers were all male and one day during their journey Sarah Cain, their daughter, cooked for the men and boys after one of the men shot a rabbit. The ten-day train trip terminated in Martinez, Contra Costa County, California where their parents met them and took them to Nortonville.

After the death of his wife, Elizabeth, James Cain married Christina Leishman Ward. Christina was widowed and had a young son. It is believed that Christina's first husband died in a mining accident in Nortonville. James and Christina Cain moved to Nanaimo, British Columbia, Canada sometime before 1891.

Census records for Canada (*1891 Census for Mountain, Vancouver, British Columbia* and *1901 Census for Nanaimo (South/Sud), Vancouver, British Columbia*) list James Cain, his wife, Christina, and their children: John L., Margaret B., Christina L., and Robert L. Cain. In the 1901 census, it states that James' date of birth was June 22, 1827, his year of immigration as 1887, and his occupation as coal miner.

The *British Columbia Death Index: 1872 to 1979*, obtained from www.ancestry.com, states that James Cain died on December 31, 1914 at age 85. He is buried in the coal mining area of Nanaimo, British Columbia, Canada.

Information obtained from "Biography in Miniature," an article regarding Marion Cain Malpass (daughter of Elizabeth Cain) that appeared in a newspaper [name and date of paper unknown]; Elizabeth's husband was born in Ireland and traveled with his parents [Bernard and Sarah (Brown) Cain] to Scotland when he was young. A few years after the birth of their children John and Mary, the James Cain family moved from Scotland to the United States, settling in Lexington, Lafayette County, Missouri. The article notes that later they settled in Somersville [the family states they settled in Nortonville], Contra Costa County, California.

Elizabeth's grandson, Percival Sidney Malpass, is also buried in Rose Hill Cemetery. See Percival Sidney Malpass.

**ADDITIONAL GRAVESITE INFORMATION:**
Zelma Myrick, who recorded information in a notebook in the 1930s during a visit to Rose Hill Cemetery, reported that the gravestone "Has six rifle shot marks otherwise in good condition." The bottom portion of the gravestone is in storage. The top half of the stone is missing. A marble footstone with the initials "E. O. C." once existed at the site. The gravestone was present in 1963 because it appears in a student term paper by Jim Rotelli. The brick wall enclosure was rebuilt in March 1988 by the East Bay Regional Park District.

**REFERENCES:** 1, 3, 4, 6, 11 (P610.117.16, P610.146.3, P610.294.8, and P610.345.1 to P610.345.5), 12, 14

Reference 345.1

Reference 345.2

Left, Elizabeth (Gavin) Cain with daughter (probably Sarah Elizabeth Cain, born 1861) and husband James Cain on right. According to a descendant, Elizabeth was born in Edinburgh, Scotland. Her husband, James Cain, was born June 21, 1829 in Derry/Londonderry, Ireland. Elizabeth Gavin married James Cain on December 30, 1853 in Glasgow, Scotland.

During the Civil War, James Cain was forced to join the Union Army when troops invaded Missouri. He was allowed to return home to harvest his crops; however upon returning to his residence he deserted the army.

James and Elizabeth (Gavin) Cain had at least six children:

- Mary, born Feb. 1, 1856, Rutherglen, Lanarkshire, Scotland; died *circa* 1861, Missouri
- John Gavin, born Feb. 26, 1859, Scotland; died March 24, 1943
- Peter G., born Jan. 25, 1860, Lexington, Lafayette County, Missouri; died May 28, 1931, Menlo Park, San Mateo County, CA
- Sarah Elizabeth, born April or May 5, 1861, Lexington, Missouri; died Aug. 1, 1946, Menlo Park, CA
- James H., born Nov. 11 or 22, 1862, Lexington, Missouri; died Jan. 22, 1940, Menlo Park, CA
- Marion J., born Sept. 10, 1864, Scott County, Illinois; died Dec. 12 or 18, 1948, Menlo Park, CA

Elizabeth O. Cain gravesite *circa* 1958.

All that remains of the Elizabeth O. Cain gravestone, June 1983. Photograph by Roger Epperson, EBRPD.

Elizabeth O. Cain gravestone standing upright in the distance in the northwest corner of Rose Hill Cemetery, *circa* 1950s.

## PERSONAL INFORMATION:

| | |
|---|---|
| SEX: | Male |
| DATE OF BIRTH: | February 7, 1875 |
| DATE OF DEATH: | May 4, 1883 |
| PLACE OF DEATH: | New York Landing, Contra Costa County, California |
| AGE AT DEATH: | 8 years, 2 months, 27 days |
| CAUSE OF DEATH: | Kicked in the head by a horse |
| BIRTHPLACE: | California |
| SPOUSE: | None |
| PARENTS: | Robert M. and Cecelia Clare |

## GRAVESITE INFORMATION:

| | |
|---|---|
| LOCATION OF GRAVESITE: | Section N-B, Plot #112 |
| GRAVESTONE: | Exists (partial – in storage) |
| TYPE OF GRAVESTONE: | Marble |
| SHAPE OF GRAVESTONE: | Tablet |
| INSCRIPTION: | *Son of* |
| EPITAPH: | *Open wide are the pearly gates* |
| | *That lead to the shining shore* |
| | *Our Walter suffered in passing through* |
| | *But his sufferings now are o'er.* |
| MOTIF: | Drapery |
| CARVER: | |
| BASE: | Exists (two of three bases) |
| TYPE OF BASE: | Sandstone with two middle marble bases |
| ENCLOSURE: | |
| TYPE OF ENCLOSURE: | |
| FENCE: | |
| TYPE OF FENCE: | |
| FENCE MOTIF: | |

# CLARE, Walter E.

**ADDITIONAL PERSONAL INFORMATION:**
According to the *History of Contra Costa County* by Slocum & Company, 1882, page 475, Walter's father, Robert Clare, was a charter member of Black Diamond Lodge, No. 29, Knights of Pythias, Nortonville, Contra Costa County, California, which organized October 24, 1874. Robert Maphfit Clare is listed as holding the office of Marshal for the Contra Costa Masonic Lodge No. 227 in Somersville in 1882.

The *1880 Census for the New York Landing, Contra Costa County, California* precinct lists Robert Clair [sic], age 42, as a native of Pennsylvania and a macheinest [sic]. Also listed are his wife Cecelia, age 37, a native of Pennsylvania; and their five children, Porter, age 16, a farmer; and Madaline, age 13, both natives of Pennsylvania; and Walter, age 5; Robert, age 2; and an infant daughter, age 1 month; all natives of California. Living with them is Frank Kinney, age 40, a native of Ireland and a laborer.

Mrs. R. M. Clara [sic] is listed in the records of the New York Congregational Church from 1883. She was removed from the church congregation on March 6, 1892. Manner of removal was a "letter of dismissal." On June 10, 1883 "Mr. R. M. Clare - whose name was presented last Sabbath - assented to Confession of Faith and Covenant and was duly declared a member of the church." On December 16, 1883 Brother R. M. Clare was nominated and duly elected a Trustee of the church.

Walter's place of death comes from the *Contra Costa Gazette* newspaper, May 26, 1883.

**ADDITIONAL GRAVESITE INFORMATION:**
Zelma Myrick, who recorded information in a notebook in the 1930s during a visit to Rose Hill Cemetery, reported the gravestone "separated and down."

Originally there were at least four pieces to Walter's gravestone: a bottom sandstone base that held two middle marble bases, each containing two lines of the epitaph. The sandstone base and one of the marble bases is missing. The other marble base is in storage.

In May 2002 most of Walter's gravestone was recovered from a home in Walnut Creek, Contra Costa County, California and returned to the East Bay Regional Park District. The gravestone was unearthed by workers using a backhoe to replace a sewer line.

In August 2001, while Rangers were removing Elias Havard's gravestone from Rose Hill Cemetery for repair, a broken footstone with the initials W. E. C. was found under Elias' gravestone. Walter E. Clare is the only individual interred in the cemetery with these initials. A photograph (the same photograph shown on page 110 of this document) of the backside of the gravestone appears in the book *Old Times in Contra Costa* by Robert Damas Tatam, page 66, Highland Publisher, Pittsburg, CA, 1993.

REFERENCES: 1, 2, 3, 4, 6, 8 (May 26, 1883), 10 (page 474), 11 (P610.98.20 and P610.294.1), 12, *Ledger Dispatch* newspaper (June 5, 2002, p.5), *Contra Costa County Historical Society Bulletin*, June/July 2002

Reference 98.20

The Walter E. Clare gravesite in 1962. Photograph by Madison Devlin.

The Community Presbyterian Church in Pittsburg, Contra Costa County, California, the descendant congregation from the Nortonville church, located church records dating to 1882. In these church records, an entry was made in reference to Walter E. Clare. The reference dated May 6, 1883 stated:

Today a dark, stormy and dreary day we assembled to pay our last respects to the memory of little Walter Clare, who died May 4th from injuries received April 28th. The little fellow was kicked in the head by a horse and lay in an unconscious state until he died. God grant the terrible blow may be given in kindness, and that good results will follow this awful warning. Mr. Fitch conducted the funeral exercises which were quite impressive. Notwithstanding the terrible state of the weather a large number followed the remains to its final resting place.

C. P. Lyndall, Clerk

Walter E. Clare gravestone sitting on a sandstone base and two marble middle bases, center front, Rose Hill Cemetery, *circa* 1954.

## PERSONAL INFORMATION:

| | |
|---|---|
| SEX: | Female |
| DATE OF BIRTH: | March 17, 1834 |
| DATE OF DEATH: | February 13, 1875 |
| PLACE OF DEATH: | Somersville, Contra Costa County, California |
| AGE AT DEATH: | 40 years, 10 months, 17 days |
| CAUSE OF DEATH: | |
| BIRTHPLACE: | South Wales |
| SPOUSE: | William H. Clement |
| PARENTS: | |

## GRAVESITE INFORMATION:

| | |
|---|---|
| LOCATION OF GRAVESITE: | Section S-F, Plot #100 |
| GRAVESTONE: | Exists |
| TYPE OF GRAVESTONE: | Marble |
| SHAPE OF GRAVESTONE: | Obelisk |
| INSCRIPTION: | *In Memory of /Our Father and Mother.* |
| | Marble base says *Clement* |
| EPITAPH: | *Where immortal spirits* |
| | *reign we shall meet again.* |
| MOTIF: | Independent Order of Odd Fellows/basket with Lilies/lily |
| CARVER: | |
| BASE: | Exists |
| TYPE OF BASE: | Granite with middle marble base |
| ENCLOSURE: | Exists |
| TYPE OF ENCLOSURE: | Sandstone |
| FENCE: | |
| TYPE OF FENCE: | |
| FENCE MOTIF: | |

# CLEMENT, Ann

**ADDITIONAL PERSONAL INFORMATION:**
The birth and death dates and age at death are listed on the gravestone. However based on the information obtained from www.timeanddate. com, Ann's age at death is calculated as 40 years, 10 months, and 27 days and not 17 days as listed on the gravestone.

The obituary in the *Contra Costa Gazette* newspaper, February 20, 1875, lists her age at death as 41 years. See William H. Clement.

**ADDITIONAL GRAVESITE INFORMATION:**
Ann shares a gravestone with her husband, William H. Clement. Ann's gravestone inscription faces east and William's faces west. The epitaph and inscription "In Memory of" and "Our Father and Mother." appear on the north side. A single lily with leaves appears on this side as well. The east, west, and south sides of the gravestone have a motif of a basket with lilies. Additionally the west side also contains an Independent Order of Odd Fellows motif.

The gravestone sits on a middle marble base. The marble base contains an ivy motif. A large granite base supports the middle base and cracked gravestone. All pieces were concreted together prior to East Bay Regional Park District acquisition.

The bottom half of a marble tablet stone (see "unknown adult" on pages 589 and 590) once rested on the south side of the Clement gravesite. The top half of the stone that once contained the name of the person interred is missing. The remaining bottom piece was put in storage for safekeeping. The individual buried here was 42 years old. They also died on February 13, 1875, the same day as Ann. This may be the stone for another individual interred in Rose Hill Cemetery or perhaps it is the original stone for Ann Clement. The date of death is the same and the age at death very similar to Ann Clement.

A photograph of the Clement gravestone appears in the *California Monthly* magazine, "Back Yard Ghost Towns," May 1949, page 23.

**REFERENCES:** 1, 2, 3, 6, 8 (Feb. 20, 1875), 11 (P610.31.135, P610.31.212, and P610.31.213), 12, 14

## DIED.

WELLS——In Moraga Valley, Feb. 4th, Ellen, infant daughter of Howard and Olive Wells, aged 1 year, 3 months and 9 days.

JONES——In Nortonville, Feb. 6th, Lewis, son of Austin and Cella Jones, aged 5 months and 6 days.

CLEMENTS——In Somersville, Feb. 13th, Ann, wife of W. Clements, aged 41 years.

From the *Contra Costa Gazette* newspaper, February 20, 1875.
Ann is the third listing in the obituary. Her name is incorrectly spelled as "Clements."

# CLEMENT,
## William H.

## PERSONAL INFORMATION:

|                    |                                               |
|--------------------|-----------------------------------------------|
| SEX:               | Male                                          |
| DATE OF BIRTH:     | July 24, 1825                                 |
| DATE OF DEATH:     | February 29, 1892                             |
| PLACE OF DEATH:    | Somersville, Contra Costa County, California  |
| AGE AT DEATH:      | 66 years, 7 months, 5 days                    |
| CAUSE OF DEATH:    | Killed by falling tree                        |
| BIRTHPLACE:        | South Wales                                   |
| SPOUSE:            | Ann Clement                                   |
| PARENTS:           |                                               |

## GRAVESITE INFORMATION:

|                       |                                                          |
|-----------------------|----------------------------------------------------------|
| LOCATION OF GRAVESITE:| Section S-F, Plot #100                                   |
| GRAVESTONE:           | Exists                                                    |
| TYPE OF GRAVESTONE:   | Marble                                                   |
| SHAPE OF GRAVESTONE:  | Obelisk                                                  |
| INSCRIPTION:          | *In Memory of/Our Father and Mother.*                   |
|                       | Marble base says *Clement*                               |
| EPITAPH:              | *Where immortal spirits*                                 |
|                       | *reign we shall meet again.*                            |
| MOTIF:                | Independent Order of Odd Fellows/basket with Lilies/lily |
| CARVER:               |                                                          |
| BASE:                 | Exists                                                   |
| TYPE OF BASE:         | Granite with middle marble base                          |
| ENCLOSURE:            | Exists                                                   |
| TYPE OF ENCLOSURE:    | Sandstone                                                |
| FENCE:                |                                                          |
| TYPE OF FENCE:        |                                                          |
| FENCE MOTIF:          |                                                          |

# CLEMENT, William H.

**ADDITIONAL PERSONAL INFORMATION:**
The County Hall of Records in Martinez, Contra Costa County, California, lists William Clement as a native of Wales, and age at death as 64 years, and not 66 years as recorded on his gravestone. He was a resident of Somersville and his cause of death was listed as "accident."

William's name appears on the *1876 Contra Costa County Voting Register*. On May 1, 1874 when William registered to vote, he was listed as a native of England, age 48, and a miner in Somersville. He was a member of Mount Diablo Lodge No. 128, Independent Order of Odd Fellows (I.O.O.F) in Somersville.

The *1880 Census for Sommersville* [sic], *Contra Costa County, California* lists William Clement, widowed, age 54, birthplace Wales. Also listed are his three children: Sarahann, housekeeper, age 17; William, age 13, and David, age 11; all natives of California.

**ADDITIONAL GRAVESITE INFORMATION:**
William Clement shares a gravestone with his wife, Ann Clement. See Ann Clement.

**REFERENCES:** 1, 2, 3, 6, 7, 9 (June 2, 1894, March 5, 1892, and March 12, 1892), 11 (P610.31.135, P610.31.212, and P610.31.213), 12, 14, *Oral History with George Vivian*, May 1978, see newpaper appendix page 686

## Fatal Accident.

Wm. Clement, an old resident of Somersville, aged about 60 years, met with a tragic death one day last week. He was out on a side hill chopping wood. He had felled a tree on the side hill and was engaged in chopping away a limb on the lower side of the hill, when the trunk of the tree suddenly rolled over and pinned him to the earth, killing him instantly. It took several men a couple of hours to dig the body from the position in which it had been pinned. The coroner was summoned and held an inquest and a verdict was returned in accordance with the above facts. The decedent was a pioneer resident of Somersville and a highly respected citizen.

This newspaper article from the *Antioch Ledger*, March 5, 1892, discusses the accident that killed William Clement.

## PERSONAL INFORMATION:

| | |
|---|---|
| SEX: | Male |
| DATE OF BIRTH: | February 1, 1877 |
| DATE OF DEATH: | November 4, 1877 |
| PLACE OF DEATH: | |
| AGE AT DEATH: | 9 months, 3 days |
| CAUSE OF DEATH: | |
| BIRTHPLACE: | |
| SPOUSE: | None |
| PARENTS: | Robert B. and Mary J. Conner |

## GRAVESITE INFORMATION:

| | |
|---|---|
| LOCATION OF GRAVESITE: | Unknown |
| GRAVESTONE: | Missing |
| TYPE OF GRAVESTONE: | Marble |
| SHAPE OF GRAVESTONE: | Block |
| INSCRIPTION: | *Son of* |
| EPITAPH: | |
| MOTIF: | |
| CARVER: | |
| BASE: | |
| TYPE OF BASE: | |
| ENCLOSURE: | |
| TYPE OF ENCLOSURE: | |
| FENCE: | Missing |
| TYPE OF FENCE: | Iron |
| FENCE MOTIF: | Shells |

# CONNER, John T.

**ADDITIONAL PERSONAL INFORMATION:**
In the *1880 Nortonville Precinct Census, Contra Costa County, California*, Robert Conner, a native of Scotland, age 29, is listed as an engineer. Also recorded are his wife, Mary, a native of Ohio, age 27, and their children: Margretta, age 5; and Albert, age 1; both natives of California. This may possibly be John Conner's family.

**ADDITIONAL GRAVESITE INFORMATION:**
John T. Conner's gravestone was missing from Rose Hill Cemetery prior to East Bay Regional Park District acquisition. The gravestone was present in 1963 because it is listed in a student term paper compiled by Jim Rotelli. This gravestone may have once stood within the iron fence at Catherine Edwards' gravesite. It is unknown as to why it was placed at this site.

Zelma Myrick, who recorded information in a notebook in the 1930s during a visit to Rose Hill Cemetery, reported the gravestone in "good condition."

**REFERENCES:** 1, 2, 3, 4, 6, 11 (P610.129.1), 12

Reference 129.1

John T. Conner's gravestone sits within what is believed to be Catherine Edwards' gravesite iron fence enclosure, *circa* 1960s.

# COOPER,
## George

**PERSONAL INFORMATION:**

| | |
|---|---|
| SEX: | Male |
| DATE OF BIRTH: | 1844 |
| DATE OF DEATH: | November 9, 1884 |
| PLACE OF DEATH: | |
| CAUSE OF DEATH: | |
| AGE AT DEATH: | 40 years |
| BIRTHPLACE: | England or Pennsylvania |
| SPOUSE: | Margaret "Maggie" (Jones) Cooper |
| PARENTS: | |

**GRAVESITE INFORMATION:**

| | |
|---|---|
| LOCATION OF GRAVESITE: | Section S-B, Plot #25 |
| GRAVESTONE: | Exists |
| TYPE OF GRAVESTONE: | Marble |
| SHAPE OF GRAVESTONE: | Obelisk |
| INSCRIPTION: | |
| EPITAPH: | *Two precious ones from us has gone,* *Two voices we loved are stilled;* *A place is vacant in our home,* *Which never can be filled.* |
| MOTIF: | Basket with lilies/ivy |
| CARVER: | |
| BASE: | Exists |
| TYPE OF BASE: | Granite with middle marble base |
| ENCLOSURE: | Exists |
| TYPE OF ENCLOSURE: | Brick |
| FENCE: | Missing |
| TYPE OF FENCE: | Wood and wire mesh |
| FENCE MOTIF: | |

# COOPER, George

**ADDITIONAL PERSONAL INFORMATION:**
The *1876 Contra Costa County Voting Register* lists George Cowper [sic], age 32, as a native of England and miner living in Nortonville.

The *1880 Census for Nortonville Precinct, Contra Costa County, California* lists George Cooper, age 37, as a native of Pennsylvania, and a miner. Also listed are his wife, Margaret, age 30, a native of California and their children Johnathon [sic], age 7, and Mary, age 2; both natives of California.

George Cooper's parents were from Wales. Margaret's father was from England and her mother from Pennsylvania. On May 17, 1886, four years after the death of her first husband, George, Maggie Cooper married William Thomas Buxton.

**ADDITIONAL GRAVESITE INFORMATION:**
George shares a gravestone with his wife, Maggie Buxton. Maggie Buxton's gravestone inscription faces west; George Cooper's inscription faces east. The epitaph appears on the south side of the gravestone. The motif appears on the north, south, east, and west sides of the stone. The finial (ornamentation on top of the stone) is missing. Marble footstones with inscriptions "G. C." and "M. B." exist at the site but are broken and were concreted flat to the ground prior to East Bay Regional Park District acquisition. This tall marble stone sits on a middle marble base. The middle base contains an ivy motif. The middle base and gravestone sit on a granite base. A brick enclosure surrounds the site. The brick work was done prior to East Bay Regional Park District acquisition and after the coal mining days. See Maggie Buxton.

**REFERENCES:** 1, 2, 3, 4, 11 (P610.31.188, P610.31.189, P610.31.206, P610.145.1, and P160.168.25), 12, 14, *Trip of Louis Stein and D. F. Myrick to Stewartsville [sic], June 24, 1967 accompanied by Mrs. James Parsons and her daughter, Mrs. Gibbel*, page 4

> STILL IMPROVING.—There is not a town in the county improving so rapidly in the addition of new buildings and growth of population as Nortonville. The force of workingmen in the Black Diamond will be doubled during the coming year. The row of business houses opposite the brick store of Morgan, Duncan & Davis, is to be removed, and the proprietors are now erecting new and substantial buildings for their goods, farther down the ravine. Nortonville will shortly be the largest town in the county.

This newspaper article, from the *Antioch Ledger*, September 13, 1873, states that "Nortonville will shortly be the largest town in the county." George Cooper was listed as living in Nortonville in the 1870s and 1880s.

**PERSONAL INFORMATION:**

SEX:                    Male

DATE OF BIRTH:

DATE OF DEATH:

PLACE OF DEATH:

AGE AT DEATH:           Unknown

CAUSE OF DEATH:

BIRTHPLACE:

SPOUSE:

PARENTS:

**GRAVESITE INFORMATION:**

LOCATION OF GRAVESITE:  Unknown

GRAVESTONE:             Missing

TYPE OF GRAVESTONE:

SHAPE OF GRAVESTONE:

INSCRIPTION:

EPITAPH:

MOTIF:

CARVER:

BASE:

TYPE OF BASE:

ENCLOSURE:

TYPE OF ENCLOSURE:

FENCE:

TYPE OF FENCE:

FENCE MOTIF:

# COOPER, John L.

**ADDITIONAL PERSONAL INFORMATION:**
Only John's name was recorded in 1922. No other personal information, such as birth date, death date, place of birth or death was documented.

**ADDITIONAL GRAVESITE INFORMATION:**
A cemetery list compiled in 1922 by John Sullenger (see page 1004) is the only source that records John's burial in Rose Hill Cemetery.

**REFERENCES:** 4, 12

Reference 3.8

Pictured above are Jonathan Cooper (left) and Wilbert (Bert) Parsons (right). Although Jonathan Cooper and John Cooper (interred in Rose Hill) share the same last name and a similar first name, it is not known if the individual pictured above is the same male buried in Rose Hill Cemetery. According to a descendant, the Jonathan Cooper pictured above was the son of Maggie (Jones) and George Cooper. The original spelling of the family name was Cowper. Jonathan left the Mount Diablo Coal Field and traveled to Victoria, British Columbia, Canada in 1899 with his sister, Mary Ellen. Jonathan eventually returned to the United States and is believed to have settled in Vacaville, Solano County, California. His mother, Maggie Cooper Buxton, and father, George Cooper, are buried in Rose Hill Cemetery.

# CROWHURST,
## Elizabeth

## PERSONAL INFORMATION:

| | |
|---|---|
| SEX: | Female |
| DATE OF BIRTH: | 1879 |
| DATE OF DEATH: | 1882 |
| PLACE OF DEATH: | Nortonville/Somersville, Contra Costa County, California |
| AGE AT DEATH: | 3 years |
| CAUSE OF DEATH: | Diphtheria |
| BIRTHPLACE: | Vallejo, Solano County, California |
| SPOUSE: | None |
| PARENTS: | William and Clarissa M. (Brusie) Crowhurst |

## GRAVESITE INFORMATION:

| | |
|---|---|
| LOCATION OF GRAVESITE: | Unknown |
| GRAVESTONE: | Missing or never placed |
| TYPE OF GRAVESTONE: | |
| SHAPE OF GRAVESTONE: | |
| INSCRIPTION: | |
| EPITAPH: | |
| MOTIF: | |
| CARVER: | |
| BASE: | |
| TYPE OF BASE: | |
| ENCLOSURE: | |
| TYPE OF ENCLOSURE: | |
| FENCE: | |
| TYPE OF FENCE: | |
| FENCE MOTIF: | |

# CROWHURST, Elizabeth

**ADDITIONAL PERSONAL INFORMATION:**
The *1870 Census for Vallejo, Solano County, California* lists Wm. Crohurst [sic], age 25, as a teacher and native of England. Also listed is his wife, Clara Crohurst [sic], age 20, a native of New York.

The *Antioch Ledger* newspaper, October 27, 1877 lists Wm. Crowhurst of Somersville, State Deputy Grand Worthy Chief Templar, as delivering a temperance lecture at the Congregational Church. He gave a condensed history of what has been accomplished in the temperance work by the Order of Good Templars.

The *1880 Census for Modesto, Stanislaus County, California* lists W. Crowhurst, age 35, as a schoolteacher and native of England. Also listed are his wife, Clara, age 30, a native of New York; and their children, Clara, age 9; Etta, age 7; William, age 4; E. (probably Elizabeth or Elmer), age 1; all natives of California. Listed with them is Alice M. Wiley, age 21, a schoolteacher and native of Kansas.

The *1900 Census for Oakland Ward, Alameda County, California* lists William Crowhurst, age 55, as a native of England. Also listed are his wife, Clara, age 50, a native of New York; and their children, George, age 16; James, age 14; Elmor [sic], age 10; all natives of California.

The *1910 Census for Seattle Ward 2, King County, Washington* lists William Crowhurst, age 63, as a native of England; his occupation was listed as "organize fraternal order." Also listed are his wife, Clara, age 60, a native of New York and their son, Elmer, age 20, a native of California.

The *1920 Census for Oakland, Alameda County, California* lists William Crowhurst, age 75, as a native of England. Also listed is his wife, Clara, age 69, a native of New York.

The birth and death dates; places of birth and death; and Elizabeth's mother's name, all come from the Family Group sheet found on www.ancestry.com.

According to descendants, Elizabeth and her parents resided in Nortonville, Contra Costa County, California. Elizabeth died during a diphtheria epidemic. Her father, William Crowhurst, was a teacher in Somersville for two to three years, *circa* 1880s [Note: Other sources state 1870s; in 1880 they were listed in the *Census for Modesto, Stanislaus County, CA.*]

According to the *Oakland Tribune* newspaper, March 26, 1950, the Crowhurst family moved from Vallejo, Solano County, California to Somersville in 1877. Both of Elizabeth's parents served as schoolteachers. There were at least seven children in the Crowhurst family: Clara, Etta, William, Elmer, Elizabeth, George, and James.

**ADDITIONAL GRAVESITE INFORMATION:**
Elizabeth's name was provided by descendants who believe she is buried in Rose Hill Cemetery. No other sources document her burial in the cemetery.

**REFERENCES:** 8 (June 8, 1878 and Nov. 30, 1878), 9 (July 21, 1877 and Oct. 27, 1877), 12, *Oakland Tribune Knave* newspaper section (March 26, 1950), see newpaper appendix page 687 and 688

SOMERSVILLE ITEMS.—We learn with regret, from a Somersville correspondent, that Mrs. William Crowhurst, wife of the Principal, and an assistant teacher in the public school at that place, was thrown from a carriage last Sunday afternoon and suffered a fracture of one leg at the ankle which will painfully disable her for some weeks, and will doubtless be months before she will be able to resume her teaching work. Mrs. Crowhurst was in attendance, with Mr. Crowhurst, and the other teachers of the County, at the Institute held here last week, the members of which, with numerous other friends here, and elsewhere, will share our regrets that this serious mishap has befallen her.

Our correspondent writes that the mines at Somersville closed down work last week, and that all the miners are now idle, but are encouraged to hope that it is only temporarily, and that work is soon to be briskly resumed with prospects of continuing more steadily than for some time past.

The Somersville Base Ball Club's Ball, given on Friday evening of last week, our correspondent reports as having gone off finely, to the satisfaction of all parties, and that the music was exceptionally excellent.

This article from *Contra Costa Gazette* newspaper, June 8, 1878, states that Elizabeth's mother, Clarissa Crowhurst, was thrown from a carriage and "suffered a fracture of one leg at the ankle."

## Fraternal Visit of Odd Fellows.

Mr. Crowhurst, in the *New Age* of last week thus reports a fraternal visit received by Mt. Diablo Lodge I. O. O. F. from representatives of the Pacheco Lodge:

SOMERSVILLE, Nov. 17, 1878.

ED. NEW AGE—*Dear Sir and Bro.:*—Last night Mount Diablo Lodge was honored with a visit from a number of members representing Pacheco Lodge who came unexpectedly and surprised many of us, but we were equal to the occasion and turned out a very respectable meeting. There are sessions of Subordinate Lodges, Encampments, Rebecca Degree Lodges, etc., that are known by the somewhat peculiar cognomen of "Crack" meetings. Such was the gathering of last night, besides being one of those occasions where everybody seems especially happy. Everything said or done was directed toward the production or continuance of a good, social feeling and the furtherance of that unity which should exist among members of the same District of any great and universal Brotherhood.

After completing the business of the evening, the announcement of Good of the Order was the signal for social action. Addresses, songs, duets, recitations, etc. were then given by Bros. P. G.'s Hendricks, Caven and Martin, of Pacheco, and T. H. McCarthy, Geo. H. Scammon, Rankin, Dillingham and Clifford of Mount Diablo, and Bros. Kline, Clayton, White, Lando, Treglown, Hollow, Carpenter, Havart and others from Somersville, Clayton and Pacheco.

The principles of Odd Fellowship were not forgotten, but were beautifully and often alluded to.

Several expressions of sorrow were given concerning the loss by removal from town of Bro. P. G., Thomas B. Brown, who has been one of the most faithful members of this Lodge for many years. The brother has been exceedingly unfortunate, having recently lost his house, furniture, clothing and valuables by fire. In this connection I would also allude that the fire element has also been at work on the property of Bro. P. G. Scammon.

After the meeting adjourned, Bro. Scammon received us pleasantly and warmly into his dining room, where we enjoyed the bountiful supply of good things so plentifully provided for the occasion in spite of the intended surprise. The chickens, too ; they came from Clayton and Concord, having preceded the brothers in their enjoyable trip.

One of the emblematic parts of the entertainment was the singing of songs in three languages English, Welsh and German. This forcibly illustrated the fact that all nations, kindreds and *tongues* of the earth shall be bound by one law —that law, the law of Universal Brotherhood.

WM. CROWHURST.

The *Contra Costa Gazette* newspaper printed this article on November 30, 1878 regarding Elizabeth's father, William Crowhurst, and the "Fraternal Visit of Odd Fellows" in Somersville on November 17, 1878.

## PERSONAL INFORMATION:

SEX:                    Male
DATE OF BIRTH:          *Circa* 1840
DATE OF DEATH:          December 16, 1873
PLACE OF DEATH:         Somersville, Contra Costa County, California
AGE AT DEATH:           Approximately 33 years
CAUSE OF DEATH:         Boiler explosion at Independent Shaft
BIRTHPLACE:             Norfolk, Virginia
SPOUSE:
PARENTS:

## GRAVESITE INFORMATION:

LOCATION OF GRAVESITE:  Unknown
GRAVESTONE:             Missing or never placed
TYPE OF GRAVESTONE:
SHAPE OF GRAVESTONE:
INSCRIPTION:
EPITAPH:
MOTIF:
CARVER:
BASE:
TYPE OF BASE:
ENCLOSURE:
TYPE OF ENCLOSURE:
FENCE:
TYPE OF FENCE:
FENCE MOTIF:

# DALEY, James

**ADDITIONAL PERSONAL INFORMATION:**
James Daley worked as a fireman for the Pittsburg Coal Mining Company at the Independent Shaft in Somersville, Contra Costa County, California. He was killed instantly in the boiler explosion at the mine site along with John Hay. The explosion occurred about 5 pm on Tuesday, December 16, 1873. Also killed as a result of the explosion was David G. Williams. Badly injured and "not expected to live" was Henry Davidson. It was reported that none of the deceased left families.

The *Antioch Ledger* newspaper, December 27, 1873, indicates that Daley was married at the time of the accident, but the article does not record his wife's name. See John Hay.

**ADDITIONAL GRAVESITE INFORMATION:**
The *Antioch Ledger* newspaper, December 20, 1873 is the only source to reference his burial in Rose Hill Cemetery. The article states: "The bodies of the deceased were buried at Somersville on Wednesday afternoon." His burial location is not known.

**REFERENCES:** 8 (Dec. 20, 1873, Dec. 27, 1873, Jan. 3, 1874 – two articles, Jan. 10, 1874 - two articles, Jan. 17, 1874, Jan. 24, 1874, and Jan. 31, 1874), 9 ( Dec. 20, 1873 and Dec. 27, 1873 – two articles), *Daily Alta California* newspaper (Dec. 18, 1873), *San Francisco Call* newspaper (Dec. 20, 1873), see newpaper appendix pages 689-692

## A Chance for a Runaway.

The furnace doors at the Independent shaft, at Somersville, face the road, and, when thrown open at night, cast a ruddy glare across the street, rendering passage there with skittish teams exceedingly risky. A gentleman and lady narrowly escaped upsetting there, a few evenings ago. The fierce light flashing in the horse's face so suddenly, frightened him and he started to run; and had it not been for the timely assistance of a gentleman who noticed the occurrence and seized the horse by the head, somebody would have got hurt. A screen placed before the furnace would be a great improvement.

CAUSE OF THE BOILER EXPLOSION AT THE INDEPENDENT MINE.—Levi F. Cole, head boiler maker of the Union Iron Works at San Francisco, after a careful investigation, makes affidavit before J. P. Abbott, Notary Public, that in his opinion, the boiler explosion at the Independent mine was caused by pumping cold water into the overheated boiler after the water had been suffered to get too low; and Robert Prutton, an accomplished engineer, makes a similar affidavit. If the judgment of these experts is reliable, as there is good reason to believe, the jury of inquest were in error, in finding that the explosion resulted from the insufficiency and defects of the boiler for which the Foreman and Superintendent were responsible.

These newspaper articles reference the Independent Mine in Somersville. The article on the left comes from the *Antioch Ledger*, July 16, 1870, and the article on the right comes from the *Contra Costa Gazette*, January 3, 1874.

## PERSONAL INFORMATION:

| | |
|---|---|
| SEX: | Male |
| DATE OF BIRTH: | July 24, 1846 |
| DATE OF DEATH: | December 23, 1876 |
| PLACE OF DEATH: | |
| AGE AT DEATH: | 30 years, 4 months, 29 days |
| CAUSE OF DEATH: | |
| BIRTHPLACE: | CWM-BACH Glanmorgenshire [sic], South Wales |
| SPOUSE: | |
| PARENTS: | |

## GRAVESITE INFORMATION:

| | |
|---|---|
| LOCATION OF GRAVESITE: | Section S-D, Plot #53 |
| GRAVESTONE: | Exists |
| TYPE OF GRAVESTONE: | Marble |
| SHAPE OF GRAVESTONE: | Tablet |
| INSCRIPTION: | *In Memory of* |
| EPITAPH: | |
| MOTIF: | Knights of Pythias |
| CARVER: | |
| BASE: | Exists |
| TYPE OF BASE: | Granite base with middle marble base |
| ENCLOSURE: | Partial |
| TYPE OF ENCLOSURE: | Sandstone |
| FENCE: | |
| TYPE OF FENCE: | |
| FENCE MOTIF: | |

# DAVIES, Evan

**ADDITIONAL PERSONAL INFORMATION:**
Evan's birth date was calculated by www.timeanddate.com, using his age of death and date of death listed on his gravestone. His birthplace is spelled exactly as it appears on the gravestone. The correct spelling is Cwmbach, Glamorganshire. Evan was a member of the Knights of Pythias, Black Diamond Lodge No. 29, Nortonville. The initials F. C. B. found on the Knights of Pythias motif stand for Friendship, Charity, and Benevolence. William Gething is the only other individual buried in Rose Hill Cemetery with the Knights of Pythias motif on the gravestone. His motif is slightly different from the one for Evan Davies, who may also be listed as Evan Davis.

According to the *1876 Contra Costa County Voting Register*, Evan was 29, a native of Wales, and a miner living in Nortonville.

**ADDITIONAL GRAVESITE INFORMATION:**
The gravestone was broken into two pieces with portions of the stone chipped. The stone was removed from the cemetery by Black Diamond Rangers and the concrete detached from the back. Holes were drilled into the ends of the broken stone and the damaged pieces were pinned (using threaded brass pins) and epoxied back together. The gravestone was placed upright by the East Bay Regional Park District *circa* 1982 by reattaching the repaired gravestone to the middle marble base. The middle base sits on a granite base. Evan's gravesite appears in a book by Sunset titled *Beautiful California*, Lane Book Company, Menlo Park, CA, 1963, pages 82 and 83.

**REFERENCES:** 1, 2, 3, 4, 6, 9 (January 27, 1877), 11 (P610.31.129, P610.168.16, P610.204.1, P610.263.9, P610.294.6, and P610.317.19), 12, 14, see newpaper appendix page 693

Reference 31.129

The vandalized gravestone for Evan Davies in July 1977. The gravestone was repaired by Black Diamond Rangers and now stands upright on it's base. Photograph by Traci (Gibbons) Parent.

# DAVIS,
## Anna

## PERSONAL INFORMATION:

| | |
|---|---|
| SEX: | Female |
| DATE OF BIRTH: | 1844 |
| DATE OF DEATH: | August 9, 1869 |
| PLACE OF DEATH: | |
| AGE AT DEATH: | 25 years |
| CAUSE OF DEATH: | |
| BIRTHPLACE: | |
| SPOUSE: | James E. Davis |
| PARENTS: | |

## GRAVESITE INFORMATION:

| | |
|---|---|
| LOCATION OF GRAVESITE: | Section S-E, Plot #90 |
| GRAVESTONE: | Exists |
| TYPE OF GRAVESTONE: | Marble |
| SHAPE OF GRAVESTONE: | Tablet |
| INSCRIPTION: | *Sacred to the Memory of/Beloved wife of* |
| EPITAPH: | *Therefore be ye also ready for* |
| | *in such an hour as ye think not* |
| | *the Son of man cometh.* |
| | *(St. Matthew 24:44v)* |
| MOTIF: | Rope with tassels |
| CARVER: | |
| BASE: | Exists |
| TYPE OF BASE: | Sandstone |
| ENCLOSURE: | |
| TYPE OF ENCLOSURE: | |
| FENCE: | |
| TYPE OF FENCE: | |
| FENCE MOTIF: | |

# DAVIS, Anna

**ADDITIONAL PERSONAL INFORMATION:**
The *Contra Costa County Assessment List 1872-73*, records Anna's husband, James Davis, as having a home in Nortonville.

The *1876 Voting Register* lists James Edward Davis, age 30, as a native of Wales, and a miner living in Nortonville.

According to the *History of Contra Costa County* published by Slocum and Company, 1882, page 475, James E. Davis was a charter member of Black Diamond Lodge, No. 29, Knights of Pythias, Nortonville, Contra Costa County, California, which was instituted December 18, 1874.

**ADDITIONAL GRAVESITE INFORMATION:**
A photograph of the Anna Davis gravestone appears in the *California Monthly* magazine, "Back Yard Ghost Towns," May 1949, page 23.

The gravestone was broken into four pieces and concreted flat to the ground prior to East Bay Regional Park District acquisition. A small portion of the gravestone sits in the sandstone base. A piece of the bottom portion of the gravestone was found in the ground in May 2005. The epitaph on Anna's gravestone comes from the *Bible*: St. Matthew, Chapter 24, verse 44.

**REFERENCES:** 1, 2, 5, 10 (page 475), 11 (P610.31.165), 12, 14

Reference 31.165

The vandalized gravestone of Anna Davis that has been pieced together and concreted to the ground. Photograph taken July 1977 by Traci (Gibbons) Parent.

## PERSONAL INFORMATION:

| | |
|---|---|
| SEX: | Male |
| DATE OF BIRTH: | October 4, 1870 |
| DATE OF DEATH: | July 3, 1878 |
| PLACE OF DEATH: | |
| AGE AT DEATH: | 7 years, 8 months, 29 days |
| CAUSE OF DEATH: | Diphtheria |
| BIRTHPLACE: | |
| SPOUSE: | None |
| PARENTS: | David B. and Ellen (Jenkins) Davis |

## GRAVESITE INFORMATION:

| | |
|---|---|
| LOCATION OF GRAVESITE: | Section N-F, Plot 102 or 103 |
| GRAVESTONE: | Missing |
| TYPE OF GRAVESTONE: | Marble |
| SHAPE OF GRAVESTONE: | Tablet |
| INSCRIPTION: | |
| EPITAPH: | |
| MOTIF: | |
| CARVER: | |
| BASE: | Exists |
| TYPE OF BASE: | Granite |
| ENCLOSURE: | Exists |
| TYPE OF ENCLOSURE: | Sandstone (partial) |
| FENCE: | |
| TYPE OF FENCE: | |
| MOTIF OF FENCE: | |

# DAVIS, David

**ADDITIONAL PERSONAL INFORMATION:**
David's death date and age come from source 2 (see page 1004), a cemetery list compiled in 1935/1936, by Ann Louchs, for the Daughters of the American Revolution. His birth date was calculated by www.timeanddate.com.

See David B. Davis, Ellen Davis, Morgan Davis, William T. Davis, and Schwartz infant #1 and #2.

**ADDITIONAL GRAVESITE INFORMATION:**
Only a granite base marks the gravesite today. David is buried next to his mother, Ellen Davis, and brothers, Morgan and William T. Davis. His father, David B. Davis, is also believed to be buried in Rose Hill Cemetery.

**REFERENCES:** 1, 2, 8 (March 30, 1907 – two articles), 12

## FUNERAL.

The funeral of David Davis will take place on Sunday from the Congregational Church at Clayton at 1 p. m. The interment is to be at Live Oak Cemetery, to which place the bodies of his wife and children who are buried at Somersville, will be removed.

From the *Contra Costa Gazette* newspaper, March 30, 1907. Although this article states that David's father, David Davis, will be interred at Live Oak Cemetery in Concord, Contra Costa County, California, it is believed that he is buried in Rose Hill Cemetery with his wife and children.

## PERSONAL INFORMATION:

| | |
|---|---|
| Sex: | Male |
| Date of Birth: | December 1828 |
| Date of Death: | March 25, 1907 |
| Place of Death: | Clayton, Contra Costa County, California |
| Age at Death: | 79 years |
| Cause of Death: | Bright's disease |
| Birthplace: | Glamorganshire, South Wales |
| Spouse: | Ellen Davis |
| Parents: | |

## GRAVESITE INFORMATION:

| | |
|---|---|
| Location of Gravesite: | Unknown |
| Gravestone: | Missing or never placed |
| Type of Gravestone: | |
| Shape of Gravestone: | |
| Inscription: | |
| Epitaph: | |
| Motif: | |
| Carver: | |
| Base: | |
| Type of Base: | |
| Enclosure: | |
| Type of Enclosure: | |
| Fence: | |
| Type of Fence: | |
| Fence Motif: | |

# DAVIS, David B.

**ADDITIONAL PERSONAL INFORMATION:**
David's month of birth comes from the *1900 Census for Clayton, Contra Costa County, California*. His middle initial, "B," comes from the *Live Oak Cemetery Records* [Concord, Contra Costa County, CA], and the *1876 Contra Costa County Voting Register*.

According to descendants, David was born in England in 1826. David and his wife Ellen traveled to America by crossing the Isthmus of Panama on mules and eventually arrived in California. David's wife, Ellen, died in 1878, and is also buried in Rose Hill Cemetery along with their two sons, David and Morgan Davis.

The *1870 Census for Township 3, Contra Costa County*, lists David Davis, age 39, born *circa* 1831, as a miner and native of Wales. Also listed are his wife, Ellen, a native of Wales, age 34, born *circa* 1836, as "Keeping House" and their children: Morgan, age 6, born *circa* 1864; and Rebecca, age 4, born *circa* 1866; both natives of California. Also living with them is Henry Harris, age 19, a native of Prussia.

The *1876 Contra Costa County Voting Register* lists David B. Davis, age 54, as a miner, native of Wales, and resident of Nortonville. His date of registration was August 16, 1875.

According to descendants, after the death of his wife, Ellen, David took their son, William, and moved to San Francisco. There he worked on the docks, remarried and had more children.

In 1876, David B. Davis served as the Administrator of the Estate for William Gething. See William Gething on pages 213-216.

The *1900 Census for Clayton, Contra Costa County, California* lists David Davis, widowed, age 71, a native of Wales, and born December 1828. His occupation is listed as farmer. Also living with him is his son, William Davis, born January 1875 in California. William is recorded as age 25, a farm laborer and married for 4 years. Boarder Richard Stevens, a widow [sic-widower], native of Wales, and farm laborer, age 63, resides with them.

David's funeral took place on Sunday, March 31, 1907. His date of death was calculated by using www.timeanddate.com.

See David Davis, Ellen Davis, William T. Davis, Morgan Davis, and Schwartz infant #1 and #2.

**ADDITIONAL GRAVESITE INFORMATION:**
The *Contra Costa Gazette* newspaper, March 30, 1907 stated that:

> The bad condition of the roads will probably prevent the burial of David Davis alongside of his wife and children, but the place and time of his burial will be noted later.

Additionally the paper stated:

> The interment is to be at Live Oak Cemetery, to which place the bodies of his wife and children who are buried at Somersville, will be removed.

However, according to Charmetta Mann, who compiled the burial record for Live Oak Cemetery, Concord, Contra Costa County, California, the 16' x 24' plot at Live Oak was purchased by William Davis (son of David B. Davis) in 1907, but the only individual buried there is William Davis ["Baby"], son of William Davis Sr. and grandson of David B. Davis.

**REFERENCES:** 8 (March 30, 1907 – two articles), 11 (P610.317.9), 12, *Live Oak Cemetery Association Records, Concord, Contra Costa County, California* compiled by Charmetta Mann, 2009, see newspaper appendix page 694

# DAVIS,
## Ellen

## PERSONAL INFORMATION:

| | |
|---|---|
| SEX: | Female |
| DATE OF BIRTH: | June 18, 1845 |
| DATE OF DEATH: | July 16, 1878 |
| PLACE OF DEATH: | Somersville, Contra Costa County, California |
| AGE AT DEATH: | 33 years, 28 days |
| CAUSE OF DEATH: | Tuberculosis |
| BIRTHPLACE: | Pembrokeshire, South Wales |
| SPOUSE: | David B. Davis (first husband - Morgan Jenkins) |
| PARENTS: | |

## GRAVESITE INFORMATION:

| | |
|---|---|
| LOCATION OF GRAVESITE: | Section N-F, Plot #101 |
| GRAVESTONE: | Exists |
| TYPE OF GRAVESTONE: | Marble |
| SHAPE OF GRAVESTONE: | Tablet |
| INSCRIPTION: | *Also her two beloved* _____ [stone broken]/*wife of David Davis and Jenkins* |
| EPITAPH: | *Y bedd yw'r anwedd-oer*<br>*Enyd*<br>*A gawn nid ein hawddfyd*<br>*Gorwedd sydd raid newn*<br>*Gweryd*<br>*I beth y carwn ni y byd.* |
| MOTIF: | |
| CARVER: | F. Field |
| BASE: | Exists |
| TYPE OF BASE: | Granite |
| ENCLOSURE: | Exists (partial) |
| TYPE OF ENCLOSURE: | Sandstone |
| FENCE: | |
| TYPE OF FENCE: | |
| FENCE MOTIF: | |

# DAVIS, Ellen

**ADDITIONAL PERSONAL INFORMATION:**
According to descendants, Ellen, age 19, married Morgan Jenkins, June 28, 1864 in Wales. On January 2, 1872, her husband, Morgan, died. After the death of her first husband, Ellen married David B. Davis on August 30, 1873.

David was born in England in 1826. They traveled to America by crossing the Isthmus of Panama on mules and eventually arrived in California.

Ellen's gravestone was vandalized and only the month of death is found on her stone; the day and year of death is missing. Information obtained from descendants state Ellen's date of death as July 3, <u>1890</u>; however, probate documents found at the Contra Costa County Historical Society History Center archives record her date of death as July 16, 1878. The marble tablet gravestone that was placed at her gravesite is typical of the 1870s period and not the 1890s. Because of the Contra Costa County probate record found and her type and style of gravestone, her date of death has been listed as July 16, 1878. The probate record dated October 18, 1879, also states that:

> ...the only heirs of the deceased is her husband the said David Davis and two infant children to wit: Rebecca Davis, aged about 13 years and William Davis aged about five years.

Ellen died the same month and year as her son David. Both her sons (David and Morgan) died of diphtheria. Ellen and David B. Davis had at least four children:

- Morgan, born September 1865
- Rebecca, born about 1866
- David, born October 1870
- William T., born January 2, 1875

Ellen's husband, David B. Davis, died in March 1907, at age 79 years, and is also believed to be interred in Rose Hill Cemetery. Her three sons David, Morgan, and William T. Davis are also buried in the cemetery beside her.

See David B. Davis, David Davis, Morgan Davis, William T. Davis, and Schwartz infant #1 and #2.

**ADDITIONAL GRAVESITE INFORMATION:**
Zelma Myrick, who recorded information in a notebook in the 1930s during a visit to Rose Hill Cemetery, reported the gravestone "so broken hard to piece together." The gravestone was broken into numerous pieces and was concreted flat to the ground prior to East Bay Regional Park District acquisition. Much of the broken stone is missing, including the piece which held the date of death. A small bottom portion of the gravestone sits inside the granite base. The broken pieces of the gravestone that were concreted flat to the ground were removed from the cemetery by Black Diamond Rangers and placed in storage for safekeeping until repairs can be made.

In March 2005, Black Diamond Rangers found small pieces of the gravestone between plots 104 and 105, and near plot 103. An old pepper tree provides shade at the gravesite. The translation of Ellen's epitaph is:

> *The grave is the cold dwelling place*
> *which we have, not our happiness.*
> *One must be under the sward.*
> *Why must we love the world.*

The word "sward" in the epitaph means a piece of ground covered by grass.

**REFERENCES:** 2, 5, 8 (March 30, 1907 – two articles), 11 (P610.31.205 and P610.317.9), 12

Reference 317.9

The vandalized gravestone of Ellen Davis. The small gravestone lying on the ground
to the right is probably the stone for one of her sons, David or Morgan Davis.
Photograph taken *circa* 1939 by Zelma Myrick.

Reference 31.205

Ellen Davis gravestone, August 1977.
Photograph by Traci (Gibbons) Parent.

The south side of Rose Hill Cemetery looking east toward Somersville town site. Ellen Davis and her two sons, David and Morgan, are buried under the pepper trees located in the lower left corner (cluster of trees shown on far left) of the cemetery. The tall "white bronze" monument seen in the center of this photograph, surrounded by a brick wall enclosure and pipe fence, is the burial site for three miners (Thomas D. James, David Watts, and Theophilus Watts) who died in the July 24, 1876 mine explosion in Nortonville. Photograph taken *circa* 1939 by Zelma Myrick.

# DAVIS,
## Margaret

**PERSONAL INFORMATION:**

| | |
|---|---|
| SEX: | Female |
| DATE OF BIRTH: | 1861 |
| DATE OF DEATH: | 1878 |
| PLACE OF DEATH: | Nortonville, Contra Costa County, California |
| AGE AT DEATH: | Approximately 17 years |
| CAUSE OF DEATH: | |
| BIRTHPLACE: | Sweetara [sic], Pennsylvania |
| SPOUSE: | |
| PARENTS: | Joseph and Mary Ann (Evans) Davis |

**GRAVESITE INFORMATION:**

| | |
|---|---|
| LOCATION OF GRAVESITE: | Unknown |
| GRAVESTONE: | Missing or never placed |
| TYPE OF GRAVESTONE: | |
| SHAPE OF GRAVESTONE: | |
| INSCRIPTION: | |
| EPITAPH: | |
| MOTIF: | |
| CARVER: | |
| BASE: | |
| TYPE OF BASE: | |
| ENCLOSURE: | |
| TYPE OF ENCLOSURE: | |
| FENCE: | |
| TYPE OF FENCE: | |
| FENCE MOTIF: | |

# DAVIS, Margaret

**ADDITIONAL PERSONAL INFORMATION:**
According to descendants, Margaret's parents, Joseph Davis and Mary Ann Evans, married on April 14, 1849, in Merthyr Tydfil, Glamorganshire, Wales. Joseph's last name was spelled as Davies on the marriage license and later on his citizenship papers was spelled as Davis.

Joseph Davis was born July 25, 1827, in Sunnyside, Carmarthenshire, Wales and died March 17, 1901, in Foresthill, Placer County, California. Mary Ann (Evans) Davis was born March 3, 1830, in Ferryside, Carmarthenshire, Wales and died October 12, 1912, in Oakland, Alameda County, California. Information obtained from www.ancestry.com, states that Joseph was born in Merthyr Tydfil, Wales and that his wife, Mary, was born March 28, 1830.

After arriving in the United States, Joseph sent for his wife, Mary, and their surviving child, Mary Jane, to join him. They settled in Pottsville, Schuylkill County, Pennsylvania, where Joseph worked as a miner. Several of their children were born while living there. The family gradually moved west, stopping in: St. Joseph, Buchanan County, Missouri; Salt Lake City, Salt Lake County, Utah; Genoa, Douglas County, Nevada; finally arriving in Foresthill, Placer County, California. Their first child born in California was Eliza in November 1863. Although it is not known when they arrived in the Mount Diablo Coal Field, one child, Alice, was born in Nortonville in 1874. Another daughter, Catherine, was already married to William Stine at the time of her death in Nortonville in 1882. Additionally, the *1876 Contra Costa County Voting Register* lists Joseph D. Davis, age 46, as a native of Wales and miner residing in Nortonville. He registered to vote on April 22, 1874.

According to the *1900 Census for Township 5, Placer County, California*, there were 13 children in the family and only nine surviving by 1900.

Their children included:

- Mary Jane, born *circa* 1854, Wales (married to John Evans in Nortonville)
- Thomas, born *circa* 1856, Pennsylvania
- David D., born Jan. 22, 1858, Pottsville, Pennsylvania; died July 13, 1936, Martinez, California
- Joseph, born *circa* 1859, Pennsylvania
- Margaret, born 1861, Sweetara, [sic-probably Swatara, Schuylkill County] Pennsylvania; died 1878, Nortonville, California (buried in Rose Hill Cemetery)
- Eliza, born Nov. 15, 1863, Foresthill, California; died Feb. 16, 1944, Pittsburg, California
- Catherine (Katie), born 1865, Foresthill, California; died 1882, Nortonville, CA (buried in Rose Hill Cemetery; see Catherine Stine)
- Annie, born *circa* 1867, California
- Edward W., born May 2, 1868, Bath, California; died Nov. 19, 1951, Napa, California
- Sarah, born Feb. 15, 1870, Bath, California; died Nov. 10, 1966, Concord, California
- Joseph, born May 9, 1872, Bath, California; died Oct. 18, 1930, Martinez, California
- Alice, born March 2, 1874, Nortonville, California; died Oct. 3, 1906, San Francisco, California

**ADDITIONAL GRAVESITE INFORMATION:**
According to descendants, Margaret and her sister, Catherine (Davis) Stine, are buried in Rose Hill Cemetery. No other source documents their burial in the cemetery. See Catherine "Katie" Stine.

**REFERENCES:** 12

## PERSONAL INFORMATION:

| | |
|---|---|
| SEX: | Male |
| DATE OF BIRTH: | September 25, 1865 |
| DATE OF DEATH: | August 30, 1874 |
| PLACE OF DEATH: | Somersville, Contra Costa County, California |
| AGE AT DEATH: | 9 years, 11 months, 26 days |
| CAUSE OF DEATH: | Diphtheria |
| BIRTHPLACE: | California |
| SPOUSE: | None |
| PARENTS: | David B. and Ellen (Jenkins) Davis |

## GRAVESITE INFORMATION:

| | |
|---|---|
| LOCATION OF GRAVESITE: | Section N-F, Plot #102 or 103 |
| GRAVESTONE: | Missing |
| TYPE OF GRAVESTONE: | Marble |
| SHAPE OF GRAVESTONE: | Tablet |
| INSCRIPTION: | |
| EPITAPH: | |
| MOTIF: | |
| CARVER: | |
| BASE: | Exists |
| TYPE OF BASE: | Granite |
| ENCLOSURE: | Exists (partial) |
| TYPE OF ENCLOSURE: | Sandstone |
| FENCE: | |
| TYPE OF FENCE: | |
| FENCE MOTIF: | |

# DAVIS, Morgan

**ADDITIONAL PERSONAL INFORMATION:**
The *Contra Costa Gazette* newspaper, September 12, 1874 (see below), lists his name as Davies and his mother's name as Eleanor.

See David Davis, David B. Davis, Ellen Davis, William T. Davis, and Schwartz infant #1 and #2.

**ADDITIONAL GRAVESITE INFORMATION:**
Zelma Myrick, who recorded information in a notebook in the 1930s during a visit to Rose Hill Cemetery, reported the gravestone was "so broken hard to piece together."

Morgan is buried beside his mother Ellen Davis, and brothers David and William T. Davis. His father, David B. Davis, is also believed to be buried in Rose Hill Cemetery.

**REFERENCES:** 2, 8 (Sept. 12, 1874), 12

## DIED.

DAVIES—In Somersville, August 30th, Morgan, son of David and Eleanor Davies, aged 9 years, 11 months and 27 days.

ROONEY—Near Concord, August 30th, Mary, wife of John Rooney, aged 40 years.

From the *Contra Costa Gazette* newspaper, September 12, 1874.
Morgan's last name is spelled as Davies.

## PERSONAL INFORMATION:

| | |
|---|---|
| SEX: | Male |
| DATE OF BIRTH: | 1820 |
| DATE OF DEATH: | March 14, 1872 |
| PLACE OF DEATH: | |
| AGE AT DEATH: | 52 years |
| CAUSE OF DEATH: | |
| BIRTHPLACE: | Carmarthen-Shire [sic], South Wales |
| SPOUSE: | |
| PARENTS: | |

## GRAVESITE INFORMATION:

| | |
|---|---|
| LOCATION OF GRAVESITE: | Section S-F, Plot #111 |
| GRAVESTONE: | Exists |
| TYPE OF GRAVESTONE: | Marble |
| SHAPE OF GRAVESTONE: | Tablet |
| INSCRIPTION: | *In Memory of* |
| EPITAPH: | *Judge not that ye be not judged.* |
| MOTIF: | |
| CARVER: | Pioneer Steam Marble Works, San Francisco |
| BASE: | Missing |
| TYPE OF BASE: | |
| ENCLOSURE: | |
| TYPE OF ENCLOSURE: | |
| FENCE: | Exists |
| TYPE OF FENCE: | Iron with granite corner blocks |
| FENCE MOTIF: | |

# DAVIS, Peter

**ADDITIONAL PERSONAL INFORMATION:**
Carmarthenshire is spelled as two words on Peter's gravestone.

**ADDITIONAL GRAVESITE INFORMATION:**
Zelma Myrick, who recorded information in a notebook in the 1930s during a visit to Rose Hill Cemetery, reported "Fence and stone broken."

The original iron fence exists at the gravesite and has a gate. The gravestone is broken into three pieces and was concreted flat to the ground prior to East Bay Regional Park District acquisition. A photograph of the gravesite appears in *Contra Costa Living* (a supplement of the *Contra Costa Sunday Times* newspaper - April 11, 1971, page 8)

**REFERENCES:** 1, 3, 5, 6, 11 (P610.8.3, P610.31.121, and P610.31.157), 12, 14

Reference 8.3

Rose Hill Cemetery 1971, looking west with the Peter Davis gravesite and iron fence visible in the right corner of the photograph. At the time this picture was taken, the cemetery was surrounded by a cyclone and barbed wire fence.
Photograph by Brian Suen.

# DAVIS,
## Thomas J.

## PERSONAL INFORMATION:

| | |
|---|---|
| SEX: | Male |
| DATE OF BIRTH: | 1844 |
| DATE OF DEATH: | April 9, 1883 |
| PLACE OF DEATH: | |
| AGE AT DEATH: | 39 years |
| CAUSE OF DEATH: | |
| BIRTHPLACE: | |
| SPOUSE: | Elizabeth (Jones) Davis |
| PARENTS: | |

## GRAVESITE INFORMATION:

| | |
|---|---|
| LOCATION OF GRAVESITE: | Section S-D, Plot #59 |
| GRAVESTONE: | Exists |
| TYPE OF GRAVESTONE: | Marble |
| SHAPE OF GRAVESTONE: | Tablet |
| INSCRIPTION: | |
| EPITAPH: | *Lost to sight but to memory dear.* |
| MOTIF: | Clasped hands/rope with tassels |
| CARVER: | |
| BASE: | |
| TYPE OF BASE: | |
| ENCLOSURE: | Exists |
| TYPE OF ENCLOSURE: | Brick with granite corner blocks |
| FENCE: | Exists |
| TYPE OF FENCE: | Iron |
| FENCE mMOTIF: | |

# DAVIS, Thos. J.

## ADDITIONAL PERSONAL INFORMATION:

Thomas J. Davis, age 35, of Nortonville, Contra Costa County, California, married Elizabeth Jones, age 39, of Nortonville, on November 13, 1880. Witnesses were John D. Williams and John M. Phillips. According to the *Index to Marriage Certificates*, located at the Contra Costa County Hall of Records in Martinez, California, Thomas J. Davis married Elizabeth Jones on November 17, 1880. They were married by Rev. John J. Powell; the information is recorded in Volume 2, page 353.

According to the *History of Contra Costa County* by Slocum and Company, 1882, page 475, Thomas J. Davis was a charter member of Social Encampment, No. 50, Independent Order of Odd Fellows (I.O.O.F.), Nortonville, Contra Costa County, California, which was instituted December 18, 1874.

## ADDITIONAL GRAVESITE INFORMATION:

Thomas shares a gravestone with J. B. (John B.) Jones and shares the gravesite with Lulu and Alfred W. Buxton. The original iron fence stands around this gravesite. The gravestone is broken into numerous pieces and has been placed in storage until repairs can be made.

Zelma Myrick, who recorded information in a notebook in the 1930s during a visit to Rose Hill Cemetery, reported "Stone riveted together."

A photograph of the gravesite appears in *Contra Costa Living* (a supplement of the *Contra Costa Sunday Times* newspaper, April 11, 1971, page 9).

See Alfred W. Buxton, Lulu Buxton, and John B. Jones.

REFERENCES: 1, 2, 3, 6, 8 (Nov. 20, 1880), 10, 11 (P610.31.123, P610.31.139, and P610.117.6), 12, 14

---

## MARRIED.

DAVIS–JONES—At Nortonville, November 13th, by Rev. John J. Powell, Thomas J. Davis and Elizabeth Jones, all of Nortonville.

This newspaper article from the *Contra Costa Gazette*, November 20, 1880, announces the marriage of Thomas J. Davis and Elizabeth Jones.

# DAVIS,
## William T.

## PERSONAL INFORMATION:

| | |
|---|---|
| Sex: | Male |
| Date of Birth: | January 2, 1875 |
| Date of Death: | May 26, 1954 |
| Place of Death: | Clayton, Contra Costa County, California |
| Age at Death: | 79 years, 4 months, 24 days |
| Cause of Death: | |
| Birthplace: | Somersville, Contra Costa County, California |
| Spouse: | Henrietta Christine (O'Conner) Davis |
| Parents: | David B. and Ellen (Jenkins) Davis |

## GRAVESITE INFORMATION:

| | |
|---|---|
| Location of Gravesite: | Section N-F, Plot #104 |
| Gravestone: | Exists |
| Type of Gravestone: | Polished granite |
| Shape of Gravestone: | Block |
| Inscription: | *Dad* |
| Epitaph: | |
| Motif: | Floral |
| Carver: | |
| Base: | Exists |
| Type of Base: | Concrete |
| Enclosure: | Exists (partial) |
| Type of Enclosure: | Sandstone |
| Fence: | |
| Type of Fence: | |
| Fence Motif: | |

# DAVIS, William T.

**ADDITIONAL PERSONAL INFORMATION:**
The *Index to Marriage Certificates*, located at the Contra Costa County Hall of Records, Martinez, California, states that William Davis married Henrietta C. O'Conner on December 3, 1893. They were married by Hugh McDonald; the information is recorded in Volume 5, page 18.

The *1900 Census for Clayton, Contra Costa County, California* lists William Davis, age 25, as a native of California and living with his father, David Davis. It states that William is a farm laborer and has been married for four years.

The *1910 Census for Township 13, Contra Costa County, California* lists William T. Davis, age 35. Also listed are his wife Henrieta [sic] Davis, age 28, and their children Melvin, age 4, and Madeline, age 8 months; all natives of California.

The birth date for William Thomas Davis comes from the *California Death Index, 1940-1997 Record*.

William Thomas Davis was buried in the family plot in 1954 and he is believed to be the last individual interred in Rose Hill Cemetery.

According to family records, William T. arrived in the coal field from Wales at age 3, though his birthplace is recorded as Somersville in the *Contra Costa Gazette* newspaper, May 27, 1954. His children were Melvin W. Davis and Madeline (Davis) Fragulia. He lived most of his life on his ranch in Mitchell Canyon, Clayton, Contra Costa County, California, where he raised almonds and grapes.

See David Davis, David B. Davis, Ellen Davis, Morgan Davis, and Schwartz infant #1 and #2.

**ADDITIONAL GRAVESITE INFORMATION:**
He is buried beside his mother, Ellen Davis, and two brothers, David and Morgan Davis. His father, David B. Davis, is also believed to be buried in Rose Hill Cemetery.

The concrete base contains two round flower receptacles.

**REFERENCES:** 1, 8 (May 27, 1954), 11 (P610.31.150), 12, 14, *History of Contra Costa County, California with Biographical Sketches, 1926*, page 573, see newspaper appendix page 695

# DAWSON,
## Mary A.

**PERSONAL INFORMATION:**

| | |
|---|---|
| SEX: | Female |
| DATE OF BIRTH: | June 1, 1879 |
| DATE OF DEATH: | October 7, 1879 |
| PLACE OF DEATH: | Nortonville, Contra Costa County, California |
| AGE AT DEATH: | 4 months, 7 days |
| CAUSE OF DEATH: | |
| BIRTHPLACE: | Nortonville, Contra Costa County, California |
| SPOUSE: | None |
| PARENTS: | William Namar & Sarah Charlotte (Green) Dawson |

**GRAVESITE INFORMATION:**

| | |
|---|---|
| LOCATION OF GRAVESITE: | Section S-F, Plot #106 |
| GRAVESTONE: | Exists |
| TYPE OF GRAVESTONE: | Marble |
| SHAPE OF GRAVESTONE: | Tablet |
| INSCRIPTION: | *Daughter of* |
| EPITAPH: | *Gone but not forgotten.* |
| MOTIF: | |
| CARVER: | |
| BASE: | Exists |
| TYPE OF BASE: | Sandstone (new) |
| ENCLOSURE: | |
| TYPE OF ENCLOSURE: | |
| FENCE: | |
| TYPE OF FENCE: | |
| FENCE MOTIF: | |

# DAWSON, Mary A.

**ADDITIONAL PERSONAL INFORMATION:**
Mary Alice Dawson was a niece to Martha J. Green and George B. Hook, both buried nearby. Although the gravestones record their names as Martha J. Green and George B. Hook, a descendant states that Martha's middle name was Ann and George's middle name was Henry.

William N. Dawson, age 23, of Amador County, California and Sarah C. Green, age 20, of Nortonville, Contra Costa County, California applied for a marriage license on September 28, 1877. The information was recorded in *Applications for Marriage Licenses, Contra Costa County, 1873-1887*, page 118, located at the Contra Costa County Historical Society History Center in Martinez, California.

The *Index to Marriage Certificates*, Contra Costa County Hall of Records, Martinez, California states that William N. Dawson married Sarah C. Green on December 26, 1877. They were married by Rev. Owen Smith and the information is recorded in Volume 2, page 208.

The *1880 Census for Township 2, Amador County, California* lists William N. Dawson, age 25, born *circa* 1855, as a native of Iowa and his occupation as "works on farm." Also recorded is his wife Sarah C., age 22, born *circa* 1858 in California.

The *1920 Census for Sacramento Assembly District 14, Sacramento County, California* lists William N. Dawson, age 66 years, and born *circa* 1854 in Iowa. Also listed are his wife Sarah C., age 63 years, a native of California and their children: Ida D. Dawson, age 37 years and single; John B. Dawson, age 19 and single; and Pearl B. (Dawson)

Richards, age 35 years and married. All are natives of California.

William Dawson was born on August 6, 1854 in Iowa, and died June 24, 1924 in Sacramento, Sacramento County, California. Sarah (Green) Dawson was born September 25, 1857 in San Bernardino, San Bernardino County, California, and died May 21, 1937 in Sacramento. They are interred in East Lawn Cemetery, Sacramento, California.

**ADDITIONAL GRAVESITE INFORMATION:**
A photograph showing Mary Dawson's broken gravestone concreted to the ground appears in the *California Monthly* magazine, May 1949, page 23.

In September 2005, Black Diamond Rangers removed the gravestone from the cemetery to make repairs and returned it to the cemetery in April 2006. Sadly, in February 2008 the gravestone was knocked down again by vandals and the original sandstone base destroyed. A new sandstone base was installed and the gravestone placed upright again in May 2009.

Two new bases were manufactured for gravestones (Mary Dawson and Georg Adam Ott) in Rose Hill Cemetery by V. Fontana and Company of Colma, California, reusing the original base of the "Baseball Player" monument. This life-sized, bronze sculpture, created by renowned artist, Douglas Tilden, was dedicated July 8, 1891 and is located in Golden Gate Park in San Francisco, California.

**REFERENCES:** 1, 2, 3, 6, 11 (P610.31.154), 12, 14

Reference 322.6

Reference 322.5

Pictured on the left is Sarah Charlotte (Green) Dawson, mother of Mary A. Dawson. Sarah was the sister of Martha J. Green, who is also buried in Rose Hill Cemetery. Pictured on the right is William Namar Dawson, father of Mary A. Dawson and husband of Sarah (Green) Dawson.

The children of Sarah C. (Green) and William N. Dawson were:

- James, born in Ione, Amador County, California
- Mary Alice, born June 1, 1879, Nortonville, Contra Costa County, California
- William Henry, born Jan. 28, 1881, Nortonville, Contra Costa County, California
- Ida Dorina, born Sept. 2, 1882, Ione, Amador County, California
- Pearl Budie, born Dec. 23, 1884, Nortonville, Contra Costa County, California
- Ruby Budie, born Dec. 23, 1884, Nortonville, Contra Costa County, California
- Annie Mae, born May 16, 1892, Alila, Tulare County, California
- Florence Olive, born Jan. 4, 1895, Alila, Tulare County, California
- John Byron, born Dec. 31, 1900, Ione, Amador County, California

## Communicated.

SOMERSVILLE, May 9th, 1877.

ED. LEDGER.—In an issue of the *Call* May 3d, I saw an account of two young gentlemen in Stockton having experimented with the telephone. Whereupon four young men of Somersville, namely, Messrs. Ralph Dawson, Matt. Orr, Wm. Pettigrew and John Coll, took it upon themselves to improve on their invention. The Stockton gentlemen could communicate at 30 or 40 feet, but the young men of this place have been able to telephone at 1,000 feet, and they are confident that they can make it work at three times the distance. Their apparratus consists of two common oyster cans, with pieces of sheep skin stretched tightly over one end. The sheep skin is slightly perforated in the center and the cord passed through and fastened to the ground, the cans are then fastened about three feet from the end, and any word being spoken in one can, can be distinctly heard at the other end. They have also two branch lines from the main line at a distance of 100 feet each, and the slightest articulation being uttered by any person can be heard distinctly at all ends. By inserting the above you will greatly oblige an old subscriber.

G. H. SCAMMON.

This article appeared in the *Antioch Ledger* newspaper on May 12, 1877. It is not known if the Ralph Dawson of Somersville, mentioned in the article, is related to the Dawson family of Nortonville. William N. Dawson and Sarah C. Green were married in December 1877, just seven months after this article appeared in the paper.

# DENNIS,
## John

## PERSONAL INFORMATION:

SEX: Male
DATE OF BIRTH:
DATE OF DEATH:
PLACE OF DEATH:
AGE AT DEATH: Approximately 10 years
CAUSE OF DEATH:
BIRTHPLACE:
SPOUSE: None
PARENTS:

## GRAVESITE INFORMATION:

LOCATION OF GRAVESITE: Unknown
GRAVESTONE: Missing
TYPE OF GRAVESTONE:
SHAPE OF GRAVESTONE:
INSCRIPTION:
EPITAPH:
MOTIF:
CARVER:
BASE:
TYPE OF BASE:
ENCLOSURE:
TYPE OF ENCLOSURE:
FENCE:
TYPE OF FENCE:
FENCE MOTIF:

# DENNIS, John

**ADDITIONAL PERSONAL INFORMATION:**
A park visitor provided the name of John Dennis and his approximate age. This name has not appeared on any prior cemetery lists.

**ADDITIONAL GRAVESITE INFORMATION:**
On October 26, 1978, a park visitor reported to Black Diamond staff that they remembered seeing a gravestone for John Dennis in the cemetery approximately twenty years prior. The marble or granite gravestone was seen "near one tall [Italian] cypress tree - close to the road."

**REFERENCES:** 12

Reference 41.37

Group gathered at the Dickinson Hotel, Somersville, *circa* 1890s. The hotel, located on the eastern or Pittsburg Mine side of Somersville, was operated by James and Mary Dickinson. Formerly the hotel was operated by Frank and Bridget Hollywood. In addition to being called the Scammon, Hollywood, and Dickinson Hotel, it was commonly known as the Pittsburg or Somersville Hotel.

# DODSWORTH,
## George Washington

**PERSONAL INFORMATION:**

| | |
|---|---|
| SEX: | Male |
| DATE OF BIRTH: | |
| DATE OF DEATH: | 1890s |
| PLACE OF DEATH | |
| AGE AT DEATH: | Adult |
| CAUSE OF DEATH: | |
| BIRTHPLACE: | Wales |
| SPOUSE: | |
| PARENTS: | _____ and Eunice Dodsworth |

**GRAVESITE INFORMATION:**

| | |
|---|---|
| LOCATION OF GRAVESITE: | Unknown |
| GRAVESTONE: | Missing or never placed |
| TYPE OF GRAVESTONE: | |
| SHAPE OF GRAVESTONE: | |
| INSCRIPTION: | |
| EPITAPH: | |
| MOTIF: | |
| CARVER: | |
| BASE: | |
| TYPE OF BASE: | |
| ENCLOSURE: | |
| TYPE OF ENCLOSURE: | |
| FENCE: | |
| TYPE OF FENCE: | |
| FENCE MOTIF: | |

# DODSWORTH , George Washington

**ADDITIONAL PERSONAL INFORMATION:**
According to descendants, the Dodsworth family traveled from Kansas to the Mount Diablo Coal Field and settled in Nortonville, Contra Costa County, California *circa* 1883. They may have originally come from Wales. George Washington Dodsworth was a coal miner.

**ADDITIONAL GRAVESITE INFORMATION:**
George Washington Dodsworth has not been recorded on any previous cemetery lists. Descendants believe George is buried in Rose Hill Cemetery.

**REFERENCES:** 12

Reference 41.32

The new Main Street located on the south side of Nortonville.
The brick structures were built after the 1878 fire.
For more information on the Nortonville fire see page 442.

# DOULTON,
## George

## PERSONAL INFORMATION:

| | |
|---|---|
| Sex: | Male |
| Date of Birth: | 1830 |
| Date of Death: | 1884 |
| Place of Death: | |
| Age at Death: | 54 years |
| Cause of Death: | |
| Birthplace: | Wales |
| Spouse: | Mary Doulton |
| Parents: | |

## GRAVESITE INFORMATION:

| | |
|---|---|
| Location of Gravesite: | Unknown |
| Gravestone: | Missing |
| Type of Gravestone: | Granite |
| Shape of Gravestone: | |
| Inscription: | |
| Epitaph: | |
| Motif: | |
| Carver: | W. H. McCormick, San Francisco, California |
| Base: | |
| Type of Base: | |
| Enclosure: | |
| Type of Enclosure: | |
| Fence: | |
| Type of Fence: | |
| Fence Motif: | |

# DOULTON, George

**ADDITIONAL PERSONAL INFORMATION:**
According to descendants, George Doulton left Wales and traveled to Pennsylvania. While in Pennsylvania, he sent for his wife to join him. They eventually resided in Birchell, (or Burchell) Pennsylvania. George's last name has also been spelled Dalton.

George and Mary Doulton had four children: Tom, Margaret, Rachel, and Mary (called May). His son, Thomas, died in San Francisco, California in January 1934 at the age of 62.

The *1876 Contra Costa County Voting Register* lists George Dalton [sic], age 36, as a native of Wales and miner living in Somersville.

The *Assessment List County of Contra Costa, 1876 – Somersville and Nortonville*, records George Dalton [sic] as a taxpayer in the town of Somersville. His description of property is listed as "House in Somersville $100, Furniture $20." The total value of his property was $120 and his total tax $2.06.

The *1880 Census for Sommersville* [sic] *Precinct, Contra Costa County, California* lists George Dalton [sic], age 50, as a miner and native of Wales. Also listed are his wife, Mary, age 45, a native of Wales and their children: Harriet, age 14; Margaret, age 9; Thomas, age 7; Mary, age 5; and Ratchel [sic], age 2; all natives of California.

**ADDITIONAL GRAVESITE INFORMATION:**
According to descendants, George is buried about 15 feet from the 1934 Native Sons and Native Daughters of the Golden West monument. He was buried above the monument (to the west) towards the fence. A stone was never placed in the cemetery at the time of his death. His grandson, C. Doulton Burner, placed a black granite slab stone years later, but descendants state it was stolen during the time that Camp Stoneman (a military facility built in 1942 for World War II in Pittsburg, Contra Costa County, California), was active.

A gravestone must have been in existence in approximately 1972 because information was recorded from the stone during this time (recorders name unknown). George Doulton's name appears on this cemetery list only. Since the list contains only 25 names, 24 of which have been referenced on previous lists, the *circa* 1972 list was not used to reference other gravesites in Rose Hill Cemetery. The gravestone carver's name was recorded on the 1972 list and was misspelled as "McCormirk."

**REFERENCES:** 8 (Jan. 30, 1934), 12, see newspaper appendix page 696

> **Busy.**—The present demand for coal appears to be quite brisk, and the coal mines are turning out unusual quantities. The shipments from the Black Diamond, Union, Pittsburgh and Central, for the month of May, aggregate, it is reported, more than 20,000 tons, equal in market value to $120,000 at least.

From the *Contra Costa Gazette* newspaper, June 6, 1874.

## PERSONAL INFORMATION:

SEX:                    Male
DATE OF BIRTH:          *Circa* 1838-1848
DATE OF DEATH:          July 25, 1876
PLACE OF DEATH:         Nortonville, Contra Costa County, California
AGE AT DEATH:           28 or 38 years
CAUSE OF DEATH:         Mine explosion
BIRTHPLACE:             Canada
SPOUSE:
PARENTS:

## GRAVESITE INFORMATION:

LOCATION OF GRAVESITE:  Section S-C, Plot #47
GRAVESTONE:             Exists
TYPE OF GRAVESTONE:     Marble
SHAPE OF GRAVESTONE:    Tablet
INSCRIPTION:
EPITAPH:
MOTIF:                  Masonic
CARVER:
BASE:                   Exists
TYPE OF BASE:           Granite
ENCLOSURE:              Exists
TYPE OF ENCLOSURE:      Brick
FENCE:
TYPE OF FENCE
FENCE MOTIF:

# DUMAS, Theophile

**ADDITIONAL PERSONAL INFORMATION:**
The *Canadian Genealogy Index, 1600s-1900s Record* lists Theophile Dumas as living in Quebec Province, in Laprairie de Madelei in 1861.

The *Contra Costa Gazette* newspaper, July 29, 1876 states that Body Dumas and seven others died as a result of an explosion which occurred at a mine in Nortonville on Monday, July 24, 1876. It is believed that "Body" may be a nickname for Theophile. According to the newspaper article, Body Dumas was initially listed as a survivor, but died on Tuesday night. He was not survived by any family.

Dumas was interred in the cemetery next to other men who died in the same explosion. The *History of Contra Costa County*, published by W. A. Slocum and Company in 1882, page 474, and the *Contra Costa Gazette*, July 29, 1876 are the only sources that list his death date.

Theophile Dumas is recorded in the *1876 Contra Costa County Voting Register*. According to the voting register, Dumas was 31 years old in 1876, a native of Canada, and miner living in Nortonville. He was born in 1845, and registered to vote on April 30, 1874. Also listed is Nortonville resident, Louis Dumas, age 31, a miner and native of Canada. He also registered to vote on April 30, 1874.

The *1880 Nortonville Precinct Census* lists a Lewis [sic] Dumas, as a native of Canada, age 44. Perhaps this is a brother to Theophile Dumas who was also a native of Canada.

See William Gething, Thomas D. James, Meredith Lewis, George. M. Reynolds, Evan Smith, David Watts, Theophilus Watts, and William L. Williams.

**ADDITIONAL GRAVESITE INFORMATION:**
The gravestone is broken into at least 13 pieces and is so badly weathered that the name and death date are barely legible. The age of death appears to be 28 or 38 years. His gravestone indicates that he belonged to the Masonic Lodge.

His gravestone, the *Contra Costa Gazette* newspaper, and the *History of Contra Costa County*, by Slocum, 1882, page 474, are the only sources that indicate Dumas is buried in Rose Hill Cemetery. His name was not recorded on any previous cemetery lists.

The gravestone was removed from Rose Hill Cemetery and placed in storage for safekeeping by Black Diamond Park Rangers *circa* early 1980s.

**REFERENCES:** 8 (July 29, 1876 and Aug. 12, 1876), 9 (July 29, 1876), 10 (page 474), 11 (P610.31.183, P610.117.7, and P610.259.1), see newspaper appendix (William Gething) pages 706 and 707

Theophile Dumas gravesite, July 1977.
Photograph by Traci (Gibbons) Parent.

Miners at the Black Diamond Mine, Nortonville, California. Theophile Dumas was working in this mine at the time the explosion occurred on Monday, July 24, 1876. Pictured third from the right is shift boss (foreman) Watkin Morgans. Watkin's brother, Morgan Morgans, was the mine's superintendent.

THE MOUNT DIABLO COAL MINES.—The Sacramento *Union* says, Professor Whitney, the State Geologist, who has just returned from a hasty examination of the mines, pronounces them one of the most valuable discoveries and deposits yet found on the coast. The Mount Diablo coal is pronounced superior in quality, and apparently inexhaustable in quantity.

From the *Contra Costa Gazette* newspaper, March 16, 1861.

East Bay Regional Park District

**PERSONAL INFORMATION:**

SEX:                          Male

DATE OF BIRTH:

DATE OF DEATH:

PLACE OF DEATH:

AGE AT DEATH:                 Infant

CAUSE OF DEATH:

BIRTHPLACE:

SPOUSE:                       None

PARENTS:                      Loren and Dora (Isadora) Dunton

**GRAVESITE INFORMATION:**

LOCATION OF GRAVESITE:        Unknown

GRAVESTONE:                   Missing

TYPE OF GRAVESTONE:

SHAPE OF GRAVESTONE:

INSCRIPTION:                  *Infant children of*

EPITAPH:

MOTIF:

CARVER:

BASE:

TYPE OF BASE:

ENCLOSURE:

TYPE OF ENCLOSURE:

FENCE:

TYPE OF FENCE:

FENCE MOTIF:

# DUNTON, Clyde C.

**ADDITIONAL PERSONAL INFORMATION:**
A sister, Lulu B. Dunton, is also buried in Rose Hill Cemetery. Clyde was the infant son of L. and D. Dunton according to Zelma Myrick, who recorded information in a notebook in the 1930s during a visit to Rose Hill Cemetery.

The parents of Clyde C. and his sister, Lulu B., are most likely Loren and Dora F. (Laport) Dunton. According to *Illinois Marriages, 1851-1900* obtained from www.ancestry.com, Loren Dunton married Dora F. Laport on January 11, 1871, in Sycamore, DeKalb County, Illinois.

According to the obituary for Loren Dunton, from the *Antioch Ledger* newspaper, February 7, 1920, Loren died on February 2, 1920. (Records from Oak View Memorial Park Cemetery, E. 18th Street, Antioch, Contra Costa County, California, where he is buried, state he died February 1, 1920.) He was born in Bath, Stuben County, New York on May 27, 1851. He married Dora Laporte [sic] at Earlville, LaSalle County, Illinois in 1872. The same year they left for California settling in Somersville, Contra Costa County. Dunton was employed in the Black Diamond Coal Mine in Nortonville. The newspaper article also states that "Loren Dunton had resided in this vicinity about thirty-five years."

The *1876 Contra Costa County Voting Register* lists Loren Dunton, age 25, as a native of New York and laborer living in Somersville, Contra Costa County, California. He registered to vote on August 9, 1875.

The *1880 Census for Judsonville, Contra Costa County, California*, lists Loren Dunton, age 30, born *circa* 1850, in New York. His occupation is recorded as carpenter. Also listed is his wife, Isadora, age 29, born *circa* 1851 in Illinois, and their children: Eva, age 3, born *circa* 1877 in California; and Maud, 1 month, born 1880 in California. The place of birth for Loren Dunton's father and mother is recorded as New York. The place of birth for Isadora's father is Canada and her mother's is New York.

The *1900 Census for Antioch, Contra Costa County, California* lists Loren Duntan [sic], age 50, born May 1850 in New York. His father's birthplace is listed as Massachusetts and his mother's as New York. The census states that he married in 1872 and has been married for 28 years. Also listed on the census is his wife, Dora, age 48, born December 1851 in Illinois and their daughter: Frances, age 17, born November 1882 in California; and their son, Adelbert, age 12, born December 1887 in California.

The *1920 Census for Antioch, Contra Costa County, California* lists Isadora F. Dunton, age 68, born *circa* 1852 in Illinois. Her father's birthplace is recorded as France and her mother's as New York. It states she is married, but her husband is not listed on the census with her. Also listed is Isadora's widowed daughter, Frances E. (Dunton) Pettus, age 37, born about 1883 in California. Isadora's single son, Adelbert L. Dunton, age 32, born *circa* 1888, is listed as the head of the house.

See Lulu B. Dunton for more information.

**ADDITIONAL GRAVESITE INFORMATION:**
Zelma Myrick, who recorded information in a notebook in the 1930s during a visit to Rose Hill Cemetery, reported that Clyde shared a gravestone with his sister Lulu.

**REFERENCES:** 1, 2, 3, 12, see newspaper appendix page 697

**PERSONAL INFORMATION:**

| | |
|---|---|
| SEX: | Female |
| DATE OF BIRTH: | |
| DATE OF DEATH: | |
| PLACE OF DEATH: | |
| AGE AT DEATH: | Infant |
| CAUSE OF DEATH: | |
| BIRTHPLACE: | |
| SPOUSE: | None |
| PARENTS: | Loren and Dora (Isadora) Dunton |

**GRAVESITE INFORMATION:**

| | |
|---|---|
| LOCATION OF GRAVESITE: | Unknown |
| GRAVESTONE: | Missing |
| TYPE OF GRAVESTONE: | |
| SHAPE OF GRAVESTONE: | |
| INSCRIPTION: | *Infant children of* |
| EPITAPH: | |
| MOTIF: | |
| CARVER: | |
| BASE: | |
| TYPE OF BASE: | |
| ENCLOSURE: | |
| TYPE OF ENCLOSURE: | |
| FENCE: | |
| TYPE OF FENCE: | |
| FENCE MOTIF: | |

# DUNTON, Lulu B.

**ADDITIONAL PERSONAL INFORMATION:**
A brother, Clyde C. Dunton, is also buried in Rose Hill Cemetery. See Clyde C. Dunton.

Based on census information (see Clyde C. Dunton), and the family gravestone at Oak View Memorial Park Cemetery in Antioch, Contra Costa County, California, there were at least six children in the Dunton family. In addition to Clyde C. and Lulu B., there were:

- Eva, born *circa* 1877, California
- Maude, born *circa* 1880, California
- Frances E., born November 1882, California
- Adelbert L., born December 1887, California and died January 14, 1962

According to cemetery records, Lulu's father, Loren, died February 1, 1920 at age 68 years. He was interred February 4, 1920 in the Masons' and Odd Fellows' Cemetery (now known as Oak View Memorial Park Cemetery).

His wife, Isadora F. Dunton, was born in 1851 and died February 27, 1927 at age 75 years and 2 months. According to the *Antioch Ledger* newspaper, Mrs. Dunton came to Somersville in 1872. She married her husband at Earlville, LaSalle County, Illinois before coming to California. Information obtained from www.ancestry.com states that they married in Sycamore, DeKalb County, Illinois.

Sharing the burial plot with Loren and Isadora Dunton is their son, Adelbert L. Dunton and his wife, Portia C. Dunton. Portia was born in 1899 and died January 14, 1965 at the age of 65.

**ADDITIONAL GRAVESITE INFORMATION:**
Zelma Myrick, who recorded information in a notebook in the 1930s during a visit to Rose Hill Cemetery, reported that Lulu shared a gravestone with her brother Clyde.

**REFERENCES:** 1, 2, 3, 12, see newspaper appendix page 697

---

## CARD OF THANKS

We desire to express our sincere thanks for all the kind assistance tendered us by our neighbors and friends during the illness and death of our beloved husband and father. Especially do we thank the members of Mizpah Rebekah Lodge and of Antioch Encampment. These many kindnesses will ever be cherished in our memory.

Mrs. Dora Dunton,
Mrs. Frances Pettus,
Adelbert Dunton.

From the *Antioch Ledger* newspaper, February 7, 1920. Mrs. Dora Dunton is presumably the mother of Lulu B. and Clyde C. Dunton. Frances (Dunton) Pettus and Adelbert Dunton were the children of Dora and Loren Dunton, and brother and sister to Clyde C. and Lulu B. Loren Dunton died February 1920 in Antioch, Contra Costa County, California.

# MRS. DUNTON ANSWERS LAST CALL SUNDAY

Mrs. Isadora Florence Dunton passed away Sunday morning about 9 o'clock at the age of seventy-five years. Death was from the infirmatives of age.

Mrs. Dunton came to Somersville in 1872 and was one of the oldest pioneers of this section. After a few years, with her husband, to whom she was married at Earlville, Ill., just before coming to California, she removed to Eureka but returned to Antioch shortly after and made her home here since. Mr. Dunton was a carpenter by trade.

Mrs. Dunton was ill for two weeks prior to her death.

She is survived by one daughter, Mrs. Frances Westover, and one son, Adellbert Dunton.

Funeral services were held Tuesday afternoon from the Preston funeral home at 2:30, Rev. Stark officiating, as she was a member of that church. The services were attended by many friends of years standing.

The pall bearers were: L. Griswold, C. T. Richey, Wm. Schmidt, Ed. Hobson, Larry Masters and Arch Waldie. Interment was in M. & O. cemetery.

This newspaper article from the *Antioch Ledger*, March 3, 1927, announces the death of Mrs. Isadora Dunton. Mr. Dunton's obituary can be found in the newspaper appendix on page 697. Her daughter, listed as Frances E. Pettus on page 166, is now listed as Mrs. Frances Westover in the above obituary.

The Dunton family gravestone at Oak View Memorial Park Cemetery (formerly called the Masons' and Odd Fellows' Cemetery). Buried at this site are Loren and Isadora Dunton, the parents of Lulu and Clyde, their son, Adelbert, and Adelbert's wife, Portia (Cox) Dunton. Photograph taken May 2010 by Traci (Gibbons) Parent.

## PERSONAL INFORMATION:

| | |
|---|---|
| SEX: | Female |
| DATE OF BIRTH: | *Circa* 1854 |
| DATE OF DEATH: | November 1886 |
| PLACE OF DEATH: | |
| AGE AT DEATH: | Approximately 32 years |
| CAUSE OF DEATH: | |
| BIRTHPLACE: | Pennsylvania |
| SPOUSE: | Robert Easton |
| PARENTS: | |

## GRAVESITE INFORMATION:

| | |
|---|---|
| LOCATION OF GRAVESITE: | Unknown |
| GRAVESTONE: | Missing or never placed |
| TYPE OF GRAVESTONE: | |
| SHAPE OF GRAVESTONE: | |
| INSCRIPTION: | |
| EPITAPH: | |
| MOTIF: | |
| CARVER: | |
| BASE: | |
| TYPE OF BASE: | |
| ENCLOSURE: | |
| TYPE OF ENCLOSURE: | |
| FENCE: | |
| TYPE OF FENCE: | |
| FENCE MOTIF: | |

# EASTON, Mary

**ADDITIONAL PERSONAL INFORMATION:**
The *Antioch Ledger* newspaper, November 27, 1886 indicated that Mary left behind a husband and three children at the time of her death.

The *Assessment List, Contra Costa County, for 1872-'73*, lists Robert Easton as being assessed $225 in the town of Somersville; $220 for other solvent debts, and $25 for furniture.

According to the *1880 Census for Judsonville, Contra Costa County, California*, Mary Easton, age 26, was born *circa* 1854 in Pennsylvania. Also listed are her husband, Robert, a miner, age 36, born *circa* 1844 in Scotland and their children: William, age 8; Gertrude, age 5; and Ellen Maud, age 3. All are natives of California.

The *Great Register of the County of Contra Costa in the State of California 1898*, page 79, lists Mary's husband, Robert Easton, as a miner, age 52, height 5 feet, 8 ½ inches, complexion dark, color of eyes brown, and color of hair black. His "Country of Nativity" is listed as Scotland and his place of residence Somersville. He was naturalized July 24, 1869 in the 15th District Court in Contra Costa County. He registered to vote on August 10, 1896.

**ADDITIONAL GRAVESITE INFORMATION:**
The *Antioch Ledger* newspaper, November 27, 1886 reported that Mrs. Mary Easton "was laid to rest in the Stewartville cemetery on the 19th of November." It is not known if she was actually buried in Stewartville (another town in the Mount Diablo Coal Field located approximately two miles east of Somersville and Rose Hill Cemetery) or if the entry of Stewartville rather than Somersville was an error in the newspaper. This is the only source to document her burial in the area.

**REFERENCES:** 9 (Nov. 27, 1886), 12, see newspaper appendix page 698

## PERSONAL INFORMATION:

| | |
|---|---|
| SEX: | Female |
| DATE OF BIRTH: | June 12, 1852 |
| DATE OF DEATH: | November 25, 1876 |
| PLACE OF DEATH: | Somersville, Contra Costa County, California |
| AGE AT DEATH: | 24 years, 5 months, 13 days |
| CAUSE OF DEATH: | |
| BIRTHPLACE: | Wisconsin |
| SPOUSE: | Hugh Edwards |
| PARENTS: | Daniel and Jane Edwards |

## GRAVESITE INFORMATION:

| | |
|---|---|
| LOCATION OF GRAVESITE: | Section N-C, Plot #31 |
| GRAVESTONE: | Exists |
| TYPE OF GRAVESTONE: | Marble |
| SHAPE OF GRAVESTONE: | Tablet |
| INSCRIPTION: | *Beloved wife of* |
| EPITAPH: | *To me to live is Christ* |
| | *and to died gine.* [sic] |
| MOTIF: | Flower/rope with tassels |
| CARVER: | |
| BASE: | Exists |
| TYPE OF BASE: | Granite |
| ENCLOSURE: | Exists |
| TYPE OF ENCLOSURE: | Brick with sandstone cornerstones |
| FENCE: | Missing |
| TYPE OF FENCE: | Iron |
| FENCE MOTIF: | Clamshell/fleur-de-lis |

# EDWARDS, Catherine

**ADDITIONAL PERSONAL INFORMATION:**
The *1860 Census for Emmet, Dodge County, Wisconsin* lists Catherine Edwards, age 8, as a native of Wisconsin. Also listed are her parents and siblings: Daniel, age 40; and Jane, age 35, both natives of Wales; Elizabeth, age 11; Margaret, age 6; Daniel, age 4; and John, age 1; natives of Wisconsin.

Catherine Edwards, age 22, of Somersville, Contra Costa County, California, and Hugh Edwards, age 30, also of Somersville, applied for a marriage license on April 26, 1876. William D. Griffiths of Somersville is listed as the individual who desired "a license to authorize" the marriage. The information was recorded in the *Applications for Marriage Licenses, Contra Costa County, 1873-1887*, page 74, located at the Contra Costa County Historical Society History Center in Martinez, California. Catherine Edwards, a native of Wisconsin married Hugh Edwards, a native of Wales, on April 26, 1876. Catherine's maiden name was also Edwards. The *Index to Marriage Certificates* located at the Contra Costa County Hall of Records, Martinez, California states that they were married by William H. Ford and that the information was recorded in Volume 2, page 118.

The *Contra Costa Gazette* newspaper, December 16, 1876, says Catherine died at age 23 years, 5 months, and 11 days, and not 24 years, 5 months, and 13 days as stated on her gravestone. Catherine died only six months after marrying Hugh Edwards.

**ADDITIONAL GRAVESITE INFORMATION:**
This gravestone was still present in the cemetery in 1963 because it is recorded in a college term paper by Jim Rotelli.

Zelma Myrick, who recorded information in a notebook in the 1930s during a visit to Rose Hill Cemetery, reported "Iron fence in good condition."

A photograph (see page 116) shows the gravestone for John T. Conner sitting at this site in the 1960s. It is not known why John's gravestone was placed at Catherine's gravesite.

A photograph of the gravesite appears in *Contra Costa Living* (a supplement of the *Contra Costa Sunday Times* newspaper, April 11, 1971, page 8). The photograph shows the iron fence existing at the site.

According to the *Alameda Times Star* newspaper, Alameda, California, November 29, 1973, the gravestone was stolen from Rose Hill Cemetery prior to East Bay Regional Park District acquisition. The stone was recovered by the Walnut Creek Police Department and remained in storage for ten years in the property department before being returned to the East Bay Regional Park District.

The concrete that was once used to embed the gravestone to the ground prior to it being stolen, was removed from the gravestone by Black Diamond Rangers. The existing granite base at the site was leveled on a sub-grade concrete pad. The gravestone was returned to the cemetery and attached to the base in July 2001. The location of the gravesite was based on a map of the cemetery drawn in 1954. The epitaph that appears on Catherine's gravestone is a variation of a *Bible* verse and comes from Philippians Chapter 1, Verse 21. The *Bible* verse is: "For to me to live is Christ, and to die is gain."

**REFERENCES:** 1, 2, 3, 5, 6, 8 (May 6, 1876 and Dec. 16, 1876), 11 (P610.117.15 and P610.362.5), 12, 14, *Alameda Times Star* newspaper (Nov. 29, 1973), see newspaper appendix page 699

**PERSONAL INFORMATION:**

| | |
|---|---|
| SEX: | Female |
| DATE OF BIRTH: | 1864 |
| DATE OF DEATH: | August 1865 |
| PLACE OF DEATH: | Somersville, Contra Costa County, California |
| AGE AT DEATH: | 1 year, 3 months |
| CAUSE OF DEATH: | Brain fever |
| BIRTHPLACE: | At sea |
| SPOUSE: | None |
| PARENTS: | John and Emma Edwards |

**GRAVESITE INFORMATION:**

| | |
|---|---|
| LOCATION OF GRAVESITE: | Unknown |
| GRAVESTONE: | Missing or never placed |
| TYPE OF GRAVESTONE: | |
| SHAPE OF GRAVESTONE: | |
| INSCRIPTION: | |
| EPITAPH: | |
| MOTIF: | |
| CARVER: | |
| BASE: | |
| TYPE OF BASE: | |
| ENCLOSURE: | |
| TYPE OF ENCLOSURE: | |
| FENCE: | |
| TYPE OF FENCE: | |
| FENCE MOTIF: | |

# EDWARDS, Clara

**ADDITIONAL PERSONAL INFORMATION:**
Clara was born aboard the ship *Black Hawk*, nine days before it arrived in San Francisco, California from Sydney Harbour, Australia. Clara's father, John, was killed by a mine cave-in in Nortonville, Contra Costa County, California in September 1870. Clara's mother, Emma, died of brain fever on February 24, 1865, in Somersville, Contra Costa County, California. Both her mother and father are buried in Rose Hill Cemetery. It is believed that Clara may be buried next to her parents. Clara died 6 months after her mother and from the same illness. The information regarding Clara comes from a family history document that was shared by descendants. See Emma Edwards and John Edwards.

**ADDITIONAL GRAVESITE INFORMATION:**
Clara's name has not been recorded on any previous cemetery lists.

**REFERENCES:** 12

EXCURSION TO-MORROW. — Parties at Nortonville have engaged the Parthenius for an excursion to San Francisco to-morrow (Sunday) and return. The boat will leave Antioch at 6:45 A. M., calling at Black Diamond, Martinez and Benicia. Excursionists will have five hours in the city. A band of music will accompany the excursion and a pleasant time is anticipated. Fare for round trip from Antioch and Black Diamond, $2; from Nortonville, $2 25; from Martinez and Benicia, $1 50.

## Summer Excursions!

THE ELEGANT AND FAST STEAMER

# PARTHENIUS,

STOWELL, MASTER.

On and after TUESDAY, MAY 1st, 1877, will resume her Daily trips (Sundays excepted), leaving Washington street Wharf, at 3½ P. M., for VALLEJO, BENICIA, MARTINEZ, NEW YORK AND PITTSBURG LANDING AND ANTIOCH, Connecting with Stages and Cars for Somersville, Nortonville, Pacheco, Concord and Clayton.
**Easiest and Most Charming Route to Mount Diablo,**
Connecting with Bennett's Elegant Six-Horse Carriages from Martinez.

Returning leaves ANTIOCH at 6 A. M., making the usual Way-Stations.
For freight and passage apply to
A. D. SHARON,
305 Sansome street, or to Purser on board Steamer.

The articles above come from the *Antioch Ledger* newspaper and describe summer excursions to San Francisco aboard the steamer *Parthenius*. The excursion fare from Nortonville in 1874 was $2.25. In 1877 the excursion included connecting stages and cars for Somersville and Nortonville. The article on the left is from July 25, 1874 and the *Parthenius* advertisement, on the right, is from May 12, 1877. Somersville residents, Clara, and her parents, Emma and John Edwards were already deceased at the time these articles appeared in the newspaper. However, they may have used similar transportation to travel from San Francisco to Somersville when they arrived in the Mount Diablo Coal Field in the 1860s.

# EDWARDS,
## Emma

## PERSONAL INFORMATION:

| | |
|---|---|
| SEX: | Female |
| DATE OF BIRTH: | February 25, 1842 |
| DATE OF DEATH: | February 24, 1865 |
| PLACE OF DEATH: | Somersville, Contra Costa County, California |
| AGE AT DEATH: | 23 years |
| CAUSE OF DEATH: | Phrenitis or Brain fever |
| BIRTHPLACE: | Castle Hills, New South Wales, Australia |
| SPOUSE: | John Edwards |
| PARENTS: | Matthew and Frances Ann (Smith) Gallard |

## GRAVESITE INFORMATION:

| | |
|---|---|
| LOCATION OF GRAVESITE: | Unknown |
| GRAVESTONE: | Missing or never placed |
| TYPE OF GRAVESTONE: | |
| SHAPE OF GRAVESTONE: | |
| INSCRIPTION: | |
| EPITAPH: | |
| MOTIF: | |
| CARVER: | |
| BASE: | |
| TYPE OF BASE: | |
| ENCLOSURE: | |
| TYPE OF ENCLOSURE: | |
| FENCE: | |
| TYPE OF FENCE: | |
| FENCE MOTIF: | |

# EDWARDS, Emma

**ADDITIONAL PERSONAL INFORMATION:**
In 1860, Emma Gallard married John Edwards. A few years prior to 1860, John Edwards left Pennsylvania and traveled to Australia. Emma's daughter, Clara, and husband, John, and are also buried in Rose Hill.

According to family records, Emma (Gallard) Edwards was one of ten children born to Matthew Gallard and Frances Ann (Smith) Gallard. Emma's father was born June 12, 1808, in Southborough, Kent, England. He was the son of Matthew and Susan Gallard. Matthew and Frances were married in 1830, at St. Martins Church, Inficle, England. Matthew died on October 29, 1850, in the county of Cumberland, near Sydney, New South Wales, Australia. The children of Matthew and Frances Ann (Smith) Gallard were:

- Robert, born May 31, 1831
- Frank, born Feb. 25, 1833 (married Susan Small)
- Edward, born Oct. 29, 1835
- George, born Dec. 28, 1837; died June 2, 1839, Sydney, Southborough, England
- Susan, born May 3, 1840 (married George Roberts; left Australia for Utah on June 27, 1857)
- Emma, born Feb. 25, 1842, Castle Hills, New South Wales, Australia; died Feb. 24, 1865, Somersville, Contra Costa County, CA (married John Edwards)
- Henry, born Oct. 17, 1844
- Rosina, born July 12, 1846, Castle Hills, New South Wales, Australia; died Aug. 28, 1929, Santa Cruz, Santa Cruz County, CA (married Henry Washington Byron)
- Mark, born April 16, 1848; died April 20, 1882
- Frances, born Dec, 15, 1849, New South Wales, Australia

Emma and John's daughter, Clara, was born aboard a ship nine days before their arrival in San Francisco. According to information obtained from descendants:

> John and Emma and their baby Johnnie, took passage on the *Black Hawk* for San Francisco, California.

The family eventually settled in Somersville and most likely arrived there sometime in 1864. The document also states that in December 1864 there was an epidemic of scarlet fever.

> Emma had worked herself into brain fever and died five days [in Somersville] after taking sick, leaving little Johnnie sick with inflammation of the bowels, and little Clara nine months old, and a sick husband. Little Clara died afterwards when she was fifteen months old. John Edwards was killed by a mine cave-in in the Nortonville mines in 1870...

Emma's sister Rosina Gallard married Henry W. Byron on February 22, 1864 and immediately took passage on the *T. W. House* to San Francisco, California. Upon arrival in California, they joined Emma and John Edwards in Somersville where Henry Byron secured work. The Byrons lived in Somersville from 1864 until 1869, except for the nine months they lived in Nortonville.

The *Contra Costa Gazette* newspaper, March 11, 1865, lists her cause of death as phrenitis or brain fever. Emma's date of birth comes from family history documents shared by descendants. See Clara Edwards and John Edwards.

**ADDITIONAL GRAVESITE INFORMATION:**
Descendants believe that Emma Edwards is buried in Rose Hill Cemetery. The *Antioch Ledger* newspaper, September 24, 1870 states that her husband, John Edwards, was buried in the cemetery beside her. John died 5½ years after the death of his wife. No other sources document Emma's burial in the cemetery.

**REFERENCES:** 8 (March 11, 1865), 12, see newspaper appendix page 700

# EDWARDS,
## John

## PERSONAL INFORMATION:

|  |  |
|---|---|
| SEX: | Male |
| DATE OF BIRTH: | *Circa* 1829 |
| DATE OF DEATH: | September 1870 |
| PLACE OF DEATH: | Nortonville, Contra Costa County, California |
| AGE AT DEATH: | 41 years |
| CAUSE OF DEATH: | Mine cave-in |
| BIRTHPLACE: | Pennsylvania |
| SPOUSE: | Emma (Gallard) Edwards |
| PARENTS: | Mr. and Mrs. Edwards |

## GRAVESITE INFORMATION:

|  |  |
|---|---|
| LOCATION OF GRAVESITE: | Unknown |
| GRAVESTONE: | Missing or never placed |
| TYPE OF GRAVESTONE: | |
| SHAPE OF GRAVESTONE: | |
| INSCRIPTION: | |
| EPITAPH: | |
| MOTIF: | |
| CARVER: | |
| BASE: | |
| TYPE OF BASE: | |
| ENCLOSURE: | |
| TYPE OF ENCLOSURE: | |
| FENCE: | |
| TYPE OF FENCE: | |
| FENCE MOTIF: | |

# EDWARDS, John

**ADDITIONAL PERSONAL INFORMATION:**
The *1870 Census for Township 3, Contra Costa County, California* lists John Edwards, age 41, as miner and a native of Wales.

According to the *Antioch Ledger* newspaper, September 24, 1870, John was a native of Wales. Family records state he was born in Pennsylvania. John's wife, Emma, and child, Clara, died before he did and are also buried in Rose Hill Cemetery. Also, according to the *Antioch Ledger*, at the time of his death, he left a son, about seven years of age, living in Tulare, Tulare County, California.

See Clara Edwards and Emma Edwards.

**ADDITIONAL GRAVESITE INFORMATION:**
The *Antioch Ledger* newspaper, September 24, 1870 states that John was buried in the cemetery beside his wife. This is the only source to document his burial in Rose Hill Cemetery.

**REFERENCES:** 9 (Sept. 24, 1870), 12, see newspaper appendix page 701

---

**The Somersville Road.**

Numerous applications have been made to us recently concerning the Somersville road, between that town and Antioch, it being in a very bad condition. We do not know of any but the Supervisors who have the authority to order the road repaired; but we do say that the complaints made are just, and we trust the matter will be attended to. On entering the canyon there is barely space to allow a coal-wagon to pass safely, and there are points on the road where passage endangers life. Surely the amount of taxes paid by the citizens of Nortonville and Somersville will justify the expenditure of a sum sufficient to render the road safe, to say nothing of comfort.

---

**Improvement.**

The shaky places on the Somersville road, in the canyon, are being repaired and rendered comparatively safe. While the workmen are about it, they should chip off the overhanging masses of earth which threaten to fall into the road, and widen the grade with the material thus obtained.

---

John Edwards and his family were living in the Mount Diablo Coal Field at the time these articles appeared in the *Antioch Ledger* newspaper. The article on the left is from the June 18, 1870 edition of the newspaper and the article on the right from July 16, 1870.

# EDWARDS,
## Joseph M.

## PERSONAL INFORMATION:

SEX: Male

DATE OF BIRTH: 1843

DATE OF DEATH: September 4, 1889

PLACE OF DEATH: Stewartville, Contra Costa County, California

AGE AT DEATH: 46 years

CAUSE OF DEATH:

BIRTHPLACE: Troedyrhiw, Cayo. [sic] Carmarthenshire, Wales

SPOUSE:

PARENTS: David and Jane Edwards

## GRAVESITE INFORMATION:

LOCATION OF GRAVESITE: Section N-B, Plot #7a

GRAVESTONE: Exists

TYPE OF GRAVESTONE: Marble

SHAPE OF GRAVESTONE: Tablet

INSCRIPTION: *In Memory of/the beloved son of/Died at Stewartsville* [sic]

EPITAPH:

MOTIF: Rope with tassels

CARVER:

BASE: Exists

TYPE OF BASE: Sandstone

ENCLOSURE:

TYPE OF ENCLOSURE:

FENCE: Exists

TYPE OF FENCE: Iron with granite blocks

FENCE MOTIF:

# EDWARDS, Joseph M.

**ADDITIONAL PERSONAL INFORMATION:**
The *1851 Wales Census Record, Llandovery Registration District* lists Joseph Edwards, age 7, as a native of Conwil Gaio, Carmarthenshire, Wales. Also listed are his parents Jane Edwards, age 35, a native of Talley, Carmarthenshire, Wales; and David Edwards, age 33, a native of Conwil Gaio, Carmarthenshire, Wales; and their children: Mary, born about 1846, and William, born about 1849.

The *1861 Wales Census Record, Llandovery Registration District* lists Joseph Edwards, age 17, as a native of Cayo, Carmarthenshire Wales. Also listed are his parents: David, age 48, a native of Cayo, Carmarthenshire, Wales, and Jane, age 46, a native of Talley, Carmarthenshire, Wales, and their children: John, born about 1855; Mary, born about 1844; and William, born about 1849.

The *1880 Census for Nortonville, Contra Costa County, California* lists Joseph Edwards, age 36, as an engineer and native of Wales.

According to the *Contra Costa Gazette* newspaper, September 7, 1889, Joseph died September 3, 1889, and not September 4, 1889 as indicated on his gravestone. According to a coal field descendant, Joseph probably died in a mine accident. He traveled from Wales with Rees G. Thomas and David E. Griffith (both buried in Rose Hill Cemetery). It is also believed that Joseph was four years old when he traveled to the United States and that he is probably related to Griffith and Thomas (although Welsh census records have him in Wales at least until age 17).

According to a deed dated May 5, 1885, Joseph Edwards sold land to David E. Griffiths [sic] for the sum of $1,500 in gold coin. See David E. Griffith.

The place of birth is spelled exactly as it appears on the gravestone. Most likely the place he was born in was Cynwyl Gaeo, Carmarthenshire, Wales.

**ADDITIONAL GRAVESITE INFORMATION:**
Zelma Myrick, who recorded information in a notebook in the 1930s during a visit to Rose Hill Cemetery, reported the "Stone broken down at bottom in the same plot as Griffith monument."

Joseph shares a gravesite with David E. Griffith. According to the *Contra Costa Gazette* newspaper, May 26, 1900, David E. Griffith is buried next to Edwards because "...He [Griffith] directs that his body be buried beside that of Joe E. [sic] Edwards in the Somersville Cemetery..."

The iron fence surrounding the gravesite was repaired by Black Diamond Rangers. Part of the fence had to be replicated. The gravestone is broken into seventeen pieces with portions missing. The pieces were concreted flat to the ground prior to East Bay Regional Park District acquisition. A sandstone base, holding a bottom portion of the stone, also exists. See David E. Griffith and Rees G. Thomas.

**REFERENCES:** 1, 2, 3, 4, 5, 6, 8 (Sept. 7, 1889 and May 26, 1900), 11 (P610.31.193, P610.31.194, P610.119.23, P610.119.24, P610.145.1, P610.168.20, P610.268.2, and P610.294.8), 12, 14, see newspaper appendix page 701 and (David E. Griffith) pages 233-236 and 709

# ENGLER,
## Annie Henrietta

## PERSONAL INFORMATION:

| | |
|---|---|
| SEX: | Female |
| DATE OF BIRTH: | May 1875 |
| DATE OF DEATH: | September 15, 1877 |
| PLACE OF DEATH: | Nortonville, Contra Costa County, California |
| AGE AT DEATH: | 2 years, 4 months |
| CAUSE OF DEATH: | |
| BIRTHPLACE: | |
| SPOUSE: | None |
| PARENTS: | John and Mary/Annie Mary (Heisler or Hausler) Engler |

## GRAVESITE INFORMATION:

| | |
|---|---|
| LOCATION OF GRAVESITE: | Unknown |
| GRAVESTONE: | Missing |
| TYPE OF GRAVESTONE: | |
| SHAPE OF GRAVESTONE: | |
| INSCRIPTION: | |
| EPITAPH: | |
| MOTIF: | |
| CARVER: | |
| BASE: | |
| TYPE OF BASE: | |
| ENCLOSURE: | |
| TYPE OF ENCLOSURE: | |
| FENCE: | |
| TYPE OF FENCE: | |
| FENCE MOTIF: | |

East Bay Regional Park District

# ENGLER, Annie Henrietta

**ADDITIONAL PERSONAL INFORMATION:**
The obituary from the *Antioch Ledger* newspaper, September 22, 1877, says Annie died on September 12, at about age 3 years. The last name appears in the obituary as "Englar." The *Contra Costa Gazette* newspaper, September 29, 1877, also states that Annie died September 12, at about age about 3 years. The last name also appears in the obituary as "Englar."

According to cemetery lists compiled in 1922, 1935/1936, 1953, and 1954, Annie died September 15, 1877, and not September 12, 1877, as stated in the newspapers. The Engler family *Bible* records Annie's birth date as April 27, 1874, and her death date as August 25, 1876. It is not known why these dates differ so much from what was recorded in the newspapers and on the gravestone.

According to the Engler family *Bible*, John and Mary (also known as Annie Mary) Engler had at least nine children. They were:

- Margaret, born Sept. 14, 1859
- Emeline Mary, born May 8, 1861 in Ohio; died 1936, San Francisco, California
- William, born Dec. 29, 1862; died Dec. 18, 1865

- Katerina Louisa, born Sept. or Nov. 14, 1864; died Dec. 27, 1947, San Francisco, California
- George Frederick, born Nov. 18, 1865; died Aug. 14, 1908
- John Wilhelm, born Dec. 7, 1869; died Aug. 8, 1929
- Charles, born Nov. 7, 1870; died Sept. 5, 1871
- Charles Henry (or Henry Charles), born July 15, 1872; died Nov. 10, 1873
- Annie Henrietta, born April 27, 1874; died Aug. 25, 1876

Annie Henrietta's father, John, and brother, Charles, are also buried in Rose Hill Cemetery. See Charles Engler and John Engler.

**ADDITIONAL GRAVESITE INFORMATION:**
According to cemetery lists compiled in 1922, 1935/1936, 1953, and 1954, Annie is buried in Rose Hill Cemetery.

**REFERENCES:** 1, 2, 4, 6, 8 (Sept. 29, 1877 and June 22, 1878), 9 (Sept. 22, 1877), 12, (see also Jeanette Parsons - "Fire at Nortonville," page 442), see newspaper appendix page 702

**DIED.**

At Somersville Sept. 12th, a son of William Hughes, age 7 years.

At Somersville Sept. 14th, Thomas Joseph Jenkins, age about 5 years.

At Nortonville Sept. 12th, youngest daughter of Mrs. Englar, age about 3 years.

From the *Antioch Ledger* newspaper, September 22, 1877.
Annie Henrietta Engler is the third entry in this obituary. Her last name was spelled as "Englar."

## PERSONAL INFORMATION:

| | |
|---|---|
| SEX: | Male |
| DATE OF BIRTH: | June 1873 |
| DATE OF DEATH: | October 6, 1874 |
| PLACE OF DEATH: | Nortonville, Contra Costa County, California |
| AGE AT DEATH: | 1 year, 4 months |
| CAUSE OF DEATH: | |
| BIRTHPLACE: | |
| SPOUSE: | None |
| PARENTS: | John and Mary/Annie Mary (Heisler or Hausler) Engler |

## GRAVESITE INFORMATION:

| | |
|---|---|
| LOCATION OF GRAVESITE: | Unknown |
| GRAVESTONE: | Missing |
| TYPE OF GRAVESTONE: | |
| SHAPE OF GRAVESTONE: | |
| INSCRIPTION: | |
| EPITAPH: | |
| MOTIF: | |
| CARVER: | |
| BASE: | |
| TYPE OF BASE: | |
| ENCLOSURE: | |
| TYPE OF ENCLOSURE: | |
| FENCE: | |
| TYPE OF FENCE: | |
| FENCE MOTIF: | |

# ENGLER, Charles

**ADDITIONAL PERSONAL INFORMATION:**
According to the *Contra Costa Gazette* newspaper, October 31, 1874, Charles Engler died on October 20, and not October 6 as recorded from the gravestone. The last name of this family has also been spelled "Englar."

The Engler family *Bible* records Charles' birth date as November 7, 1870, and his death date as September 5, 1871. It is not known why these dates differ so much from what was recorded in the newspapers and on the gravestone.

His father, John, and sister, Annie Henrietta, are also buried in Rose Hill. See Annie Henrietta Engler and John Engler.

**ADDITIONAL GRAVESITE INFORMATION:**
According to cemetery lists compiled in 1935, 1935/1936, 1953, and 1954, Charles is buried in Rose Hill Cemetery.

**REFERENCES:** 1, 2, 3, 8 (Oct. 31, 1874), 12, see newspaper appendix page 702

Reference 41.29

Main Street, Nortonville, looking north. A fire in June 1878 destroyed much of Main Street including the Engler family shoe store and dwelling.

**PERSONAL INFORMATION:**

SEX: Male

DATE OF BIRTH: November 26, 1832

DATE OF DEATH: September 4, 1875

PLACE OF DEATH: Nortonville, Contra Costa County, California

AGE AT DEATH: 42 years, 9 months, 9 days

CAUSE OF DEATH: Suicide

BIRTHPLACE: Germany

SPOUSE: Mary/Annie Mary (Heisler or Hausler) Engler

PARENTS:

**GRAVESITE INFORMATION:**

LOCATION OF GRAVESITE: Unknown

GRAVESTONE: Missing

TYPE OF GRAVESTONE:

SHAPE OF GRAVESTONE:

INSCRIPTION:

EPITAPH:

MOTIF:

CARVER:

BASE:

TYPE OF BASE:

ENCLOSURE:

TYPE OF ENCLOSURE:

FENCE:

TYPE OF FENCE:

FENCE MOTIF:

# ENGLER, John

**ADDITIONAL PERSONAL INFORMATION:**

The last name of this family has also been spelled Englar. John's date of birth was calculated by www.timeanddate.com, using his date of death and age of death from the reference lists. The Engler family *Bible* records John's birth date as March 3, 1834, and his death date as September 4, 1875. Based on these dates, John would have been 41 years, 6 months, and 1 day old at the time of his death. *The Antioch Ledger* newspaper, September 11, 1875, says John's age at death was 45 years and not 42 years as recorded from his gravestone.

John Engler, age 28, was enrolled as a private in Company C, 107th Regiment of the Ohio Volunteer Infantry on the 5th day of August 1862 at Richland County, Ohio. He was honorably discharged for physical disability at Washington D. C. in December 1862. At the time of his enlistment he was living in Shelby, Richland County, Ohio.

According to a Claimants Affidavit in the State of California, City and County of San Francisco (in the matter of the claim for widows pension of Annie M. Griffiths, formerly Annie M. Engler), dated August 20, 1917:

> John Engler was a shoemaker by occupation, was about five feet eleven inches tall in height, dark brown hair and eyes and dark complexion. Wore a goete [sic] had very heavy lips.

The *Pacific Coast Business Directory for 1876-78*, page 195, lists John Engler as a boot and shoe maker in Nortonville. The *Contra Costa Gazette* newspaper, June 22, 1878 states that the shoe store and dwelling for Mrs. Engler was destroyed during a fire at Nortonville. (See article "Fire at Nortonville" on page 442.)

The *1880 Census for Nortonville Precinct, Contra Costa County, California* lists Mary Engler, age 40, as a nurse and native of Germany. Also listed are her children: Emma, age 19, a native of Ohio and also a nurse; Kate, age 15, a native of Ohio; George, age 13, a native of Missouri; and John, age 11, a native of Illinois. Two of their children, Annie (died Sept. 15, 1877, age 2 years, 4 months) and Charles (died Oct. 6, 1874, age 1 year, 4 months), are also buried in Rose Hill Cemetery. After the death of her husband, Mary married Griffith L. Griffiths on December 25, 1886.

According to information recorded in an Engler family *Bible* in the possession of Engler descendants, John married Mary (Annie Mary) Heisler or Hausler on December 13, 1858. Mary (Annie Mary) was born in Germany on May 5, 1839 and died April 1, 1924 in San Francisco, California at the age of 84 years, 10 months, and 27 days. There were at least nine children in the Engler family. See Annie Henrietta and Charles Engler.

**ADDITIONAL GRAVESITE INFORMATION:**

According to cemetery lists compiled in 1935, 1935/1936, 1953, and 1954, John is buried in Rose Hill Cemetery. Nothing exists in the cemetery today to mark the burial location for this family.

**REFERENCES:** 1, 2, 3, 6, 8 (Sept. 11, 1875 and June 22, 1878), 9 (Sept. 11, 1875), 11 (P610.307.1, P610.307.3, and P610.307.5), 12, see newspaper appendix page 702

Reference 307.1

Reference 307.5

Left, John Engler of Nortonville, Contra Costa County, California, date unknown. Right, Mary/Annie Mary Engler (widow of John Engler) and Griffith L. Griffiths. After the death of her husband, John Engler, Mary/Annie Mary (Heisler) Engler married Mr. Griffiths in 1886.

Reference 307.3

Annie Mary (Heisler) Engler Griffiths and three of her children, left to right:  Katerina (Kate) Louisa, married William A. Adams; Emeline (Emma) Mary, married William P. Hughes; and John Wilhelm Engler. According to the family *Bible* there were nine children in the John and Annie Mary (Heisler) Engler family: The children were:

- Margaret, born Sept. 14, 1859
- Emeline Mary, born May 8, 1861
- William, born Dec. 29, 1862
- Katerina Louisa, born Sept. or Nov. 1864
- George Frederick, born Nov. 18, 1865
- John Wilhelm., born Dec. 7, 1869
- Charles, born Nov. 7, 1870
- Charles Henry (or Henry Charles), born July 15, 1872
- Annie Henrietta, born April 27, 1874

# ENO,
## Susan J.

## PERSONAL INFORMATION:

| | |
|---|---|
| SEX: | Female |
| DATE OF BIRTH: | June 5, 1873 |
| DATE OF DEATH: | February 3, 1880 |
| PLACE OF DEATH: | Judsonville, Contra Costa County, California |
| AGE AT DEATH: | 6 years, 7 months, 28 days |
| CAUSE OF DEATH: | |
| BIRTHPLACE: | |
| SPOUSE: | None |
| PARENTS: | John W. and Elizabeth (Reed) Eno |

## GRAVESITE INFORMATION:

| | |
|---|---|
| LOCATION OF GRAVESITE: | Section N-F, Plot #71 |
| GRAVESTONE: | Exists |
| TYPE OF GRAVESTONE: | Marble |
| SHAPE OF GRAVESTONE: | Tablet |
| INSCRIPTION: | *Dau. of* |
| EPITAPH: | *Alas how changed that lovely flower,* |
| | *Which bloomed and cheered our heart.* |
| | *Fair fleeting comforts of an hour* |
| | *How soon were called to part.* |
| MOTIF: | Nipped rosebud |
| CARVER: | |
| BASE: | Exists |
| TYPE OF BASE: | Sandstone |
| ENCLOSURE: | |
| TYPE OF ENCLOSURE: | |
| FENCE: | |
| TYPE OF FENCE: | |
| FENCE MOTIF: | |

# ENO, Susan J.

**ADDITIONAL PERSONAL INFORMATION:**
According to the *Antioch Ledger* newspaper, February 7, 1880, "Susie" died at age 7 years, and not 6 years, 7 months, and 28 days as stated on her gravestone.

The *1876 Contra Costa County Voting Register* lists John Willis Eno, age 26, as a native of England and miner living in Somersville. His date of registration was June 22, 1867.

The *1880 Census for Township Five, Judsonville, Contra Costa County, California* lists John W. Eno, age 40, as a miner and native of England. Also listed are his wife, Elizabeth, age 37, a native of England, and their children: Mary F., age 9, a native of Illinois; Annie, age 5, a native of England; John, age 3, a native of California; and Elizabeth, age 1 month, a native of California.

According to descendants, Susan's father, John Willis Eno, was born about 1840, in Lincolnshire, England. He married Elizabeth Reed (born September 2, 1842 in London, England) in March 1870 in Boston, Lincolnshire, England. John died on June 30, 1884, in South Wellington, British Columbia, Canada in a mine explosion. His wife died on November 23, 1919, in Toronto, York County, Ontario, Canada. John and Elizabeth (Reed) Eno had at least six children. The places of birth come from descendants and the 1880 census. Their children were:

- Mary Frances, born about 1871, Illinois (1880 census)
- Susan J., born June 5, 1873
- Annie, born about 1875, England (1880 census)
- John Willis, born December 17, 1876, Contra Costa County, California
- Elizabeth, born June 1880, Contra Costa County, California
- Violet Ella, born August 19, 1884, Wellington, British Columbia, Canada

**ADDITIONAL GRAVESITE INFORMATION:**
The gravestone was stolen from Rose Hill Cemetery prior to East Bay Regional Park District acquisition and was eventually returned. The lower left corner of the gravestone has been broken off and is missing. Part of the epitaph is missing because of this. The missing part of the epitaph was provided by Zelma Myrick, who recorded information in a notebook in the 1930s during a visit to Rose Hill Cemetery.

In August 2004, Black Diamond Rangers located the Eno burial site by taking the small gravestone from storage and matching it to the piece of marble still sitting in the base at the gravesite. A marble encasement was made by the Black Diamond Rangers to support the broken stone. The gravestone was repaired and placed in the encasement and returned to the cemetery in April 2009.

A photograph of the gravestone appears in *The Bear Facts*, "Nortonville and Somersville Ghost Coal Mining Towns," February 1947, page 6, published by the Dow Chemical Company, Pittsburg, California.

**REFERENCES:** 1, 2, 3, 6, 8 (Feb. 14, 1880), 9 (Feb. 7, 1880), 11 (P610.117.12), 12, 14, *Pittsburg Post Dispatch* newspaper (Wednesday, June 15, 1955, page 9), see newspaper appendix page 703

Judsonville social hall and school, 1890. Susan Eno died in Judsonville on February 3, 1880.
The Eno family was listed as living in this community in the 1880 census.

Reference 329.1                                               Reference 329.2

Left: Mary Frances Eno, born *circa* 1872 in Illinois and sister to Susan Eno. Right: Pictured left to right are three generations of Eno family members in 1935; Mary Eno, sister to Susan Eno; Charlotte Horrobin, daughter of Mary Eno; and Rena Mary Blackburn, daughter of Charlotte Horrobin.

## PERSONAL INFORMATION:

| | |
|---|---|
| SEX: | Female |
| DATE OF BIRTH: | |
| DATE OF DEATH: | |
| PLACE OF DEATH: | |
| AGE AT DEATH: | 6 years |
| CAUSE OF DEATH: | |
| BIRTHPLACE: | |
| SPOUSE: | None |
| PARENTS: | John H. and Araminta/Arminta A. (Prosser) Evans |

## GRAVESITE INFORMATION:

| | |
|---|---|
| LOCATION OF GRAVESITE: | Unknown |
| GRAVESTONE: | Missing or never placed |
| TYPE OF GRAVESTONE: | |
| SHAPE OF GRAVESTONE: | |
| INSCRIPTION: | |
| EPITAPH: | |
| MOTIF: | |
| CARVER: | |
| BASE: | |
| TYPE OF BASE: | |
| ENCLOSURE: | |
| TYPE OF ENCLOSURE: | |
| FENCE: | |
| TYPE OF FENCE: | |
| FENCE MOTIF: | |

# EVANS, Elizabeth

**ADDITIONAL PERSONAL INFORMATION:**
Elizabeth's father, John H. Evans, came to the Mount Diablo Coal Field from Rhos, Clwyd, Wales. He arrived in the United States in 1872 with his sister Sarah. (Sarah later married a Mr. Griffiths.) Their mother had died when John was five years old.

John Evans, age 22, of Nortonville, Contra Costa County, California, and Mannty Prosser, age 19, also of Nortonville, applied for a marriage license on December 28, 1874. The information was recorded in the *Applications for Marriage Licenses, Contra Costa County, 1873-1887*, page 41, located at the Contra Costa County Historical Society History Center in Martinez, California. John Evans, a native of North Wales, married Araminta Prosser, a native of California, on December 28, 1874. Witnesses were Nortonville residents Henry Thomas and Mary Thomas. William H. Ford, Justice of the Peace, performed the ceremony.

According to descendants, Araminta (perhaps nicknamed "Mannty" - see marriage license application information above) was the stepdaughter of Watkin Prosser. Watkin's wife was Margaret. (Note: Watkin had a brother, William Prosser, who also lived in the coal field. William's wife, Mary Prosser, is buried in Rose Hill Cemetery, Section S-E, Plot #78.) John H. and Araminta Evans had eleven children, two of whom died at birth. Elizabeth is the only child of the family known to be buried at Rose Hill Cemetery. In 1900, the family moved to Antioch, Contra Costa County, California. John died on April 12, 1924 and was interred in Oak View Cemetery on East 18th Street in Antioch. According to his obituary in the *Antioch Ledger* newspaper on April 17, 1924, John passed away at his home on Sixth Street in Antioch. He arrived in the United States when he was 17 years of age. He mined in Wales and British Columbia, Canada prior to arriving in the Mount Diablo Coal Field. At the time of his death, three sons and five daughters were living. They were:

William Evans, Watkin Evans, Ellis Evans, Sarah E. (Evans) Brown, Minta (Evans) Olsen, Margaret (Evans) Murrey, Frances (Evans) Murrey, and Mrs. Haudashalt (perhaps this was Maud (Evans) Haudashalt).

The *1880 Census for Judsonville, Contra Costa County, California* lists John H. Evans, age 24, a miner, born *circa* 1856 in Wales. Also listed in the census are his wife Aminta [sic], age 24, a native of California; and their children: Sarah E. M., age 4; Watkin, age 3; and Maggie May, age 1; all natives of British Columbia.

The *1900 Census for Antioch, Contra Costa County, California* lists John Evans, age 44, born *circa* 1856 in Wales. Also listed are his wife Aminta [sic], age 43, born *circa* 1857 in "Canada English" and their children: Watkin, age 23, born in "Canada English"; Frances, age 15; Aminta, age 12; Ellis, age 10; William, age 6; and Maud, age 3; natives of California.

The *1920 Census for Antioch, Contra Costa County, California* lists John H. Evans, age 64, as a native of Wales. Also listed are his wife, Araminta A. Evans, age 63, a native of California and their daughter, T. Maude Evans, age 23, a native of California.

Elizabeth's parents are buried at Oak View Memorial Park Cemetery in Antioch, California. John H. Evans died April 12, 1924, at the age of 69 years. His wife, Arminta, died January 5, 1936, at the age of 80 years.

**ADDITIONAL GRAVESITE INFORMATION:**
In March 1996, great granddaughters of John H. and Araminta Evans reported to park staff that Elizabeth Evans, age 6, was buried in Rose Hill Cemetery. The descendants also provided the names of Elizabeth's parents and stated that no gravestone was placed at her gravesite.

**REFERENCES:** 9 (April 17, 1924), 12

## John H. Evans Buried Monday

### Was Resident of This County Forty Years Ago—Odd Fellows Officiate at Grave

John H. Evans, long a resident of this community, passed away at his home on Sixth street Saturday, April 12th, at the age of 69 years. The deceased, who was born in Wales, came to America when he was 17 years of age. During most of his life he followed mining, beginning when a boy in Wales, later following the same pursuit in British Columbia and then coming to the coal mines near Antioch. He passed nearly forty years of his life in Contra Costa county. Mr. Evans leaves to mourn his passing his wife, Araminta A. Evans, three sons, William, Watkins and Ellis Evans; five daughters, Mrs. Sarah E. Brown, Mrs. Minta Evans Olsen, Mrs. Margaret Murrey, Mrs. Frances Murrey and Mrs. Haudashalt, eight grandchildren and one great-grandchild.

The funeral services were held Monday afternoon at 2 o'clock at the family residence, Rev. John D. Voce of the First Methodist church conducting the services. At the conclusion of the services by the minister, the sorrowing relatives and friends followed the hearse to the Masons and Odd Fellows' cemetery, where the last earthly remains were consigned to rest. The services at the cemetery were conducted by members of the San Joaquin lodge in honor of their departed brother, long a member of the lodge.

The funeral was largely attended and the floral tributes were beautiful, varied and numerous. H. G. Preston had charge of the funeral arrangements.

The pall bearers were George and Mark Fields, and four brother members of San Joaquin lodge, I. O. O. F. Henry Taylor. C. T. Ritchie, J. A. King and A. A. Waldie, Jr.

This obituary for Elizabeth's father, John H. Evans, appeared in the *Antioch Ledger* newspaper, April 17, 1924. In the article the name of John's wife is splled "Araminta." However on her gravestone her name is spelled "Arminta."

Reference 379.11

The gravestones for Elizabeth's parents at Oak View Memorial Park Cemetery, Antioch, California. Photographs taken May 2010 by Traci (Gibbons) Parent.

Reference 379.12

Nortonville, looking west, 1870s. John H. Evans, and his wife, Araminta A. (Prosser) Evans, were listed as residents of Nortonville when they married in December 1874.

## PERSONAL INFORMATION:

| | |
|---|---|
| SEX: | Male |
| DATE OF BIRTH: | January 22, 1869 |
| DATE OF DEATH: | January 22, 1877 |
| PLACE OF DEATH: | Nortonville, Contra Costa County, California |
| AGE AT DEATH: | 8 years |
| CAUSE OF DEATH: | Diphtheria |
| BIRTHPLACE: | Nortonville, Contra Costa County, California |
| SPOUSE: | None |
| PARENTS: | John R. and Mary (Morgan) Evans |

## GRAVESITE INFORMATION:

| | |
|---|---|
| LOCATION OF GRAVESITE: | Section S-E, Plot #94 |
| GRAVESTONE: | Missing |
| TYPE OF GRAVESTONE: | Marble |
| SHAPE OF GRAVESTONE: | Tablet |
| INSCRIPTION: | *Father's Grave* |
| EPITAPH: | |
| MOTIF: | Fleur-de-lis |
| CARVER: | |
| BASE: | |
| TYPE OF BASE: | |
| ENCLOSURE: | |
| TYPE OF ENCLOSURE: | |
| FENCE: | |
| TYPE OF FENCE: | |
| FENCE MOTIF: | |

# EVANS, John

**ADDITIONAL PERSONAL INFORMATION:**
John was the son of John R. and Mary (Morgan) Evans of Nortonville, Contra Costa County, California. John and Mary came to California in 1860. Sometime between 1866 and 1869 the Evans family moved to Nortonville.

The *1870 Census for Township 3, Contra Costa County, California* lists John Evans, age 39, as a miner and native of England. Also listed are his wife, Mary, age 35, and their son, John Evans, age 5, both natives of England.

The other children of John and Mary Evans were:

- William Rodrick
- Margaret Jane
- Thomas Richard
- David John
- Sarah
- Mary
- Williee (twin to Fredie)
- Fredie (twin to Williee)

John's father died on February 2, 1877, just a short time after John died. The *Antioch Ledger* newspaper, January 27, 1877, states that John died on January 20, 1877 at age 9 years and not January 22 at age 8 years as indicated on his gravestone. See John R. Evans.

**ADDITIONAL GRAVESITE INFORMATION:**
John shares a gravestone with his father, John R. Evans and brother, William Evans. At one time this stone sat next to the gravestone of his other brother, William Rodrick Evans. The gravestone was present in 1963 because it is listed on a student term paper by Jim Rotelli.

See John R. Evans, William Evans, and William Rodrick Evans.

**REFERENCES:** 1, 2, 3, 5, 6, 9 (Jan. 27, 1877), 11 (P610.116.4, P610.116.6, P610.151.2, and P610.362.6), 12

### DIED.

At Nortonville, January 17, 1877, only son of Martin Bonzagui, aged about 2 years, of diphtheria.

At Nortonville, January 20, 1877, ———, son ( John R. Evans, aged 9 years, of diphtheria.

In this obituary from the *Antioch Ledger* newspaper, January 27, 1877, John's name was not listed. He is only referred to as the son of John R. Evans.

David Morgan gravestone (left), lying flat; John R. Evans and sons, John and William, gravestone (middle), lying flat; and William Rodrick Evans gravestone (right), standing, in November, 1967. Photograph by Frank Norris.

Reference 116.6

Gravestone for John Evans, his brother William Evans, and father, John R. Evans.
Photograph taken by Frank Norris on November 5, 1967.

# EVANS,
## John R.

## PERSONAL INFORMATION:

| | |
|---|---|
| SEX: | Male |
| DATE OF BIRTH: | February 1832 |
| DATE OF DEATH: | February 3, 1877 |
| PLACE OF DEATH: | Nortonville, Contra Costa County, California |
| AGE AT DEATH: | 45 years |
| CAUSE OF DEATH: | |
| BIRTHPLACE: | Llanybri, Carmarthenshire, South Wales |
| SPOUSE: | Mary (Morgan) Evans |
| PARENTS: | Thomas and Jane (Richard) Evans |

## GRAVESITE INFORMATION:

| | |
|---|---|
| LOCATION OF GRAVESITE: | Section S-E, Plot #94 |
| GRAVESTONE: | Missing |
| TYPE OF GRAVESTONE: | Marble |
| SHAPE OF GRAVESTONE: | Tablet |
| INSCRIPTION: | *Father's Grave* |
| EPITAPH: | |
| MOTIF: | Fleur-de-lis |
| CARVER: | |
| BASE: | |
| TYPE OF BASE: | |
| ENCLOSURE: | |
| TYPE OF ENCLOSURE: | |
| FENCE: | |
| TYPE OF FENCE: | |
| FENCE MOTIF: | |

# EVANS, John R.

**ADDITIONAL PERSONAL INFORMATION:**
According to descendants, John R. Evans:

> ...came to California in 1860 with Frederick and Margaret Howell. They came to New York, left there on the steamer *Baltic*, came to the Isthmus of Panama, crossed on the train, took the steamer, *Sierra Nevada*, on the Pacific to San Francisco arriving on February 2, 1860. They then took a steamer up the river to Sacramento, went by railroad to Folsom and by stagecoach to Auburn and on to Forest Hill, Placer County, California. They reached Forest Hill on the 7th of February 1860.

John married Mary Morgan on April 8, 1861. Also according to descendants, John's wife,

> Mary Morgan was the daughter of William Morgan and Margaret Howell. She was born the 13th of March 1839 in Merthyr Tydfil, Wales. She came to the Untied States from Wales in 1860 with her Uncle Morgan Howell and his wife, Betsy. Morgan Howell's brother was Frederick Howell. Frederick was married to Margaret Evans, the sister of John R. Evans.

Sarah and Thomas M. Howell, children of Frederick and Margaret, are also buried in Rose Hill Cemetery (Section N-C, plot #8). Buried near John R. Evans is his wife's uncle, David Morgan, who died in Nortonville in 1882 (Section S-E, plot #92).

The *1870 Census for Township 3, Contra Costa County, California* lists John Evans, age 39, as a miner and native of England. Also listed are his wife, Mary, age 35, and their son, John Evans, age 5; both natives of England. The *1876 Contra Costa County Voting Register* lists John's occupation as a miner and residence as Nortonville.

The *Contra Costa Gazette* newspaper, February 17, 1877, states that John R. Evans died on February 3, 1877, aged 44 years, 11 months, and 28 days and not 45 years as recorded on his gravestone. The *Antioch Ledger* newspaper, February 10, 1877, states that John R. Evans died on February 2, 1877, aged about 35 years.

The Evans family resided in Nortonville until 1877 or 1878 when they relocated to Placer County, California. John R. and Mary Evans had eight children, five of whom were born in Nortonville. Three of their children are buried in Rose Hill Cemetery: William Rodrick (died Feb. 8, 1870); John (died Jan. 22, 1877); and William (died Feb. 16, 1877).

According to a descendant, John's wife, Mary (Morgan) Evans, died December 5, 1923 in Penryn, and is buried in Newcastle, Placer County, California. John's sister, Elizabeth (Evans) Jones, died in Nortonville in 1881, and is also buried in Rose Hill Cemetery. John also had a brother named Brigham Evans.

See Sarah Howell, Thomas M. Howell, Elizabeth Jones (died Sept. 1881), and David Morgan.

**ADDITIONAL GRAVESITE INFORMATION:**
John R. Evans shares a gravestone with his sons, John and William Evans. Originally this stone sat next to the gravestone of his other son, William Rodrick Evans.

The gravestone inscription *Father's Grave*, comes from Zelma Myrick, who recorded information in a notebook in the 1930s during a visit to Rose Hill Cemetery.

**REFERENCES:** 1, 2, 3, 5, 6, 8 ( Feb. 17, 1877), 9 (Feb. 10, 1877 and March 3, 1877), 11 (P610.116.4, P610.116.6, P610.317.14, P610.151.2, and P610.362.6), 12, see newspaper appendix page 704

## PERSONAL INFORMATION:

| | |
|---|---|
| SEX: | Female |
| DATE OF BIRTH: | February 1, 1853 |
| DATE OF DEATH: | March 24, 1886 |
| PLACE OF DEATH: | Nortonville or Concord, Contra Costa County, California |
| AGE AT DEATH: | 33 years, 1 month, 23 days |
| CAUSE OF DEATH: | |
| BIRTHPLACE: | Pennsylvania |
| SPOUSE: | John Butler Evans |
| PARENTS: | David and Elizabeth Jones |

## GRAVESITE INFORMATION:

| | |
|---|---|
| LOCATION OF GRAVESITE: | Section S-B, Plot #27 |
| GRAVESTONE: | Exists |
| TYPE OF GRAVESTONE: | Marble |
| SHAPE OF GRAVESTONE: | Obelisk |
| INSCRIPTION: | *Beloved wife of/and daughter of/* *EVANS (on middle base)* |
| EPITAPH: | *Lost to sight but to* *memory dear.* |
| MOTIF: | Ivy |
| CARVER: | |
| BASE: | Exists [Middle marble base with "EVANS" name is missing] |
| TYPE OF BASE: | Granite with middle marble base |
| ENCLOSURE: | Exists |
| TYPE OF ENCLOSURE: | Brick |
| FENCE: | |
| TYPE OF FENCE: | |
| FENCE MOTIF: | |

# EVANS, Rebecca

**ADDITIONAL PERSONAL INFORMATION:**
Rebecca was the daughter of David and Elizabeth Jones of Scranton, Lackawanna County, Pennsylvania. David was a coal miner. Rebecca and her husband, John B. Evans, moved from Scranton, Pennsylvania to Nortonville, Contra Costa County, California where, in 1872, they paid a property tax of $30 for their home.

According to family records, Rebecca had 10 children before she was 30. Her children were: Melvin, Tal, Sarah, Elizabeth, Winefred (Winifred), Mozzie, Shadrack Butler, Damaris, and two others, names unknown.

According to the *Index to Marriage Certificates*, located at the Contra Costa County Hall of Records, Martinez, California, Rebecca Jones married John B. Evans on September 12, 1870. Rev. John Price performed the ceremony; the information is recorded in Volume 1, page 182.

The *Assessment List, Contra Costa County, for 1872-73*, lists John B. Evans as being assessed for a home in Nortonville, furniture and other solvent debts for $185.00.

The *1880 Census for Nortonville Precinct, Contra Costa County, California* records John Evans, age 40, as a miner and native of Wales. Also listed are his wife, Rebecca, age 27, a native of Pennsylvania, and their children: Taliesan [sic], age 9; Shadrick [sic], age 7; Damaris, age 5; Lizzie, age 3; and Sarah, age 6 months. All are natives of California.

After Rebecca's death, her husband, J. B. Evans, moved to the coal mining community of Black Diamond, King County, Washington. In 1887, J. B. Evans, age 46, was listed as a miner and native of Wales in Black Diamond, Washington. Also living with him were his children, all born in California: Taliesen [sic], age 16; Shadrack [sic], age 14; Damaris, age 12; Elizabeth, age 10; Sarah, age 8; and Melville, age 5.

According to *Black Diamond Cemetery* records, Black Diamond, Washington, John died January 24, 1897 at age 56 years, 11 months, and 24 days. Sharing the gravesite with him is Taliesyn Evans, who died February 10, 1899 at age 27 years, 10 months, and 27 days. According to John's death certificate, he died January 25, 1897 of "sclerosis of Liver."

**ADDITIONAL GRAVESITE INFORMATION:**
A marble middle base inscribed with the name "EVANS" is missing. The marble obelisk gravestone sits on a granite base. A brick enclosure, built prior to East Bay Regional Park District acquisition and after the coal mining days, is present at this site. A wooden footstone once existed at the gravesite.

**REFERENCES:** 1, 2, 3, 4, 6, 8 (March 27, 1886), 11 (P610.14.2, P610.14.3, P610.31.181, P610.168.15, P610.260.12, P610.260.13, and P610.317-11), 12, 14, *Black Diamond Cemetery* records, Black Diamond, Washington, see newspaper appendix page 705

Rebecca Evans gravesite, *circa* 1930. The middle marble base
with the name "Evans" is missing from the cemetery today.

Reference 260.14

Reference 260.13

Pictured is the gravestone for John B. Evans and Taliesyn Evans (husband and daughter of Rebecca Evans), Black Diamond Cemetery, King County, Washington. John B. Evans died January 24, 1897, age 56 years, 11 months, and 24 days (photograph on left). Sharing the same stone is his daughter, Taliesyn Evans (photograph on right), who died February 10, 1899, age 27 years, 10 months, and 27 days. Photographs by Traci (Gibbons) Parent, August 2001.

## PERSONAL INFORMATION:

|  |  |
|---|---|
| SEX: | Male |
| DATE OF BIRTH: | October 12, 1874 |
| DATE OF DEATH: | February 18, 1877 |
| PLACE OF DEATH: | Nortonville, Contra Costa County, California |
| AGE AT DEATH: | 2 years, 4 months, 6 days |
| CAUSE OF DEATH: |  |
| BIRTHPLACE: | Nortonville, Contra Costa County, California |
| SPOUSE: | None |
| PARENTS: | John R. and Mary (Morgan) Evans |

## GRAVESITE INFORMATION:

|  |  |
|---|---|
| LOCATION OF GRAVESITE: | Section S-E, Plot #94 |
| GRAVESTONE: | Missing |
| TYPE OF GRAVESTONE: | Marble |
| SHAPE OF GRAVESTONE: | Tablet |
| INSCRIPTION: | *Father's Grave* |
| EPITAPH: |  |
| MOTIF: | Fleur-de-lis |
| CARVER: |  |
| BASE: |  |
| TYPE OF BASE: |  |
| ENCLOSURE: |  |
| TYPE OF ENCLOSURE: |  |
| FENCE: |  |
| TYPE OF FENCE: |  |
| FENCE MOTIF: |  |

# EVANS, William

**ADDITIONAL PERSONAL INFORMATION:**
Family records indicate "Williee" (twin to Fredie) was born October 10, 1874 in Nortonville. He died February 16, 1877 in Nortonville, and not February 18, as indicated on his gravestone. William died shortly after the death of his father, John R. Evans (died Feb. 3, 1877) and brother John (died Jan. 22, 1877).

**ADDITIONAL GRAVESITE INFORMATION:**
William shares a gravestone with his father John R. Evans and brother John. At one time, this stone sat next to the stone of his other brother, William Rodrick Evans. See John R. Evans, John Evans, and William Rodrick Evans.

**REFERENCES:** 1, 2, 3, 5, 6, 9 (March 3, 1877), 11 (P610.116.4, P610.116.6, P610.151-2, and P610.362.6), 12, see newspaper appendix page 704

Reference 317.14

The vandalized gravesites of David Morgan (top), William Rodrick Evans (center), and John R. Evans, and sons, John and William Evans (bottom). Photograph taken *circa* 1939 by Zelma Myrick.

# EVANS,
## William Rodrick

## PERSONAL INFORMATION:

| | |
|---|---|
| SEX: | Male |
| DATE OF BIRTH: | January 22, 1862 |
| DATE OF DEATH: | February 8, 1870 |
| PLACE OF DEATH: | Nortonville, Contra Costa County, California |
| AGE AT DEATH: | 8 years, 17 days |
| CAUSE OF DEATH: | |
| BIRTHPLACE: | Foresthill, Placer County, California |
| SPOUSE: | None |
| PARENTS: | John R. and Mary (Morgan) Evans |

## GRAVESITE INFORMATION:

| | |
|---|---|
| LOCATION OF GRAVESITE: | Section S-E, Plot #93 |
| GRAVESTONE: | Missing |
| TYPE OF GRAVESTONE: | Marble |
| SHAPE OF GRAVESTONE: | |
| INSCRIPTION: | *Son of* |
| EPITAPH: | *Let not the foot of pride come against me, and let not the hand of the wicked remove me.* |
| MOTIF: | |
| CARVER: | |
| BASE: | Exists |
| TYPE OF BASE: | Sandstone |
| ENCLOSURE: | |
| TYPE OF ENCLOSURE: | |
| FENCE: | |
| TYPE OF FENCE: | |
| FENCE MOTIF: | |

# EVANS, William Rodrick

**ADDITIONAL PERSONAL INFORMATION:**
William's age at death was calculated by www.timeanddate.com, based on the birth and death dates listed on his gravestone. See John R. Evans.

**ADDITIONAL GRAVESITE INFORMATION:**
Zelma Myrick, who recorded information in a notebook in the 1930s during a visit to Rose Hill Cemetery, reported "stone off base." The epitaph on the gravestone comes from the *Bible*, Psalms 36:11.

William Rodrick is buried next to his brothers, John and William, and his father, John R. Evans. See John R. Evans, John Evans, and William Evans.

**REFERENCES:** 1, 2, 3, 6, 11 (P610.114.2, P610.116.4, P610.116.8, P610.151.1, P610.317.14, and P610.362.6), 12

Reference 116.8

William Rodrick Evans gravestone, November 5, 1967.
Photograph by Frank Norris.

## PERSONAL INFORMATION:

| | |
|---|---|
| SEX: | Female |
| DATE OF BIRTH: | 1793 |
| DATE OF DEATH: | September 11, 1874 |
| PLACE OF DEATH: | |
| AGE AT DEATH: | 81 years |
| CAUSE OF DEATH: | |
| BIRTHPLACE: | |
| SPOUSE: | Jacob French |
| PARENTS: | |

## GRAVESITE INFORMATION:

| | |
|---|---|
| LOCATION OF GRAVESITE: | Section N-F, Plot #115 |
| GRAVESTONE: | Exists |
| TYPE OF GRAVESTONE: | Marble |
| SHAPE OF GRAVESTONE: | Tablet |
| INSCRIPTION: | *Farewell/Wife of* |
| EPITAPH: | |
| MOTIF: | Clasped hands/rope with tassels |
| CARVER: | |
| BASE: | Missing |
| TYPE OF BASE: | |
| ENCLOSURE: | |
| TYPE OF ENCLOSURE: | |
| FENCE: | |
| TYPE OF FENCE: | |
| FENCE MOTIF: | |

# FRENCH, Ruth

**ADDITIONAL PERSONAL INFORMATION:**
Ruth French is one of the oldest individuals buried in Rose Hill Cemetery.

**ADDITIONAL GRAVESITE INFORMATION:**
Zelma Myrick, who recorded information in a notebook in the 1930s during a visit to Rose Hill Cemetery, reported the "stone badly broken."

The gravestone is broken into five pieces and was concreted flat to the ground prior to Park District acquisition. A portion of the clasped hand motif is missing. This gravestone was hidden under the soil for many years until accidentally discovered by East Bay Regional Park District Rangers in the late 1970s.

A small piece of a marble footstone was found by Black Diamond Rangers in March 2005. The piece was found between plots 104 and 105 and might have belonged to the Ruth French gravesite.

**REFERENCES:** 1, 2, 6, 11 (P610.168.13), 12, 14, *Pittsburg Post Dispatch* newspaper (Wednesday, June 15, 1955, page 12)

# GETHING (GETHIN),
## William

## PERSONAL INFORMATION:

| | |
|---|---|
| SEX: | Male |
| DATE OF BIRTH: | February 1, 1839 |
| DATE OF DEATH: | July 24, 1876 |
| PLACE OF DEATH: | Nortonville, Contra Costa County, California |
| AGE AT DEATH: | 36 years [sic] |
| CAUSE OF DEATH: | Burns and/or suffocation caused by a mine explosion |
| BIRTHPLACE: | Glamorganshire, South Wales |
| SPOUSE: | |
| PARENTS: | Owen and Sarah Gethin |

## GRAVESITE INFORMATION:

| | |
|---|---|
| LOCATION OF GRAVESITE: | Section S-C, Plot #46 |
| GRAVESTONE: | Exists |
| TYPE OF GRAVESTONE: | Marble |
| SHAPE OF GRAVESTONE: | Tablet |
| INSCRIPTION: | |
| EPITAPH: | |
| MOTIF: | Independent Order of Odd Fellows/Knights of Pythias/ rope with tassels |
| CARVER: | Pioneer Steam Marble Works, San Francisco |
| BASE: | Exists |
| TYPE OF BASE: | Sandstone |
| ENCLOSURE: | Exists |
| TYPE OF ENCLOSURE: | Brick |
| FENCE: | Missing |
| TYPE OF FENCE: | Iron |
| FENCE MOTIF: | Shell/fleur-de lis |

# GETHING (GETHIN), William

**ADDITIONAL PERSONAL INFORMATION:**
In a document sent from Wales titled *Declaration of Mr. Owen Gethin*, filed August 11, 1877, regarding his son William Gethin [sic], deceased: William's father indicated that the last name was spelled Gethin not Gething (as stated on his gravestone) and his date of birth as February 1, 1839. (Note: Based on the birth date provided by his family, and the death date listed on his gravestone, William would have been 37 yrs., 5 mos., and 23 days old at the time of his death. His gravestone states he was 36 years old.) William left England for America about 1870. In or about the month of August 1876, William's father received a letter from Mr. David B. Davis of Nortonville, Contra Costa County, California, informing him that his son had been killed in a mine explosion. David B. Davis served as the Administrator of the Estate for William Gething (see David B. Davis pages 133 and 134). A voucher from Nortonville, dated August 3, 1876, indicates a payment received regarding William Gething to Woodruff and Guy (undertakers at Nortonville). The voucher says: "July 26 To Coffin Box ($)75.00. Coffin trimmed with moulding. Received payment. Woodruff."

The *History of Contra Costa County*, by Slocum and Company, 1882, page 474, states that William Gething, age 35, and six others were killed by a powder explosion which occurred in Nortonville on July 24, 1876. Gething was interred in the cemetery by members of the Odd Fellows Lodge, of which he was a member. An Independent Order of Odd Fellows Lodge existed both in Somersville (Mount Diablo Lodge No. 128, instituted October 27, 1866) and in Nortonville (Social Encampment No. 50, instituted December 18, 1874). Gething was also a member of the Knights of Phythias. The "K. P." initials that appear under the motif stand for Knights of Phythias. Evan Davies is the only other individual interred in the cemetery with the Knights of Phythias motif on the gravestone.

According to a baptism document dated February 7, 1877, William Gethin [sic] was baptized February 3, 1839 at Neath in the County of Glamorgan, South Wales. The *Declaration of Mr. Owen Gethin*, filed August 11, 1877 states that William Gethin was a widower at the time of his death. He had no children. See Theophile Dumas, David W. Griffiths, Thomas D. James, Meredith Lewis, George M. Reynolds, Evan Smith, David Watts, Theophilus Watts, and William L. Williams.

**ADDITIONAL GRAVESITE INFORMATION:**
Zelma Myrick, who recorded information in a notebook in the 1930s during a visit to Rose Hill Cemetery, reported William's "stone broken." The gravestone was broken in at least four pieces and was concreted flat to the ground. It was buried under the soil and not visible prior to East Bay Regional Park District acquisition. The lower portion of the stone was embedded in a sandstone base. Black Diamond Rangers removed the gravestone from the cemetery in 1999 for repairs. The rough concrete encasement was removed. The stone was repaired by drilling and pinning the pieces back together using white epoxy adhesive. The missing section of the gravestone was filled with white cement mortar. The sandstone base was leveled and a concrete sub-grade slab was poured under the base. In 2000, the stone was reattached to the base with epoxy. A footstone with the initials "W. G." was found and removed from the site for safekeeping when the gravestone was brought down for repair. A partial sandstone rock wall sits nearby.

According to Contra Costa County probate records, the iron fence which once surrounded William's grave cost $90. Freight on the fence alone was $13 [?]. Labor for the fence and brick work was $6.

A photograph of William Gething's gravesite can be seen on page 244.

**REFERENCES:** 1, 6, 8 (July 29, 1876 and Aug. 12, 1876), 9 (July 29, 1876), 10 (page 474), 11 (P610.5.2, P610.31.207 to P610.31.209, P610.267.3, P610.363.1, and P610.363.2), 12, 13, 14, *Pittsburg Post Dispatch* newspaper (Wed., June 15, 1955, page 9), see newspaper appendix pages 706 and 707

This receipt, dated December 20, 1876, from Michael Heverin, gravestone carver and proprietor of the Pioneer Steam Marble Works in San Francisco, was for work done on the William Gething gravestone and footstone. David B. Davis served as the Administrator of the Estate for William Gething. The receipt says:

| | |
|---|---|
| *For 1 headstone and foot-stone* | $25.00 |
| *Extra cutting 3 links* | 3.00 |
| *For cutting the emblem "Knights* | |
| *of Phais"* [sic] | 2.00 |
| | $30.00 |

East Bay Regional Park District

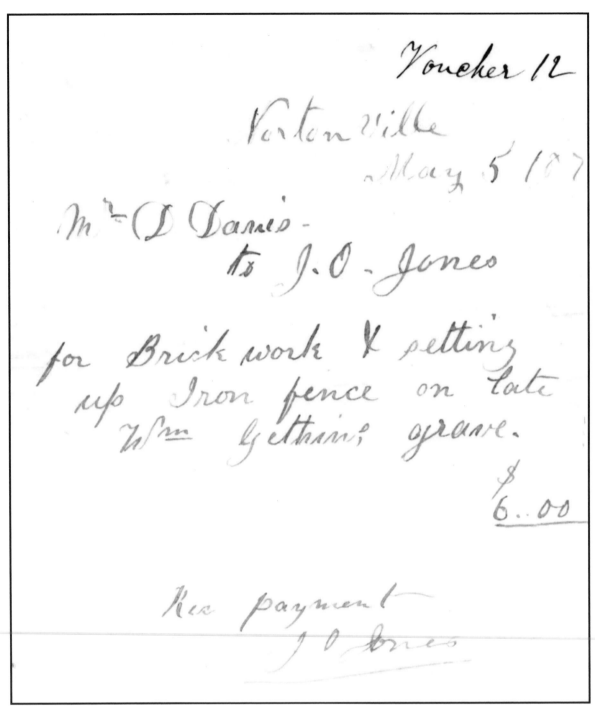

The May 5, 1877 receipt from J. O. Jones to
Mr. D. Davis (Administrator of the Estate for William Gething)
was for brick work and iron fence installation at the William Gething gravesite.

# GOULDING,
## Fanny Sarah

**PERSONAL INFORMATION:**

| | |
|---|---|
| SEX: | Female |
| DATE OF BIRTH: | July 2, 1859 |
| DATE OF DEATH: | April 30, 1865 |
| PLACE OF DEATH: | Somersville, Contra Costa County, California |
| AGE AT DEATH: | 5 years, 9 months, 28 days |
| CAUSE OF DEATH: | |
| BIRTHPLACE: | Newcastle, New South Wales, Australia |
| SPOUSE: | None |
| PARENTS: | Daniel and Elizabeth Merrifield (Pratten) Goulding |

**GRAVESITE INFORMATION:**

| | |
|---|---|
| LOCATION OF GRAVESITE: | Unknown |
| GRAVESTONE: | Missing or never placed |
| TYPE OF GRAVESTONE: | |
| SHAPE OF GRAVESTONE: | |
| INSCRIPTION: | |
| EPITAPH: | |
| MOTIF: | |
| CARVER: | |
| BASE: | |
| TYPE OF BASE: | |
| ENCLOSURE: | |
| TYPE OF ENCLOSURE: | |
| FENCE: | |
| TYPE OF FENCE: | |
| FENCE MOTIF: | |

# GOULDING, Fanny Sarah

## ADDITIONAL PERSONAL INFORMATION:

Fanny died three months after her brother, Thomas Pratten Goulding. Her brother, Thomas P., and two cousins (sons of her father's brother John) are buried in Rose Hill. Fanny's age at death was calculated by www.timeanddate.com.

The *1851 Wales Census for Machen, Lower Machen, Monmouthshire, Wales* lists Fanny's grandparents, parents, aunt, and uncles:

- John Goulding, born *circa* 1798, in Wesley, Gloucestershire, England
- Rasannah Goulding, born *circa* 1801, in Beaufort, Monmouthshire, Wales
- Sarah Goulding, born *circa* 1828, in Blaenavon, Monmouthshire, Wales
- Daniel Goulding (father of Fanny), born *circa* 1831, in Winterborne, Gloucestershire, England
- Elizabeth Goulding (wife of Daniel), born *circa* 1832, in Hightelleter, Somerset, England
- George Goulding, born *circa* 1835, in Blaina, Monmouthshire, Wales
- Thomas Goulding, born *circa* 1840, in Abersychan, Monmouthshire, Wales

The *1880 Census for Cannonville, Iron County, Utah* lists Fanny's father, Daniel Goulding, as a stone mason and native of England, age 49, born *circa* 1831. Also listed are his two wives: Elizabeth, age 47, born *circa* 1833 in England and Fanny, age 37, born *circa* 1843 in England. Ten children are listed: Rose A., age 19, born in Australia; George J., age 17, born in Australia; John, age 15, born in California; Henrietta, age 11, born in Nevada; Clara E., age 7, born in Utah Territory; Lucy B., age 7, born in Utah Territory; William E., age 5, born in Utah Territory; James A., age 5, born in Utah Territory; Samuel E., age 4, born in Utah Territory; and Zina E., age 2, born in Utah Territory.

The *1900 Census for Henrieville, Garfield County, Utah* records Daniel Goulding as a farmer, age 69, born March 1831 in England. Also listed is his wife Elisabeth [Elizabeth], age 67, born May 1833 in England. The census records their immigration year as 1863 and lists Elizabeth as the mother of 12 children, with the number of living children as 5.

Daniel Goulding died on August 1, 1905 and is buried in Henrieville Cemetery located in Henrieville, Garfield County, Utah. His first spouse, Elizabeth (mother of Fanny Sarah Goulding and Thomas Pratten Goulding) died July 18, 1918 in Panguitch, Garfield County, Utah.

See Joseph Goulding, Thomas John Goulding, and Thomas Pratten Goulding.

## ADDITIONAL GRAVESITE INFORMATION:

A descendant believes that Fanny Sarah Goulding is buried in Rose Hill Cemetery. Her source of information comes from other Goulding descendants and the *Family Group Sheet* compiled by a Goulding family member.

No previous cemetery lists record Fanny's burial in Rose Hill Cemetery.

**REFERENCES: 12**

# GOULDING,
## Joseph

## PERSONAL INFORMATION:

| | |
|---|---|
| SEX: | Male |
| DATE OF BIRTH: | December 18, 1852 |
| DATE OF DEATH: | October 6, 1871 |
| PLACE OF DEATH: | Contra Costa County, California |
| AGE AT DEATH: | 19 years |
| CAUSE OF DEATH: | |
| BIRTHPLACE: | Risca, Monmouthshire, Wales |
| SPOUSE: | |
| PARENTS: | John and Cladice (Jones) Goulding |

## GRAVESITE INFORMATION:

| | |
|---|---|
| LOCATION OF GRAVESITE: | Section N-F, Plot #72 |
| GRAVESTONE: | Missing |
| TYPE OF GRAVESTONE: | Marble |
| SHAPE OF GRAVESTONE: | Tablet |
| INSCRIPTION: | *Children of* |
| EPITAPH: | |
| MOTIF: | Clasped hands |
| CARVER: | |
| BASE: | Exists |
| TYPE OF BASE: | Granite |
| ENCLOSURE: | |
| TYPE OF ENCLOSURE: | |
| FENCE: | |
| TYPE OF FENCE: | |
| FENCE MOTIF: | |

# GOULDING, Joseph

**ADDITIONAL PERSONAL INFORMATION:**
According to information from www.ancestry.com, Joseph's middle name was Hyrum and his date of birth was December 18, 1852. Joseph's date of death and age at death was provided by Zelma Myrick who recorded information in a notebook in the 1930s during a visit to Rose Hill Cemetery. Using the date of birth provided from www.ancestry.com, Joseph's age at death would have been 18 years, 9 months, and 18 days, and not 19 years as recorded on his gravestone.

Other information obtained from this website states that Joseph's father, John Goulding, was born July 9, 1821 in Shiroway, Bedwellty, Monmouthshire, Wales and died July 18, 1895 in Henrieville, Garfield County, Utah. John Goulding married Cladice Jones on February 15, 1848, in Bedwellty, Monmouthshire, Wales.

Also according to the family group sheet from *Ancestry.com* Cladice (Jones) Goulding was born in 1821 in Trefechan, Brecon, Wales. She died in Contra Costa County in 1870. John and Cladice Goulding had at least eight children:

- Sarah, born Feb. 21, 1849, Upper Machen, Monmouthshire, Wales
- Mary, born Oct. 24, 1850, Upper Machen, Monmouthshire, Wales
- Joseph, born Dec. 18, 1852, Risca, Monmouthshire, Wales (buried in Rose Hill)
- Rosanna, born Dec. 1, 1854, Lower Machen, Monmouthshire, Wales
- Brigham Lawrence, born Jan. 14, 1856, Lower Machen, Monmouthshire, Wales

- Margerite (Maggie), born 1861, Weathersfield, Trumbull County, Ohio
- Daniel, born 1865, Ohio
- Thomas John, born Nov. 10, 1866, Weathersfield, Trumbull County, Ohio (buried in Rose Hill)

According to information obtained from a descendant, John Goulding was naturalized at Trumbull County, Ohio in 1858, and he registered to vote in Contra Costa County in 1872.

Two cousins (children of their father's brother Daniel), are also believed to be buried in Rose Hill Cemetery.

See Fanny Sarah Goulding and Thomas Pratten Goulding. For additional information on the John and Cladice Goulding family see Thomas John Goulding.

**ADDITIONAL GRAVESITE INFORMATION:**
Joseph shares a gravestone with his brother Thomas Goulding. The gravestone was present in 1963 because it is listed in a student term paper by Jim Rotelli. The section and plot location of the gravesite was determined by comparing a photograph of the gravestone taken at the burial location to the current site. The base on site appears to match the base in the photograph. See Thomas John Goulding.

**REFERENCES:** 1, 2, 3, 6, 11 (P610.146.4), 12, *Pittsburg Post Dispatch* newspaper (Wed., June 15, 1955, page 9 and 12)

Joseph and Thomas Goulding gravesite, *circa* 1958.

**WORK SUSPENDED AT THE MINES.—** The customary price for cutting coal on this coast has been one dollar per yard. In a few mines, where unusual obstructions existed, the price has been one dollar and twenty-five cents. On Saturday last the coal companies of Somersville and Nortonville, comprising the Black Diamond and Pittsburg, notified their employees that from the first day of October the price for cutting coal would be reduced twenty-five cents. To this the miners demurred, and on consultation determined not to go to work. A meeting for consultation was held by the miners of Somersville and Nortonville on the summit of the hill separating the two towns on Monday. We are not advised as to the subject matter discussed, or the nature of their deliberations; but they were evidently not of a conciliatory spirit, as, we understand, all work is suspended at these two mines. The companies claim that with the dull market and extremely low price of coal, by reason of great competition, they cannot afford to keep up the old established rates of one dollar per yard for cutting. Many of these miners have been engaged in the business all their lives, and it will be difficult to fill their places by new hands. On the other hand, many of them have large families dependent for support upon their daily earnings, and it is uncertain what may be the final result of the present unpleasantness.

From the *Antioch Ledger* newspaper, October 7, 1876.

# GOULDING,
## Thomas John

**PERSONAL INFORMATION:**

| | |
|---|---|
| SEX: | Male |
| DATE OF BIRTH: | 1862 |
| DATE OF DEATH: | August 15, 1875 |
| PLACE OF DEATH: | Nortonville, Contra Costa County, California |
| AGE AT DEATH: | 13 years |
| CAUSE OF DEATH: | |
| BIRTHPLACE: | Newcastle, New South Wales, Australia |
| SPOUSE: | None |
| PARENTS: | John and Cladice (Jones) Goulding |

**GRAVESITE INFORMATION:**

| | |
|---|---|
| LOCATION OF GRAVESITE: | Section N-F, Plot #72 |
| GRAVESTONE: | Missing |
| TYPE OF GRAVESTONE: | Marble |
| SHAPE OF GRAVESTONE: | Tablet |
| INSCRIPTION: | *Children of* |
| EPITAPH: | |
| MOTIF: | Clasped hands |
| CARVER: | |
| BASE: | Exists |
| TYPE OF BASE: | Granite |
| ENCLOSURE: | |
| TYPE OF ENCLOSURE: | |
| FENCE: | |
| TYPE OF FENCE: | |
| FENCE MOTIF: | |

# GOULDING, Thomas John

**ADDITIONAL PERSONAL INFORMATION:**
According to family group sheets obtained from www.ancestry.com, Thomas John Goulding was born November 10, 1866, in Weathersfield, Trumbull County, Ohio. If Thomas was born in 1866, he would only have been 9 years old at the time of his death in 1875. His death date (Aug. 15, 1875) and age of death (13 years) was recorded on reference lists 1, 2, and 3. Additionally, Zelma Myrick, who recorded information in a notebook in the 1930s during a visit to Rose Hill Cemetery, reported his age at death as 13 years and date of death as August 15, 1875.

The *1851 Wales Census for Upper Machen, Monmouthshire, Wales* lists Thomas' father, John Goulding, a coal miner, age 27, born *circa* 1824 in Monmouthshire, Wales. Also listed are his wife, Gladice [sic], age 27, born *circa* 1824 in Breconshire, Wales; and their 5 month old daughter, Mary, born *circa* 1850 in Monmouthshire, Wales. George Evance, a coal miner, age 23, was recorded as living with them as a lodger.

The *1860 Census for Weathersfield, Trumbull, Ohio* lists Jno [sic] Golden [sic], age 37, born *circa* 1823 and a native of Wales. Also listed are his wife and three children: Letitia [sic], age 35, born *circa* 1825 in Wales; Sarah, age 11, born *circa* 1849 in Wales; Joseph, age 7, born *circa* 1853 in Wales; and Brigham, age 4, born *circa* 1856 in Wales.

The *1870 Census for Township Three, Contra Costa County, California* lists John Golden [sic], age 50, a miner and birthplace England; his wife Glatine [sic], age 51, birthplace England; Joseph, age 18, a miner, birthplace England; Brigham, age 15, birthplace England; Margaret, age 9, birthplace Ohio; Daniel, age 5, birthplace Ohio; and Thomas, age 6, birthplace Ohio.

The *1880 Census for Panguitch, Iron County, Utah* lists John Golden [sic] as a laborer, age 59, and a native of Wales. Also listed are Glaticia [sic] his wife, age 59, birthplace Wales; and their son Daniel, age 15, birthplace Ohio.

Two cousins (children of their father's brother Daniel), are also believed to be buried in Rose Hill Cemetery.

See Fanny Sarah Goulding and Thomas Pratten Goulding. See Joseph Goulding for additional information on the John and Cladice Goulding family.

**ADDITIONAL GRAVESITE INFORMATION:**
Thomas shares a gravestone with his brother Joseph. See Joseph Goulding.

**REFERENCES:** 1, 2, 3, 6, 8 (February 25, 1865), 11 (P610.146.4), 12, *Pittsburg Post Dispatch* newspaper (Wed. June 15, 1955, pages 9 and 12)

# GOULDING,
## Thomas Pratten

## PERSONAL INFORMATION:

| | |
|---|---|
| SEX: | Male |
| DATE OF BIRTH: | June 13 or 14, 1857 |
| DATE OF DEATH: | January 31, 1865 |
| PLACE OF DEATH: | Somersville, Contra Costa County, California |
| AGE AT DEATH: | 7 years, 7 months, 17 days |
| CAUSE OF DEATH: | Scarlatina Maligna (scarlet fever) |
| BIRTHPLACE: | Newcastle, Astria, New South Wales, Australia |
| SPOUSE: | None |
| PARENTS: | Daniel and Elizabeth Merrifield (Pratten) Goulding |

## GRAVESITE INFORMATION:

| | |
|---|---|
| LOCATION OF GRAVESITE: | Unknown |
| GRAVESTONE: | Missing or never placed |
| TYPE OF GRAVESTONE: | |
| SHAPE OF GRAVESTONE: | |
| INSCRIPTION: | |
| EPITAPH: | |
| MOTIF: | |
| CARVER: | |
| BASE: | |
| TYPE OF BASE: | |
| ENCLOSURE: | |
| TYPE OF ENCLOSURE: | |
| FENCE: | |
| TYPE OF FENCE: | |
| FENCE MOTIF: | |

# GOULDING, Thomas Pratten

**ADDITIONAL PERSONAL INFORMATION:**
The only source that lists Thomas' death in Somersville is the *Contra Costa Gazette* newspaper, February 25, 1865. The other children listed in the same newspaper article that died from the disease scarlatina maligna (scarlet fever) in Somersville during February 1865 were: Elizabeth Richmond, died Feb. 17; Annie Tregellas, died Feb. 19; Joseph Tregellas, died Feb. 18; and Charles W. Blackburn, died Feb. 20.

Thomas' date of birth was calculated by www.timeanddate.com, based on the date of death and age of death listed in the *Contra Costa Gazette* newspaper, February 25, 1865. Information on www.ancestry.com, lists his date of birth as June 13, 1857. The newspaper lists his date of death as January 31, 1865. Information obtained from *Ancestry.com*, lists his date of death as January 27, 1865. See Fanny Goulding, Joseph Goulding, and Thomas John Goulding.

According to a descendant, Thomas' father, Daniel, was born in Wales. In 1854, at age 23, he traveled on the ship *Araminta* to Australia. Daniel and his family spent approximately eleven years in Australia before traveling to California. They were in California for about three years and then traveled to Nevada and eventually to Utah. Descendants also state that Daniel Goulding (born March 31, 1831) and Elizabeth Merrifield Pratten (born May 16, 1833) were married on February 19, 1851, in Risca, Newport, Monmouthshire, England. [Note: Monmouthshire is a border county between England and Wales.] They had at least 14 children:

- William, born Dec. 21, 1851, Buckfarm Hill, Lower Machen, Monmouthshire, England
- Sarah Arminta, born Sept. 13, 1854, Newhandle-Sydney, New South Wales, Australia
- Elijah, born Oct. 16, 1855, Sydney, New South Wales, Australia
- Thomas Pratten, born June 13 or 14, 1857, Newcastle, Astria, New South Wales, Australia
- Fanny Sarah, born July 2, 1859, Sydney, New South Wales, Australia
- Rose Ann, born July 31, 1861, Sydney, New South Wales, Australia
- George Joseph, born May 18, 1863, Newhandle-Sydney, New South Wales, Australia
- John, born May 2, 1865, Somersville, Contra Costa County, California
- Henery [sic], born Nov. 1868, Big Muddy, Clark County, Nevada
- Henrietta, born Nov. 20, 1868, Big Muddy, Clark County, Nevada
- Clara Elizabeth, born Dec. 22, 1872, Pleasant Grove, Utah County, Utah
- Lucy Beatrice, born Jan. 16, 1873, Pleasant Grove, Utah County, Utah
- James Arthur, born May 26, 1875, Pleasant Grove, Utah County, Utah

Daniel married his second spouse, Fanny Pratten, on May 16, 1870, in Salt Lake City, Salt Lake County, Utah. With his second wife he had five children: William Eelan, Samuel Evan, Zina Emmeline, Fanny Edelia, and Pheobe Elzada Goulding. Information from www.ancestry.com lists Clara Elizabeth as the daughter of both Elizabeth and Fanny Goulding.

**ADDITIONAL GRAVESITE INFORMATION:**
Since two other Goulding males (cousins to this Thomas Goulding) are buried in Rose Hill (Joseph died October 1871 and Thomas John died August 1875), it is likely that Thomas is buried in Rose Hill Cemetery as well. Descendants also believe that Thomas' sister, Fanny, is buried in Rose Hill although there are no documents recording Thomas' or Fanny's burial there.

**REFERENCES:** 8 (February 25, 1865), 12, see newspaper appendix (Elizabeth Richmond) page 749

## PERSONAL INFORMATION:

| | |
|---|---|
| SEX: | Female |
| DATE OF BIRTH: | April 19, 1879 |
| DATE OF DEATH: | December 8, 1879 |
| PLACE OF DEATH: | Nortonville, Contra Costa County, California |
| AGE AT DEATH: | 7 months, 19 days |
| CAUSE OF DEATH: | |
| BIRTHPLACE: | Nortonville, Contra Costa County, California |
| SPOUSE: | None |
| PARENTS: | Henry Sheldon and Mary Ann (Hulme) Green |

## GRAVESITE INFORMATION:

| | |
|---|---|
| LOCATION OF GRAVESITE: | Section S-F, Plot #107 |
| GRAVESTONE: | Exists |
| TYPE OF GRAVESTONE: | Marble |
| SHAPE OF GRAVESTONE: | Tablet |
| INSCRIPTION: | *Dau. of* |
| EPITAPH: | *Gone but not forgotten.* |
| MOTIF: | |
| CARVER: | |
| BASE: | Exists |
| TYPE OF BASE: | Granite (new) |
| ENCLOSURE: | |
| TYPE OF ENCLOSURE: | |
| FENCE: | |
| TYPE OF FENCE: | |
| FENCE MOTIF: | |

# GREEN, Martha J.

**ADDITIONAL PERSONAL INFORMATION:**
The *1860 Census for San Bernardino, San Bernardino County, California* lists Henry Green, age 30, as a farmer and a native of Ohio. Also listed are his wife Mary Ann, age 22, a native of England; and their children Mary Ann, age 5; Sarah C., age 2; and Eliza A., age 2 months; all natives of California. Also listed as living at the household is Harry Green, age 53, a schoolteacher. The *1880 Census for the Nortonville Precinct, Contra Costa County, California* lists Henry Green, age 50, as a native of Ohio and stable keeper. His father was from New York and his mother from Germany (a descendant states New York). Also listed is his wife Mary, age 42, native of England. Her mother and father were also from England. Their five children are listed: Eliza, age 20, a housekeeper; Henry, age 17; William, age 12; Joseph, age 7; and John, age 5. All are natives of California.

A descendant states that her name was Martha Ann Green and not Martha J. as recorded on her gravestone. Additionally, the descendant lists Martha's father's name as Hervey Sheldon Green and not Henry Green. According to family records, Martha's father, Henry (Hervey) Sheldon Green, was born May 18, 1830 in Huron, Erie County, Ohio and died July 18, 1896 in Alila, Tulare County, California. Martha's mother, Mary Ann (Hulme) Green, was born July 19, 1838 in Stoke On Trent, Staffordshire, England and died January 5, 1920, in Sacramento, Sacramento County, California. Henry (Hervey) Green married Mary Ann Hulme on January 29, 1853 in San Bernardino, San Bernardino County, California. Martha's seven siblings were:

- Mary Ann, born April 17, 1855, San Bernardino, California; died Jan. 8, 1933, Sacramento, California

- Sarah Charlotte, born Sept. 25, 1857, San Bernardino, California; died May 21, 1937, Sacramento, California

- Eliza Alice, born April 9, 1860, San Bernardino, California; died May 27, 1893, Sacramento, California

- Henry Hervey, born March 17, 1865, San Bernardino, California; died June 15, 1895, Sacramento, California

- William Ammon, born July 2, 1867, The Whippies (Tulare County), California; died April 11, 1958, Sacramento, California

- Joseph Charles, born June 2, 1873, Nortonville, California; died June 24, 1940, Portland, Oregon

- John Holmes, born August 13, 1876, Nortonville, California; died March 30, 1914, Sacramento, California

*The Pacific Coast Directory 1883-1884*, lists Martha's father, H. S. Green, as constable and operating a livery stable in Somersville, Contra Costa County, California. The *History of Contra Costa County* by Slocum and Company, 1882, pages 251 and 253 list H. S. Green as a constable in 1879-1880 and 1881-1882 for Township 4 (the area including Somersville and Nortonville).

**ADDITIONAL GRAVESITE INFORMATION:**
The Green family was related to the Hook family. Martha is buried beside George Hook and his daughter Alice Hook. See George B. Hook and Alice Hook.

Zelma Myrick, who recorded information in a notebook in the 1930s during a visit to Rose Hill Cemetery, reported "stone on ground." The original base for this gravestone was missing at the time of Park District acquisition. A new granite base was purchased by Black Diamond Rangers in 2003. The gravestone was broken into three sections and had been concreted flat to the ground prior to Park District acquisition. In 1982, the stone was removed from the cemetery by park staff and the concrete backing carefully detached from the gravestone. A marble encasement was added to strengthen the original gravestone. In August 2003, the stone was returned to the cemetery and attached to the new granite base.

**REFERENCES:** 1, 2, 3, 10 (pages 251, 253), 11 (P610.31.153), 12, 14

Henry (Hervey) Sheldon Green and his wife,
Mary Ann (Hulme) Green, parents of Martha J. Green.

Reference 322.4

Reference 322.7

Reference 322.2

Reference 322.9

Henry (Hervey) S. Green and wife, Mary Ann (Hulme) Green (above left), and children (right, top to bottom): Eliza Alice Green, William Ammon Green, and Joseph Charles Green.

Reference 322.10

# GRIFFITH,
## (Infant)

## PERSONAL INFORMATION:

| | |
|---|---|
| SEX: | Male |
| DATE OF BIRTH: | |
| DATE OF DEATH: | December 13, 1893 |
| PLACE OF DEATH: | |
| AGE AT DEATH: | Infant |
| CAUSE OF DEATH: | |
| BIRTHPLACE: | |
| SPOUSE: | None |
| PARENTS: | John (Jack) and Emma Griffith |

## GRAVESITE INFORMATION:

| | |
|---|---|
| LOCATION OF GRAVESITE: | Unknown |
| GRAVESTONE: | Missing |
| TYPE OF GRAVESTONE: | |
| SHAPE OF GRAVESTONE: | |
| INSCRIPTION: | |
| EPITAPH: | |
| MOTIF: | |
| CARVER: | |
| BASE: | |
| TYPE OF BASE: | |
| ENCLOSURE: | |
| TYPE OF ENCLOSURE: | |
| FENCE: | |
| TYPE OF FENCE: | |
| FENCE MOTIF: | |

# GRIFFITH, (Infant)

**ADDITIONAL PERSONAL INFORMATION:**
This infant's parents, Jack and Emma Griffith, are also buried in Rose Hill Cemetery. Since no death dates are given for the infant and the mother, it is not known for certain if this is the infant who died while Emma was giving birth.

See Emma Griffith and Jack Griffith.

The *Contra Costa County Register of Deaths* lists an infant, age 3 days, as the son of John J. Griffiths [sic] of Somersville, who died December 13, 1893. This may be the same infant.

**ADDITIONAL GRAVESITE INFORMATION:**
The burial location for Jack and Emma Griffith and their infant is not known.

**REFERENCES:** 3, 7, 12

# GRIFFITH,
## David E.

## PERSONAL INFORMATION:

| | |
|---|---|
| SEX: | Male |
| DATE OF BIRTH: | 1824 |
| DATE OF DEATH: | May 20, 1900 |
| PLACE OF DEATH: | Near Cornwall, Contra Costa County, California |
| AGE AT DEATH: | 76 years |
| CAUSE OF DEATH: | Fell off horse from exhaustion and landed on fence post |
| BIRTHPLACE: | Cardiganshire, Wales |
| SPOUSE: | Margaret (Edwards) Thomas Griffith |
| PARENTS: | Mr. and Mrs. Griffith |

## GRAVESITE INFORMATION:

| | |
|---|---|
| LOCATION OF GRAVESITE: | Section N-B, Plot #7b |
| GRAVESTONE: | Exists |
| TYPE OF GRAVESTONE: | Polished granite |
| SHAPE OF GRAVESTONE: | Obelisk |
| INSCRIPTION: | Polished middle granite base says *Griffith* |
| EPITAPH: | |
| MOTIF: | |
| CARVER: | |
| BASE: | Exists |
| TYPE OF BASE: | Granite base with polished middle granite base |
| ENCLOSURE: | |
| TYPE OF ENCLOSURE: | |
| FENCE: | Exists |
| TYPE OF FENCE: | Iron with granite blocks |
| FENCE MOTIF: | |

# GRIFFITH, David E.

**ADDITIONAL PERSONAL INFORMATION:**
The *1870 Census for Township Three, Contra Costa County*, California, lists David Griffiths [sic] as a native of Wales, age 40, and a butcher. On November 12, 1891 in Somersville, Contra Costa County, California, David E. Griffiths [sic] loaned William Dainty $2,200 in United States gold coins. In 1892, D. E. Griffith loaned $180 to the church for the "benefit of Church." The "church" was the Nortonville Church that was relocated to Black Diamond (now Pittsburg), Contra Costa County, California for the use of the New York Landing Congregational Church and Society.

The *Great Register of Contra Costa County, California, 1894*, page 18, lists David E. Griffith, age 68, as 5' 9" tall, dark complexion, gray hair and eyes. He was a stock raiser and a native of Great Britain living in Nortonville. The *Great Register of the County of Contra Costa in the State of California, 1898* for Somersville precinct lists David E. Griffiths [sic], age 71, of Nortonville, Contra Costa County, California, as a stock raiser. He was 5' 9" with dark complexion and gray eyes and hair. He was a native of Wales and naturalized into the United States on October 15, 1860. In the last will and testament left by Griffith dated April 7, 1899, he directed that he be buried beside the body of his friend, Joe Edwards. Griffith died at his home near Cornwall, Contra Costa County, California, between Nortonville and present day Pittsburg. His siblings included: Elizabeth, William, Evan, John, Thomas, Griffith and at least two other brothers, names unknown.

A Superior Court document from Contra Costa County dated October 8, 1900, regarding the estate of David E. Griffith states that $10 was charged to dig two graves for Griffith (two graves at $5 each).

> The first grave being dug, it was afterwards learned from the will of D. E. Griffith deceased that it was not where his wish to be buried was hence the digging of a second grave.

Contra Costa County probate records dated October 20, 1900, ordered the following articles of personal property be left to his surviving wife Margaret:

> Two horses named "Ben" and "Nell" and their harness; Three cows "Blossom," "Lily" and "Rose" and their sucking calves; one spring wagon; all the farming utensils and implements consisting of two single plows, three harrows, two cultivators.

Also, an allowance of $100 per month for maintenance of the family out of the estate. In a Superior Court of Contra Costa County document dated May 1, 1901, regarding the matter of a claim against the Estate of David Griffith it states that on May 27, 1900, $12 was charged for carriages for the funeral. Griffith's widow, Margaret, was formerly married to his best friend Rees G. Thomas.

The *1910 Census for Township 6, Contra Costa County, California*, lists Margurete [sic] Griffb [sic], age 74, as a widow and native of Wales. Also listed is her son Rees J. Thomas, age 35, a native of California. See Joseph M. Edwards and Rees G. Thomas.

**ADDITIONAL GRAVESITE INFORMATION:**
Zelma Myrick, who recorded information in a notebook in the 1930s during a visit to Rose Hill Cemetery, reported "Stone down, iron fence around plot." David shares a gravesite with Joseph M. Edwards. A polished middle granite base, inscribed "Griffith" sits on larger granite base. It is chipped in a few places. The iron fence sits on granite blocks. The fence was repaired by the Black Diamond Rangers in 1988. See Joseph M. Edwards.

**REFERENCES:** 1, 2, 3, 4, 5, 6, 8 (July 14, 1900 and May 26, 1900), 9 (May 26, 1900 and April 13, 1901), 11 (P610.31.193, P610.31.195, P610.119.24, P610.145.1, P610.168.20, P610.268.2, P610.312.1, P610.317.20, and P610.349.1), 12, 13 (April 7, 1899), 14, *Contra Costa Times* newspaper (November 7, 1999, page C 9), see newspaper appendix pages 708-710

# ACME MARKET,

Front Street,

## ANTIOCH,

## NORTONVILLE AND SOMERSVILLE.

---

The above Meat Markets are fitted up in first class style, with everything convenient and necessary. Fresh meats of all kinds, and always the VERY BEST the country affords.

## Dried, Smoked, and Salted Meats

### Of every kind. Also:

## Fresh Sausage, Head Cheese, Etc.

---

The proprietors will ever do their best to please and satisfy their customers.

ALEXANDER MOORE. ) Proprietors at Somers-
DAVID E. GRIFFITH. ) ville and Nortonville.

ALEXANDER MOORE. )
DAVID E. GRIFFITH. ) Proprietors at
CHARLES LUPPA. ) Antioch.

This *Antioch Ledger* newspaper article from December 25, 1875 lists David E. Griffith as one of the Proprietors of the Acme Market in Nortonville, Somersville, and Antioch. According to the *Contra Costa Gazette* newspaper, May 26, 1900 (see page 709):

> The deceased left an estate worth $25,000, consisting of the Starr Hotel at Crockett, $8,000; 480 acres of land near Cornwall, $6,000; a lot in the town of Paso Robles, at $1,000; live stock, $500; money in bank, $6,000, and claims against the estate of John E. Hughes, $2,000.

Photograph above: Nortonville resident, David E. Griffith, 1898. Photograph on left: Rees Thomas, son of Rees G. and Margaret Thomas, and stepson of David E. Griffith, *circa* 1880s.

On May 20, 1900, David Griffith rode his horse from Nortonville to Somersville to order coal and get his mail. According to the *Antioch Ledger* newspaper of May 26, 1900:

> Mr. Griffiths [sic] was in the habit of throwing his right leg around the horn of the saddle at times for relief, and on his left foot he wore a spur. It is supposed the sharp points of the spur irritated the horse and he broke into a gallop. When in front of the house Mr. Griffiths [sic] fell off the horse, probably from exhaustion after riding so hard and fell heavily against a barbed wire fence post, knocking it out of the ground and breaking three ribs on his right side near the arm pit. The force of the concussion must have been terrific. Hugh Medill and Rees Thomas, his stepson, who witnessed the accident, went to his assistance with a cart but he refused help and got into the cart alone. When they reached the house he got out alone crawled in on his hands and went to bed. Dr. George of Antioch was summoned and dressed his wounds. He was beyond medical aid, however, for he lingered until 8 o'clock the next evening, Sunday, when he expired.

**PERSONAL INFORMATION:**

| | |
|---|---|
| SEX: | Female |
| DATE OF BIRTH: | |
| DATE OF DEATH: | |
| PLACE OF DEATH: | |
| AGE AT DEATH: | Adult |
| CAUSE OF DEATH: | Childbirth |
| BIRTHPLACE: | |
| SPOUSE: | Jack Griffith |
| PARENTS: | |

**GRAVESITE INFORMATION:**

| | |
|---|---|
| LOCATION OF GRAVESITE: | Unknown |
| GRAVESTONE: | Missing |
| TYPE OF GRAVESTONE: | |
| SHAPE OF GRAVESTONE: | |
| INSCRIPTION: | |
| EPITAPH: | |
| MOTIF: | |
| CARVER: | |
| BASE: | |
| TYPE OF BASE: | |
| ENCLOSURE: | |
| TYPE OF ENCLOSURE: | |
| FENCE: | |
| TYPE OF FENCE: | |
| FENCE MOTIF: | |

# GRIFFITH, Emma

**ADDITIONAL PERSONAL INFORMATION:**
According to a cemetery list compiled in 1935 by Eva Roath Olcott, for the Daughters of the American Revolution (reference 3; see page 1004), Emma died while giving birth. Emma's husband, Jack, and their infant child are also buried in Rose Hill Cemetery. See Jack and (infant) Griffith.

**ADDITIONAL GRAVESITE INFORMATION:**
The burial location for Emma and Jack Griffith and their infant child is not known.

**REFERENCES:** 3, 12

Reference 362.6

Rose Hill Cemetery looking northwest in January 1968.
At the time this photograph was taken, the cemetery was surrounded by a cyclone fence.

# GRIFFITH,
## Jack

## PERSONAL INFORMATION:

SEX:    Male

DATE OF BIRTH:

DATE OF DEATH:

PLACE OF DEATH:

AGE AT DEATH:    Adult

CAUSE OF DEATH:

BIRTHPLACE:

SPOUSE:    Emma Griffith

PARENTS:

## GRAVESITE INFORMATION

LOCATION OF GRAVESITE    Unknown

GRAVESTONE:    Missing

TYPE OF GRAVESTONE:

SHAPE OF GRAVESTONE:

INSCRIPTION:

EPITAPH:

MOTIF:

CARVER:

BASE:

TYPE OF BASE:

ENCLOSURE:

TYPE OF ENCLOSURE:

FENCE:

TYPE OF FENCE:

FENCE MOTIF:

# GRIFFITH, Jack

**ADDITIONAL PERSONAL INFORMATION:**
Jack Griffith may also have been known as John J. Griffith. Jack's wife, Emma, and their infant child are also buried in Rose Hill Cemetery. See Emma and (infant) Griffith.

**ADDITIONAL GRAVESITE INFORMATION:**
The burial location for Jack and Emma Griffith and their infant child is not known.

**REFERENCES:** 3, 12

Courtesy of CCCHS

Miners at the Pittsburg Mine, Somersville, *circa* 1898. The Jack Griffith family may have lived in Somersville in the 1890s during the time that the Pittsburg Mine was active.

# GRIFFITHS,
## David W.

**PERSONAL INFORMATION:**

| | |
|---|---|
| SEX: | Male |
| DATE OF BIRTH: | 1834 |
| DATE OF DEATH: | July 25, 1876 |
| PLACE OF DEATH: | Nortonville, Contra Costa County, California |
| AGE AT DEATH: | 42 years |
| CAUSE OF DEATH: | Burns and/or suffocation caused by a mine explosion |
| BIRTHPLACE: | Monmouthshire, South Wales |
| SPOUSE: | Emma (?) Griffiths |
| PARENTS: | |

**GRAVESITE INFORMATION:**

| | |
|---|---|
| LOCATION OF GRAVESITE: | Section S-D, Plot #49 |
| GRAVESTONE: | Exists |
| TYPE OF GRAVESTONE: | Marble |
| SHAPE OF GRAVESTONE: | Tablet |
| INSCRIPTION: | Middle marble base says *Griffiths* |
| EPITAPH: | *In the morning it flourisheth, and groweth up.* |
| | *In the evening it is cut down and witherd.*[sic] |
| MOTIF: | |
| CARVER: | Excelsior Marble Works, San Jose, California |
| BASE: | Exists |
| TYPE OF BASE: | Sandstone with middle marble base |
| ENCLOSURE: | Exists |
| TYPE OF ENCLOSURE: | Brick (partial) |
| FENCE: | Missing |
| TYPE OF FENCE: | Iron |
| FENCE MOTIF: | Shell and fleur-de lis |

East Bay Regional Park District

# GRIFFITHS, David W.

**ADDITIONAL PERSONAL INFORMATION:**
The *History of Contra Costa County*, by Slocum and Company, 1882, page 474, states that David Griffiths and five others were killed by a powder explosion which occurred in the Black Diamond Mine at Nortonville on July 24, 1876.

According to the *Contra Costa Gazette* newspaper, July 29, 1876, David Griffiths left behind a wife and several children. He was interred in the cemetery next to other men who died in the same explosion by the Cambrian Mutual Aid Society, of which he was a member.

See Theophile Dumas, William Gething, Thomas D. James, Meredith Lewis, George M. Reynolds, Evan Smith, David Watts, Theophilus Watts, and William L. Williams.

**ADDITIONAL GRAVESITE INFORMATION:**
The gravestone was broken from the base and concreted flat to the ground prior to East Bay Regional Park District acquisition. The stone was removed from the cemetery by Black Diamond Rangers for repairs on February 27, 1997. The rough concrete encasement was removed. The bottom sandstone base was leveled and a sub-grade concrete footing poured. The repaired stone was returned to the cemetery and re-attached to the base with brass pins and white epoxy in March 1997. The gravestone sits on the middle base that is inscribed "Griffiths." The middle marble base sits on a larger sandstone base.

David's epitaph comes from the *Bible*: Psalms, Chapter 90, Verse 6. The epitaph recorded on the gravestone is a slight variation from the *Bible* verse that says: "In the morning it flourisheth, and groweth up; in the evening it is cut down, and withereth." See William Gething.

**REFERENCES:** 1, 2, 3, 4, 5, 6, 8 ( July 29, 1876 and Aug. 12, 1876), 9 (July 29, 1876), 10 (pages 474), 11 (P610.5.2, P610.8.10, P610.31.182, P610.84.2, P610.267.3, P610.312.3, P610.363.1, and P610.363.2), 12, 14, *Pittsburg Post Dispatch* newspaper (Wed., June 15, 1955, pages 9 and 12), see newspaper appendix (William Gething) pages 706 and707

Reference 8.10

The vandalized gravestone of David W. Griffiths, knocked from its base and concreted to the ground, 1971. Photograph by Brian Suen.

## Probate Court.

### Hon. Thomas A. Brown, Judge.

Monday, August 7th 1876.

In the matter of the estate of Willim Gething, deceased. D. B. Davis, was appointed administrator of said estate on executing and filing bonds in the sum of $3,200, and taking the oath of office.

In the same estate an order was made directing the administrator to cause notice to the creditors of the deceased to be given by posting and publication of notice, requiring creditors to present their claims within four months.

In the matter of the estate of David W. Griffith deceased. A petition was filed by Emma Griffith praying for letters of administration on said estate an order was made fixing the hearing of the petition for the 19th, instant at 10 o'clock A. M.

In the matter of the guardianship of George Brenzel, and Earnest Brenzel, minors. The petition of E. W. Hiller to be appointed guardian of said miners came on to be heard and an order was made appointing E. W. Hiller to be appointed guardian for said minors of his executing and filing a good sufficient bond to each of said minors in the penal sum of three hundred dollars, and taking the oath of office.

In matter of the estate of Sarah P. Minor, deceased. The executors of said estate filed an account of sales of certain real property of the deceased, the matter on the petition of the executors praying for an order confirming the sale came on to be heard and testimony was taken and the further hearing was continued until the 12th instant, at 10 o'clock A. M.

In the matter of the guardianship of J. W. Stephens, a minor. The hearing and settlement of the annual account of John Larkey guardian of said minor having been fixed for this day after hearing testimony in the case an order was made settling said account.

This "Probate Court" article from the *Contra Costa Gazette* newspaper of August 12, 1876, states that:

In the matter of the estate of David W. Griffith [sic] deceased. A petition was filed by Emma Griffith [sic] praying for letters of administration on said estate an order was made fixing the hearing of the petition for the 19th, instant at 10 o'clock A. M.

Also listed in this article is William Gething who died in the same mining accident in Nortonville on July 24, 1876.

Above, David W. Griffiths' gravesite with gravestone and iron fence on right. An unknown gentleman stands next to the burial site for three miners who died in the July 24, 1876 mine explosion in Nortonville. The date of the photograph is unknown. Below, David W. Griffiths' gravestone and vandalized fence stand next to the defaced gravesite of William Gething, April 1960.

Reference 346.1

# HABENICHT,
## Wilhelm C.

**PERSONAL INFORMATION:**

| | |
|---|---|
| SEX: | Male |
| DATE OF BIRTH: | March 29, 1863 |
| DATE OF DEATH: | February 25, 1882 |
| PLACE OF DEATH: | |
| AGE AT DEATH: | 18 years, 10 months, 27 days |
| CAUSE OF DEATH: | |
| BIRTHPLACE: | Illinois |
| SPOUSE: | |
| PARENTS: | Henry and Leana Habenicht |

**GRAVESITE INFORMATION:**

| | |
|---|---|
| LOCATION OF GRAVESITE: | Section N-A, Plot #4 |
| GRAVESTONE: | Missing |
| TYPE OF GRAVESTONE: | Marble |
| SHAPE OF GRAVESTONE: | |
| INSCRIPTION: | *Son of* |
| EPITAPH: | *Tis hard to part* |
| | *With the one so dear as thee* |
| | *Our loved and gentle boy* |
| | *No more on earth thy smiles to see* |
| | *Thy smiles that gave us joy.* |
| MOTIF: | |
| CARVER: | |
| BASE: | Bottom base exists/middle base missing |
| TYPE OF BASE: | Granite (bottom)/marble (middle) |
| ENCLOSURE: | Exists |
| TYPE OF ENCLOSURE: | Brick |
| FENCE: | |
| TYPE OF FENCE: | |
| FENCE MOTIF: | |

# HABENICHT, Wilhelm C.

**ADDITIONAL PERSONAL INFORMATION:**
Wilhelm's age at death was calculated based on his birth date and death date that were listed on his gravestone. Although census records list his mother's name as Lena, his gravestone indicates her name was Leana. According to an interview with historian Louis Stein in 1974, Mr. Habenicht worked in Sam Brown's store in Somersville.

According to information obtained by www.ancestry.com: Henry Habenicht Sr. was born in 1833 in Hannover, Niedersachsen, Germany and died 1915 in Black Diamond, King County, Washington. His wife, Caroline "Lena" Habenicht, was born in 1835 and died in 1916. They were married in 1854 and had eleven children. Their children were:
- August, born 1856; died June 2, 1894
- Henry, born 1858; died March 2, 1897
- Emma, born 1858
- Albert, born 1860; died 1941
- Wilhelm, born 1863; died Feb. 25, 1882
- Annie, born 1867; died 1947
- Lizzie, born 1872
- Frederick August, born 1873; died 1942
- Amelia, born 1875
- Mary, born 1878
- Pauline, birth date unknown

The *1880 Census for Sommersville* [sic] *Precinct, Contra Costa County, California*, lists Henry Habeniche [sic], age 46, as a miner and native of Germany. Also recorded are his wife, Lena, age 44, a native of Germany and their children: August, age 24, a miner and native of Pennsylvania; Henry, age 21, a miner and native of Missouri; Albert, age 19, a laborer and native of Missouri; William [sic], age 17, a laborer and native of Illinois; Annie, age 12, a housekeeper and native of Iowa; Lizzie, age 8, a native of Iowa; Fred, age 6, a native of Iowa; Amelia, age 4, a native of California; and Mary, age 2, a native of California.

The *Washington State and Territorial Censuses, 1857-1892*, lists Lena Habenicht as married and living in Black Diamond, King County, Washington on June 10, 1887. The *Seattle, Washington City Directories, 1899-90*, lists Henry Habenicht as a miner in 1889 living in King County, Washington.

The *1900 Census for Black Diamond, King County, Washington* lists Lena Habenicht, age 65, as a native of Germany. Also listed are her husband, Henry Habenicht, age 66, a native of Germany and John Jacky, age 23, a native of Michigan and boarder.

The *1910 Census for Black Diamond, King County, Washington* lists Lina [sic] Habenicht, age 73, as a native of Germany. Also recorded is her husband Heinrich [Henry], age 76, a native of Germany.

According to *Black Diamond, Washington Cemetery* records, page 23, Wilhelm's parents, Henry and Lena [sic] Habenicht, are buried in Black Diamond, King County, Washington. Wilhelm's father, Henry, was born in 1833 and died in 1915. His mother, Lena (Leana), was born in 1835 and died in 1916. Vernon Habenicht, grandson of Henry Habenicht, was interviewed July 18, 1982 in Black Diamond, Washington. The transcription can be found in the Black Diamond Mines Regional Preserve archives.

**ADDITIONAL GRAVESITE INFORMATION:**
Zelma Myrick, who recorded information in a notebook in the 1930s during a visit to Rose Hill Cemetery, reported Wilhelm's stone in "Good condition."

The brick wall enclosure was rebuilt in 2003 by the East Bay Regional Park District. In April 2004, the granite base was re-leveled. A photograph of the gravestone appeared in *The Pittsburg Post Dispatch* newspaper, June 5, 1955, page 9.

**REFERENCES:** 1, 2, 3, 4, 6, 11 (P610.260.16, P610.267.2, P610.294.8, and P610.317.2), 12, *The Pittsburg Post Dispatch* newspaper (Wed., June 15, 1955, pages 9 and 12)

Wilhelm C. Habenicht gravestone, *circa* 1939. Photograph by Zelma Myrick.

The stone says:

SON OF
HENRY & LEANA
HABENICHT
Native of Illinois
BORN
March 29, 1863
DIED
Feb. 25, 1882

Pictured are Henry Habenicht Jr. and his family. Henry was the brother of Wilhelm Habenicht. Identified left to right are: Henry III (born Nov. 24, 1881, Contra Costa County, California); Henry's wife, Ellen (McVary) Habenicht (born 1860); William Joseph (born June 26, 1886, King County, Washington); Henry (born July 26, 1858 in Putnam County, Missouri); and John (born Sept. 6, 1883, Contra Costa County, California).

Henry F. Habenicht, age 22, of Somersville, Contra Costa County, California, and Ellen McVary, age 20, also of Somersville, applied for a marriage license on February 2, 1881. The information was recorded in the *Applications for Marriage Licenses, Contra Costa County, 1873-1887*, page 231, located at the Contra Costa County Historical Society History Center in Martinez, California.

# HAVARD,
## Elias

**PERSONAL INFORMATION:**

| | |
|---|---|
| SEX: | Male |
| DATE OF BIRTH: | October 10, 1870 |
| DATE OF DEATH: | August 27, 1875 |
| PLACE OF DEATH: | Nortonville, Contra Costa County, California |
| AGE AT DEATH: | 4 years, 10 months, 17 days |
| CAUSE OF DEATH: | |
| BIRTHPLACE: | Port Wine, Sierra County, California |
| SPOUSE: | None |
| PARENTS: | Thomas D. and Margaret (Davies) Havard |

**GRAVESITE INFORMATION:**

| | |
|---|---|
| LOCATION OF GRAVESITE: | Section N-D, Plot #39 |
| GRAVESTONE: | Exists |
| TYPE OF GRAVESTONE: | Marble |
| SHAPE OF GRAVESTONE: | Tablet |
| INSCRIPTION: | *To the Memory of/Native of California* |
| EPITAPH: | *He left this earth to bloom in heaven.* |
| MOTIF: | |
| CARVER: | W. H. McCormick, 827 Market St., San Francisco |
| BASE: | Exists |
| TYPE OF BASE: | Granite with middle marble base |
| FENCE: | |
| ENCLOSURE: | |
| TYPE OF ENCLOSURE: | |
| TYPE OF FENCE: | |
| FENCE MOTIF: | |

# HAVARD, Elias

**ADDITIONAL PERSONAL INFORMATION:**
Elias' age was calculated by www.timeanddate.com, based on the birth and death date listed on his gravestone. The place of birth and death comes from descendants. According to information obtained from descendants, Elias' mother, Margaret Davies, was born July 28, 1834 in Wales, and died June 28, 1919. His father, Thomas David Havard, was born March 14, 1831 in Wales, and died October 30, 1893. Margaret and Thomas are interred in Alhambra Cemetery, Martinez, Contra Costa County, California. Margaret Davies married Thomas D. Havard on July 8, 1856 in New York City, New York. Havard came to California in 1862. Elias' siblings were: Richard D., born March 11, 1859, Scranton, Lackawanna County, PA; David John, born Sept. 21, 1860, Scranton, PA; Annie, born Aug. 10, 1865, Port Wine, Sierra County, CA; Evan, born Dec. 24, 1867, Port Wine, CA; and Lydia, born Aug. 9, 1873, Port Wine, CA. They also had a two year old who died in Scranton, Pennsylvania and a one day old daughter who died in California.

The *1870 Census for Sears, Sierra County, California* lists Thos. D. Havard, age 39, as a miner and native of Wales. Also listed are his wife Margaret, age 35, a native of Wales and their children, Richard, age 11; David J., age 9, both natives of Pennsylvania; Anna, age 4, and Evan, age 2, both natives of California. Elias' name does not appear on the 1870 census because he was born in October and the census was taken in June 1870. In 1876, Thomas D. Havard operated a store that sold wines, liquors and cigars on Main Street, Nortonville, Contra Costa County, California. The *Business Directory of San Francisco and Principal Towns of California and Nevada, 1877*, page 50, under the "Nortonville" heading lists T. D. Havard as selling liquors. The *Antioch Ledger* newspaper, February 13, 1879, lists Thomas D. Havard as a Trustee of the Carbondale School District in Nortonville.

The *1880 Census for Nortonville Precinct, Contra Costa County, California* records Thomas Havard, age 49, as a native of Wales and a miner. Also listed are his wife Margaret, age 45, a native of Wales and their children: Richard, age 21, a miner and native of Pennsylvania; David, age 19, a laborer and native of Pennsylvania; Annie, age 15; Evan, age 13; and Liddia [sic], age 6. All are natives of California. The *Contra Costa Gazette* newspaper, December 19, 1888, lists T. D. Havard as the proprietor of the Exchange Hotel in Martinez, Contra Costa County. According to the *Contra Costa Gazette*, November 4, 1893, Thomas D. Havard located in Nortonville in 1874, eventually settling in Martinez, Contra Costa County, California, where he died and is buried. At the time of his death he left a widow and four children.

The *1900 Census for Oakland Ward, Alameda County, California* lists Margaret Havard, age 65, as a native of Wales and the head of the house. Also listed are her children: Richard D., age 41, a native of Pennsylvania; Annie, age 34; Evan, age 32; Ludia [sic], age 26, all natives of California.

**ADDITIONAL GRAVESITE INFORMATION:**
In August 2001, a broken marble footstone with the initials "W. E. C." (for Walter E. Clare) was found under Elias Havard's gravestone when it was removed for repairs. Walter E. Clare is interred in Section N-B, plot 112 in Rose Hill Cemetery. Elias' gravestone was broken in two pieces and concreted flat to the ground prior to East Bay Regional Park District acquisition. The gravestone was repaired and set upright by Black Diamond Rangers in August 2002. The gravestone sits on a middle marble base.

**REFERENCES:** 2, 3, 4, 8 (Dec. 19, 1888, Nov. 4, 1893 – two articles, Aug. 27, 1898 – two articles), 9 (July 1, 1876, July 15, 1876, and Feb. 13, 1879), 11 (P610.31.178, P610.119.28, and P610.263.4), 12, 14, see newspaper appendix page 711

From the *Antioch Ledger* newspaper, July 15, 1876.

From the *Contra Costa Gazette* newspaper, December 19, 1888.

## THOMAS D. HAVARD.

Death has been busy in our community within the past week, and among those to whom the final summons came was the subject of this notice, an old and highly esteemed citizen, an affectionate husband and parent, and an honest and upright man. Mr. Havard numbered among his friends all who made his acquaintance. Courteous in manner, though retiring in disposition, he won and retained the confidence of all who knew him, and his loss will be deplored not only by his bereaved family, who have the sympathy of all, but by a wide circle of friends, who knew and appreciated his unobtrusive ways and steadfast friendship. He had been an invalid for a considerable time and the end had been anticipated for several weeks. Mr. Havard was a native of Wales, and early in life came to America, residing for a period in the east, and finally removing to California. He came to Contra Costa in 1874 and located at Nortonville, at that time the center of a large and prosperous coal mining industry. Here he engaged in business until about ten years since, when he removed to Martinez and made it his home during the remainder of his life. He leaves a widow and four children. The funeral services were held at Odd Fellows Hall on Friday afternoon, and a long procession followed the remains to the cemetery.

This obituary for Elias Havard's father, Thomas D. Havard, appeared in the *Contra Costa Gazette* newspaper on November 4, 1893.

## PERSONAL INFORMATION:

| | |
|---|---|
| SEX: | Male |
| DATE OF BIRTH: | *Circa* 1833 |
| DATE OF DEATH: | December 16, 1873 |
| PLACE OF DEATH: | Somersville, Contra Costa County, California |
| AGE AT DEATH: | Approximately 40 years |
| CAUSE OF DEATH: | Boiler explosion at Independent Shaft |
| BIRTHPLACE: | Scotland |
| SPOUSE: | |
| PARENTS: | |

## GRAVESITE INFORMATION:

| | |
|---|---|
| LOCATION OF GRAVESITE: | Unknown |
| GRAVESTONE: | Missing or never placed |
| TYPE OF GRAVESTONE: | |
| SHAPE OF GRAVESTONE: | |
| INSCRIPTION: | |
| EPITAPH: | |
| MOTIF: | |
| CARVER: | |
| BASE: | |
| TYPE OF BASE: | |
| ENCLOSURE: | |
| TYPE OF ENCLOSURE: | |
| FENCE: | |
| TYPE OF FENCE: | |
| FENCE MOTIF: | |

# HAY, John

**ADDITIONAL PERSONAL INFORMATION:**
John Hay was one of at least three men killed in the boiler explosion at the Independent Mine in Somersville, Contra Costa County, California, which occurred about 5 pm on Tuesday, December 16, 1873. It was reported that none of the deceased left families.

**ADDITIONAL GRAVESITE INFORMATION:**
The *Antioch Ledger* newspaper, December 20, 1873 is the only source to reference his burial in Rose Hill Cemetery. The article states: "The

bodies of the deceased were buried at Somersville on Wednesday afternoon." His burial location is not known. See James Daley.

**REFERENCES:** 8 (Dec. 20, 1873, Dec. 27, 1873, Jan. 3, 1874, Jan. 10, 1874 - two articles, Jan. 17, 1874, Jan. 24, 1874, and Jan. 31, 1874), 9 (Dec. 20, 1873 and Dec. 27, 1873 - two articles) and *Daily Alta California* newspaper (Dec. 18, 1873), *San Francisco Call* newspaper (Dec. 20, 1873), see newspaper appendix pages 689, 690, and 712

Reference 297.1

Independent Mine, Somersville, no date. The mine, shown here partially obscured by exhaust steam from the hoist machinery, was the northernmost mine in the coal field. James Daley was killed instantly in the boiler explosion that occurred at this mine on December 16, 1873.

# HEYCOCK,
## Richard

## PERSONAL INFORMATION:

| | |
|---|---|
| SEX: | Male |
| DATE OF BIRTH: | December 4, 1868 |
| DATE OF DEATH: | November 14, 1877 |
| PLACE OF DEATH: | Nortonville, Contra Costa County, California |
| AGE AT DEATH: | 8 years, 11 months, 10 days |
| CAUSE OF DEATH: | |
| BIRTHPLACE: | California |
| SPOUSE: | None |
| PARENTS: | Job and Catherine Heycock |

## GRAVESITE INFORMATION:

| | |
|---|---|
| LOCATION OF GRAVESITE: | Section N-D, Plot #35 |
| GRAVESTONE: | Exists |
| TYPE OF GRAVESTONE: | Marble |
| SHAPE OF GRAVESTONE: | Tablet |
| INSCRIPTION: | *Son of* |
| EPITAPH: | *Y bore Y blodeua ac y tyf* |
| | *prydnawn y torrir ymaith,* |
| | *ac y gwywa.* |
| MOTIF: | |
| CARVER: | Aitken and Fish, Sacramento, California |
| BASE: | Exists |
| TYPE OF BASE: | Granite |
| ENCLOSURE: | |
| TYPE OF ENCLOSURE: | |
| FENCE: | |
| TYPE OF FENCE: | |
| FENCE MOTIF: | |

# HEYCOCK, Richard

**ADDITIONAL PERSONAL INFORMATION:**
Richard's date of birth was calculated by www.timeanddate.com, based on his date of death and age at death. According to the *Antioch Ledger* newspaper, November 17, 1877 and the *Contra Costa Gazette* newspaper, November 24, 1877, Richard was 9 years old at the time of his death. The *1870 Census for Township Three, Contra Costa County, California* lists Job Heycock, age 30, as a miner and native of Wales. Also listed are his wife, Catherine, age 30, a native of Wales and children: William, age 7, a native of Pennsylvania; Reese, age 4, a native of Pennsylvania; and Richard, age 1, a native of California. Richard's father, Job Heycock, was listed in the *Contra Costa County Directory 1871-2* as a miner in Nortonville. In the *Assessment List, Contra Costa County, for 1872-73*, Jobe [sic] Hecock [sic] is assessed $240 for a house, furniture and other solvent debts in Nortonville. The *1880 Census for Nortonville, Contra Costa County, California* lists a married female Heacock [sic], as 40 years old and a housekeeper. Also listed with her are her children: Edward, age 17 and Reese, age 13, both natives of Pennsylvania. Edward was also listed as having brain fever. Richard's brother, William Edward Heycock, age 17, died in Nortonville on June 9, 1880. He was 17 years of age and a native of Carbon County, Pennsylvania according to his obituary that appeared in the *Contra Costa Gazette* newspaper on June 19, 1880.

In the *History of Contra Costa County* by Slocum and Company, 1882, page 360, it states:

> A Welchman [sic] named Peter Peters was shot and mortally wounded by a fellow-countryman named Job Heycock on Thursday, March 14, 1872. From the testimony given before the Coroner's jury it appears that Heycock was aroused from his sleep on Thursday morning between the hours of four and five o'clock by a great noise in the room adjoining his bedroom. He got up, went into the next room, taking with him a loaded, double-barreled shot-gun [sic]. It was quite dark there; but he thought he noticed somebody going upstairs; he called out to him to stop, but receiving no answer, he fired. The deceased fell down to the bottom of the stairs. Heycock approached him, found him to be Peter Peters, a very particular friend of his...

In 1884, Job Heycock gave his testimony in the murder case, *The People vs. William Bennett*. Job stated he had lived in Stewartville, Contra Costa County, California for two years. By 1887, both Job, age 50, and his wife, Catherine, age 49, were living in Black Diamond, King County, Washington, where Job worked as a miner.

**ADDITIONAL GRAVESITE INFORMATION:**
Zelma Myrick, who recorded information in a notebook in the 1930s during a visit to Rose Hill Cemetery, reported "Stone broken and down." Richard's gravestone was broken into two pieces and concreted flat to ground prior to East Bay Regional Park District acquisition. A brick enclosure was also placed around the gravesite after the coal mining period and prior to Park District acquisition. The brick enclosure was photographed, measured, and removed by Black Diamond Rangers in 2009 so that the gravestone could be placed upright in its original location. The enclosure had been built on top of the buried gravestone base. Richard's epitaph is written in Welsh. The translation is: *In the morning it flourisheth, and groweth up; in the evening it is cut down, and withereth.* The epitaph is from the *Bible*, Psalms, Chapter 90, Verse 6.

**REFERENCES:** 1, 2, 3, 6, 8 (Nov. 24, 1877), 9 (Nov. 17, 1877), 11 (P610.31.177), 12, 13, 14, *The Move of Coal Miners From Nortonville, California to Black Diamond, Washington Territory, 1885*, by Jacqueline Byer Dial, Senior Honors Thesis, June 1980, page 81, see newspaper appendix page 713

**PERSONAL INFORMATION:**

| | |
|---|---|
| SEX: | Male |
| DATE OF BIRTH: | April 1, 1873 |
| DATE OF DEATH: | January 1, 1882 |
| PLACE OF DEATH: | |
| AGE AT DEATH: | 8 years, 9 months |
| CAUSE OF DEATH: | |
| BIRTHPLACE: | |
| SPOUSE: | None |
| PARENTS: | Isaac H. and Julia (Canify) Holt |

**GRAVESITE INFORMATION:**

| | |
|---|---|
| LOCATION OF GRAVESITE: | Section N-B, Plot #10 |
| GRAVESTONE: | Exists |
| TYPE OF GRAVESTONE: | Marble |
| SHAPE OF GRAVESTONE: | Tablet |
| INSCRIPTION: | *Son of* |
| EPITAPH: | |
| MOTIF: | |
| CARVER: | |
| BASE: | Exists |
| TYPE OF BASE: | Granite |
| ENCLOSURE: | |
| TYPE OF ENCLOSURE: | |
| FENCE: | |
| TYPE OF FENCE: | |
| FENCE MOTIF: | |

# HOLT, Walter L.

**ADDITIONAL PERSONAL INFORMATION:**
Walter's birth was calculated by <u>www.timeanddate.com</u>, based on his date at death and age at death. Mr. and Mrs. I. H. Holt are listed in the records of the New York Congregational Church for 1883. (Although not stated, the church was most likely located at New York Landing, now Pittsburg, Contra Costa County, California.) Mrs. Holt was a charter member. On December 16, 1883, Brother Holt was nominated and duly elected as a trustee of the church. He received eight votes and his competitor received three. Mr. and Mrs. Holt were removed from the church congregation on February 12, 1886. Manner of removal was "letter of dismissal." Under the column listed "organization" it is written "Letter M. E. Church San Francisco."

Walter was born after the 1870 census and before the 1880 census was taken. No information could be found on Walter in the 1880 census. The *1900 Census for Woodland, Yolo County, California* lists Isaac H. Holt, age 49, as a native of Connecticut, born May 1851 and occupation bricklayer. His father's birthplace was England and mother's birthplace Scotland. Also listed is his wife, Julia, age 46, a native of New York, born March 1854. Her parents were born in New York. Julia and Isaac were married in 1873 and the census states that Julia is the mother of four children and that two are living. Included on the census is their daughter Grace Holt, age 20, born February 1880 in California and listed as single. The *1910 Census for Woodland Ward 2, Yolo County, California* lists Isaac H. Holt, age 58, as a native of Massachusetts, born about 1852. His wife, Julia, age 55, a native of New York is also listed. The *1920 Census for Woodland, Yolo County, California* lists Isaac Henry Holt, age 68, as a native of Connecticut, born about 1852 and occupation as brick mason, general work. Also listed is his wife, Julia, age 55, born about 1865 and a native of New York. The *1930 Census for Woodland, Yolo County, California* lists Issac [sic] H. Holt, age 78, widowed, born about 1853 in Massachusetts.

The *Woodland Daily Democrat* newspaper, June 3, 1929 reported that Mrs. Holt died at age 75 years and was a resident of Woodland, Yolo County, California for 41 years. The article also states that:

> Mrs. Holt was a native of New York and was formerly Miss Julia Canify. She married Holt at New Haven, Connecticut, in 1872, and they came to California and settled in Martinez two years later. In 1886 they moved to Woodland.

The *Woodland Daily Democrat*, July 7, 1932, reported the death of Isaac H. Holt. The article states he was a retired brick mason who was one of the pioneer residents of Woodland. He died in Honolulu on June 29 at the home of his daughter, Mrs. Grace Holt Hedeman. His daughter Grace and son Arthur E. Holt of Oakland, Alameda County, California were his only children living at the time of his death. According to their gravestones at the City of Woodland Cemetery (Yolo County, California), Julia was born March 2, 1854 and died June 3, 1929. Isaac H. Holt was born May 31, 1851 and died June 29, 1932. Located next to their gravesite in the cemetery is the gravestone for Mildred D. Holt who died on October 26, 1898 at age 20 years. Mildred is presumably their daughter.

**ADDITIONAL GRAVESITE INFORMATION:**
Zelma Myrick, who recorded information in a notebook in the 1930s during a visit to Rose Hill Cemetery, reported "Stone broken." The gravestone was broken into two pieces, concreted flat to the ground and secured by two metal pieces prior to East Bay Regional Park District acquisition and after the coal mining period.

**REFERENCES:** 1, 2, 3, 4, 6, 8 (Sept. 26, 1896), 11 (P610.31.196 and P610.119.6), 12, 14, *Woodland Daily Democrat* newspaper (June 3, 1929 and July 7, 1932), *History of New York/Pittsburg Congregational Church*, and *History and Directory of the Pittsburg Congregational Church, Pittsburg, Contra Costa County, California*, January 1913

## ACCIDENTAL SHOOTING.

Last night about twilight, Arthur Holt, who lives with his parents on Cross street, near Cleveland, shot his sister in the right ankle with a No. 22 Ballard rifle. Both claim that the shooting was accidental. The little girl suffered very much from the hurt. Dr. Beebe was called, but did not remove the ball, as it had entered near the ankle joint, and he thought it best to allow it to remain a day or two.

Arthur Holt is about sixteen years of age, and enjoys a very unenviable reputation. The neighbors describe him as being the worst boy that Woodland has ever had the pleasure of raising. The shooting occurred in this way, according to the statement of one of the neighbors, who seems to think that it was not altogether accidental :

Mrs. Holt had sent the boy on an errand, and he took the gun with him. As he remained away much longer than was necessary, the mother sent her little girl to find him. She is about ten years old. She met him on Cleveland street near Clanton's corner, and asked him why he had been gone so long. He commenced cursing and said it was none of her business. They walked along together, she expostulating with him and he abusing her, when the gun was suddenly discharged. The little girl screamed, and Mr. and Mrs. Clanton ran out to see what had happened. The little girl was lying in the street, and said she was shot. The boy said, "Oh, for God's sake shut up your crying. You are not hurt. It would not go through your shoe." Nevertheless, she was hurt, and the blood was flowing freely from the wound. The little girl was taken to her home, and Dr. Beebe called. Both claimed the shooting to be accidental.

These articles from the *Woodland Daily Democrat* newspaper, discuss Walter's brother, Arthur. The Holt family moved to Woodland, Yolo County, California in 1886. The article on the left is dated April 28, 1891 and the one below, August 27, 1891.

Readers of the DEMOCRAT will remember the incident of the Holt boy shooting his sister with a parlor rifle not long ago. As was stated at that time, young Holt enjoys the unenviable reputation of being the worst boy in the town, and it seems that he is trying his best to keep up his record.

For sometime he has been frequenting the warehouses and using vile language, cursing the men and otherwise making himself obnoxious. A few days ago Bob Hill, the foreman at the warehouses, told him to keep away, but the boy persisted in coming, and yesterday he grew so insulting that Hill picked him up and gave him a spanking.

This morning the boy complained to Judge Ruggles of the conduct of Hill, and a warrant was issued for the arrest of the latter. Hill gave bonds immediately went before Judge Fisher and swore to a warrant charging the boy with disturbing the peace, and, as a consequence, young Holt is now behind the bars.

Hill's trial will take place this evening at 8 o'clock, and Holt will have his hearing before Judge Fisher to-morrow at 9 o'clock.

## Mrs. Holt, 75, Resident of Woodland for 41 Years, Dies

Mrs. Julia Holt, 75, for 41 years a resident of Woodland, died at her home here Monday afternoon. Mrs. Holt had been unconscious since she was stricken with paralysis last Wednesday and her death was not unexpected.

Mrs. Holt was a native of New York and was formerly Miss Julia Canify. She married Holt at New Haven, Connecticut, in 1872, and they came to California and settled in Martinez two years later. In 1886 they moved to Woodland.

She is survived by her widower, I. N. Holt; a son, Arthur Holt of Oakland, and a daughter, Mrs. Grace Hedemann of Honolulu. During her long residence in Woodland she has made many friends who will mourn her passing. During the war period, she was active as a Red Cross worker.

Funeral arrangements are under the direction of the Krellenberg Co. Services will be held Wednesday morning at 10 o'clock at the home, 320 Cross street. Interment will be in the Woodland cemetery.

## Pioneer Of Woodland Dies In Honolulu

Isaac H. Holt, retired brick mason who was one of the pioneer resident of Woodland, died in Honolulu June 29th at the home of his daughter, Mrs. Grace Holt Hedeman.

News of his death came in a brief message from Mrs. Hedeman. No particulars were given in the letter.

During his residence in Woodland, Holt lived at 320 Cross street. His wife died years ago and three years ago he left for Honolulu, where he has since resided with his daughter, Mrs. Hedeman.

Fireplaces and chimneys in many of the older residences in Woodland were constructed by Mr. Holt, who was regarded as an expert in his line.

He was a member of Woodland lodge No. 156, F. and A. M.

The only survivors are his daughter, Mrs. Hedeman, and a son, Arthur E. Holt, of Oakland.

The articles above are from the *Woodland Daily Democrat* newspaper.
The article on the left is dated June 3, 1929, and the article on the right is from July 7, 1932.

# HOOK,
## Alice J.

## PERSONAL INFORMATION:

| | |
|---|---|
| SEX: | Female |
| DATE OF BIRTH: | November 16, 1874 |
| DATE OF DEATH: | February 20, 1875 |
| PLACE OF DEATH: | Nortonville, Contra Costa County, California |
| AGE AT DEATH: | 3 months, 4 days |
| CAUSE OF DEATH: | |
| BIRTHPLACE: | Nortonville, Contra Costa County, California |
| SPOUSE: | None |
| PARENTS: | George and Mary Ann (Green) Hook |

## GRAVESITE INFORMATION:

| | |
|---|---|
| LOCATION OF GRAVESITE: | Section S-F, Plot #108 |
| GRAVESTONE: | Exists |
| TYPE OF GRAVESTONE: | Marble |
| SHAPE OF GRAVESTONE: | Tablet |
| INSCRIPTION: | *Dau. of* |
| EPITAPH: | *God took thee from a world of care.* |
| MOTIF: | |
| CARVER: | |
| BASE: | Exists |
| TYPE OF BASE: | Sandstone |
| ENCLOSURE: | |
| TYPE OF ENCLOSURE: | |
| FENCE: | |
| TYPE OF FENCE: | |
| FENCE MOTIF: | |

# HOOK, Alice J.

**ADDITIONAL PERSONAL INFORMATION:**
According to family history records provided by a descendant, Alice J. Hook was born November 20, 1877 and not November 16, 1874 as indicated on her gravestone. Additionally, these records indicate that she died February 20, 1878 and not February 20, 1875 as indicated on her gravestone. Descendant records also list Alice's father as George Henry Hook and not George B. Hook.

**ADDITIONAL GRAVESITE INFORMATION:**
The gravestone was broken into three pieces and concreted flat to the ground prior to East Bay Regional Park District acquisition and after the coal mining period. The gravestone was removed and repaired by Black Diamond Rangers. A marble encasement was added to strengthen the original gravestone. The repaired stone was returned to the cemetery in September 2006.

The Hook family was related to the Green family. Alice is buried beside Martha Green and her father, George B. Hook. See George B. Hook and Martha Green.

REFERENCES:  1, 2, 3, 11 (P610.31.130), 12, 14

Reference 31.130

The Alice J. Hook vandalized gravestone as it appeared in 1977. The gravestone has been repaired by Black Diamond Rangers and now stands upright on its base in Rose Hill Cemetery.
Photograph by Traci (Gibbons) Parent.

# HOOK,
## George B.

**PERSONAL INFORMATION:**

| | |
|---|---|
| SEX: | Male |
| DATE OF BIRTH: | 1849 |
| DATE OF DEATH: | December 16, 1880 |
| PLACE OF DEATH: | Nortonville, Contra Costa County, California |
| AGE AT DEATH: | 31 years |
| CAUSE OF DEATH: | |
| BIRTHPLACE: | Ohio |
| SPOUSE: | Mary Ann (Green) Hook |
| PARENTS: | |

**GRAVESITE INFORMATION:**

| | |
|---|---|
| LOCATION OF GRAVESITE: | Section S-F, Plot #109 |
| GRAVESTONE: | Exists |
| TYPE OF GRAVESTONE: | Marble |
| SHAPE OF GRAVESTONE: | Tablet (partial) |
| INSCRIPTION: | *Beloved Husband of* |
| EPITAPH: | |
| MOTIF: | |
| CARVER: | |
| BASE: | Exists |
| TYPE OF BASE: | Granite |
| ENCLOSURE: | |
| TYPE OF ENCLOSURE: | |
| FENCE: | Exists |
| TYPE OF FENCE: | Iron |
| FENCE MOTIF: | |

# HOOK, George B.

**ADDITIONAL PERSONAL INFORMATION:**
George Hook, age 26, of Nortonville, Contra Costa County, California, and Mary Ann Green, age 19, also a resident of Nortonville applied for a marriage license on October 17, 1874. The information was recorded in the *Applications for Marriage Licenses, Contra Costa County, 1873-1887*, page 31, located at the Contra Costa County Historical Society History Center in Martinez, California.

According to the *Index to Marriage Certificates* located at the Contra Costa County Hall of Records, Martinez, California, George Hook married Mary Ann Green on November 11, 1874. They were married by William H. Ford and the information is listed is Volume 2, page 67.

The *1870 Census for Township Three, Contra Costa County, California* lists George Hook, age 21, as a resident of the "Hotel and Mines Boarding House." The census also states that he is a laborer and native of Ohio.

In the *1871 Contra Costa County Directory*, George Hook was listed as a laborer in Somersville.

The *1880 Nortonville Precinct Census, Contra Costa County, California* lists George, age 29 years, a butcher and native of Ohio. Also listed are his wife Mary, a native of California, age 25, and their daughter, Sarah, age 4, and son, Henry, age 6 months. Both children are natives of California.

According to descendants, they also had a daughter Zayda C. (born Feb. 7, 1876).

George's wife, Mary Ann, died in Sacramento, Sacramento County, California on January 8, 1933. The *Sacramento Bee* newspaper, January 9, 1933, states that Mary Ann Hook was a native of California and died at age 76 years, 8 months, and 21 days. She was interred at East Lawn Cemetery in Sacramento.

George's daughter, Alice J. Hook, is buried beside him. His sister-in-law, Martha J. Green, is buried near him. George Hook's gravestone lists him as George B. Hook. According to a descendant, he was George Henry Hook. See Alice J. Hook and Martha J. Green.

**ADDITIONAL GRAVESITE INFORMATION:**
Zelma Myrick, who recorded information in a notebook in the 1930s during a visit to Rose Hill Cemetery, reported "Stone broken in 4 pieces on ground."

The iron gate for the iron fence is missing. The top spire on the left, south facing side of the iron fence says "WAYNE." Only the top half of gravestone exists. The gravestone is broken into two pieces and was concreted to the ground prior to East Bay Regional Park District acquisition.

See "Additional Gravesite Information" for Dora Pohl on page 448 and 449.

**REFERENCES:** 1, 2, 3, 6, 11 (P610.31.155 and P610.31.202), 12, 14

# HOWELL,
## Sarah

## PERSONAL INFORMATION:

|  |  |
|---|---|
| SEX: | Female |
| DATE OF BIRTH: | January 9, 1866 |
| DATE OF DEATH: | October 9, 1870 |
| PLACE OF DEATH: | Nortonville, Contra Costa County, California |
| AGE AT DEATH: | 4 years, 9 months |
| CAUSE OF DEATH: | Diphtheria |
| BIRTHPLACE: | California |
| SPOUSE: | None |
| PARENTS: | Frederick and Margaret (Evans) Howell |

## GRAVESITE INFORMATION:

|  |  |
|---|---|
| LOCATION OF GRAVESITE: | Section N-C, Plot #8 |
| GRAVESTONE: | Exists |
| TYPE OF GRAVESTONE: | Marble |
| SHAPE OF GRAVESTONE: | Tablet |
| INSCRIPTION: | *Sacred to the Memory of/Children of Frederick and Margaret Howell* |
| EPITAPH: | *May their souls rest in Peace.* |
| MOTIF: | Rope with tassels |
| CARVER: | M. Heverin, 422 Jackson St., San Francisco, California |
| BASE: | Missing |
| TYPE OF BASE: |  |
| ENCLOSURE: | Exists |
| TYPE OF ENCLOSURE: | Brick; evidence of sandstone wall near brick wall |
| FENCE: |  |
| TYPE OF FENCE: |  |
| FENCE MOTIF: |  |

# HOWELL, Sarah

**ADDITIONAL PERSONAL INFORMATION:**
Sarah's date of birth was calculated by www.timeanddate.com, based on her date of death and age at death listed on her gravestone. According to information provided by a descendant regarding Sarah's parents: Margaret Evans married Frederick Howell in the United States in 1860. By 1861 they were living in Placer County, California, where Frederick worked as a miner in Michigan Bluff. They moved to Utah by 1863 and were back in California by 1866.

The *1870 Census for Township 3, Contra Costa County, California* lists Fredrick [sic] Howell, age 42, as a miner and a native of Wales. Also listed are his wife Maggie, age 28, a native of Wales and their children: Thomas, age 9, and Sarah, age 4; both natives of California; and Frederick, age 7, a native of Utah.

The *1880 Census for Forest Hill [sic], Placer County, California* lists Frederick Howell, age 51, as a miner, and his wife, Margaret, age 38; both natives of Wales. Also listed are their children: Frederick, age 17, a miner and native of Utah Territory; Jane Edith, age 4, a native of California; and Brigham Evans, age 29, a miner and native of Wales and brother-in-law to Frederick Howell.

The Howell family died during a diphtheria epidemic while living in Contra Costa County. According to cemetery year list #3, "there were graves indicating a large family" in 1936. According to a handwritten note found in cemetery reference list 2 at the California State Library in Sacramento:

> ...the bodies of Sarah and Thomas M. Howell were removed by their father and taken to Forest Hill [sic], Placer County, California. The headstone was buried in the Nortonville Cemetery but uncovered by erosion. It was eventually removed from the Howell plot to the Davis plot.

By 1880, the family was living in Foresthill, Placer County, where they eventually owned a gold mine. The *Placer Herald* (Placer County, California) newspaper states that Sarah's father, Frederick Howell, died August 10, 1900 at Centerville, aged 71 years. He was a native of Wales. According to the *Oakland Tribune* newspaper, her mother, Margaret Howell, died in Oakland, Alameda County, California on April 10, 1926. She was a native of Wales, aged 84 years. Interment was at Foresthill Cemetery, Placer County, California. Both of Sarah's parents are buried in Foresthill, Placer County, California. Sarah's brother, Thomas M. Howell and aunt, Elizabeth (Evans) Jones (wife of Evan D. Jones; Elizabeth died Sept. 17, 1881) are also buried in Rose Hill Cemetery. See John R. Evans, Thomas M. Howell, Elizabeth Jones (died 1881), and David Morgan.

**ADDITIONAL GRAVESITE INFORMATION:**
Sarah shares a gravestone with her brother, Thomas M. Howell. The stone was broken and concreted flat to the ground prior to East Bay Regional Park District acquisition. Evidence of a sandstone rock wall surrounds this gravesite.

Zelma Myrick, who recorded information in a notebook in the 1930s during a visit to Rose Hill Cemetery, reported footstones with the initials "S. H. and T. M. H." at this gravesite. She also noted "stone gone on base" perhaps meaning that only the footstones and gravestone base remained at the site. Myrick probably found the gravestone near the Thomas Jones (died Nov. 10, 1878; age 16 months) plot since she recorded information from the Howell gravestone and the Thomas gravestone on the same page in her notebook. Maybe the gravestone had been moved from its original location to an area near the Thomas Jones gravesite.

**REFERENCES:** 1, 2, 3, 6, 11 (P610.31.192, P610.168.14, and P610.285.8), 12, 14

# HOWELL,
## Thomas M.

## PERSONAL INFORMATION:

| | |
|---|---|
| SEX: | Male |
| DATE OF BIRTH: | July 21, 1860 |
| DATE OF DEATH: | September 2, 1870 |
| PLACE OF DEATH: | Nortonville, Contra Costa County, California |
| AGE AT DEATH: | 10 years, 1 month, 12 days |
| CAUSE OF DEATH: | Diphtheria |
| BIRTHPLACE: | California |
| SPOUSE: | None |
| PARENTS: | Frederick and Margaret (Evans) Howell |

## GRAVESITE INFORMATION:

| | |
|---|---|
| LOCATION OF GRAVESITE: | Section N-C, Plot #8 |
| GRAVESTONE: | Exists |
| TYPE OF GRAVESTONE: | Marble |
| SHAPE OF GRAVESTONE: | Tablet |
| INSCRIPTION: | *Sacred to the Memory of/Children of Frederick and Margaret Howell* |
| EPITAPH: | *May their souls rest in Peace.* |
| MOTIF: | Rope with tassels |
| CARVER: | M. Heverin, 422 Jackson St., San Francisco, California |
| BASE: | Missing |
| TYPE OF BASE: | |
| ENCLOSURE: | Exists |
| TYPE OF ENCLOSURE: | Brick; evidence of sandstone wall near brick wall |
| FENCE: | |
| TYPE OF FENCE: | |
| FENCE MOTIF: | |

# HOWELL, Thomas M.

**ADDITIONAL PERSONAL INFORMATION:**
Thomas' date of birth was calculated by www.timeanddate.com, based on the date of death and age of death listed on the gravestone.

The children of Frederick and Margaret (Evans) Howell were:

- Thomas M., born July 21, 1860, Nortonville, Contra Costa County, California
- Frederick Jr., born 1862, Utah
- Sarah, born Jan. 9, 1866, Nortonville, Contra Costa County, California
- Jane Edith, born *circa* 1876, California
- Walter N., born 1886, California

Thomas' father, Frederick, was the uncle of Mary Morgan. Mary Morgan was married to John R. Evans, who is also buried in Rose Hill Cemetery (Section S-E, plot 115), along with their children. Buried near the John R. Evans gravesite is David Morgan, brother to Mary Morgan. Thomas' mother, Margaret, was the sister of John R. Evans.

Thomas' sister, Sarah Howell and aunt, Elizabeth (Evans) Jones (wife of Evan D. Jones; Elizabeth died Sept. 17, 1881), are also buried in Rose Hill Cemetery. See John R. Evans, Sarah Howell, Elizabeth Jones (died 1881), and David Morgan.

**ADDITIONAL GRAVESITE INFORMATION:**
Thomas shares a gravestone with his sister, Sarah Howell. The gravestone was broken into two pieces and concreted flat to ground prior to Park District acquisition.

Zelma Myrick, who recorded information in a notebook in the 1930s during a visit to Rose Hill Cemetery, reported a footstone with the initials "T. M. H."

**REFERENCES:** 1, 2, 3, 6, 11 (P610.31.192, P610.168.14, and P610.285.8), 12, 14

Reference 379.13

The Howell family gravesite, Foresthill Protestant Cemetery, Foresthill, Placer County, California, May 2010. Buried at this site and listed on the obelisk gravestone are Thomas' parents: Margaret Howell, born 1842 in Wales and died 1926; and Frederick Howell, born March 13, 1829 in Merthyr Tydfil, Wales and died at Centerville, California on August 10, 1900, age 71 years, 4 months and 8 days. Also listed is Jane R. Evans (most likely Margaret's mother), born October 30, 1806 in Llanharan, Glamorganshire, Wales and died January 9, 1887 at Foresthill, California. Located to the left of the obelisk is a grave marker for their son, Walter N., born 1886 and died 1941. Located to the right of the obelisk is a marker for their other son, Fred Jr., born 1862, died 1931. Photograph by Traci (Gibbons) Parent.

## PERSONAL INFORMATION:

| | |
|---|---|
| SEX: | Male |
| DATE OF BIRTH: | |
| DATE OF DEATH: | 187? |
| PLACE OF DEATH: | |
| AGE AT DEATH: | 53 years |
| CAUSE OF DEATH: | |
| BIRTHPLACE: | |
| SPOUSE: | |
| PARENTS: | |

## GRAVESITE INFORMATION:

| | |
|---|---|
| LOCATION OF GRAVESITE: | Section N-F, Plot #73 |
| GRAVESTONE: | Exists |
| TYPE OF GRAVESTONE: | Marble |
| SHAPE OF GRAVESTONE: | Tablet (partial) |
| INSCRIPTION: | *In Memory of* |
| EPITAPH: | |
| MOTIF: | |
| CARVER: | |
| BASE: | Exists |
| TYPE OF BASE: | Granite |
| ENCLOSURE: | |
| TYPE OF ENCLOSURE: | |
| FENCE: | |
| TYPE OF FENCE: | |
| FENCE MOTIF: | |

# HOWELLS, Isaac

**ADDITIONAL PERSONAL INFORMATION:**
According to the *Oakland Tribune* newspaper, October 29, 1933, Mrs. Isaac Howell [sic] was a washerwoman and probably the outstanding singer of the Nortonville chorus (most likely the Welsh choir). In her youth, she had been decorated by Queen Victoria, who presented her with a silver replica of the Welsh National Flower. Concerts in San Francisco won her wide acclaim. This is most likely the wife of Isaac Howells who is interred in Rose Hill Cemetery.

**ADDITIONAL GRAVESITE INFORMATION:**
Isaac's stone was broken according to Zelma Myrick, who recorded information in a notebook in the 1930s during a visit to Rose Hill Cemetery.

The inscription *In Memory of* also comes from Myrick's notebook.

Only a small top portion of the gravestone remains in the cemetery today. The stone is badly weathered and the name barely readable. The lower portion of the gravestone is in storage. A granite base, which sits nearby, may or may not be the base for this gravestone.

**REFERENCES:** 1, 3, 5, 8 (March 6, 1875), 11 (P610.31.149), 12, 14, *Oakland Tribune* newspaper (Oct. 29, 1933), *Pittsburg Post Dispatch* newspaper (Wed., June 15, 1955, pages 9 and 12), see newspaper appendix pages 714-716

Reference 31.149

All that remains of Isaac Howells' gravestone in Rose Hill Cemetery, July 1977.
Photograph by Traci (Gibbons) Parent.

## PERSONAL INFORMATION:

| | |
|---|---|
| SEX: | Male |
| DATE OF BIRTH: | 1851 |
| DATE OF DEATH: | March 12, 1888 |
| PLACE OF DEATH: | Concord, Contra Costa County, California |
| AGE AT DEATH: | 37 years |
| CAUSE OF DEATH: | |
| BIRTHPLACE: | Wales |
| SPOUSE: | Maggie (Hughes) Hughes |
| PARENTS: | Mr. and Mrs. Hughes |

## GRAVESITE INFORMATION:

| | |
|---|---|
| LOCATION OF GRAVESITE: | Section S-B, Plot #12 |
| GRAVESTONE: | Exists |
| TYPE OF GRAVESTONE: | Marble |
| SHAPE OF GRAVESTONE: | Obelisk |
| INSCRIPTION: | |
| EPITAPH: | *Absent, But Not Forgotten* |
| MOTIF: | Shells and ivy |
| CARVER: | |
| BASE: | Exists |
| TYPE OF BASE: | Granite with middle marble base |
| ENCLOSURE: | Exists |
| TYPE OF ENCLOSURE: | Brick |
| FENCE: | |
| TYPE OF FENCE: | |
| FENCE MOTIF: | |

# HUGHES, David M.

**ADDITIONAL PERSONAL INFORMATION:**
David M. Hughes, age 26, of Nortonville, Contra Costa County, California, and Maggie Hughes, age 20, also of Nortonville, were issued a marriage license on October 21, 1878. The information was recorded in the *Applications for Marriage Licenses, Contra Costa County, 1873-1887*, page 151, located at the Contra Costa County Historical Society History Center in Martinez, California. David M. Hughes married Maggie Hughes on October 31, 1878. They were married by minister John J. Powell at the Nortonville Congregational Church. Witnesses were William W. Davis of Nortonville and Thomas Davis of Nortonville.

According to the *Index to Marriage Certificates*, located at the Contra Costa County Hall of Records in Martinez, California, David M. Hughes married Maggie Hughes on November 5, 1878. The information is recorded in Volume 2, page 249.

The *1880 Census for Nortonville Precinct, Contra Costa County, California* lists David Hughes, age 28, as a miner and native of Wales. Also listed are his wife, Maggie, age 21, a native of Ohio and their son, George, age 3 months, a native of California.

The *Contra Costa Gazette* newspaper, March 14, 1888, states that David was about 40 years old at the time of his death.

After David's death, Margaret (Maggie) Hughes married Mr. Lambert. In 1891, Maggie (Hughes) Lambert petitioned The Superior Court, Contra Costa County, State of California regarding the estate and guardianship of her children: George W. Hughes, David Hughes, Rosanna Hughes, and Camilla Hughes.

**ADDITIONAL GRAVESITE INFORMATION:**
Zelma Myrick, who recorded information in a notebook in the 1930s during a visit to Rose Hill Cemetery, reported the "Top broken off of stone."

A marble obelisk stone sits on a middle marble base that contains the epitaph. The middle base sits on a much larger granite base. A brick enclosure was built before East Bay Regional Park District acquisition and after the coal mining days. A marble footstone with the initials "D. H." exists and may be the footstone for David Hughes. The footstone has been placed in storage for safekeeping. The shell and ivy motif exists on all sides of the gravestone. This motif is similar to the one found on the Rebecca Evans (Section S-B, Plot #27) gravestone.

**REFERENCES:** 1, 2, 3, 4, 5, 8 (March 14, 1888 and Nov. 16, 1878), 11 (P610.31.191 and P610.145.1), 12, 13, 14, see newspaper appendix page 717

## Died.

HUGHES—In Concord, March 12th, 1888, David Hughes, a native of Wales, aged about 40 years.

From the *Contra Costa Gazette* newspaper, March 14, 1888.

## PERSONAL INFORMATION:

|  |  |
|---|---|
| SEX: | Female |
| DATE OF BIRTH: | June 6, 1838 |
| DATE OF DEATH: | May 11, 1876 |
| PLACE OF DEATH: | |
| AGE AT DEATH: | 37 years, 11 months, 5 days |
| CAUSE OF DEATH: | Dropsy |
| BIRTHPLACE: | Wales |
| SPOUSE: | W. J. Hughes |
| PARENTS: | |

## GRAVESITE INFORMATION:

|  |  |
|---|---|
| LOCATION OF GRAVESITE: | Section S-D, Plot #54 |
| GRAVESTONE: | Exists |
| TYPE OF GRAVESTONE: | Marble |
| SHAPE OF GRAVESTONE: | Tablet |
| INSCRIPTION: | *Wife of* |
| EPITAPH: | *For me to live is Christ and to die is gain.* |
| MOTIF: | Open *Bible*/hand with finger pointing to Heaven/ acorns/rosette |
| CARVER: | Excelsior Marble Works, San Jose, California |
| BASE: | Exists |
| TYPE OF BASE: | Sandstone (broken) |
| ENCLOSURE: | Exists |
| TYPE OF ENCLOSURE: | Brick |
| FENCE: | Missing |
| TYPE OF FENCE: | Iron |
| FENCE MOTIF: | |

# HUGHES, Margaret

**ADDITIONAL PERSONAL INFORMATION:**
Margaret's date of birth was calculated by www.timeanddate.com, based on the date of death and age at death listed on her gravestone.

The County Hall of Records in Martinez, Contra Costa County, California, lists her date of death as May 13, 1876 and not May 11 as stated on her stone and indicates she is a native of "Wales-England." The Hall of Records also lists her age as 37 years, 11 months, and 7 days, and not 37 years, 11 months, and 5 days as stated on her gravestone. She was a resident of Contra Costa County for nearly four years.

The *Assessment List, Contra Costa County, for 1872-73*, lists Margaret's husband, William Hughes, as being assessed for property and improvements valued at $545.

The *Business Directory of San Francisco and Principal Towns of California and Nevada 1877*, page 104, lists Margaret's husband, W. J. Hughes, as operating a general merchandise store in Somersville.

According to *Applications for Marriage Licenses, Contra Costa County, 1873-1887*, page 194, Somersville residents, W. J. Hughes, age 45, and Mrs. Mary Watkins, age 42, applied for a marriage license on December 24, 1879. This indicates (if it is the same W. J. Hughes) that Margaret's husband remarried after her death.

**ADDITIONAL GRAVESITE INFORMATION:**
The gravestone was concreted flat to the ground prior to East Bay Regional Park District acquisition. The epitaph is inscribed on the open *Bible*. The epitaph comes from the King James Version; Philippians 1:21. The *Bible* verse reads: "For to me to live is Christ, and to die is gain."

Margaret Hughes' gravestone appears in a Sunset book titled *Beautiful California*, Lane Book Company, Menlo Park, California, 1963, page 83.

The brick wall enclosure was rebuilt by an East Bay Regional Park District contractor in March 1988.

**REFERENCES:** 1, 2, 3, 4, 5, 6, 7, 8 (Nov. 16, 1878), 11 (P610.31.136, P610.31.203, P610.98.19, P610.117.8, P610.139.1, P610.139.3, P610.168.23, P610.207.1, P610.294.6, P610.312.4, P610.362.3, and P610.362.5), 12, 14, *Alameda Times-Star* newspaper (May 18, 1974, page 10)

This advertisement for the J. W. Hughes general merchandise store in Somersville appeared in the *Antioch Ledger* newspaper on July 15, 1876. Margaret's husband was W. J. Hughes and not J. W. Hughes as printed in this advertisement. It is presumed that the initials were reversed and incorrectly printed in the newspaper.

Reference 349.5

Reference 139.1

The top photograph, date unknown, shows the backside of the Margaret Hughes gravesite with iron fence. The photograph was taken looking east toward Somersville town site. The bottom photograph shows the Margaret Hughes gravestone in 1953.

Reference 207.1

Reference 362.3

The top photograph shows the Margaret Hughes gravesite (foreground) with remains of the iron fence in 1964. The bottom photograph shows the broken Margaret Hughes gravestone *circa* 1967.

## PERSONAL INFORMATION:

| | |
|---|---|
| SEX: | Male |
| DATE OF BIRTH: | 1871 |
| DATE OF DEATH: | 1877 |
| PLACE OF DEATH: | |
| AGE AT DEATH: | 6 years |
| CAUSE OF DEATH: | |
| BIRTHPLACE: | |
| SPOUSE: | None |
| PARENTS: | David and Mary Humphreys |

## GRAVESITE INFORMATION:

| | |
|---|---|
| LOCATION OF GRAVESITE: | Section S-C, Plot #43 |
| GRAVESTONE: | Exists |
| TYPE OF GRAVESTONE: | Brick with mortar covering |
| SHAPE OF GRAVESTONE: | |
| INSCRIPTION: | |
| EPITAPH: | |
| MOTIF: | |
| CARVER: | |
| BASE: | |
| TYPE OF BASE: | |
| ENCLOSURE: | Exists |
| TYPE OF ENCLOSURE: | Brick with mortar covering |
| FENCE: | |
| TYPE OF FENCE: | |
| FENCE MOTIF: | |

# HUMPHREYS, Gwelym (Gwylym)

**ADDITIONAL PERSONAL INFORMATION:**
Gwelym (Gwylym) is the Welsh spelling for William. According to court documents found at the Contra Costa County Historical Society History Center, Martinez, California, *Mary Humphreys vs. David Humphreys*, the Humphreys family resided in Somersville, Contra Costa County, California and operated a saloon there. Mary and David Humphreys were married on February 25, 1854 in Glamorganshire, Wales. David and Mary divorced in January 1894. They are believed to be the parents of Gwelym. Mary Humphreys died February 2, 1917 and was interred at the Oak View Memorial Park Cemetery in Antioch, Contra Costa County, California.

The *1880 Census for Somersville Precinct, Contra Costa County, California* lists David Humphreys, age 49, as a miner and native of Wales. Also listed are his wife, Mary, age 48, a native of Wales and their daughters: Lavinia, age 17, a native of Wales; Amelia, age 13, a native of Pennsylvania; Sarah, age 11; and Mary, age 3; both natives of California.

The *1890 Great Register of Voters in Contra Costa County, California* records David Humphreys, age 53, as a native of Wales and a resident of Somersville. His occupation is listed as miner and his registration date August 24, 1884. It also states that he naturalized on September 18, 1881 in Siskiyou County, California.

The *1900 Census for Somersville, Contra Costa County, California* lists Mary Humphreys, age 68, as the head of the household and a native of Wales. Also listed are her daughter, Emma Harris, a native of California, age 20, and Harry Ober, a boarder and native of Germany, age 38. The census also indicates Mary is a widow with a total of 11 children, 4 living. Year of immigration was listed as 1863.

Humphreys' Saloon is listed on the memory map of Somersville, California compiled *circa* 1950s by former coal field resident Austin Mortimore.

**ADDITIONAL GRAVESITE INFORMATION:**
Gwelym's name, birth date, and death date are etched in the mortar marker.

**REFERENCES:** 1, 6, 9 (Feb. 3, 1917 and Feb. 10, 1917), 11 (P610.31.186 and P610.363.2), 12, 13, 14, *Pittsburg Pride* newspaper (Feb. 9, 1917)

## MRS. HUMPHREYS DEAD

### Mother of Mrs. Ben Scott Had Also Resided in Pittsburg.

Old age and a general breakdown in health, resulted in the death of Mrs. Mary Humphreys of this place at the Commercial Hotel yesterday morning. She had been ailing about three years, but a change for the worse came several days ago.

Funeral services will be conducted at the hotel tomorrow, Sunday afternoon, at 2:00 o'clock, by Rev. C. C. Champlin of the Congregational Church of Pittsburg, of which the deceased had long been a faithful and devout member. The interment will be in the Mason's and Odd Fellows' Cemetery.

Mrs. Humphreys was born in Glenmorganshire, Wales, in 1831, and came to California by way of the Isthmus of Panama, in the early sixties, enduring many of the hardships experienced by all pioneers, and had resided in this state since that time. She was a good, Christian woman and loved by all with whom she came in contact on account of her kindly ways. Previous to coming to Antioch, she had resided with her daughter, Mrs. Ben Scott, at Pittsburg, and had also made her home with Mr. and Mrs. Scott at the hotel.

There survive three daughters, Mrs. John Nicholas of San Francisco, Mrs. Ben Scott of this place, and Mrs. Hannah Clement of Pittsburg, and also nine grandchildren and three great grandchildren, who have the sympathy of many in their sorrow.

## ASHES THE CAUSE.

Somersville was visited by fire this week. It was a serious one and did much damage. Mrs. Humphreys' two story dwelling and contents were destroyed by fire at 2 o'clock Thursday morning. But few personal effects were saved. The fire was caused by ashes. The ashes were taken up and placed in a wooden box the evening before. The box was then placed outside near the building, and it is supposed the wind fanned the "dead coals," which set the box on fire and then ignited the building. The loss is estimated at between $1500 and $2000; no insurance.

This obituary (left) for Mary Humphreys, Gwelym (Gwylym) Humphreys' mother, appeared in the *Antioch Ledger* newspaper on Saturday, February 2, 1917. The article states she was born in Glenmorganshire [sic], Wales. The correct spelling is Glamorganshire. The two story dwelling that is described in this article (right) from the April 6, 1901, *Antioch Ledger* newspaper, can be seen in the photograph on the following page.

Reference 41.13

The west side of Somersville, Contra Costa County, California, *circa* 1900. This area of Somersville was also called the Union side because the Union Mine was located near the number 5 shown in the upper portion of this photograph. The Humphreys family saloon is pictured in the lower left corner of the photograph (number 11). The other features shown include: (2) Jack Latimore Saloon; (3) unknown; (4) the Joe Buffo family home; (5) the waste rock from the Union Mine; (6) the Daley family home; (7) Hunter family home; (8) the Evans family home; (9) Somersville School; and (10) Rose Hill Cemetery.

## CARD OF THANKS

We feel the deepest gratitude and our sincere thanks are extended all the dear friends who assisted during our recent sad bereavement, caused by the sickness and death of our beloved mother. The tender sympathy expressed, and the love and esteem shown by the many friends, have brought more comfort than words can express, but we assure all their thoughtfulness will ever be gratefully remembered.

Ben Scott and Wife,
Mrs. Levina Nicholls,
Mrs. Hannah Clement,
Mrs. Amy McAvoy.

Reference 379.14

The article above from the *Antioch Ledger* newspaper, April 10, 1917, regards Gwelym's mother, Mary Humphreys. According to the *Antioch Ledger*, February 2, 1917, Mrs. Humphreys died on February 1, 1917. The individuals listed in the above "Card of Thanks" are her children. Pictured above is the gravestone for Mary Humphreys. She is buried at Oak View Memorial Park Cemetery, Antioch, California. Photograph taken May 2010 by Traci (Gibbons) Parent.

## PERSONAL INFORMATION:

| | |
|---|---|
| SEX: | Female |
| DATE OF BIRTH: | April 1, 1857 |
| DATE OF DEATH: | October 1, 1877 |
| PLACE OF DEATH: | Nortonville, Contra Costa County, California |
| AGE AT DEATH: | 20 years, 6 months |
| CAUSE OF DEATH: | Childbirth (?) |
| BIRTHPLACE: | Pennsylvania |
| SPOUSE: | Morgan E. James |
| PARENTS: | William and Mary (Reese) Cook |

## GRAVESITE INFORMATION:

| | |
|---|---|
| LOCATION OF GRAVESITE: | Section N-C, Plot #28 |
| GRAVESTONE: | Missing |
| TYPE OF GRAVESTONE: | Marble |
| SHAPE OF GRAVESTONE: | |
| INSCRIPTION: | *Wife of* |
| EPITAPH: | *We miss thee at home.* |
| MOTIF: | Rosette |
| CARVER: | Excelsior Marble Works, San Jose, California |
| BASE: | Exists |
| TYPE OF BASE: | Granite |
| ENCLOSURE: | |
| TYPE OF ENCLOSURE: | |
| FENCE: | |
| TYPE OF FENCE: | |
| FENCE MOTIF: | |

# JAMES, Mary Ann

**ADDITIONAL PERSONAL INFORMATION:**
Mary Ann's birth date was calculated by www.timeanddate.com, based on her date of death and age at death listed on her gravestone. The *Antioch Ledger* newspaper states that Mrs. Morgan James died October 2, 1877 and not October 1, 1877 as indicated on her gravestone. According to descendants, Mary Ann's father was William Cook of London, England. Mary Ann's parents, William and Mary (Reese) Cook, came to the United States traveling around Cape Horn from London in a sailing ship. They settled in Nortonville, Contra Costa County, California and various sources including the *Assessment List, Contra Costa County, for 1872-'73* and the *1876 Contra Costa County Voting Register*, document William's existence there.

The *1870 Census for Township Three, Contra Costa County, California* lists Mary Ann's parents and siblings: William Cook, age 45, a native of Wales; Mary, age 35, a native of Wales; Mary, age 13; David, age 11; Ellen, age 9; and Maggie, age 2. All are natives of California. The *1870 Census for Township Three, Contra Costa County, California* also lists Morgan James (future husband of Mary Ann James), age 20, as a miner and a native of Wales.

Mary Ann Cook, age 17, a resident of Nortonville, and Morgan E. James, age 27, also a resident of Nortonville, applied for a marriage license on June 27, 1874. The information was recorded in the *Applications for Marriage Licenses, Contra Costa County, 1873-1887*, page 22, located at the Contra Costa County Historical Society History Center in Martinez, California. According to the *Index to Marriage Certificates*, located at the Contra Costa County Hall of Records, Martinez, California, Mary Ann Cook married Morgan E. James on July 23, 1874. They were married by Rev. William Parry and the information is recorded in Volume 2, page 49.

Information obtained by a descendant state that:

> Mary Ann married a man named Morgan James and they had two daughters. Mary Ann died in 1877 when her youngest daughter was born. Morgan James [her husband] took the girls to Oregon as the William Cook family [Mary Ann's father] was moving there. William Cook died in Oregon in 1882 or 1883 and his widow Mary Rees Cook, took her youngest daughter Verina and her youngest granddaughter Lavinia James (Mary Ann's and Morgan's youngest daughter) to Australia to live as she (Mary Rees Cook) had two brothers living there.

Morgan James died in Clayton, Contra Costa County, California on September 3, 1890 and is also buried in Rose Hill Cemetery. According to family records, Mary Ann James shares a gravesite with Thomas R. James who died July 24, 1876. Thomas was probably the brother of Mary Ann's husband. Thomas <u>D.</u> not Thomas <u>R.</u> James is buried in Rose Hill Cemetery. Thomas D. James was one of the miners killed in the July 24, 1876 mine explosion in Nortonville. See Morgan E. James and Thomas D. James.

**ADDITIONAL GRAVESITE INFORMATION:**
The epitaph comes from Zelma Myrick, who recorded information in a notebook in the 1930s during a visit to Rose Hill Cemetery. Also according to Myrick, this is an Odd Fellows plot. Myrick reported the stone in "Good condition." Mary Ann's stone was present in 1963 because it is listed on a term report compiled by Jim Rotelli for a California History class. Additionally it was photographed in the cemetery in 1969.

**REFERENCES:** 1, 2, 3, 6, 8 (July 4, 1874, Oct. 20, 1877, and Oct. 11, 1879), 9 (Oct. 13, 1877), 11 (P610.263.15 to P610.263.24, and P610.285.1), 12, see newspaper appendix page 718

Pictured is the granite base and broken marble gravestone for Mary Ann James in March 1969. A descendant remembered that the gravesite was located in the shade of the Italian Cypress tree. This photograph showing the base and partial gravestone also confirms her burial site. Today, a small piece of the gravestone, with a barely visible portion of the carver's name, sits in the base. A bronze plaque listing Mary Ann's name, date of birth, and date of death was placed in the cemetery in 2002 by her descendants to mark the grave location. Photograph by David Stogner. The plaque says:

*MARY ANN JAMES*
*1857 – 1877*
PLAQUE PLACED IN 2002

Nortonville looking south, *circa* 1880. Seven unidentified children pose in front of the fence that surrounds the Black Diamond Coal Company stables. The brick stack and coal bunker for the Mount Hope slope can be seen in the center back. A waste rock pile stands beside the three-story Black Diamond Exchange Hotel on the left. Mary Ann Cook who married Morgan E. James were residents of this community in the 1870s.

# JAMES,
## Morgan E.

## PERSONAL INFORMATION:

| | |
|---|---|
| SEX: | Male |
| DATE OF BIRTH: | *Circa* 1847 |
| DATE OF DEATH: | September 3, 1890 |
| PLACE OF DEATH: | Clayton, Contra Costa County, California |
| AGE AT DEATH: | Approximately 43 years |
| CAUSE OF DEATH: | Pulmonary congestion |
| BIRTHPLACE: | Wales |
| SPOUSE: | Mary Ann (Cook) James |
| PARENTS: | |

## GRAVESITE INFORMATION:

| | |
|---|---|
| LOCATION OF GRAVESITE: | Unknown |
| GRAVESTONE: | Missing or never placed |
| TYPE OF GRAVESTONE: | |
| SHAPE OF GRAVESTONE: | |
| INSCRIPTION: | |
| EPITAPH: | |
| MOTIF: | |
| CARVER: | |
| BASE: | |
| TYPE OF BASE: | |
| ENCLOSURE: | |
| TYPE OF ENCLOSURE: | |
| FENCE: | |
| TYPE OF FENCE: | |
| FENCE MOTIF: | |

# JAMES, Morgan E.

**ADDITIONAL PERSONAL INFORMATION:**
According to the *Contra Costa Gazette* newspaper, July 4, 1874, Nortonville residents, Morgan James and Mary Ann Cook were married by Rev. W. Parry on June 30, 1874.

The *1870 Census for Township Three, Contra Costa County, California* lists Morgan James, age 20, as a miner and a native of Wales. According to descendants, after the death of his wife, Morgan went north to work in the Oregon coal mines. Descendants also state that Mary Ann and Morgan had two daughters. Mary Ann died in 1877, when her youngest daughter was born. Morgan James took the girls to Oregon as the William Cook family (Mary Ann's family) was moving there. He must have stayed in Oregon for a short time since he was back in California by 1879.

According to the *Contra Costa Gazette* newspaper, October 11, 1879, Morgan E. James was sent as the messenger from Clayton (located just southeast of Nortonville) to obtain Sarah Norton from Nortonville on October 5, 1879. Mrs. Norton was a midwife and her services were needed in Clayton. The return trip that Morgan James made to Clayton with Sarah Norton resulted in the death of Mrs. Norton. The *Antioch Ledger* newspaper, October 11, 1879 stated that:

> Morgan James of Clayton, rode a saddle horse to Nortonville to procure the services of Mrs. Norton as midwife. The saddle horse was hitched to a buggy and the old lady reluctantly consented to accompany Mr. James ... When descending the steep hill going toward Clayton the horse became unmanageable and ran down a steep embankment throwing both occupants to the ground. Mr. James was somewhat bruised. Mrs. Norton had both arms, both legs, and her neck broken dying instantly.

According to *Contra Costa County Register of Deaths*, Morgan James of Clayton was married at the time of his death and was 42 years old when he died. (Note: Morgan remarried after the death of his first wife, Mary Ann James, in 1877.)

Morgan James, age 34, of Clayton, Contra Costa County, California, and Margaret Atkins, age 34, also of Clayton, applied for a marriage license on April 5, 1880. The information was recorded in the *Applications for Marriage Licenses, Contra Costa County, 1873-1887*, page 199, located at the Contra Costa County Historical Society History Center in Martinez, California.

Morgan's obituary in the *Contra Costa Gazette* newspaper, September 10, 1890, states he was 43 years old when he died.

See Mary Ann James, Thomas D. James, and Sarah Norton.

**ADDITIONAL GRAVESITE INFORMATION:**
According to the *Contra Costa Gazette*, September 6, 1890, Morgan's "remains were taken to Somersville for interment." This is the only source to indicate his burial there.

**REFERENCES:** 7, 8 (July 4, 1874, Oct. 11, 1879, Sept. 6, 1890, and Oct. 10, 1890), 9 (Oct. 11, 1879), 12, see newspaper appendix page 719, and (Sarah Norton) pages 741 and 742

# JAMES,
## Thomas D.

## PERSONAL INFORMATION:

| | |
|---|---|
| SEX: | Male |
| DATE OF BIRTH: | *Circa 1847 - 1849* |
| DATE OF DEATH: | July 24, 1876 |
| PLACE OF DEATH: | Nortonville, Contra Costa County, California |
| AGE AT DEATH: | 27 or 29 years |
| CAUSE OF DEATH: | Scorched by fire in mine explosion |
| BIRTHPLACE: | Carmarthenshire, South Wales |
| SPOUSE: | |
| PARENTS: | |

## GRAVESITE INFORMATION:

| | |
|---|---|
| LOCATION OF GRAVESITE: | Section S-D, Plot #50 |
| GRAVESTONE: | Missing |
| TYPE OF GRAVESTONE: | White bronze (zinc) with moveable tablets |
| SHAPE OF GRAVESTONE: | Obelisk |
| INSCRIPTION: | *In Memory of/Native of/Erected by the Citizens of Nortonville* |
| EPITAPH: | |
| MOTIF: | Clasped hands/leaves |
| CARVER: | |
| BASE: | Exists |
| TYPE OF BASE: | Concrete |
| ENCLOSURE: | Exists |
| TYPE OF ENCLOSURE: | Brick |
| FENCE: | Exists |
| TYPE OF FENCE: | Iron (replica) |
| FENCE MOTIF: | Urns and vases (missing) |

# JAMES, Thomas D.

**ADDITIONAL PERSONAL INFORMATION:**

*Nortonville Memories* written by Ellis Griffiths (no date) states:

> The three best singers of the village were two brothers, David Watts, Theophilus Watts, and their companion, Thomas James. These boys lead all the entertainments and also the choir of the church.

Thomas D. James served as a witness to the marriage of Charles Baker, age 30, a native of England and resident of Somersville; and Elizabeth Miller, age 25, a widow and native of Pennsylvania and resident of Nortonville. The couple were married August 9, 1874. Another witness was Morgan Morgan.

According to the *History of Contra Costa County*, by Slocum and Company, 1882, page 474, T. James was burned following an explosion that occurred in the Nortonville mines on July 24, 1876. This source lists him as a survivor of the accident.

Three early cemetery lists (sources 2, 3, and 6; see page 1004) state he died July 24, 1876. According to the article titled "The New Monument" in the *Contra Costa Gazette* newspaper, November 23, 1878, Thomas D. James is recorded as Thomas D. Jones. Two years after the death of these miners, the people of Nortonville raised nearly $300 to erect a "white bronze monument" to the memory of the three men. The monument was 60" high with four moveable tablets - one for each of the men and one that said "Erected by the citizens of Nortonville."

A cemetery list (source 2) compiled in 1936 lists the name as Thomas D. Jones and not James. Cemetery reference list 3 records his age at death as 27 years. Cemetery reference lists 2 and 6 and Zelma Myrick record his age at death as 29 years.

**ADDITIONAL GRAVESITE INFORMATION:**

Zelma Myrick, who recorded information in a notebook in the 1930s during a visit to Rose Hill Cemetery, reported "Iron Stone, Brick and iron fence poor condition." A concrete base which once held the monument, pieces of the monument, and one section of iron fence are all that remain. Vandals destroyed the remains of the white bronze monument in 1994.

On April 5, 1980, the Joaquin Murrieta Chapter 13 of E Clampus Vitus placed a plaque at this site to commemorate the men buried here. The plaque was removed in 2003 when the brick wall was rebuilt. The original section of iron fence that once stood at the site has been placed in storage and a replicated fence (based on the original piece) was manufactured and placed at the site by Black Diamond Rangers in September 2007. Through additional research it was determined that Thomas D. James is buried at the site and not Thomas D. Jones.

A volunteer Italian Cypress tree grew at this site but it died and was removed in July 2009. The fence that once existed at this site appears in a photograph in a book by Sunset titled *Beautiful California*, Lane Book Company, Menlo Park, California, 1963, page 83. See Theophile Dumas, William Gething, David W. Griffiths, Mary Ann James, Morgan James, Meredith Lewis, George M. Reynolds, Evan Smith, David Watts, Theophilus Watts, and William L. Williams.

**REFERENCES:** 2, 3, 6, 8 (Nov. 23, 1878), 9 (July 29, 1876), 10 (page 474), 11 (P610.5.2, P610.31.128, P610.31.204, P610.43.4, P610.84.2, P610.139.2, P610.207.1, P610.247.1, P610.248.1, P610.294.6, P610.312.3, P610.312.4, P610.317.3, P610.317.7, P610.363.1, and P610.363.2), 12, *Pittsburg Daily Independent* newspaper (April 30, 1941), *Nortonville Memories* by Ellis Griffiths (no date), see newspaper appendix page 720 and (William Gething) pages 706 and 707

Reference 317.7

White bronze miners' monument erected in 1878 by the citizens of Nortonville in memory of Thomas D. James, David Watts, and Theophilus Watts. Note the bullet marks in the upper portion of the obelisk. Photograph taken *circa* 1939 by Zelma Myrick. See additional photographs of the monument on pages 138 and 631.

Black Diamond Mine, Nortonville, California, *circa* 1880. The Black Diamond was the largest mine in the Mount Diablo Coal Field. The home for mine superintendent, Morgan Morgans, can be seen in the upper left corner.

## GREENHOOD, NEWBAUER & KLEIN,
### DEALERS IN
# ALL KINDS OF COAL,
### AND OFFICE OF THE
# MOUNT DIABLO COAL MINES,
## 207 & 209 SANSOM STREET,
BETWEEN CALIFORNIA AND PINE,                     SAN FRANCISCO.

General Depot—on Market Street, opposite the Old Railroad Depot.

From the *San Francisco Directory, 1866*, page 662.

# JENKINS,
## (infant)

## PERSONAL INFORMATION:

| | |
|---|---|
| SEX: | Female |
| DATE OF BIRTH: | April 14, 1880 |
| DATE OF DEATH: | April 15, 1880 |
| PLACE OF DEATH: | |
| AGE AT DEATH: | 1 day |
| CAUSE OF DEATH: | |
| BIRTHPLACE: | |
| SPOUSE: | None |
| PARENTS: | Thomas H. and Elizabeth Jenkins |

## GRAVESITE INFORMATION:

| | |
|---|---|
| LOCATION OF GRAVESITE: | Section N-B, Plot #9 |
| GRAVESTONE: | Exists (only a small piece) |
| TYPE OF GRAVESTONE: | Marble |
| SHAPE OF GRAVESTONE: | Tablet |
| INSCRIPTION: | *Born in Wales/Infant daughter of* |
| EPITAPH: | *Gone but not forgotten.* |
| MOTIF: | Clasped hands |
| CARVER: | |
| BASE: | Exists |
| TYPE OF BASE: | Sandstone |
| ENCLOSURE: | Exists (partial) |
| TYPE OF ENCLOSURE: | Brick |
| FENCE: | |
| TYPE OF FENCE: | |
| FENCE MOTIF: | |

East Bay Regional Park District

# JENKINS, (infant)

**ADDITIONAL PERSONAL INFORMATION:**
Although the first name of the Jenkins infant is not known, the gravestone indicates it was an infant daughter.

The family of this infant is listed in the 1880 census. The *1880 Census for Nortonville Precinct, Contra Costa County, California* lists Thomas Jenkins, age 49, as a miner and native of Wales. Also recorded are his wife, Elizabeth, age 44, a native of Pennsylvania and his stepson, Charles, age 15, a native of Pennsylvania.

See Thomas H. Jenkins

**ADDITIONAL GRAVESITE INFORMATION:**
The gravestone inscription "Born in Wales," refers to her father, Thomas H. Jenkins.

Zelma Myrick, who recorded information in a notebook in the 1930s during a visit to Rose Hill Cemetery, reported "Stone in good condition."

A gravestone rubbing exists. The infant shares a gravestone with her father, Thomas H. Jenkins (died March 24, 1882). The gravestone was still present in 1963 because it is listed on a student term paper by Jim Rotelli. Additionally the vandalized gravestone was photographed in 1971. See pages 299 and 300.

A brass plaque was placed at the site in 2004 to mark the burial site. The location of the gravesite is documented in numerous photographs. The plaque says:

> *THOMAS H. JENKINS*
> *1830 – 1882*
> *AND*
> *INFANT DAUGHTER*
> *APRIL 14 – APRIL 15, 1880*
> *PLAQUE PLACED IN 2004*

**REFERENCES:** 1, 2, 3, 6, 11 (P610.8.1, P610.98.17, and P610.312.8), 12, *Pittsburg Post Dispatch* newspaper (Wed., June 15, 1955, pages 9 and 12)

# JENKINS,
## Ebenezer Harris

**PERSONAL INFORMATION:**

| | |
|---|---|
| SEX: | Male |
| DATE OF BIRTH: | December 4, 1866 |
| DATE OF DEATH: | June 23, 1874 |
| PLACE OF DEATH: | Nortonville, Contra Costa County, California |
| AGE AT DEATH: | 7 years, 6 months, 19 days |
| CAUSE OF DEATH: | |
| BIRTHPLACE: | |
| SPOUSE: | None |
| PARENTS: | Thomas W. and Mary Jenkins |

**GRAVESITE INFORMATION:**

| | |
|---|---|
| LOCATION OF GRAVESITE: | Section S-D, Plot #88 |
| GRAVESTONE: | Exists (two markers exist at this site) |
| TYPE OF GRAVESTONE: | Marble (original stone)/Marble encased in concrete granite aggregate (newer marker) |
| SHAPE OF GRAVESTONE: | Obelisk (original stone)/concrete tile aggregate covering (newer marker) |
| INSCRIPTION: | *Children of* (on original stone)/*Jenkins* (on newer marker) |
| EPITAPH: | *Gone but not forgotten.* (on original stone) |
| MOTIF: | |
| CARVER: | |
| BASE: | Exists |
| TYPE OF BASE: | Marble (on original stone) |
| ENCLOSURE: | |
| TYPE OF ENCLOSURE: | |
| FENCE: | |
| TYPE OF FENCE: | |
| FENCE MOTIF: | |

# JENKINS, Ebenezer Harris

**ADDITIONAL PERSONAL INFORMATION:**
Ebenezer's death age was calculated by www.timeanddate.com, using the birth and death dates listed on his gravestone.

The *Contra Costa Gazette* newspaper, July 4, 1874, lists his age of death as 7 years, 7 months, and 19 days, and not 8 years, and 6 months, as listed on his gravestone. Ebenezer was the oldest son of Thomas W. and Mary Jenkins.

The *Antioch Ledger* newspaper, June 6, 1874, lists Aaron Senderman and Thomas W. Jenkins (Ebenezer's father), both residents of Nortonville, as organizing themselves into a co-partnership for the purpose of carrying on and conducting a mercantile business for the buying and selling of general merchandise in the town of Nortonville.

*The Business Directory of San Francisco and Principal Towns of California and Nevada, 1877*, page 104, under the "Somersville" heading lists T. W. Jenkins as operating a general merchandise business.

See Elizabeth Ann Jenkins, Thomas Joseph Jenkins (born 1869 and died 1870), and Thomas Joseph Jenkins (born 1872 and died 1877).

**ADDITIONAL GRAVESITE INFORMATION:**
There are two monuments for this family. The original stone is a small marble obelisk and the newer marker a large slab of concrete tile aggregate in checkerboard pattern, resembling granite and marble. The original stone lists only three names. The newer stone lists four names (a second Thomas Joseph is listed).

Ebenezer shares the gravestone with sister Elizabeth Ann, and two brothers, both named Thomas Joseph Jenkins. The newer marker, slab of concrete tile aggregate in checkerboard pattern, is believed to have been placed in the cemetery during the 1940s or 1950s. The epitaph, "Gone, but not forgotten," is on the east side of the marble base on the original stone. The marble base probably had a bottom base at one time.

One tile is missing from the newer monument. The original obelisk marble stone sits next to and just west of newer marker.

**REFERENCES:** 1, 2, 3, 6, 8 (July 4, 1874), 9 (June 6, 1874 and July 1, 1876), 11 (P610.31.122, P610.31.167 to P610.31.169, P610.119.60 to P610.119.65, P610.139.3, P610.285.2, and P610.362.5), 12, 14, *Pittsburg Post Dispatch* newspaper (Wed., June 15, 1955, pages 9 and 12), see newspaper appendix pages 721 and 722

---

SCHOOL EXHIBITION.—The Nortonville public school, one of the largest in the county, under charge of Mr. T. H. McCarthy as Principal, has been through a course of rigid written examinations during the past ten days and was to close, for a vacation, with a public exhibition last evening, the 26th instant.

---

Ebenezer Harris Jenkins died just a few days prior to the publication of this article in the June 27, 1874 edition of the *Contra Costa Gazette* newspaper. Most likely Ebenezer attended this school before his death.

# JENKINS,
## Elizabeth Ann

## PERSONAL INFORMATION:

| | |
|---|---|
| SEX: | Female |
| DATE OF BIRTH: | August 2, 1870 |
| DATE OF DEATH: | September 22, 1870 |
| PLACE OF DEATH: | |
| AGE AT DEATH: | 1 month, 20 days |
| CAUSE OF DEATH: | |
| BIRTHPLACE: | |
| SPOUSE: | None |
| PARENTS: | Thomas W. and Mary Jenkins |

## GRAVESITE INFORMATION:

| | |
|---|---|
| LOCATION OF GRAVESITE: | Section S-D, Plot #88 |
| GRAVESTONE: | Exists (two markers exist at this site) |
| TYPE OF GRAVESTONE: | Marble (original stone)/Marble encased in concrete granite aggregate (newer marker) |
| SHAPE OF GRAVESTONE: | Obelisk (original stone)/concrete tile aggregate covering (newer marker) |
| INSCRIPTION: | *Children of* (on original stone)/*Jenkins* (on newer marker) |
| EPITAPH: | *Gone but not forgotten.* (on original stone) |
| MOTIF: | |
| CARVER: | |
| BASE: | Exists |
| TYPE OF BASE: | Marble (on original stone) |
| ENCLOSURE: | |
| TYPE OF ENCLOSURE: | |
| FENCE: | |
| TYPE OF FENCE: | |
| FENCE MOTIF: | |

# JENKINS, Elizabeth Ann

**ADDITIONAL PERSONAL INFORMATION:**
See Ebenezer Harris Jenkins, Thomas Joseph Jenkins (born 1869 and died 1870), and Thomas Joseph Jenkins (born 1872 and died 1877).

**ADDITIONAL GRAVESITE INFORMATION:**
There are two gravestones for this family. Elizabeth Ann shares a stone with brothers Thomas Joseph (died 1870), Ebenezer, and Thomas Joseph Jenkins (died 1877). The older marble stone states that Elizabeth A. Jenkins died on October 22, 1870, aged 2 months and 2 days and not September 22 as stated on the newer stone.

The newer marker, a slab of concrete tile aggregate in checkerboard pattern, is believed to have been placed in the cemetery during the 1940s or 1950s.

**REFERENCES:** 1, 2, 3, 6, 9 (July 1, 1876), 11 (P610.31.167 to P610.31.169, P610.119.60 to P610.119.65, P610.139.3, and P610.362.5), 12, 14, *Pittsburg Post Dispatch* newspaper (Wed., June 15, 1955, pages 9 and 12), see newspaper appendix page 722

**T. W. JENKINS.**

Dealer in

**DRY GOODS, GROCERIES,**

BOOTS & SHOES, ETC.

A GENERAL ASSORTMENT OF

MERCHANDISE.

MAIN STREET, SOMERSVILLE.

7 1 76 tf

**Somerville,**

CONTRA COSTA COUNTY,

A small town situated near Mount Diablo, and supported by coal mining.

Brown P, liquors
Coll John, bootmaker
Cox John T, blacksmith
Craft L F, brickyard
Dellingham E, liquors
**GAMBS F,** General merchandise
Hammond T G, butcher
Haroxhurst George, mining superintendent
Hughes W J, general merchandise
Jenkins T W, general merchandise
Lando J, general merchandise
**MAGUIRE P,** Blacksmith
Mills & Bagley, liquors
Philips William, Union hotel
Pinkerton John W, supt Pittsburg Coal Co.
Prosser W, liquors
Riddle J R, physician
Scammon G H, agent Gilpatrick express
    postmaster
Scammon J E, hotel
**TURNVULL A,** Butcher
Ward H E, livery stable

The advertisement (left) for T. W. Jenkins comes from the *Antioch Ledger* newspaper, July 15, 1876. On the right, the T. W. Jenkins general merchandise store is advertised on page 104, in the *Business Directory of San Francisco and Principal Towns of California and Nevada, 1877*.

# JENKINS,
## Thomas H.

## PERSONAL INFORMATION:

| | |
|---|---|
| SEX: | Male |
| DATE OF BIRTH: | February 5, 1830 |
| DATE OF DEATH: | March 24, 1882 |
| PLACE OF DEATH: | |
| AGE AT DEATH: | 52 years, 1 month, 19 days |
| CAUSE OF DEATH: | |
| BIRTHPLACE: | Wales |
| SPOUSE: | Elizabeth Jenkins |
| PARENTS: | |

## GRAVESITE INFORMATION:

| | |
|---|---|
| LOCATION OF GRAVESITE: | Section N-B, Plot #9 |
| GRAVESTONE: | Exists (only a small piece) |
| TYPE OF GRAVESTONE: | Marble |
| SHAPE OF GRAVESTONE: | Tablet |
| INSCRIPTION: | *Born in Wales/Infant Daughter of* |
| EPITAPH: | *Gone but not forgotten.* |
| MOTIF: | Clasped hands |
| CARVER: | |
| BASE: | Exists |
| TYPE OF BASE: | Sandstone |
| ENCLOSURE: | Exists (partial) |
| TYPE OF ENCLOSURE: | Brick |
| FENCE: | |
| TYPE OF FENCE: | |
| FENCE MOTIF: | |

# JENKINS, Thomas H.

**ADDITIONAL PERSONAL INFORMATION:**
Thomas' death age was calculated by www.timeanddate.com, based on the birth and death dates that appeared on his gravestone.

The *1880 Census for Nortonville Precinct, Contra Costa County, California* lists Thomas Jenkins, age 49, as a miner and native of Wales. Also listed are his wife, Elizabeth, age 44, a native of Pennsylvania and his stepson, Charles, age 15, also a native of Pennsylvania.

See Jenkins infant.

**ADDITIONAL GRAVESITE INFORMATION:**
Zelma Myrick, who recorded information about Rose Hill Cemetery in a notebook in the 1930s, reported "Stone in good condition."

A gravestone rubbing exists. Thomas shares the gravestone with his infant daughter. The gravestone was still present in 1963 because it is listed on a student term paper by Jim Rotelli. Additionally the vandalized gravestone was photographed in 1971.

A 1957 photograph of the Thomas H. Jenkins gravesite appears on the front cover, and on page 9, of *Ansel Adams Singular Images*, Text by Edwin Land, David H. McAlpin, Jon Homes, and Ansel Adams, New York Graphic Society, Boston, MA, 1974.

Park staff determined the location of the gravesite based on photographs. The size of the stone in the photographs and the small piece that remains appears to match the size of the base at Plot #9.

The tilted and cracked sandstone base was epoxied together and leveled in April 2004 by Black Diamond Rangers. A brass plaque was placed at the site to mark the burial location. The plaque says:

*THOMAS H. JENKINS*
*1830 – 1882*
*AND*
*INFANT DAUGHTER*
*APRIL 14 – 15, 1880*
*PLAQUE PLACED IN 2004*

**REFERENCES:** 1, 2, 3, 4, 5, 6, 11 (P610.8.1, P610.98.17, and P610.312.8), 12

The gravestone of Thomas H. Jenkins and infant daughter, 1962.
Photograph by Madison Devlin.

Reference 8.1

The vandalized gravestone of Thomas H. Jenkins and his one day old infant daughter, 1971.
Photograph by Brian Suen.

# JENKINS,
## Thomas Joseph

## PERSONAL INFORMATION:

| | |
|---|---|
| SEX: | Male |
| DATE OF BIRTH: | March 2, 1869 |
| DATE OF DEATH: | August 5, 1870 |
| PLACE OF DEATH: | |
| AGE AT DEATH: | 1 year, 5 months, 3 days |
| CAUSE OF DEATH: | |
| BIRTHPLACE: | |
| SPOUSE: | None |
| PARENTS: | Thomas W. and Mary Jenkins |

## GRAVESITE INFORMATION:

| | |
|---|---|
| LOCATION OF GRAVESITE: | Section S-D, Plot #88 |
| GRAVESTONE: | Exists (two markers exist at this site) |
| TYPE OF GRAVESTONE: | Marble (original stone)/Marble encased in concrete granite aggregate (newer marker) |
| SHAPE OF GRAVESTONE: | Obelisk (original stone)/concrete tile aggregate covering (newer marker) |
| INSCRIPTION: | *Children of* (on original stone)/*Jenkins* (on newer marker) |
| EPITAPH: | *Gone, but not forgotten.* (on original stone) |
| MOTIF: | |
| CARVER: | |
| BASE: | Exists |
| TYPE OF BASE: | Marble (on original stone) |
| ENCLOSURE: | |
| TYPE OF ENCLOSURE: | |
| FENCE: | |
| TYPE OF FENCE: | |
| FENCE MOTIF: | |

# JENKINS, Thomas Joseph

**ADDITIONAL PERSONAL INFORMATION:**
See Ebenezer Harris Jenkins, Elizabeth Ann Jenkins, and Thomas Joseph Jenkins (born 1872 and died 1877).

**ADDITIONAL GRAVESITE INFORMATION:**
There are two markers for this family. The newer marker, a slab of concrete tile aggregate in checkerboard pattern, is believed to have been placed in the cemetery during the 1940s or 1950s.

**REFERENCES:** 1, 3, 6, 11 (P610.31.167 to P610.31.169, P610.119.60 to P610.119.65, P610.139.3, and P620.362.5), 12, 14, *Pittsburg Post Dispatch* newspaper (Wed., June 15, 1955, pages 9 and 12), see newspaper appendix pages 721 and 722

Reference 139.3

Rose Hill Cemetery looking northwest in 1953. The large concrete tile aggregate flat monument for the Jenkins family can be seen near the center of the photograph. It is believed that this newer marker for the Jenkins family was placed in the cemetery in the 1940s or early 1950s.

# JENKINS,
## Thomas Joseph

## PERSONAL INFORMATION:

| | |
|---|---|
| Sex: | Male |
| Date of Birth: | July 30, 1872 |
| Date of Death: | September 5, 1877 |
| Place of Death: | Somersville, Contra Costa County, California |
| Age at Death: | 5 years, 1 month, 6 days |
| Cause of Death: | |
| Birthplace: | |
| Spouse: | None |
| Parents: | Thomas W. and Mary Jenkins |

## GRAVESITE INFORMATION:

| | |
|---|---|
| Location of Gravesite: | Section S-D, Plot #88 |
| Gravestone: | Exists (two markers exist at this site) |
| Type of Gravestone: | Marble (original stone)/Marble encased in concrete granite aggregate |
| Shape of Gravestone: | Obelisk (original stone)/concrete tile aggregate covering (newer marker) |
| Inscription: | *Children of* (on original stone)/*Jenkins* (on newer marker) |
| Epitaph: | *Gone, but not forgotten.* (on original stone) |
| Motif: | |
| Carver: | |
| Base: | Exists |
| Type of Base: | Marble (on original stone) |
| Enclosure: | |
| Type of Enclosure: | |
| Fence: | |
| Type of Fence: | |
| Fence Motif: | |

# JENKINS, Thomas Joseph

**ADDITIONAL PERSONAL INFORMATION:**
Thomas Joseph's age of death was calculated by www.timeanddate.com, based on the birth and death dates listed on his gravestone.

The *Contra Costa Gazette* newspaper, September 29, 1877, and the *Antioch Ledger* newspaper, September 22, 1877, state that Thomas Joseph Jenkins died September 14 and not September 5 as stated on the gravestone. (See page 182 for obituary notice.)

**ADDITIONAL GRAVESITE INFORMATION:**
There are two markers for this family. See Ebenezer Harris Jenkins, Elizabeth Ann Jenkins, and Thomas Joseph Jenkins (born 1869 and died 1870).

The newer marker, a slab of concrete tile aggregate in checkerboard pattern, is believed to have been placed in the cemetery during the 1940s or 1950s.

**REFERENCES:** 1, 6, 8 (Sept. 29, 1877), 9 (Sept. 22, 1877), 11 (P610.31.167 to P610.31.169, P610.119.60 to P610.119.65, P610.139.3, and P610.362.5), 12, 14, *Pittsburg Post Dispatch* newspaper (Wed., June 15, 1955, pages 9 and 12), (see also Annie Henrietta Engler pages 181 and 182), see newspaper appendix page 722

Reference 362.5

Rose Hill Cemetery looking southeast in January 1968.
The Jenkins family large concrete tile aggregate marker rests next to the Italian Cypress tree.

**PERSONAL INFORMATION:**

| | |
|---|---|
| SEX: | Female |
| DATE OF BIRTH: | September 11, 1825 |
| DATE OF DEATH: | January 14, 1883 |
| PLACE OF DEATH: | Somersville, Contra Costa County, California |
| AGE AT DEATH: | 57 years, 4 months, 3 days |
| CAUSE OF DEATH: | |
| BIRTHPLACE: | Ohio |
| SPOUSE: | Henry Jewett |
| PARENTS: | |

**GRAVESITE INFORMATION:**

| | |
|---|---|
| LOCATION OF GRAVESITE: | Unknown |
| GRAVESTONE: | Exists |
| TYPE OF GRAVESTONE: | Marble |
| SHAPE OF GRAVESTONE: | |
| INSCRIPTION: | *Wife of/Mother* |
| EPITAPH: | |
| MOTIF: | Shells and flowers |
| CARVER: | |
| BASE: | |
| TYPE OF BASE: | |
| ENCLOSURE: | |
| TYPE OF ENCLOSURE: | |
| FENCE: | |
| TYPE OF FENCE: | |
| FENCE MOTIF: | |

# JEWETT, Emeline F.

**ADDITIONAL PERSONAL INFORMATION:**
Milton and Walter S. Jewett, the sons of Emeline F. and Henry Jewett, are also buried in Rose Hill Cemetery.

The *1870 Census for Township Three, Contra Costa County, California* lists Henry Jewett, age 46, as a native of Ohio and a laborer. Also listed are his wife, Emily, age 44, a native of Ohio and their daughter, Adelade [sic], age 16, and son, Milton, age 12; both natives of California.

The *Contra Costa Directory 1871-2*, page 344, lists Henry Jewett as a laborer in Somersville.

The *1880 Somersville Precinct Census, Contra Costa County, California*, lists Henry, age 56, a native of Ohio and laborer; Emeline, age 54, a native of Ohio; daughter, Adaleine [sic], age 26, a native of California and housekeeper; and Nelson Jewett, age 11, a native of California.

**ADDITIONAL GRAVESITE INFORMATION:**
The gravestone for Emeline F. Jewett is currently in storage. It was present in the cemetery in 1963 because it is listed on a student term paper by Jim Rotelli. See Milton and Walter S. Jewett.

**REFERENCES:** 1, 2, 3, 6, 8 (Jan. 27, 1883), 11 (P610.31.34), 12, 14, *Pittsburg Post Dispatch* newspaper (Wed., June 15, 1955, pages 9 and 12)

## DIED.

GERMAIN—In Oakland, January 13, Parker Germain, aged 67 years.

RAINS in Petaluma, January 4, Margaret Rains, a native of Kentucky, mother-in-law of R. R. Veale and I. W. Gann, aged 75 years.

JEWETT—In Somersville, January 14, Emeline F., wife of Henry Jewett, aged 57 years.

From the *Contra Costa Gazette* newspaper, January 27, 1883.
Emeline F. Jewett is the last entry in this obituary.

Reference 31.35

Reference 31.34

The front side of the Emeline F. Jewett gravestone (left) and backside (right).
Photographs by Roger Epperson, EBRPD, 1983.

## PERSONAL INFORMATION:

| | |
|---|---|
| SEX: | Male |
| DATE OF BIRTH: | 1858 |
| DATE OF DEATH: | August 20, 1874 |
| PLACE OF DEATH: | |
| AGE AT DEATH: | 16 years |
| CAUSE OF DEATH: | |
| BIRTHPLACE: | California |
| SPOUSE: | |
| PARENTS: | Henry and Emeline Jewett |

## GRAVESITE INFORMATION:

| | |
|---|---|
| LOCATION OF GRAVESITE: | Section N-F, Plot #105 |
| GRAVESTONE: | Exists |
| TYPE OF GRAVESTONE: | Marble |
| SHAPE OF GRAVESTONE: | Tablet |
| INSCRIPTION: | *Farewell/Sons of H. & E. Jewett* |
| EPITAPH: | |
| MOTIF: | Clasped hands with "farewell"/rope with tassels |
| CARVER: | Excelsior Marble Works, San Jose, California |
| BASE: | Exists |
| TYPE OF BASE: | Concrete |
| ENCLOSURE: | |
| TYPE OF ENCLOSURE: | |
| FENCE: | |
| TYPE OF FENCE: | |
| FENCE MOTIF: | |

# JEWETT, Milton

**ADDITIONAL PERSONAL INFORMATION:**
See Emeline F. and Walter S. Jewett.

**ADDITIONAL GRAVESITE INFORMATION:**
Zelma Myrick, who recorded information about Rose Hill Cemetery in a notebook in the 1930s, reported this "Stone broken."

The gravestone is broken into four pieces and concreted flat to ground. The bottom portion of the gravestone sits in the sandstone base. Milton shares a gravestone with his brother, Walter S. Jewett.

**REFERENCES:** 1, 2, 11 (P610.31.200), 12, 14, *Pittsburg Post Dispatch* newspaper (Wed., June 15, 1955, pages 9 and 12)

## Antioch Correspondence.

### Sudden Death at Somersville—Accident to an Antioch Citizen.

On Friday, the 23d inst., Henry Jewett of Somersville dropped dead in the presence of his daughter, at about 5 o'clock P. M. He had been in his usual health during the first part of the day, and had been down to S. Brown's store at about 1 o'clock. Shortly before he expired, he was in the wood shed preparing kindling for a fire when, all of a sudden he threw up his hands and said to his daughter who was near by, " I am dying," and fell into her arms a corpse. Dr. Parkison was telephoned for at once, but on reaching the body, found life to be extinct. The supposed cause of death was paralysis of the heart. Deceased was about 65 years of age. a man of steady habits and was one of our best citizens. He leaves a daughter, the only survivor of his entire family, to whom the entire community tender their heart-felt sympathy.

From the *Contra Costa Gazette* newspaper, December 31, 1887. The article above discusses the death of Henry Jewett, the father of Milton and Walter S. Jewett, and the husband of Emeline F. Jewett. By 1887, there must have been telephone service in Somersville since the article states "Dr. Parkison was telephoned for at once, but on reaching the body, found life to be extinct."

## PERSONAL INFORMATION:

| | |
|---|---|
| SEX: | Male |
| DATE OF BIRTH: | 1850 |
| DATE OF DEATH: | April 21, 1869 |
| PLACE OF DEATH: | Somersville, Contra Costa County, California |
| AGE AT DEATH: | 19 years |
| CAUSE OF DEATH: | Consumption |
| BIRTHPLACE: | |
| SPOUSE: | |
| PARENTS: | Henry and Emeline Jewett |

## GRAVESITE INFORMATION:

| | |
|---|---|
| LOCATION OF GRAVESITE: | Section N-F, Plot #105 |
| GRAVESTONE: | Exists |
| TYPE OF GRAVESTONE: | Marble |
| SHAPE OF GRAVESTONE: | Tablet |
| INSCRIPTION: | *Farewell/Sons of H. & E. Jewett* |
| EPITAPH: | |
| MOTIF: | Clasped hands with "farewell"/rope with tassels |
| CARVER: | Excelsior Marble Works, San Jose, California |
| BASE: | Exists |
| TYPE OF BASE: | Concrete |
| ENCLOSURE: | |
| TYPE OF ENCLOSURE: | |
| FENCE: | |
| TYPE OF FENCE: | |
| FENCE MOTIF: | |

## JEWETT, Walter S.

**ADDITIONAL PERSONAL INFORMATION:**
The *Contra Costa Gazette* newspaper, June 19, 1869, lists Walter's age at death as 21 years, and not 19 years as stated on his gravestone. See Emeline F. Jewett and Milton Jewett.

**ADDITIONAL GRAVESITE INFORMATION:**
Walter shares the gravestone with his brother, Milton Jewett. A footstone was found by Black Diamond Rangers in March 2005 between plots 104 and 105. The footstone says "W S J".

**REFERENCES:** 1, 2, 8 (June 19, 1869), 11 (P610.31.200), 12, 14, *Pittsburg Post Dispatch* newspaper (Wed., June 15, 1955, pages 9 and 12)

DIED.

At San Francisco, on the 12th inst., from the effects of a tumor, JOHN KELLY, of Martinez, aged 44 years.

At Somersville, on the 12th inst., an infant son of Mr. and Mrs. Samuel Brown.

[Published by request.]

In Somersville, April 21st, of consumption, WALTER JEWETT, eldest son of Henry and Emeline Jewett, in the 21st year of his life.

Ye have gone in manhood's earliest hour,
Ye have passed away with the spring's sweet flowers,
When wild birds were trilling notes that ye loved,
And all things were bright where thy footsteps had
    roved.

Ye have gone from the scenes of pleasure and mirth
Ye have passed away from the beautiful earth,
And places ye loved shall know you no more,
Thy bark is afloat on the the other shore.

Ye died in life's morn, when thy spirit was free.
Ere dark pages in life were unfolded to thee,
When flower's of affection seemed everywhere found,
And Hope's rose tinted hues clothed all things around.

Death passed unto life, aye, with a sweet trust !
Thy soul to its Heaven—dust unto dust,
With such glory around—with thy parting breath,
We could not but whisper, can this be death ?

Ye have gone—and a pall is over our hearts,
We mourn that the noble of earth should depart;
But 'round thy remembrance a halo is set,
And words ye have uttered we cannot forget.

R. P. B.

From the *Contra Costa Gazette* newspaper, June 19, 1869.
Walter Jewett is the third entry in this obituary.

## PERSONAL INFORMATION:

| | |
|---|---|
| SEX: | Male |
| DATE OF BIRTH: | 1834 |
| DATE OF DEATH: | November 20, 1880 |
| PLACE OF DEATH: | Nortonville, Contra Costa County, California |
| AGE AT DEATH: | 46 years |
| CAUSE OF DEATH: | |
| BIRTHPLACE: | England |
| SPOUSE: | Celia (Spill) Jones |
| PARENTS: | |

## GRAVESITE INFORMATION:

| | |
|---|---|
| LOCATION OF GRAVESITE: | Section S-C, Plot #23 |
| GRAVESTONE: | Exists |
| TYPE OF GRAVESTONE: | Marble |
| SHAPE OF GRAVESTONE: | Tablet |
| INSCRIPTION: | *Sacred to the Memory of* |
| EPITAPH: | *I Fear Not Death.* |
| MOTIF: | Rope with tassels |
| CARVER: | |
| BASE: | |
| TYPE OF BASE: | |
| ENCLOSURE: | |
| TYPE OF ENCLOSURE: | |
| FENCE: | Missing |
| TYPE OF FENCE: | Wooden picket/later a pipe fence |
| FENCE MOTIF: | |

# JONES, Austin

## ADDITIONAL PERSONAL INFORMATION:

According to descendants, Austin left his wife, Ceila (Spill) Jones, and two small children in Maryland while he traveled to California to look for work. His family joined him in 1862 traveling by ship around Cape Horn. Austin worked as a miner and the family lived in Stewartville and Nortonville. Austin and Celia had nine children. Their first two children were born in Maryland, and the others were born in California.

The *1870 Census for Washington, Plumas County, California* lists Austin Jones, age 36, as a placer miner and native of England. Also listed are his wife, Celia, age 38, a native of England and their children: James, age 16, and Sarah Ann, age 14, both natives of Maryland; Charles, age 5; Lizzie, age 3; and Martha, age 2, all natives of California.

The *1880 Census for Nortonville Precinct, Contra Costa County, California* lists, Austin Jones, age 46, as a native of Wales, a miner and as having paralysis. Also listed are his wife, Celia, age 47, a native of England and their children: Charles, age 15, a laborer; Elizabeth, age 13; Martha, age 12; and Georganna [sic], age 9. All are natives of California.

Austin suffered from consumption and a stroke before passing away. He was the husband of Celia Spill of England. The obituary from the *Contra Costa Gazette* newspaper, November 27, 1880 says Austin was a native of South Wales and 45 years of age at the time of his death. After his death, Austin's wife traveled to King County, Washington with her daughter and son-in-law.

The *1910 Census for Black River, King County, Washington* lists Celia Jones, age 79, as a native of England. Also listed is: her daughter, Georgia Buxton, age 39, a native of California; her husband, Thomas Buxton, a native of California; and their son, Carroll, age 13; daughter, Florence E., age 11; and son, Walter, age 9. All are natives of California.

Austin's three children and son-in-law, Richard Mortimore, are also buried in Rose Hill Cemetery. See Jennie Jones, Lewis James Jones, Martha Jones, and Richard Mortimore.

## ADDITIONAL GRAVESITE INFORMATION:

Austin shares a gravesite with three of his children and three members of the Mortimore family.

The gravestone was broken into three pieces prior to East Bay Regional Park District acquisition. The stone was repaired by Black Diamond Rangers and placed upright in the cemetery in May 2005. The stone was repaired by placing it in a marble encasement to strengthen the original gravestone.

A wooden picket fence originally surrounded this gravesite and the nearby gravesite of the Mortimore family. After the wooden fence disappeared, a pipe fence was installed at the site in the 1930s by family members. The pipe fence was removed *circa* 1978. A badly-cracked concrete pad covers the site today. A broken footstone is embedded in the concrete pad.

**REFERENCES:** 1, 2, 3, 4, 5, 6, 8 (Feb. 20, 1875 and Nov. 27, 1880), 11 (P610.31.126, P610.31.170, P610.145.1, and P610.263.8), 12, 14, see newspaper appendix page 723

Celia (Spill) Jones, wife of Austin Jones. According to descendants, Celia continued to live in Nortonville after the death of her husband and bake bread for miners in order to make money to support her family. *Circa* 1901 Celia traveled to Renton, King County, Washington with her daughter, Georgia, and son-in-law, Thomas Buxton, and lived with them. She was confined to a wheelchair much of the time due to dropsy. Celia Jones died in Earlington, King County, Washington on November 20, 1910, and was buried November 22 in Mount Olivet Cemetery, Renton, Washington.

Reference 343.1

The granite obelisk gravestone for Celia (Spill) Jones, wife of Austin Jones, Mount Olivet Cemetery, Renton, King County, Washington, 2007. Also buried at this gravesite are two of her daughters: Georgia (Jones) Buxton and Elizabeth (Jones) Thomas and their husbands, Tom Buxton and John Thomas. Photograph by June DeJong.

# JONES,
## Benjamin A.

## PERSONAL INFORMATION:

SEX:                  Male

DATE OF BIRTH:        December 9, 1840

DATE OF DEATH:        January 22, 1911

PLACE OF DEATH:       Oakland, Alameda County, California

AGE AT DEATH:         71 years

CAUSE OF DEATH:       Suicide

BIRTHPLACE:           Wales

SPOUSE:               Mary Ann Thomas (Jones) Jones

PARENTS:

## GRAVESITE INFORMATION:

LOCATION OF GRAVESITE:    Unknown

GRAVESTONE:               Missing or never placed

TYPE OF GRAVESTONE:

SHAPE OF GRAVESTONE:

INSCRIPTION:

EPITAPH:

MOTIF:

CARVER:

BASE:

TYPE OF BASE:

ENCLOSURE:

TYPE OF ENCLOSURE:

FENCE:

TYPE OF FENCE:

FENCE MOTIF:

# JONES, Benjamin A.

**ADDITIONAL PERSONAL INFORMATION:**
The date of birth and death were calculated by www.timeanddate.com, based on the information provided in the *Contra Costa Gazette* newspaper, January 28, 1911.

Benjamin's wife, Mary Ann, was the adopted daughter of John Davidson and Gwellyan Jones. Mary Ann and her adoptive parents lived in Placer County, California in the mid 1860s. In 1866, Benjamin Jones arrived in the area.

The *1870 Census for Township 6, Placer County, California* lists Benjamin Jones, age 31, born *circa* 1839 in Wales. His occupation was listed as miner.

Benjamin Jones, age 35 and a resident of Nortonville, and Mary Ann Thomas, age 18, also a resident of Nortonville, applied for a marriage license on August 19, 1874. The information was recorded in the *Applications for Marriage Licenses, Contra Costa County, 1873-1887*, page 26, located at the Contra Costa County Historical Society History Center in Martinez, California.

According to the *Index to Marriage Certificates* located in Contra Costa County Hall of Records, Martinez, California, Benjamin Jones married Mary Ann Thomas on September 8, 1874. They were married by Rev. William Parry; the information is recorded in Volume 2, page 70. The newspaper article from the *Contra Costa Gazette*, September 5, 1874, states they were married August 24, 1874 (see page 317).

The *1880 Census for Nortonville, Contra Costa County, California* lists Benjamon [sic] Jones, age 40, as a native of Wales. Also listed are his wife Maryann, age 25, a native of Wales, and their children Gwenney, age 3, and Richard, age 9 months, both natives of California.

The *1900 Census for Clayton, Contra Costa County, California* lists Benja. A. Jones, age 59, born *circa* 1841, and a native of Wales. His immigration year is listed as 1858. Also listed are his wife, Mary, age 44, born *circa* 1856 in Wales and immigration year as 1860; Gwennie Jones (mother-in-law to Benjamin Jones), age 82, born *circa* 1818 in Wales; and children John W., age 18; Ben B., age 15; Owen O., age 13; Robert W., age 10; Mary L., age 7; and Earl L., age 5. All are natives of California.

After his wife, Mary Ann, died in 1907, Benjamin and his children moved to Oakland. The *1910 Census for Oakland Ward 1, Alameda County, California* lists Benjamin Jones, age 71, as a widower. Also listed are his children: Benjamin, age 25; Mary, age 17; and Earl, age 16.

**ADDITIONAL GRAVESITE INFORMATION:**
The *Contra Costa Gazette* newspaper, January 28, 1911, states that "...the remains were carried to Clayton where the interment took place in Live Oak Cemetery." Descendants, however, believe Benjamin A. Jones is buried in Rose Hill Cemetery.

**REFERENCES:** 8 (Sept. 5, 1874 and Jan. 28, 1911), 11 (P610.336.3 to P610.336.13), 12, see newspaper appendix page 724

Reference 336.3

Benjamin A. and Mary Ann Thomas (Jones) Jones, date unknown. The September 5, 1874 *Contra Costa Gazette* newspaper article (above) states that they were married August 24, 1874 in Nortonville, Contra Costa County, by the Rev. W. Parry. Benjamin and Mary Ann had eight children. The first child was born in San Francisco, the next three were born in Nortonville, and the four youngest were born in Irish Canyon, an area located south of Nortonville.

Reference 336.4

Reference 336.7

Above left, Benjamin A. Jones; and above right, Mary Ann Jones with her adoptive parents, John Davidson Jones and Gwellyan Jones.

Reference 336.13

Pictured above is the abandoned Jones home in Irish Canyon, south of Nortonville. According to a descendant, John D. Jones, adoptive father of Mary Ann, died January 16, 1896. After his death, the land the family owned in Irish Canyon passed to Gwenllyan (Gwennie), his widow. Gwenllyan died in 1902. Contra Costa County probate records state she owned 160 acres, $1500 in improvements, 80 cultivatable acres, the rest pasture land; a one-story, seven room dwelling in fairly good condition; two barns and several small outbuildings.

# JONES,
## Catherine

## PERSONAL INFORMATION:

SEX: Female

DATE OF BIRTH: 1833

DATE OF DEATH: May 27, 1867

PLACE OF DEATH:

AGE AT DEATH: 34 Years

CAUSE OF DEATH:

BIRTHPLACE:

SPOUSE: Benj. R. Jones

PARENTS:

## GRAVESITE INFORMATION:

LOCATION OF GRAVESITE: Section S-E, Plot #82

GRAVESTONE: Exists

TYPE OF GRAVESTONE: Marble

SHAPE OF GRAVESTONE: Tablet

INSCRIPTION: *In Memory of/wife of*

EPITAPH: *My wife how fondly shall thy memory*

*Be shrined within the chambers of my heart.*

*Thy virtuous worth was only known to me*

*And I can feel how sad it is to part.*

MOTIF: Clasped hands

CARVER:

BASE: Exists

TYPE OF BASE: Granite

ENCLOSURE:

TYPE OF ENCLOSURE:

FENCE:

TYPE OF FENCE:

FENCE MOTIF:

# JONES, Catherine

**ADDITIONAL PERSONAL INFORMATION:**
Catherine was one of the earliest burials in Rose Hill Cemetery.

**ADDITIONAL GRAVESITE INFORMATION:**
The gravestone is broken at the start of the epitaph. The epitaph was obtained from Eugene Prince and Kathryn Crabtree, who have been researching and documenting epitaphs from gravestones in many cemeteries throughout the American West.

The lower portion of the gravestone sits in a granite base. The remaining portion of gravestone was concreted flat to the ground prior to East Bay Regional Park District acquisition. A photograph showing the gravestone broken in half appears in *Sunset Magazine*, June 1952, page 26.

**REFERENCES:**  1, 2, 3, 4, 6, 11 (P610.31.161, P610.168.20, and P610.211.6), 12, 14

Reference 211.6

Catherine Jones' broken marble tablet gravestone (foreground), 1973.

# JONES,
## Davied [sic] R.

## PERSONAL INFORMATION:

| | |
|---|---|
| SEX: | Male |
| DATE OF BIRTH: | April 1, 1875 |
| DATE OF DEATH: | October 29, 1875 |
| PLACE OF DEATH: | Somersville, Contra Costa County, California |
| AGE AT DEATH: | 6 months, 28 days |
| CAUSE OF DEATH: | |
| BIRTHPLACE: | Somersville, Contra Costa County, California |
| SPOUSE: | None |
| PARENTS: | Richard Hugh and Elizabeth (Jones) Jones |

## GRAVESITE INFORMATION:

| | |
|---|---|
| LOCATION OF GRAVESITE: | Section S-E, Plot #83 |
| GRAVESTONE: | Exists |
| TYPE OF GRAVESTONE: | Marble |
| SHAPE OF GRAVESTONE: | Tablet |
| INSCRIPTION: | |
| EPITAPH: | *Coffawdwriaeth y Cfiawn* [sic] |
| | *Sydd fendegedig* [sic] |
| MOTIF: | Nipped flower/rope with tassels |
| CARVER: | |
| BASE: | Exists |
| TYPE OF BASE: | Sandstone with new middle marble base |
| ENCLOSURE: | Exists |
| TYPE OF ENCLOSURE: | Brick |
| FENCE: | Missing |
| TYPE OF FENCE: | Iron |
| FENCE MOTIF: | |

# JONES, Davied [sic] R.

**ADDITIONAL PERSONAL INFORMATION:**
Davied shares a gravestone with his mother, Elizabeth Jones. Buried nearby are his grandparents, Hugh R. and Ellen Jones. An aunt, Ellen (Jones) Van Amringe, is also buried in Rose Hill Cemetery, however her burial location is unknown. A brother, George, was two years old at the time of Davied's birth. See Elizabeth Jones, Hugh R. Jones, Ellen Jones, and Ellen Van Amringe.

**ADDITIONAL GRAVESITE INFORMATION:**
Note the different spelling of his first name. Additionally, died is spelled as *deid* on the gravestone. Two Welsh words in the epitaph are incorrectly spelled. The correct spelling is *Cyfiawn* in the first line and *fendigedig* in the second line. The translation of the epitaph is: "The memory of the righteous is blessed." It comes from the *Bible*, Proverbs (10:7).

**REFERENCES:** 1, 2, 3, 5, 6, 11 (P610.14.1, P610.31.160, and P610.268.6), 12, 14

Reference 14.1

Rose Hill Cemetery looking northwest *circa* 1930s. The gravestone and iron fence surrounding the gravesite of Davied and his mother, Elizabeth Jones (or that of Annie Williams, see page 326), can be seen on the far left just above the man standing in the cemetery.

# JONES,
## David Thomas

**PERSONAL INFORMATION:**

| | |
|---|---|
| SEX: | Male |
| DATE OF BIRTH: | January 19, 1872 |
| DATE OF DEATH: | July 10, 1874 |
| PLACE OF DEATH: | |
| AGE AT DEATH: | 2 years, 5 months, 21 days |
| CAUSE OF DEATH: | |
| BIRTHPLACE: | |
| SPOUSE: | None |
| PARENTS: | D. J. and C. Jones |

**GRAVESITE INFORMATION:**

| | |
|---|---|
| LOCATION OF GRAVESITE: | Unknown |
| GRAVESTONE: | Missing |
| TYPE OF GRAVESTONE: | |
| SHAPE OF GRAVESTONE: | |
| INSCRIPTION: | |
| EPITAPH: | |
| MOTIF: | |
| CARVER: | |
| BASE: | |
| TYPE OF BASE: | |
| ENCLOSURE: | |
| TYPE OF ENCLOSURE: | |
| FENCE: | |
| TYPE OF FENCE: | |
| FENCE MOTIF: | |

# JONES, David Thomas

**ADDITIONAL PERSONAL INFORMATION:**
David Thomas' date of birth was calculated by www.timeanddate.com, based on his recorded death date and age at death.

The *1880 Census for Nortonville Precinct, Contra Costa County, California* lists David Jones, age 39, as a miner and native of Wales. Also listed are his wife Catherine, age 32, a native of Wales and their son, Echvin, age 13, a native of Iowa. David and Catherine Jones may possibly be the parents of David Thomas Jones.

**ADDITIONAL GRAVESITE INFORMATION:**
Zelma Myrick, who recorded information about Rose Hill Cemetery in a notebook in the 1930s, reported "Stone on ground, not broken."

The gravestone was present in 1963, because it was listed in a student term paper by Jim Rotelli.

**REFERENCES:** 1, 2, 3, 12

Reference 41.21

Nortonville, May Day picnic, no date. Townspeople are leaving by train from the Black Diamond Coal Mine and Railroad Company freight depot (center) at Nortonville and traveling six miles north to Pittsburg Landing on the San Joaquin River for a May Day celebration. A converted horse car, barely visible behind the timber car on the right, served as the coach. The timber cars hauled the rest of the passengers. The *Antioch Ledger* newspaper, January 16, 1875 reported:

> For the convenience of the traveling public the Black Diamond Coal Company run a passenger car between Nortonville and the Landing. The passenger car comes down the grade unaided by an engine, but rarely has sufficient momentum to reach the wharf. It is customary to run out an engine to meet the morning passenger car, which approaches within a few hundred yards of the landing...

## PERSONAL INFORMATION:

| | |
|---|---|
| SEX: | Female |
| DATE OF BIRTH: | 1851 |
| DATE OF DEATH: | March 10, 1876 |
| PLACE OF DEATH: | Somersville, Contra Costa County, California |
| AGE AT DEATH: | 25 years |
| CAUSE OF DEATH: | |
| BIRTHPLACE: | Steuben, Oneida County, New York |
| SPOUSE: | Richard Hugh Jones |
| PARENTS: | Hugh Richard and Ellen Jones |

## GRAVESITE INFORMATION:

| | |
|---|---|
| LOCATION OF GRAVESITE: | Section S-E, Plot #83 |
| GRAVESTONE: | Exists |
| TYPE OF GRAVESTONE: | Marble |
| SHAPE OF GRAVESTONE: | Tablet |
| INSCRIPTION: | *Beloved Wife of* |
| EPITAPH: | *Coffawderiaeth y Cfiawn* [sic] |
| | *Sydd fendegedig* [sic] |
| MOTIF: | Nipped flower/rope with tassels |
| CARVER: | |
| BASE: | Exists |
| TYPE OF BASE: | Sandstone with new middle marble base |
| ENCLOSURE: | Exists |
| TYPE OF ENCLOSURE: | Brick |
| FENCE: | Missing |
| TYPE OF FENCE: | Iron |
| FENCE MOTIF: | |

# JONES, Elizabeth

**ADDITIONAL PERSONAL INFORMATION:**
The *1860 Census for Steuben, Oneida, New York* lists Elizabeth's father, Hugh R. Jones, age 34, as a farmer and native of Wales. Also listed are Elizabeth, age 9; her mother, Ellen, age 38, a native of Wales; and Elizabeth's siblings: Prissilia [sic], age 6 months; Ellen, age 11; and Saphora [sic], age 3. All are natives of Wales.

The *1870 Census for Township 3, Contra Costa County, California* lists Ella [sic], age 44, a native of England and her daughters: Elizabeth, age 17; Sofia [sic], age 12; Precelia [sic], age 8; and Jennie, age 6. All are natives of New York. [Note: The place of birth for the 1860 census record differs from the information provided in the 1870 and 1880 census records.]

The obituary in the *Contra Costa Gazette* newspaper, March 18, 1876, lists Elizabeth's age at death as 22 years, and not 25 years as stated on gravestone.

Elizabeth married Richard Hugh Jones (son of Catherine and Hugh Jones) on October 21, 1871 in Somersville. According to the *Index to Marriage Certificates* located at the Contra Costa County Hall of Records, Martinez, California, Elizabeth and Richard Jones were married by C. W. Lander; the information is recorded in Volume 1, page 203.

Elizabeth's parents, Hugh R. and Ellen Jones, are buried near her. A polished granite obelisk stone marks her parent's grave. A sister, Ellen (Jones) Van Amringe, is also buried in Rose Hill Cemetery, but the gravesite location is unknown. See Davied R. Jones, Ellen Jones, Hugh R. Jones, and Ellen Van Amringe.

**ADDITIONAL GRAVESITE INFORMATION:**
A photograph in "Back Yard Ghost Towns," by William Berk, *California Monthly* magazine, May 1949, pages 22 and 23, shows the Annie Williams gravestone standing upright at this site, indicating that Elizabeth's stone may not presently be at her actual burial location.

Elizabeth shares a gravestone with her infant son, Davied, who died October 29, 1875. Elizabeth had another son, George, who was born April 8, 1873. Note the spelling of "deid" (died) on the gravestone.

Two Welsh words in the epitaph are incorrectly spelled. The correct spelling is *Cyfiawn* in the first line and *fendigedig* in the second line. The translation of the epitaph is: "The memory of the righteous is blessed." It comes from the *Bible*, Proverbs (10:7).

The gravestone was concreted flat to the ground and a brick enclosure was placed around the gravesite prior to East Bay Regional Park District acquisition and after the coal mining days. The gravestone was removed from the cemetery in October 2002 for repairs. The cement backing was detached, the base was leveled, and the stone was placed upright on a new middle marble base in March 2003 by Black Diamond Rangers.

Based on historic photographs, the iron fence that once existed at the site appears to have had two iron crosses on the west side cornerstones of the fence.

This is one of the few stones with a Welsh epitaph that remains in the cemetery today.

**REFERENCES:** 1, 2, 3, 5, 6, 8 (March 18, 1876), 11 (P610.14.1, P610.31.160, P610.119.48, P610.119.49, P610.268.6, P610.268.12, and P610.268.16), 12, 14, see newspaper appendix page 725

Elizabeth Jones, wife of Richard Hugh Jones and mother of Davied R.
and George Jones. Date unknown.

Reference 268.6                                                      Reference 268.12

Left: Richard Hugh Jones, husband of Elizabeth Jones with their son, George. Right: Richard Hugh Jones. Elizabeth's husband was a native of Llanllechid, Caernarvonshire, Wales, and a coal miner in Somersville. When he arrived in America sometime after the Civil War, he settled in Arizona, eventually traveling to Somersville. After his wife's death, Richard lived in Somersville for a short time before returning to Arizona. Richard Hugh Jones died October 3, 1907, in Bloomfield, Sonoma County, California. According to his obituary that appeared in the *Contra Costa Gazette* newspaper on October 26, 1907, Richard Jones was buried on October 13, at Bloomfield, near Petaluma, Sonoma County, California. The article states:

> Dick Jones, as he was familiarly called, drove the stage from Martinez to San Ramon before the branch road was built between these two towns. He also worked in the coal mines at Somersville in early days, thence going to San Ramon where he drove the stage. After the San Ramon branch road was completed, Dick Jones moved to Oakland and from there to Petaluma at which place he resided until his death.

**PERSONAL INFORMATION:**

|   |   |
|---|---|
| SEX: | Female |
| DATE OF BIRTH: | *Circa* 1838 |
| DATE OF DEATH: | September 17, 1881 |
| PLACE OF DEATH: | Nortonville, Contra Costa County, California |
| AGE AT DEATH: | 43 years |
| CAUSE OF DEATH: | |
| BIRTHPLACE: | Aberdare, Glamorganshire, South Wales |
| SPOUSE: | Evan D. Jones |
| PARENTS: | Thomas and Jane R. Evans |

**GRAVESITE INFORMATION:**

|   |   |
|---|---|
| LOCATION OF GRAVESITE: | Unknown |
| GRAVESTONE: | Missing |
| TYPE OF GRAVESTONE: | |
| SHAPE OF GRAVESTONE: | |
| INSCRIPTION: | |
| EPITAPH: | |
| MOTIF: | |
| CARVER: | |
| BASE: | |
| TYPE OF BASE: | |
| ENCLOSURE: | |
| TYPE OF ENCLOSURE: | |
| FENCE: | |
| TYPE OF FENCE: | |
| FENCE MOTIF: | |

# JONES, Elizabeth

**ADDITIONAL PERSONAL INFORMATION:**
Elizabeth Jones lived in Nortonville, Contra Costa County, California. Reference 2 records the name of her husband as Ivan [sic] Jones.

The *1870 Census for Empire Township, Ormsby County, Nevada* lists Elizabeth, age 31, as native of Wales and "keeping house." Also listed are her husband, E. D. Jones, age 33, a native of Wales and a laborer; and their daughters: K. J., age 8, a native of Pennsylvania; M. M., age 6, a native of Nevada; and Elizabeth, age 1, a native of Nevada.

The *1880 Census for Nortonville Precinct, Contra Costa County, California* lists Evan Jones, age 43, as a miner and native of Wales. Also listed are his wife, Eliza Jones, age 40, a native of Wales, and their three children: Mary, age 15; Elizabeth, age 11; and David, age 8. All are natives of Nevada.

According to information obtained by a descendant, Elizabeth Evans immigrated to the United States with her parents in 1855 and was living in Cressona, Schuylkill County, Pennsylvania about 1860. There she married William Roderick. After his death about 1862, she married Evan D. Jones. Evan was born in Wales in May 1835 and immigrated to the United States in 1860. He was working as a wagon master in Pennsylvania when he met Elizabeth (Evans) Roderick.

By 1863, Evan and Elizabeth moved to Empire Township, Ormsby County, Nevada. Sometime between 1872 and 1876, they moved to Nortonville, Contra Costa County, California.

In 1876, Evan was listed in the Assessment list for Contra Costa County - Somersville and Nortonville as owning a cabin valued at $50, a horse and wagon valued at $30, and one dog. He is also listed in the *1876 Contra Costa County Voting Register* as a miner in Nortonville.

Elizabeth's sister, Margaret (Evans) Howell, was already living in Nortonville. Elizabeth had a least four children: Katie J., born 1862, Pennsylvania; Mary M., born 1864, Nevada; Elizabeth, born 1869, Nevada; and David, born 1872, Nevada.

Elizabeth's niece and nephew, Thomas M. Howell and Sarah Howell (children of her sister Margaret (Evans) Howell), are also buried in Rose Hill Cemetery. Additionally Elizabeth's brother, John R. Evans and John's three sons (John, William, and William Rodrick Evans) are also buried in Rose Hill Cemetery. Elizabeth's grandson, Alexander Morris, is buried in Rose Hill as well.

See John Evans, John R. Evans, William Evans, William Rodrick Evans, Sarah Howell, Thomas M. Howell, David Morgan, and Alexander Morris.

After Elizabeth died, her husband, Evan, moved to Black Diamond, King County, Washington with their daughter, Elizabeth, in 1885.

The *1889 Seattle Washington City Directories* lists Evan D. Jones as a miner in King County. By 1910, he was living with stepdaughter, Katie Jane (Roderick) Davies, in Black Diamond, Washington.

Evan died in October 1910, and is buried in the Black Diamond, Washington Cemetery.

**ADDITIONAL GRAVESITE INFORMATION:**
According to cemetery lists compiled in 1922, 1934, 1935/1936, and 1954, Elizabeth is buried in Rose Hill Cemetery. Nothing exists in the cemetery today to mark her burial location.

**REFERENCES:** 2, 4, 5, 11 (P610.328.1 and P610.328.2), 12

Elizabeth (Evans) Roderick Jones, Nortonville resident.

East Bay Regional Park District

Reference 328.2

Evan D. Jones, husband of Elizabeth (Evans) Roderick Jones.

# JONES,
## Ellen

**PERSONAL INFORMATION:**

| | |
|---|---|
| SEX: | Female |
| DATE OF BIRTH: | 1820 |
| DATE OF DEATH: | August 15, 1890 |
| PLACE OF DEATH: | Somersville, Contra Costa County, California |
| AGE AT DEATH: | 69 years |
| CAUSE OF DEATH: | Cancer |
| BIRTHPLACE: | Pwllheli, Caernarvon, North Wales |
| SPOUSE: | Hugh R. Jones |
| PARENTS: | |

**GRAVESITE INFORMATION:**

| | |
|---|---|
| LOCATION OF GRAVESITE: | Section S-E, Plot #89 |
| GRAVESTONE: | Exists |
| TYPE OF GRAVESTONE: | Polished granite |
| SHAPE OF GRAVESTONE: | Obelisk |
| INSCRIPTION: | Middle base with *JONES* |
| EPITAPH: | *Gone but not forgotten.* |
| MOTIF: | Sheaf of wheat wrapped with ivy |
| CARVER: | |
| BASE: | Exists |
| TYPE OF BASE: | Middle granite base sits on larger granite base |
| ENCLOSURE: | |
| TYPE OF ENCLOSURE: | |
| FENCE: | Missing |
| TYPE OF FENCE: | Wood and wire mesh |
| FENCE MOTIF: | |

# JONES, Ellen

**ADDITIONAL PERSONAL INFORMATION:**
The *1860 Census for Steuben, Oneida, New York* lists Hugh R. Jones, age 34, as a farmer and native of Wales. Also listed are his wife, Ellen, age 38, a native of Wales and their children: Prissilia [sic], age 6 months; Ellen, age 11; Elizabeth, age 9; and Saphora [sic], age 3. All are natives of Wales. [Note: The place of birth for the 1860 census record differs from the information provided in the 1870 and 1880 census records.]

The *1870 Census for Township 3, Contra Costa County, California* lists Ella [sic], age 44, a native of England and her daughters: Elizabeth, age 17; Sofia [sic], age 12; Precelia [sic], age 8; and Jennie, age 6. All are natives of New York.

The *1880 Census for Somersville Precinct, Contra Costa County, California* lists Ellen Jones, housekeeper, age 60, and a native of Wales. Also listed are her daughters: Zipporia [sic], age 22, a dressmaker; Pricilla, age 20; and Jane, age 18. All are natives of New York.

The obituary from the *Contra Costa Gazette* newspaper, August 27, 1890 states Ellen's age at death as 70 years, and not 69 years as listed on her gravestone. The *Contra Costa County, California, Registers of Death* lists her age at death as 70 years. W. S. George was her doctor.

Ellen's daughters, Ellen Van Amringe and Elizabeth Jones, and grandson, Davied R. Jones are also buried in Rose Hill Cemetery.

See Davied R. Jones, Elizabeth Jones, Hugh R. Jones, and Ellen Van Amringe.

**ADDITIONAL GRAVESITE INFORMATION:**
Ellen shares a gravestone with her husband, Hugh R. Jones. A polished granite stone sits on a middle base with the "JONES" inscription. The middle base sits on larger granite base. The gravestone is chipped in a few places. Inscriptions for both husband and wife appear on the east side of the gravestone.

**REFERENCES:** 1, 2, 3, 4, 6, 8 (Aug. 27, 1890 – two articles), 11 (P610.14.1, P610.31.166, P610.108.13, P610.168.10, P610.265.17, P610.317.4, and P610.317.6), 12, 14, see newspaper appendix page 725

## Died.

JONES—In Somersville, August 16, 1890, Ellen Jones, relict of the late Hugh Jones, a native of Wales, aged 70 years.

From the *Contra Costa Gazette* newspaper, August 27, 1890.

Ellen Jones, Somersville resident, date unknown. Ellen was the mother of seven daughters.

- Ellen, born 1849
- Elizabeth, born 1851
- Zippora, born 1856
- Jennie, born 1856 (twin to Zippora; died of measles as an infant)
- Priscilla, born 1860
- Jennie, born 1861 (died of whopping cough as a small child)
- Jennie (called Janie), born 1862

All daughters, except Ellen, were born in New York. Ellen (Jones) Van Amringe, named after her mother, was born in Caernarvon, North Wales.

Left to right: Sisters, Jennie "Janie" (Jones) Brown, wife of Samuel Brown, and Zippora (Jones) Williams, wife of Daniel Williams, at the gravesite of their parents, Hugh R. and Ellen Jones, *circa* 1920.

# JONES,
## George T.

## PERSONAL INFORMATION:

| | |
|---|---|
| SEX: | Male |
| DATE OF BIRTH: | August 12, 1871 |
| DATE OF DEATH: | March 21, 1876 |
| PLACE OF DEATH: | Nortonville, Contra Costa County, California |
| AGE AT DEATH: | 4 years, 7 months, 9 days |
| CAUSE OF DEATH: | Typhoid or diphtheria |
| BIRTHPLACE: | Somersville, Contra Costa County, California |
| SPOUSE: | None |
| PARENTS: | Thomas M. and Annie Jones |

## GRAVESITE INFORMATION:

| | |
|---|---|
| LOCATION OF GRAVESITE: | Near Section N-E, Plot #70 |
| GRAVESTONE: | Missing or never placed |
| TYPE OF GRAVESTONE: | |
| SHAPE OF GRAVESTONE: | |
| INSCRIPTION: | |
| EPITAPH: | |
| MOTIF: | |
| CARVER: | |
| BASE: | |
| TYPE OF BASE: | |
| ENCLOSURE: | |
| TYPE OF ENCLOSURE: | |
| FENCE: | |
| TYPE OF FENCE: | |
| FENCE MOTIF: | |

# JONES, George T.

**ADDITIONAL PERSONAL INFORMATION:**
George's birth and death dates come from family records. His age at death was calculated by www.timeanddate.com, based on these dates.

George T. and two other children are buried next to their father, Thomas M. Jones. The names are listed in the family *Bible*.

According to information obtained from a descendant and the *1880 Census for Sommersville* [sic], *Contra Costa County, California*, Thomas M. and Annie Jones had at least seven children. All were born in Somersville, Contra Costa County, California. Their children were:

- John, born July 13, 1869; died July 14, 1869
- Henry, born June 7, 1870; died August 27, 1870
- George T., born August 12, 1871; died March 21, 1876

- Etta Margaret, born Jan. 24, 1875
- Albert T., born Jan. 19, 1877; died 1951
- George, born *circa* 1877 (from 1880 census records)
- George Washington, born Feb. 23, 1880; died approximately 1946

See Henry Jones, John Jones, and Thomas M. Jones.

**ADDITIONAL GRAVESITE INFORMATION:**
George is buried in the vicinity of Thomas M. Jones, Section N-E, Plot #70.

**REFERENCES:** 12, Black *Diamond Oral History – Mayme (Joers) Jones and Margaret (Jones) Gunnell*, January 27, 1981, by Karana Hattersley-Drayton, pages 2, 4, and 34

Reference 318.48

Mule-powered coal car at the Pittsburg Mine in Somersville, *circa* 1880. George's father, Thomas M. Jones, was a miner and resident of Somersville during the time that this mine was active.

## PERSONAL INFORMATION:

| | |
|---|---|
| Sex: | Male |
| Date of Birth: | June 7, 1870 |
| Date of Death: | August 27, 1870 |
| Place of Death: | |
| Age at Death: | 2 months, 20 days |
| Cause of Death: | Typhoid or diphtheria |
| Birthplace: | Somersville, Contra Costa County, California |
| Spouse: | None |
| Parents: | Thomas M. and Annie Jones |

## GRAVESITE INFORMATION:

| | |
|---|---|
| Location of Gravesite: | Near Section N-E, Plot #70 |
| Gravestone: | Missing or never placed |
| Type of Gravestone: | |
| Shape of Gravestone: | |
| Inscription: | |
| Epitaph: | |
| Motif: | |
| Carver: | |
| Base: | |
| Type of Base: | |
| Enclosure: | |
| Type of Enclosure: | |
| Fence: | |
| Type of Fence: | |
| Fence Motif: | |

# JONES, Henry

**ADDITIONAL PERSONAL INFORMATION:**
Henry and two other children are buried next to their father, Thomas M. Jones. The names are listed in the family *Bible*.

**ADDITIONAL GRAVESITE INFORMATION:**
Henry is buried in the vicinity of Thomas M. Jones, Section N-E, Plot #70. See George T. Jones, John Jones, and Thomas M. Jones.

**REFERENCES:** 12, *Black Diamond Oral History – Mayme (Joers) Jones and Margaret (Jones) Gunnell*, January 27, 1981, by Karana Hattersley-Drayton, pages 2, 4, and 34

Reference 358.2

Rose Hill Cemetery, looking east toward Somersville town site, 1963.
A barbed wire fence surrounds the cemetery. Photograph by Ray Sullivan.

## PERSONAL INFORMATION:

| | |
|---|---|
| SEX: | Male |
| DATE OF BIRTH: | May 22, 1825 |
| DATE OF DEATH: | November 1869 |
| PLACE OF DEATH: | Somersville, Contra Costa County, California |
| AGE AT DEATH: | 44 years |
| CAUSE OF DEATH: | Typhoid or diphtheria |
| BIRTHPLACE: | Caernarvon, North Wales |
| SPOUSE: | Ellen Jones |
| PARENTS: | |

## GRAVESITE INFORMATION:

| | |
|---|---|
| LOCATION OF GRAVESITE: | Section S-E, Plot #89 |
| GRAVESTONE: | Exists |
| TYPE OF GRAVESTONE: | Polished granite |
| SHAPE OF GRAVESTONE: | Obelisk |
| INSCRIPTION: | Middle base says *JONES* |
| EPITAPH: | *Gone but not forgotten.* |
| MOTIF: | Sheaf of wheat wrapped with ivy |
| CARVER: | |
| BASE: | Exists |
| TYPE OF BASE: | Middle granite base sits on larger granite base |
| ENCLOSURE: | |
| TYPE OF ENCLOSURE: | |
| FENCE: | Missing |
| TYPE OF FENCE: | Wood and wire mesh |
| FENCE MOTIF: | |

# JONES, Hugh R.

ADDITIONAL PERSONAL INFORMATION:
The *1860 Census for Steuben, Oneida, New York* lists Hugh R. Jones, age 34, as a farmer and native of Wales. Also listed are his wife, Ellen, age 38, a native of Wales and their children: Prissilia [sic], age 6 months; Ellen, age 11; Elizabeth, age 9; and Saphora [sic], age 3. All are recorded as natives of Wales.

Hugh Richard Jones, a resident of Somersville, was the father of seven daughters (two died at a young age). He died during an outbreak of either typhoid or diphtheria. His occupations included a bricklayer in Wales and miner in Somersville. A daughter, Elizabeth (Jones) Jones, and grandson, Davied R. Jones, share a gravestone nearby. Another daughter, Ellen (Jones) Van Amringe, is also buried in Rose Hill Cemetery, but the gravesite location is unknown.

See Davied R. Jones, Elizabeth Jones, Ellen Jones, and Ellen Van Amringe.

ADDITIONAL GRAVESITE INFORMATION:
Hugh shares a gravestone with his wife, Ellen Jones.

REFERENCES: 1, 2, 3, 4, 6, 11 (P610.14.1, P610.31.166, P610.108.12, P610.168.10, P610.265.17, P610.317.4, and P610.317.6), 12, 14

---

GOOD FOR SOMERSVILLE.—The mines at this place contributed $105 to the Sanitary Fund on election day. As there were only 96 voters, this is equal to $1 09 for each man. This beats any precinct in the county. All honor to the men of Somersville; they are generous and patriotic!

Hugh R. Jones was not yet living in Somersville when this article
appeared in the *Contra Costa Gazette* newspaper on September 12, 1863.
Hugh arrived in Somersville in 1869.

Reference 108.12

Hugh R. Jones, Somersville resident, date unknown. Hugh and his wife, Ellen, left Wales by ship about 1850 with 2-year-old daughter Ellen, and settled in Steuben Corners, Oneida County, New York. Eventually they went west to San Francisco, settling in the Telegraph Hill vicinity and later in May 1869, located in Somersville. According to family history documents:

> The journey, made by water, was a long and tedious passage around Cape Horn, on to the Pacific, and San Francisco, then a thriving port of interest. When they entered the Golden Gate, the coming of the vessel was advanced by primitive methods to the Port of Embarkation from where stands the Coit Tower or Telegraph Hill - either embarked by a flare of light, or the booming of a small cannon, as with all the other vessels. The vessel was owned by one of a number of companies organized in Massachusetts. Each company in its own sailing ship, furnished provisions and mining tools to every member. The boat was probably named "Crescent City" as it had sailed this route since 1849. Religious services were conducted on the boat by Albert Williams who organized the first Presbyterian Church in S. F. on April 1, 1849, and in 1853 received the Welsh Church into the Presbytery.

## NORTONVILLE.

We put the population of this town at from four to five hundred, including children, the latter no inconsiderable item, for the foreign population, chiefly Welsh, Scotch and Irish, are proverbially prolific; and, it is not too much to say, make up largely the sinew of the nation. They bring with them, too, their old home associations of morality and religion, elements contributing to make good and patriotic citizens. Take the Welsh, in illustration, who sustain a preacher in their own vernacular. All these will be found members of some of the social or charitable orders, either Masons, Odd Fellows, R.d Men, Good Templars, or other organizat.on. The business of the town is represented by three general merchandise stores—a fourth now in progress, of brick, projected by the enterprise of Mr. Scammon, will be stocked in a few days. There are three hotels, the principal being the Black Diamond Exchange, the present site of which being required by the Coal Company, the house will be shortly removed, and the lessees, Messrs. Tyler & Gwynn (among the most popular caterers of the place), will build at once a first class establishment, and continue the business.

Besides hotels proper, there are four private boarding houses, six saloons, a livery stable, Good Templars' Hall and a church, both elegant structures, reflecting credit upon the liberality and good taste of the people; also, a well conducted school, averaging from seventy-five to one hundred scholars. Communication with the city is direct, a special car being dispatched daily to connect with the boats at New York Landing. If the demand for coal were only brisk and sustained, it would be the liveliest and most money-making place in the State. As it is, judging from the improvements going on, public confidence seems to paint to such consummation as not improbable or very distant.

"Jones" is the most abundant name in Rose Hill Cemetery. At least twenty-one individuals with the Welsh last name of "Jones" are interred in Rose Hill Cemetery. This newspaper article regarding Nortonville, from the *Antioch Ledger,* June 4, 1870, states:

> We put the population of this town at from four to five hundred, including children, the latter no inconsiderable item, for the foreign population, chiefly Welsh, Scotch and Irish, are proverbially prolific; and, it is not too much to say, make up largely the sinew of the nation.

# JONES,
## Isabella

**PERSONAL INFORMATION:**

| | |
|---|---|
| SEX: | Female |
| DATE OF BIRTH: | April 1868 |
| DATE OF DEATH: | February 5, 1872 |
| PLACE OF DEATH: | |
| AGE AT DEATH: | 3 years, 10 months |
| CAUSE OF DEATH: | |
| BIRTHPLACE: | |
| SPOUSE: | None |
| PARENTS: | James and Ellen Jones |

**GRAVESITE INFORMATION:**

| | |
|---|---|
| LOCATION OF GRAVESITE: | Section S-E, Plot #84 |
| GRAVESTONE: | Exists (top portion with motif missing) |
| TYPE OF GRAVESTONE: | Marble |
| SHAPE OF GRAVESTONE: | Tablet |
| INSCRIPTION: | *Daughter of* |
| EPITAPH: | *Weep not for me my parents dear.* |
| | *I am not dead but sleeping here,* |
| | *I am not your's but Jesus alone.* |
| | *He thought it best to take me home.* |
| MOTIF: | Rope with tassels/Weeping willow with obelisk monument |
| CARVER: | |
| BASE: | Missing |
| TYPE OF BASE: | |
| ENCLOSURE: | |
| TYPE OF ENCLOSURE: | |
| FENCE: | |
| TYPE OF FENCE: | |
| FENCE MOTIF: | |

# JONES, Isabella

**ADDITIONAL PERSONAL INFORMATION:**
Isabella is one of the youngest individuals to be buried in Rose Hill Cemetery.

**ADDITIONAL GRAVESITE INFORMATION:**
Zelma Myrick, who recorded information about Rose Hill Cemetery in a notebook in the 1930s, reported "Stone flat on ground."

The top portion of the gravestone containing the motif was broken off and is missing. The remaining piece of the gravestone was concreted flat to the ground prior to East Bay Regional Park District acquisition.

**REFERENCES:** 1, 2, 3, 6, 11 (P610.31.159, P610.119.47, and P610.268.1), 12, 14

Reference 268.1

Isabella Jones gravestone, *circa* 1950s.

## PERSONAL INFORMATION:

|  |  |
|---|---|
| SEX: | Female |
| DATE OF BIRTH: | |
| DATE OF DEATH: | |
| PLACE OF DEATH: | |
| AGE AT DEATH: | Infant |
| CAUSE OF DEATH: | |
| BIRTHPLACE: | |
| SPOUSE: | None |
| PARENTS: | Austin and Celia (Spill) Jones |

## GRAVESITE INFORMATION:

|  |  |
|---|---|
| LOCATION OF GRAVESITE: | Section S-C, Plot #117 |
| GRAVESTONE: | Missing or never placed |
| TYPE OF GRAVESTONE: | |
| SHAPE OF GRAVESTONE: | |
| INSCRIPTION: | |
| EPITAPH: | |
| MOTIF: | |
| CARVER: | |
| BASE: | |
| TYPE OF BASE: | |
| ENCLOSURE: | |
| TYPE OF ENCLOSURE: | |
| FENCE: | |
| TYPE OF FENCE: | |
| FENCE MOTIF: | |

# JONES, Jennie

**ADDITIONAL PERSONAL INFORMATION:**
Jennie was one of nine children of Austin and Celia (Spill) Jones. Jennie's father Austin, sister Martha, and brother Lewis are also buried in Rose Hill Cemetery. See Austin Jones, Lewis James Jones, and Martha Jones.

**ADDITIONAL GRAVESITE INFORMATION:**
A plaque was purchased by descendants and placed at the site to mark the area where it is believed Jennie, and her brother Lewis James, may be buried. The plaque says:

*LEWIS JAMES JONES*
*OCT. 26, 1874 – FEB. 6, 1875*
*AND*
*JENNIE JONES*
*INFANT CHILDREN OF*
*AUSTIN AND CELIA JONES*
*PLAQUE PLACED IN 2005*

**REFERENCES:** 12

Reference 314.1

Reference 308.21

Left, Georgia Jones and her brother, James Jones, right, siblings of Jennie Jones and children of Austin and Celia (Spill) Jones. The Jones children were:

- James, born July 8, 1854, Frostburg, Allegany County, Maryland
- Sarah Ann, born Jan. 26, 1857, Frostburg, Allegany County, Maryland
- Charles, born May 1865, California
- Elizabeth, born Nov. 26, 1866, Gibsonville, Sierra County, California
- Martha, born March 14, 1868, California
- Georgia, born May 29, 1871, Sawpit Flats, Plumas County, California
- Austin, born 1879, La Porte, Plumas County, California
- Lewis James, born Oct. 26, 1874, Nortonville, Contra Costa County, California
- Jennie, born in California

## PERSONAL INFORMATION:

| | |
|---|---|
| SEX: | Male |
| DATE OF BIRTH: | July 13, 1869 |
| DATE OF DEATH: | July 14, 1869 |
| PLACE OF DEATH: | Somersviile, Contra Costa County, California |
| AGE AT DEATH: | 1 day |
| CAUSE OF DEATH: | Typhoid or diphtheria |
| BIRTHPLACE: | Somersville, Contra Costa County, California |
| SPOUSE: | None |
| PARENTS: | Thomas M. and Annie Jones |

## GRAVESITE INFORMATION:

| | |
|---|---|
| LOCATION OF GRAVESITE: | Near Section N-E, Plot #70 |
| GRAVESTONE: | Missing or never placed |
| TYPE OF GRAVESTONE: | |
| SHAPE OF GRAVESTONE: | |
| INSCRIPTION: | |
| EPITAPH: | |
| MOTIF: | |
| CARVER: | |
| BASE: | |
| TYPE OF BASE: | |
| ENCLOSURE: | |
| TYPE OF ENCLOSURE: | |
| FENCE: | |
| TYPE OF FENCE: | |
| FENCE MOTIF: | |

# JONES, John

**ADDITIONAL PERSONAL INFORMATION:**
Although John was only one day old, descendants state he died from typhoid or diphtheria. John and two other children are buried next to their father, Thomas M. Jones. The names are listed in the family *Bible*.

See George Jones, Henry Jones, and Thomas M. Jones.

**ADDITIONAL GRAVESITE INFORMATION:**
The family *Bible* is the only source that documents John's burial in Rose Hill Cemetery.

**REFERENCES:** 12, *Black Diamond Oral History – Mayme (Joers) Jones and Margaret (Jones) Gunnell*, January 27, 1981, by Karana Hattersley-Drayton, pages 2, 4, and 34

## A Cave at the Mines.

On Saturday afternoon last the earth overhead in the old Eureka slope, at Somersville, commenced giving way. The earth in this stope is of soft sandstone, and is not completely timbered. The discovery caused considerable excitement, and orders were issued to cease work in that portion of the mine. Arrangements are being made to timber the insecure portion.

This newspaper article from the *Antioch Ledger*, May 21, 1870, discusses the Eureka slope coal mine. Five coal mines existed in Somersville. In addition to the Eureka mine there was the Pittsburg, Independent, Manhattan, and Union. John's father, Thomas M. Jones, worked as a miner in the coal field and died in Somersville.

# JONES,
## John B.

**PERSONAL INFORMATION:**

| | |
|---|---|
| SEX: | Male |
| DATE OF BIRTH: | May 1840 |
| DATE OF DEATH: | February 9, 1879 |
| PLACE OF DEATH: | Nortonville, Contra Costa County, California |
| AGE AT DEATH: | 38 years, 9 months |
| CAUSE OF DEATH: | |
| BIRTHPLACE: | Tredegar, Monmouthshire, South Wales |
| SPOUSE: | |
| PARENTS: | |

**GRAVESITE INFORMATION:**

| | |
|---|---|
| LOCATION OF GRAVESITE: | Section S-D, Plot #59 |
| GRAVESTONE: | Exists |
| TYPE OF GRAVESTONE: | Marble |
| SHAPE OF GRAVESTONE: | Tablet |
| INSCRIPTION: | |
| EPITAPH: | *Gone But Not Forgotten* |
| MOTIF: | Clasped hands/rope with tassels |
| CARVER: | |
| BASE: | |
| TYPE OF BASE: | |
| ENCLOSURE: | Exists |
| TYPE OF ENCLOSURE: | Brick with granite corner blocks |
| FENCE: | Exists |
| TYPE OF FENCE: | Iron |
| FENCE MOTIF: | |

# JONES, John B.

**ADDITIONAL PERSONAL INFORMATION:**
The obituary from *Contra Costa Gazette* newspaper, February 15, 1879 and the *Antioch Ledger* newspaper, February 15, 1879, state his age at death as 39 years, and not 38 years and 9 months as listed on his gravestone.

According to the *History of Contra Costa County* by Slocum and Company, 1882, page 251, J. B. (John B.) Jones served as a constable for Township No. 4 (includes the Nortonville and Somersville area) in 1876-1877.

The *Business Directory of San Francisco and Principal Towns of California and Nevada*, 1877, page 50, under the "Nortonville" heading lists John B. Jones as a constable.

**ADDITIONAL GRAVESITE INFORMATION:**
Zelma Myrick, who recorded information about Rose Hill Cemetery in a notebook in the 1930s, reported "Stone riveted together."

The remaining portion of the gravestone is broken into four pieces. The pieces were removed from the cemetery *circa* 1986 and placed in storage for safekeeping. The gravestone was bolted flat to the ground prior to East Bay Regional Park District acquisition. J. B. Jones shares a gravestone with Thomas J. Davis. Buried at the same gravesite, and within the same original iron fence, are Lulu and Alfred W. Buxton.

A photograph of the gravesite appears in *Contra Costa Living* (a supplement of the *Contra Costa Sunday Times* newspaper, April 11, 1971, page 9).

See Alfred W. Buxton, Lulu Buxton, and Thomas J. Davis.

**REFERENCES:** 1, 2, 3, 4, 6, 8 (Feb. 15, 1879), 9 (Feb. 15, 1879), 10 (page 251), 11 (P610.31.139, P610.31.123, P610.117.6, and P610.263.7), 12, 14, see newspaper appendix page 726

Reference 31.139

The gravestone for J. B. (John B.) Jones and Thomas J. Davis as it appeared in July 1977.
Photograph by Traci (Gibbons) Parent.

# JONES,
## Lewis James

## PERSONAL INFORMATION:

| | |
|---|---|
| SEX: | Male |
| DATE OF BIRTH: | October 26, 1874 |
| DATE OF DEATH: | February 6, 1875 |
| PLACE OF DEATH: | |
| AGE AT DEATH: | 3 months, 11 days |
| CAUSE OF DEATH: | |
| BIRTHPLACE: | Nortonville, Contra Costa County, California |
| SPOUSE: | None |
| PARENTS: | Austin and Celia (Spill) Jones |

## GRAVESITE INFORMATION:

| | |
|---|---|
| LOCATION OF GRAVESITE: | Section S-C, Plot #117 |
| GRAVESTONE: | Missing or never placed |
| TYPE OF GRAVESTONE: | |
| SHAPE OF GRAVESTONE: | |
| INSCRIPTION: | |
| EPITAPH: | |
| MOTIF: | |
| CARVER: | |
| BASE: | |
| TYPE OF BASE: | |
| ENCLOSURE: | |
| TYPE OF ENCLOSURE: | |
| FENCE: | |
| TYPE OF FENCE: | |
| FENCE MOTIF: | |

# JONES, Lewis James

**ADDITIONAL PERSONAL INFORMATION:**
Lewis was one of nine children of Austin and Celia (Spill) Jones. Lewis' father, Austin, and his sisters, Jennie and Martha, are also buried in Rose Hill Cemetery.

See Austin Jones, Jennie Jones, and Martha Jones.

**ADDITIONAL GRAVESITE INFORMATION:**
A plaque was purchased by descendants and placed at the site to mark the area where it is believed Lewis James, and his sister, Jennie, may be buried. The plaque says:

*LEWIS JAMES JONES*
*OCT. 26, 1874 – FEB. 6, 1875*
*AND*
*JENNIE JONES*
*INFANT CHILDREN OF*
*AUSTIN AND CELIA JONES*
*PLAQUE PLACED IN 2005*

**REFERENCES:** 12, 8 (Feb. 20, 1875)

---

## DIED.

WELLS——In Moraga Valley, Feb. 4th, Ellen, infant daughter of Howard and Olive Wells, aged 1 year, 3 months and 9 days.

JONES——In Nortonville, Feb. 6th, Lewis, son of Austin and Celia Jones, aged 5 months and 6 days.

---

From the *Contra Costa Gazette* newspaper, February 20, 1875. Lewis Jones is the second entry in this obituary. The obituary lists Lewis' age at death as 5 months and 6 days. Descendants provided Lewis' birthdate. His age at death (listed on the previous page) was calculated using the date of birth and death provided by descendants.

## GRAVESTONE INFORMATION:

|  |  |
|---|---|
| SEX: | Female |
| DATE OF BIRTH: | March 14, 1868 |
| DATE OF DEATH: | October 27, 1886 |
| PLACE OF DEATH: | Martinez, Contra Costa County, California |
| AGE AT DEATH: | 18 years, 7 months, 13 days |
| CAUSE OF DEATH: | Diphtheria |
| BIRTHPLACE: | California |
| SPOUSE: | None |
| PARENTS: | Austin and Celia (Spill) Jones |

## GRAVESITE INFORMATION:

|  |  |
|---|---|
| LOCATION OF GRAVESITE: | Section S-C, Plot #22 |
| GRAVESTONE: | Exists |
| TYPE OF GRAVESTONE: | Marble |
| SHAPE OF GRAVESTONE: | Tablet |
| INSCRIPTION: | *Beloved daughter of* |
| EPITAPH: | |
| MOTIF: | |
| CARVER: | |
| BASE: | Exists |
| TYPE OF BASE: | Sandstone |
| ENCLOSURE: | |
| TYPE OF ENCLOSURE: | |
| FENCE: | Missing |
| TYPE OF FENCE: | Wooden picket/later a pipe fence |
| FENCE MOTIF: | |

# JONES, Martha

**ADDITIONAL PERSONAL INFORMATION:**
The *Contra Costa Gazette* newspaper, October 30, 1886, lists Martha's age of death as 18 years and 9 months, and not 18 years, 7 months, and 13 days, as listed on her gravestone.

According to descendants, Martha was born March 14, 1868. She did millinery and dressmaking work. Martha died of diphtheria.

See Austin Jones, Jennie Jones, Lewis James Jones, and Richard Mortimore.

**ADDITIONAL GRAVESITE INFORMATION:**
Martha shares the gravesite with: her father, Austin Jones; two siblings, Jennie and Lewis James Jones; and three members of the Mortimore family, Richard, and his children, Harriet and Alvin Mortimore. Austin Jones was the father-in-law of Richard Mortimore. The gravestone was broken into eight pieces with some missing pieces.

In 1988 the gravestone was placed in storage until repairs could be made. A marble encasement was made by Black Diamond Rangers to support the stone. The gravestone was repaired and placed in the encasement and returned to the cemetery in October 2004.

**REFERENCES:** 1, 2, 3, 4, 6, 8 (Oct. 30, 1886), 11 (P610.2.18, P610.31.126, P610.31.171, P610.43.4, P610.117.17, P610.145.1, P610.285.11, and P610.290.1), 12, 14, see newspaper appendix page 726

Reference 290.1

Martha Jones, daughter of Austin and Celia (Spill) Jones, *circa* 1880s.

## PERSONAL INFORMATION:

| | |
|---|---|
| SEX: | Female |
| DATE OF BIRTH: | May 1865 |
| DATE OF DEATH: | August 21, 1865 |
| PLACE OF DEATH: | |
| AGE AT DEATH: | 3 months |
| CAUSE OF DEATH: | |
| BIRTHPLACE: | |
| SPOUSE: | None |
| PARENTS: | Joseph and Joanna Jones |

## GRAVESITE INFORMATION:

| | |
|---|---|
| LOCATION OF GRAVESITE: | Section S-E, Plot #79 |
| GRAVESTONE: | Exists |
| TYPE OF GRAVESTONE: | Marble |
| SHAPE OF GRAVESTONE: | Tablet |
| INSCRIPTION: | *Infant daughter of* |
| EPITAPH: | *Two pilgrims for the holy land* |
| | *Have left our lonely door,* |
| | *Two sinless angels, hand in hand* |
| | *Have reached promised shore.* |
| MOTIF: | Hand with finger pointing toward Heaven |
| CARVER: | |
| BASE: | Exists |
| TYPE OF BASE: | New granite base with new middle marble base |
| ENCLOSURE: | |
| TYPE OF ENCLOSURE: | |
| FENCE: | |
| TYPE OF FENCE: | |
| FENCE MOTIF: | |

# JONES, Mary E.

**ADDITIONAL PERSONAL INFORMATION:**
The *1870 Census for Township Three* (includes Nortonville, Clayton, Pittsburg Landing, and Somersville) lists Joseph Jones, age 37, as a quartz miner and native of Wales. Also listed are his wife, Johanna [sic], age 26, a native of Wales, and their son, William, age 4, a native of Ohio.

The *1880 Census for Sutter Creek, Amador County, California* lists Joseph Jones, age 45, as a native of Ohio. Also recorded are his wife, Johanna, age 35, a native of Wales and their sons, William, age 14, a native of Ohio, and John, age 5, a native of California.

**ADDITIONAL GRAVESITE INFORMATION:**
Mary E. shares a stone with a 3-day-old unnamed infant. The gravestone was broken into two pieces and concreted flat to the ground in the marble base prior to East Bay Regional Park District acquisition. Another base (bottom base) most likely existed at one time. The 3-day-old infant is the youngest person buried in the cemetery with an existing stone. See Unknown "Infant Babe."

In 2003, the Mary E. Jones gravestone was removed for repairs. A new bottom granite base was purchased to hold the middle marble base and gravestone. The gravestone was returned to the cemetery and placed upright on the middle marble base in July 2004. Sadly, on September 14, 2007, the stone was vandalized, and the gravestone was broken again. The original middle marble base, which held the stone, was broken beyond repair. A new middle marble base was purchased and installed in July 2009. A marble encasement was added to strengthen the original gravestone. The repaired stone was returned to the cemetery in 2009.

**REFERENCES:** 1, 2, 3, 6, 11 (P610.31.163, P610.119.54, and P610.31.163), 12, 14

Reference 317.4

Rose Hill Cemetery facing northwest. The broken gravestone for Mary E. Jones and "Infant Babe" can seen lying on the ground in the center of the photograph. Photograph taken *circa* 1939 by Zelma Myrick.

# JONES,
## Thomas

**PERSONAL INFORMATION:**

| | |
|---|---|
| Sex: | Male |
| Date of Birth: | July 1877 |
| Date of Death: | November 10, 1878 |
| Place of Death: | Nortonville, Contra Costa County, California |
| Age at Death: | 16 months |
| Cause of Death: | |
| Birthplace: | Nortonville, Contra Costa County, California |
| Spouse: | None |
| Parents: | Joseph H. and Elizabeth Jones |

**GRAVESITE INFORMATION:**

| | |
|---|---|
| Location of Gravesite: | Section S-C, Plot #113 |
| Gravestone: | Exists |
| Type of Gravestone: | Marble |
| Shape of Gravestone: | Block |
| Inscription: | *In Memory of/Son of/Nortonville* |
| Epitaph: | *To us for sixteen anxious months* |
| | *His infant smile was given:* |
| | *And then he bade farewell to earth and went to live in Heaven.* |
| Motif: | |
| Carver: | |
| Base: | Exists |
| Type of Base: | Granite |
| Enclosure: | |
| Type of Enclosure: | |
| Fence: | |
| Type of Fence: | |
| Fence Motif: | |

# JONES, Thomas

**ADDITIONAL PERSONAL INFORMATION:**
The *Contra Costa Gazette* newspaper, November 16, 1878, lists Thomas' age at death as 1 year and 3 months, and not 16 months as listed on his gravestone.

The *1880 Census for Judsonville Precinct, Contra Costa County, California*, lists Thomas' father, Joseph H. Jones, age 35, as a miner and native of Wales. Also listed are his mother, Elizabeth, age 30, a native of Wales, and their children: Joseph, age 5, a native of Indiana; and Margaret, age 1, a native of California. Perhaps the family moved from Nortonville to Judsonville after the death of their youngest son Thomas.

The *1900 Census for Renton, King County, Washington* lists Joseph Jones, age 55, as a native of Wales. Also listed are his wife, Elizabeth, age 50, a native of Wales, and their children: Arthur, age 26, a native of Oregon [Arthur was not listed with them in the 1880 census]; Joseph, age 25, a native of Indiana; Homer, age 19, a native of California; and Walter D., age 10, a native of Washington. This same document states that Joseph and Elizabeth Jones immigrated to the United States in 1874.

**ADDITIONAL GRAVESITE INFORMATION:**
This small marble stone is concreted to a chipped granite base. The gravestone says "Son of Joseph H. and Elizabeth Jones, Nortonville." It is not certain if this stone is sitting in its original location.

**REFERENCES:** 1, 2, 3, 6, 8 (Nov. 16, 1878), 11 (P610.31.185 and P610.285.4), 12, 14

---

### DIED.

BOWEN—At St. Mary's Hospital, San Francisco, Nov. 11th, Nathan S. Bowen, of Martinez, aged 55 years.

The remains were brought to this place for interment, and the funeral services were conducted by the Masonic Fraternity, of which he was an honored member. A devoted husband, kind and indulgent parent and good citizen, has gone to his rest. To his afflicted family the loss falls with crushing force, and a large circle of friends who knew and appreciated his uprightness and integrity of character, deeply sympathise with them in their bereavement.

COLLINS—In Pacheco, November 14th, W. W. Collins, of Clayton, a native of Manchester, England, aged 67 years.

JONES—In Nortonville, November 10th, Thomas, youngest son of Joseph and Elizabeth Jones, aged 1 year and 3 months.

Thomas Jones is listed as the last entry in this obituary from the *Contra Costa Gazette* newspaper, November 16, 1878.

# JONES,
## Thomas M.

## PERSONAL INFORMATION:

| | |
|---|---|
| SEX: | Male |
| DATE OF BIRTH: | February 17, 1838 |
| DATE OF DEATH: | March 19, 1896 |
| PLACE OF DEATH: | Somersville, Contra Costa County, California |
| AGE AT DEATH: | 58 years, 1 month, 2 days |
| CAUSE OF DEATH: | Pneumonia or black lung |
| BIRTHPLACE: | Wales |
| SPOUSE: | Annie (Jones) Jones |
| PARENTS: | |

## GRAVESITE INFORMATION:

| | |
|---|---|
| LOCATION OF GRAVESITE: | Section N-E, Plot #70 |
| GRAVESTONE: | Exists |
| TYPE OF GRAVESTONE: | Polished granite |
| SHAPE OF GRAVESTONE: | Block |
| INSCRIPTION: | |
| EPITAPH: | |
| MOTIF: | |
| CARVER: | |
| BASE: | Exists |
| TYPE OF BASE: | Concrete |
| ENCLOSURE: | |
| TYPE OF ENCLOSURE: | |
| FENCE: | |
| TYPE OF FENCE: | |
| FENCE MOTIF: | |

# JONES, Thomas M.

**ADDITIONAL PERSONAL INFORMATION:**
Thomas' birth date was calculated by www.timeanddate.com, based on his date of death and age at death.

The *1880 Census for Sommersville* [sic], *Contra Costa County, California* lists Thomas Jones, age 41, a native of Wales, and his wife Annie, age 28, a native of Pennsylvania. Also listed are their children: Etta, age 5; Albert, age 3; and George, age 3 months; all are natives of California.

The *1890 Great Register of Voters in Contra Costa County, California* records Thomas M. Jones, age 31, as a native of Wales and resident of Somersville. His occupation is listed as miner. This record also lists his date of registration as July 24, 1869.

*The Great Register of Contra Costa County, California, 1894*, page 25, lists Thomas M. Jones age 54, 5' 5" tall, fair complexion, blue eyes, and brown hair. He was a miner and native of Wales residing in West Hartley, Contra Costa County, California. He was naturalized July 24, 1869.

The *Contra Costa Gazette* newspaper, March 28, 1896, lists Thos. M. Jones' age at death as 58 years, 1 month, and 21 days, and not 58 years, 1 month, and 2 days as listed on his gravestone.

Thomas' wife, Annie, was the daughter of John Philpot and Margaret Jones. When Annie was 2 years old, the family left Pennsylvania and arrived in Nevada County, California, where her father worked as a hard rock miner. Annie and her two sisters, Libby and Mary (Mayme), were raised in Nevada County. The family eventually moved to Contra Costa County, settling in Somersville, circa 1870. Annie Jones married Thomas M. Jones in Somersville. Their six children [a seventh child, George, born *circa* 1877, is listed in the 1880 census] were born in Somersville including three buried in Rose Hill Cemetery: George T., Henry, and John Jones.

According to the *Index to Marriage Certificates* located at the Contra Costa County Hall of Records, Martinez, California, Thomas M. Jones married Ann Jones on May 25, 1868. They were married by Rev. John J. Powell and the information is listed in Volume 1, page 128.

According to a descendant of Thomas M. Jones who attended a former resident's picnic in October 1980, George and Albert T. (Bert) Jones were the sons of Thomas. At age 16, George dug his father's grave. The family *Bible* lists three of Thomas' children buried near him: John, born 1869, died 1869; Henry, born 1870, died 1870; and George T., born 1871, died 1876. The inscription states that they died of either typhoid or diphtheria. According to *the Black Diamond Oral History – Mayme (Joers) Jones and Margaret (Jones) Gunnell, January 27, 1981*, page 4, Annie Jones married Thomas "Tommy" Jones in Somersville, Contra Costa County, California.

See George Thomas Jones, Henry Jones, and John Jones.

**ADDITIONAL GRAVESITE INFORMATION:**
An iron pipe sticks out of the ground just north of the gravesite and might be the remains of a fence. According to a descendant, the existing gravestone was probably placed in the cemetery in the 1920s. Prior to that time, nothing existed at the site.

**REFERENCES:** 1, 2, 3, 5, 6, 8 (March 28, 1896), 11 (P610.31.148 and P610.119.35), 12, 14, *Black Diamond Oral History – Mayme (Joers) Jones and Margaret (Jones) Gunnell*, Jan. 27, 1981, by Karana Hattersley-Drayton, pages 2, 4, 7, and 34, see newspaper appendix page 726

# JONES,
## Thomas S.

## PERSONAL INFORMATION:

SEX: Male

DATE OF BIRTH: 1830

DATE OF DEATH: January 5, 1875

PLACE OF DEATH: Somersville or Briones Valley, Contra Costa County, California

AGE AT DEATH: 45 years

CAUSE OF DEATH:

BIRTHPLACE: Aberdare, Glamorganshire, South Wales

SPOUSE: Mary (Botting) Jones

PARENTS:

## GRAVESITE INFORMATION:

LOCATION OF GRAVESITE: Section N-E, Plot #69

GRAVESTONE: Exists

TYPE OF GRAVESTONE: Marble

SHAPE OF GRAVESTONE: Tablet

INSCRIPTION: *Also two infant children.*/Middle base says *JONES*

EPITAPH: *Though lost to sight to memory dear.*

MOTIF: Masonic & Odd Fellows emblems/rope with tassels

CARVER: Excelsior Marble Works, San Jose, California

BASE: Exists

TYPE OF BASE: Sandstone with middle marble base

ENCLOSURE:

TYPE OF ENCLOSURE:

FENCE:

TYPE OF FENCE:

FENCE MOTIF:

# JONES, Thomas S.

**ADDITIONAL PERSONAL INFORMATION:**
According to information obtained from a descendant, Thomas Samuel and Mary (Botting) Jones were from Aberdare, Glamorganshire, South Wales. Mary was the daughter of a mine owner. They married in Wales *circa* 1850 and then traveled to the United States, settling with relatives in Missouri. While there, Thomas joined the Masonic Lodge. When they left Missouri they sailed around Cape Horn to San Francisco. Upon arrival they traveled to and settled in the town of Port Wine, Sierra County, California where Thomas' aunt and family were living. Thomas worked in the gold mines as a blacksmith until 1866 when the family moved to Nortonville. Thomas became master of the Masonic Lodge while living in Nortonville, and was serving as chaplain at the time of his death in 1873. Descendants state that Thomas died suddenly on the ranch they had bought near Brentwood, Contra Costa County, California. Thomas and Mary had eight children, five of whom died at a young age. One baby died in Missouri and another was born prematurely while on the ship traveling to California. A girl and two boys died during a diphtheria epidemic in Nortonville. Surviving children were: William D. Jones, born 1862 in Port Wine, Sierra County, California, died 1913; Elizabeth Jones, born July 9, 1864 in Port Wine, Sierra County, died 1943; Paul Jones, born 1870 in Nortonville, Contra Costa County, died 1899.

The *1870 Census for Township 3, Contra Costa County, California* lists Thomas Jones, age 40, as a miner and a native of England. Also listed are his wife, Mary, age 39, a native of England, and their children: William, age 8; and Lizzie, age 6; both natives of California. According to descendants, Thomas was either a miner or a blacksmith who created tools for the miners. Family records for Thomas S. Jones indicate his birth as 1825 and death as 1873. Thomas' wife, Mary, was forty-four when Thomas died. Also surviving at the time of his death were his children: William D., age 12; Elizabeth, age 10; and Paul, age 3. According to

the *History of Contra Costa County*, W. A. Slocum and Company, San Francisco, 1882, page 477, Thomas was a charter member of the Mount Diablo No. 128 Independent Order of Odd Fellows (I.O.O.F.) in Somersville, Contra Costa County, California. According to the *Contra Costa Gazette* newspaper, January 9, 1875, Thomas was also an active member in good standing of the Masons and Working Men's Association. Contra Costa County probate records show that at the time of his death he owned land, a house, barn, and cattle. James Dainty bought the property in August 1882 after Thomas' death. According to the *Contra Costa Gazette* newspaper, January 19, 1875, Thomas died in Briones Valley in east Contra Costa County. The *Antioch Ledger* and *Contra Costa Gazette* newspapers, both dated January 9, 1875, state that he died in Somersville. The *Contra Costa Gazette* states he died at age 44 years, 11 months, and 5 days.

**ADDITIONAL GRAVESITE INFORMATION:**
Zelma Myrick, who recorded information about Rose Hill Cemetery in a notebook in the 1930s, reported the "Stone down." A photograph of the gravestone appears in *The Bear Facts*, "Nortonville and Somersville Ghost Coal Mining Towns," February 1947, page 6, published by the Dow Chemical Company, Pittsburg, Contra Costa County, California. Thomas shares a gravestone with two infant children. The stone was concreted flat to the ground prior to East Bay Regional Park District acquisition. A small piece of the lower left corner of the gravestone is missing. The carver was probably Excelsior Marble Works of San Jose, California, but the stone is broken in this spot. The marble base for this stone was found and the stone was returned to the cemetery and placed in its base by Black Diamond Rangers in May 2001.

**REFERENCES:** 1, 2, 3, 5, 6, 8 (Jan. 9, 1875, January 19, 1875), 9 (Jan. 9, 1875- two articles, Jan. 16, 1875), 10 (page 477), 11 (P610.31.147, P610.119.33, P610.119.34, P610.168.22, P610.263.3, P610.317.10, and P610.317.15), 12, 13, 14, see newspaper appendix pages 727 and 728

# LEAM,
## Margaret

## PERSONAL INFORMATION:

| | |
|---|---|
| SEX: | Female |
| DATE OF BIRTH: | December 25, 1836 |
| DATE OF DEATH: | October 3, 1884 |
| PLACE OF DEATH: | Stewartville, Contra Costa County, California |
| AGE AT DEATH: | 47 years, 9 months, 8 days |
| CAUSE OF DEATH: | Pneumonia |
| BIRTHPLACE: | Pennsylvania |
| SPOUSE: | Robert Leam |
| PARENTS: | Mr. and Mrs. Richardson |

## GRAVESITE INFORMATION:

| | |
|---|---|
| LOCATION OF GRAVESITE: | Section S-E, Plot #91 |
| GRAVESTONE: | Exists |
| TYPE OF GRAVESTONE: | Marble |
| SHAPE OF GRAVESTONE: | Tablet |
| INSCRIPTION: | *Sacred to the Memory of/Wife of/who departed this life* |
| EPITAPH: | *We will not mourn,* |
| | *For her tasks are done,* |
| | *Her trials are ended,* |
| | *And Glory won.* |
| MOTIF: | Weeping willow tree |
| CARVER: | W. H. McCormick, San Francisco |
| BASE: | Exists |
| TYPE OF BASE: | Sandstone |
| ENCLOSURE: | |
| TYPE OF ENCLOSURE: | |
| FENCE: | |
| TYPE OF FENCE: | |
| FENCE MOTIF: | |

# LEAM, Margaret

**ADDITIONAL PERSONAL INFORMATION:**
Margaret's date of birth was calculated by using www.timeanddate.com, based on the date of death and age of death provided on her gravestone.

According to information obtained from www.ancestry.com, Margaret's date of birth was December 27, 1836.

Margaret Leam may have been a midwife in Somersville. Former Somersville resident, Gertrude (Anderson) Young, talked about an Auntie Leam who was a midwife in Somersville (*Oral History Interview With Gertrude Anderson Young*, February 5, 1979, by Traci Gibbons and John Waters, page 8). It is unknown if this is the same person that Gertrude is referring to, or a relative of Margaret Leam. [Note: Since Margaret Leam died in 1884, the year before Gertrude was born, and Gertrude didn't move to Somersville until 1890, it is unlikely that this is the Auntie Leam that Gertrude refers to.]

In the document *Trip of Louis Stein and D. F. Myrick to Stewartville, June 24, 1967*, located in the Black Diamond archives, it states "Mrs. Leam lived across the way from the store in Stewartville."

According to family history documents provided by Margaret's descendants, her maiden name was Richardson.

See May Leam and Robert Leam.

**ADDITIONAL GRAVESITE INFORMATION:**
Margaret shares a gravestone with daughter, May Leam. The gravestone was broken into four pieces and concreted flat to the ground prior to East Bay Regional Park District acquisition.

The upper half of a footstone with the initials "M. L." was found by Black Diamond Rangers in the lower north corner of the cemetery *circa* 2000 and may be the footstone for Margaret or May Leam.

The gravestone was removed from the cemetery for repairs in July 2001. A marble encasement was added to strengthen the original gravestone. The repaired stone was returned to the cemetery in October 2008.

**REFERENCES:** 1, 2, 3, 6, 8 (Oct. 18, 1884), 9 (Nov. 6, 1875 and Oct. 4, 1884), 11 (P610.31.142, P610.119.56, P610.168.21, and P610.235.1), 12, 14, see newspaper appendix page 729 and (Maggie Buxton) page 685

Reference 235.1

Margaret and Robert Leam, date unknown.

**BURGLARS ABOUT.**—Contra Costa seems at present to be inflicted with a band of peregrinating burglars. On Wednesday night of last week they entered both the Clayton hotels carrying off the money drawer from one containing nearly three hundred dollars. From Clayton they proceeded to Nortonville where they entered the saloon of Robert Leam, but finding no coin, consoled themselves by a gin cocktail. They next attempted a raid upon the Brick store of Dodge & Co, removed three tier of brick when they were disturbed by passing miners and skedadled. On the following night, Friday, they burglarized the gunsmith shop of S. P. Page at this place, leaving him no portion of his tools. He is also minus a shot gun and several other articles in his keeping for repairs. Page estimates his loss at one hundred dollars. Constable Chapman, of Clayton, was in town Staturday seeking the whereabouts of the robbers, but returned without learning aught that would lead to discovery. A crowd of six genuine looking hoodlums, men grown, have been lurking about town for a few days past, arousing the suspicion of our business men somewhat; yet it is not known they are in anywise connected with the burglars above mentioned. A night watchman to guard the town during the winter months is in order.

This November 6, 1875, *Antioch Ledger* newspaper article states that burglars entered Robert Leam's saloon in Nortonville, "but finding no coin, consoled themselves by a gin cocktail."

# LEAM,
## May

**PERSONAL INFORMATION:**

| | |
|---|---|
| SEX: | Female |
| DATE OF BIRTH: | May 4, 1860 |
| DATE OF DEATH: | September 7, 1870 |
| PLACE OF DEATH: | Stewartville, Contra Costa County, California |
| AGE AT DEATH: | 10 years, 4 months, 4 days |
| CAUSE OF DEATH: | |
| BIRTHPLACE: | Pennsylvania |
| SPOUSE: | None |
| PARENTS: | Robert and Margaret (Richardson) Leam |

**GRAVESITE INFORMATION:**

| | |
|---|---|
| LOCATION OF GRAVESITE: | Section S-E, Plot #91 |
| GRAVESTONE: | Exists |
| TYPE OF GRAVESTONE: | Marble |
| SHAPE OF GRAVESTONE: | Tablet |
| INSCRIPTION: | *Sacred to the Memory of/daughter of /who departed this life* |
| EPITAPH: | *We will not mourn,* |
| | *For her tasks are done,* |
| | *Her trials are ended,* |
| | *And Glory won.* |
| MOTIF: | Weeping willow tree |
| CARVER: | W. H. McCormick, San Francisco, California |
| BASE: | Exists |
| TYPE OF BASE: | Sandstone |
| ENCLOSURE: | |
| TYPE OF ENCLOSURE: | |
| FENCE: | |
| TYPE OF FENCE: | |
| FENCE MOTIF: | |

East Bay Regional Park District

# LEAM, May

**ADDITIONAL PERSONAL INFORMATION:**
In family history documents provided by descendants, her name is listed as Mary and not May as stated on her gravestone. She is also listed as Mary in the *1870 Census for Township Three, Contra Costa County, California.*

May was the third child born in the Leam family. She had seven siblings. May's birth date and place of birth comes from family history documents provided by descendants. According to www. timeanddate.com, May's birth date would have been May 3, 1860, based on the date of death and age of death provided by the gravestone.

The *1870 Census for Township Three, Contra Costa County, California,* lists May's father, Robert Leam, age 35, as a miner and native of England. The census also listed May, her mother, and her siblings: Margaret, age 24, a native of Pennsylvania: Rebecca, age 13, a native of Pennsylvania; Annie, age 12, a native of New Jersey; Mary, age 10, a native of Pennsylvania; John, age 2; and Henry, age 1; both natives of California.

The *1880 Census for Township 5, Judsonville, Contra Costa County, California* lists Robert Leam, age 45, a miner and native of England; his wife, Margaret, age 44, a native of Pennsylvania, and their children Annie, age 21, a native of New Jersey; John, age 13; Henry, age 11; Margaret, age 8; Robert, age 6; and Violet, age 3; all are natives of California.

In the *1900 Federal Census for Tesla, Alameda County, California,* Robert's wife, Mary A., is listed along with her children: Jacob D., age 21; Joseph J., age 19; and Ethel M., age 9. Apparently Robert remarried after the death of his first wife, Margaret. See Margaret Leam and Robert Leam.

**ADDITIONAL GRAVESITE INFORMATION:**
May shares a gravestone with her mother, Margaret Leam. May died before her mother.

**REFERENCES:** 1, 2, 3, 4, 6, 9 (Nov. 6, 1875), 11 (P610.31.142, P610.119.56, and P610.168.21), 12, 14

Reference 31.142

The Margaret and May Leam gravestone before repair, July 1977.
Photograph by Traci (Gibbons) Parent.

## PERSONAL INFORMATION:

| | |
|---|---|
| SEX: | Male |
| DATE OF BIRTH: | May 1, 1836 |
| DATE OF DEATH: | February 27, 1900 |
| PLACE OF DEATH: | Tesla, Alameda County, California |
| AGE AT DEATH: | 63 years, 9 months, 26 days |
| CAUSE OF DEATH: | Cancer/complications from pneumonia |
| BIRTHPLACE: | Manchester, Lancashire, England |
| SPOUSE: | Margaret (Richardson) Leam (1st wife); Mary A. Leam (2nd wife) |
| PARENTS: | Robert and Rebecca Leam |

## GRAVESITE INFORMATION:

| | |
|---|---|
| LOCATION OF GRAVESITE: | Believed to be in Section S-E, near Plot #91 |
| GRAVESTONE: | Missing or never placed |
| TYPE OF GRAVESTONE: | |
| SHAPE OF GRAVESTONE: | |
| INSCRIPTION: | |
| EPITAPH: | |
| MOTIF: | |
| CARVER: | |
| BASE: | |
| TYPE OF BASE: | |
| ENCLOSURE: | |
| TYPE OF ENCLOSURE: | |
| FENCE: | |
| TYPE OF FENCE: | |
| FENCE MOTIF: | |

# LEAM, Robert

**ADDITIONAL PERSONAL INFORMATION:**
Robert was the second of five children in his family. His siblings included: Anthony, born 1833; Henry or Harry, born 1839; Martha, born 1841; and Thomas, born 1844.

Robert's date of birth comes from his obituary in the *Livermore Echo* newspaper, March 1, 1900. According to the newspaper article, Robert came to California in 1862 and settled in Somersville where he became the superintendent of the Pittsburg Mine. Later, he was employed in mines in Amador and Alameda counties. The article reports that he ran the Cosmopolitan Hotel in Livermore and during the two years prior to his death he resided in Tesla, Alameda County, California. At the time of his death he left a wife, five daughters, and three sons. Robert was a member of the Odd Fellows order for 30 years. The article states that, "His remains were shipped by the 1-o'clock train Wednesday to Summerville [sic], Contra Costa County for interment." Robert died in Tesla in February 1900 at age 64 years, but was interred in Rose Hill Cemetery.

On May 28, 1874, Robert Leam served as a witness to the marriage of his daughter. George Thomas, age 28, a native of Cornwall, England and resident of Nortonville married Rebecca Leam, age 17, a native of Porterville, Tulare County, California and resident of Nortonville. [Note: The *1870 Census* states she was a native of Pennsylvania.] The other witness was David Richards of Nortonville. William Parry served as the minister. According to the *Antioch Ledger* newspaper, November 6, 1875, Robert Leam operated a saloon in Nortonville, Contra Costa County, California.

Information obtained by Robert's descendants, census records 1870-1900, and other documents from www.ancestry.com, record at least eight children in the Leam family:

- Rebecca—born Aug. 2, 1856 in Pennsylvania and died Nov. 4, 1943 in Sacramento, Sacramento County, California; married George Thomas on May 23, 1874

- Annie Hannah Elizabeth—born Sept. 24, 1858 in Jefferson Twp., Passaic County, New Jersey and died April 16, 1923 in Sacramento, Sacramento County, California; married Robert McLay on June 1, 1885

- May—born May 4, 1860 in Pennsylvania and died Sept. 7, 1870 in Nortonville, Contra Costa County, California; buried in Rose Hill Cemetery

- John W.— born Dec. 1866 in California; married Louise in 1896

- Harry (Henry)—born 1869 in California; married Gwennie Jones

- Margaret—born 1872 in California

- Robert—born April 5, 1874 in California; married Mildred May Wise in 1902 in California

- Violet—born Oct. 1876 in California

**ADDITIONAL GRAVESITE INFORMATION:**
It is presumed that Robert Leam was interred next to his daughter May and first wife Margaret. It is uncertain if a gravestone was ever placed in the cemetery for Robert. See Margaret Leam and May Leam.

**REFERENCES:** 8 (March 5, 1881, March 3, 1900, and March 10, 1900), 9 (Nov. 6, 1875, Jan. 5, 1901, March 3, 1900 - two articles), *The Livermore Herald* newspaper (Feb. 24, 1900 and March 3, 1900 - two articles), Livermore *Echo* newspaper (March 1, 1900), 12, see newspaper appendix pages 730-732

After four mouths' illness suffering from pneumonia and cancer of the stomach, Robert Leam, one of the pioneers of the State, died at Tesla on Tuesday, at the age of over 63 years. Deceased was a native of Manchester, England, where he was born May 1, 1836. He came to California in 1852 and settled at Summerville in 1862, where he became superintendent of the Pittsburg Mine. He was afterwards employed in mines in Amador and Alameda counties. For several years he ran the Cosmopolitan Hotel, in this place, which has since been destroyed by fire; but for the past two years he has resided at Tesla. Deceased leaves a wife, five daughters, and three sons to mourn his loss. He has been a member of the Odd Fellows' order for 30 years. His remains were shipped by the 1-o'clock train Wednesday to Summerville, Contra Costa county, for interment.

This newspaper article, from the *Livermore Echo*, March 1, 1900, states that Robert Leam died at Tesla, Alameda County, California.

Pictured below is the community of Tesla *circa* 1910 facing northwest. Tesla Plaza, with the bandstand, flagpole, and various shops can be seen left of center in the photograph. The managers, engineers, and foremen lived in the string of homes called "Treadwell Row." Jimtown can be seen on the far left against the hill. According to *The Livermore Hearld* newspaper, March 3, 1900, Robert Leam died in Jimtown. Mount Carmel Catholic Church is situated on the hill on the far right. The mine office (far right), hospital (center) and general store sit just below the church. The two-story bunkhouses for singe men are seen along the bottom right of the photograph.

Reference 233.2

Pictured on the right is Robert Leam's daughter, Annie Hannah E. (Leam) McLay and her husband Robert McLay. Annie was one of eight children in the Leam family. According to the *Contra Costa Gazette* newspaper, June 6, 1885, Annie Leam of Stewartville, California and Robert McLay, a native of British Columbia, Canada, were married on June 1, 1885 in Martinez, Contra Costa County, California by Rev. W. H. Tubb.

Robert was born April 3, 1859 and died December 5, 1940 in Sacramento, Sacramento County, California. Annie was born in New Jersey on September 24, 1858, and died April 16, 1923 in Sacramento, California.

Reference 235.2

HAZARDOUS SERVICE:—We take the following from the Antioch *Ledger* of last Saturday :

The Empire coal company have had considerable difficulty in expelling the surplus water from the mine. The steam pipes connect with the pump, still under water below and by reason of a leak in the elbow the water in the sump about two feet in depth, was heated almost to the degree of boiling. A few days ago a small skiff was taken into the mine and Robert Leam rowed over the scalding water and through the steam to a point near the pump. He soon discovered that to longer inhale the steam would be fatal. To manage a boat in the narrow passage was difficult, and realizing that his life depended on instant action, he leaped into the hot water and walked to the bottom of the slope, a distance of one hundred feet. He was taken out of the mine nearly insensible. Both legs were badly scalded to a point half way from the knee to the hip. Doctor Wemple was called, the limbs were dressed and the Doctor informs us that his patient will be out again in a couple of weeks. It was a narrow escape from death. Mr. Leam has for many years been engaged in coal mining and has had several narrow escapes.

This newspaper article, from the *Contra Costa Gazette*, March 5, 1881, discusses an incident Robert Leam had with scalding water in a Mount Diablo Coal Field mine operated by the Empire Coal Mining Company.

# LEWIS,
## David John

## PERSONAL INFORMATION:

| | |
|---|---|
| SEX: | Male |
| DATE OF BIRTH: | *Circa* 1877 |
| DATE OF DEATH: | *Circa* 1881 |
| PLACE OF DEATH: | |
| AGE AT DEATH: | 4 years |
| CAUSE OF DEATH: | Diphtheria |
| BIRTHPLACE: | |
| SPOUSE: | None |
| PARENTS: | William D. and Mary (Bowen) Lewis |

## GRAVESITE INFORMATION:

| | |
|---|---|
| LOCATION OF GRAVESITE: | Unknown |
| GRAVESTONE: | Missing or never placed |
| TYPE OF GRAVESTONE: | |
| SHAPE OF GRAVESTONE: | |
| INSCRIPTION: | |
| EPITAPH: | |
| MOTIF: | |
| CARVER: | |
| BASE: | |
| TYPE OF BASE: | |
| ENCLOSURE: | |
| TYPE OF ENCLOSURE: | |
| FENCE: | |
| TYPE OF FENCE | |
| FENCE MOTIF: | |

East Bay Regional Park District

# LEWIS, David John

**ADDITIONAL PERSONAL INFORMATION:**
David John's death age comes from the *History of Contra Costa County with Biographical Sketches*, page 551. This same source lists the children of William D. and Mary Lewis:

- Elizabeth (Mrs. George Bloching), born in Wales

- Phoebe (Mrs. F. N. Myrick), born in Wales

- Martha, born in Missouri [this Martha died at 17 months]

- Seth, born in Missouri

- a second Martha (Mrs. Rumgay)

- Margaret (Mrs. Llewellyn)

- Edith (Mrs. Costello)

- William C.

The family moved from Concord to Black Diamond, King County, Washington in 1880 where William worked as a coal miner until his retirement.

Passport information obtained from www.ancestry.com, states that William D. Lewis was born on June 10, 1840. He emigrated to the United States sailing on board the Steamship *Palmyra* from Wales about March 1, 1869. The document also states that he had resided 51 years uninterruptedly in the U. S. from 1869 to 1902 in Pennsylvania, Missouri, California, and Black Diamond, Washington. He was naturalized as a U. S. citizen on July 1, 1880. His occupation was listed as coal miner. He sailed from New York on board the Steamship *Muretania* on April 17, 1920. The "object of visit" of his three month trip was to "visit near relatives enroute."

After his wife died on september 8, 1925, William went to live with his daughter, Phoebe (Lewis) Myrick, in Clayton, Contra Costa County, California (near Concord) where he passed away. The death certificate for William D. Lewis states he was born June 10, 1840 in Fishgard [sic], Wales and died on December 30, 1931 at 91 years, 6 months, and 20 days. According to the *Standard Certificate of Death*, his cause of death was Broncho [sic] Pneumonia.

He was listed as a retired miner and length of residence at place of death, near Clayton, Contra Costa County, California as 5 years, and 57 years in California. According to descendants, William D. Lewis was a charter member of the Independent Order of Odd Fellows in Missouri, being a 75-year member at the time of his death.

William D. was buried next to his wife in Enumclaw, King County, Washington. See Seth John Lewis.

**ADDITIONAL GRAVESITE INFORMATION:**
According to descendants, David John Lewis, and his brother, Seth John Lewis, are buried in Rose Hill Cemetery. No other source documents their burial there.

**REFERENCES:** 11 (P610.82.1, P610.176.1, and P610.260.21), 12, *History of Contra Costa County with Biographical Sketches*, Historic Record Company, Los Angeles, 1926, pages 548 and 551, *Live Oak Cemetery Association Records, Concord, Contra Costa County, California* compiled by Charmetta Mann, 2009

William D. and Mary (Bowen) Lewis, natives of Fishguard, Wales and
parents of David John Lewis and Seth John Lewis, date unknown.

Reference 82.1

Reference 176.2

Left: Elizabeth Ann (Lewis) Bloching and George Bloching (sister and brother-in-law of David John and Seth John Lewis), standing beside William D. Lewis, father of Elizabeth. Right: Elizabeth Ann (Lewis) Bloching was born February 6, 1867 in Wales and died April 27, 1897 in Clayton, Contra Costa County, California at age 30 years, 2 months, and 21 days. Her husband, George Bloching, was born April 12, 1851 in Wurttemberg, Germany and died June 3, 1927 in Martinez, Contra Costa County, California. Elizabeth Ann and George are buried in Live Oak Cemetery, Concord, Contra Costa County, California. George purchased the burial plot there in April 1897.

**PERSONAL IN FORMATION:**

| | |
|---|---|
| SEX: | Male |
| DATE OF BIRTH: | 1838 |
| DATE OF DEATH: | July 24, 1876 |
| PLACE OF DEATH: | Nortonville, Contra Costa County, California |
| AGE AT DEATH: | 38 years |
| CAUSE OF DEATH: | Suffocation from mine explosion |
| BIRTHPLACE: | Wales |
| SPOUSE: | Elizabeth Lewis |
| PARENTS: | |

**GRAVESITE INFORMATION:**

| | |
|---|---|
| LOCATION OF GRAVESITE: | Unknown |
| GRAVESTONE: | Missing or never placed |
| TYPE OF GRAVESTONE: | |
| SHAPE OF GRAVESTONE: | |
| INSCRIPTION: | |
| EPITAPH: | |
| MOTIF: | |
| CARVER: | |
| BASE: | |
| TYPE OF BASE: | |
| ENCLOSURE: | |
| TYPE OF ENCLOSURE: | |
| FENCE: | |
| TYPE OF FENCE | |
| FENCE MOTIF: | |

# LEWIS, Meredith

**ADDITIONAL PERSONAL INFORMATION:**
*The 1871-72 Contra Costa County Directory*, page 350, lists M. Lewis, as a miner residing in Nortonville.

The *Contra Costa Gazette* newspaper, July 29, 1876, states that Meredith Lewis and seven others died as a result of an explosion which occurred at a mine in Nortonville on July 24, 1876. He left behind a wife and five children. The *Antioch Ledger* newspaper of July 29, 1876 says Meredith left behind a wife and seven children.

According to a descendant of Meredith Lewis, there were six daughters in the family: Margaret, Jane, and Annie, born in Wales; Emma, Sarah, and Maud, born in California. Meredith's wife, Elizabeth, would have been pregnant with Maud when Meredith was killed. Meredith Lewis was interred in Rose Hill Cemetery by the Cambrian Mutual Aid Society, of which he was a member.

*The Move of Coal Miners from Nortonville, California to Black Diamond, Washington Territory, 1885*, a senior honor thesis compiled by Jacqueline Byer Dial, June 1980, page 82, lists Elizabeth Lewis, age 48, birthplace Wales. She was recorded as living in California in 1880 and in Washington Territory in 1887. Listed with her are her children: Annie, age 20, a native of Wales; Sarah, age 13, a native of California; and Maud, age 10, a native of California.

The *1900 Census for Black Diamond, King County, Washington* lists Elizabeth Lewis, age 60, as a native of Wales. Also listed with her are her son-in-law, Samuel Boxill, age 34, a native of California; her daughter, Annie Boxill, age 32, a native of Wales; and their children Loran, age 9, and Lizzie M., age 6; both natives of Washington.

See Theophile Dumas, William Gething, Thomas D. James, George M. Reynolds, Evan Smith, David Watts, Theophilus Watts, and William L. Williams.

**ADDITIONAL GRAVESITE INFORMATION:**
The *Contra Costa Gazette* newspaper, July 29, 1876 and the *History of Contra Costa County*, by Slocum and Company, 1882, page 474, are the only sources that indicate Meredith Lewis is buried in Rose Hill Cemetery. His name was not recorded on any previous cemetery lists.

**REFERENCES:** 8 (July 29, 1876 and Aug. 12, 1876), 9 (July 29, 1876), 10 (page 474), 12, *History of Contra Costa County, California*, W. A. Slocum and Co., San Francisco, 1882, page 474, see newspaper appendix (William Gething) pages 706 and 707

## PERSONAL INFORMATION:

| | |
|---|---|
| SEX: | Male |
| DATE OF BIRTH: | |
| DATE OF DEATH: | |
| PLACE OF DEATH: | |
| AGE AT DEATH: | Infant |
| CAUSE OF DEATH: | Diphtheria |
| BIRTHPLACE: | Missouri |
| SPOUSE: | None |
| PARENTS: | William D. and Mary (Bowen) Lewis |

## GRAVESITE INFORMATION:

| | |
|---|---|
| LOCATION OF GRAVESITE: | Unknown |
| GRAVESTONE: | Missing or never placed |
| TYPE OF GRAVESTONE: | |
| SHAPE OF GRAVESTONE: | |
| INSCRIPTION: | |
| EPITAPH: | |
| MOTIF: | |
| CARVER: | |
| BASE: | |
| TYPE OF BASE: | |
| ENCLOSURE: | |
| TYPE OF ENCLOSURE: | |
| FENCE: | |
| TYPE OF FENCE: | |
| FENCE MOTIF: | |

# LEWIS, Seth John

**ADDITIONAL PERSONAL INFORMATION:**
The source for Seth John's birthplace comes from *History of Contra Costa County with Biographical Sketches*, pages 548 and 551.

The *1870 Census for Bevier, Macon County, Missouri* lists Wm. D. Lewis, a native of Wales, age 29, born *circa* 1841; his occupation is mining coal. Also listed are Mary Lewis, age 25, born *circa* 1845, a native of Wales and their daughters: Elizabeth, age 4, born *circa* 1866, and Phebe [sic], age 1, born *circa* 1869; both were born in Wales. Living with them is Wm. Howard, a native of Wales, age 30. His occupation is listed as "diging [sic] coal."

In the *Contra Costa County Directory, 1871-2*, Wm. Lewis is listed as a miner in Nortonville.

The *1880 Census for Nortonville, Contra Costa County, California*, lists William Lewis, age 39, as a miner from Wales. Also listed are his wife, Mary, age 36, a native of Wales and their children: Elizabeth, age 13; Phoebe, age 11; both natives of Wales; Martha, age 5; David, age 3; and Margaret, age 1; natives of California.

The *1900 Census for Concord, Contra Costa County, California*, lists Mary B. Lewis, age 56, born May 1844 in Wales. She is listed as married and also the Head of the house. The census states she was married in 1866 and is the mother of nine children; four are living. Her year of immigration was 1862. Also listed are her married daughter, Eddith Downer, age 17; and her husband, Leonard B. Downer, age 23, and their daughter, Eddith Downer, age 1. Mary's son, William Lewis, age 14, and granddaughter Martha Blocking [sic - Bloching], age 7, are recorded as well. Martha Bloching was the daughter of Elizabeth (Lewis) and George Bloching.

The *1920 Census for Black Diamond, King County, Washington* lists William D. Lewis, age 80, as a native of Wales. His year of immigration is listed as 1869. Also listed is his wife Mary D. Lewis, age 74, a native of Wales.

See David John Lewis.

**ADDITIONAL GRAVESITE INFORMATION:**
According to descendants, Seth John Lewis and his brother, David John Lewis, are buried in Rose Hill Cemetery. No other source documents their burial there.

**REFERENCES:** 11 (P610.82.1, P610.176.1, and P610.260.21), 12, *History of Contra Costa County with Biographical Sketches*, Historic Record Company, Los Angeles, 1926, pages 548 and 551

## PERSONAL INFORMATION:

SEX: Male

DATE OF BIRTH: August 14, 1835

DATE OF DEATH: March 3, 1877

PLACE OF DEATH:

AGE AT DEATH: 41 years, 6 months, 17 days

CAUSE OF DEATH:

BIRTHPLACE: Scotland

SPOUSE: Margaret "Maude" (Thomas, Mucklow) Love

PARENTS: Mr. and Mrs. Love

## GRAVESITE INFORMATION:

LOCATION OF GRAVESITE: Section N-C, Plot #30

GRAVESTONE: Exists

TYPE OF GRAVESTONE: Marble

SHAPE OF GRAVESTONE: Tablet

INSCRIPTION:

EPITAPH:
*Farewell my wife and my children all.*
*From you a Father Christ doth call.*
*Mourn not for me it is in vain.*
*To call me to your sight again.*

MOTIF: Clasped hands

CARVER:

BASE: Exists

TYPE OF BASE: Sandstone

ENCLOSURE: Exists

TYPE OF ENCLOSURE: Brick

FENCE:

TYPE OF FENCE:

FENCE MOTIF:

# LOVE, John

**ADDITIONAL PERSONAL INFORMATION:**
The date of birth was calculated by www.timeanddate.com, based on his age of death and date of death recorded on his gravestone.

According to the *Index to Marriage Certificates*, located at the Contra Costa County Hall of Records, Martinez, California, John Love married Margaret Lloyd on July 14, 1865. It is not certain if this is the same John Love buried in Rose Hill Cemetery, since the name on the certificate for his wife is Margaret Lloyd and not Margaret Thomas. Additionally, her name from a previous marriage was Mucklow. John Love and Margaret Lloyd were married by Rev. H. R. Avery; the information is recorded in Volume 1, page 91.

The *Assessment List for Contra Costa County, 1872-1873*, lists John Love assessed $130 for improvements in the town of Somersville.

According to family records, John was a stagecoach driver. After his death, his wife, Margaret "Maude," operated a hotel in Somersville. Maude did the cooking in the hotel. In June 1988, descendants donated to the Preserve an iron skillet that was used by Maude for cooking in the hotel. Maude was born in 1825 [according to 1870, 1880, and 1900 census records, she would have been born in 1835] and died in 1913. She is buried in Oak View Memorial Park Cemetery, Antioch, Contra Costa County, California.

According to *History of Contra Costa County, California with Biographical Sketches*, page 506, Margaret (Thomas) Love was a native of Illinois. This source states she passed away in Contra Costa County in 1912. Her obituary in the *Antioch Ledger* newspaper, February 1, 1913, states she passed away January 30, 1913.

John Love came to California in the late 1850s and was "interested with his brother in the cattle business in Inyo County. Later he took up ranching and cattle-raising in the Diablo Valley and on Marsh Creek, where he had valuable holdings."

In the *1870 Census for Township Three, Contra Costa County, California*, John Love, age 36, is listed as a laborer and native of Scotland. Also listed are his wife Margarete [sic], age 35, a native of Scotland and their children, Annie, age 4, and Robert, age 2; both natives of California and Margaret's children from a previous marriage: Mary Mucklow, age 17; Elizabeth, age 13; and Josephine, age 10; all natives of Pennsylvania.

The *1880 Census for Township Five (Judsonville), Contra Costa County, California* lists, Margaret Love, age 45, a native of Scotland and keeper of Boarding House. Her children, Annie L., age 14; Robert, age 12; and sister [sic] Agnes Love, age 9; all natives of California and five boarders (four miners and one carpenter) were also listed.

The *1900 Census for Somersville, Contra Costa County, California* lists Margaret Love, age 65, as a native of Scotland and born January 1835. She is recorded as widowed and living as a boarder with Samuel and Jennie Brown and family.

**ADDITIONAL GRAVESITE INFORMATION:**
The clasped hands motif on the gravestone are carved upside down. It is not known if this was an error or intentionally done by the carver. The gravestone is broken into six pieces, with a portion missing. The stone sits in its sandstone base and was concreted flat to ground prior to East Bay Regional Park District acquisition. A brick enclosure was also placed around the gravesite prior to Park District acquisition.

**REFERENCES:** 1, 2, 3, 4, 6, 11 (P610.119.24), 12, 13, 14, *History of Contra Costa County, California with Biographical Sketches*, Historic Record Company, 1926, page 506

# DEATH OF MRS. LOVE

## Had Been a Resident of the County Over Fifty Years.

Mrs. Margaret Love passed away at her home on Seventh street Thursday afternoon, death being due to a general breaking down in health. she being 88 years of age. Mrs. Love was a noble Christian woman and her many friends will mourn her death.

The deceased was a native of Glasgow, Scotland, but came to the United States when a young woman. Previous to making California her home, which was over fifty years ago, she resided in Pottsville, Pennsylvania, for a number of years. After removing to this state she spent practically all of the time in the coal mining district south of town, where she conducted various hotels successfully. She was well and favorably known to all throughout the eastern part of the county and in addition to being highly respected was considered a good business woman. The last twelve years were spent in Antioch.

Mrs. Love was a devout and faithful member of the Methodist Church, with which denomination she had been affiliated many years.

There are left to mourn one son and two daughters, being Robert Love of this place, Mrs. James Hawkes of Chehallis, Washington and Mrs. Thomas P. Shine of this place.

The funeral arrangements had not been completed last night.

This obituary for John Love's wife, Margaret Love, appeared in the *Antioch Ledger* newspaper, February 1, 1913. According to this article, Margaret died January 30, 1913.

# ROBERT LOVE SUES FOR SHARE OF ESTATE

## CONVEYANCE OF MOTHER'S PROPERTY TO DAUGHTER CAUSES CIVIL ACTION.

Robert Love of Antioch on Wednesday instituted suit against his sister, Mrs. Agnes Shine, wife of Marshal Tom Shine of that place, to have a conveyance of certain property from his mother, the late Mrs. Margaret Love, to her daughter set aside, alleging that the daughter exerted undue influences to have her mother convey her property. Love seeks an order of the court vesting him with a one-htird interest in the property, the other interests going to his sisters, Mrs. Shine and Mrs. Josephine Hawkes.

This *Contra Costa Gazette* newspaper article from February 8, 1913, states that Robert Love (son of John Love), instituted suit against his sister, Agnes Shine, regarding the property of their deceased mother, Margaret Love.

# MACLEOD,
## John

**PERSONAL INFORMATION:**

| | |
|---|---|
| SEX: | Male |
| DATE OF BIRTH: | *Circa* 1873-1874 |
| DATE OF DEATH: | *Circa* 1874 |
| PLACE OF DEATH: | |
| AGE AT DEATH: | 6 months |
| CAUSE OF DEATH: | Scarlet fever |
| BIRTHPLACE: | Somersville, Contra Costa County, California |
| SPOUSE: | None |
| PARENTS: | Edward and Elizabeth MacLeod |

**GRAVESITE INFORMATION:**

| | |
|---|---|
| LOCATION OF GRAVESITE: | Unknown |
| GRAVESTONE: | Missing or never placed |
| TYPE OF GRAVESTONE: | |
| SHAPE OF GRAVESTONE: | |
| INSCRIPTION: | |
| EPITAPH: | |
| MOTIF: | |
| CARVER: | |
| BASE: | |
| TYPE OF BASE: | |
| ENCLOSURE: | |
| TYPE OF ENCLOSURE: | |
| FENCE: | |
| TYPE OF FENCE: | |
| FENCE MOTIF: | |

# MACLEOD, John

**ADDITIONAL PERSONAL INFORMATION:**
The last name has also been spelled McLeod.

According to a descendant, John's father, Edward MacLeod, "was a stationary engineer in the mines at or near Airdrie, Scotland and came to California in 1872." His wife, Elizabeth MacLeod, arrived in Somersville, Contra Costa County, in the summer *circa* 1873 with their three year old son, James, and a six month old daughter, Elizabeth. John was born after the family arrived in Somersville. Another daughter, Winifred, was born in Somersville in June of 1875 or 1876.

The *History of Contra Costa County, California*, page 477, lists Edward McLeod [sic] as a member of Mount Diablo Lodge No. 128, Independent Order of Odd Fellows in Somersville. Edward was also a member of Contra Costa Masonic Lodge No. 227 in Somersville.

The *1880 Census for Sommersville* [sic], *Contra Costa County, California* lists Edward McLeod [sic] age 32, as a native of Scotland. The birthplace for his parents is recorded as Scotland. He was listed as married and his occupation as engineer.

See the *Contra Costa Gazette* newspaper article on page 524 for additional information on a McLeod [sic] family in Somersville.

**ADDITIONAL GRAVESITE INFORMATION:**
According to a descendant, John MacLeod is buried in Rose Hill Cemetery. No other source documents his burial there.

**REFERENCES:** 10 (page 477), 11 (P610.177.1), 12

Edward and Elizabeth MacLeod, parents of John MacLeod, with daughter Winifred, *circa* 1876.

## Nortonville Correspondence.

NORTONVILLE, January 2d. 1875.

EDS. GAZETTE: An abundance of miscellaneous home items has transpired during this and the preceding week, some of which may be deemed worthy of record; but awaiting their notice by some other correspondents who possess a more descriptive talent, I have thus far refrained until patience ceases to be a virtue. Consequently my audacious pen receives fresh impetus to once again encroach on your columns. As the items are somewhat compounded of malicious and benevolent, I may as well repeat them in succession.

Christmas was generally observed here as a holiday, all work in and around the mines were suspended. On the afternoon the modern disciples of Bacchus assembled at the Lava Beds, (a place so anathematized from the frequent eruptions that occur 'twixt the inebriates that rendevouz in that sanctified locality), to perform their sacreligious and profane office of arranging in battle innocent poultry, and rend the air with vociferous yells when the bleeding fowls lay gasping for breath. Their chivalry may be better described in the following satire:

We'll keep our Christmas merry still,
Tho' blood of jaded birds may flow at will;
And dancing 'round the cock-pit vile,
We make such barbarous mirth the while,
As best might to the mind recall·
The boisterous joys of Odin's hall.

The officers of Contra Costa Lodge, No. 227, F. A. M., were duly installed this week by the Grand Worthy State Lecturer, J. W. Schaeffer.' The following are the officers elect: J. W. Rankin, M.; M. Body, S. W.; W. Prutton, J. W.; J. Cox, S. D.; R. Clare, J. D.; S. Brown, Treas.; Messrs. Gambs, Jones and McLoud, Stewards; P. Martin, Tyler. Though young, the Lodge figuratively speaking displays a healthy appearance in finance and members, which may be attributed to its good discipline and rigid scrutiny of character and morals of candidates for initiation. The ex-Master, Mr. J. F. Deomer, who has labored most assiduously for the last year in promoting the interests of the honorable and ancient cause of Masonry, now retires from office, having gained the universal approbation of his fellow-brethren.

ALEET.

In this article from the *Contra Costa Gazette* newspaper, January 2, 1875, Somersville resident, Edward MacLeod (spelled as McLoud above), is listed as one of the Stewards for Contra Costa Masonic Lodge No. 227 in Somersville.

# MADDIN,
## Ella

**PERSONAL INFORMATION:**

| | |
|---|---|
| Sex: | Female |
| Date of Birth: | January 18, 1878 |
| Date of Death: | July 28, 1880 |
| Place of Death: | Nortonville, Contra Costa County, California |
| Age at Death: | 2 years, 6 months, 10 days |
| Cause of Death: | Effects of fire |
| Birthplace: | Oregon |
| Spouse: | None |
| Parents: | Archibald "Archie" and Sarah (Leach) Maddin |

**GRAVESITE INFORMATION:**

| | |
|---|---|
| Location of Gravesite: | Unknown |
| Gravestone: | Missing |
| Type of Gravestone: | |
| Shape of Gravestone: | |
| Inscription: | *Daughter of* |
| Epitaph: | |
| Motif: | |
| Carver: | |
| Base: | |
| Type of Base: | |
| Enclosure: | |
| Type of Enclosure: | |
| Fence: | |
| Type of Fence: | |
| Fence Motif: | |

# MADDIN, Ella

**ADDITIONAL PERSONAL INFORMATION:**
The last name has also been spelled Madden. Ella's cause of death comes from the article titled "Sad Accident" in the *Contra Costa Gazette* newspaper, August 7, 1880.

Ella's parents, Archibald Madden, age 24, of Nortonville, Contra Costa County, California and Sarah Leach, age 17, of Nortonville applied for a marriage license on December 17, 1876. The information was recorded in the *Applications for Marriage Licenses, Contra Costa County, 1873-1887*, page 96, located at the Contra Costa County Historical Society History Center in Martinez, California. According to the *Index to Marriage Certificates*, located in Contra Costa County Hall of Records in Martinez, Archibald Madden married Sarah Leach on December 20, 1876. They were married by Rev. William Parry; the information is recorded in Volume 2, page 149.

The *1880 Census for Nortonville Precinct, Contra Costa County, California*, lists Mrs. Madden, age 21, as a housekeeper and native of California. Also listed are children: Maryann, age 8, a stepdaughter and native of Nova Scotia; Ella, age 2, a native of Oregon; and a son, Archie, age 3 months, a native of California. Her mother, Mrs. Hughes, age 56, a midwife and native of Wales is also living with her. Perhaps her husband died prior to 1880. Ella is listed on the census because it was taken on June 2, 1880, slightly over a month before she died.

**ADDITIONAL GRAVESITE INFORMATION:**
Zelma Myrick, who recorded information about Rose Hill Cemetery in a notebook in the 1930s, reported the "stone down" and her name as "Etta."

**REFERENCES:** 1, 2, 3, 6, 8 (Aug. 7, 1870 and Dec. 23, 1876), 12

---

**MARRIED.**

MADDEN—LEACH—In Nortonville, December 17th, by Rev. W. Parry, Mr. A. Madden and Miss S. Leach.

From the *Contra Costa Gazette* newspaper, December 23, 1876.

---

**Sad Accident.**

Another of those sad and terrible kerosene accidents occurred here last Tuesday evening. Mrs. Archie Madden left the children in the house with a lighted lamp on the table. The little ones, while playing, overturned the table so that the lamp broke. One of the children, a little girl about two years old, died the next morning about 4 o'clock from the effects of the fire.

J. J. P.

From the *Contra Costa Gazette* newspaper, August 7, 1880.

## PERSONAL INFORMATION:

| | |
|---|---|
| SEX: | Male |
| DATE OF BIRTH: | October 10, 1895 |
| DATE OF DEATH: | *Circa* June 1897 |
| PLACE OF DEATH: | Somersville, Contra Costa County, California |
| AGE AT DEATH: | 1 year, 8 months |
| CAUSE OF DEATH | |
| BIRTHPLACE: | Nanaimo, British Columbia, Canada |
| SPOUSE: | None |
| PARENTS: | Joseph and Marion (Cain) Malpass |

## GRAVESITE INFORMATION:

| | |
|---|---|
| LOCATION OF GRAVESITE: | Unknown |
| GRAVESTONE: | Missing or never placed |
| TYPE OF GRAVESTONE: | |
| SHAPE OF GRAVESTONE: | |
| INSCRIPTION: | |
| EPITAPH: | |
| MOTIF: | |
| CARVER: | |
| BASE: | |
| TYPE OF BASE: | |
| ENCLOSURE: | |
| TYPE OF ENCLOSURE: | |
| FENCE: | |
| TYPE OF FENCE: | |
| FENCE MOTIF: | |

# MALPASS, Percival Sidney

**ADDITIONAL PERSONAL INFORMATION:**
Percival was the grandson of James and Elizabeth Cain of Somersville and/or Nortonville, Contra Costa County, California. Elizabeth Cain is also buried in Rose Hill Cemetery (Section N-A, Plot #2). Marion (Percival's mother), was one of six children of James and Elizabeth Cain.

After the death of Elizabeth Cain (died October 27, 1881), her daughter Marion, who was in bad health, and her sister, Sarah Elizabeth, left Nortonville and went to live with their brother Peter in Nanaimo, British Columbia, Canada. In 1883 Marion Cain married Joseph Malpass in Nanaimo, British Columbia, Canada. They had four children; all were born in Nanaimo:

- Sarah Elizabeth, born April 25, 1886; died 1979 in Tacoma, Washington (married Guy Byron)
- John Leonard, born July 18, 1889; died September 5, 1898, Nanaimo, British Columbia, Canada
- Wilfred Arthur, born August 27, 1892; died 1916
- Percival Sidney, born October 10, 1895; died *circa* June 1897

Sarah returned to California shortly after her sister Marion's wedding. Marion and her husband eventually returned to Somersville to stay with Sarah and assist her with her two sick children. Marion's son, Percival, died six months after the family returned to Somersville. Six months after Percival's death, Marion returned to Nanaimo and on September 5, 1898, another son, John Leonard Malpass, died after being sick for several months. He was buried in the Nanaimo Cemetery.

See Elizabeth O. Cain.

**ADDITIONAL GRAVESITE INFORMATION:**
According to descendants, Percival Sidney Malpass is buried in Rose Hill Cemetery. No other source documents his burial there.

**REFERENCES:** 11 (P610.345.1 to P610.345.5), 12

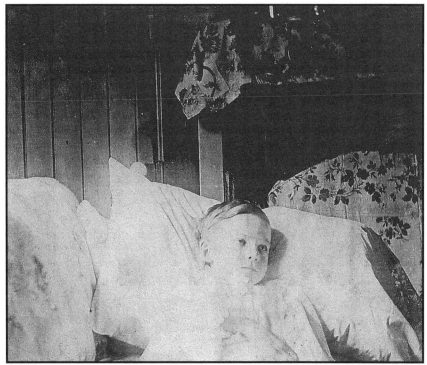

Reference 345.3

Percival Malpass at rest on what appears to be a couch or large chair. This photograph may have been taken just prior to his death. Descendants believe that this photograph was taken at his aunt Sarah's (Sarah Elizabeth (Cain) Byron) home at Pittsburg Landing (near present-day Pittsburg, Contra Costa County, California).

Reference 345.4

Percival's siblings, brother Wilfred (left) and sister, Sarah Elizabeth Malpass.

Reference 345.5

Marion (Cain) and Joseph Malpass, parents of Percival Sidney Malpass.
Marion was the daughter of James and Elizabeth O. Cain. Marion's mother
is also buried in Rose Hill Cemetery.

# MARKLEY,
## Andrew Jackson (A. J.)

## PERSONAL INFORMATION:

| | |
|---|---|
| SEX: | Male |
| DATE OF BIRTH: | December 2, 1829 |
| DATE OF DEATH: | May 2, 1870 |
| PLACE OF DEATH: | Martinez, Contra Costa County, California |
| AGE AT DEATH: | 40 years |
| CAUSE OF DEATH: | Heart disease |
| BIRTHPLACE: | Near West Field, Champaign County, Ohio |
| SPOUSE: | Margarette Markley |
| PARENTS: | David and Susannah (Faidley) Markley |

## GRAVESITE INFORMATION:

| | |
|---|---|
| LOCATION OF GRAVESITE: | Section N-E, Plot #67 |
| GRAVESTONE: | Exists |
| TYPE OF GRAVESTONE: | Marble |
| SHAPE OF GRAVESTONE: | Tablet |
| INSCRIPTION: | *In Memory of/a native of Ohio/Erected by Somersville Division No. 43 Sons of Temperance* |
| EPITAPH: | |
| MOTIF: | Weeping willow tree |
| CARVER: | |
| BASE: | Exists |
| TYPE OF BASE: | Sandstone |
| ENCLOSURE: | |
| TYPE OF ENCLOSURE: | |
| FENCE: | |
| TYPE OF FENCE: | |
| FENCE MOTIF: | |

# MARKLEY, Andrew Jackson (A. J.)

**ADDITIONAL PERSONAL INFORMATION:**
The *1860 Census for Township Three, Contra Costa County, California* lists Andrew J. Markley, age 30, as a native of Illinois and a stock raiser. Also listed are his wife, Margaret, age 28, a native of England and their daughter, Eliza J., age 4. Living at the same household is Josephus Gifford, laborer, age 30, and a native of Ohio. Family records list A. J. Markley's age of death as 41 years and not 40 years as stated on his gravestone.

The *Contra Costa Gazette*, May 7, 1870, states that A. J. Markley was about 45 years of age at the time of his death. He served as Clerk for Contra Costa County 1869-1870. After Markley's death, Margarette married Mr. Talleyrand, who worked as an engineer in the coal field. Markley Creek in Somersville, Contra Costa County, California is named for A. J. Markley.

Markley's gravestone states that he was a member of the Sons of Temperance, Somersville Division No. 43. Additionally since the *Contra Costa Gazette* newspaper of May 7, 1878 states that members of the Odd Fellows Lodge attended his service, it is presumed he was a member of the Independent Order of Odd Fellows.

A. J. Markley's parents' names come from the Family Data Collection – Individual Records at www.ancestry.com. This same source also states A. J. was born in Ashland, Ashland County, Ohio. Information written in the family *Bible* states that A. J. Markley was born in Champaine [sic] County, Ohio. The correct spelling is Champaign. A handwritten inscription in the family *Bible* indicates that his wife's name was spelled Margarette.

See David Markley and Eliza Jane Markley.

**ADDITIONAL GRAVESITE INFORMATION:**
Zelma Myrick, who recorded information about Rose Hill Cemetery in a notebook in the 1930s, reported "Stone down, good condition."

A. J. shares a gravestone with his children, Eliza Jane and David Markley. The gravestone was erected by Somersville Division No. 43 Sons of Temperance. The gravestone was broken into two pieces and concreted flat to ground prior to East Bay Regional Park District acquisition.

**REFERENCES:** 1, 2, 3, 6, 8 (Nov. 7, 1863, Nov. 19, 1864, and May 7, 1870 – two articles), 9 (May 7, 1870 – two articles), 10 (pages 141, 246, 703), 11 (P610.31.141, P610.168.30, and P610.168.31), 12, 14, *Pittsburg Post Dispatch* newspaper (Wed., June 15, 1955, pages 9 and 12), family *Bible*, see newspaper appendix pages 733-735

---

## BIRTHS.

In Green Valley near Alamo, Oct. 31st., to Mr. and Mrs. Andrew Inman, a son.

In Somersville, Nov. 2d, to Mr. and Mrs. A. J. Markley, a son.

In Mitchel's Cañon, 4th inst., to Mr. and Mrs. J. W. Cassidy, a daughter.

---

This article, from the *Contra Costa Gazette* newspaper, November 7, 1863, announces the birth of son, Andrew James Markley.

# MARKLEY,
## David

## PERSONAL INFORMATION:

| | |
|---|---|
| SEX: | Male |
| DATE OF BIRTH: | December 8, 1868 |
| DATE OF DEATH: | April 19, 1869 |
| PLACE OF DEATH: | Somersville, Contra Costa County, California |
| AGE AT DEATH: | 4 months, 11 days |
| CAUSE OF DEATH: | |
| BIRTHPLACE: | Somersville, Contra Costa County, California |
| SPOUSE: | None |
| PARENTS: | Andrew Jackson and Margarette Markley |

## GRAVESITE INFORMATION:

| | |
|---|---|
| LOCATION OF GRAVESITE: | Section N-E, Plot #67 |
| GRAVESTONE: | Exists |
| TYPE OF GRAVESTONE: | Marble |
| SHAPE OF GRAVESTONE: | Tablet |
| INSCRIPTION: | *In Memory of/And his Infant Son* |
| EPITAPH: | |
| MOTIF: | Weeping willow tree |
| CARVER: | |
| BASE: | Exists |
| TYPE OF BASE: | Sandstone |
| ENCLOSURE: | |
| TYPE OF ENCLOSURE: | |
| FENCE: | |
| TYPE OF FENCE: | |
| FENCE MOTIF: | |

# MARKLEY, David

**ADDITIONAL PERSONAL INFORMATION:**
The birth date and place of birth come from the family *Bible*. See Andrew Jackason (A. J.) Markley and Eliza Jane Markley.

**ADDITIONAL GRAVESITE INFORMATION:**
David shares a gravestone with his father, A. J. Markley and sister, Eliza Jane Markley.

**REFERENCES:** 1, 2, 3, 6, 8 (Nov. 7, 1863, Nov. 19, 1864, April 24, 1869, and May 7, 1870), 9 (May 7, 1870), 10 (pages 141, 246, 703), 11 (P610.31.141, P610.168.30, and P610.168.31), 12, 14, *Pittsburg Post Dispatch* newspaper (Wed., June 15, 1955, pages 9 and 12), family *Bible*, see newspaper appendix page 736

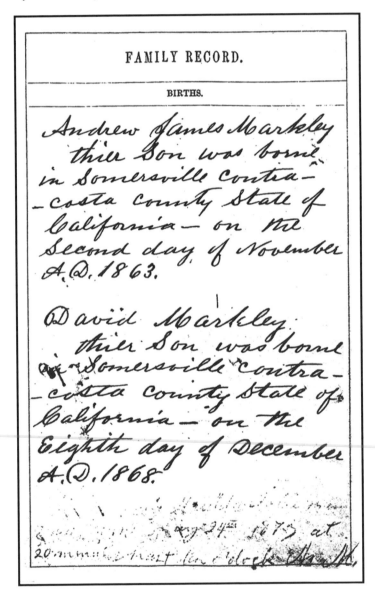

This birth information for David Markley and his brother, Andrew James Markley, was recorded in the family *Bible* (*The Holy Bible, containing the Old and New Testaments*, New York, American Bible Society, 1864).

# MARKLEY,
## Eliza Jane

**PERSONAL INFORMATION:**

| | |
|---|---|
| SEX: | Female |
| DATE OF BIRTH: | December 2, 1855 |
| DATE OF DEATH: | March 26, 1869 |
| PLACE OF DEATH: | Somersville, Contra Costa County, California |
| AGE AT DEATH: | 13 years, 3 months, 23 days |
| CAUSE OF DEATH: | Black Measles |
| BIRTHPLACE: | Near Antioch, Contra Costa County, California |
| SPOUSE: | None |
| PARENTS: | Andrew Jackson and Margarette Markley |

**GRAVESITE INFORMATION:**

| | |
|---|---|
| LOCATION OF GRAVESITE: | Section N-E, Plot #67 |
| GRAVESTONE: | Exists |
| TYPE OF GRAVESTONE: | Marble |
| SHAPE OF GRAVESTONE: | Tablet |
| INSCRIPTION: | *In Memory of/Also his Daughter* |
| EPITAPH: | |
| MOTIF: | Weeping willow tree |
| CARVER: | |
| BASE: | Exists |
| TYPE OF BASE: | Sandstone |
| ENCLOSURE: | |
| TYPE OF ENCLOSURE: | |
| FENCE: | |
| TYPE OF FENCE: | |
| FENCE MOTIF: | |

# MARKLEY, Eliza Jane

**ADDITIONAL PERSONAL INFORMATION:**
The date of birth comes from the family *Bible*. See Andrew Jackson (A. J.) Markley and David Markley.

**ADDITIONAL GRAVESITE INFORMATION:**
Eliza Jane shares a gravestone with her father, A. J. Markley and brother, David Markley.

**REFERENCES:** 1, 2, 3, 6, 8 (Nov. 7, 1863, Nov. 19, 1864, April 10, 1869, and May 7, 1870), 9 (May 7, 1870), 10 (pages 141, 246, 703), 11 (P610.31.141, P610.168.30, and P610.168.31), 12, 14, *Pittsburg Post Dispatch* newspaper (Wed., June 15, 1955, pages 9 and 12), family *Bible*, see newspaper appendix page 736

## FAMILY RECORD.

### BIRTHS.

Andrew Jackson Markley was borne near Westfield Champaine county State of Ohio — on the Second day of December A.D. 1829.

Margarette Markley was borne in Charnock county of Lancashire England — on the Sixteenth day of March A.D. 1831.

Eliza Jane Markley their Daughter was borne near Antioch contra—costa county State of California—on the Second day of December A.D. 1855.

This birth information for Eliza Jane Markley, her father and mother, was recorded in the family *Bible* (*The Holy Bible, containing the Old and New Testaments*, New York, American Bible Society, 1864).

# MILLS,
## Charles W.

## PERSONAL INFORMATION:

| | |
|---|---|
| SEX: | Male |
| DATE OF BIRTH: | November 3, 1879 |
| DATE OF DEATH: | November 3, 1881 |
| PLACE OF DEATH: | Black Diamond, Contra Costa County, California |
| AGE AT DEATH: | 2 years, 1 month |
| CAUSE OF DEATH: | |
| BIRTHPLACE: | California |
| SPOUSE: | None |
| PARENTS: | John X. and Lizzie (Elizabeth) A. (Lewis) Mills |

## GRAVESITE INFORMATION:

| | |
|---|---|
| LOCATION OF GRAVESITE: | Section N-B, Plot #11 |
| GRAVESTONE: | Exists (partial) |
| TYPE OF GRAVESTONE: | Marble |
| SHAPE OF GRAVESTONE: | Tablet |
| INSCRIPTION: | *Son of* |
| EPITAPH: | |
| MOTIF: | Lamb |
| CARVER: | |
| BASE: | Exists |
| TYPE OF BASE: | Granite |
| ENCLOSURE: | Exists (partial) |
| TYPE OF ENCLOSURE: | Brick |
| FENCE: | |
| TYPE OF FENCE: | |
| FENCE MOTIF: | |

# MILLS, Charles W.

**ADDITIONAL PERSONAL INFORMATION:**
The November 3 birth date comes from a list compiled by Jim Rotelli for a California History class term paper, 1963. According to the *Contra Costa Gazette* newspaper, November 12, 1881, Charles died at age 2 years and 1 month. Charles Walter Mills was the only son of John Xerxes and Elizabeth Mills. J. X. Mills, age 27, of Nortonville, Contra Costa County, California, and Elizabeth Lewis, age 17, also of Nortonville, applied for a marriage license on January 31, 1878. The application states "The consent of the Mother is filed in this Office this 31st day of January 1878." The information was recorded in the *Applications for Marriage Licenses, Contra Costa County, 1873-1887*, page 132, located at the Contra Costa County Historical Society History Center in Martinez, California. The *Index to Marriage Certificates* located at the Contra Costa County Hall of Records in Martinez states that John X. Mills married Elizabeth Lewis on February 12, 1878. They were married by Rev. John J. Powell; the information is located in Volume 2, page 218. Descendants provided Elizabeth's middle initial.

Also according to descendants, Elizabeth lost her father when he was killed in Nortonville's largest mine explosion. The only known Lewis killed in the July 24, 1876 mine explosion in Nortonville was Meredith Lewis. Elizabeth's name, however, has not been recorded as one of his daughters. See Meredith Lewis.

John moved to Black Diamond, Washington Territory after being offered a job as pump man by mine superintendent, Morgan Morgans. Shortly after arriving in Black Diamond, John Mills purchased a cabin on Log Cabin Hill which he rented to Welsh coal miner, David Lewis. Elizabeth Mills and her two children arrived in Seattle by ship in the fall of 1885. They were greeted by Nortonville friends. Charles' father also paid the ship passage of his widowed mother-in-law and her minor children.

The *1900 Census for Black Diamond, King County, Washington* lists John Mills, age 49, as a native of Missouri. Also listed are his daughters, Annie, age 19, a native of California, and Edna, age 13, a native of Washington.

The *1910 Census for Black Diamond, King County, Washington* lists John Mills, age 59, as a native of Missouri and widowed. John's parents are listed as natives of Scotland.

John's wife, Lizzie, died in Black Diamond, King County, Washington. Their children were: Charles, Annie, and Luther, born in Nortonville, Contra Costa County, California; and Edna, born in Black Diamond, King County, Washington. According to the document *Black Diamond Cemetery* records, Black Diamond, Washington, page 12, Charles' parents are buried in this cemetery. Listed is John X. Mills, died September 16, 1920, age 70 years. Also listed on the same stone is his wife, Elizabeth, who died March 12, 1892, age 32 years (see page 406).

**ADDITIONAL GRAVESITE INFORMATION:**
Zelma Myrick, who recorded information about Rose Hill Cemetery in a notebook in the 1930s, reported the stone in "Good condition." The small piece of the gravestone that remains today was placed in storage for safekeeping.

**REFERENCES:** 1, 2, 3, 4, 6, 8 (Nov. 12, 1881), 11 (P610.260.24, P610.261.21, P610.261.22, P610.285.5, and P610.294.2), 12, 14, *Black Diamond Cemetery* records, Black Diamond, WA; *Green River Coal Fields*, C. William Thorndale, May 28, 1965, pages 114-125; *The Post Intelligencer* newspaper, Seattle, WA (Sept. 19, 1920, page 9, and Sept. 20, 1920, page 13), *Pittsburg Post Dispatch* newspaper (Wed., June 15, 1955, pages 9 and 12), see newspaper appendix pages 737 and 738

STEIN
BLACK DIAMOND COAL CARS MACHINE SH

The Black Diamond Coal Company wharf at New York Landing, Contra Costa County, California. The Black Diamond Coal and Railroad Company transported coal from the mines in Nortonville to the San Joaquin River at New York Landing. Visible are coal cars on the wharf (left) and a machine shop (adjacent to the cars). The home of the railroad superintendent is surrounded by trees. John X. Mills worked as a conductor on this railroad. The *1880 Census for New York Landing Precinct, Contra Costa County, California*, lists John Mills, age 30, and his occupation "Brakesman" [sic]. Also listed are his wife, Lizzy, [sic] age 20, a native of Wales and son, Charles, age 7 months, a native of California.

Reference 285.5

Reference 260.24

Left: Charles Mills' gravesite in Rose Hill Cemetery, March 1969, Section N-B, Plot #11. Photograph by David Stogner. Right: John and Elizabeth Mills' gravestone (parents of Charles Mills), Black Diamond Cemetery, King County, Washington, August 2001. John X. Mills died September 16, 1920, age 70 years. Elizabeth Mills died March 12, 1892, age 32 years. Photograph by Traci (Gibbons) Parent.

## PERSONAL INFORMATION:

| | |
|---|---|
| SEX: | Male |
| DATE OF BIRTH: | 1841 |
| DATE OF DEATH: | May 27, 1866 |
| PLACE OF DEATH: | Somersville, Contra Costa County, California |
| AGE AT DEATH: | 25 years |
| CAUSE OF DEATH: | |
| BIRTHPLACE: | Warwickshire, England |
| SPOUSE: | |
| PARENTS: | |

## GRAVESITE INFORMATION:

| | |
|---|---|
| LOCATION OF GRAVESITE: | Section N-E, Plot #66 |
| GRAVESTONE: | Exists |
| TYPE OF GRAVESTONE: | Marble |
| SHAPE OF GRAVESTONE: | Tablet |
| INSCRIPTION: | *In Memory of/Erected by the Somersville Division #43 Sons of T [Temperance]* |
| EPITAPH: | *Write the errors of your Brother in sand, but engrave his Virtues on the tablets of enduring memory.* |
| MOTIF: | |
| CARVER: | J. Daniel, 421 Pine St., San Francisco, California |
| BASE: | Exists |
| TYPE OF BASE: | Sandstone |
| ENCLOSURE: | |
| TYPE OF ENCLOSURE: | |
| FENCE: | |
| TYPE OF FENCE: | |
| FENCE MOTIF: | |

# MINETT, William C.

**ADDITIONAL PERSONAL INFORMATION:**
William's place of birth and place of death come from the *Contra Costa Gazette* newspaper, June 2, 1866. His date of birth was calculated based on his date of death and age at death listed on his gravestone.

**ADDITIONAL GRAVESITE INFORMATION:**
Zelma Myrick, who recorded information in a notebook in the 1930s during a visit to Rose Hill Cemetery, reported "Stone broken and down." The gravestone was broken into four pieces and concreted flat to the ground prior to East Bay Regional Park District acquisition.

**REFERENCES:** 1, 2, 6, 8 (June 2, 1866), 11 (P610.31.146 and P610.119.31), 12, 14

**DIED.**

In Somersville, May 27th, WILLIAM C. MINETT, native of Warwickshire, Eng., aged 25 years.

From the *Contra Costa Gazette* newspaper, June 2, 1866.

# MORGAN,
## Ann

## PERSONAL INFORMATION:

|  |  |
|---|---|
| SEX: | Female |
| DATE OF BIRTH: | 1847 |
| DATE OF DEATH: | September 19, 1873 |
| PLACE OF DEATH: | |
| AGE AT DEATH: | 26 years |
| CAUSE OF DEATH: | |
| BIRTHPLACE: | Merthyr Tydfil, Glamorganshire, Wales |
| SPOUSE: | Richard Morgan |
| PARENTS: | |

## GRAVESITE INFORMATION:

|  |  |
|---|---|
| LOCATION OF GRAVESITE: | Unknown |
| GRAVESTONE: | Missing |
| TYPE OF GRAVESTONE: | |
| SHAPE OF GRAVESTONE: | |
| INSCRIPTION: | *In memory of/A native of/wife of* |
| EPITAPH: | *Fy Nyddiau a Aeth Heibio,* |
| | *Fy Amcanion A Dynned* |
| | *Ymaeth: Sef Meddyliau* |
| | *Fy nghalon.* |
| MOTIF: | |
| CARVER: | |
| BASE: | |
| TYPE OF BASE: | |
| ENCLOSURE: | |
| TYPE OF ENCLOSURE: | |
| FENCE: | |
| TYPE OF FENCE: | |
| FENCE MOTIF: | |

# MORGAN, Ann

**ADDITIONAL PERSONAL INFORMATION:**
Ann's birthplace in Wales was spelled as Mirtha-Tidvill [sic] on her gravestone according to Zelma Myrick who recorded information in a notebook in the 1930s during a visit to Rose Hill Cemetery. Myrick also recorded Ann's date of death, age at death, and the name of Ann's husband.

**ADDITIONAL GRAVESITE INFORMATION:**
The epitaph is written in Welsh and was translated by Idris Evans of the Welsh American

Society of Northern California. Some words may be missing from the first line of her epitaph. The translation of the epitaph is:

> My days have gone by
> My aspirations have been taken away
> That is, the meditations
> of my heart.

**REFERENCES:** 1, 2, 3, 4, 6, 12

Reference 19.1

A map of burial locations for Rose Hill Cemetery, drawn by Jim Rotelli in 1963 for a California history class, indicates that Ann Morgan may be interred at Section S-E, Plot #87. This site is located to the left of the Italian Cypress tree pictured in this photograph. The iron fence for this gravesite is visible. Several photographs were taken of this gravesite prior to East Bay Regional Park District acquisition. All the photographs were taken from a distance and some show a marble tablet gravestone within an iron fence enclosure. Since no photographs exist showing a close-up view of the gravestone, it can not be confirmed that Ann Morgan is buried at this site. At the time this photograph was taken in the early 1970s, a cyclone fence surrounded the cemetery. See Unknown on pages 585-588.

# MORGAN,
## David

**PERSONAL INFORMATION:**

| | |
|---|---|
| SEX: | Male |
| DATE OF BIRTH: | September 27, 1846 |
| DATE OF DEATH: | May 16, 1882 |
| PLACE OF DEATH: | Nortonville, Contra Costa County, California |
| AGE AT DEATH: | 35 years, 7 months, 19 days |
| CAUSE OF DEATH: | Heart attack |
| BIRTHPLACE: | The Dyffryn near Merthyr Tydfil, Glamorganshire, South Wales |
| SPOUSE: | Mary Morgan |
| PARENTS: | William and Margaret (Howell) Morgan |

**GRAVESITE INFORMATION:**

| | |
|---|---|
| LOCATION OF GRAVESITE: | Section S-E, Plot #92 |
| GRAVESTONE: | Exists |
| TYPE OF GRAVESTONE: | Marble |
| SHAPE OF GRAVESTONE: | Tablet |
| INSCRIPTION: | *In Memory of/Died at Nortonville* |
| EPITAPH: | |
| MOTIF: | Rope with tassels |
| CARVER: | |
| BASE: | Exists |
| TYPE OF BASE: | Granite |
| ENCLOSURE: | |
| TYPE OF ENCLOSURE: | |
| FENCE: | |
| TYPE OF FENCE: | |
| FENCE MOTIF: | |

# MORGAN, David

**ADDITIONAL PERSONAL INFORMATION:**
According to the birth certificate acquired by David's descendants, David was born October 28, 1846. However David's gravestone says he was born September 27, 1846.

The *1851 Census for Merthyr-Tydfil, Glamorgan, Wales* lists David's father, William Morgan, age 37, as an Engine Tender and his mother, Margaret Morgan, age 33. Also listed are David, age 4, and his siblings: Mary, age 12; and Jennet [sic], age 9.

The *1861 Census for Merthyr-Tydfil, Glamorgan, Wales* lists David's father, William Morgan, age 47, and his mother, Margaret, age 43, both natives of Merthyr-Tydril, Glamorgan, Wales. Also listed are their children: Jannet [sic], age 20; David, age 14; Morgan, age 10; Sarah Ann, age 7; Fredrick [sic], age 4; all natives of Merthyr-Tydfil, Glamorgan, Wales. Also listed are boarders Morgan Morgan, age 53, and Thomas Morgan, age 41, both are natives of Merthyr-Tydfil, Glamorgan, Wales.

The *List of Voters 1871-72* for Merthyr Tydfil Lower, lists David Morgan living at 8, Taibach, Pentrebach in Wales.

David was the brother of Mary Morgan, who married John R. Evans (also buried in Rose Hill Cemetery) of Nortonville, Contra Costa County, California.

According to family history documents compiled by a descendant of David Morgan, David's father and mother were married November 12, 1836. David's father, William, died June 18, 1870. His mother, Margaret, died January 21, 1862. William Morgan's parents (David's grandparents) were Morgan and Mary (Richards) Howell. David's siblings included: Mary, born March 16, 1839; Janet (Jennet, Jannet), born October 5, 1841; Margaret, born September 10, 1844; Morgan,

born September 5, 1851; Sarah Anne, born April 22, 1854; and Frederick, born February 11, 1857.

The *1880 Census for Lackawanna County, Pennsylvania, Scranton Township* lists David D. Morgan, age 33, a native of Wales, and his occupation as "working in coal mines." Also listed are his wife, Mary, age 33, a native of Wales and their children: Mary E., age 7; Emma, age 5; David G., age 3; and Sarah Ann, age 1. All are natives of Pennsylvania.

**ADDITIONAL GRAVESITE INFORMATION:**
The place of birth is incorrectly spelled as "Glammorgan Shire" on the gravestone.

Zelma Myrick, who recorded information in a notebook in the 1930s during a visit to Rose Hill Cemetery, reported "Large white stone on ground not broken." The right bottom corner of gravestone is broken and missing.

A photograph of David Morgan's gravestone appears in the *California Monthly* magazine, "Back Yard Ghost Towns," May 1949, page 23.

The granite base was found buried below the gravestone by Black Diamond Rangers in the winter of 1996. The gravestone was placed upright on the base by Park staff in July 1997. During repair work, a coal miner's pick and wood fragments were found underneath the gravestone. David is buried next to his brother-in-law, John R. Evans, and John's children. See John R. Evans, Sarah Howell, Thomas M. Howell, and Elizabeth Jones (died Sept. 17, 1881).

**REFERENCES:** 1, 2, 3, 5, 6, 11 (P610.31.211, P610.119.91, P610.151.3, P610.168.27, P610.263.2, and P610.317.14), 12, 14, *California Monthly* magazine, May 1949, pages 22 and 23

## PERSONAL INFORMATION:

| | |
|---|---|
| SEX: | Male |
| DATE OF BIRTH: | March 30, 1867 |
| DATE OF DEATH: | April 19, 1875 |
| PLACE OF DEATH: | |
| AGE AT DEATH: | 8 years, 20 days |
| CAUSE OF DEATH: | |
| BIRTHPLACE: | California |
| SPOUSE: | None |
| PARENTS: | William and Martha Morris |

## GRAVESITE INFORMATION:

| | |
|---|---|
| LOCATION OF GRAVESITE: | Section N-D, Plot #38 |
| GRAVESTONE: | Missing |
| TYPE OF GRAVESTONE: | Marble |
| SHAPE OF GRAVESTONE: | Tablet |
| INSCRIPTION: | *Son of* |
| EPITAPH: | *Farewell my Father and Mother dear* |
| | *My love for you is very near* |
| | *Dry up your tears & do not weep* |
| | *I hope in heaven we shall meet.* |
| MOTIF: | Dove with rosebud |
| CARVER: | |
| BASE: | Exists (marble middle base missing) |
| TYPE OF BASE: | Concrete bottom base with marble middle base |
| ENCLOSURE: | |
| TYPE OF ENCLOSURE: | |
| FENCE: | |
| TYPE OF FENCE: | |
| FENCE MOTIF: | |

# MORRIS, Alexander

**ADDITIONAL PERSONAL INFORMATION:**
The birth date was calculated by www.timeanddate.com, based on the date of death and age of death listed on the gravestone.

The *1860 Census for Mason, Mason County, Virginia* lists Alexander's father, William Morris, as a miner, age 30, and his mother, Martha, age 25, as natives of Wales. Also listed are their children: Mary, age 8; Margaret, age 4; and Edward, age 2.

The *1870 Census for Scott Valley, Siskiyou County, California* lists Alexander Morris, age 3, as a native of California. Also listed are his father, William, age 42, a miner; mother, Martha Morris, age 35; both natives of Wales; and his siblings Margaret, age 14; Edwin, age 12, natives of Virginia; and William, age 5, a native of California.

The *1880 Nortonville Precinct Census, Contra Costa County, California,* lists William Morris, age 53, as a native of Wales and a miner. Also listed are his wife, Martha, a native of Wales, age 44, and their five children and two grandchildren: Margaret, age 24, a housekeeper and native of Virginia; Edwin, age 22, a miner and native of Virginia; William, age 16, a laborer and native of California; Ebenezar [sic], age 10, a native of California; and Martha, age 4, a native of California. The grandchildren of William and Martha were: William McCoy, age 4, and Nellie McCoy, age 2, natives of California. Their father was a native of Ohio and their mother a native of Virginia. Also listed with them are four male boarders: one clerk BBCCR, William Tingman, age 27, a native of California; 2 bakers, Nicholas Borrfilio, age 26, a native of Italy and Isadore Istrub, age 31, a native of France; and one laborer, Domnick Malatesta, age 30, a native of Italy.

The *1900 Census for Albion, Cassia County, Idaho,* lists William Morris, age 73, his wife, Martha, age 64, and their grandson, Edwin E. Smart, age 14, a native of Idaho.

Alexander's brother, Edwin Morris, was married to Mary M. (Jones) Morris. Mary was the daughter of Evan D. and Elizabeth (Evans) Jones. Elizabeth Jones (died Sept. 17, 1881) is also buried in Rose Hill Cemetery.

See John Evans, John R. Evans, William Evans, William Rodrick Evans, Sarah Howell, Thomas M Howell, and Elizabeth Jones (died 1881).

**ADDITIONAL GRAVESITE INFORMATION:**
Zelma Myrick, who recorded information in a notebook in the 1930s during a visit to Rose Hill Cemetery, reported "Stone off base." The gravestone was missing from Rose Hill Cemetery prior to East Bay Regional Park District acquisition. A gravestone rubbing exists.

The epitaph was not readable in the photograph taken in 1962 by Madison Devlin. The epitaph was recorded by Cecelia Trueman on July 28, 1963, during a visit to Rose Hill Cemetery. A marble footstone was found buried under the soil at the gravesite by Black Diamond Rangers on March 3, 2006. It was broken in half but contains the initials "A. M." The footstone has been placed in storage for safekeeping. A brass plaque was purchased and placed at the site. The plaque says:

> ALEXANDER MORRIS
> MAR. 30,1867 – APR. 19,1875
> AGED 8 YEARS, 20 DAYS
> PLAQUE PLACED IN 2007

**REFERENCES:** 1, 2, 3, 5, 6, 11 (P610.98.14 and P610.146.2), 12

Alexander Morris gravesite, 1962. This gravestone is now missing from Rose Hill Cemetery.
Photograph by Madison Devlin.

BLACK DIAMOND COAL MINE.—This property appears to be in fine and prosperous condition. The works at Nortonville were visited recently by the editor of the Antioch *Ledger*, who furnishes some interesting details of the company's operations. He says: The apparatus at the mines is in a high state of perfection. During our visit, between the hours of 1 and 4 o'clock P. M., on Saturday last, there were hoisted from the main shaft 212 cars of coal, containing each one ton, besides 200 men and boys and twelve horses, the men and horses, as we were informed, being equal to about 32 cars of coal. Mr. Morgan informed us that between 500 and 600 tons of coal would be taken out of the mine that day, for which a ready market is found, as was shown by the bunkers, which were, at the time of our visit, nearly empty. Some 8 or 10 boys and men were engaged in screening, and nothing but pure coal was allowed to pass into the bunkers. Probably there is no coal mine on the coast which has such extensive machinery and complete arrangements for work. To those who have never examined anything of the kind, it is well worth a trip to Nortonville.

This article from the publication, *Mining and Scientific Press*, August 28, 1880, page 136, was written during the time that Alexander's father, William Morris, was working as a miner and living in Nortonville.

# MORTIMORE,
## Alvin

## PERSONAL INFORMATION:

| | |
|---|---|
| SEX: | Male |
| DATE OF BIRTH: | July 5, 1892 |
| DATE OF DEATH: | August 3, 1893 |
| PLACE OF DEATH: | Somersville, Contra Costa County, California |
| AGE AT DEATH: | 1 year, 1 month |
| CAUSE OF DEATH: | Brain and spinal disease |
| BIRTHPLACE: | Somersville, Contra Costa County, California |
| SPOUSE: | None |
| PARENTS: | Richard and Sarah Ann (Jones) Mortimore |

## GRAVESITE INFORMATION:

| | |
|---|---|
| LOCATION OF GRAVESITE: | Section S-C, Plot #21 |
| GRAVESTONE: | Exists |
| TYPE OF GRAVESTONE: | Marble |
| SHAPE OF GRAVESTONE: | Obelisk |
| INSCRIPTION: | Middle marble base says *MORTIMORE/Son of* |
| EPITAPH: | |
| MOTIF: | Masonic emblem |
| CARVER: | |
| BASE: | Exists |
| TYPE OF BASE: | Middle marble base sits on granite base |
| ENCLOSURE: | |
| TYPE OF ENCLOSURE: | |
| FENCE: | Missing |
| TYPE OF FENCE: | Wooden picket; later a pipe fence |
| FENCE MOTIF: | |

# MORTIMORE, Alvin

**ADDITIONAL PERSONAL INFORMATION:**
The Contra Costa County Hall of Records in Martinez, California, lists Alvin's date of death as August 5, 1893 and not August 3, 1893 as stated on his gravestone. Alvin's doctor was Frank Rattan. See Harriet Mortimore and Richard Mortimore.

**ADDITIONAL GRAVESITE INFORMATION:**
Alvin shares a gravestone with his sister, Harriet and father, Richard Mortimore. He shares the gravesite with his grandfather, Austin Jones and aunt, Martha Jones. Alvin's mother, Sarah, was sister to Martha Jones. Austin and Celia Jones were the parents of Sarah and Martha. A wooden picket fence originally stood around this gravesite and the nearby Austin Jones and Martha Jones gravesites. After the wooden fence disappeared, a pipe fence and a cement pad were installed at the site by family members *circa* 1937. The pipe fence was removed *circa* 1978.

**REFERENCES:** 1, 2, 3, 6, 7, 11 (P610.2.18, P610.31.126, P610.31.172, P610.31.179, P610.43.4, P610.145.1, P610.277.2, P610.285.12, and P610.312.5), 12, 14, *Pittsburg Post Dispatch* newspaper (Wed., June 15, 1955, page 9)

Reference 277.2

The children of Richard and Sarah Ann (Jones) Mortimore, left to right: Charles, William and Walter. The youngest, Austin Mortimore, stands in front. Date unknown.

# MORTIMORE,
## Harriet

## PERSONAL INFORMATION:

| | |
|---|---|
| Sex: | Female |
| Date of Birth: | December 8, 1876 |
| Date of Death: | January 15, 1885 |
| Place of Death: | Nortonville, Contra Costa County, California |
| Age at Death: | 8 years, 1 month, 7 days |
| Cause of Death: | |
| Birthplace: | Nortonville, Contra Costa County, California |
| Spouse: | None |
| Parents: | Richard and Sarah Ann (Jones) Mortimore |

## GRAVESITE INFORMATION:

| | |
|---|---|
| Location of Gravesite: | Section S-C, Plot #21 |
| Gravestone: | Exists |
| Type of Gravestone: | Marble |
| Shape of Gravestone: | Obelisk |
| Inscription: | Middle marble base says MORTIMORE/*Daughter of* |
| Epitaph: | |
| Motif: | Masonic emblem |
| Carver: | |
| Base: | Exists |
| Type of Base: | Middle marble base sits on granite base |
| Enclosure: | |
| Type of Enclosure: | |
| Fence: | Missing |
| Type of Fence: | Wooden picket; later a pipe fence |
| Fence Motif: | |

# MORTIMORE, Harriet

**ADDITIONAL PERSONAL INFORMATION:**
See Alvin Mortimore and Richard Mortimore.

**ADDITIONAL GRAVESITE INFORMATION:**
Harriet shares a gravestone with her brother, Alvin and father, Richard Mortimore. She shares the gravesite with her grandfather, Austin Jones and aunt, Martha Jones. Harriet's mother, Sarah, was sister to Martha Jones. Austin and Celia Jones were the parents of Sarah and Martha.

A footstone may have existed at this site. On the 1936 Ann Louchs Chapter D. A. R. Cemetery list (source 2; see page 1004), page 8 it states, "There was one footstone marked J. E. one marked H. A. M. and a third marked W. E. C." The H. A. M. footstone may have belonged to Harriet.

REFERENCES: 1, 2, 3, 6, 11 (P610.2.18, P610.31.126, P610.31.172, P610.31.179, P610.43.4, P610.145.1, P610.277.1, P610.285.12, and P610.312.5), 12, 14, *Pittsburg Post Dispatch* newspaper (Wed., June 15, 1955, page 9)

Reference 277.1

Sarah Ann Mortimore, wife of Richard Mortimore and mother of Alvin and Harriet Mortimore. Date unknown. Sarah is buried in Oak View Cemetery, Antioch, Contra Costa County, California.

# MORTIMORE,
## Richard

**PERSONAL INFORMATION:**

| | |
|---|---|
| SEX: | Male |
| DATE OF BIRTH: | March 6, 1843 |
| DATE OF DEATH: | September 4, 1895 |
| PLACE OF DEATH: | Somersville, Contra Costa County, California |
| AGE AT DEATH: | 52 years, 5 months, 29 days |
| CAUSE OF DEATH: | Consumption (Tuberculosis) |
| BIRTHPLACE: | Tavistock, Devonshire, England |
| SPOUSE: | Sarah Ann (Jones) Mortimore |
| PARENTS: | Richard and Harriet Mortimore |

**GRAVESITE INFORMATION:**

| | |
|---|---|
| LOCATION OF GRAVESITE: | Section S-C, Plot #21 |
| GRAVESTONE: | Exists |
| TYPE OF GRAVESTONE: | Marble |
| SHAPE OF GRAVESTONE: | Obelisk |
| INSCRIPTION: | Middle base says MORTIMORE/*In Memory of* |
| EPITAPH: | |
| MOTIF: | Masonic emblem |
| CARVER: | |
| BASE: | Exists |
| TYPE OF BASE: | Middle marble base sits on granite base |
| ENCLOSURE: | |
| TYPE OF ENCLOSURE: | |
| FENCE: | Missing |
| TYPE OF FENCE: | Wooden picket; later a pipe fence |
| FENCE MOTIF: | |

# MORTIMORE, Richard

**ADDITIONAL PERSONAL INFORMATION:**
The *1851 England Census* Record lists Richard's parents Richard Mortimore, age 33, and his wife, Harriet, age 33, both natives of Tavistock, Devon, England. Also listed are their children: Richard, age 7; John, age 5; and Elizabeth, age 3.

The *1861 England Census* lists Richard's parents, Richard Mortimore, age 45, and his wife, Harriot [sic], age 45, both natives of Tavistock, Devon, England. Also listed are their children: John, age 15; Mary, age 9; and William H., age 3.

The *1870 Census for Washington, Plumas County, California* lists Richard Mortimer [sic], age 27, as a placer miner and native of England.

The *1890 Great Register of Voters in Contra Costa County, California* records Richard Mortimore, as age 38, a native of England, and resident of Somersville. His occupation is listed as miner and his registration date as August 1, 1882. This record states that he was naturalized on August 1, 1882 in Martinez, California.

*The Great Register of Contra Costa County, California, 1894*, page 31, lists Richard Mortimer [sic], age 49, as 5' 10" tall, dark complexion, gray eyes, and black hair. He was a miner and native of England living in Somersville. This record states that he was naturalized in the Contra Costa Superior Court on August 1, 1892.

The Contra Costa County Hall of Records in Martinez, California, lists Richard's death year as 1894 and not 1895 as inscribed on his gravestone. The *Contra Costa Gazette* newspaper lists his age at death as 50 years and not 52 years as stated on his gravestone. He was a miner in Somersville, Contra Costa County, California. W. S. George was his doctor. Richard's wife, Sarah, died on October 17, 1917 and was interred in Oak View Cemetery, Antioch, Contra Costa County, California. Richard is the son-in-law of Austin Jones, also buried in Rose Hill Cemetery.

The *1900 Census for Somersville Precinct, Contra Costa County, California*, lists Richard's widow, Sarah A. Mortimore, age 43, a native of California and her four sons, all natives of California: William, age 19, a coal miner; Charley, age 16, a coal miner; Walter, age 13, a student; and Austin, age 10, a student.

According to descendants, after the coal mines closed, William and Austin Mortimore took their home in Somersville apart and hauled the lumber to Pittsburg, Contra Costa County, California where they used the lumber to build a home on E. 15th Street. See Alvin Mortimore and Harriet Mortimore.

**ADDITIONAL GRAVESITE INFORMATION:**
Richard Mortimore shares a gravestone with his children, Alvin and Harriet Mortimore. He shares a gravesite with his father-in-law, Austin Jones and sister-in-law, Martha Jones. Richard's wife, Sarah, was sister to Martha Jones. Austin and Celia Jones were the parents of Sarah and Martha. A wooden picket fence originally stood around this gravesite and the nearby Austin Jones and Martha Jones gravesites. After the wooden fence disappeared, a pipe fence and a cement pad were placed at the site by descendants *circa* 1937. The pipe fence was removed *circa* 1978. Richard's inscription, the Masonic motif, and the family name "MORTIMORE" appear on the middle base and face east. The inscription for his children, Alvin and Harriet, appear on the south side of the stone.

**REFERENCES:** 1, 2, 3, 6, 7, 8 (Sept. 15, 1895), 11 (P610.2.18, P610.31.126, P610.31.172, P610.43.4, P610.94.1, P610.285.12, and P610.312.5), 12, 14, Oak View Cemetery records, *Pittsburg Post Dispatch* newspaper (June 15, 1955, page 9), see newspaper appendix page 739

Reference 94.1

Richard Mortimore, Somersville resident. Date unknown. Richard traveled by ship from England to San Francisco. Upon arrival he went to La Porte, Plumas County, California to mine gold. From La Porte he went to Nortonville and Somersville, in Contra Costa County, married Sarah Ann Jones and settled in Somersville. Richard and Sarah Ann had six children. Richard was a member of Contra Costa Masonic Lodge No. 227 in Somersville.

The Jones and Mortimore family gravesites. Buried here are Austin Jones and his daughter, Martha Jones. It is also believed that Lewis James Jones (age 3 months, 11 days) and Jennie Jones (infant), children of Austin and Celia Jones, are buried here. Most likely no markers were placed to mark their gravesites at the time of their death. The marble tablet gravestones for Austin and Martha can be seen lying flat on the cement pad. Austin's son-in-law, Richard Mortimore, and Richard's children, Alvin and Harriet Mortimore, are also buried at this site. The Mortimore marble obelisk gravestone sits beside the bottom granite base and middle marble base. The cement pad and pipe fence were installed by descendants *circa* 1937. Photograph taken August 1977 by Traci (Gibbons) Parent.

## PERSONAL INFORMATION:

| | |
|---|---|
| SEX: | Female |
| DATE OF BIRTH: | *Circa* 1860 or 1861 |
| DATE OF DEATH: | January 4, 1865 |
| PLACE OF DEATH: | Somersville, Contra Costa County, California |
| AGE AT DEATH: | 4 years, 9 months |
| CAUSE OF DEATH: | Scarlet fever? |
| BIRTHPLACE: | |
| SPOUSE: | None |
| PARENTS: | Thomas and Susan Muir |

## GRAVESITE INFORMATION:

| | |
|---|---|
| LOCATION OF GRAVESITE: | Unknown |
| GRAVESTONE: | Missing or never placed |
| TYPE OF GRAVESTONE: | |
| SHAPE OF GRAVESTONE: | |
| INSCRIPTION: | |
| EPITAPH: | |
| MOTIF: | |
| CARVER: | |
| BASE: | |
| TYPE OF BASE: | |
| ENCLOSURE: | |
| TYPE OF ENCLOSURE: | |
| FENCE: | |
| TYPE OF FENCE: | |
| FENCE MOTIF: | |

# MUIR, Jane Russel

**ADDITIONAL PERSONAL INFORMATION:**
The names of Jane's parents, her date of death, and age at death come from her obituary in the *Contra Costa Gazette* newspaper, January 14, 1865. It is believed that Jane died from scarlet fever. Her obituary stated that she died "of the same fatal disease." Numerous other children died of scarlet fever during the same period of time and are buried in, or believed to be buried in, Rose Hill Cemetery. Other children who died in 1865 (see pages 749 and 765) of this disease include:

- Charles W. Blackburn, died February 20, 1865, age 9 years, 7 months
- Thomas Pratten Goulding, died January 31, 1865, age 7 years, 7 months, 17 days
- Elizabeth Richmond, died February 17, 1865, age 8 years, 5 months, 11 days
- John Tonkins, died December 29, 1864, age 16 years, 3 months
- Annie Tregellas, died February 19, 1865, age 7 years, 7 months
- James Tregellas, died December 28, 1864, age 2 years, 21 days
- Joseph Tregellas, died February 18, 1865, age 5 years, 1 month
- John Edmund Wright, died December 28, 1864, age 9 years, 10 months
- Mary Elizabeth Wright, died December 25, 1864, age 1 year, 6 months

According to information obtained through www.ancestry.com, Jane's father, Thomas, was born in Edinburgh, Scotland and her mother, Susan, was born in Glasgow, Lanarkshire, Scotland. Thomas immigrated to the United States (Pennsylvania) in 1845. The 1860 census states he was living in Allegheny Township, Armstrong County, Pennsylvania. The *1863 Tax Book for Contra Costa County, California* lists Thomas Muir for improvements in the town of Somersville valued at $100. The *Contra Costa Gazette* newspaper, January 27, 1863 states that T. Muir was chosen as an officer for the newly established Mount Diablo Lodge, No. 195 of the International Order of Good Templars (I. O. G. T.) in Somersville.

The *1864 Assessment Property 9th School District, Contra Costa County, California* lists Thomas Muir for improvements at the Independent Mine (Somersville) valued at $75.

The *1870 Census for Township Three Contra Costa County, California* lists Jane Russel's father, Thomas Muir, age 55, born *circa* 1815, as a miner and native of Scotland. Also recorded are his wife, Susan, age 54, born *circa* 1816, a native of Scotland, and their children: James, age 32, a miner and native of British America [sic]; Thomas, age 22, a miner and native of Pennsylvania; and Robert, age 15, a native of Pennsylvania.

The *1876 Contra Costa County Voting Register* lists Tom Russell [sic] Muir, age 21, as a miner and native of Pennsylvania. He was a resident of Somersville and registered to vote on June 19, 1868. According to the *Contra Costa Gazette* newspaper, June 15, 1872 (see page 524), "...a fire broke out in the house of Thomas Muir, but was soon subdued, damage about twenty dollars; cause, hot ashes."

The *1880 Census for Clayton, Contra Costa County, California* lists Thomas Muir, age 65, born *circa* 1815 in Scotland. Also listed are his wife, Susan, age 64, born *circa* 1816 in Scotland, and their son, James, age 42, a miner and native of Nova Scotia.

Jane's father, Thomas Muir, died at age 66 years near Clayton, California on March 9, 1881. According to the obituary that appeared in the *Contra Costa Gazette* newspaper, Thomas had resided in Contra Costa County since 1864.

**ADDITIONAL GRAVESITE INFORMATION:**
Although no source documents Jane Russel's burial in Rose Hill Cemetery, it is possible she is interred there along with the other children listed in the same newspaper account from the *Contra Costa Gazette*, January 14, 1865.

**REFERENCES:** 8 (Jan. 14, 1865 and June 15, 1872), 12, see newspaper appendix page 739

# DIED.

WOOD—In Lower Lake, Lake county, February 26th, Henry Wood, aged about 55 years, a native of the State of New York. [New York papers please copy.]

MUIR—Near Clayton, March 9, Thomas Muir, aged 66 years.

The deceased was a native of Ayrshire, Scotland, who emigrated to Canada in 1838, and in 1842 went to Pennsylvania, where his practical knowledge was employed in opening up some of the most important coal mining properties in that State, among others, the Tuscarora mine. In 1848 he went to Missouri, and there opened the mines on the Bellville tract, on Muddy river, one of the finest coal fields yet opened in the country. He came to California in 1856, and, has resided with his sons in this county since 1864.,

COM.

WILDER—At Byron, March 12, Harriet E., daughter of William R. and Frances E. Wilder, born in Sacramento City, California, aged 21 years, 6 months and 16 days. [Cincinnati papers please copy.]

The deceased, after long and painful suffering for twelve and a half years, quietly passed away to receive her promised reward. Her severe afflictions were borne to the last with great patience and consideration for those about her. She was a good daughter, and a kind and affectionate sister. COM.

This obituary for Thomas Muir, Jane Russel's father, appeared in the *Contra Costa Gazette* newspaper, March 19, 1881. Thomas Muir is the second entry in the article. By 1880, census records document the family living in Clayton, Contra Costa County, California.

## Letter from Somersville.

SOMERSVILLE, Sept. 3, 1872.

EDS. GAZETTE: In your last issue of the GAZETTE I noticed an article headed: "A Coal Scare in England," and I have been prompted to figure a little on our resources in this coal region, and have arrived at the following conclusion. As I do not recollect of ever having seen an estimate made at any previous time, I will let you know what I know about coal mining in Somersville. Now England's estimated depth is 4,000 feet, and we can dig just as deep here, with proper ventilation, as they do in England; for according to scientific statements proven to be facts, the natural increase of heat beyond any solar influence is about one degree in every fifty feet in depth, which would give us at 4,000ft. about 80 degrees Farenheit, and there are now places in some of these mines where men are, and have been working from eight to ten hours per day, where the mercury reached 120 degrees. So, taking the Union mine for a basis, which has been working for about ten years, a perpendicular shaft of 500 feet in depth would reach the second lift which is worked out, on the Clark vein, and allowing ten years time to work out these two levels, and another ten years to work out the coal in the other two veins, on these same two levels, (and there can be as much more coal obtained from the remaining two veins as there was from the Clark veins on the same levels) that would give us just 20 years coal on 500 feet of depth—and presuming that more discoveries may be made, of course it would average more; but calling it an average 500 feet for 20 years, of course 4.000 feet would give us, or somebody else, just 160 years, or 116 years less than the Alabama folks who are going to get their work done in 276 years. Now some folks have an idea that the coal mines around here are about worked out. And this is just an estimate by one who has been around here and seen some things, and if any of these figures are to large or small, I would be very much pleased to have some one else give a verdict.

JIMMY LEOS.

This article, regarding coal mining in Somersville, appeared in the *Contra Costa Gazette* newspaper on September 7, 1872. In the 1870s, Thomas Muir, the father of Jane Russel Muir, was listed as a miner and resident of Somersville.

NORTON,
Sarah

**PERSONAL INFORMATION:**

| | |
|---|---|
| SEX: | Female |
| DATE OF BIRTH: | 1811 |
| DATE OF DEATH: | October 5, 1879 |
| PLACE OF DEATH: | Near Clayton, Contra Costa County, California |
| AGE AT DEATH: | 68 years |
| CAUSE OF DEATH: | Runaway horse; thrown from buggy |
| BIRTHPLACE: | Canada |
| SPOUSE: | Noah Norton |
| PARENTS: | |

**GRAVESITE INFORMATION:**

| | |
|---|---|
| LOCATION OF GRAVESITE: | Section N-B, Plot #6 |
| GRAVESTONE: | Exists |
| TYPE OF GRAVESTONE: | Marble |
| SHAPE OF GRAVESTONE: | Tablet |
| INSCRIPTION: | *In Memory of/Erected by Her Son* |
| EPITAPH: | *Our head and stay has left us,* |
| | *And we are left alone.* |
| | *Our mother dear, who was so near,* |
| | *Is fled away and gone.* |
| | *It breaks our heart; it is hard to part.* |
| | *With one who was so kind,* |
| | *Where shall we go to ease our woe,* |
| | *Or soothe our troubled mind?* |
| MOTIF: | Rope with tassels |
| CARVER: | |
| BASE: | Exists |
| TYPE OF BASE: | Granite with new middle marble base |
| ENCLOSURE: | Exists |
| TYPE OF ENCLOSURE: | Sandstone block (new) |
| FENCE: | |
| TYPE OF FENCE: | |
| FENCE MOTIF: | |

# NORTON, Sarah

**ADDITIONAL PERSONAL INFORMATION:**
Sarah is listed on the gravestone as "Mrs. Sarah Norton." She was a widow at the time of her death. Sarah was a midwife and according to the *Daily Alta California* newspaper, October 6, 1879, she delivered over 600 babies.

The *1870 Census for Township Three, Contra Costa County, California* lists Sarah Norton, age 54, as keeping house and born at sea. Sarah's husband, Noah, was from Lenawee County, Michigan. He was recorded living there as early as 1825. In 1828, Noah, his first wife (also named Sarah) and their children located in Adrian, Michigan. After the death of his first wife, Noah married Mrs. Sarah Miller on June 27, 1858. Sarah Miller was a widow.

Noah is listed in the first directory for Adrian, Michigan, 1859-1860. Since he is not listed in the next directory, it is believed he moved to California, settling in Nortonville, Contra Costa County, California, the town named for this family. It has been recorded that Noah built the first house in Nortonville in 1861. Noah, age 84, died January 31, 1871, at his grandson's home in Oakland, Alameda County, California and is buried in Mountain View Cemetery, in Oakland.

Sarah had at least six children from her previous marriage to Mr. Miller. Her children were:

- Sarah V. Williams, wife of Charles Williams, Nortonville
- Theodora Cecil, wife of Thomas W. Cecil, Nortonville
- George S. Miller, husband of Carolina W. (Olfermann) Thomas, Nortonville
- Jane R. Holmes, wife of William Holmes, West Tilbury, Essex County, Ontario, Canada
- Adam George Miller, East Palestine, Columbiana County, Ohio
- John Miller, Pottersville, Pennsylvania.

**ADDITIONAL GRAVESITE INFORMATION:**
Zelma Myrick, who recorded information in a notebook in the 1930s during a visit to Rose Hill Cemetery, reported "Stone down." The gravestone was broken in two pieces and concreted flat to the ground prior to East Bay Regional Park District acquisition.

A brick enclosure was placed around the gravesite by Park District staff and volunteers in September 1979 (see *Contra Costa Times* newspaper, September 16, 1979, page 21) and repaired in 1981. The brick wall enclosure was removed in 2004 and replaced with a sandstone block wall enclosure by Black Diamond Rangers.

A photograph (P610.294.8) documenting a marble middle base was located, and a new marble middle base was purchased to place the stone on.

The gravestone was removed for repairs in April 2004 and placed back in the cemetery in July 2005. Sarah is buried beside John Thomas and John's son, Frederick Elias Thomas. After John's death, his widow, Carolina W. (Olfermann) Thomas, married George Miller, son of Sarah (Miller) Norton.

See Frederick Elias Thomas and John Thomas.

**REFERENCES:** 1, 2, 3, 4, 6, 8 (Oct. 11, 1879- two articles; Feb. 28, 1880), 9 (Oct. 11 and 18, 1879), 11 (P610.31.197, P610.119.9, P610.119.10, P610.238.1, P610.285.3, P610.294.8, and P610.312.7), 12, 13, 14, *Daily Alta California* newspaper (October 6, 1879), *Oakland Tribune* newspaper (Oct. 29, 1933, and March 26, 1950), *Pittsburg Post Dispatch* newspaper (Wed., June 15, 1955, pages 9 and 12), *The Bear Facts*, Feb. 1947, page 6, see newspaper appendix pages 740-743

Sarah Norton, right, in dark dress, with a member of the Gordon family of Clayton, date unknown. At the time of her death in 1879, Sarah owned four houses in Nortonville (the house she lived in, one adjoining house not occupied, one house occupied by Mr. Powell, and another not occupied). Listed among her possessions were: a bedspread, spring mattress, feather bed, six chairs, rocking chair, clock, light stand, wash stand, ten dresses, one box herbs, two cupboards, crockery, three quilts, two blankets, Japanese cabinet, earthenware spittoon, one box of towels, feather pillow, cooking stove, two tables, a cow, and calf.

Carolina Wilhemina (Olfermann) Thomas Miller and husband George Miller, son of Sarah (Miller) Norton. After the death of her first husband, John Thomas, Carolina married George Miller. Carolina's first husband, John Thomas, and their son, Frederick Elias Thomas, are buried in Rose Hill Cemetery beside Sarah Norton. George S. Miller was appointed to serve as executor of his mother's estate, but after objections of his siblings, Sarah Norton's son-in-law, Charles Williams, served as the executor.

The village Welsh choir in front of the Congregational Church in Nortonville (church not visible). The choir master was Evan Meredith. Sarah Norton's home can be seen in the top right corner of the photograph, *circa* 1870s.

# OLIVER,
## Jane

**PERSONAL INFORMATION:**

| | |
|---|---|
| SEX: | Female |
| DATE OF BIRTH: | September 17, 1840 |
| DATE OF DEATH: | March 17, 1880 |
| PLACE OF DEATH: | Nortonville, Contra Costa County, California |
| AGE AT DEATH: | 39 years, 6 months |
| CAUSE OF DEATH: | |
| BIRTHPLACE: | Merthyr Tydfil, Glamorganshire, South Wales |
| SPOUSE: | Thomas J. Oliver |
| PARENTS: | |

**GRAVESITE INFORMATION:**

| | |
|---|---|
| LOCATION OF GRAVESITE: | Section S-D, Plot #95 |
| GRAVESTONE: | Exists |
| TYPE OF GRAVESTONE: | Marble |
| SHAPE OF GRAVESTONE: | Block |
| INSCRIPTION: | In memory of/Wife of |
| EPITAPH: | *Blessed are the dead* |
| | *who die in the Lord.* |
| MOTIF: | |
| CARVER: | |
| BASE: | Exists |
| TYPE OF BASE: | Granite |
| ENCLOSURE: | |
| TYPE OF ENCLOSURE: | |
| FENCE: | |
| TYPE OF FENCE: | |
| FENCE MOTIF: | |

# OLIVER, Jane

**ADDITIONAL PERSONAL INFORMATION:**
Jane's birth date was calculated by www.timeanddate.com, based on the date of death and age of death listed on the gravestone. According to a descendant, Jane Llewelyn married Thomas J. Oliver in 1866. See Thomas J. Oliver.

**ADDITIONAL GRAVESITE INFORMATION:**
Zelma Myrick, who recorded information in a notebook in the 1930s during a visit to Rose Hill Cemetery, reported "Pointed stone on ground broken." According to photographs located in the Black Diamond archives, an obelisk once sat on the top of this stone.

The gravestone was present in 1963 because it is listed on a student term paper by Jim Rotelli. It was stolen from Rose Hill Cemetery prior to Park District acquisition and was eventually found on a road near Concord, Contra Costa County, California, by a California Highway Patrol officer (see *Oakland Tribune* newspaper, November 6, 1973).

The epitaph comes from the *Bible*, Revelation 14:13. Jane's place of birth comes from the *Contra Costa Gazette* newspaper, March 27, 1880; and the *Oakland Tribune* newspaper, November 6, 1973.

The stone was returned to the cemetery by Black Diamond Rangers and sits on a granite base. The granite base was leveled with a sub-grade concrete pad poured under the base. The stone was attached to the base with pins and epoxy *circa* 1980s. The top portion of the stone, an obelisk, is missing.

**REFERENCES:** 1, 2, 4, 5, 6, 8 (March 27, 1880), 11 (P610.186.1 and P610.317.4), 12, 14, *Oakland Tribune* newspaper (Nov. 3, 1973, page 22-E, and Nov. 6, 1973), *Alameda Times Star* newspaper (Nov. 29, 1973), see newspaper appendix page 744

Reference 117.9

The Jane Oliver gravestone, June 1983, before it was returned to the cemetery and placed on the granite base. Photograph by Roger Epperson, EBRPD.

# OLIVER,
## Thomas J.

## PERSONAL INFORMATION:

| | |
|---|---|
| SEX: | Male |
| DATE OF BIRTH: | *Circa* 1840 |
| DATE OF DEATH: | December 10, 1885 |
| PLACE OF DEATH: | San Francisco, San Francisco County, California |
| AGE AT DEATH: | Approximately 45 years |
| CAUSE OF DEATH: | |
| BIRTHPLACE: | Abernant, Carmarthenshire, Wales |
| SPOUSE: | Jane (Llewelyn) Oliver |
| PARENTS: | John and Anna (Thomas) Oliver |

## GRAVESITE INFORMATION:

| | |
|---|---|
| LOCATION OF GRAVESITE: | Beside S-D, Plot #95 |
| GRAVESTONE: | Missing or never placed |
| TYPE OF GRAVESTONE: | |
| SHAPE OF GRAVESTONE: | |
| INSCRIPTION: | |
| EPITAPH: | |
| MOTIF: | |
| CARVER: | |
| BASE: | |
| TYPE OF BASE: | |
| ENCLOSURE: | |
| TYPE OF ENCLOSURE: | |
| FENCE: | |
| TYPE OF FENCE: | |
| FENCE MOTIF: | |

# OLIVER, Thomas J.

**ADDITIONAL PERSONAL INFORMATION:**
According to information provided by a descendant, Thomas Oliver married Jane Llewelyn in 1866. Also according to the descendant, Oliver was appointed Postmaster at Carbondale in Los Angeles County on August 31, 1881.

The *1841 Wales Census* lists Thomas Oliver, age 1, and his parents Annah [sic], age 25, and John, age 25. Also listed are his sisters, Annah [sic], age 7, and Ester, age 4.

The *1851 Wales Census* lists Thomas Oliver, age 12, born *circa* 1839 in Abernant, Carmarthenshire, Wales. Also listed are his siblings: John, age 5; James, age 2; and Eliza, age 7; and parents, Annah [sic], age 38, and John, age 37.

The *1861 Wales Census* lists Thomas, age 22, living in Merthyr Tydfil and working as a grocer's assistant.

The *1870 Census for North East, Yuba County, California* lists Thomas J. Oliver, age 30, as a miner and native of Wales born *circa* 1840. Sharing a residence with him is William S. Miles, also age 30, a miner and native of Wales.

In 1873, Thomas was a clerk and resident of Nortonville, Contra Costa County, California. The *Antioch Ledger* newspaper, February 13, 1879, lists Thomas as a Trustee of the Carbondale School District in Nortonville.

The *1880 Nortonville Precinct Census, Contra Costa County, California*, lists Thomas Oliver, age 40, as a native of Wales, widower (his wife Jane died March 17, 1880), and a boarder in Watkin Williams Hotel in Nortonville. His occupation was an ASA cleark [sic] in store.

According to the *History of Contra Costa County*, published by W. A. Slocum and Company, 1882, page 475, T. J. Oliver was a charter member of Black Diamond Lodge, No. 29, Knights of Pythias, Nortonville, organized October 24, 1874. He was also a member of Contra Costa Masonic Lodge No. 227 in Somersville, Contra Costa County, California.

The *Contra Costa Gazette* newspaper, December 19, 1885, states that Thomas J. Oliver was interred in the Somersville cemetery next to his wife, Jane. Thomas' age at death and date of birth is based on information from the 1880 census. Jane and Thomas had at least one daughter. See Jane Oliver.

**ADDITIONAL GRAVESITE INFORMATION:**
Thomas J. Oliver's name has not been recorded on any previous cemetery lists. The only source that mentions his burial in Rose Hill Cemetery is the 1885 newspaper article from the *Contra Costa Gazette*. It is possible that a gravestone was never placed at his gravesite.

**REFERENCES:** 8 (Dec. 19, 1885), 9 (Feb. 13, 1879), 10 (page 475), 12, *Oakland Tribune* newspaper (Nov. 3, 1973, page 22-E, and Nov. 6, 1973), *Alameda Times Star* newspaper (Nov. 29, 1973), see newspaper appendix 744

## PERSONAL INFORMATION:

| | |
|---|---|
| Sex: | Male |
| Date of Birth: | August 1873 |
| Date of Death: | November 7, 1873 |
| Place of Death: | |
| Age at Death: | 3 months |
| Cause of Death: | |
| Birthplace: | |
| Spouse: | None |
| Parents: | Adam and Isabella (Mary Isabelle Davis) Ott |

## GRAVESITE INFORMATION:

| | |
|---|---|
| Location of Gravesite: | Section S-E, Plot #76 |
| Gravestone: | Exists |
| Type of Gravestone: | Marble |
| Shape of Gravestone: | Tablet |
| Inscription: | *Sacred to the Memory of/Son of* |
| Epitaph: | *To [sic] Sweet a flower to bloom on earth, he is gone to bloom in Heaven.* |
| Motif: | Weeping willow tree and lamb |
| Carver: | |
| Base: | Exists |
| Type of Base: | Sandstone (new) |
| Enclosure: | |
| Type of Enclosure: | |
| Fence: | |
| Type of Fence: | |
| Fence Motif: | |

# OTT, Georg Adam

## ADDITIONAL PERSONAL INFORMATION:

According to the *MacPhee Family History* document, Georg's mother, Mary Isabelle Davis, was born at Coal Brook Mines, Luzerne County, Pennsylvania on February 24, 1854. Mary Isabelle Davis married Adam Ott in 1876. However, according to the *Index to Marriage Certificates*, located at Contra Costa County Hall of Records, Martinez, California, Adam Ott married Maria [sic] I. Davis on September 19, 1872. The document states they were married by W. H. Ford; the information is recorded in Volume 1, page 232.

Adam and Isabella/Mary Isabelle Ott had four children in addition to Georg Adam. Their other children were Jeanette, Isabel, Charles, and Elsie.

The *1870 Census for Township Three, Contra Costa County, California* lists Georg's father, Adam Ott, age 23, as a tinsmith and native of Hessia, Germany.

According to information obtained by The University of California, Berkeley archaeology students, Georg's father, Adam Ott, was listed as a tinsmith in Somersville, Contra Costa County, California in 1872. His tin shop was valued at $200.

The *Assessment List, Contra Costa County, for 1872-'73*, page 126, states that Adam Ott owned other solvent debts valued at $100 and merchandise valued at $1,000, making his total assessment value $1,100.

The *Pacific Coast Directory for 1871-73*, page 229, lists Adam Ott as a tinner in the town of Nortonville.

The *Pacific Coast Business Directory for 1876-78*, page 195, lists A. Ott as operating a "stoves and tinware" business in Nortonville.

## ADDITIONAL GRAVESITE INFORMATION:

Zelma Myrick who recorded information in a notebook in the 1930s during a visit to Rose Hill Cemetery reported "Stone broken." The white marble tablet stone was broken into two pieces. The gravestone was removed by Black Diamond Rangers and placed in storage for repair work.

In September 1999, the stone was backed with white cement mortar. The original sandstone base that once held the stone was so damaged it was unusable. The sandstone base was flipped over so that the bottom surface could be used as the top. The base was leveled, a sub-grade pad was poured under the base. The gravestone was attached to the base with pins and epoxy and placed back in the cemetery October 27, 1999. Sadly, on February 29, 2008, vandals knocked down the Ott gravestone, breaking the original base beyond repair.

Two new bases were manufactured for gravestones (Georg Adam Ott and Mary A. Dawson) in Rose Hill Cemetery by V. Fontana and Company of Colma, California, reusing the original base of the "Baseball Player" monument. This life-sized, bronze sculpture, created by renowned artist, Douglas Tilden, was dedicated July 8, 1891 and is located in Golden Gate Park in San Francisco, California.

**REFERENCES:** 1, 2, 3, 6, 8 ( July 27, 1872), 11 (P610.31.143 and P610.117.18), 12, 14, *MacPhee Family History*, Prepared by Chester Riddoch MacPhee and Marjorie Young Otton MacPhee, June 5, 1983

## PERSONAL INFORMATION:

| | |
|---|---|
| SEX: | Female |
| DATE OF BIRTH: | 1878 |
| DATE OF DEATH: | 1878 |
| PLACE OF DEATH: | Somersville, Contra Costa County, California |
| AGE AT DEATH: | Infant |
| CAUSE OF DEATH: | |
| BIRTHPLACE: | |
| SPOUSE: | None |
| PARENTS: | Walter and Emma Henrietta (Saddler) Parsons |

## GRAVESITE INFORMATION:

| | |
|---|---|
| LOCATION OF GRAVESITE: | Unknown |
| GRAVESTONE: | Missing or never placed |
| TYPE OF GRAVESTONE: | |
| SHAPE OF GRAVESTONE: | |
| INSCRIPTION: | |
| EPITAPH: | |
| MOTIF: | |
| CARVER: | |
| BASE: | |
| TYPE OF BASE: | |
| ENCLOSURE: | |
| TYPE OF ENCLOSURE: | |
| FENCE: | |
| TYPE OF FENCE: | |
| FENCE MOTIF: | |

# PARSONS, Jeanette

**ADDITIONAL PERSONAL INFORMATION:**
Family history documents provided by descendants indicate that Jeanette Parsons died as an infant in Somersville, Contra Costa County, California. The information also states that she was the daughter of Emma Henrietta (Saddler) Parsons, born 1853, Benicia, Solano County, California and Walter Parsons, born 1845 in Cornwall, England. Jeannette had at least one sister, Emma Harriett Parsons, born March 12, 1871, and two brothers: George Walter Parsons, born March 1873; and Wilbert (Bert) A. Parsons, born 1875. Wilbert Parsons married Irene Waters, and Emma Parsons married Francis William Bussey Jr. Jeanette's aunt, Mary Frances Saddler (sister of Emma Henrietta (Saddler) Parsons), married Peter Lassesen Vestnys. Their daughter, Lorenda A. Vestnys, is buried in Rose Hill Cemetery. Also buried in the cemetery is Jeanette's grandmother, Harriet A. Saddler. For additional information on family members interred in Rose Hill Cemetery see: Joseph Bussey, Saddler (male child), Harriet A. Saddler, Lorenda A. Vestnys, Edna Isabella Waters, John Robert Waters, and William (Willie) Waters.

According to the *Contra Costa Gazette* newspaper, June 11, 1870, Mr. Walter Parsons of Nortonville married Miss Emma H. Saddler of Nortonville at the residence of the bride's father in Nortonville, on June 5, 1870. The *1870 Census for Township 3, Contra Costa County, California* lists Walter Parson [sic], age 25, born *circa* 1845 in England. Also listed are his wife, Emma, age 17, born *circa* 1853 in California, and Emma's family: her mother, Harriet Saddler, age 46, a native of Virginia; her father, Frederick Saddler, age 46, a native of New York; her brother, Frederick, age 9, a native of California; and sister, Hattie, age 14, a native of California.

The *1880 Census for New York Landing, Contra Costa County, California* lists Walter Parsons, as a clerk and native of England, age 35. Walter is listed as a boarder at the hotel of Fredrick Hunds. Emma divorced Walter Parsons, and on August 30, 1885 she married Joseph Fowler Bussey.

The *1900 Census for Black Diamond, King County, Washington* lists Emma Bussey, age 46, born January 1854 in California. The census states that she married in 1885 and has been married for 15 years. Also listed is her husband Joseph Bussey, a coal miner, age 44, born August 1855, in Wisconsin; her daughter, Mable [sic] Bussey, age 13, born May 1887, in California; and her son from her first marriage, George Parsons, a coal miner, age 28, born March 1878, in California. (Note: A descendant has the birthdate for George recorded as May 29, 1873.)

The *1910 Census for Black Diamond, King County, Washington* lists Joe Bussey, age 54, as a native of Washington. His occupation is recorded as "miner, coal mines." He is noted as "widowed." Also listed are his daughter, Edna, age 9, born *circa* 1901 in Washington; his daughter, Maybell [sic] (Bussey) Purington, a native of California, age 23; and her husband, Leroy Purington, a native of Colorado, age 22.

**ADDITIONAL GRAVESITE INFORMATION:**
Jeanette Parsons' name was added to this burial record based on information written, "Jeannette [sic] Parsons buried in 1878," by an unknown individual on a Rose Hill Cemetery list compiled by Traci (Gibbons) Parent in 1977. This handwritten addition to the cemetery list was found at the Contra Costa County Historical Society History Center in Martinez, California. It appears that the same individual wrote the names of Joseph Bussey and Harriet (Langley) Saddler on the list. The source for this information is not known. No other reference source is listed for this individual.

**REFERENCES:** 8 (June 11, 1870), 11 (P610.3.5 and P610.352.3), 12

## BIRTHS.

At Willow Pass, on the 10th inst., to Mr. and Mrs. Ronian, a daughter.

## MARRIED.

At the residence of the bride's father, in Nortonville, June 5th, by Rev. R. Kernick, Mr. WALTER PARSONS and Miss EMMA H. SADDLER, both of Nortonville.

## DIED.

Near New York Landing, in this county, June 7th, JAMES HENRY McCLOSKY, son of James and Catherine McClosky, aged 3 years, 2 months and 16 days.

San Francisco and Virginia (Nevada,) papers please copy.

This article from the *Contra Costa Gazette* newspaper, June 11, 1870, announces the marriage of Mr. Walter Parsons and Miss Emma H. Saddler, both of Nortonville.

Pictured right is Emma Henrietta (Saddler) Parsons Bussey, the mother of Jeanette Parsons. Emma married Walter Parsons in Martinez, Contra Costa County, California in 1870. She divorced Walter Parsons and married Joseph Fowler Bussey in 1885. Emma was the mother of Emma Harriet Parsons, born 1871; George Walter Parsons, born 1873; Wilbert Augustus Parsons, born 1875; Jeanette Parsons, born 1878; Maybelle Bussey, born 1887; and Edna Bussey (adopted), born 1900.

Reference 3.5

East Bay Regional Park District

**FIRE AT NORTONVILLE.**—A fire broke out in Noakes' butcher shop at Nortonville about one o'clock last Thursday morning which resulted in the destruction of some fourteen buildings, two or three of which were blown up or torn down to arrest the spread of the fire. The loss of property, if estimated at its cost, is probably not less than from $25,000 to $30,000, and would not perhaps have been estimated at less than half that value at the time. There was little or no insurance to offset the loss. As it cannot be otherwise accounted for the fire is presumed to have had an incendiary origin. Following are some of the reported losses: C. H. Gordon, saloon building; Howell Thomas, hotel and dwelling; Fred Hund, barber shop and dwelling; G. H. Swartz, saloon and dwelling; Noakes & Son, market and public hall; Wesley Sharp, saloon; A. Senderman, store and dwelling; Mrs. Engler, shoe store and dwelling; Wesley Sharp, dwelling; James Sharp, dwelling; Walter Parsons, dwelling; F. A. Saddler, dwelling. There was no organization or appliances for contending with fire, but, with assistance from Somersville, the citizens made good use of all the means at hand to check the spread of the fire which threatened to sweep off all the buildings on the west side of the ravine, and but for these efforts little of that side of the town would have escaped.

The dwelling of Walter Parsons was one of many structures destroyed in a fire at Nortonville on Thursday, June 20, 1878. This article from the *Contra Costa Gazette* newspaper, June 22, 1878, describes the incident.

**PERSONAL INFORMATION:**

| | |
|---|---|
| SEX: | Female |
| DATE OF BIRTH: | December 29, 1867 |
| DATE OF DEATH: | December 7, 1870 |
| PLACE OF DEATH: | Nortonville, Contra Costa County, California |
| AGE AT DEATH: | 2 years, 11 months, 8 days |
| CAUSE OF DEATH: | |
| BIRTHPLACE: | |
| SPOUSE: | None |
| PARENTS: | John H. and Julia Piercy |

**GRAVESITE INFORMATION:**

| | |
|---|---|
| LOCATION OF GRAVESITE: | Section S-F, Plot #85 |
| GRAVESTONE: | Exists |
| TYPE OF GRAVESTONE: | Marble |
| SHAPE OF GRAVESTONE: | Tablet |
| INSCRIPTION: | *Daughter of* |
| EPITAPH: | *Too sweet a flower to bloom on Earth* |
| | *she is gone to bloom in Heaven.* |
| MOTIF: | Weeping willow tree and lamb/rope with tassels |
| CARVER: | A. Paltenghi, 812 Montgomery St., San Francisco, California |
| BASE: | Exists (original marble base is broken and in storage) |
| TYPE OF BASE: | Sandstone with new middle marble base |
| ENCLOSURE: | |
| TYPE OF ENCLOSURE: | |
| FENCE: | |
| TYPE OF FENCE: | |
| FENCE MOTIF: | |

# PIERCY, Julia Etta

**ADDITIONAL PERSONAL INFORMATION:**
Julia's birth date was calculated by www. timeanddate.com, based on her date of death and age listed on her gravestone.

Julia's father, John H. Piercy, was born in Ireland in 1829. He was listed as a resident of Nortonville, Contra Costa County, California, in October 1869.

According to the *History of Contra Costa County*, page 475, John Piercy was a charter member of Black Diamond Lodge No. 29, Knights of Pythias in Nortonville which was organized October 24, 1874. John Hay Piercy was also a member of Contra Costa Masonic Lodge No. 227 in Somersville.

By 1889, John, age 67, and his wife, Julia, a native of New York, age 63, had moved to Black Diamond, King County, Washington where John worked as a boilermaker.

The *Seattle, Washington City Directories, 1888-90 Record* lists John H. Piercy as a boilermaker.

**ADDITIONAL GRAVESITE INFORMATION:**
The gravestone was broken into two pieces and concreted flat to ground prior to East Bay Regional Park District acquisition. The gravestone was removed for repairs in February 2003. The original middle marble base is broken and contains the carver's name. The base was not able to be reused at the gravesite and was placed in storage for safekeeping.

The concrete backing from the stone was removed, the bottom sandstone base was leveled and a new middle marble base purchased. A small piece of redwood and a metal hinge were found in the ground at the back of the base in May 2003 by Black Diamond Rangers while re-leveling the base. Many small pieces of burnt wood were found around the hinge and wood piece. The stone was placed upright in the cemetery in July 2003.

**REFERENCES:** 1, 2, 3, 6, 8 (Dec. 17, 1870 and April 24, 1875), 9 (July 8, 1871), *Contra Costa Times* newspaper (May 13, 1969, page 8A), 10 (page 475), 11 (P610.31.158, P610.119.46, P610.292.144, P610.292.145, and P610.294.9), 12, 14, see newspaper appendix pages 745 and 746

The vandalized gravestone of Julia Etta Piercy, *circa* late 1960s to early 1970s. The broken middle marble base, containing the carver's name (A. Paltenghi), sits at the foot of the gravestone. The sandstone bottom base sits at the top of the gravestone.

## Local Option.

EDS. GAZETTE: A number of the citizens of Somersville, Nortonville and Clayton precincts, assembled in Good Templars' Hall, Nortonville, on Saturday evening, the 28th ult. John Piercy called the meeting to order, and stated that the object was to take steps toward the enforcement of the Local Option law in the Township. C. M. Chapman of Somersville, was appointed Chairman, and T. H. McCarthy of Clayton, Secretary. It was ordered that a committee of three be appointed to draft a petition to present to the Supervisors. T. H. McCarthy, Wm. Parry, and T. R. Muir, were appointed such committee. They proposed the following, which was adopted:

To the Hon. the Board of Supervisors of Contra Costa County, State of California: The undersigned, residents and citizens of Supervisor Township No. 4, in said county, respectfully petition your honorable body to order an election according to the provisions of the law known as the Local Option Law, and for the purposes therein mentioned.

Walter Nellis and George Copeland, of Somersville, Wm. Prosser and John Lane of Nortonville, and T. R. Muir and D. S. Carpenter of Clayton, were appointed committees to obtain the signatures of the voters to the above petition in their respective precincts. John H. Piercy and John R. Davis were appointed a committee to receive the petitions and forward them to the County Clerk, according to the provisions of the law. The Rev. Wm. Parry made some appropriate remarks, after which the meeting adjourned *sine die*.

LOCAL OPTION.

This article from the *Contra Costa Gazette* newspaper, April 4, 1874, discusses John Piercy's involvement "toward the enforcement of the Local Option law in the Township." The Local Option law allowed voters to decide if or how alcohol would be sold in their community. John Piercy was the father of Julia Etta Piercy who is buried in Rose Hill Cemetery.

## PERSONAL INFORMATION:

| | |
|---|---|
| SEX: | Female |
| DATE OF BIRTH: | January 1874 |
| DATE OF DEATH: | July 14, 1874 |
| PLACE OF DEATH: | |
| AGE AT DEATH: | 6 months |
| CAUSE OF DEATH: | |
| BIRTHPLACE: | |
| SPOUSE: | None |
| PARENTS: | O. and M. Pohl |

## GRAVESITE INFORMATION:

| | |
|---|---|
| LOCATION OF GRAVESITE: | Section S-F, Plot #110 |
| GRAVESTONE: | Exists |
| TYPE OF GRAVESTONE: | Marble |
| SHAPE OF GRAVESTONE: | Block |
| INSCRIPTION: | *Children of O. & M. Pohl* |
| EPITAPH: | |
| MOTIF: | Cross |
| CARVER: | Aitken and Luce |
| BASE: | |
| TYPE OF BASE: | |
| ENCLOSURE: | |
| TYPE OF ENCLOSURE: | |
| FENCE: | |
| TYPE OF FENCE: | |
| FENCE MOTIF: | |

# POHL, Dora

**ADDITIONAL PERSONAL INFORMATION:**
Oliver Pohl was most likely the father of Dora and Millie Pohl.

The *Assessment List, Contra Costa County, for 1872-73*, lists Oliver Pohl living in Nortonville with furniture valued at $50.

The *Assessment List, County of Contra Costa, 1876 – Somersville and Nortonville*, lists Oliver Pohl as owning a house in Nortonville valued at $250 and furniture at $30.

**ADDITIONAL GRAVESITE INFORMATION:**
Zelma Myrick, who recorded information in a notebook in the 1930s during a visit to Rose Hill Cemetery, reported, "Cross stone with tree stump inside of fence." She also reported it as an Odd Fellows plot.

A distant photograph of the Pohl cross appears in the *California Monthly* magazine, "Back Yard Ghost Towns," May 1949, page 23. According to the *Oakland Tribune* newspaper, May 28, 1944 article, "a little white cross with the names 'Millie' and 'Dora' engraved on the faces" once existed at the site.

Based on a photograph in the Black Diamond archives (see photograph on page 450), the actual burial location may either be on the west side of the George Hook site, or where the George Hook gravestone sits today. Dora shares the gravestone with sister, Millie Pohl. The gravestone was present in 1963 when it was listed in a student term paper by Jim Rotelli. Additionally, Rotelli's map indicates a fence was surrounding the gravestone. The *Valley Pioneer* newspaper, March 20, 1974, page 1, contains a photograph of the Pohl stone in what appears to be the iron fence where the gravestone and base for George B. Hook stands today.

The Pohl gravestone is broken and missing pieces, and is currently in storage for safekeeping.

A plaque was purchased by descendants and placed at the site in May 2007 to mark the burial location for Dora and her sister Millie. See Millie Pohl. The plaque says:

> MILLIE POHL
> JAN. 12, 1872 - JAN. 16, 1875
> AND
> DORA POHL
> JAN. 1874 - JULY 14, 1874
> PLAQUE PLACED IN 2007

**REFERENCES:** 1, 11 (P610.31.156, P610.31.202, P610.117.10, P610.163.16, P610.317.16, and P610.362.5), 12, *Oakland Tribune* newspaper (May 28, 1944), 14

Reference 117.10

The only remaining piece of the Dora and Millie Pohl gravestone, June 1983. This marker was sitting at Section S-F, plot #110 when the area became an East Bay Regional Park. The original placement of this stone may have been at Section S-F, plot #109. The gravestone for George B. Hook sits at plot #109 today. Photograph by Roger Epperson, EBRPD.

Rose Hill Cemetery looking east toward Somersville town site. The Dora and Millie Pohl cross stone is believed to be pictured on the far left next to or inside the iron fence. In *circa* 1939 it was reported that "cross stone with tree stump inside of fence." Photograph taken *circa* 1940s to 1950s.

## PERSONAL INFORMATION:

| | |
|---|---|
| SEX: | Female |
| DATE OF BIRTH: | January 12, 1872 |
| DATE OF DEATH: | January 16, 1875 |
| PLACE OF DEATH: | |
| AGE AT DEATH: | 3 years, 4 days |
| CAUSE OF DEATH: | |
| BIRTHPLACE: | |
| SPOUSE: | None |
| PARENTS: | O. and M. Pohl |

## GRAVESITE INFORMATION:

| | |
|---|---|
| LOCATION OF GRAVESITE: | Section S-F, Plot #110 |
| GRAVESTONE: | Exists |
| TYPE OF GRAVESTONE: | Marble |
| SHAPE OF GRAVESTONE: | Block |
| INSCRIPTION: | *Children of O. & M. Pohl* |
| EPITAPH: | |
| MOTIF: | Cross |
| CARVER: | Aitken and Luce |
| BASE: | |
| TYPE OF BASE: | |
| ENCLOSURE: | |
| TYPE OF ENCLOSURE: | |
| FENCE: | |
| TYPE OF FENCE: | |
| FENCE MOTIF: | |

# POHL, Millie

**ADDITIONAL PERSONAL INFORMATION:**
See Dora Pohl.

**ADDITIONAL GRAVESITE INFORMATION:**
Millie shares a gravestone with her sister, Dora Pohl.

**REFERENCES:** 1, 3, 6, 11 (P610.31.156, P610.31.202, P610.117.10, P610.163.16, P610.317.16, and P610.362.5), 12, *Oakland Tribune* newspaper (May 28, 1944), 14

Reference 31.202

The Dora and Millie Pohl gravestone (far left) as it appeared in July 1977. The gravestone currently sits in storage for safekeeping. A brass plaque has been placed at the site to mark the burial location for the Pohl girls. The iron fence sits nearby at the gravesite of George B. Hook. In 1974, The *Valley Pioneer* newspaper printed a photograph of the Pohl stone sitting inside this iron fence. Photograph by Traci (Gibbons) Parent.

# POWELL,
## Mary

## PERSONAL INFORMATION:

| | |
|---|---|
| SEX: | Female |
| DATE OF BIRTH: | 1818 |
| DATE OF DEATH: | April 7, 1878 |
| PLACE OF DEATH: | |
| AGE AT DEATH: | 60 years |
| CAUSE OF DEATH: | |
| BIRTHPLACE: | |
| SPOUSE: | David Powell |
| PARENTS: | |

## GRAVESITE INFORMATION:

| | |
|---|---|
| LOCATION OF GRAVESITE: | Section S-C, Plot #42 |
| GRAVESTONE: | Exists |
| TYPE OF GRAVESTONE: | Marble |
| SHAPE OF GRAVESTONE: | Tablet |
| INSCRIPTION: | *Gone Home/Wife of* |
| EPITAPH: | *Gone but not forgotten.* |
| MOTIF: | Hand with finger pointing toward Heaven |
| CARVER: | |
| BASE: | Exists |
| TYPE OF BASE: | Granite |
| ENCLOSURE: | |
| TYPE OF ENCLOSURE: | |
| FENCE: | |
| TYPE OF FENCE: | |
| FENCE MOTIF: | |

# POWELL, Mary

**ADDITIONAL PERSONAL INFORMATION:**
The *1880 census for the Nortonville Precinct, Contra Costa County, California* lists David Powell, age 54, as a miner and native of Wales. This is most likely the spouse of Mary Powell. Also listed as residing with him is his nephew, David Powell, age 14, a native of Pennsylvania.

**ADDITIONAL GRAVESITE INFORMATION:**
The gravestone was broken into two pieces and concreted flat to ground prior to East Bay Regional Park District acquisition.

**REFERENCES:** 1, 2, 3, 4, 6, 11 (P610.8.14, P610.31.127, and P610.168.12), 12, 14, *Contra Costa Times* newspaper (May 13, 1969, page 8A)

Reference 8.14

The vandalized Mary Powell gravestone, 1971, prior to East Bay Regional Park District acquisition. The stone was knocked from the granite base and concreted to the ground. Photograph by Brian Suen.

# PRICE,
## Hazel

## PERSONAL INFORMATION:

SEX: Female
DATE OF BIRTH:
DATE OF DEATH:
PLACE OF DEATH:
AGE AT DEATH:
CAUSE OF DEATH:
BIRTHPLACE:
SPOUSE:
PARENTS: George and Martha Price

## GRAVESITE INFORMATION:

LOCATION OF GRAVESITE: Unknown
GRAVESTONE: Missing
TYPE OF GRAVESTONE:
SHAPE OF GRAVESTONE:
INSCRIPTION:
EPITAPH:
MOTIF:
CARVER:
BASE:
TYPE OF BASE:
ENCLOSURE:
TYPE OF ENCLOSURE:
FENCE:
TYPE OF FENCE:
FENCE MOTIF:

# PRICE, Hazel

**ADDITIONAL PERSONAL INFORMATION:**
George and Martha Price are most likely Hazel's parents.

The *1870 Census for Township Three, Contra Costa County, California* lists George Price, age 24, as a native of England and miner. Also listed are his wife, Martha, age 23, a native of England; and their daughters, Mary, age 3, a native of England and Elizabeth, age 3 months, a native of California.

The *Assessment List for Contra Costa County, 1872-73* lists George Price as owning a house in Nortonville valued at $75.

The *1880 Nortonville Precinct Census, Contra Costa County, California* lists George Price, age 34, as a native of Wales and a miner. Also listed are his wife, Martha, age 33, a native of Wales and their five children: Mary Jane, age 13, a native of Wales; Lizzie, age 10; George, age 8; David, age 5; Lotta, age 3; all natives of California.

The *1900 Census for Spokane Ward 1, Spokane County, Washington* lists George Price, age 53, and his wife, Martha, age 53, as natives of Wales. Also listed are their children: David, age 24, and Maud, age 18, both natives of California; and Charley, age 16, a native of Washington.

**ADDITIONAL GRAVESITE INFORMATION:**
A cemetery list (reference 2; see page 1004) compiled in 1935/1936 by Ann Louchs of the Daughters of the American Revolution, is the only source that records Hazel's burial in Rose Hill Cemetery.

**REFERENCES:** 2, 8 (Nov. 23, 1878), 12

Reference 1.11

Nortonville school on School Hill, *circa* 1880s. The *Contra Costa Gazette* newspaper, July 1, 1876 stated that "The school is the largest in the county."

## PERSONAL INFORMATION:

| | |
|---|---|
| SEX: | Female |
| DATE OF BIRTH: | *Circa* 1880 |
| DATE OF DEATH: | *Circa* 1880 |
| PLACE OF DEATH: | Nortonville, Contra Costa County, California |
| AGE AT DEATH: | Infant, approximately 3 months |
| CAUSE OF DEATH: | Stillborn (according to descendants) |
| BIRTHPLACE: | Most likely Nortonville, Contra Costa County, CA |
| SPOUSE: | None |
| PARENTS: | Thomas and Mary (Perfecta Lopez) Pritchard |

## GRAVESITE INFORMATION:

| | |
|---|---|
| LOCATION OF GRAVESITE: | Unknown |
| GRAVESTONE: | Missing or never placed |
| TYPE OF GRAVESTONE: | |
| SHAPE OF GRAVESTONE: | |
| INSCRIPTION: | |
| EPITAPH: | |
| MOTIF: | |
| CARVER: | |
| BASE: | |
| TYPE OF BASE: | |
| ENCLOSURE: | |
| TYPE OF ENCLOSURE: | |
| FENCE: | |
| TYPE OF FENCE: | |
| FENCE MOTIF: | |

# PRITCHARD, Lupyester

**ADDITIONAL PERSONAL INFORMATION:**
Lupyester's father, Thomas Pritchard, was born April 18, *circa* 1846 in Pwllheli, Caernarvonshire, North Wales. He died on March 17, 1898 in Martinez, Contra Costa County, California and is presumed to be buried in Alhambra Cemetery in Martinez. Thomas was a coal miner. Originally the name was spelled Pritchett. Pritchard is the spelling that the family uses today. This spelling was documented on a Union Navy enlistment roll found by a family member at the National Archives in Washington D. C. Thomas Pritchett was enlisted in the Union Navy from October 1, 1862 to October 7, 1863. He was listed as an "ordinary seaman" and served aboard four different ships: *North Carolina, Seneca, Flag*, and *Princeton*. Thomas Pritchard married Mary (Maria) Perfecta Lopez on February 8, 1874 at Saint Francis Church in San Francisco. Mary's father was John Lopez and her mother was Florence Vega. Mary was born April 18, 1858 in Monterey, California and died December 17, 1946 in San Francisco. She is buried in Holy Cross Cemetery in Colma, San Mateo County, California. According to family she was called Grandma Roberts because after her first husband, Thomas Pritchard, died in 1898, she married Julius Roberts in San Francisco on April 13, 1908. Thomas and Mary Pritchard had at least seven children; all were born in Contra Costa County, California:

- Lydia (daughter), born *circa* 1878 (October 1877 newspaper articles in the *Contra Costa Gazette* and the *Antioch Ledger* report a daughter born in Nortonville on Oct. 8, 1877; the name of the child was not provided.)
- Lupyester (daughter), born *circa* 1880
- Ruby Estelle (daughter), born February 14, 1881 in Nortonville
- Wespie Thomas (son), born 1882
- Gracie (daughter), born July 27, 1886 in Nortonville
- Grover Clarence (son; called Clay), born June 8, 1888 in Concord
- William Raymond (son), born June 13, 1891 in Concord

According to descendants, one of the children was stillborn. The family believes the stillborn child was Lupyester, one of the children listed on the 1880 census. This child does not appear on the 1900 census so it is likely that she was the stillborn child. However, the *1880 Census for Nortonville, Contra Costa County, California* lists Lupyester as 3 months old at the time of the census – not a stillborn. The Pritchard family eventually left Contra Costa County and moved to San Francisco. In the publication *Assessment Lists 1876 and 1886 County of Contra Costa, California, Somersville and Nortonville, Township No. 4*, page 17, Thomas Prichard [sic], is listed as owning a house in Nortonville valued at $300 and furniture valued at $50 in 1876. The *1880 Nortonville Precinct Census, Contra Costa County, California* lists Thomas Pricktett [sic], age 34, born *circa* 1846 in Wales. Also listed are his wife, Mary, age 21, born *circa* 1859 in Oregon and their children: Lidda [sic], age 2, born *circa* 1878 in California; Lupyester, age 3 mos., born *circa* 1880; and Robert Roberts, age 57, a native of Wales, single and a Bar Keeper [sic]. *McKenney's Pacific Coast Directory for 1886-7*, page 604, lists Thomas Pritchard as selling liquors in Nortonville. The *1900 Census for Concord, Contra Costa County, California* lists Mary Pritchard, age 41, born April 1859 in California and widowed. Mexico is listed as the birthplace for her father and mother. Also listed are Mary's children: Lydia, age 22; Ruby, age 25; Westley [sic], age 18; Grace, age 14; Grover, age 12; and William, age 8. The *1930 Census for Oakland, Alameda County, California* lists Mary with her new spouse, Julius. Mary is recorded as age 71, and born *circa* 1859. Julius is 58 years, born *circa* 1872, and a native of Michigan.

**ADDITIONAL GRAVESITE INFORMATION:**
Descendants believe that Lupyester is buried in Rose Hill Cemetery. No other source documents her burial there.

**REFERENCES:** 8 (Oct. 20, 1877), 9 (Oct. 13, 1877), 12

# PROSSER,
## Mary

## PERSONAL INFORMATION:

SEX: Female

DATE OF BIRTH: 1824

DATE OF DEATH: September 24, 1876

PLACE OF DEATH: Somersville, Contra Costa County, California

AGE AT DEATH: 52 years

CAUSE OF DEATH:

BIRTHPLACE: Troedyrhiw Merthyr, Glamorganshire, Wales

SPOUSE: William Prosser

PARENTS:

## GRAVESITE INFORMATION:

LOCATION OF GRAVESITE: Section S-E, Plot #78

GRAVESTONE: Exists

TYPE OF GRAVESTONE: Marble

SHAPE OF GRAVESTONE: Tablet

INSCRIPTION: *Farewell/Wife of*

EPITAPH: *"Take ye heed, watch and pray,*
*for ye know not when the time is."*

MOTIF: Clasped hands

CARVER: Excelsior Marble Works, San Jose, California

BASE: Exists

TYPE OF BASE: Sandstone with new middle marble base

ENCLOSURE:

TYPE OF ENCLOSURE:

FENCE:

TYPE OF FENCE:

FENCE MOTIF:

# PROSSER, Mary

## ADDITIONAL PERSONAL INFORMATION:

The *1860 Census for Mount Pleasant, Sierra County, California*, lists William Prosser, a miner, age 38, and his wife, Mary, age 35, as natives of Wales. Also listed are their children: Joanna, age 16; Thomas, age 12; John J., age 9; all natives of Pennsylvania; and William H., age 2, a native of California. In August 1866, Mary's husband, William (born 1832 in Wales), was listed as a miner and resident of Somerville.

The *1870 Census for Township Three, Contra Costa County, California* lists William Prosser, age 50, as a miner and native of Wales. Also listed are his wife, Mary, age 45, a native of Wales and their children: Thomas, age 22; John, age 18; both miners and natives of Pennsylvania; and William, age 12, a native of California.

The *Assessment List, Contra Costa County, for 1872-73*, lists William Prosser owning land valued at $640 and improvements in Nortonville School District valued at $250.

In July 1876, William Prosser was listed in the *Antioch Ledger* newspaper as a dealer in wines, liquors and cigars on Main Street, Somersville. The ad states, "Keeps nothing but the best." W. Prosser is listed as selling liquors in *The Business Directory of San Francisco and Principal Towns of California and Nevada, 1877*, page 104, under the "Somersville" heading.

According to an *Interview with William Tornheim regarding the History of the Mt. Diablo Coal Field*, March 4, 1974, William's brother was Watkin Prosser. Tornheim, an Antioch historian, states that Watkin and William were both members of the Contra Costa Masonic Lodge No. 227 in Somersville. In 1882, William Prosser was listed as "withdrawn" from the lodge.

See Elizabeth Evans, daughter of John H. and Araminta A. Evans, pages 193-196. Araminta Evans was the stepdaughter of Watkin Prosser.

## ADDITIONAL GRAVESITE INFORMATION:

The gravestone was broken in half and concreted flat to the ground prior to East Bay Regional Park District acquisition. It was removed from the cemetery by Black Diamond Rangers in 1994 for repair. A small section was missing from the back center of the stone. The middle base was also missing. To repair the stone and place it upright, the broken pieces were drilled, pinned, and epoxied together. The missing section of the gravestone was filled with white cement mortar. A new replicated middle marble base was manufactured. In September 2000, the original bottom sandstone base was leveled with a sub grade concrete pad poured under the base. The gravestone was reattached to the base on August 10, 2001 during the Association for Gravestone Studies workshop held at Black Diamond Mines Regional Preserve.

REFERENCES: 1, 2, 3, 6, 8 (Oct. 7, 1876), 9 (July 1, 1876), 11 (P610.31.164, P610.117.13, P610.261.24, and P610.261.25), 12, 14, *Contra Costa Times* newspaper (Aug. 11, 2001, page A3), *William Tornheim, Historian , Regarding the History of the Mt. Diablo Coal Field*, March 4, 1974, see newspaper appendix pages 747

# Fourth of July
# CELEBRATION
## AT NORTONVILLE.

The Committee appointed to make arrangements for the Celebration, take pleasure in making known to the people of the County the Programme of the Day:

The Procession will form in front of the Temperance Hall promptly at 10 A. M., and march from thence to the Picnic Grounds.

The following are the officers of the day.

**Chairman:**
## WILLIAM PROSSER.
**Orator:**
## DR. DAVIS,
OF CHICO.

**Reader of Declaration of Independence:**
## H. GARNHAM.
**Chaplain:**
## REV. JOHN PRICE.
**Marshal:**
### WILLIAM CANTRILL.

A GOOD BAND OF MUSIC has been engaged for the occasion. A platform for dancing will be erected on the Grounds.

After the Exercises, FREE LUNCH will be served up to all who may wish to partake.

We extend a cordial invitation to the people of the County to unite with us, and we assure them that no effort will be spared to make this a grand affair.

In the Evening a BALL will be given at Good Templars' Hall. The following are the Committees:

*Invitation Committee.*—H. Loring, Concord; C. D. Porter, S. W. Johnson; Pacheco; Alex. Riddock, T. W. Richmond, Somersville; R. B. Hard, A. Banks, Antioch; J. W. Pinkerton, Pittsburgh; Frank Maxon, New York; Geo. Wall, Chas. Rhine, Clayton; W. P. Morgans, Asher Tyler, Nortonville.

*Floor Managers*—T. H. McCarthy, and A. Banks.

**Tickets, including Supper, $3.**
Nortonville, June 11, 1870.

William Prosser is listed as the chairman of the 4th of July celebration at Nortonville in this June 11, 1870, *Contra Costa Gazette* newspaper article.

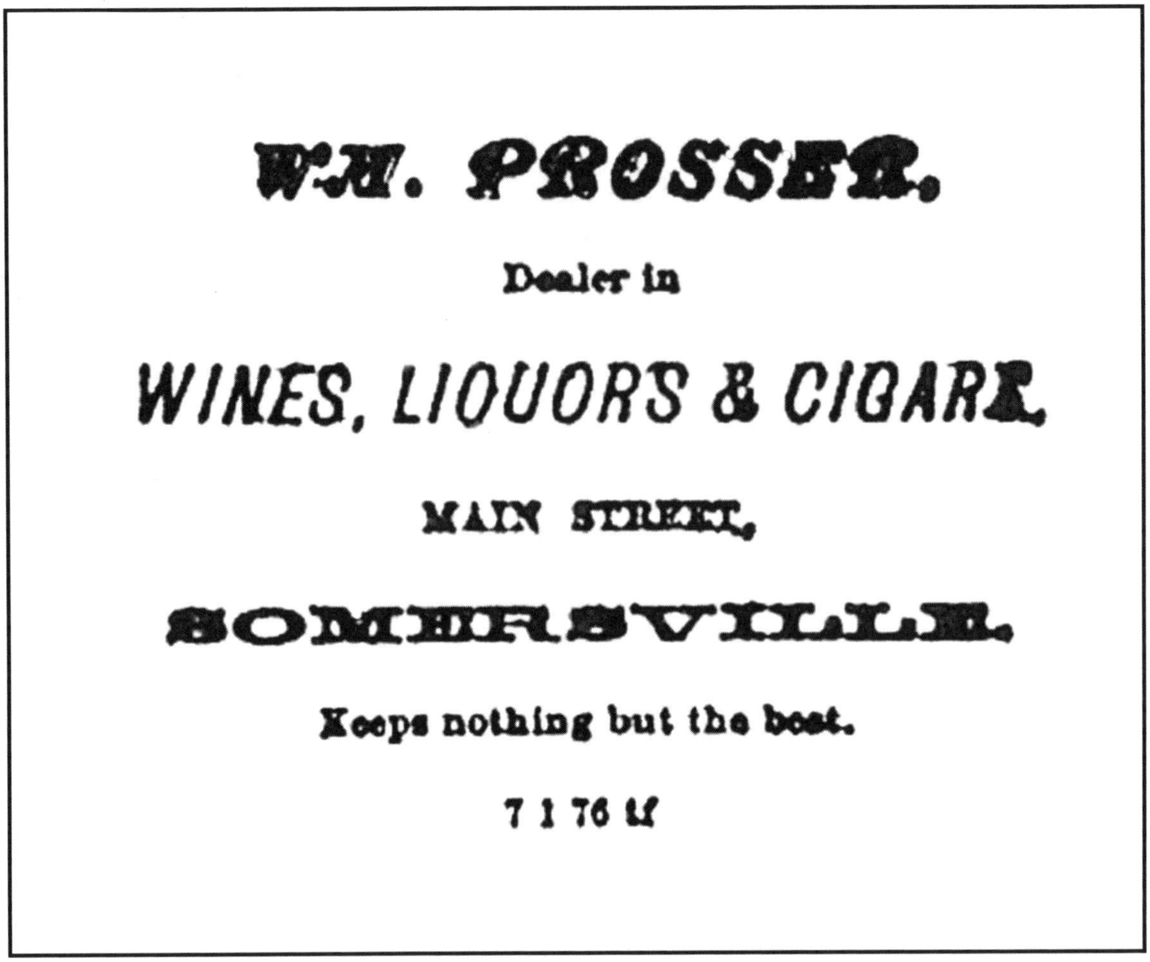

# WM. PROSSER,

Dealer in

## WINES, LIQUORS & CIGARS,

MAIN STREET,

## SOMERSVILLE.

Keeps nothing but the best.

7 1 76 tf

This advertisement from the *Antioch Ledger,* July 15, 1876, lists
Wm. Prosser as a dealer in wines, liquors and cigars in Somersville.

**PERSONAL INFORMATION:**

|  |  |
|---|---|
| SEX: | Male |
| DATE OF BIRTH: | |
| DATE OF DEATH: | |
| PLACE OF DEATH: | |
| AGE AT DEATH: | Child |
| CAUSE OF DEATH: | |
| BIRTHPLACE: | |
| SPOUSE: | None |
| PARENTS: | Joseph and Sarah Ramsay |

**GRAVESITE INFORMATION:**

|  |  |
|---|---|
| LOCATION OF GRAVESITE: | Unknown |
| GRAVESTONE: | Missing  or never placed |
| TYPE OF GRAVESTONE: | |
| SHAPE OF GRAVESTONE: | |
| INSCRIPTION: | |
| EPITAPH: | |
| MOTIF: | |
| CARVER: | |
| BASE: | |
| TYPE OF BASE: | |
| ENCLOSURE: | |
| TYPE OF ENCLOSURE: | |
| FENCE: | |
| TYPE OF FENCE: | |
| FENCE MOTIF: | |

# RAMSAY, (child)

**ADDITIONAL PERSONAL INFORMATION:**
Descendants provided the spelling of the name as "Ramsay." The name has been spelled as "Ramsey" in the 1870 Census and in the *Antioch Ledger* and *Contra Costa Gazette* newspapers.

Descendants believe that a male child, born before 1873, and the first of ten children born to the Ramsay family, is buried in Rose Hill Cemetery. The Ramsay family later moved to Washington state after the Mount Diablo Coal Field ceased to operate.

The *1870 Census for Township Three, Contra Costa County, California* lists Joseph Ramsey, [sic] an engineer, age 27, and his wife, Sarah Ramsey, age 24, both natives of Scotland. Also listed are their children: Lizzie, age 4, and Jennie, age 2, both natives of Scotland and John, age 4 months, a native of California. This is probably the family of the child buried in Rose Hill Cemetery.

In a sworn statement by Joseph Ramsay in the *Antioch Ledger* newspaper article, December 20, 1873, regarding a boiler explosion at the Independent Mine in Somersville, Ramsay (spelled as "Ramsey" in the article) stated:

> I have been engaged as an engineer ten years. I was engaged at the Independent shaft til the 3d of November last.

**ADDITIONAL GRAVESITE INFORMATION:**
Descendants believe that the Ramsay child is buried in Rose Hill Cemetery. No other sources document the burial of this child in the cemetery. Descendants provided this information to park staff in 1977/1978.

**REFERENCES:** 9 (Dec. 20, 1873), 12

ACCIDENT AT SOMERSVILLE.—We learn that J. Ramsey, a laborer in the shaft of the Independent mine at Somersville, fell down the shaft on Tuesday last, breaking his jaw bone, and otherwise severely injuring his person.

This article about J. Ramsey [sic] comes from the *Antioch Ledger* newspaper, March 14, 1874.

# REES,
## Elizabeth Ann

## PERSONAL INFORMATION:

| | |
|---|---|
| SEX: | Female |
| DATE OF BIRTH: | July 22, 1870 |
| DATE OF DEATH: | April 6, 1877 |
| PLACE OF DEATH: | |
| AGE AT DEATH: | 6 years, 8 months, 15 days |
| CAUSE OF DEATH: | |
| BIRTHPLACE: | California |
| SPOUSE: | None |
| PARENTS: | William J. and Elizabeth Rees |

## GRAVESITE INFORMATION:

| | |
|---|---|
| LOCATION OF GRAVESITE: | Section S-C, Plot #19 |
| GRAVESTONE: | Exists |
| TYPE OF GRAVESTONE: | Marble |
| SHAPE OF GRAVESTONE: | Tablet |
| INSCRIPTION: | *To the Memory of/Daughter of* |
| EPITAPH: | *Forever with Christ* |
| MOTIF: | Dove with rosebud |
| CARVER: | |
| BASE: | |
| TYPE OF BASE: | |
| ENCLOSURE: | |
| TYPE OF ENCLOSURE: | |
| FENCE: | |
| TYPE OF FENCE: | |
| FENCE MOTIF: | |

# REES, Elizabeth Ann

**ADDITIONAL PERSONAL INFORMATION:**
Elizabeth's date of birth was calculated by www.timeanddate.com, based on her date of death and age at death listed on her gravestone. The last name for this family has also been spelled as Reese.

The *1870 Census for Cottonwood, Siskiyou County, California*, lists Elizabeth's parents, William Rees, age 35, a miner and native of Wales, and Elizabeth, age 35, a native of Wales. Also listed is their daughter, Ann E. Rees, 1 month, a native of California. Since the census was taken August 3, 1870, and Elizabeth Ann was born July 23, 1870, the one-month-old Ann E. listed on the census may be Elizabeth Ann.

The *1880 Census for Nortonville Precinct, Contra Costa County, California*, lists William Reese [sic], age 35 [Note: he was listed as age 35 in the 1870 census], a miner and native of Wales. Also listed is his wife, Eliza, age 35, a native of Wales. "Boarding House" is listed as her occupation. Their two sons, Edmond, age 13, and John,

age 5, both natives of California, are listed as well. Additionally, eight borders are recorded: five miners, and a saloon keeper, tinsmith, and laborer. This may be the same family, although the last name is spelled differently and William's age is listed as 35 years in both the 1870 and 1880 census records.

According to the *Contra Costa Gazette* newspaper, June 20, 1880, William J. Rees built a boarding house near Mr. Lando's store in Nortonville.

William J. Rees, was listed as the proprietor of the Nortonville Hotel, Nortonville, Contra Costa County, California in the *McKenney's Pacific Coast Directory for 1886-7*, page 699.

**ADDITIONAL GRAVESITE INFORMATION:**
The gravestone was removed from the cemetery *circa* 1983 and placed in storage by Black Diamond Rangers until repairs can be made.

**REFERENCES:** 1, 2, 3, 4, 6, 8 (June 20, 1880), 11 (P610.31.173 and P610.117.19), 12, 14

---

## NORTONVILLE.

CONTRA COSTA COUNTY. A post and express town. Reached by S. P. Co.'s Western Division to Cornwall, thence by Black Diamond Railroad. It is an important coal mining town. Freight and express are addressed to Cornwall. Martinez is its nearest banking town. Population, 1,000.

Clifford Frank, justice of the peace
Green Henry S, livery stable
Holladay George, butcher
Howell E J, liquors
Hughes John M, coal dealer
Pritchard Thomas, liquors
Rankin Jones, notary public
Rees W J, liquors

W. J. Rees is listed as selling "liquors" in Nortonville on page 604 of the *McKenney's Pacific Coast Directory for 1886-7*.

The broken gravestone of Elizabeth Ann Rees, June 1983.
Photograph by Roger Epperson, EBRPD.

East Bay Regional Park District

# Nortonville Correspondence.

NORTONVILLE, Nov. 14th, 1880.

### THE LAST GUN.

EDS. GAZETTE:—The Republicans of Nortonville turned out last Saturday evening in full force for the purpose of celebrating in an appropriate manner the grand victory won in the election of Garfield and Arthur. The first thing on the programme was a salute of one hundred guns, and their deep thundering sound struck terror to the hearts of the defeated seventeen advocates of a "tariff for revenue only." About half past seven the procession formed in front of the Black Diamond Hotel and marched through town for an hour, then retired to the headquarters of the Club, where the band played patriotic music. The Glee Club sung "Garfield at the Fron," as well as other pieces; John J. Powell delivered a speech appropriate to the occasion; music by the band; Prof. Phalin made some remarks, and enough cash was raised on the spot to pay all outstanding obligations, as well as for powder fuse and caps for the canonading. The whole demonstration was a success. No accident occurred to mar the pleasure of the evening, and we are satisfied with the result of the election. We look forward with special interest for years of peace, prosperity, and progress in the right direction.

### THE COAL TRADE.

All the coal mines of our county are running full force all the time. The coal trade, as far as the demand goes, has never been better. The Black Diamond Company cannot supply the increasing demand for their excellent quality of coal. Though hundreds of tons are shipped away every day, yet they could sell hundreds more if they could get it out of the mines. If the demand continues as it is now, the company doubtless will work nights as well as days. It is very gratifying to all connected with the coal mines that consumers are beginning to appreciate the home article in preference to the imported article.

### IMPROVEMENTS.

The Black Diamond Company have just put on a new and elegant passenger car on the Black Diamond Railroad. It is twenty-two feet long, and a little less than average width of passenger cars. It was manufactured by Carter Bros., Newark, Alameda County. It is finished in the highest style, and reflects credit on the manufacturers as well as the company.

The Central Pacific Railroad Company are busily engaged now in putting in a new switch at Cornwell station to connect the C. P. with the Black Diamond railway, so that they can get their cars loaded at the bunkers at the mine in Nortonville instead of dumping it into the cars at Cornwall station, as they do at present when shipping by rail. The company are preparing to build a new depot at this station also.

Mr. William J. Rees is building a neat and commodious boarding house near Mr. Lando's store. The carpenters and paper-hangers are putting the finishing touches on it now. They expect to open the new caravansary in about two weeks. Success to the enterprise.                    J. J. P.

Under the "IMPROVEMENTS" heading in this *Contra Costa Gazette*, November 20, 1880 newspaper article, Elizabeth's father, William J. Rees, is mentioned as "building a neat and commodious boarding house."

## PERSONAL INFORMATION:

| | |
|---|---|
| SEX: | Female |
| DATE OF BIRTH: | June 17, 1874 |
| DATE OF DEATH: | October 22, 1875 |
| PLACE OF DEATH: | Nortonville, Contra Costa County, California |
| AGE AT DEATH: | 1 year, 4 months, 5 days |
| CAUSE OF DEATH: | Epidemic (possibly scarlet fever) |
| BIRTHPLACE: | Nortonville, Contra Costa County, California |
| SPOUSE: | None |
| PARENTS: | David W. and Jane (Richards) Rees |

## GRAVESITE INFORMATION:

| | |
|---|---|
| LOCATION OF GRAVESITE: | Unknown |
| GRAVESTONE: | Missing or never placed |
| TYPE OF GRAVESTONE: | |
| SHAPE OF GRAVESTONE: | |
| INSCRIPTION: | |
| EPITAPH: | |
| MOTIF: | |
| CARVER: | |
| BASE: | |
| TYPE OF BASE: | |
| ENCLOSURE: | |
| TYPE OF ENCLOSURE: | |
| FENCE: | |
| TYPE OF FENCE: | |
| FENCE MOTIF: | |

# REES, Margaret

**ADDITIONAL PERSONAL INFORMATION:**
According to descendants, Margaret may have died of scarlet fever. Also according to descendants, Margaret's father, David Rees, was born January 11, 1840, in Morgan Parish, Glamorganshire, Wales. He died July 4, 1914, in Roslyn, Kittitas County, Washington. His wife, Jane (Richards) Rees, was born April 11, 1840, in Maesteg, Glamorganshire, Wales. She died July 27, 1919, in Roslyn, Kittitas County, Washington. According to the descendant, they are both buried in the Roslyn Cemetery, Roslyn, Kittitas County, Washington. David and Jane were married on November 30, 1861 in Morgan Parish, Glamorganshire, Wales and had eight children. Their children were:

- Mary Ann, born July 26, 1862, Wales; died April 18, 1939, Seattle, Washington

- Dave J., born March 1, 1864, Wales; died May 27, 1927, Marshfield, Oregon

- Thomas, born Feb. 11, 1866, Wales; died Jan. 11, 1867, Tomaqua, Pennsylvania

- Joseph, born July 17, 1868, Nortonville, California; died June 19, 1888, Washington Territory

- Sarah Jane, born June 26, 1870, Nortonville, California; died May 8, 1963, Washington

- Elizabeth, born March 25, 1872, Nortonville, California; died May 14, 1957, Monroe, Washington

- Margaret, born June 17, 1874, Nortonville, California; died Oct. 22, 1875, Nortonville, California

- Maud, born Aug. 23, 1878, Nortonville, California; died Feb. 20, 1957, Cle Elum, Washington

After leaving the Mount Diablo Coal Field, the Rees family moved to Oregon and then Washington state. The *Roster of California Pioneers*, compiled by the Native Daughters of the Golden West, 1985, page 71, states that Margaret's mother, Jane (Richards) Rees, was born in 1840 in Wales. She arrived in San Francisco, California in 1866 and resided in Somersville. This source lists six children: Mary Ann, born 1863 in Wales; David J., born March 1, 1865 in Wales; Joseph, born 1868 in Somersville; Sarah, born May 1870 in Somersville; Elizabeth and Maude [sic], both with birth dates unknown and both born in Somersville.

The *1870 Census for Township Three, Contra Costa County*, California lists Margaret's parents, David Reese [sic], a miner, age 30, and Jane, age 30, both natives of Wales. Also listed are their children: Mary, age 7, a native of Wales; David, age 5, a native of Wales; Joseph, age 2, a native of California; and Sarah, age 1 month, a native of California.

The *1876 Contra Costa County Voting Register*, lists David W. Rees, age 30, as a native of Wales and miner living in Nortonville. His date of registration was July 18, 1871.

The *1880 Census for Nortonville, Contra Costa County, California* lists Mrs. Reese [sic] (no first name listed), age 40, as a native of Wales. Listed with her are her children: Mary Ann, age 17, a housekeeper and native of Wales; Dave, age 16, a native of Wales; Joseph, age 11, a native of California; Sarah Jane, age 10, a native of California; Lizzy, age 8, a native of California; and Margaret, age 1, a native of California. [Since the first Margaret died in 1875, it is likely they may have given another child the same name.]

**ADDITIONAL GRAVESITE INFORMATION:**
According to descendants, Margaret's burial place is recorded as "Nortonville" in the family *Bible*. The family believes she is buried in Rose Hill Cemetery. This is the only source that documents her burial there.

**REFERENCES:** 12

## PERSONAL INFORMATION:

| | |
|---|---|
| SEX: | Male |
| DATE OF BIRTH: | 1847 |
| DATE OF DEATH: | July 24, 1876 |
| PLACE OF DEATH: | Nortonville, Contra Costa County, California |
| AGE AT DEATH: | 29 years |
| CAUSE OF DEATH: | Burns and/or suffocation caused by a mine explosion |
| BIRTHPLACE: | England |
| SPOUSE: | |
| PARENTS: | |

## GRAVESITE INFORMATION:

| | |
|---|---|
| LOCATION OF GRAVESITE: | Unknown |
| GRAVESTONE: | Missing or never placed |
| TYPE OF GRAVESTONE: | |
| SHAPE OF GRAVESTONE: | |
| INSCRIPTION: | |
| EPITAPH: | |
| MOTIF: | |
| CARVER: | |
| BASE: | |
| TYPE OF BASE: | |
| ENCLOSURE: | |
| TYPE OF ENCLOSURE: | |
| FENCE: | |
| TYPE OF FENCE | |
| FENCE MOTIF: | |

# REYNOLDS, George M.

**ADDITIONAL PERSONAL INFORMATION:**
The *1876 Contra Costa County Voting Register* lists George M. Reynolds as a native of England, and a miner living in Nortonville. He registered to vote on September 1, 1875.

The *Contra Costa Gazette* newspaper, July 29, 1876, states that G. M. Reynolds and seven others died as a result of an explosion which occurred at a mine in Nortonville on July 24, 1876. The article states that he left behind a wife and three young children. George M. Reynolds was interred in the cemetery by the Knights of Pythias Lodge No. 29 of Nortonville, of which he was a member.

See Theophile Dumas, William Gething, Thomas D. James, Meredith Lewis, Evan Smith, David Watts, Theophilus Watts, and William L. Williams.

**ADDITIONAL GRAVESITE INFORMATION:**
The *Contra Costa Gazette* newspaper and the *History of Contra Costa County,* by Slocum and Company, 1882, page 474, are the only sources that indicate George M. Reynolds is buried in Rose Hill Cemetery. His name was not recorded on any previous cemetery lists.

**REFERENCES:** 8 (July 29, 1876 and August 12, 1876), 9 (July 29, 1876), 10 (pages 474 and 475), see newspaper appendix (William Gething) pages 706 and 707

## The Nortonville Calamity.

NORTONVILLE, Aug. 8th, 1876.
EDS. GAZETTE: It has been make known to the public, through the columns of the GAZETTE and other papers, that a terrible disaster occurred at Nortonville, July 24th, resulting in the death of eleven person, and leaving four wives widows and twelve children fatherless. On Friday evening last a meeting was held at Good Templars' Hall in this place, for the purpose of devising the best means for the relief of the orphans and widows. A committee of seven persons was elected for such purpose. After the adoption of certain Resolutions, a subscription list was opened, when the sum of $496 was promised. Since then the members of said committee have collected $713, making a total of $1,209.

The magnitude of this calamity makes it desirable to appeal to the community at large for help. We confidently trust that a liberal and generous response will be made, particularly by the inhabitants of Contra Costa. All contributions to be sent to Mr. L. Abrams, Treasurer of the Committee, ot Nortonville.

Yours truly,

C. GWYNN, Sec'y.

This article from the *Contra Costa Gazette* newspaper, August 12, 1876 states that four wives were left as widows and twelve children left fatherless as a result of the July 24, 1876 mine explosion at the Black Diamond Mine in Nortonville. George M. Reynolds died in the accident and left behind a wife and three children.

# RICHARDS,
## Daniel

## PERSONAL INFORMATION:

| | |
|---|---|
| SEX: | Male |
| DATE OF BIRTH: | July 20, 1821 |
| DATE OF DEATH: | September 11, 1890 |
| PLACE OF DEATH: | Somersville, Contra Costa County, California |
| AGE AT DEATH: | 69 years, 1 month, 22 days |
| CAUSE OF DEATH: | Bright's disease |
| BIRTHPLACE: | Merthyr Tydvil [sic], Glamorganshire, South Wales |
| SPOUSE: | Mary (Thomas) Ritchards [sic] |
| PARENTS: | |

## GRAVESITE INFORMATION:

| | |
|---|---|
| LOCATION OF GRAVESITE: | Section S-C, Plot #15 |
| GRAVESTONE: | Exists |
| TYPE OF GRAVESTONE: | Marble |
| SHAPE OF GRAVESTONE: | Tablet |
| INSCRIPTION: | |
| EPITAPH: | *Gone by sight but not by memory.* |
| MOTIF: | |
| CARVER: | |
| BASE: | Exists |
| TYPE OF BASE: | Middle marble base (new) sits on larger bottom granite base |
| ENCLOSURE: | Exists |
| TYPE OF ENCLOSURE: | Sandstone |
| FENCE: | |
| TYPE OF FENCE: | |
| FENCE MOTIF: | |

# RICHARDS, Daniel

**ADDITIONAL PERSONAL INFORMATION:**
The place of birth, listed on Daniel's gravestone, is misspelled. The correct spelling is Merthyr Tydfil.

The Contra Costa County Hall of Records in Martinez, Contra Costa County, California, lists Daniel's death as age 69 years, 1 month, and 20 days, and not 69 years, 1 month, and 22 days, as stated on his gravestone. His doctor was W. S. George.

The *1870 Census for Township Three, Contra Costa County, California* lists Daniel Richards, age 40, as a miner and native of England. Also listed is his wife, Mary, age 40, a native of England.

The *Assessment List for Contra Costa County, 1872-73*, lists Daniel Richards being assessed $175 for one house and furniture in Somersville.

The *1880 Census for Somersville Precinct, Contra Costa County, California* lists Daniel Richards, age 59, as a miner and native of Wales. Also listed is his wife, Mary, age 52, a native of Wales.

Daniel's wife, Mary, died before he did, in December 1888. According to the *Antioch Ledger* newspaper, September 20, 1890, Richards had no children and no relatives except a cousin of his deceased wife. Because of this, at his death he left his house in Somersville, with the furniture and appurtenances and $500 cash, to John H. and Margaret Thomas of Somersville. The Thomas family apparently nursed him during his illness. John Thomas and David Rees served as executors of his will. The total value of his estate at the time of death was $4,197.85. Daniel gave the balance of his estate ($2,857.21) to twenty people. Each individual listed received $142.86.

Daniel was buried beside his wife on September 14, 1890. According to Contra Costa County probate Records, it cost $2.50 to dig Daniel's grave and $53.00 for the coffin. See Mary Ritchards (Richards).

**ADDITIONAL GRAVESITE INFORMATION:**
Zelma Myrick, who recorded information in a notebook in the 1930s during a visit to Rose Hill Cemetery, reported "Stone off base." Daniel's gravestone was concreted flat to the ground prior to East Bay Regional Park District acquisition. The middle marble base was missing. A new middle marble base was purchased in 2002 by park staff. A larger bottom granite base exists. The stone was placed upright by Black Diamond Rangers in April 2003.

**REFERENCES:** 1, 2, 3, 4, 5, 6, 7, 8 (Sept. 17, 1890), 9 (Sept. 20, 1890), 11 (P610.31.134, P610.43.4, P610.145.1, P610.232.4, and P610.285.15), 12, 13, 14, see newspaper appendix page 748

# RICHARDS,
## John

## PERSONAL INFORMATION:

| | |
|---|---|
| SEX: | Male |
| DATE OF BIRTH: | 1844 |
| DATE OF DEATH: | August 4, 1874 |
| PLACE OF DEATH: | |
| AGE AT DEATH: | 30 years |
| CAUSE OF DEATH: | |
| BIRTHPLACE: | South Wales |
| SPOUSE: | Mary Richards |
| PARENTS: | |

## GRAVESITE INFORMATION:

| | |
|---|---|
| LOCATION OF GRAVESITE: | Section N-E, Plot #64 |
| GRAVESTONE: | Exists |
| TYPE OF GRAVESTONE: | Marble |
| SHAPE OF GRAVESTONE: | Tablet |
| INSCRIPTION: | *In Memory of* |
| EPITAPH: | *Mewn bedd o dan gudd, mewn arch o goed.* |
| | *Allan nis gellir fy nganfod,* |
| | *Na dyn byw fy nwys abnabod,* |
| | *Nol cau fy medd ond cof fy mod.* |
| MOTIF: | Dove with olive branch/rope with tassels |
| CARVER: | Pioneer Steam Marble Works, 422 & 424 Jackson St., San Francisco, California |
| BASE: | Exists |
| TYPE OF BASE: | Sandstone |
| ENCLOSURE: | |
| TYPE OF ENCLOSURE: | |
| FENCE: | |
| TYPE OF FENCE: | |
| FENCE MOTIF: | |

# RICHARDS, John

**ADDITIONAL PERSONAL INFORMATION:**
The *1870 Census for Township Three, Contra Costa County, California*, lists John Richards, age 27, as a miner and native of Wales.

The *Assessment List for Contra Costa County for 1872-73*, lists John Richards living in the town of Nortonville and property assessed at $25.

**ADDITIONAL GRAVESITE INFORMATION:**
Zelma Myrick, who recorded information in a notebook in the 1930s during a visit to Rose Hill Cemetery, reported "Stone down."

The epitaph is written in Welsh and was translated by Idris Evans of the Welsh American Society of Northern California. The translation is:

> Hidden in a grave,
> In a wooden coffin.
> Not perceived from the outside
> Nor recognized by anyone,
> After closing my grave I am but a memory.

John shares a gravestone with his son, William Timothy Richards. The stone was concreted flat to the ground prior to East Bay Regional Park District acquisition.

In June 2001, the gravestone was removed from the cemetery for repairs. The concrete was detached from the stone and the sandstone base was leveled with a sub-grade concrete footing. The base that was broken into two pieces, was repaired with epoxy. The stone was placed upright in the base on August 2, 2001 by Black Diamond Rangers.

An Italian Cypress tree was planted at this site by park staff sometime between the 1980s and 1990s. See William Timothy Richards.

**REFERENCES:** 1, 2, 3, 5, 6, 11 (P610.13.11, P610.31.145, P610.151.4, P610.168.11, P610.168.32, P610.255.16 to P610.255.26, and P610.263.5), 12, 14

# RICHARDS,
## William Timothy

**PERSONAL INFORMATION:**

| | |
|---|---|
| SEX: | Male |
| DATE OF BIRTH: | January 1873 |
| DATE OF DEATH: | June 2, 1874 |
| PLACE OF DEATH: | |
| AGE AT DEATH: | 17 months |
| CAUSE OF DEATH: | |
| BIRTHPLACE: | |
| SPOUSE: | None |
| PARENTS: | John and Mary Richards |

**GRAVESITE INFORMATION:**

| | |
|---|---|
| LOCATION OF GRAVESITE: | Section N-E, Plot #64 |
| GRAVESTONE: | Exists |
| TYPE OF GRAVESTONE: | Marble |
| SHAPE OF GRAVESTONE: | Tablet |
| INSCRIPTION: | *In Memory of/Son of* |
| EPITAPH: | *Mewn bedd o dan gudd, mewn arch o goed.* |
| | *Allan nis gellir fy nganfod,* |
| | *Na dyn byw fy nwys abnabod,* |
| | *Nol cau fy medd ond cof fy mod.* |
| MOTIF: | Dove with olive branch/rope with tassels |
| CARVER: | Pioneer Steam Marble Works, |
| | 422 & 424 Jackson St., San Francisco, California |
| BASE: | Exists |
| TYPE OF BASE: | Sandstone |
| ENCLOSURE: | |
| TYPE OF ENCLOSURE: | |
| FENCE: | |
| TYPE OF FENCE: | |
| FENCE MOTIF: | |

# RICHARDS, William Timothy

**ADDITIONAL PERSONAL INFORMATION:**
See John Richards.

**ADDITIONAL GRAVESITE INFORMATION:**
William Timothy shares a gravestone with his father, John Richards. See the gravestone information for John Richards.

**REFERENCES:** 1, 2, 3, 6, 11 (P610.13.11, P610.31.145, P610.151.4, P610.168.11, P610.168.32, P610.255.16 to P610.255.26, P610.259.1 to P610.259.5, and P610.263.5), 12, 14

Reference 13.11

The vandalized John and William Timothy Richards gravestone, *circa* 1950s, lies on the ground prior to East Bay Regional Park District acquisition. Black Diamond Rangers repaired the gravestone and placed it back upright in the base in 2001.

# RICHMOND,
## Anne

## PERSONAL INFORMATION:

| | |
|---|---|
| SEX: | Female |
| DATE OF BIRTH: | January 10, 1826 |
| DATE OF DEATH: | May 31, 1882 |
| PLACE OF DEATH: | |
| AGE AT DEATH: | 56 years, 4 months, 21 days |
| CAUSE OF DEATH: | |
| BIRTHPLACE: | Aberystruth, Monmouthshire, South Wales |
| SPOUSE: | Thomas Richmond |
| PARENTS: | Mr. and Mrs. Jones |

## GRAVESITE INFORMATION:

| | |
|---|---|
| LOCATION OF GRAVESITE: | Section S-E, Plot #80 |
| GRAVESTONE: | Missing |
| TYPE OF GRAVESTONE: | Marble |
| SHAPE OF GRAVESTONE: | |
| INSCRIPTION: | *Father and Mother/Both Natives of Monmouthshire South Wales* |
| EPITAPH: | *WE HOPE TO MEET AGAIN.* (on marble middle base) |
| MOTIF: | Flowers and shells |
| CARVER: | |
| BASE: | Exists |
| TYPE OF BASE: | Middle marble base with epitaph, sits on larger granite base |
| ENCLOSURE: | |
| TYPE OF ENCLOSURE: | |
| FENCE: | |
| TYPE OF FENCE: | |
| FENCE MOTIF: | |

# RICHMOND, Anne

**ADDITIONAL PERSONAL INFORMATION:**
Anne died seven days after her husband, Thomas. Family members believe she died of a broken heart. See Elizabeth Richmond and Thomas Richmond.

Thomas Richmond married Anne Jones in Wales. On August 17, 1862, Thomas and Anne, and their son, Thomas, departed on the *S. S. Great Eastern* and sailed from Liverpool, England with 820 other passengers to the United States. As they approached New York Harbor the *Great Eastern* hit a submerged rock; however the vessel managed to reach New York. The ship continued to California via Panama and from Panama they traveled on another ship bound for California.

Once in California the Richmonds headed to Morristown, Sierra County. The family arrived in Somersville, Contra Costa County, California, *circa* 1864. Their daughter, Margaret, was the first of their children born in California (at least three children were born prior in Wales). Margaret was named for her father's sister, Margaret, who lived in Wales.

Thomas was a member of Mount Diablo Lodge No. 128, Independent Order of Odd Fellows (I.O.O.F.) in Somersville, Contra Costa County, California. He was seriously injured when a coal car ran off the track and struck him. Thomas died a short time later.

**ADDITIONAL GRAVESITE INFORMATION:**
A broken bottom granite base is all that remains at this gravesite today. Part of the middle marble base with the epitaph exists and was placed in storage for safekeeping. The gravestone disappeared prior to East Bay Regional Park District acquisition. It was present in 1963 because it appears on a list in a student term paper by Jim Rotelli. Additionally it was photographed in the cemetery *circa* 1965.

The gravestone was still present in the cemetery in 1971; a distant view of the stone appears in *Contra Costa Living* (a supplement to the *Contra Costa Sunday Times* newspaper, April 11, 1971, page 8).

A plaque was purchased by descendants and placed at the site in August 2005. The plaque says:

> *THOMAS RICHMOND*
> *1825 – 1882*
> *ANNE RICHMOND*
> *1826 – 1882*
> *PLAQUE PLACED IN 2005*

**REFERENCES:** 1, 2, 3, 6, 11 (P610.14.1, P610.25.1, P610.31.201, P610.129.2, P610.268.15, P610.285.14, P610.317.4, P610.317.6, P610.362.2, P610.362.5, and P610.362.6), 12; *Black Diamond – Somersville, Interview with Helen Branstetter King*, May 15, 1979, (by Patrice Jeppson and John Liversidge, page 9); *The Richmond Story in Calif.*, (no author or date, 10 pages)

Margaret Richmond (left) with parents Thomas and Anne (Jones) Richmond. Date unknown.

Reference 268.5

Reference 268.7

Margaret Richmond, daughter of Anne and Thomas Richmond, and sister to Elizabeth Richmond; left, as a young woman and right, later in life.

According to family records, Margaret, was attending San Jose Normal School in 1882, studying to become a teacher, when she was notified about her father's accident. Her father, Thomas Richmond, died April 7, 1882 in Somersville and is buried in Rose Hill Cemetery. At the time of his death, Thomas owned two houses in Somersville, valued at $500.

*The Richmond Story in Calif.*, page 7, states:

> The family sent word that her father [Thomas Richmond] had been hurt. She [Margaret] immediately took a train to get home as soon as possible. A man got on the train carrying a newspaper and sat down beside her. He opened the paper to read the news. Margaret, sitting next to him too read the headlines. 'Tom Richmond Killed in the Mine.'

## PERSONAL INFORMATION:

| | |
|---|---|
| SEX: | Female |
| DATE OF BIRTH: | September 6, 1856 |
| DATE OF DEATH: | February 17, 1865 |
| PLACE OF DEATH: | Somersville, Contra Costa County, California |
| AGE AT DEATH: | 8 years, 5 months, 11 days |
| CAUSE OF DEATH: | Mountain Fever/scarlatina maligna |
| BIRTHPLACE: | Somersville, Contra Costa County, California |
| SPOUSE: | None |
| PARENTS: | Thomas and Anne (Jones) Richmond |

## GRAVESITE INFORMATION:

| | |
|---|---|
| LOCATION OF GRAVESITE: | Section S-E, Plot #81 |
| GRAVESTONE: | Exists |
| TYPE OF GRAVESTONE: | Marble |
| SHAPE OF GRAVESTONE: | Tablet |
| INSCRIPTION: | *In Memory of/Daughter of Thos. & Anne Richmond of Somersville* |
| EPITAPH: | *Farewell dear Lizzie, she is gone the way we all must go, And may we be at peace with God. Before it happens so.* |
| MOTIF: | Clasped hands |
| CARVER: | Aitken and Luce, Sacramento, California |
| BASE: | Exists |
| TYPE OF BASE: | Granite |
| ENCLOSURE: | |
| TYPE OF ENCLOSURE: | |
| FENCE: | |
| TYPE OF FENCE: | |
| FENCE MOTIF: | |

# RICHMOND, Elizabeth

**ADDITIONAL PERSONAL INFORMATION:**
Family records state that the Richmond family arrived in Somersville in 1863 or 1864, and that Elizabeth died of mountain fever (a form of meningitis).

The *Contra Costa Gazette* newspaper, February 25, 1865, says Elizabeth died of the disease scarlatina maligna (scarlet fever). The article lists her age of death as 8 years and 6 months, and not 8 years, 5 months, and 11days as stated on her gravestone. Elizabeth is buried next to her parents, Anne and Thomas Richmond.

Numerous other children died from scarlet fever during the same period of time and are buried in, or are believed to be buried in, Rose Hill Cemetery. Other children who died in 1865 of scarlet fever include:

- Charles W. Blackburn, died February 20, 1865, age 9 years, 7 months
- Thomas Pratten Goulding, died January 31, 1865, age 7 years, 7 months, 17 days
- Jane Russel Muir, died January 4, 1865, age 4 years, 3 (?) months
- John Tonkins, died December 29, 1865, age 16 years, 3 months
- Annie Tregellas, died February 19, 1865, age 7 years, 7 months

- James Tregellas, died December 28, 1865, age 2 years, 21 days
- Joseph Tregellas, died February 18, 1865, age 5 years, 1 month
- John Edmund Wright, died December 28, 1865, age 9 years, 10 months
- Mary Elizabeth Wright, died December 25, 1865, age 1 year, 6 months

See Anne Richmond and Thomas Richmond.

**ADDITIONAL GRAVESITE INFORMATION:**
Elizabeth is believed to be one of the first individuals buried in Rose Hill Cemetery, or at least it is the oldest gravestone in the cemetery today. The gravestone was broken in six places and concreted flat to the ground prior to East Bay Regional Park District acquisition. A granite base, previously buried, was discovered by Black Diamond Rangers in the 1990s.

**REFERENCES:** 1, 2, 3, 4, 8 (Feb. 25, 1865), 11 (P610.14.1, P610.25.1, P610.31.162, P610.119.51, P610.119.52, and P610.317.6), 12, 14; *Black Diamond – Somersville, Interview with Helen Branstetter King,* May 15, 1979, (by Patrice Jeppson and John Liversidge, page 9); *The Richmond Story in Calif.,* (no author or date, 10 pages); see newspaper appendix page 749

## PERSONAL INFORMATION:

| | |
|---|---|
| SEX: | Male |
| DATE OF BIRTH: | July 16, 1825 |
| DATE OF DEATH: | April 7, 1882 |
| PLACE OF DEATH: | Somersville, Contra Costa County, California |
| AGE AT DEATH: | 57 years, 8 months, 22 days |
| CAUSE OF DEATH: | Run over by coal car |
| BIRTHPLACE: | Aberystruth, Monmouthshire, South Wales |
| SPOUSE: | Anne (Jones) Richmond |
| PARENTS: | Mr. and Mrs. William Richmond |

## GRAVESITE INFORMATION:

| | |
|---|---|
| LOCATION OF GRAVESITE: | Section S-E, Plot #80 |
| GRAVESTONE: | Missing |
| TYPE OF GRAVESTONE: | Marble |
| SHAPE OF GRAVESTONE: | |
| INSCRIPTION: | *Father and Mother/Both Natives of Monmouthshire South Wales* |
| EPITAPH: | *WE HOPE TO MEET AGAIN.* (on marble middle base) |
| MOTIF: | Flowers and shells |
| CARVER: | |
| BASE: | Exists |
| TYPE OF BASE: | Middle marble base with epitaph, sits on larger granite base |
| ENCLOSURE: | |
| TYPE OF ENCLOSURE: | |
| FENCE: | |
| TYPE OF FENCE: | |
| FENCE MOTIF: | |

# RICHMOND, Thomas

**ADDITIONAL PERSONAL INFORMATION:**
The *1861 Census for Wales* lists Thomas Richmond, age 35, as a native of Aberystruth, Monmouthshire, Wales. Thomas and his family are listed as living with his father, William Richmond, age 63, a native of Cwmder, Breconshire, Wales. Also listed are Thomas' wife, Anne, age 34, and their children: Thomas, age 14; Mary, age 6; and Elizabeth, age 4. All are natives of Aberystruth, Monmouthsire, Wales.

The *1876 Contra Costa County Voting Register* lists Thomas Richmond, age 43, as a native of Wales and miner in Somersville. He registered to vote on July 23, 1868.

In the *1880 Census for Somersville Precinct, Contra Costa County, California*, Thomas Richmond, age 54, is listed as a miner and native of Wales. Also listed are his wife, Anne, age 53, a native of Wales, and their children: William, age 14 and Margaret Ann, age 16. Both are natives of California. Also residing with them are Cornelies Royal, age 62, from Ireland and Lawrance Power, age 35, a miner from Ireland.

Listed as his children at the time of his death were: Thomas W. Richmond, age 36, of Eureka, Humboldt County, California; Mary (Richmond) Alford, age 28, of Ferndale, Humboldt County, California; Margaret Richmond, age 18, of Somersville, Contra Costa County, California;

and William A. Richmond, age 16, of Somersville, Contra Costa County, California. Thomas' wife, Anne, died seven days after his death. A daughter, Elizabeth, is buried beside them. See Anne Richmond and Elizabeth Richmond.

**ADDITIONAL GRAVESITE INFORMATION:**
Thomas shares a gravestone with his wife, Anne Richmond. A broken granite bottom base is all that remains at this gravesite. A middle marble base, which contained the epitaph, once existed at the site and sat on top of the granite base. Portions of the middle marble base are in storage. A plaque was purchased by descendants and placed at the burial site in August 2005. The plaque says:

> THOMAS RICHMOND
> 1825 – 1882
> ANNE RICHMOND
> 1826 – 1882
> PLAQUE PLACED IN 2005

**REFERENCES:** 1, 2, 3, 6, 8 (April 15, 1882), 11 (P610.14.1, P610.25.1, P610.31.201, P610.129.2, P610.268.15, P610.279.2, P610.285.14, P610.317.4, P610.317.6, P610.362.2, P610.362.5, and P610.362.6), 12; *Black Diamond – Somersville, Interview with Helen Branstetter King*, May 15, 1979, (by Patrice Jeppson and John Liversidge, page 9); *The Richmond Story in Calif.*, (no author or date, 10 pages); see newspaper appendix pages 750 and 751

---

**DIED.**

RICHMOND—At Somersville, April 7th, Thomas Richmond, a native of Wales; aged 57 years.

---

This article from the *Contra Costa Gazette* newspaper, April 15, 1882, announces the death of Thomas Richmond.

Elizabeth Richmond's gravestone and footstone (left) sits beside the
gravestone of her parents, Anne and Thomas Richmond.
Photograph taken *circa* 1939 by Zelma Myrick.

The front side of the Anne and Thomas Richmond gravestone, 1963.
The gravestone sits on a middle marble base that says *WE HOPE TO MEET AGAIN.*

The backside of the Thomas and Anne Richmond gravestone, *circa* 1965.

# RIDDOCK,
## Mary Jane

## PERSONAL INFORMATION:

| | |
|---|---|
| SEX: | Female |
| DATE OF BIRTH: | *Circa* 1858 |
| DATE OF DEATH: | March 2, 1865 |
| PLACE OF DEATH: | |
| AGE AT DEATH: | 7 years |
| CAUSE OF DEATH: | |
| BIRTHPLACE: | |
| SPOUSE: | None |
| PARENTS: | Alexander and Jessie (Davis) Riddock |

## GRAVESITE INFORMATION:

| | |
|---|---|
| LOCATION OF GRAVESITE: | Unknown |
| GRAVESTONE: | Missing or never placed |
| TYPE OF GRAVESTONE: | |
| SHAPE OF GRAVESTONE: | |
| INSCRIPTION: | |
| EPITAPH: | |
| MOTIF: | |
| CARVER: | |
| BASE: | |
| TYPE OF BASE: | |
| ENCLOSURE: | |
| TYPE OF ENCLOSURE: | |
| FENCE: | |
| TYPE OF FENCE: | |
| FENCE MOTIF: | |

# RIDDOCK, Mary Jane

**ADDITIONAL PERSONAL INFORMATION:**
Mary Jane's date of birth was calculated by www.timeanddate.com, based on her date of death and age at death reported in the *Contra Costa Gazette* newspaper, March 11, 1865. The newspaper article also states that Mary Jane was the oldest daughter of Alexander and Jesse Reddock [sic].

In a sworn statement by A. Riddock in the *Antioch Ledger* newspaper, December 20, 1873, regarding a boiler explosion at the Independent Mine in Somersville, Riddock stated:

> Am an engineer; have been employed as such for 25 years. I was within 30 feet of the boiler when the explosion occurred. The boilers were repaired about one year ago; they were not very good at that time. I would not have dared to run over fifty-five pounds of steam a year ago. The boilers were leaking and in a bad condition generally at that time, generally defective and worn out. The rivets were very bad. The adding of fifteen pounds weight to the bar would require about 30 pounds additional steam.

The *1870 Census for Township Three, Contra Costa County, California* lists Alex Riddock, age 43, born *circa* 1827 in Scotland. His occupation is listed as engineer. Also listed with him are his wife, Jemie [sic], age 33, born *circa* 1837 in "British America" and their children: Lizzie, age 11, born in Pennsylvania; Jenet [sic], age 5; Wingate, age 3; and Alex, age nine months. All were born in California.

The *1871-1872 Contra Costa County Directory*, page 374, lists A. Riddock as an engineer in Somersville.

The *1880 Census for Judsonville, Contra Costa County, California* lists Alex Riddock, age 50, born *circa* 1830 in Scotland. His occupation is listed as engineer. Also recorded are his wife, Jessie, age 43, born *circa* 1837 in "B America" and their children: Nettie, age 15; Wingate, age 12; Alixander [sic], age 10; George, age 8; Jessie Q., age 6; and Margie, age 3. All are natives of California.

The *1900 Census for San Francisco, San Francisco County, California* lists Alexander Riddock, age 70, born December 1829 in Scotland and married in 1857. It also states his year of immigration as 1852 and his occupation as "collector." Also listed on the census is his wife, Jessie, age 62, born June 1837 in "Canada English" and a mother of 12 children. Four children are listed on the census: Alexander S., single, age 30, born October 1869 in California with his occupation as engineer – stationary; George H., single, age 28, born March 1872 in California with his occupation as plumber; Margaret A., single, age 23, born January 1877 in California with her occupation as saleslady – dry goods; and Grace E., single, age 17, born August 1882 in California.

In a document compiled by a descendant, it states that three children died from the "black plague." See Robert Riddock (died Feb. 1865), Robert Riddock (died 1867), and William Riddock (died 1865).

**ADDITIONAL GRAVESITE INFORMATION:**
A descendant believes that members of the Riddock family are buried in Rose Hill Cemetery. No other cemetery list or source documents their burial there.

**REFERENCES:** 8 (March 11, 1865), 9 (Dec. 20, 1873, July 26, 1877, Nov. 24, 1877, April 25, 1885, and Feb. 14, 1891), 12, see newspaper appendix (Emma Edwards) page 700

Reference 3.12

Pictured above is Alexander Riddock, most likely the son of Alexander and Jessie (Davis) Riddock. According to a descendant, Alexander, age 28, married Jessay [sic] Davis, age 19, at Coal Brook, Pennsylvania on November 13, 1856. Alexander and Jessie Riddock arrived in Somersville, Contra Costa County, California on July 27, 1863. The Riddocks owned the only house in Somersville with a brick chimney. This home was later moved to New York Landing, near present-day Pittsburg, and rebuilt. The Riddocks also moved to New York Landing. Alexander and Jessie Riddock had twelve children. They were:

- Mary Jane, born *circa* 1858; died March 2, 1865 (possibly buried in Rose Hill)
- Elizabeth, born *circa* 1859
- William, born *circa* 1861; died 1865 (possibly buried in Rose Hill)
- Robert, born *circa* 1865; died Feb. 27, 1865 (possibly buried in Rose Hill)
- Jeanette, born April 26, 1866, Somersville, California; died 1886, San Francisco, California
- Wingate (twin to Robert), born July 17, 1867, Somersville, California; died 1939
- Robert (twin to Wingate), born July 17, 1867, Somersville, California; died 1867 (possibly buried in Rose Hill)
- Alexander S., born Oct. 26, 1869, Somersville, California
- George H., born March 1872, Somersville, California
- Jessie, born *circa* 1874, Somersville, California; died *circa* 1893, San Francisco, California
- Margaret A., born Jan. 11, 1877, Judsonville, California; died Nov. 26, 1960, San Francisco, California
- Grace Ethel, born Aug. 13, 1882, Judsonville, California

The Pittsburg Mine, Somersville, *circa* 1897. On the left is the headframe for the hoist that lifted coal out of the mine. The Pittsburg was the largest of the five mines in Somersville. Alexander Riddock worked at this mine in the 1870s as a stationary engineer and later worked at a coal mine in the neighboring town of Judsonville. Riddock also owned and operated a hotel in Somersville called "Riddock's Hotel."

## PERSONAL INFORMATION:

SEX:                    Male

DATE OF BIRTH:          *Circa* April 1863

DATE OF DEATH:          February 27, 1865

PLACE OF DEATH:

AGE AT DEATH:           1 year, 10 months

CAUSE OF DEATH:

BIRTHPLACE:

SPOUSE:                 None

PARENTS:                Alexander and Jessie (Davis) Riddock

## GRAVESITE INFORMATION:

LOCATION OF GRAVESITE:  Unknown

GRAVESTONE:             Missing or never placed

TYPE OF GRAVESTONE:

SHAPE OF GRAVESTONE:

INSCRIPTION:

EPITAPH:

MOTIF:

CARVER:

BASE:

TYPE OF BASE:

ENCLOSURE:

TYPE OF ENCLOSURE:

FENCE:

TYPE OF FENCE:

FENCE MOTIF:

# RIDDOCK, Robert

**ADDITIONAL PERSONAL INFORMATION:**
The date of birth for Robert was calculated by www.timeanddate.com, based on his date of death and age at death reported in the *Contra Costa Gazette* newspaper, March 11, 1865. The newspaper article also states that Robert was the only son of Alexander and Jesse Reddock [sic]. The Riddocks would eventually have six sons and six daughters. See Mary Jane Riddock, Robert Riddock (died 1867), and William Riddock.

**ADDITIONAL GRAVESITE INFORMATION:**
A descendant believes that members of the Riddock family are buried in Rose Hill Cemetery. No other cemetery list or source documents their burial there.

**REFERENCES:** 8 (March 11, 1865), 12, see newspaper appendix (Emma Edwards) page 700

THE EMPIRE COAL MINE.—The work for developing the Empire Coal Mine, as we are informed by Mr. Alexander Riddock, is being prosecuted by the owners with unflagging energy and large outlay of capital for the advantageous cutting and raising of the coal. The slope is already down nine hundred feet, with gangway turned in the vein on that level, where a water lodgment is to be sunk forty feet and a pump set for raising the water, one being already at work in the six hundred feet gangway. The slope is to be immediately extended down three hundred feet further on the vein where another gangway will be run, and an air shaft driven from that depth which will be also permanently used for raising the water and coal from the mine. The hoisting drum of the engine is also about to be changed from one of seven to one of twelve feet in diameter, with a 40-inch face, capable of carrying rope enough for hoisting from a depth of 2,200 feet. The railroad of three feet gauge for delivering the coal into barges at Antioch, is completed, and equipped with cars and a Baldwin locomotive of the most approved construction for a heavy grade road. Messrs. Judson and Belshaw, the principal owners of the mine, are large consumers of coal in their powder, candle, chemical and other manufacturing works, and will soon be able to supply themselves with fuel from their own mine as well as to furnish other customers.

This newspaper article from the *Contra Costa Gazette*, November 24, 1877, references the involvement of Alexander Riddock at the Empire Coal Mine. The Empire Mine was located in the eastern section of the Mount Diablo Coal Field.

## PERSONAL INFORMATION:

| | |
|---|---|
| SEX: | Male |
| DATE OF BIRTH: | July 17, 1867 |
| DATE OF DEATH: | 1867 |
| PLACE OF DEATH: | |
| AGE AT DEATH: | 3 weeks |
| CAUSE OF DEATH: | |
| BIRTHPLACE: | Somersville, Contra Costa County, California |
| SPOUSE: | None |
| PARENTS: | Alexander and Jessie (Davis) Riddock |

## GRAVESITE INFORMATION:

| | |
|---|---|
| LOCATION OF GRAVESITE: | Unknown |
| GRAVESTONE: | Missing or never placed |
| TYPE OF GRAVESTONE: | |
| SHAPE OF GRAVESTONE: | |
| INSCRIPTION: | |
| EPITAPH: | |
| MOTIF: | |
| CARVER: | |
| BASE: | |
| TYPE OF BASE: | |
| ENCLOSURE: | |
| TYPE OF ENCLOSURE: | |
| FENCE: | |
| TYPE OF FENCE: | |
| FENCE MOTIF: | |

# RIDDOCK, Robert

**ADDITIONAL PERSONAL INFORMATION:**
See Mary Jane Riddock, Robert Riddock (died Feb. 27, 1865), and William Riddock. This was the second Robert Riddock born to Alexander and Jessie Riddock.

**ADDITIONAL GRAVESITE INFORMATION:**
A descendant believes that members of the Riddock family are buried in Rose Hill Cemetery. No other source documents their burial there.

**REFERENCES:** 12

SOMERSVILLE.—We learn from an obliging correspondent at Somersville, that the Mt. Diablo Lodge, No. 128, I. O. O. F., instituted at that place in November last, now numbers thirty-two members and is in very prosperous condition in finances and fellowship character, with the following officers : N. G., John Williams ; V. G., Thomas S. Jones ; Rec. Sec., John G. Davis ; Fin. Sec., Thomas Brown ; Treas., Wm. Prosser ; P. N. G., Alexander Riddock.

Saturday last was signalized by the raising of a handsome new liberty pole—which was to have been raised on Washington's birth-day anniversary had the weather not been so unpropitious. The new staff, nicely painted, stands 95 feet out of the ground, and it will speak well for the public spirited and patriotic citizens of our mountain coal mining town.

This *Contra Costa Gazette* newspaper article from March 23, 1867, states that Alexander Riddock served as an officer of the Mount Diablo Lodge, No. 128, Independent Order of Odd Fellows (I.O. O. F.) in Somersville.

## PERSONAL INFORMATION:

| | |
|---|---|
| SEX: | Male |
| DATE OF BIRTH: | *Circa* 1861 |
| DATE OF DEATH: | 1865 |
| PLACE OF DEATH: | |
| AGE AT DEATH: | 4 years |
| CAUSE OF DEATH: | |
| BIRTHPLACE: | |
| SPOUSE: | None |
| PARENTS: | Alexander and Jessie (Davis) Riddock |

## GRAVESITE INFORMATION:

| | |
|---|---|
| LOCATION OF GRAVESITE: | Unknown |
| GRAVESTONE: | Missing or never placed |
| TYPE OF GRAVESTONE: | |
| SHAPE OF GRAVESTONE: | |
| INSCRIPTION: | |
| EPITAPH: | |
| MOTIF: | |
| CARVER: | |
| BASE: | |
| TYPE OF BASE: | |
| ENCLOSURE: | |
| TYPE OF ENCLOSURE: | |
| FENCE: | |
| TYPE OF FENCE: | |
| FENCE MOTIF: | |

# RIDDOCK, William

**ADDITIONAL PERSONAL INFORMATION:**
See Mary Jane Riddock, Robert Riddock (died 1865), and Robert Riddock (died 1867). See newspaper article "The Stewartville Concert" from the *Contra Costa Gazette*, July 26, 1884 on page 685, regarding a Nellie Riddock.

**ADDITIONAL GRAVESITE INFORMATION:**
A descendant believes that members of the Riddock family are buried in Rose Hill Cemetery. No other source documents their burial there.

**REFERENCES:** 12

### Dance at Judsonville.

A social dance will be given at Hobson's Hall in Judsonville, on Monday evening, Feb 23d in honor of Washington's birthday. The members of the committee of arrangements are James Hobson, James Golden and Alex Riddock; Floor Managers, Thos. Golden and John McAvoy. First class music has been secured for the occasion and a good time is guarenteed. Tickets, including lunch, 75 cents. The dance will undoubtedly be well patronized by the devotees of terpsichore in Antioch, for the last time they went to Judsonville to a party they all came home reporting a royal good time.

William's father, Alexander Riddock, participated in many community events in the coal field. This article from the *Antioch Ledger*, February 14, 1891, mentions the involvement of Riddock in the social dance given at Hobson's Hall in Judsonville on February 23, in honor of Washington's birthday.

## A Red Letter Day for Stewartville.

The Odd Fellows celebration and picnic at Stewartville was a grand success, and the most enjoyable affair of the season. Antioch turned out en masse, and the excursion train was loaded down. In fact there were probably twice as many people from Antioch as from the mines. The Odd Fellows who were active in getting the encampment removed to Martinez instead of Antioch, would do well to make note of this fact. How many came up from Martinez, to attend their festival? At the appointed hour, lead by the Antioch brass band Mount Diablo and San Joaquin Lodges formed in Stewartville and marched to the grove, where a large number of people had congregated. On arrival at the grove the open air, ritualistic exercises were carried out by Noble Grand Laird, when the President of the Day A. Riddock took charge of affairs. He introduced H. D. Rowe, who made a short and pointed address, when the orator of the day, J. E. Cahenour was introduced, and delivered an eloquent and logical oration. After the literary exercises the company dispersed to explore well filled baskets. Those who desired to dance occupied the platform, and the Antioch Brass Band furnished the music. All who attended agree that it was a well conducted picnic, and that Grand Marshal Samuel Brown was the right man in the right place. The festivities wound up with a grand ball in the evening, with excellent music by the Stewartville String Band. Harry Treglown, and in fact all the miners, made the party a pleasure long to be remembered by all visitors. A great many more would have stayed to the party, but there was no night train and no way to get home. All in all it was a happy time, and one long to be remembered.

This article from the *Antioch Ledger* newspaper, May 2, 1885 indicates that:

A. Riddock took charge of the affairs during the Odd Fellows celebration and picnic at Stewartville. He introduced H. D. Rowe, who made a short and pointed address...

## Anniversary of Somersville I. O. R. M.

SOMERSVILLE, Feb. 5, 1867.

EDS. GAZETTE :

In default of any more competent correspondent I am moved to let you hear that the Manhattan Tribe No. 2, Independent Order of Red Men, celebrated the Anniversay of the Order, at our little town last evening, in style that reflects the highest credit upon the liberal spirit of the members and the good taste of the managers. The supper tables— three in number, spread in the nicely carpeted and tastefully decorated hall—were arranged under the supervision of Mr. and Mrs. R. Talfor, and their handsome appearance as well as the ample display of tempting edibles, was greatly admired

Alexander Riddock and William Prosser Esqrs. discharged their duties as President and Vice President of the evening, to entire satisfaction of the guests.

An interesting and appropriate feature of the exercises was the reading of an historical sketch of the origin of the I. O. R. M. by I. A. Iredale, Esq.

Abraham Lobree, Esq.,responded in a handsome manner to the first regular toast : " The great Council, I. O. R. M. of the United States."

The songs, sentiments, mirth and music that filled the measure of the evening, lighted as they were, by the bright, approving smiles of the ladies, will long be pleasently remembered by the guests, and it is proper to say that the Somersville Brass Band and Messrs. Talfor and Webster are entitled to special mention for their contributions of music and song to the entertainment. *  *

The *Contra Costa Gazette* newspaper of February 9, 1867, notes that Alexander Riddock "discharged" his duties as president at the Manhattan Tribe No. 2, Independent Order of Red Men (I. O. R. M.) anniversary celebration in Somersville during their February 5th event.

# RITCHARDS (RICHARDS),
## Mary

**PERSONAL INFORMATION:**

| | |
|---|---|
| SEX: | Female |
| DATE OF BIRTH: | 1825 |
| DATE OF DEATH: | December 13, 1888 |
| PLACE OF DEATH: | Somersville, Contra Costa County, California |
| AGE AT DEATH: | 63 years |
| CAUSE OF DEATH: | Consumption |
| BIRTHPLACE: | South Wales |
| SPOUSE: | Daniel Richards [sic] |
| PARENTS: | |

**GRAVESITE INFORMATION:**

| | |
|---|---|
| LOCATION OF GRAVESITE: | Section S-C, Plot #14 |
| GRAVESTONE: | Exists |
| TYPE OF GRAVESTONE: | Marble |
| SHAPE OF GRAVESTONE: | Tablet |
| INSCRIPTION: | *Wife of* |
| EPITAPH: | *Asleep in Jesus.* |
| MOTIF: | |
| CARVER: | |
| BASE: | Exists |
| TYPE OF BASE: | Middle marble base sits on top of granite base |
| ENCLOSURE: | Exists |
| TYPE OF ENCLOSURE: | Sandstone |
| FENCE: | |
| TYPE OF FENCE: | |
| FENCE MOTIF: | |

# RITCHARDS (RICHARDS), Mary

**ADDITIONAL PERSONAL INFORMATION:**
Mary's last name (Ritchards) is spelled differently on her gravestone than her husband's name of Richards.

The Contra Costa County Hall of Records in Martinez, Contra Costa County, California lists her date of death as November 13, 1888, and not December 13, 1888 as listed on her gravestone.

The *Contra Costa Gazette* newspaper, December 21, 1888, lists her age at death as 62 years and 5 months. See Daniel Richards.

Mary Thomas, age 58, of Somersville, Contra Costa County, California, and Daniel Richards, age 65, also of Somersville, applied for a marriage license most likely in 1886 or 1887. The prior entry in the ledger lists the year as 1886 and the entry following the Richards (also on page 444) appears to be 1887. The information was recorded in the *Applications for Marriage Licenses, Contra Costa County, 1873-1887*, page 444, located at the Contra Costa County Historical Society History Center in Martinez, California. The entry does not contain a date and a message under the entry appears to say "(Error No go.) Glass." F. L. Glass served as a Deputy Clerk for Contra Costa County.

**ADDITIONAL GRAVESITE INFORMATION:**
Zelma Myrick, who recorded information in a notebook in the 1930s during a visit to Rose Hill Cemetery, reported "Stones off base."

Mary is buried beside her husband, Daniel Richards. The gravestone was concreted flat to the ground prior to East Bay Regional Park District acquisition. The stone was removed by Black Diamond Rangers in July 2001 for repairs. The base was re-leveled, the concrete was removed from the gravestone, and the stone was reattached to the middle base. An inscription from the stone carver, found on the bottom of the base, reads "Daniel Richards." The gravestone was placed back upright in the cemetery in August 2001, during the Association for Gravestone Studies Conservation Workshop held at Black Diamond Mines Regional Preserve.

**REFERENCES:** 1, 2, 3, 4, 5, 6, 7, 8 (Dec. 19, 1888-two articles), 9 (Nov. 13, 1886), 11 (P610.31.133, P610.43.4, P610.145.1, P610.232.4, and P610.285.15), 12, 14; *Regional Park News*, East Bay Regional Park District (Vol. 15, Issue 2, July, August, September 2001); see newspaper appendix page 752

Reference 8.11

The vandalized gravestones of Mary Ritchards (Richards) and Daniel Richards, 1971. Photograph by Brian Suen.

# ROGERS (RODGERS),
## Elizabeth

## PERSONAL INFORMATION:

SEX:                    Female
DATE OF BIRTH:          *Circa* 1856
DATE OF DEATH:          1884
PLACE OF DEATH:         Clayton, Contra Costa County, California
AGE AT DEATH:           28 years
CAUSE OF DEATH:
BIRTHPLACE:             Pottsville, Schuylkill County, Pennsylvania
SPOUSE:                 Thomas Rogers (Rodgers)
PARENTS:                Mr. and Mrs. Mucklow

## GRAVESITE INFORMATION:

LOCATION OF GRAVESITE:  Unknown
GRAVESTONE:             Missing
TYPE OF GRAVESTONE:
SHAPE OF GRAVESTONE:
INSCRIPTION:
EPITAPH:
MOTIF:
CARVER:
BASE:
TYPE OF BASE:
ENCLOSURE:
TYPE OF ENCLOSURE:
FENCE:
TYPE OF FENCE:
FENCE MOTIF:

# ROGERS (RODGERS), Elizabeth

**ADDITIONAL PERSONAL INFORMATION:**
According to a descendant, Elizabeth (Mucklow) Rogers' son, Thomas Andrew Rogers, was born November 22, 1876 in Clayton, Contra Costa County, California and lived in Nortonville for a while.

Thomas Rogers, believed to be Elizabeth's husband, was a hotelkeeper in Nortonville in 1872. Thomas Rogers was also listed as a member of the Contra Costa Masonic Lodge No. 227 in Somersville in 1873 and a Master Mason in 1882.

*The Pacific Coast Business Directory for 1876-78*, page 195, lists T. M. Rogers as operating a "boarding and liquor saloon" in Nortonville.

The *1890 Great Register of Voters in Contra Costa County, California* lists Thomas M. Rogers, age 48, as a native of Wales and resident of Nortonville.

His occupation is recorded as saloonkeeper [sic] and his date of registration as April 10, 1879. This record indicates that his naturalization papers were lost.

**ADDITIONAL GRAVESITE INFORMATION:**
A coal field descendant provided the name of Elizabeth Rogers (Rodgers) and states he saw the gravestone for Elizabeth in Rose Hill Cemetery years ago. No other source documents her burial there.

The coal field descendant who provided the information about Elizabeth, the 1876-78 Business Directory, as well as the information recorded on the back of the photograph (pictured below), records the spelling of the last name as Rogers. The newspaper article below and the 1890 Great Register spell the last name as Rodgers.

**REFERENCES:** 8 (Jan. 13, 1874), 12, *Fifty Years of Masonry in California, Volume 1*, Edwin A. Sherman, San Francisco, California, George Spaulding and Company Publishers, 1898

Courtesy of CCCHS

MAHEM AT NORTONVILLE.—Hugh Pugh and Richard Pritchard had a difficulty at the boarding house of Thomas Rodgers in Nortonville, some time in the early part of this week. Rodgers intervened to make peace, when both the others turned and attacked him savagely, biting one of his cheeks quite off in the encounter. A warrant has been issued for the arrest of Pugh on charge of mayhem. But at last report he was still at large, having as is supposed, set off at once for San Francisco after commission of the offense.

The two individuals on the left are identified only as Grandma Abrams and Tom Rogers. Thomas Rogers operated a hotel in Nortonville. It is not known if this is the same Thomas Rogers that was married to Elizabeth Rogers. The above newspaper article concerning Thomas comes from the *Contra Costa Gazette*, January 31, 1874.

# SADDLER,
## (male child)

**PERSONAL INFORMATION:**

| | |
|---|---|
| SEX: | Male |
| DATE OF BIRTH: | |
| DATE OF DEATH: | |
| PLACE OF DEATH: | |
| AGE AT DEATH: | Approximately 2-3 years |
| CAUSE OF DEATH: | |
| BIRTHPLACE: | |
| SPOUSE: | None |
| PARENTS: | Frederick Augustus & Harriet A. (Langley) Saddler |

**GRAVESITE INFORMATION:**

| | |
|---|---|
| LOCATION OF GRAVESITE: | Unknown |
| GRAVESTONE: | Missing |
| TYPE OF GRAVESTONE: | |
| SHAPE OF GRAVESTONE: | |
| INSCRIPTION: | |
| EPITAPH: | |
| MOTIF: | |
| CARVER: | |
| BASE: | |
| TYPE OF BASE: | |
| ENCLOSURE: | |
| TYPE OF ENCLOSURE: | |
| FENCE: | |
| TYPE OF FENCE: | |
| FENCE MOTIF: | |

# SADDLER, (male child)

**ADDITIONAL PERSONAL INFORMATION:**
According to a descendant, a male Saddler child is buried in Rose Hill Cemetery. Descendants also believe his mother, Harriet A. Saddler, is buried in Rose Hill Cemetery. See Harriet A. Saddler for more information.

The *1860 Census for Benicia, Solano County, California* lists the child's father, Frederick Saddler, age 34, as a native of New York and a laborer. Also listed are his mother, Harriet, age 34, a native of Virginia and his siblings: Mary F., age 14, a native of Virginia; Emma H., age 7; and Harriet L., age 4; both natives of California.

The *1870 Census for Township Three, Contra Costa County, California* lists Frederick Saddler, age 46, as a laborer and native of New York. Also listed are his wife, Harriet, age 46, a native of Virginia and their children, Hattie, age 14, and Fredrick [sic], age 9; both natives of California.

The *1880 Census for Nortonville Precinct, Contra Costa County, California* lists Fredrick [sic] Saddler, age 56, as a carpenter and native of New York. Also listed are his wife Harriet, age 56, a native of Virginia and their son, Freddy Saddler, age 18, a laborer and native of California.

This family is also related to the Bussey, Parsons, and Vestnys families. See Joseph Bussey, Jeanette Parsons, and Lorenda A. Vestnys.

**ADDITIONAL GRAVESITE INFORMATION:**
A descendant recalled that the gravestone for this child was adorned with a lamb. No other source documents the Saddler child's burial in Rose Hill Cemetery.

**REFERENCES:** 8 (June 22, 1878 and March 15, 1884), 12

## PERSONAL INFORMATION:

|                  |                                               |
|------------------|-----------------------------------------------|
| SEX:             | Female                                        |
| DATE OF BIRTH:   | October 2, 1823                               |
| DATE OF DEATH:   | March 6, 1884                                 |
| PLACE OF DEATH:  | Nortonville, Contra Costa County, California  |
| AGE AT DEATH:    | 60 years, 5 months, 4 days                    |
| CAUSE OF DEATH:  |                                               |
| BIRTHPLACE:      | Yorktown, Virginia                            |
| SPOUSE:          | Frederick Augustus Saddler                    |
| PARENTS:         | Mr. and Mrs. Langley                          |

## GRAVESITE INFORMATION:

|                       |                         |
|-----------------------|-------------------------|
| LOCATION OF GRAVESITE:| Unknown                 |
| GRAVESTONE:           | Missing or never placed |
| TYPE OF GRAVESTONE:   |                         |
| SHAPE OF GRAVESTONE:  |                         |
| INSCRIPTION:          |                         |
| EPITAPH:              |                         |
| MOTIF:                |                         |
| CARVER:               |                         |
| BASE:                 |                         |
| TYPE OF BASE:         |                         |
| ENCLOSURE:            |                         |
| TYPE OF ENCLOSURE:    |                         |
| FENCE:                |                         |
| TYPE OF FENCE:        |                         |
| FENCE MOTIF:          |                         |

# SADDLER, Harriet A.

**ADDITIONAL PERSONAL INFORMATION:**
The *Contra Costa County Directory 1871-2*, page 376, lists Harriet's husband, Fred'k A. Sadler [sic], as a laborer in Nortonville.

The *1876 Contra Costa County Voting Register*, lists Fred Augustus Saddler, age 40, as a native of New York, his occupation carpenter and his residence as Nortonville. His date of registration was July 14, 1866.

The *Antioch Ledger* newspaper, August 18, 1877 reported that during the Republican primary election, F. A. Saddler was one of eight delegates chosen from Nortonville to attend the nominating convention at Pacheco, Contra Costa County, California.

According to the *Contra Costa Gazette* newspaper, June 22, 1878, the dwelling of F. A. Saddler was destroyed during a fire in Nortonville. See article on page 442.

The *Contra Costa Gazette*, October 11, 1879, reported that F. A. Saddler served on an inquest jury with nine other men regarding the fatal accident of Mrs. Sarah Norton. (See Sarah Norton, pages 429-432 and 742.)

In the *History of Contra Costa County, California*, published by W. A. Slocum and Company, 1882, page 476, Saddler is listed as a member and original officer of Carbondale Lodge No. 288, International Order of Good Templars, which was instituted in 1867 in Nortonville.

The *Great Register of Contra Costa County, State of California, 1894*, lists Frederick Augustus Saddler as age 69, 5' 5½" tall, dark complexion, gray eyes and hair. He was a carpenter and native of New York living in West Hartley (one of five communities in the Mount Diablo Coal Field).

This family is also related to the Bussey, Parsons, and Vestnys families. See Joseph Bussey, Jeanette Parsons, and Lorenda A. Vestnys. See the Saddler male child (page 506) for census information regarding this family.

**ADDITIONAL GRAVESITE INFORMATION:**
Information was written by an unknown individual on a Rose Hill Cemetery list compiled by Traci (Gibbons) Parent in 1977, stating "Harriet Langley Parker Saddler buried by back fence, no marker." This handwritten addition to the cemetery list was found at the Contra Costa County Historical Society History Center in Martinez, California. It appears that the same individual wrote the names of Joseph Bussey and Jeanette Parsons on the list. The source for this information is not known. No other reference source is listed for this individual.

**REFERENCES:** 8 (June 22, 1878, Oct. 11, 1879, and March 15, 1884), 9 (Aug. 18, 1877), 12, see newspaper appendix page 753

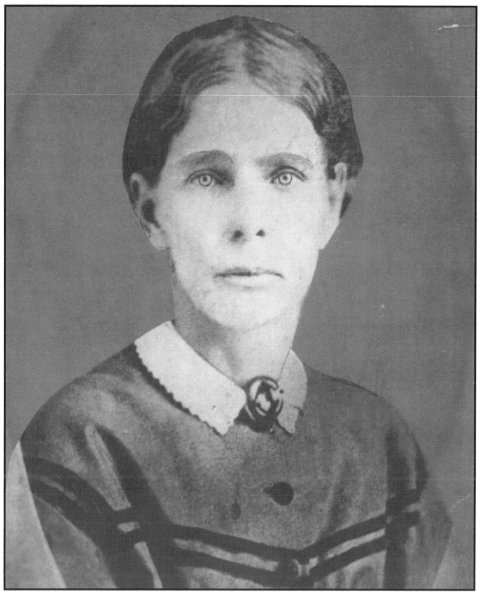

Harriet A. (Langley) Saddler was the wife of Frederick Augustus Saddler of Nortonville. Harriet married Frederick Augustus Saddler in Virginia in 1845. Langley was her maiden name according to her daughter, Mary's, death certificate. Harriet was born October 2, 1823 in Yorktown, York County, Virginia. She died March 6, 1884 in Nortonville, Contra Costa County, California. Harriet and Frederick Augustus Saddler had at least five children. They were:

- Mary Frances, born May 4, 1847, Yorktown, York County, Virginia
- Emma Henrietta, born 1853, Benicia, Solano County, California
- Harriet Louise (Hattie), born 1856, Benicia, Solano County, California
- Frederick William, born 1861, Benicia, Solano County, California
- Male child, died age 2-3 years

Frederick Augustus Saddler, husband of Harriet (Langley) Saddler. Frederick was born in New York *circa* 1823. According to genealogical information compiled by descendants, Frederick Saddler was a carpenter in Nortonville in 1866. He fought six battles in Mexico and later was stationed at the Benicia (Solano County, California) Arsenal. The *Contra Costa Gazette* newspaper, March 15, 1884, states that Frederick Saddler was a Mexican war veteran and then a sergeant in the regular army. According to the *U.S. Army, Register of Enlistments, 1798-1914*, Saddler served in the regular army and was discharged in December 1853 at Benicia Barracks, Solano County, California. Frederick and Harriet Saddler lived in Nortonville for 19 years.

According to *Washington Deaths, 1891-1907* (Register of Deaths in King County, State of Washington, page 236, record no. 3005), Frederick died October 23, 1897, in Black Diamond, King County, Washington. This source records his last name as "Sadler" and states that he was a widower at the time of his death. His cause of death was listed as embolism. His father's birthplace is recorded as Germany and his mother's birthplace, France.

## PERSONAL INFORMATION:

|  |  |
|---|---|
| SEX: | Unknown |
| DATE OF BIRTH: | *Circa* 1870s |
| DATE OF DEATH: | *Circa* 1870s |
| PLACE OF DEATH: | Somersville, Contra Costa County, California |
| AGE AT DEATH: | Infant |
| CAUSE OF DEATH: | |
| BIRTHPLACE: | Somersville, Contra Costa County, California |
| SPOUSE: | None |
| PARENTS: | George Herman and Martha Elizabeth (Saxe) Schwartz |

## GRAVESITE INFORMATION:

|  |  |
|---|---|
| LOCATION OF GRAVESITE: | Unknown |
| GRAVESTONE: | Missing or never placed |
| TYPE OF GRAVESTONE: | |
| SHAPE OF GRAVESTONE: | |
| INSCRIPTION: | |
| EPITAPH: | |
| MOTIF: | |
| CARVER: | |
| BASE: | |
| TYPE OF BASE: | |
| ENCLOSURE: | |
| TYPE OF ENCLOSURE: | |
| FENCE: | |
| TYPE OF FENCE: | |
| MOTIF OF FENCE: | |

East Bay Regional Park District

# SCHWARTZ, (Infant #1)

**ADDITIONAL PERSONAL INFORMATION:**
According to a descendant and Live Oak Cemetery Records (Concord, Contra Costa County, California), two Schwartz infants are buried in Rose Hill Cemetery. These are the only sources that document their burial there. The parents of these infants were George Herman Schwartz and Martha Elizabeth (Saxe) Schwartz. Martha, was born May 1842 in Black Forest, Germany and died June 21, 1910 in Clayton, Contra Costa County, California. She operated a candy store in the Mount Diablo Coal Field. The Davis family of Nortonville owned a candy store, but it is not certain if this is the store where Martha was employed. George and Martha E. (Saxe) Schwartz had thirteen children. They were:

- Infant #1 (buried in Rose Hill Cemetery)

- Infant #2 (buried in Rose Hill Cemetery)

- George John, born 1859, Hazelton, Luzerne County, Pennsylvania; died April 20, 1908, Richmond, Contra Costa County, California

- Elizabeth, born 1865, Hazelton, Pennsylvania; died July 1898, Clayton, Contra Costa County, California

- Catherine, born *circa* 1865, Pennsylvania

- Martha, born *circa* 1866, Pennsylvania

- Anna, born *circa* 1868, Pennsylvania

- Harietta, born *circa* 1869, California

- William, born 1874; died September 28, 1920, Clayton, California

- Otto, born Jan. 27, 1879, Clayton, California; died December 31, 1951, Clayton, California

- Alice, born 1880; died 1904

- Dorothy, buried in St. Stephens Cemetery, Concord, Contra Costa County, California

George, Martha, and three of their children (Elizabeth, George, and William) are buried in Live Oak Cemetery, Concord, Contra Costa County, California. Also buried in Live Oak Cemetery is infant Violet Eleanor Schwartz. Violet may be the child of George and Martha Schwartz or perhaps she is the daughter of George and Rebecca (Davis) Schwartz, the son and daughter-in-law of George and Martha Schwartz. Their son, George John Schwartz, married Rebecca Davis, daughter of Ellen and David B. Davis of Somersville. Rebecca's mother, father, and three brothers are buried in Rose Hill Cemetery. See Schwartz infant #2 for additional information.

See David Davis, David B. Davis, Ellen Davis, Morgan Davis, and William T. Davis.

**ADDITIONAL GRAVESITE INFORMATION:**
According to a descendant, two Schwartz infants are buried in Rose Hill Cemetery.

**REFERENCES:** 8 ( June 22, 1878), 9 ( July 2, 1870 – two articles), 12, see John Tierney (newspaper article "Somersville Notes" – *Antioch Ledger*, July 26, 1890 on page 569)

## The Strawberry Festival

At Somersville, on the 22d, was a grand success, in every respect. A large number were present on the occasion. In the early part of the evening some fears were entertained that it would be a Strawberry Festival only in name, as, owing to some mistake, the berries were not delivered as per agreement. For some time D. R. Ward, the proprietor of the Pittsburg House, to whom had been entrusted the ordering of the berries, was literally bewildered by eager inquiries as to the why and wherefore of the delay. Ward, who is a peaceful man, ensconsed himself in a corner, behind two chairs, and whistled, "There's a good time coming, girls, wait a little longer;" but the company could not see this in a philosophical light, so the floor was cleared for dancing, and for a time Professors Parker and Schwartz made all forget that such things as Strawberries ever existed. Waltzes, Polkas and Quadrilles followed each other in rapid succession, and all went "merry as a marriage bell," when, hark! there was a sound as of a stage wagon coming up the canyon. Joe Bernard was the first to hear it, and made a frantic rush for the door, and Mr. Black, the Postmaster, tells us he was first at the Postoffice. Joe Spaulding surrendered at discretion, and the way the treasure boxes—no, strawberry boxes, we mean—were handed out, was a caution to snakes. A line was formed and it took just 0005 minutes to pass the fruit to the Hall. Dancing ceased, and as fast as the nimble fingers of eight or ten ladies could prepare them, strawberries, covered with rich cream were given away at two bits a dish, and we hesitate to say how many boxes were so disposed of. The receipts of the evening amounted to $94, an amount which more than realized the expectations of the most sanguine: The committee appointed on the occasion carried out the arrangements most effectively, and the expense incurred was very light. We are informed that the receipts exceed those of the theatrical entertainments. Ladies try another one, and let some of us Antioch folks come and see you. The proceeds are to be devoted to church purposes.

This article from the *Antioch Ledger* newspaper, July 2, 1870 describes the participation of musicians "Professors Parker and Schwartz" in the Strawberry Festival at Somersville:

> ...the floor was cleared for dancing...Waltzes, Polkas and Quadrilles followed each other in rapid succession...

George Schwartz was born May 14, 1836 in Rothenburg, Germany and worked as a miner in Somersville. Prior to arriving in Somersville, George worked in the mines in Luzerne County, Pennsylvania. He was an accomplished musician and bandleader in Somersville and later in nearby Clayton, Contra Costa County, California, where he was the founder of Clayton's first brass band. He also served as a saloonkeeper in Clayton. The Schwartz family moved to Clayton after leaving the Mount Diablo Coal Field. George died in Clayton on November 28, 1889.

## The Nortonville Celebration

Is looked forward to with great interest by all classes in this section of country. The orator of the day, Wm. H. Rhodes (Caxton), is famed for his eloquent addresses. In consequence, we look for a rare treat in this respect. The Committee of arrangements are providing, too, for outdoor sports. The Base Ball Clubs will have an opportunity to distinguish themselves. A purse has been subscribed, and seven horses entered for a race, which will take place on a flat below the picnic ground. There will be also races for minor prizes after this. Long ropes have been purchased for the good old game of Copenhagen. A platform has been erected for dancing. Schwartz is getting his instrument in tune. In fact, to tell all the preparations that are being made would fill a column, so we will stop right here, and recommend one and all to see for themselves on Monday. Depend upon this the Nortonville people are whole-souled, and never do things by halves. Let there be a general rally.

## Nortonville,

### CONTRA COSTA COUNTY,

A small town near Mount Diablo, supported by coal mining.

---

**BERRY J L**, Physician
Christensen N, hardware
Conro & Dodge, general merchandise
Danziger H, tailor
Davis Mrs W E D, hotel and saloon
Davis B, boarding house
Gagen John, livery stable
Gwynn & Tyler, hotel
Havard T D, liquors
Hund Fred, barber
Jones John B, constable
Moore & Co, butchers
Morgans Morgan, superintendent Black Diamond Coal Co
Nooks William G, butcher
**ROZSAS H**, Physician
**SCHWARTZ G H**, Liquors
**SENDERMANN A**, General merchandise
Sharp W, liquors
**SHRADER S R**, Bootmaker
Thomas H, bootmaker
Thomas H M, hotel
Tingman William J, agt W, F & Co, postmaster and telegraph operator
**WATSON A P**, Liquors
Woodruff D S, druggist & justice of peace

This July 2, 1870 *Antioch Ledger* newspaper article (left) discusses the involvement of Mr. Schwartz in the July 4th Nortonville celebration: "A platform has been erected for dancing. Schwartz is getting his instrument in tune."

The information on the right comes from the *Business Directory of San Francisco and Principal Towns of California and Nevada, 1877*, page 50. G. H. Schwartz was listed as operating a business dealing in liquors in Nortonville, California.

## PERSONAL INFORMATION:

| | |
|---|---|
| SEX: | Unknown |
| DATE OF BIRTH: | *Circa* 1870s |
| DATE OF DEATH: | *Circa* 1870s |
| PLACE OF DEATH: | Somersville, Contra Costa County, California |
| AGE AT DEATH: | Infant |
| CAUSE OF DEATH: | |
| BIRTHPLACE: | Somersville, Contra Costa County, California |
| SPOUSE: | None |
| PARENTS: | George Herman and Martha Elizabeth (Saxe) Schwartz |

## GRAVESITE INFORMATION:

| | |
|---|---|
| LOCATION OF GRAVESITE: | Unknown |
| GRAVESTONE: | Missing or never placed |
| TYPE OF GRAVESTONE: | |
| SHAPE OF GRAVESTONE: | |
| INSCRIPTION: | |
| EPITAPH: | |
| MOTIF: | |
| CARVER: | |
| BASE: | |
| TYPE OF BASE: | |
| ENCLOSURE: | |
| TYPE OF ENCLOSURE: | |
| FENCE: | |
| TYPE OF FENCE: | |
| FENCE MOTIF: | |

# SCHWARTZ, (Infant #2)

**ADDITIONAL PERSONAL INFORMATION:**
See Schwartz infant #1 for additional information.

The *1870 Census for Township Three, Contra Costa County, California* lists George Swartz [sic], age 35, born *circa* 1835 in Germany, and his occupation as miner. Also listed are his wife, Martha, age 28, born *circa* 1842 in Germany, and their children: George, age 10; Catherine, age 5; Martha, age 4; and Anna, age 2; all natives of Pennsylvania. Harietta, age 1, is listed as a native of California.

George H. Schwartz is listed as operating a "confectionery and fruits" business in Nortonville in *The Pacific Coast Business Directory, 1871-73,* page 229.

The *Assessment List, Contra Costa County, for 1872-'73,* lists George H. Schwartz's property as "1 House in Town of Nortonville, valued at $300; other solvent debts $50; furniture $20; cows - 1 American $40, 1 mixed $30." Total value of his property was recorded as $440.

The *Contra Costa Gazette* newspaper, June 22, 1878, states that the saloon and dwelling for G. H. Swartz [sic] was destroyed during a fire at Nortonville. (See article "Fire at Nortonville on page 442).

The *Pacific Coast Business Directory for 1876-78,* page 195, lists George H. Schwartz as operating a "liquor saloon" in Nortonville.

The *Business Directory of San Francisco and Principal Towns of California and Nevada, 1877,* page 50, records G. H. Schwartz as operating a liquor business in Nortonville.

See Schwartz infant #1, David Davis, David B. Davis, Ellen Davis, Morgan Davis, and William T. Davis.

**ADDITIONAL GRAVESITE INFORMATION:**
According to a descendant, two Schwartz infants are buried in Rose Hill Cemetery. No other source documents their burial there.

**REFERENCES:** 8 ( June 22, 1878), 9 ( July 2, 1870 - two articles), 12, see John Tierney (newspaper article "Somersville Notes" - *Antioch Ledger,* July 26, 1890, on page 569)

Reference 56.3

The Davis family owned the two-story lodging house and candy store on the left. The structure on the right was a boardinghouse. The cook, in his white apron, is resting against the right corner of the building. Martha Schwartz, the infant's mother, operated a candy store in the Mount Diablo Coal Field; however it is not certain that this is the candy store where she was employed.

# SHAW,
## Hazel Beatrice

## PERSONAL INFORMATION:

| | |
|---|---|
| SEX: | Female |
| DATE OF BIRTH: | October 22, 1891 |
| DATE OF DEATH: | March 17, 1892 |
| PLACE OF DEATH: | Somersville, Contra Costa County, California |
| AGE AT DEATH: | 4 months,  24 days |
| CAUSE OF DEATH: | |
| BIRTHPLACE: | |
| SPOUSE: | None |
| PARENTS: | John and Katie Shaw |

## GRAVESITE INFORMATION:

| | |
|---|---|
| LOCATION OF GRAVESITE: | Unknown |
| GRAVESTONE: | Missing |
| TYPE OF GRAVESTONE: | |
| SHAPE OF GRAVESTONE: | |
| INSCRIPTION: | |
| EPITAPH: | |
| MOTIF: | |
| CARVER: | |
| BASE: | |
| TYPE OF BASE: | |
| ENCLOSURE: | |
| TYPE OF ENCLOSURE: | |
| FENCE: | |
| TYPE OF FENCE: | |
| FENCE MOTIF: | |

# SHAW, Hazel Beatrice

**ADDITIONAL PERSONAL INFORMATION:**
According to the *Antioch Ledger* newspaper, March 19, 1892, John and Katie Shaw, parents of Hazel Beatrice, were from Nanaimo, British Columbia, Canada.

The birth date for Hazel was calculated by www.timeanddate.com, based on Hazel's date of death and age at death.

**ADDITIONAL GRAVESTIE INFORMATION:**
A cemetery list compiled in 1922 (see page 1004) by John Sullenger is the only source that records Hazel's burial in Rose Hill Cemetery.

**REFERENCES:** 4, 9 (March 19, 1892), 12

## DIED.

JUNTA—At Black Diamond, March 15, 1892, Assunta Junta, beloved wife of J. Junta, a native of Italy, aged 43 years, 10 months and 29 days.

SHAW—At Somersville, California, March 17, 1892, Hazel Beatrice, infant daughter of John and Katie Shaw, of Nanaimo, B. C., aged 4 months and 24 days. [British Columbia papers please copy.]

From the *Antioch Ledger* newspaper, March 19, 1892.
The second entry in this obituary is for Hazel Beatrice Shaw.

# SMITH,
## Evan

## PERSONAL INFORMATION:

| | |
|---|---|
| SEX: | Male |
| DATE OF BIRTH: | 1849 |
| DATE OF DEATH: | July 30, 1876 |
| PLACE OF DEATH: | Nortonville, Contra Costa County, California |
| AGE AT DEATH: | 27 years |
| CAUSE OF DEATH: | Mine explosion |
| BIRTHPLACE: | |
| SPOUSE: | |
| PARENTS: | |

## GRAVESITE INFORMATION:

| | |
|---|---|
| LOCATION OF GRAVESITE: | Section S-C, Plot #48 |
| GRAVESTONE: | Exists |
| TYPE OF GRAVESTONE: | Marble |
| SHAPE OF GRAVESTONE: | Tablet |
| INSCRIPTION: | *Farewell/Died at Nortonville* |
| EPITAPH: | |
| MOTIF: | Clasped hands with "farewell"/rope with tassels |
| CARVER: | Excelsior Marble Works, San Jose, California |
| BASE: | Exists |
| TYPE OF BASE: | Sandstone |
| ENCLOSURE: | Exists (partial) |
| TYPE OF ENCLOSURE: | Brick |
| FENCE: | |
| TYPE OF FENCE: | |
| FENCE MOTIF: | |

# SMITH, Evan

**ADDITIONAL PERSONAL INFORMATION:**
Evan Smith was injured and eventually died as a result of the July 24, 1876 mine explosion in Nortonville, Contra Costa County, California. Evan Smith and the other victims killed in the explosion are buried in the same area in Rose Hill Cemetery.

See Theophile Dumas, William Gething, David W. Griffiths, Thomas D. James, Meredith Lewis, George M. Reynolds, David Watts, Theophilus Watts, and William L. Williams.

**ADDITIONAL GRAVESITE INFORMATION:**
Zelma Myrick who recorded information in a notebook in the 1930s during a visit to Rose Hill Cemetery reported "Stone on ground."

Evan's gravestone was broken into two pieces and concreted flat to the ground prior to East Bay Regional Park District acquisition. The lower portion of the stone was embedded in the sandstone base. A portion of a brick enclosure, also done prior to the Park District acquisition, surrounds the gravesite. The carver's name (Excelsior Marble Works, San Jose, California) has been broken from the gravestone but can be found on the small piece of stone remaining in the base.

**REFERENCES:** 1, 2, 3, 4, 6, 8 (July 29, 1876 and Aug. 12, 1876), 9 (July 29, 1876), 10 (page 474), 11 (P610.5.2 and P610.31.184), 12, 14, see newspaper appendix (William Gething) pages 706 and 707

Reference 31.184

The vandalized gravestone of Evan Smith. The marble tablet stone was pieced together and concreted to the ground prior to the area becoming an East Bay Regional Park. The partial brick enclosure, somewhat visible on the left, is not original to the gravesite. Photograph by Traci (Gibbons) Parent, July 1977.

# SPOWART,
## Annie

## PERSONAL INFORMATION:

| | |
|---|---|
| SEX: | Female |
| DATE OF BIRTH: | December 16, 1860 |
| DATE OF DEATH: | June 7, 1872 |
| PLACE OF DEATH: | Somersville, Contra Costa County, California |
| AGE AT DEATH: | 11 years, 6 months |
| CAUSE OF DEATH: | Smallpox |
| BIRTHPLACE: | Australia |
| SPOUSE: | None |
| PARENTS: | David and Grace (Morgan) Spowart |

## GRAVESITE INFORMATION:

| | |
|---|---|
| LOCATION OF GRAVESITE: | Section N-D, Plot #68 |
| GRAVESTONE: | Exists |
| TYPE OF GRAVESTONE: | Marble |
| SHAPE OF GRAVESTONE: | Tablet |
| INSCRIPTION: | *Sacred to the Memory of/Daughter of/Born in Australia* |
| EPITAPH: | *Here lies the darling of my heart,* |
| | *It was hard oh yes, it was hard to part,* |
| | *But I hope to meet at mansions door,* |
| | *My Annie dear and part no more.* |
| MOTIF: | |
| CARVER: | |
| BASE: | Exists |
| TYPE OF BASE: | Sandstone |
| ENCLOSURE: | |
| TYPE OF ENCLOSURE: | |
| FENCE: | |
| TYPE OF FENCE: | |
| FENCE MOTIF: | |

# SPOWART, Annie

**ADDITIONAL PERSONAL INFORMATION:**
The *Contra Costa Gazette* newspaper, June 15, 1872, lists Annie's age at death as 13 years, and not 11 years and 6 months as stated on her gravestone.

The *1870 Census for Township Three, Contra Costa County, California*, lists Ann Spowart, age 9, as a native of Australia. Also listed are her parents, David Spowart, age 33, a native of Scotland and his wife, Grace Spowart, age 32, also a native of Scotland and their children: Eliza, age 7, a native of Australia; Robert, age 5; Maggie, age 3; and David, age 2; all natives of California.

The *1871-2 Contra Costa County Directory* records Annie's father, David Spowart, as a miner in Somersville.

The *Assessment List, Contra Costa County,* for 1872-73, documents David Spowart as being assessed $175 on improvements in Somersville.

The *1876 Contra Costa County Voting Register*, lists David Spowart, age 33, as a native of Scotland and miner living in Somersville. He registered to vote on July 23, 1870.

The *Pacific Coast Directory 1880-81*, page 823, records David Spowart as selling "liquors" in Somersville. *The Pacific Coast Directory 1883-84*, lists D. Spowart operating a saloon in Somersville.

The *1880 Census for Somersville Precinct, Contra Costa County, California*, records David Spowart, age 44, as a miner and native of Scotland. Also listed are his wife, Grace, age 42, a native of Scotland and their children: Robert, age 15; Margaret, age 13; David, age 11; Grace, age 9; Hannah, age 7; Jane, age 5; John, age 3; and Mabel, age 1; all natives of California. David Spowart was a member of the Contra Costa Masonic Lodge No. 227 in Somersville.

The *1900 Census for San Francisco, San Francisco County, California* lists David Spourt [sic], age 64, a native of Scotland and his wife, Grace, age 62, also a native of Scotland. Also recorded are their children: Maggie, age 32, a native of California; Hannah, age 27; John, age 24; Mabel, age 21; Harry, age 19; Jennie Hanley (daughter), age 26; Walter Hanley (son-in-law), age 24; and their son, William Hanley, age 3.

The *1910 Census for Oakland Ward 1, Alameda County, California* lists David Spowart, age 78 [Note: he should be age 74 if he was born in 1836], as a native of Scotland. His year of immigration was 1870. Also listed is his wife, Grace, age 72, a native of Scotland and year of immigration as 1870; and their daughter, Mary Spowart, single, age 28 and a native of California; and a single, white female boarder, Josie Baptiste, age 25.

The *1920 Census for Berkeley, Alameda County, California* records David Spowart, age 84, as a native of Scotland, and a widow [sic], living with his daughter, Margaret Webster, age 52, a native of California and her family: Thomas E. Webster, age 58; Willard, age 17; Helen, age 15; and Dorothy, age 13.

According to a descendant who attended a former resident's picnic at Black Diamond Mines Regional Preserve in October 1980, David and Grace Spowart came from Scotland by way of Australia to California. The family owned a mine in Scotland. They may have arrived in Somersville in the early 1860s. See Eliza Spowart.

**ADDITIONAL GRAVESITE INFORMATION:**
The gravestone was broken in three places and concreted flat to ground prior to East Bay Regional Park District acquisition. A small portion is missing. Zelma Myrick, who recorded information in a notebook in the 1930s during a visit to the cemetery, reported "Stone down and broken."

**REFERENCES:** 1, 2, 3, 6, 8 (June 15, 1872 – two articles), 9 (June 8, 1872, June 15, 1872, and Sept. 19, 1874), 11 (P610.31.140 and P610.119.29), 12, 13, 14, *Pittsburg Post Dispatch* newspaper (Wed., June 15, 1955, pages 9 and 12), see newspaper appendix pages 754 and 755

**SMALL POX.**—It is reported that there is a case of small pox at Somersville, and as this dreaded disease is now epidemic in a portion of Solano county and elsewhere in the State, it is well that seasonable precautions against it should be taken. Vaccination and fumigation with sulphur are the most potent preventives; and high scientific authorities assert that nothing will so effectually destroy the germs of the disease in infected houses and clothing, as the fumes of sulphur.

This newspaper article from the *Contra Costa Gazette*, June 1, 1872, discusses the spread of smallpox, the "dreaded disease." Annie Spowart died of smallpox on June 7, 1872.

## Small Pox at Somersville.

**SOMERSVILLE, June 13th, 1872.**

EDS. GAZETTE : I regret to say the small pox has again visited this place, and has already carried to the grave Annie Spourt, aged twelve years; a very intelligent young girl, whose recitations at public examination received marked attention. As soon as the disease made itself known, the citizens appointed a Board of Health to endeavor to prevent the spread of the scourge. Mrs. Spourt, (the mother of the deceased) with her five other children, was taken from the house and sent to the farm of Alexander Nelson, two miles distant: but too late, for another little sister was taken with it last Tuesday. It is believed that Mrs. McLeod, who arrived here from Scotland some four weeks ago, brought the disease with her, as she was sick when she came, but it being a mild case it was not believed to be the small pox, and Annie Spourt took care of her baby, who was also sick.

Last Monday a fire broke out in the house of Thomas Muir, but was soon subdued, damage about twenty dollars; cause, hot ashes.

ORION.

The last name for Annie Spowart has been spelled as "Spourt" in this *Contra Costa Gazette* newspaper article from June 15, 1872. For additional information on a MacLeod (spelled as McLeod in this article) family in Somersville, see pages 387-390.

## PERSONAL INFORMATION:

| | |
|---|---|
| SEX: | Female |
| DATE OF BIRTH: | *Circa* 1863 |
| DATE OF DEATH: | *Circa* June 11, 1872 |
| PLACE OF DEATH: | Somersville, Contra Costa County, California |
| AGE AT DEATH: | Approximately 9 years |
| CAUSE OF DEATH: | Smallpox |
| BIRTHPLACE: | Australia |
| SPOUSE: | None |
| PARENTS: | David and Grace (Morgan) Spowart |

## GRAVESITE INFORMATION:

| | |
|---|---|
| LOCATION OF GRAVESITE: | Unknown |
| GRAVESTONE: | Missing or never placed |
| TYPE OF GRAVESTONE: | |
| SHAPE OF GRAVESTONE: | |
| INSCRIPTION: | |
| EPITAPH: | |
| MOTIF: | |
| CARVER: | |
| BASE: | |
| TYPE OF BASE: | |
| ENCLOSURE: | |
| TYPE OF ENCLOSURE: | |
| FENCE: | |
| TYPE OF FENCE: | |
| FENCE MOTIF: | |

# SPOWART, Eliza

**ADDITIONAL PERSONAL INFORMATION:**
Descendants believe that Eliza might be the "little sister" who died of smallpox mentioned in the June 15, 1872 *Contra Costa Gazette* newspaper article on page 524.

According to a descendant, David Spowart was born in 1836, and married Grace Morgan (daughter of Robert and Annie Morgan) on December 8, 1856, in Dunfermline, County of Fife, Scotland. On June 19, 1858, David, age 21, and Grace, age 20, sailed from Liverpool, England aboard the ship *Alfred* and arrived in Moreton Bay, Brisbane, Queensland, Australia on September 19, 1858. Sailing with them were Grace's mother, father, two brothers, sister-in-law, and infant niece. Eliza's oldest brother, Thomas, was born in Australia in 1858.

The *1870 Census for Township 3, Contra Costa County, California* reports Eliza Spowart's age as 7 years old. Her sister, Annie, was reported as 9 years old in the census. Since Eliza's name does not appear in the 1880 census, it is likely that she is the other Spowart child who died of the disease. No sources document Eliza's burial in Rose Hill Cemetery. See Annie Spowart.

There were at least 11 children in the Spowart family:

- Thomas, born 1858 in Australia
- Ann, born December 16, 1860, Australia; died June 7, 1872, Somersville, Contra Costa County, California
- Eliza, born *circa* 1863, Australia; most likely died June 11, 1872, Somersville
- Robert, born *circa* 1865, California
- Maggie, born *circa* 1867, California
- David, born *circa* 1869, California
- Grace, born *circa* 1871, California
- Hannah, born *circa* 1873, California
- Jane, born *circa* 1875, California
- John, born *circa* 1877, California
- Mabel, born *circa* 1879, California

**ADDITIONAL GRAVESITE INFORMATION:**
A gravestone exists for her sister, Annie Spowart (Section N-D, Plot #68). It is likely that Eliza is buried next to her sister.

**REFERENCES:** 8 (June 15, 1872 – two articles), 9 (June 15, 1872), 12, see newspaper appendix page 755

## Small Pox.

We are informed that another daughter of Mr. Spowart is down with the small pox, and is at present at Mr. Nelson's, between Antioch and Somersville. As the members of the family continue to come to Antioch, every precautionary measure should be adopted by our citizens to prevent the further spread of this loathsome contagion. No one should fail to be vaccinated, or to make use of other appliances regarded as preventatives of the disease. Many foolishly remark that they do not fear the small pox, but every sensible person knows that it should be feared and guarded against.

This newspaper article from the *Antioch Ledger*, June 15, 1872, discusses the smallpox disease. This article may regard Eliza or another member of her family. Eliza died *circa* June 11 and this article is dated June 15. See page 524.

## PERSONAL INFORMATION:

| | |
|---|---|
| SEX: | Male |
| DATE OF BIRTH: | July 1890 |
| DATE OF DEATH: | January 18, 1891 |
| PLACE OF DEATH: | Somersville, Contra Costa County, California |
| AGE AT DEATH: | 6 months |
| CAUSE OF DEATH: | Scarlatina (scarlet fever)/congestion of brain |
| BIRTHPLACE: | |
| SPOUSE: | None |
| PARENTS: | Thomas and Mary Hannah (Barker) Spratt |

## GRAVESITE INFORMATION:

| | |
|---|---|
| LOCATION OF GRAVESITE: | Unknown |
| GRAVESTONE: | Missing or never placed |
| TYPE OF GRAVESTONE: | |
| SHAPE OF GRAVESTONE: | |
| INSCRIPTION: | |
| EPITAPH: | |
| MOTIF: | |
| CARVER: | |
| BASE: | |
| TYPE OF BASE: | |
| ENCLOSURE: | |
| TYPE OF ENCLOSURE: | |
| FENCE: | |
| TYPE OF FENCE: | |
| FENCE MOTIF: | |

# SPRATT, William Gladstone

**ADDITIONAL PERSONAL INFORMATION:**
The *Contra Costa County, California Registers of Death* recorded Wm. G. Spratt's date of death as January 17, 1891 in Somersville and not January 18 as listed in the *Antioch Ledger* newspaper. W. S. George was listed as his doctor. The cause of death was recorded as congestion of brain.

Thomas Spratt, age 28, of Somersville married Mary Hannah Barker, age 21, of Somersville on November 28, 1887. Thomas Gray and Jennie Jones, both of Somersville, served as witnesses. According to the *Index to Marriage Certificates*, located at Contra Costa County Hall of Records, Martinez, Contra Costa County, California, Thomas and Mary H. (Barker) Spratt were married by Rev. Charles S. Vaile; the information is recorded in Volume 3, page 378.

**ADDITIONAL GRAVESITE INFORMATION:**
The *Contra Costa Gazette* newspaper, January 24, 1891, is the only source that indicates William Spratt is buried in Rose Hill Cemetery. The article states: "On Tuesday the remains of the little one were deposited in their final resting place in the Somersville cemetery."

**REFERENCES:** 8 (Jan. 24, 1891), 9 (Feb. 7, 1891), 12, see newspaper appendix page 756

> ## DIED.
>
> SPRATT—In Somersville, January 18, 1891, Wm. Gladstone, infant son of Mr. and Mrs. Thos. Spratt, aged 6 months.
>
> # Dr. C. J. Grant
>
> RESPECTFULLY CALLS THE ATTENTION OF the inhabitants of Antioch, the mines and surrounding districts to his advertisement in this issue. He has commenced the practice of his profession in all its branches, and earnestly hopes, by strict attention and *moderate charges*, combined with his knowledge and experience gained in almost all the climates and countries of the world; to merit a share of their patronage and support.                d 20

From the *Antioch Ledger* newspaper, February 7, 1891. This advertisement for Dr. C. J. Grant, appearing just below the obituary for William Gladstone Spratt, states "Respectfully calls the attention of the inhabitants of Antioch, the mines and surrounding districts to his advertisement in this issue." According to information obtained from the *Registration of Deaths in Contra Costa County*, located at the Contra Costa County Hall of Records in Martinez, California, Spratt's doctor was W. S. George.

# STINE,
## Catherine "Katie"

## PERSONAL INFORMATION:

| | |
|---|---|
| SEX: | Female |
| DATE OF BIRTH: | 1865 |
| DATE OF DEATH: | 1882 |
| PLACE OF DEATH: | Nortonville, Contra Costa County, California |
| AGE AT DEATH: | Approximately 17 years |
| CAUSE OF DEATH: | |
| BIRTHPLACE: | Foresthill, Placer County, California |
| SPOUSE: | William Stine |
| PARENTS: | Joseph and Mary Ann (Evans) Davis |

## GRAVESITE INFORMATION:

| | |
|---|---|
| LOCATION OF GRAVESITE: | Unknown |
| GRAVESTONE: | Missing or never placed |
| TYPE OF GRAVESTONE: | |
| SHAPE OF GRAVESTONE: | |
| INSCRIPTION: | |
| EPITAPH: | |
| MOTIF: | |
| CARVER: | |
| BASE: | |
| TYPE OF BASE: | |
| ENCLOSURE: | |
| TYPE OF ENCLOSURE: | |
| FENCE: | |
| TYPE OF FENCE: | |
| FENCE MOTIF: | |

# STINE, Catherine "Katie"

**ADDITIONAL PERSONAL INFORMATION:**
According to information obtained from descendants, Catherine married William Stine in Clayton, Contra Costa County, California in 1881.

The *1860 Census for Pottsville, North West Ward, Schuylkill, Pennsylvania* lists Catherine's family. Recorded are Joseph Davis, age 32, born *circa* 1828 in Wales, occupation miner. Also listed are his wife, Mary, age 30, born *circa* 1830 in Wales, and their children: Mary J., age 6, born *circa* 1854 in Wales; Thomas, age 4, born *circa* 1856 in Pennsylvania; and Joseph, age 1, born *circa* 1859 in Pennsylvania.

The *1870 Census for Township 6, Placer County, California* lists Catherine Davis, age 5, born *circa* 1865 in California. Also listed are her father, Joseph D. Davis, age 42, born *circa* 1828 in Wales; her mother, Mary Davis, age 40, born *circa* 1830 in Wales; and siblings Mary J., age 17, born *circa* 1853, in Wales; Thomas, age 14, born *circa* 1856 in Pennsylvania; David, age 12, born *circa* 1858 in Pennsylvania; Margaret, age 10, born *circa* 1860 in Pennsylvania; Elizabeth, age 7, born *circa* 1863 in California; Ann, age 4, born *circa* 1866 in California; Edward, age 2, born *circa* 1868 in California; and Sarah, age 4 months, born *circa* 1870 in California.

The *1880 Census for Nortonville, Contra Costa County, California* lists Joseph Davis, age 53, a miner, born *circa* 1827 in Wales. Also recorded are his wife, Mary, age 50, born *circa* 1830 in Wales; and their children David, age 22, a miner, born *circa* 1858 in Pennsylvania; Lizza, age 16, born *circa* 1864; Kate, age 15, born *circa* 1865; Annie, age 13, born *circa* 1867; William, age 12, born *circa* 1868; Sarah, age 10, born *circa* 1870; Joseph, age 8, born *circa* 1872; and Alice, age 6, born *circa* 1874; all are natives of California.

The *1900 Census for Township 5, Placer County, California* lists Joseph D. Davis, age 79, born July 1827 in Wales. His year of marriage was 1843 and he is listed as being married for 57 years. Joseph's occupation is recorded as gold miner. Also listed is his wife, Mary, age 70, born March 1830 in Wales. The census states that she had 13 children, and 9 were living. Recorded as living with them are two of their children: David D. Davis, age 42, born January 1858, in Pennsylvania, occupation gold miner; and Alice Davis, age 26, born March 1874 in California, and single. See Margaret Davis.

**ADDITIONAL GRAVESITE INFORMATION:**
According to descendants, Catherine and her sister, Margaret Davis, are buried in Rose Hill Cemetery. No other source documents their burial there.

**REFERENCES:** 12

# THOMAS,
## Charles Morgan

## PERSONAL INFORMATION:

| | |
|---|---|
| SEX: | Male |
| DATE OF BIRTH: | September 18, 1871 |
| DATE OF DEATH: | August 12, 1877 |
| PLACE OF DEATH: | Nortonville, Contra Costa County, California |
| AGE AT DEATH: | 5 years, 10 months, 25 days |
| CAUSE OF DEATH: | Diphtheria |
| BIRTHPLACE: | |
| SPOUSE: | None |
| PARENTS: | William and Catherine Thomas |

## GRAVESITE INFORMATION:

| | |
|---|---|
| LOCATION OF GRAVESITE: | Unknown (see following page) |
| GRAVESTONE: | Missing or never placed |
| TYPE OF GRAVESTONE: | |
| SHAPE OF GRAVESTONE: | |
| INSCRIPTION: | |
| EPITAPH: | |
| MOTIF: | |
| CARVER: | |
| BASE: | |
| TYPE OF BASE: | |
| ENCLOSURE: | |
| TYPE OF ENCLOSURE: | |
| FENCE: | |
| TYPE OF FENCE: | |
| FENCE MOTIF: | |

# THOMAS, Charles Morgan

**ADDITIONAL PERSONAL INFORMATION:**
According to a gravestone in Holy Cross Cemetery, Antioch, Contra Costa County, California, the three children of William and Catherine Thomas are buried in this Catholic cemetery. However according to Kate (Thomas) Latimer, who reminisced about her father (William Thomas) and brothers (Charles, John, and Peter Thomas) in *The Pittsburg Post Dispatch* newspaper, March 11, 1938 article "As I Remember Pittsburg," her three brothers are buried in Rose Hill Cemetery:

> My father was a Welch [sic] singer, and he used to sing at all the funerals. I go to the hills regularly, and when I sit in that little cemetery there I can almost here [sic] him singing again, where he sang so often. In that graveyard one hot summer three small brothers of Mrs. Latimer [Kate (Thomas) Latimer] were buried. Two died in one day in the diphtheria epidemic that descended upon the little mining community, and another died the day they were buried in the hillside cemetery. That epidemic, and the others that seemed to come out of the warmest, bluest day, claimed many small lives that summer of '77, and left the coal miners stunned and bewildered.

The gravestone at Holy Cross Cemetery is weathered and it is difficult to decipher the information on the stone. A gravestone rubbing was done to reveal the names, dates of death, and ages of death. Also listed as buried at this site in Holy Cross Cemetery are Katherine [sic], (Mrs. Thomas) who was interred March 1, 1902 and William A. Thomas, who was interred July 15, 1931 at the age of 70 years. Since the *Antioch Ledger* newspaper, March 8, 1902 refers to the burial of Mrs. Thomas it is most likely the mother Catherine is buried at this site. William A. Thomas was her son. A footstone with the initials "C. N. T." sits next to the gravestone for Charles, John, and Peter Thomas. William Thomas, listed as buried at this site, is the brother of Charles, John, and Peter Thomas. No gravestone could be found for William. No information recording the burial of Charles, John, and Peter Thomas

was found in records maintained by Holy Cross Cemetery.

According to the Thomas gravestone and census records (see Peter Benjamin Thomas on pages 561 and 562), the children of William and Catherine Thomas were:
- James, born *circa* 1858
- Mary, born *circa* 1860
- William (Willie), born *circa* 1861
- Katie, born *circa* 1865
- Peter Benjamin, born September 1868
- Charles Morgan, born September 1871
- John H., born May 1874
- Frank P., born January 1877
- Francis, born *circa* 1878 (perhaps this is the same person as Frank P.; if so, the name of the ninth child is not known.)

Charles' date of birth was calculated by using www.timeanddate.com. His name and age of death come from the gravestone in Holy Cross Cemetery. The *Antioch Ledger* newspaper, August 18, 1877, lists the death of Charles Morgan, aged 6 years at Nortonville on August 12. This entry appears following the entry for Peter Benjamin Thomas. Since Peter and his brother died on the same day, most likely this is the listing for Charles Morgan Thomas (the last name was not included in the obituary for Charles). Additionally, the age of death listed in the newspaper for Charles is similar to the age listed on his gravestone at Holy Cross Cemetery. See John H. Thomas and Peter Benjamin Thomas.

**ADDITIONAL GRAVESITE INFORMATION:**
The only reference to the three Thomas boys buried in Rose Hill Cemetery is the *Pittsburg Post Dispatch* newspaper article, March 11, 1938. If they were buried in Rose Hill Cemetery, their burial locations are unknown.

**REFERENCES:** 9 (Aug. 25, 1877 and March 8, 1902), *The Pittsburg Post Dispatch* newspaper (July 13 and 15, 1931 and March 11, 1938, pages 1 and 2), *Martinez Herald* July 15, 1931, see newspaper appendix pages 762-764, Holy Cross Cemetery, Antioch, CA

Photograph by Traci (Gibbons) Parent

The Thomas gravestone at Holy Cross Cemetery, Antioch, Contra Costa County, California, May 2010. The *Pittsburg Post Dispatch* newspaper, March 11, 1938 states that three brothers of Kate (Thomas) Latimer are buried in Rose Hill Cemetery. No marker exists for them in Rose Hill. It is possible that this marker is a cenotaph – a monument placed in memory of the Thomas boys whose remains are elsewhere. It is unclear why the father is listed as M. Thomas on the gravestone since most sources record his name as William Thomas. The 1860 census lists him as W. M. Thomas. The gravestone reads:

PETER B.
Died
Aug. 12, 1877
Aged
8 ys. 11 ms. 4 dys.

CHARLES M.
Died
Aug. 12, 1877
Aged
5 ys. 10 ms. 25 ds

JOHN H.
Died Aug. 16, 1877
Aged 3 yrs. 2 ms. 20 ds.

CHILDREN OF M. & C. THOMAS

*Our sweet little children have gone*
*To mansions above yonder sky,*
*To gaze on the beautiful throne,*
*Of Him who is seated on high.*

This newspaper article, from the *Antioch Ledger*, April 14, 1877, lists W. Thomas (possibly the father of the Thomas child) as a Catcher for the Union Base Ball [sic-Baseball] Club of Somersville. At the time this article appeared in the paper, William Thomas was living in Nortonville. Three of his children died in August 1877. By 1900, Thomas was listed as living in Somersville.

## PERSONAL INFORMATION:

| | |
|---|---|
| SEX: | Female |
| DATE OF BIRTH: | June 17, 1875 |
| DATE OF DEATH: | June 27, 1876 |
| PLACE OF DEATH: | |
| AGE AT DEATH: | 1 year, 10 days |
| CAUSE OF DEATH: | |
| BIRTHPLACE: | |
| SPOUSE: | None |
| PARENTS: | Howell J. and Elizabeth Thomas |

## GRAVESITE INFORMATION:

| | |
|---|---|
| LOCATION OF GRAVESITE: | Unknown |
| GRAVESTONE: | Missing |
| TYPE OF GRAVESTONE: | Marble |
| SHAPE OF GRAVESTONE: | Tablet |
| INSCRIPTION: | *Children of* |
| EPITAPH: | |
| MOTIF: | Rope with tassels |
| CARVER: | |
| BASE: | |
| TYPE OF BASE: | |
| ENCLOSURE: | |
| TYPE OF ENCLOSURE: | |
| FENCE: | |
| TYPE OF FENCE: | |
| FENCE MOTIF: | |

# THOMAS, Elizabeth Ann

**ADDITIONAL PERSONAL INFORMATION:**
The *1870 Census for Township Three, Contra Costa County, California* lists Elizabeth's father, Howell Thomas, age 35, as a miner and native of Wales. Also listed are her mother, Eliza Thomas, age 23, a native of Wales, and her siblings, Joseph, age 2, and Lucretia, age 1, both natives of California.

The *1880 Census for Nortonville Precinct, Contra Costa County, California* lists Howell Thomas, age 45, as a miner and native of Wales. Also recorded are his wife, Elizabeth, age 34, a native of Wales and their children: Lucrecia [sic], age 11; Anna, age 9; Lizzy, age 4; and John, age 1. All are natives of California.

The *Washington State and Territorial Censuses, 1857-1892*, lists Howell J. Thomas as a resident of Cedar River, King County, Washington in 1885.

The *1900 Census for Black Diamond, King County, Washington*, records Howell Thomas, age 65, living with his daughter, Lucratia [sic] (Thomas) Davies, age 30, and son-in-law, Thomas Davies, age 36. Also listed are the children of Thomas and Lucratia [sic] Davies: Alvin H., age 10; Catherine E., age 8; Elizabeth, age 5; and Milton, age 6 ½. Listed as living with them is Henery [sic] Griffith, age 55, a boarder.

*Black Diamond Cemetery* records, Black Diamond, King County, Washington, documents burials for members of the Thomas family. Listed is Elizabeth's father, Howell Thomas, a native of Wales, born April 25, 1834, and died January 28, 1902, age 68 years. His epitaph says: "Lifes labor done." Also listed on a separate stone is her mother, Elizabeth, born 1843, and died 1943. Her two brothers: Joseph J. Thomas, died March 6, 1890, age 9 years and 8 months; and

Tommy T. Thomas, died February 24, 1887, age 4 years, 1 month, 17 days. Her two brothers share a gravestone with her father.

Howell and Elizabeth Thomas had at least nine children:

- Joseph, born 1867; died 1870 (buried in Rose Hill Cemetery)
- Lucretia, born *circa* 1869
- Anna, born *circa* 1871
- John D., born 1873; died 1876 (buried in Rose Hill Cemetery)
- Elizabeth Ann, born 1875; died 1876 (buried in Rose Hill Cemetery)
- Elizabeth, born February 1877
- John, born *circa* 1879
- Joseph J., born *circa* 1881; died 1890 (buried in Black Diamond, King County, Washington)
- Tommy T., born *circa* 1883; died 1887 (buried in Black Diamond, King County, Washington)

**ADDITIONAL GRAVESITE INFORMATION:**
Elizabeth Ann shares a gravestone with her brothers, John D. Thomas and Joseph Thomas. The gravestone was present in 1963 because it was listed on a student term paper by Jim Rotelli. To see a photograph of part of the gravestone, refer to page 77. See John D. Thomas and Joseph Thomas.

**REFERENCES:** 1, 2, 3, 4, 6, 11 (P610.98.15, P610.260.5, P610.260.6, and P610.261.14), 12, *Black Diamond Cemetery* records, Black Diamond, King County, Washington, page 16

## PERSONAL INFORMATION:

| | |
|---|---|
| SEX: | Female |
| DATE OF BIRTH: | February 7, 1869 |
| DATE OF DEATH: | July 18, 1870 |
| PLACE OF DEATH: | |
| AGE AT DEATH: | 1 year, 5 months, 11 days |
| CAUSE OF DEATH: | |
| BIRTHPLACE: | |
| SPOUSE: | None |
| PARENTS: | Rees G. and Margaret (Edwards) Thomas |

## GRAVESITE INFORMATION:

| | |
|---|---|
| LOCATION OF GRAVESITE: | Section S-D, Plot #56 |
| GRAVESTONE: | Exists |
| TYPE OF GRAVESTONE: | Marble |
| SHAPE OF GRAVESTONE: | Tablet |
| INSCRIPTION: | *Farewell/Dau. Of* |
| EPITAPH: | *We miss thee at home.* |
| MOTIF: | Clasped hands with "Farewell" |
| CARVER: | Excelsior Marble Works, San Jose, California |
| BASE: | Exists |
| TYPE OF BASE: | Granite |
| ENCLOSURE: | Exists |
| TYPE OF ENCLOSURE: | Brick |
| FENCE: | Missing |
| TYPE OF FENCE: | Iron |
| FENCE MOTIF: | Weeping willow tree and lamb |

# THOMAS, Elvira

**ADDITIONAL PERSONAL INFORMATION:**
Elvira's parents, Rees G. and Margaret Thomas, had at least ten children. The birth years for the children listed below come from 1860 and 1880 census records. Some birth and death dates were also obtained from the family gravestones in Oak View Memorial Park Cemetery, East 18th Street, Antioch, Contra Costa County, California.

The children were:

- Mary Ann (two daughters named Mary Ann were born to this family; the birth date of this daughter is unknown)
- Margaret Jane (two daughters named Margaret Jane were born to this family; the birth date of this daughter is unknown)
- William, born *circa* 1859
- Margaret Jane, born 1861; died 1956
- Evan E., born May 23, 1863; died July 5, 1948
- Mary Ann, born *circa* 1865
- Joan, born *circa* 1867
- Elvira, born February 7, 1869; died July 18, 1870
- Elvira, born *circa* 1871
- Rees, born April 14, 1875; died August 8, 1955

See Rees G. Thomas.

**ADDITIONAL GRAVESITE INFORMATION:**
Elvira shares a gravestone with her father, Rees G. Thomas.

**REFERENCES:** 1, 2, 3, 5, 6, 9 (Dec. 4, 1995), 11 (P610.98.13, P610.139.3, P610.157.1, P610.157.2, P610.186.3, P610.204.10 to P610.204.15, P610.312.2, P610.312.4, P610.340.4, and P610.349.3), 12, 14, *Ledger Dispatch* newspaper (Dec. 4, 1995), *Contra Costa Times* newspaper (Nov. 9, 1999, page C9)

Reference 98.13

Weeping willow tree and lamb iron fence motif at the
Rees G. and Elvira Thomas gravesite, 1962. Photograph by Madison Devlin.

Reference 348.4

Reference 348.6

Reference 348.5

Reference 348.7

Elvira Thomas, the daughter of Rees G. and Margaret (Edwards) Thomas, was born February 7, 1869, and died July 18, 1870. She was interred in Rose Hill Cemetery. After her death, Rees and Margaret had another daughter, born *circa* 1871, and also named her Elvira. Pictured above is the second Elvira Thomas, photographed during various periods of her life. According to an article in the *Contra Costa Times* newspaper, November 21, 1999:

> When it came to chocolate Easter eggs, school clothes and Christmas presents, it was Aunt Elvira who sent them from her home in New York. The boxes of gifts that Elvira Thomas Owen mailed from Buffalo would send her brother's children into a joyful frenzy every Easter and Christmas. Dolores Thomas, granddaughter of Rees G. Thomas, spoke about her aunt Elvira: 'She'd always send us clothes. She didn't have any children, and she liked to go shopping. So she'd send us a big box of clothes on Christmas.'

Above, coal field descendants, members of the Lougher and Sorgenfrey families, gather at the Elvira Thomas and Rees G. Thomas gravesite, *circa* 1932. Below, the Rees G. Thomas and Elvira Thomas gravesite, 1954. Photograph below taken by Mary-Ellen Jones.

## PERSONAL INFORMATION:

| | |
|---|---|
| SEX: | Male |
| DATE OF BIRTH: | |
| DATE OF DEATH: | October 9 [no year given on gravestone] |
| PLACE OF DEATH: | |
| AGE AT DEATH: | 2 months |
| CAUSE OF DEATH: | Smallpox |
| BIRTHPLACE: | |
| SPOUSE: | None |
| PARENTS: | John and Carolina Wilhemina (Olfermann) Thomas |

## GRAVESITE INFORMATION:

| | |
|---|---|
| LOCATION OF GRAVESITE: | Section N-B, Plot #5 |
| GRAVESTONE: | Missing |
| TYPE OF GRAVESTONE: | Marble |
| SHAPE OF GRAVESTONE: | Obelisk |
| INSCRIPTION: | *In Memory of* |
| EPITAPH: | |
| MOTIF: | Nipped rose |
| CARVER: | |
| BASE: | Exists |
| TYPE OF BASE: | Concrete (middle marble base missing) |
| ENCLOSURE: | |
| TYPE OF ENCLOSURE: | |
| FENCE: | |
| TYPE OF FENCE: | |
| FENCE MOTIF: | |

# THOMAS, Frederick Elias

**ADDITIONAL PERSONAL INFORMATION:**
According to descendants, Frederick Elias died of smallpox.

See John Thomas and Sarah Norton.

**ADDITIONAL GRAVESITE INFORMATION:**
Frederick shares a gravestone with his father, John Thomas. No death year is listed on the stone for Frederick Elias. Since a month and day is given, it is likely that he died the same year as his father (1876). A middle marble base which held the gravestone once sat on top of a concrete base.

**REFERENCES:** 1, 2, 3, 5, 6, 11 (P610.250.1 and P610.317.22), 12, *Pittsburg Post Dispatch* newspaper (Wed., June 15, 1955, pages 9 and 12)

Reference 268.2

The John Thomas and Frederick Elias Thomas marble obelisk gravestone sits on a marble middle base in the upper left corner of the photograph, *circa* 1930s. At the time this photograph was taken, the cemetery was surrounded by a barbed wire fence. The gravestones for David E. Griffith and Joseph M. Edwards sit in the foreground surrounded by an iron fence.

Reference 250.1

The John Thomas and Frederick Elias Thomas gravestone, *circa* 1960. This marble obelisk appears to have been moved on the base. The inscription on the stone is facing south, but originally the inscription (front side of the gravestone) would most likely have faced east. The photograph on page 544, taken by Zelma Myrick, *circa* 1939, shows the gravestone in the correct position.

Reference 317.22

Bullet holes in the south side of the John Thomas and Frederick Elias Thomas gravestone.
Photograph taken *circa* 1939 by Zelma Myrick.

## PERSONAL INFORMATION:

| | |
|---|---|
| SEX: | Male |
| DATE OF BIRTH: | March 12, 1875 |
| DATE OF DEATH: | April 10, 1924 |
| PLACE OF DEATH: | Pittsburg, Contra Costa County, California |
| AGE AT DEATH: | 49 years, 29 days |
| CAUSE OF DEATH: | |
| BIRTHPLACE: | Nortonville, Contra Costa County, California |
| SPOUSE: | |
| PARENTS: | Howell and Mary Thomas |

## GRAVESITE INFORMATION:

| | |
|---|---|
| LOCATION OF GRAVESITE: | Unknown |
| GRAVESTONE: | Missing or never placed |
| TYPE OF GRAVESTONE: | |
| SHAPE OF GRAVESTONE: | |
| INSCRIPTION: | |
| EPITAPH: | |
| MOTIF: | |
| CARVER: | |
| BASE: | |
| TYPE OF BASE: | |
| ENCLOSURE: | |
| TYPE OF ENCLOSURE: | |
| FENCE: | |
| TYPE OF FENCE: | |
| FENCE MOTIF: | |

# THOMAS, Handel

**ADDITIONAL PERSONAL INFORMATION:**
The *1880 Census for the Nortonville Precinct, Contra Costa County, California*, lists Handel Thomas, age 5, as a native of California; and his parents, Howell, age 40, a miner and native of Wales; and Mary, age 35, a native of Wales. Also listed is his sister, Sarah, age 9, a native of California.

Handel is recorded in the *Index of Voters Somersville Precinct, Contra Costa County, 1902*, as age 26, and a resident of Nortonville.

He is recorded in the *Index of Voters, Somersville Precinct, Contra Costa County, 1904*, as age 28, and a resident of Nortonville. The *Index to the Great Register of Contra Costa County for 1906 and 1908*, lists Handel Thomas as a miner in Nortonville.

The *Index to the Great Register of Contra Costa County, 1910*, records Handel Thomas, age 35, as a miner and resident of Nortonville and belonging to the Socialist party.

The *1910 Census for Township 6, Contra Costa County, California* lists Howell M. Thomas, age 73, as a native of Wales. His date of immigration was 1840. Also recorded are his wife, Mary, age 69, a native of Wales and date of immigration as 1840; and their son, Handel, age 35, a native of California. Handel's marital status is listed as single.

Handel's date of birth comes from *World War I Draft Registration Cards, 1917-1918 Record*. Handel was born March 12, 1875 and his permanent home address was listed as "Nortonville, near Pittsburg, Co. Co. Calif." It also stated he had no occupation, but was formerly a coal miner. At the time the registration card was completed on October 12, 1918, he was 43 years old with a slender build, blue eyes and dark brown hair. He was also listed with "3 crippled fingers on right hand. Trigger finger O.K. Bruised Kidneys. Inability to work since Oct. 23, 1914 [?]. Spine partially effected [sic]."

See Howell Thomas.

**ADDITIONAL GRAVESITE INFORMATION:**
A cemetery list (source 3; see page 1004), compiled in 1935, by Eva Roath Olcott, with the Daughters of the American Revolution, for the *Vital Records from Cemeteries in California's Northern Counties, Vol. 111*, is the only source that records Handel's burial in Rose Hill Cemetery. It is believed that a gravestone was never placed in the cemetery for Handel.

**REFERENCES:** 3, 8 (June 22, 1878, Dec. 2, 1922, page 8, and Jan. 29, 1924), 9 (April 17, 1924, page 2), 11 (P610.109.43), 12, *Pittsburg Post* newspaper (April 12, 1924, page 1), see newspaper appendix page 757 and 758

Pictured on the left is Nortonville resident, Handel Thomas, date unknown. Handel, according to some sources, was the last Welshman to live in Nortonville, Contra Costa County, California. He lived with his mother who had come from Wales with her husband, Howell Thomas, in 1869. Handel's father, Howell Thomas, worked in the mines until his death. After his death, Handel took his place mining coal shortly before the final closing of the mines.

Courtesy of CCCHS

Courtesy of CCCHS

Mary Thomas and her son Handel Thomas of Nortonville, Contra Costa County, California, February 14, 1915. According to conversations with former coal field residents [Oral History with *Johnny Buffo and Amelia Peel, Recollections of the Mining Days*, April 27, 1985, page 16], Handel had consumption. Handel and his mother, Mary, were so weak that they couldn't chop wood for a fire. Former Nortonville resident, Amelia (Ginochio) Peel stated:

> She [Mrs. Thomas] had rugs on the floor and it was cold at night and they put a big log in the stove, the wood stove. Of course it kept burning and it dropped on the rug and caught fire, and she got on fire. And they took her to Martinez. And she died down there in Martinez...

Handel's mother burned to death in January 1924 and is buried in Alhambra Cemetery, Martinez, Contra Costa County, California. The fire badly burned Handel and he was taken to a hospital. This was the second time the Thomas family experienced fire. According to the *Contra Costa Gazette* newspaper, June 22, 1878, they lost their hotel and dwelling in a fire in Nortonville. See page 442.

Pictured from left to right are John Haggerty, William "Butch" Williams, Ned Griffiths, Howell Thomas, and Leyshon Lougher at the Ginochio saloon and ranch in Nortonville, *circa* 1909. Howell Thomas was the husband of Mary Thomas. He died in May 1915 and was buried at an unknown site in Rose Hill Cemetery.

Howell Thomas lived in Nortonville, Contra Costa County, California, first settling there in 1861. He was the father of Handel Thomas and Sarah (Thomas) Davies. According to coal field descendant Elmer (Jack) Lougher (son of Leyshon Lougher pictured above on far right), Howell Thomas served as a mine superintendent for many years with the Black Diamond Coal Mining Company of Nortonville.

## PERSONAL INFORMATION:

| | |
|---|---|
| SEX: | Male |
| DATE OF BIRTH: | *Circa* 1836 |
| DATE OF DEATH: | May 14, 1915 |
| PLACE OF DEATH: | Nortonville, Contra Costa County, California |
| AGE AT DEATH: | 78 years |
| CAUSE OF DEATH: | Hemorrhage of the lungs |
| BIRTHPLACE: | Wales |
| SPOUSE: | Mary Thomas |
| PARENTS: | |

## GRAVESITE INFORMATION:

| | |
|---|---|
| LOCATION OF GRAVESITE: | Unknown |
| GRAVESTONE: | Missing or never placed |
| TYPE OF GRAVESTONE: | |
| SHAPE OF GRAVESTONE: | |
| INSCRIPTION: | |
| EPITAPH: | |
| MOTIF: | |
| CARVER: | |
| BASE: | |
| TYPE OF BASE: | |
| ENCLOSURE: | |
| TYPE OF ENCLOSURE: | |
| FENCE: | |
| TYPE OF FENCE: | |
| FENCE MOTIF: | |

# THOMAS, Howell

**ADDITIONAL PERSONAL INFORMATION:**
In June 1867, Howell Thomas was listed as a miner and resident of Nortonville. The *1870 Census for Township Three, Contra Costa County, California* lists Howell Thomas, age 30, as a miner and native of Wales. Also listed is his wife, Mary, age 26, a native of Wales.

The *1871 Contra Costa County Directory* records Howell Thomas as a miner in Nortonville.

The *Assessment List, Contra Costa County, for 1872-73*, lists Howell M. Thomas as owning houses and furniture in the town of Nortonville valued at $750.

The *Business Directory of San Francisco and Principal Towns of California and Nevada, 1877*, page 50, lists H. M. Thomas as operating a hotel in Nortonville. The *Contra Costa Gazette* newspaper, June 22, 1878 states that the hotel and dwelling for Howell Thomas was destroyed during a fire at Nortonville. (See article "Fire at Nortonville" on page 442.)

The *1880 Nortonville Precinct Census, Contra Costa County, California* lists Howell Thomas, age 40, as a native of Wales and a miner. Also recorded are his wife, Mary, age 35, a native of Wales and their children, Sarah, age 9, and Handel, age 5; both are natives of California.

The *1890 Great Register of Voters in Contra Costa County, California*, lists Howell M. Thomas, age 48, as a miner, a native of Wales, and a resident of Nortonville. He registered to vote on September 12, 1884 and was naturalized on November 7, 1864 in Martinez, California.

The *Great Register of Contra Costa County, California, 1894*, page 50, records Howell M. Thomas, age 56, as 5' 4" tall with light complexion, gray eyes, and sandy color hair. He was a miner and native of Great Britain living in Nortonville. He is also listed in the *Great Register of Contra Costa County, California, 1898*, in the Somersville Precinct.

The *Index to the Great Register of Contra Costa County 1906 and 1908* records Howell M. Thomas as a miner and resident of Nortonville.

The *1910 Census for Township 6, Contra Costa County, California* lists Howell M. Thomas, age 73, as a native of Wales. His date of immigration was 1840. Also listed are his wife, Mary, age 69, a native of Wales and date of immigration as 1840; and their son, Handel, age 35, a native of California.

The *Contra Costa Gazette* newspaper, December 2, 1922, featured Mary and Handel Thomas in an article about the deserted town of Nortonville.

According to the *Daily Gazette* newspaper, January 29, 1924, Howell's wife, Mary, died at age 86 from burns when she rescued her son, Handel, from their burning home. She is buried at Alhambra Cemetery, Martinez, Contra Costa County, California. See Handel Thomas.

**ADDITIONAL GRAVESITE INFORMATION:**
According to an oral history interview conducted with former coal field resident Leo (Ike) Latimer on August 16, 1979, by Karana Hattersley-Drayton, there probably was no marker placed in the cemetery for Howell. He is most likely buried in the northeast corner of the cemetery.

**REFERENCES:** 3, 8 (June 22, 1878, Oct. 6, 1894, April 9, 1904, May 15, 1915, May 22, 1915, Dec. 2, 1922, and Jan. 29, 1924), 11 (P610.26.1), 12, *Johnny Buffo/Amelia Peel Oral History*, April 27, 1985, page 18; *Pittsburg Post* newspaper (May 22, 1915, page 4); *Elmer (Jack) Lougher, History of the Mt. Diablo Coal Field*, August 31, 1977, page 2; see newspaper appendix pages 759-761

# THOMAS,
## John

## PERSONAL INFORMATION:

| | |
|---|---|
| SEX: | Male |
| DATE OF BIRTH: | 1853 |
| DATE OF DEATH: | September 29, 1876 |
| PLACE OF DEATH: | Nortonville, Contra Costa County, California |
| AGE AT DEATH: | 23 years |
| CAUSE OF DEATH: | Smallpox |
| BIRTHPLACE: | Wales |
| SPOUSE: | Carolina Wilhemina (Olfermann) Thomas |
| PARENTS: | |

## GRAVESITE INFORMATION:

| | |
|---|---|
| LOCATION OF GRAVESITE: | Section N-B, Plot #5 |
| GRAVESTONE: | Missing |
| TYPE OF GRAVESTONE: | Marble |
| SHAPE OF GRAVESTONE: | Obelisk |
| INSCRIPTION: | *In Memory of* |
| EPITAPH: | |
| MOTIF: | Nipped rose |
| CARVER: | |
| BASE: | Exists |
| TYPE OF BASE: | Concrete (middle marble base missing) |
| ENCLOSURE: | |
| TYPE OF ENCLOSURE: | |
| FENCE: | |
| TYPE OF FENCE: | |
| FENCE MOTIF: | |

# THOMAS, John

**ADDITIONAL PERSONAL INFORMATION:**
According to descendants, after John Thomas died, his wife, Carolina, married George S. Miller, son of Sarah (Miller) Norton of Nortonville. John Thomas is buried beside Sarah Norton. Also according to descendants, Frederick Elias Thomas, the son of John and Carolina Thomas, died of smallpox. John Thomas shares a gravestone with his 2 month old son, Frederick Elias.

See Frederick Elias Thomas and Sarah Norton.

**ADDITIONAL GRAVESITE INFORMATION:**
Zelma Myrick, who recorded information in a notebook in the 1930s during a visit to Rose Hill Cemetery, reported "Ten bullet marks on stone, otherwise in good condition."

The marble obelisk gravestone as well as the middle marble base that once sat at this site are missing. See photographs on pages 542 - 544.

**REFERENCES:** 1, 2, 3, 4, 5, 6, 9 (Oct. 7, 1876 and Aug. 25, 1877), 11 (P610.250.1 and P610.317.22), 12

> SMALL POX.—Mr. Thomas, who was last week reported sick with the small pox at Nortonville, died on Friday last. No other cases have been reported, and it is believed there will be no further spread of the disease.

From the *Antioch Ledger* newspaper, October 7, 1876.

## PERSONAL INFORMATION:

| | |
|---|---|
| Sex: | Male |
| Date of Birth: | 1873 |
| Date of Death: | August 3, 1876 |
| Place of Death: | |
| Age at Death: | 3 years |
| Cause of Death: | |
| Birthplace: | |
| Spouse: | |
| Parents: | Howell J. and Elizabeth Thomas |

## GRAVESITE INFORMATION:

| | |
|---|---|
| Location of Gravesite: | Unknown |
| Gravestone: | Missing |
| Type of Gravestone: | Marble |
| Shape of Gravestone: | Tablet |
| Inscription: | *Children of* |
| Epitaph: | |
| Motif: | Rope with tassels |
| Carver: | |
| Base: | |
| Type of Base: | |
| Enclosure: | |
| Type of Enclosure: | |
| Fence: | |
| Type of Fence: | |
| Fence Motif: | |

# THOMAS, John D.

**ADDITIONAL PERSONAL INFORMATION:**
A sister, Elizabeth Ann Thomas, and brother, Joseph Thomas, are also buried in Rose Hill Cemetery. See Elizabeth Ann Thomas and Joseph Thomas.

**ADDITIONAL GRAVESITE INFORMATION:**
John shares a gravestone with his sister, Elizabeth Ann and brother, Joseph. To see a photograph of part of the gravestone, refer to page 77.

**REFERENCES:** 1, 2, 3, 6, 11 (P610.98.15, P610.260.5, P610.260.6, and P610.261.14), 12, *Black Diamond Cemetery* records, Black Diamond, King County, Washington, page 16

---

## DEATH OF OLE THOMAS

### Was the Oldest Pioneer of Black Diamond

BLACK DIAMOND, Jan. 31.—Ole Thomas, the oldest pioneer of Black Diamond, died Tuesday morning, after a lingering illness of three months. He was 68 years of age.

He was a native of Wales and came to the United States when a boy of 8. He spent a part of his early life in New York, and moved to California in 1849, where he lived until 1880, when he moved to Washington, and seventeen years ago he moved to Black Diamond, where he has resided since. He leaves a widow, three married daughters and a son. He was buried Thursday in Black Diamond cemetery. An impressive funeral service was conducted at the residence of his daughter, Mrs. Joseph Upton, where Mr. Thomas died.

---

This newspaper article from the Seattle *Post-Intelligencer*, Saturday, February 1, 1902, page 8, does not mention Howell J. Thomas' name, but refers to him as "Ole Thomas." Howell died on Tuesday, January 28, 1902, in Black Diamond, King County, Washington and is buried in the cemetery there. He was the father of at least nine children, including Elizabeth Ann, John D., and Joseph Thomas, who are buried in Rose Hill Cemetery. The above article states that he leaves behind a widow, three married daughters, and a son. These children were most likely Lucretia (born 1869); Anna (born *circa* 1871); Elizabeth (Mrs. Joseph Upton, born 1877); and John Thomas (born *circa* 1879). Howell's wife, Elizabeth, died in 1943, and is also buried in the Black Diamond, King County, Washington cemetery. See page 558.

# THOMAS,
## John H.

**PERSONAL INFORMATION:**

SEX:                     Male

DATE OF BIRTH:           May 27, 1874

DATE OF DEATH:           August 16, 1877

PLACE OF DEATH:          Nortonville, Contra Costa County, California

AGE AT DEATH:            3 years, 2 months, 20 days

CAUSE OF DEATH:          Diphtheria

BIRTHPLACE:

SPOUSE:                  None

PARENTS:                 William and Catherine Thomas


**GRAVESITE INFORMATION:**

LOCATION OF GRAVESITE:   Unknown (see Charles M. Thomas)

GRAVESTONE:              Missing or never placed

TYPE OF GRAVESTONE:

SHAPE OF GRAVESTONE:

INSCRIPTION:

EPITAPH:

MOTIF:

CARVER:

BASE:

TYPE OF BASE:

ENCLOSURE:

TYPE OF ENCLOSURE:

FENCE:

TYPE OF FENCE:

FENCE MOTIF:

# THOMAS, John H.

**ADDITIONAL PERSONAL INFORMATION:**
A gravestone at Holy Cross Cemetery (a Catholic cemetery), Antioch, Contra Costa County, California, contains a gravestone for the three Thomas children supposedly buried in Rose Hill Cemetery.

See Charles Morgan Thomas and Peter Benjamin Thomas.

**ADDITIONAL GRAVESITE INFORMATION:**
The only reference to the three Thomas boys buried in Rose Hill Cemetery is the *Pittsburg Post Dispatch* newspaper article, March 11, 1938. If they were buried in Rose Hill Cemetery, their burial locations are unknown.

See pages 532 and 533 for additional information regarding John's burial location.

**REFERENCES:** 9 (Aug. 25, 1877), *The Pittsburg Post Dispatch* newspaper (July 13 and 15, 1931, and March 11, 1938, pages 1 and 2), see newspaper appendix pages 763 and 764, Holy Cross Cemetery, Antioch, CA

---

## Letter from Nortonville.

### NORTONVILLE, June 28th, 1880.
### School Exhibition.

EDS. GAZETTE: The Good Templars' Hall was filled to its utmost capacity last Friday evening with happy children, blooming youth, silvery age, professors, school-ma'ams, trustees, doctors, preachers, &c., to witness the closing exercises of the last term of the Carbondale school. This is one of the largest schools in the county. Four efficient teachers were engaged to instruct the rising generation here during the last term. It is the aim and desire of our intelligent trustees to make it in every respect one of the best schools in the State. There is no object more worthy than to endow the world with sound and fruitful knowledge. The singing was excellent – performance brilliant – all that the most fastidious taste could have desired. Prof. William Thomas deserves great credit for the manner in which he trained the school to sing. And the sweet toned instrument issued forth sweet melodious strains under the artistic touch of Miss Annie Morgans. All seemed to be well pleased with the exercises of the evening. They will have a vacation for about two months.

---

This portion of the article, "Letter from Nortonville" comes from the *Contra Costa Gazette* newspaper, July 3, 1880. The article states "Prof. William Thomas deserves great credit for the manner in which he trained the school to sing."

## PERSONAL INFORMATION:

| | |
|---|---|
| SEX: | Male |
| DATE OF BIRTH: | August 27, 1867 |
| DATE OF DEATH: | August 2, 1870 |
| PLACE OF DEATH: | |
| AGE AT DEATH: | 2 years, 11 months, 6 days |
| CAUSE OF DEATH: | |
| BIRTHPLACE: | California |
| SPOUSE: | None |
| PARENTS: | Howell J. and Elizabeth Thomas |

## GRAVESITE INFORMATION:

| | |
|---|---|
| LOCATION OF GRAVESITE: | Unknown |
| GRAVESTONE: | Missing |
| TYPE OF GRAVESTONE: | Marble |
| SHAPE OF GRAVESTONE: | Tablet |
| INSCRIPTION: | *Children of* |
| EPITAPH: | |
| MOTIF: | Rope with tassels |
| CARVER: | |
| BASE: | |
| TYPE OF BASE: | |
| ENCLOSURE: | |
| TYPE OF ENCLOSURE: | |
| FENCE: | |
| TYPE OF FENCE: | |
| FENCE MOTIF: | |

# THOMAS, Joseph

**ADDITIONAL PERSONAL INFORMATION:**
Joseph's birth date was calculated by www.timeanddate.com, based on his death date and age at death.

A sister, Elizabeth Ann Thomas, and brother, John D. Thomas, are also buried in Rose Hill Cemetery. See Elizabeth Ann Thomas and John D. Thomas.

**ADDITIONAL GRAVESITE INFORMATION:**
Joseph shares a gravestone with his siblings Elizabeth Ann Thomas and John D. Thomas. To see a photograph of part of the gravestone, refer to page 77.

This gravestone was present in 1963 because it is listed on a student term paper by Jim Rotelli.

**REFERENCES:** 2, 3, 4, 6, 11 (P610.98.15, P610.260.5, P610.260.6, and P610.261.14), 12, *Black Diamond Cemetery* records, Black Diamond, King County, Washington, page 16

Reference 260.2

The gravestone for Howell Thomas, Black Diamond Cemetery, Black Diamond, King County, Washington, August 2001. His two sons, Tommy T. (died February 24, 1887, age 4 years, 1 month, and 17 days) and Joseph (died March 6, 1890, age 8 months), are listed on the other sides of this stone. A gravestone for his wife, Elizabeth, is located nearby. Howell and Elizabeth Thomas were also the parents of three children buried in Rose Hill Cemetery: Elizabeth Ann (died June 27, 1876, age 1 year, 10 months), John D. (died August 3, 1876, age 3 years), and Joseph Thomas (died August 2, 1870, age 2 years, 11 months, 6 days). Photograph by Traci (Gibbons) Parent.

# THOMAS,
## Joseph

## PERSONAL INFORMATION:

SEX: Male

DATE OF BIRTH: 1861

DATE OF DEATH: October 6, 1871

PLACE OF DEATH:

AGE AT DEATH: 10 years

CAUSE OF DEATH:

BIRTHPLACE:

SPOUSE:

PARENTS:

## GRAVESITE INFORMATION:

LOCATION OF GRAVESITE: Unknown

GRAVESTONE: Missing

TYPE OF GRAVESTONE:

SHAPE OF GRAVESTONE:

INSCRIPTION:

EPITAPH:

MOTIF:

CARVER:

BASE:

TYPE OF BASE:

ENCLOSURE:

TYPE OF ENCLOSURE:

FENCE:

TYPE OF FENCE:

FENCE MOTIF:

# THOMAS, Joseph

**ADDITIONAL PERSONAL INFORMATION:**
The parents of Joseph Thomas are not known.

**ADDITIONAL GRAVESITE INFORMATION:**
Only two sources (cemetery lists compiled in 1922

and 1935; see references 3 and 4 on page 1004)
document Joseph's burial in Rose Hill Cemetery.

**REFERENCES:** 3, 4, 12

Reference 186.1

Rose Hill Cemetery, *circa* late 1950s, looking northwest showing vandalized broken gravestones. Sadly, by the time this photograph was taken, the burial location for Joseph Thomas was unknown. His gravestone was documented in the cemetery in 1922 and 1935, but no longer remains today.

# THOMAS,
## Peter Benjamin

## PERSONAL INFORMATION:

| | |
|---|---|
| SEX: | Male |
| DATE OF BIRTH: | September 8, 1868 |
| DATE OF DEATH: | August 12, 1877 |
| PLACE OF DEATH: | Nortonville, Contra Costa County, California |
| AGE AT DEATH: | 8 years, 11 months, 4 days |
| CAUSE OF DEATH: | Diphtheria |
| BIRTHPLACE: | California |
| SPOUSE: | None |
| PARENTS: | William and Catherine Thomas |

## GRAVESITE INFORMATION:

| | |
|---|---|
| LOCATION OF GRAVESITE: | Unknown (See Charles M. Thomas) |
| GRAVESTONE: | Missing or never placed |
| TYPE OF GRAVESTONE: | |
| SHAPE OF GRAVESTONE: | |
| INSCRIPTION: | |
| EPITAPH: | |
| MOTIF: | |
| CARVER: | |
| BASE: | |
| TYPE OF BASE: | |
| ENCLOSURE: | |
| TYPE OF ENCLOSURE: | |
| FENCE: | |
| TYPE OF FENCE: | |
| FENCE MOTIF: | |

# THOMAS, Peter Benjamin

**ADDITIONAL PERSONAL INFORMATION:**
A gravestone at Holy Cross Cemetery (a Catholic cemetery), Antioch, California, contains a gravestone for the three Thomas children supposedly buried in Rose Hill Cemetery. See Charles Morgan Thomas and John H. Thomas.

According to an article in the March 11, 1938, *Pittsburg Post Dispatch* newspaper, the Thomas family lived in Nortonville. Peter's father, William Thomas, immigrated to Wisconsin and traveled across the plains to California when he was 24 years old. He married in San Francisco in 1857 and mined gold in Downieville, Sierra County, California. After leaving Downieville he moved his family to Nortonville, Contra Costa County, California where he worked in the Cumberland coal mine.

In the *1860 Census for Excelsior, Sierra County, California*, Peter's father, W. M. Thomas, is listed as age 31, a native of England, and born *circa* 1829. Listed with him are his wife, Kate, age 24, a native of Ireland born *circa* 1836, and their children: James, age 2, and Mary, age 8 months; both natives of California. Living with them are two miners from England: J. J. Thomas and J. M. Bucherman.

The *1870 Census for Township 3, Contra Costa County, California* lists William Thomas, age 41, as a native of England, born *circa* 1829, and his wife, Catherine Thomas, age 33, born *circa* 1837, a native of Ireland. Also listed are their children: James, age 12, born *circa* 1858; Mary, age 10, born *circa* 1860; Willie, age 8, born *circa* 1862; Katie, age 5, born *circa* 1865; and Peter, age 1, born *circa* 1869. All are natives of California.

The *1880 Census for Nortonville, Contra Costa County, California* lists William Thomas, age 52, born *circa* 1828. Listed with him are his wife, Catherine, age 45, born *circa* 1835 and their children: James, age 22, a miner; Mary, age 21, a housekeeper; William, age 19, a laborer; Kate, age 15, at school; and a son, Francis, age 2, born *circa* 1878 in California.

The *1900 Census for Somersville, Contra Costa County, California* lists William Thomas, age 72, and his birth date as December 1827. His year of marriage is recorded as 1857 and it states he has been married for 43 years. Thomas immigrated to the United States in 1847. His wife, Catherine, is listed as age 63, and born December 1836. Her year of immigration was 1855. The census states that she had 9 children, and that 5 were living at the time the census was taken. Recorded as living with them is their single son, Frank Thomas, age 23, born January 1877 in California.

**ADDITIONAL GRAVESITE INFORMATION:**
The only reference to the three Thomas boys buried in Rose Hill Cemetery is the *Pittsburg Post Dispatch* newspaper article, March 11, 1938. If they were buried in Rose Hill Cemetery, their burial locations are unknown. See pages 532 and 533 for additional information.

**REFERENCES:** 9 (Aug. 25, 1877), *The Pittsburg Post Dispatch* newspaper (July 13 and 15, 1931, and March 11, 1938, pages 1 and 2), see newspaper appendix pages 762-764, Holy Cross Cemetery, Antioch, CA

## PERSONAL INFORMATION:

| | |
|---|---|
| SEX: | Male |
| DATE OF BIRTH: | August 30, 1827 |
| DATE OF DEATH: | December 6, 1875 |
| PLACE OF DEATH: | San Francisco, San Francisco County, California |
| AGE AT DEATH: | 48 years, 3 months, 6 days |
| CAUSE OF DEATH: | Hernia or ruptured appendix |
| BIRTHPLACE: | Wales |
| SPOUSE: | Margaret (Edwards) Thomas |
| PARENTS: | |

## GRAVESITE INFORMATION:

| | |
|---|---|
| LOCATION OF GRAVESITE: | Section S-D, Plot #56 |
| GRAVESTONE: | Exists |
| TYPE OF GRAVESTONE: | Marble |
| SHAPE OF GRAVESTONE: | Tablet |
| INSCRIPTION: | *Farewell* |
| EPITAPH: | *We miss thee at home.* |
| MOTIF: | Clasped hands with "farewell" |
| CARVER: | Excelsior Marble Works, San Jose, California |
| BASE: | Exists |
| TYPE OF BASE: | Granite |
| ENCLOSURE: | Exists |
| TYPE OF ENCLOSURE: | Brick |
| FENCE: | Missing |
| TYPE OF FENCE: | Iron |
| FENCE MOTIF: | Weeping willow tree and lamb |

# THOMAS, Rees G.

**ADDITIONAL PERSONAL INFORMATION:**
Rees' birth date was calculated by www.timeanddate.com, based on his death date and age at death.

The *1860 Census for Mauch Chunk, Carbon County, Pennsylvania* lists Reese [sic] Thomas, age 32, as a miner and native of Wales. Also listed are his wife Marg [sic], age 25, a native of Wales and Wm. Thomas, age 1, a native of Pennsylvania.

The *Assessment List, Contra Costa County, for 1872-73*, lists Reese [sic] G. Thomas possessing property valued at $676. In March 1875, Rees G. Thomas was listed as a resident and miner in Nortonville.

The *1880 Census for Nortonville Precinct, Contra Costa County, California* records Margaret Thomas, age 44, as a housekeeper and native of Wales. Also listed are her children: Margaret, age 19, a native of Pennsylvania; Evan, age 17, a laborer; Maryann, age 15; Joan, age 13; Elvira, age 9; and Reese [sic], age 5. All are natives of California.

After the death of her husband Rees, Margaret married family friend, David E. Griffith in Nortonville in 1883. David E. Griffith died in May 1900 and is also buried in Rose Hill Cemetery (Section N-B, Plot 7b).

The *1910 Census for Township 6, Contra Costa County, California* records Margurete Griffb [sic], age 74, as a native of Wales and widowed. Her year of immigration is listed as 1848. Also listed is her son, Rees J. Thomas, age 35, a native of California; marital status as single. Margaret died in 1921 and is buried in Oak View Memorial Park Cemetery, Antioch, Contra Costa County, California. See Elvira Thomas and David E. Griffith.

**ADDITIONAL GRAVESITE INFORMATION:**
Rees shares the gravestone with daughter, Elvira Thomas. The gravestone was broken into three pieces and removed from the cemetery by a Thomas family descendant in the 1960s to protect it from further destruction by vandals prior to East Bay Regional Park District acquisition. The gravestone was returned in 1994 by Wayne Thomas, grandson of Rees G. Thomas. It was repaired and placed upright by Black Diamond Rangers and volunteers in November 1995. The brick enclosure was rebuilt by a stone mason in 1993.

**REFERENCES:** 1, 2, 3, 4, 5, 6, 11 (P610.98.13, P610.139.3, P610.157.1, P610.157.2, P610.186.3, P610.204.10 to P610.204.15, P610.312.2 to P610.312.4, and P610.340.4), 12, 14, *Ledger Dispatch* newspaper (Dec. 4, 1995), *Contra Costa Times* newspaper (Nov. 7, 1999, page C9 and Nov. 14, 1999, page C8), *San Ramon Valley Times* newspaper (Nov. 21, 1999, page C8)

Reference 348.1

Rees G. Thomas, husband of Margaret (Edwards) Thomas. According to descendants, Rees G. Thomas, and his friend, David E. Griffith, left Wales in the early 1850s. They stopped in Pennsylvania where other Welsh folks were living and working in the coal mines. It was there that Rees married Margaret Edwards in April 1854. In 1862, the family arrived in California by way of the Isthmus of Panama. They settled in Sierra County, California, to seek gold and remained there for five years.

In 1867, after failing to find investors for his gold mine, Rees moved to Nortonville, Contra Costa County, California. In Nortonville there were many Welsh neighbors, his good friend David E. Griffith among them. On their 160 acre homestead the Thomas family raised horses, cows, pigs, and chickens. According to family members, Rees died in 1875 in a San Francisco hospital, suffering from either a hernia or ruptured appendix. Also according to descendants, Rees was a bookkeeper for the Black Diamond Coal Mining Company of Nortonville.

East Bay Regional Park District

Reference 348.2

Margaret (Edwards) Thomas, wife of Rees G. Thomas. After the death of Rees G. Thomas, Margaret married family friend David E. Griffith. Griffith is also buried in Rose Hill Cemetery. Margaret Griffith died May 13, 1921, at age 85 years, 10 months, and 29 days, and is buried at Oak View Memorial Park Cemetery, East 18th Street, Antioch, California.

This newspaper article regarding Margaret (Edwards) Thomas Griffith from the *Pittsburg Post*, October 21, 1916, records her last name as "Griffin."

## A REAL PIONEER

Mrs. Margaret Griffin returned to her home at Nortonville from San Francisco last Monday where she had been visiting relatives. She also attended the wedding of her granddaughter, Miss Mona Jones, which took place September 30th. At the gathering were four generations of the family, they being Mrs. Griffith, Evan Thomas and wife and Walter Bloomfield, wife and son Donald. Mrs. Griffith is hale and hearty, although 81 years of age, and attends to business affairs the same as when she had passed half that number of life's milestones. She has resided on the ranch at Nortonville 47 years, and is a real pioneer of the county.

## PERSONAL INFORMATION:

| | |
|---|---|
| SEX: | Male |
| DATE OF BIRTH: | |
| DATE OF DEATH: | |
| PLACE OF DEATH: | |
| AGE AT DEATH: | Approximately 4 years |
| CAUSE OF DEATH: | |
| BIRTHPLACE: | |
| SPOUSE: | None |
| PARENTS: | John and Mary Tierney |

## GRAVESITE INFORMATION:

| | |
|---|---|
| LOCATION OF GRAVESITE: | Unknown |
| GRAVESTONE: | Missing or never placed |
| TYPE OF GRAVESTONE: | |
| SHAPE OF GRAVESTONE: | |
| INSCRIPTION: | |
| EPITAPH: | |
| MOTIF: | |
| CARVER: | |
| BASE: | |
| TYPE OF BASE: | |
| ENCLOSURE: | |
| TYPE OF ENCLOSURE: | |
| FENCE: | |
| TYPE OF FENCE: | |
| FENCE MOTIF: | |

# TIERNEY, John

**ADDITIONAL PERSONAL INFORMATION:**
It is believed that John was the son of John and Mary Tierney. According to descendants, the elder John Tierney (originally spelled O'Tierney) was a miner in the Mount Diablo Coal Field.

Since the family was Irish and they had involvement with the Catholic Church in Somersville (see *Antioch Ledger* newspaper article July 26, 1890 on page 569) it would be more likely that John's son was buried in a Catholic cemetery rather than the Protestant Rose Hill Cemetery.

The *Assessment List, Contra Costa County for 1872-'73*, records John Tierney being assessed for "Improvements in Town of Somersville" in May 1872.

The *Assessment Lists 1876 and 1886, County of Contra Costa, California, Somersville and Nortonville, Township No. 4*, page 22, records John Tierney being assessed $200 for a house in Somersville, $50 for furniture, and $20 for a cow in 1876.

The *1876 Contra Costa County Voting Register*, lists John Tierney, age 27, as a native of Ireland and a miner living in Somersville. This same document indicates he registered to vote on June 29, 1867.

The *1880 Census for Judsonville, Contra Costa County, California* records John Tierney, age 37, born *circa* 1843 in Ireland. His occupation is miner. Also listed are his wife, Mary, age 33, born *circa* 1847 in Ireland and their children, Anna, age 9, and Rose, age 5; both are natives of California.

According to descendants, John's sister, Rose Tierney, was born in Somersville on October 21, 1874 and died in San Francisco, California on September 23, 1964.

**ADDITIONAL GRAVESITE INFORMATION:**
Descendant's believe that John Tierney is buried in Rose Hill Cemetery. No other source documents his burial there.

**REFERENCES:** 9 (July 26, 1890 and June 25, 1898), 12

## Somersville Notes.

The festival held here Wednesday evening for the purpose of securing funds to repair the Catholic Church, was a social and financial success. During the early part of the evening the grab box, donated by the ladies of Antioch, awakened much interest, which was not allowed to flag until Mr. J. Houlihan had disposed of every article. The ladies hovered around the fancy work table, upon which was seen an elegant sofa pillow, donated by Miss Etta Brown, a handsome wax doll, given by Mrs. J. C. McDermott, a very pretty pin cushion, presented by Mrs. J. Houlihan, an elegant red plush photograph album, from Mrs. Timm, of Antioch, a gentleman's ring, donated by Miss Annie Tierney, of Somersville, and a crazy pin cushion, given by one of the young ladies of Antioch. Being anxious to learn why the gentlemen all flocked to one corner of the room, we went to see the cause thereof. It was the postoffice department, presided over by Misses Annie and Kate Wagner. Here the gentlemen received letters from all parts of the world at the postal rate of ten cents each. The fish pond was in charge of Misses Rose Tierney and Mollie Gillespie. These young ladies reaped a small fortune. Mrs. James Noakes, of Antioch, in her customary jovial manner, disposed of a set of tidies, by raffle. They were won by Miss Kate Carey, of Antioch. The ice cream booth was presided over by Mrs. James Nolan, of Antioch, who spared no effort to please those who patronized her. After the articles in the grab box and fish pond had been disposed of dancing was inaugurated. The "men and maidens fair" trod the mazy measures of the waltz to the music furnished by Schwartz and son, of Concord, until the "wee sma' hours." We were unable to ascertain the amount secured. Antioch, West Hartley, Black Diamond and Nortonville were well represented. The ladies of Somersville extend their sincere thanks to those who assisted them in making the festival a success.                       FAIRFAX.

According to this *Antioch Ledger* newspaper article from July 26, 1890, Miss Annie Tierney of Somersville donated a gentleman's ring for the festival held in Somersville for the purpose of securing funds to repair the Catholic Church. The article also states, "The fish pond was in charge of Misses Rose Tierney and Mollie Gillespie." Music was furnished by Schwartz and son. For more information on Schwartz see pages 511 to 516.

## Somersville Items.

Professor French's entertainment was a success. The church was crowded to the door. After the interesting program, which every one enjoyed, ice cream was served for the benefit of the Sunday school.

Harvey and Miss Mollie Gillespie of Los Angeles and Miss Rose Tierney of San Francisco paid Somersville a visit last Sunday. Harvey is a soldier belonging to the Seventh California Volunteers, and was up to see all his old friends before sailing for Manilla.

There was a social dance in Dickinson's Hotel Monday night.

Miss Lillian Russelman of Clayton is visiting at Mrs. H. Roughs.

Mrs. M. M. Clifford is quite ill and is confined to her bed.

Miss Marguerite Brown returned from Woodland last Saturday, where she was attending the Grand Parlor of N. D. G. W.

School closed Friday, June 17th. Quite a number attended the exercises in the afternoon.

On June 18, 1898, Miss Rose Tierney of San Francisco visited Somersville according to this *Antioch Ledger* newspaper article from June 25, 1898.

# TOLAN,
## (child #1)

**PERSONAL INFORMATION:**

SEX: Unknown

DATE OF BIRTH:

DATE OF DEATH: 1870

PLACE OF DEATH: Nortonville, Contra Costa County, California

AGE AT DEATH: Child

CAUSE OF DEATH: Scarlet fever

BIRTHPLACE:

SPOUSE: None

PARENTS: Possibly Frank and Eliza Tolan

**GRAVESITE INFORMATION:**

LOCATION OF GRAVESITE: Unknown

GRAVESTONE: Missing or never placed

TYPE OF GRAVESTONE:

SHAPE OF GRAVESTONE:

INSCRIPTION:

EPITAPH:

MOTIF:

CARVER:

BASE:

TYPE OF BASE:

ENCLOSURE:

TYPE OF ENCLOSURE:

FENCE:

TYPE OF FENCE:

FENCE MOTIF:

# TOLAN, (child #1)

**ADDITIONAL PERSONAL INFORMATION:**
The parents of this child were most likely Frank and Eliza Tolan.

The *1870 Census for Township 3, Contra Costa County, California* (taken July 29, 1870, after the deaths of the two Tolan children), records Frank Tolen [sic], a miner and native of New York, age 30, born *circa* 1840. Also listed are his wife, Eliza, born *circa* 1841, a native of Ireland, age 29, and their son, Frank, a native of California, age six months.

The *Contra Costa County Directory 1871-2*, page 387, lists F. Tolan as a miner in Nortonville. The next entry on the same page lists Frank Tolen [sic] as a miner in Nortonville.

The *1880 Census for Judsonville, Contra Costa County, California* records Frank Toland [sic], age 43, born *circa* 1837, as a miner and native of New York. Also listed are his wife, Eliza Toland [sic], a native of Ireland, age 43, born *circa* 1837, and their children: Charles, age 10; Elizabeth Ann, age 7; and Rosanna, age 5. All are natives of California. Living with them is Frank's younger brother, William Toland [sic], a single miner, age 39, also a native of New York.

According to the census records listed above, the Tolan family most likely had at least six children in the family. In addition to the two unnamed children who died of scarlet fever, there were:

- Frank, born *circa* 1869 (1870 census)
- Charles, born *circa* 1870 (1880 census)
- Elizabeth Ann, born *circa* 1873 (1880 census)
- Rosanna, born *circa* 1875 (1880 census)

Records at Holy Cross Cemetery, Antioch, Contra Costa County, California indicate that Frank Toland/Tolund [sic] is buried in this Catholic cemetery. No marker could be located for him at the burial site. According to their cemetery records, Frank was interred there on January 23, 1879. (Note: If this is the same Frank Tolan, he was recorded in the 1880 Census and therefore could not be interred in 1879.)

See Tolan child #2.

**ADDITIONAL GRAVESITE INFORMATION:**
The *Contra Costa Gazette* newspaper, July 9, 1870, is the only source that records the death of the Tolan children in Nortonville. According to the newspaper article "Somersville Correspondence":

> Mr. Tolan of Nortonville, has buried two, all of scarlet fever.

Although no source documents the burial of the Tolan child in Rose Hill Cemetery, it is likely that this child is buried there. Additonally, no record exists indicating the burial of a Tolan child in Holy Cross Cemetery.

**REFERENCES:** 8 (July 9, 1870), 12, see newspaper appendix (Violette I. Bowman) page 683

## PERSONAL INFORMATION:

SEX:                    Unknown
DATE OF BIRTH:
DATE OF DEATH:          1870
PLACE OF DEATH:         Nortonville, Contra Costa County, California
AGE AT DEATH:           Child
CAUSE OF DEATH:         Scarlet fever
BIRTHPLACE:
SPOUSE:                 None
PARENTS:                Possibly Frank and Eliza Tolan

## GRAVESITE INFORMATION:

LOCATION OF GRAVESITE:  Unknown
GRAVESTONE:             Missing or never placed
TYPE OF GRAVESTONE:
SHAPE OF GRAVESTONE:
INSCRIPTION:
EPITAPH:
MOTIF:
CARVER:
BASE:
TYPE OF BASE:
ENCLOSURE:
TYPE OF ENCLOSURE:
FENCE:
TYPE OF FENCE:
FENCE MOTIF:

# TOLAN, (child #2)

**ADDITIONAL PERSONAL INFORMATION:**
See Tolan child #1.

**ADDITIONAL GRAVESITE INFORMATION:**
The *Contra Costa Gazette* newspaper, July 9, 1870, is the only source that records the death of the Tolan children in Nortonville.

Although no source documents the burial of the Tolan child in Rose Hill Cemetery, it is likely that this child is buried there.

**REFERENCES:** 8 (July 9, 1870), 12, see newspaper appendix (Violette I. Bowman) page 683

---

## From Somersville.

SOMERSVILLE, Sept. 24th, 1872.

EDS. GAZETTE: We are still living up here. The hot summer's sun nor the terrific fall winds could exterminate us. So, now, we are having a freezing spell. I do not yet know how we will come out. It looks wintry very much; and we would welcome it quite heartily; we would like a little free water again; for you must recollect we have a little water monoply here. Not a drop of God's pure San Joaquin element can we get here, except at the rate of 50 cents per barrel. Here would be a lay out for Von Schmidt and Lake Bigtaholer Water Company. Every body seems to be busy patching up troughs and roofs for the coming wet season for water is money with us. As for our Coal miner-farmers, that is, those who own small farms from four to six miles away, and do both mining and farming, they are about discouraged. Freidlander's Ring is too much for them; $1 50 per cental for wheat will not pay, hence they cannot stand the press. The coal business never was in a more prosperous state. The Union Mine Company paid off for the month of July on the 10th inst. The Pittsburgh, Eureka and Central, paid off on the 18th, for the month of August.

Politics is at a discount around here, only for a few newspapers we would not know whether we were to have any more elections or not. Every one seems disposed to let the "Bloody Chasm" remain unfilled; and keep old Horace in the newspaper business, as he is quite at home there, and knows all about the business. JIMMY LEGS.

From the *Contra Costa Gazette* newspaper, September 28, 1872.

## PERSONAL INFORMATION:

| | |
|---|---|
| SEX: | Male |
| DATE OF BIRTH: | *Circa* September 29, 1848 |
| DATE OF DEATH: | December 29, 1864 |
| PLACE OF DEATH: | Somersville, Contra Costa County, California |
| AGE AT DEATH: | 16 years, 3 months |
| CAUSE OF DEATH: | Scarlatina Maligna (scarlet fever) |
| BIRTHPLACE: | |
| SPOUSE: | None |
| PARENTS: | John and Nancy Tonkins |

## GRAVESITE INFORMATION:

| | |
|---|---|
| LOCATION OF GRAVESITE: | Unknown |
| GRAVESTONE: | Missing or never placed |
| TYPE OF GRAVESTONE: | |
| SHAPE OF GRAVESTONE: | |
| INSCRIPTION: | |
| EPITAPH: | |
| MOTIF: | |
| CARVER: | |
| BASE: | |
| TYPE OF BASE: | |
| ENCLOSURE: | |
| TYPE OF ENCLOSURE: | |
| FENCE: | |
| TYPE OF FENCE: | |
| FENCE MOTIF: | |

# TONKINS, John

**ADDITIONAL PERSONAL INFORMATION:**
John was one of at least four children who died in Somersville in December 1865 from scarlatina maligna (scarlet fever). Numerous other children died in 1865 from the same disease and are buried in, or believed to be buried in, Rose Hill Cemetery. The other children who died in 1864/1865 of this disease include:

- Charles W. Blackburn, died February 20, 1865, age 9 years, 7 months
- Thomas Pratten Goulding, died January 31, 1865, age 7 years, 7 months, 17 days
- Jane Russel Muir, died January 4, 1865, age 4 years, 3 (?) months
- Elizabeth Richmond, died February 17, 1865, age 8 years, 5 months, 11 days
- Annie Tregellas, died February 19, 1865, age 7 years, 7 months
- James Tregellas, died December 28, 1864, age 2 years, 21 days
- Joseph Tregellas, died February 18, 1865, age 5 years, 1 month
- John Edmund Wright, died December 28, 1864, age 9 years, 10 months
- Mary Elizabeth Wright, died December 25, 1864, age 1 year, 6 months

John's date of birth was calculated by using www.timeanddate.com, based on his age at death and date of death reported in the *Antioch Ledger* newspaper, January 7, 1865.

**ADDITIONAL GRAVESITE INFORMATION:**
The *Antioch Ledger* newspaper, January 7, 1865, is the only source that records the death of the Tonkin child in Somersville. Although no source documents the burial of this child in Rose Hill Cemetery, it is likely that the Tonkins' child is buried there.

**REFERENCES:** 9 (January 7, 1865), 12, see newspaper appendix page 765

# TREGELLAS (TREGALLAS),
## Annie

**PERSONAL INFORMATION:**

| | |
|---|---|
| SEX: | Female |
| DATE OF BIRTH: | July 1857 |
| DATE OF DEATH: | February 19, 1865 |
| PLACE OF DEATH: | Somersville, Contra Costa County, California |
| AGE AT DEATH: | 7 years, 7 months |
| CAUSE OF DEATH: | Scarlatina Maligna (scarlet fever) |
| BIRTHPLACE: | |
| SPOUSE: | None |
| PARENTS: | Possibly Samuel and Sarah Tregellas |

**GRAVESITE INFORMATION:**

| | |
|---|---|
| LOCATION OF GRAVESITE: | Unknown |
| GRAVESTONE: | Missing or never placed |
| TYPE OF GRAVESTONE: | |
| SHAPE OF GRAVESTONE: | |
| INSCRIPTION: | |
| EPITAPH: | |
| MOTIF: | |
| CARVER: | |
| BASE: | |
| TYPE OF BASE: | |
| ENCLOSURE: | |
| TYPE OF ENCLOSURE: | |
| FENCE: | |
| TYPE OF FENCE: | |
| FENCE MOTIF: | |

# TREGELLAS (TREGALLAS), Annie

**ADDITIONAL PERSONAL INFORMATION:**
The last name for this family has been spelled various ways (Tregellis, Treggelas, Tregallas, Tregellas, Tregillas, Tergelais). See page 580.

Annie was one of many children who died in Somersville in 1864/1865 from scarlatina maligna (scarlet fever) and are buried in, or believed to be buried in, Rose Hill Cemetery. Other children who died of scarlet fever during this same period of time include:

- Charles W. Blackburn, died February 20, 1865, age 9 years, 7 months
- Thomas Pratten Goulding, died January 31, 1865, age 7 years, 7 months, 17 days
- Jane Russel Muir, died January 4, 1865, age 4 years, 3 (?) months
- Elizabeth Richmond, died February 17, 1865, age 8 years, 5 months, 11 days
- John Tonkins, died December 29, 1864, age 16 years, 3 months
- James Tregellas, died December 28, 1864, age 2 years, 21 days
- Joseph Tregellas, died February 18, 1865, age 5 years, 1 month
- John Edmund Wright, died December 28, 1864, age 9 years, 10 months
- Mary Elizabeth Wright, died December 25, 1864, age 1 year, 6 months

Annie's date of birth was calculated by www.timeanddate.com, based on the date of death and age at death reported in the *Contra Costa Gazette* newspaper, February 25, 1865.

Annie's brother, Joseph Tregellas, died in February 1865, also from scarlatina maligna. James Tregellas, believed to be another brother, died on December 28, 1864 from the same disease.

The *Antioch Ledger* newspaper, January 7, 1865 stated that James' parents were Samuel and Sarah Tergelais [sic]. It is possible that they were the parents of Annie as well.

See James Tregellas and Joseph Tregellas.

**ADDITIONAL GRAVESITE INFORMATION:**
The *Contra Costa Gazette* newspaper, February 25, 1865, is the only source that records the death of Annie Tregellas in Somersville. Although no source documents her burial in Rose Hill Cemetery it is likely she is buried there.

**REFERENCES:** 8 (Feb. 25, 1865), 12, see newspaper appendix (Elizabeth Richmond) page 749

# TREGELLAS (TREGALLAS), James

## PERSONAL INFORMATION:

| | |
|---|---|
| SEX: | Male |
| DATE OF BIRTH: | *Circa* December 7, 1862 |
| DATE OF DEATH: | December 28, 1864 |
| PLACE OF DEATH: | Somersville, Contra Costa County, California |
| AGE AT DEATH: | 2 years, 21 days |
| CAUSE OF DEATH: | malignant scarlatina [sic] (scarlet fever) |
| BIRTHPLACE: | |
| SPOUSE: | None |
| PARENTS: | Samuel and Sarah Tregellas |

## GRAVESITE INFORMATION:

| | |
|---|---|
| LOCATION OF GRAVESITE: | Unknown |
| GRAVESTONE: | Missing or never placed |
| TYPE OF GRAVESTONE: | |
| SHAPE OF GRAVESTONE: | |
| INSCRIPTION: | |
| EPITAPH: | |
| MOTIF: | |
| CARVER: | |
| BASE: | |
| TYPE OF BASE: | |
| ENCLOSURE: | |
| TYPE OF ENCLOSURE: | |
| FENCE: | |
| TYPE OF FENCE: | |
| FENCE MOTIF: | |

# TREGELLAS (TREGALLAS), James

**ADDITIONAL PERSONAL INFORMATION:**
James was one of at least four children who died in Somersville in December 1864 from scarlatina maligna (scarlet fever). Numerous other children died from the same disease during the same period of time and are buried in, or believed to be buried in, Rose Hill Cemetery. Other children who died in 1864/1865 of this disease include:

- Charles W. Blackburn, died February 20, 1865, age 9 years, 7 months
- Thomas Pratten Goulding, died January 31, 1865, age 7 years, 7 months, 17 days
- Jane Russel Muir, died January 4, 1865, age 4 years, 3 (?) months
- Elizabeth Richmond, died February 17, 1865, age 8 years, 5 months, 11 days
- John Tonkins, died December 29, 1864, age 16 years, 3 months
- Annie Tregellas, died February 19, 1865, age 7 years, 7 months
- Joseph Tregellas, died February 18, 1865, age 5 years, 1 month
- John Edmund Wright, died December 28, 1864, age 9 years, 10 months
- Mary Elizabeth Wright, died December 25, 1864, age 1 year, 6 months

James' date of birth was calculated by using www.timeanddate.com, based on his age at death and date of death reported in the *Antioch Ledger* newspaper, January 7, 1865.

The *1864 Tax Book for Contra Costa County, California* lists James' father, Samuel Tregellis [sic], for improvements in Somersville valued at $75.

The last name for this family has been spelled various ways (Tregellis, Treggelas, Tregallas, Tregellas, Tregillas, Tergelais).

S. Treggelas [sic] is listed as an officer elect for the Somersville Division, Sons of Temperance in the *Contra Costa Gazette* newspaper, April 9, 1864.

The *Contra Costa Directory 1871-2*, page 388, lists Samuel Tregallas [sic], as an engineer in Somersville.

The *Assessment List, Contra Costa County, for 1872-'73*, page 183, records Samuel Tregellas as owning houses in the town of Somersville.

The *1876 Contra Costa County Voting Register* lists Samuel Tregillas [sic], age 35, as a blacksmith and native of England living in Somersville. He registered to vote on June 27, 1867.

Annie and Joseph Tregellas, who died in February 1865, also from scarlatina maligna, are believed to be the sister and brother of James. See Annie Tregellas and Joseph Tregellas.

**ADDITIONAL GRAVESITE INFORMATION:**
The *Antioch Ledger* newspaper, January 7, 1865 (see page 765), is the only source that lists James' death in Somersville. Although no source documents his burial in Rose Hill Cemetery, it is likely that James is buried there.

**REFERENCES:** 9 (Jan. 7, 1865), 12, see newspaper appendix (John Tonkins) page 765

# TREGELLAS (TREGALLAS),
## Joseph

**PERSONAL INFORMATION:**

| | |
|---|---|
| SEX: | Male |
| DATE OF BIRTH: | January 1860 |
| DATE OF DEATH: | February 18, 1865 |
| PLACE OF DEATH: | Somersville, Contra Costa County, California |
| AGE AT DEATH: | 5 years, 1 month |
| CAUSE OF DEATH: | Scarlatina Maligna (scarlet fever) |
| BIRTHPLACE: | |
| SPOUSE: | None |
| PARENTS: | Possibly Samuel and Sarah Tregellas |

**GRAVESITE INFORMATION:**

| | |
|---|---|
| LOCATION OF GRAVESITE: | Unknown |
| GRAVESTONE: | Missing or never placed |
| TYPE OF GRAVESTONE: | |
| SHAPE OF GRAVESTONE: | |
| INSCRIPTION: | |
| EPITAPH: | |
| MOTIF: | |
| CARVER: | |
| BASE: | |
| TYPE OF BASE: | |
| ENCLOSURE: | |
| TYPE OF ENCLOSURE: | |
| FENCE: | |
| TYPE OF FENCE: | |
| FENCE MOTIF: | |

East Bay Regional Park District

# TREGELLAS (TREGALLAS), Joseph

**ADDITIONAL PERSONAL INFORMATION:**
The last name for this family has been spelled various ways (Tregellis, Treggelas, Tregallas, Tregellas, Tregillas, Tergelais). See page 580.

Joseph's obituary from the *Antioch Ledger*, January 7, 1865 spelled his last name as Tergelais [sic]. It is believed that his last name is spelled Tregellas or Tregallas.

Joseph was one of many children who died in Somersville in 1864/1865 from scarlatina maligna (scarlet fever) and are buried in, or believed to be buried in, Rose Hill Cemetery. The other children who died in 1864/1865 of this disease include:

- Charles W. Blackburn, died February 20, 1865, age 9 years, 7 months
- Thomas Pratten Goulding, died January 31, 1865, age 7 years, 7 months, 17 days
- Jane Russel Muir, died January 4, 1865, age 4 years, 3 (?) months
- Elizabeth Richmond, died February 17, 1865, age 8 years, 5 months, 11 days
- John Tonkins, died December 29, 1864, age 16 years, 3 months
- Annie Tregellas, died February 19, 1865, age 7 years, 7 months
- James Tregellas, died December 28, 1864, age 2 years, 21 days
- John Edmund Wright, died December 28, 1864, age 9 years, 10 months
- Mary Elizabeth Wright, died December 25, 1864, age 1 year, 6 months

Joseph's date of birth was calculated by www.timeanddate.com, based on the date of death and age at death reported in the *Contra Costa Gazette* newspaper, February 25, 1865.

Joseph's sister, Annie Tregellas, died in February 1865, also from scarlatina maligna. James Tregellas, believed to be a brother, died on December 28, 1864 from the same disease.

The *Antioch Ledger* newspaper, January 7, 1865 stated that James' parents were Samuel and Sarah Tergelais [sic]. See Annie Tregellas and James Tregellas.

**ADDITIONAL GRAVESITE INFORMATION:**
The *Contra Costa Gazette* newspaper February 25, 1865, is the only source that records the death of Joseph Tregellas in Somersville. Although no source documents his burial in Rose Hill Cemetery, it is likely that he is buried there.

**REFERENCES:** 8 (Feb. 25, 1865), 12, see appendix newspaper (Elizabeth Richmond) page 749

# TULLY,
## Mary

**PERSONAL INFORMATION:**

| | |
|---|---|
| SEX: | Female |
| DATE OF BIRTH: | December 26, 1826 |
| DATE OF DEATH: | November 10, 1879 |
| PLACE OF DEATH: | |
| AGE AT DEATH: | 52 years, 10 months, 15 days |
| CAUSE OF DEATH: | |
| BIRTHPLACE: | |
| SPOUSE: | |
| PARENTS: | |

**GRAVESITE INFORMATION:**

| | |
|---|---|
| LOCATION OF GRAVESITE: | Section S-C, Plot #18 |
| GRAVESTONE: | Exists |
| TYPE OF GRAVESTONE: | Marble |
| SHAPE OF GRAVESTONE: | Tablet |
| INSCRIPTION: | *Our Mother* |
| EPITAPH: | *Rest Mother rest, in quiet sleep,* |
| | *While friends in sorrow o'er the [sic] weep.* |
| MOTIF: | Clasped hands |
| CARVER: | |
| BASE: | Exists |
| TYPE OF BASE: | Sandstone |
| ENCLOSURE: | |
| TYPE OF ENCLOSURE: | |
| FENCE: | |
| TYPE OF FENCE: | |
| FENCE MOTIF: | |

# TULLY, Mary

**ADDITIONAL PERSONAL INFORMATION:**
The epitaph and inscription on Mary's gravestone indicates she was a mother. Her birth date was calculated by www.timeanddate.com, based on the age at death and date of death listed on her gravestone.

The *1880 Census for Somersville Precinct, Contra Costa County, California* lists Lawrence Tully, age 20, as a miner and native of California. His mother was born in Virginia and his father born in Massachusetts. He may possibly be Mary Tully's son.

**ADDITIONAL GRAVESITE INFORMATION:**
Zelma Myrick, who recorded information in a notebook in the 1930s during a visit to Rose Hill Cemetery, reported "Stone broken in half." Mary's gravestone was broken in half prior to East Bay Regional Park District acquisition. Her stone was removed from the cemetery by Black Diamond Rangers and placed in storage in November 1980 until repairs could be made.

In August 2003 a new marble slab was purchased and cut to the shape of the original gravestone. Using epoxy, the new piece was laminated to the back of the original stone to provide support. In September 2005 the gravestone was returned to the cemetery and the stone placed upright on the base.

**REFERENCES:** 1, 3, 4, 6, 11 (P610.31.174, P610.117.3, and P610.263.1), 14

Reference 117.3

The broken Mary Tully gravestone before repair, June 1983.
Photograph by Roger Epperson, EBRPD.

# UNKNOWN

## PERSONAL INFORMATION:

| | |
|---|---|
| Sex: | Unknown |
| Date of Birth: | |
| Date of Death: | |
| Place of Death: | |
| Age at Death: | |
| Cause of Death: | |
| Birthplace: | |
| Spouse: | |
| Parents: | |

## GRAVESITE INFORMATION:

| | |
|---|---|
| Location of Gravesite: | Section S-E, Plot #87 |
| Gravestone: | Missing |
| Type of Gravestone: | Marble |
| Shape of Gravestone: | Tablet |
| Inscription: | |
| Epitaph: | |
| Motif: | |
| Carver: | |
| Base: | Exists |
| Type of Base: | Granite |
| Enclosure: | |
| Type of Enclosure: | |
| Fence: | Exists |
| Type of Fence: | Iron hoop (replica) with sandstone corner blocks |
| Fence Motif: | Acorn finials |

# UNKNOWN

**ADDITIONAL PERSONAL INFORMATION:**
Because the gravestone containing the name is missing, it is not known who is buried at this plot.

**ADDITIONAL GRAVESITE INFORMATION:**
Several photographs were taken of this gravesite prior to East Bay Regional Park District acquisition. All the photographs were taken from a distance and some show a marble tablet gravestone within an iron fence enclosure. Since no photographs exist showing a close-up view of the gravestone, it remains a mystery as to who is buried at this site.

A map of burial locations for Rose Hill Cemetery drawn by Jim Rotelli in 1963 for a California history class, indicates that Ann Morgan may be interred at this site. See Ann Morgan.

Two sections of the iron hoop fence were found at the gravesite when the area became an East Bay Regional Park. The original fence sections have been placed in storage. In 2004, a replica iron hoop fence was fabricated by the blacksmith at Ardenwood Historic Farm in Fremont, Alameda County, California based on existing sections of the original iron fence. Three new acorn finials were fabricated and placed on the fence with the one original finial.

A photograph of this gravesite appears in the *California Monthly* magazine, "Back Yard Ghost Towns," May 1949, page 22.

**REFERENCES:** 6, 11 (P610.14.1, P610.139.3, P610.147.18, and P610.317.6), *California Monthly* magazine, "Back Yard Ghost Towns," May 1949, page 22

Rose Hill Cemetery looking west. Plot #87 can be seen on the left, next to the Italian Cypress tree. The iron fence is intact and contains the gravestone of the unknown individual(s) interred. Photograph taken *circa* 1939 by Zelma Myrick.

Unknown burial, plot #87, date unknown.

# UNKNOWN,
## (Adult)

**PERSONAL INFORMATION:**

| | |
|---|---|
| SEX: | Unknown |
| DATE OF BIRTH: | 1833 |
| DATE OF DEATH: | February 13, 1875 |
| PLACE OF DEATH: | |
| AGE AT DEATH: | 42 years |
| CAUSE OF DEATH: | |
| BIRTHPLACE: | |
| SPOUSE: | |
| PARENTS: | |

**GRAVESITE INFORMATION:**

| | |
|---|---|
| LOCATION OF GRAVESITE: | Section S-F, Plot #99 |
| GRAVESTONE: | Exists (partial) |
| TYPE OF GRAVESTONE: | Marble |
| SHAPE OF GRAVESTONE: | Tablet |
| INSCRIPTION: | |
| EPITAPH: | *In the Midst of life we are in Death* |
| | *Tis God lifts our comforts high* |
| | *Or sinks them in the grave,* |
| | *He gives and when he takes away,* |
| | *He takes but what he gave.* |
| MOTIF: | Rope with tassels |
| CARVER: | |
| BASE: | Exists |
| TYPE OF BASE: | Sandstone |
| ENCLOSURE: | Exists |
| TYPE OF ENCLOSURE: | Sandstone |
| FENCE: | |
| TYPE OF FENCE: | |
| FENCE MOTIF: | |

# UNKNOWN, (Adult)

**ADDITIONAL PERSONAL INFORMATION:** Because the top half of the stone with the name is missing, it is not known who is buried at this plot.

**ADDITIONAL GRAVESITE INFORMATION:** The top half of the gravestone is missing and the bottom portion of the stone was concreted flat to ground prior to East Bay Regional Park District acquisition. The stone once sat next to the gravestone of Ann and William H. Clement. Ann Clement also died February 13, 1875. See Ann Clement.

In 2004 the gravestone piece was placed in storage for safekeeping.

**REFERENCES:** 11 (P610.31.152), 12, 14

Reference 31.152

The bottom half of a gravestone for an unknown adult, 42 years old, as it appeared in the summer of 1977. The top half of the gravestone is missing. Photograph by Traci (Gibbons) Parent.

# UNKNOWN,
## (Infant #1)

## PERSONAL INFORMATION:

| | |
|---|---|
| SEX: | Unknown |
| DATE OF BIRTH: | |
| DATE OF DEATH: | |
| PLACE OF DEATH: | |
| AGE AT DEATH: | Infant |
| CAUSE OF DEATH: | |
| BIRTHPLACE: | |
| SPOUSE: | None |
| PARENTS: | |

## GRAVESITE INFORMATION:

| | |
|---|---|
| LOCATION OF GRAVESITE: | Section N-E, Plot #69 |
| GRAVESTONE: | Exists |
| TYPE OF GRAVESTONE: | Marble |
| SHAPE OF GRAVESTONE: | Tablet |
| INSCRIPTION: | *Also two infant children.* |
| EPITAPH: | *Though lost to sight to memory dear.* |
| MOTIF: | Masonic & Odd Fellows emblems/rope with tassels |
| CARVER: | Excelsior Marble Works, San Jose, California |
| BASE: | Exists |
| TYPE OF BASE: | Sandstone with middle marble base |
| ENCLOSURE: | |
| TYPE OF ENCLOSURE: | |
| FENCE: | |
| TYPE OF FENCE: | |
| FENCE MOTIF: | |

# UNKNOWN, (Infant #1)

**ADDITIONAL PERSONAL INFORMATION:**
According to a descendant, Thomas S. and Mary Jones had eight children. Three of these children, a girl and two boys, died in Nortonville during a diphtheria epidemic. It is possible that two of these children are the ones interred with Thomas S. Jones.

**ADDITIONAL GRAVESITE INFORMATION:**
One of two unnamed infants buried with Thomas S. Jones. See Thomas S. Jones and unknown infant #2.

**REFERENCES:** 1, 2, 3, 6, 11 (P610.31.147, P610.168.22, and P610.317.15), 12, 14

Reference 317.15

The vandalized gravestone for Thomas S. Jones and two infants, *circa* 1939.
Photograph by Zelma Myrick.

# UNKNOWN,
## (Infant #2)

**PERSONAL INFORMATION:**

| | |
|---|---|
| SEX: | Unknown |
| DATE OF BIRTH: | |
| DATE OF DEATH: | |
| PLACE OF DEATH: | |
| AGE AT DEATH: | Infant |
| CAUSE OF DEATH: | |
| BIRTHPLACE: | |
| SPOUSE: | None |
| PARENTS: | |

**GRAVESITE INFORMATION:**

| | |
|---|---|
| LOCATION OF GRAVESITE: | Section N-E, Plot #69 |
| GRAVESTONE: | Exists |
| TYPE OF GRAVESTONE: | Marble |
| SHAPE OF GRAVESTONE: | Tablet |
| INSCRIPTION: | *Also two infant children.* |
| EPITAPH: | *Though lost to sight to memory dear.* |
| MOTIF: | Masonic & Odd Fellows emblems/rope with tassels |
| CARVER: | Excelsior Marble Works, San Jose, California |
| BASE: | Exists |
| TYPE OF BASE: | Sandstone with middle marble base |
| ENCLOSURE: | |
| TYPE OF ENCLOSURE: | |
| FENCE: | |
| TYPE OF FENCE: | |
| FENCE MOTIF: | |

# UNKNOWN, (Infant #2)

**ADDITIONAL PERSONAL INFORMATION:**
One of two unnamed infants buried with Thomas S. Jones. According to a descendant, Thomas S. and Mary Jones had eight children. Three of these children, a girl and two boys, died in Nortonville during a diphtheria epidemic. It is possible that two of these children are the ones interred with Thomas S. Jones.

**ADDITIONAL GRAVESITE INFORMATION:**
One of two unnamed infants buried with Thomas S. Jones. See Thomas S. Jones and unknown infant #1.

**REFERENCES:** 1, 2, 3, 6, 11 (P610.31.147, P610.168.22, and P610. 317.15), 12, 14

# UNKNOWN
## ("Infant Babe")

**PERSONAL INFORMATION:**

| | |
|---|---|
| SEX: | Unknown |
| DATE OF BIRTH: | |
| DATE OF DEATH: | |
| PLACE OF DEATH: | |
| AGE AT DEATH: | 3 days |
| CAUSE OF DEATH: | |
| BIRTHPLACE: | |
| SPOUSE: | None |
| PARENTS: | Unknown |

**GRAVESITE INFORMATION:**

| | |
|---|---|
| LOCATION OF GRAVESITE: | Section S-E, Plot #79 |
| GRAVESTONE: | Exists |
| TYPE OF GRAVESTONE: | Marble |
| SHAPE OF GRAVESTONE: | Tablet |
| INSCRIPTION: | *Infant Babe* |
| EPITAPH: | *Two pilgrims for the holy land* |
| | *Have left our lonely door,* |
| | *Two sinless angels, hand in hand* |
| | *Have reached promised shore.* |
| MOTIF: | Hand with finger pointing toward Heaven |
| CARVER: | |
| BASE: | Exists |
| TYPE OF BASE: | New granite and middle marble bases |
| ENCLOSURE: | |
| TYPE OF ENCLOSURE: | |
| FENCE: | |
| TYPE OF FENCE: | |
| FENCE MOTIF: | |

# UNKNOWN, ("Infant Babe")

**ADDITIONAL PERSONAL INFORMATION:**
It is unknown if this is a member of the Jones family. The baby is only referred to as "Infant Babe" on the gravestone.

**ADDITIONAL GRAVESITE INFORMATION:**
This unnamed infant shares the stone with Mary E. Jones. See Mary E. Jones.

**REFERENCES:** 1, 2, 6, 11 (P610.31.163 and P610.119.54), 12, 14

Reference 31.163

The Mary E. Jones and "Infant Babe" gravestone as it appeared in July 1977. The gravestone has been repaired by Black Diamond Rangers and now stands upright in the cemetery. Photograph by Traci (Gibbons) Parent.

# VAN AMRINGE,
## Ellen

**PERSONAL INFORMATION:**

| | |
|---|---|
| SEX: | Female |
| DATE OF BIRTH: | August 13, 1849 |
| DATE OF DEATH: | April 2, 1872 |
| PLACE OF DEATH: | Near Antioch, Contra Costa County, California |
| AGE AT DEATH: | 22 years, 7 months, 20 days |
| CAUSE OF DEATH: | |
| BIRTHPLACE: | Caernarvon, North Wales |
| SPOUSE: | Benjamin F. Van Amringe |
| PARENTS: | Hugh Richard and Ellen Jones |

**GRAVESITE INFORMATION:**

| | |
|---|---|
| LOCATION OF GRAVESITE: | Unknown |
| GRAVESTONE: | Missing |
| TYPE OF GRAVESTONE: | |
| SHAPE OF GRAVESTONE: | |
| INSCRIPTION: | |
| EPITAPH: | |
| MOTIF: | |
| CARVER: | |
| BASE: | |
| TYPE OF BASE: | |
| ENCLOSURE: | |
| TYPE OF ENCLOSURE: | |
| FENCE: | |
| TYPE OF FENCE: | |
| FENCE MOTIF: | |

# VAN AMRINGE, Ellen

**ADDITIONAL PERSONAL INFORMATION:**
Ellen was the daughter of Hugh R. and Ellen Jones, sister of Elizabeth Jones, and aunt to Davied [sic] R. Jones, all buried in Rose Hill Cemetery. According to family records, her husband's first name was Frank. Family records also state that Ellen was born August 13, 1849, and that she was married in Somersville before July 1870.

According to the *Index to Marriage Certificates*, located at the Contra Costa County Hall of Records, Martinez, California, Ben F. Von [sic] Amringe married Ellen Jones on April 14, 1869. They were married by J. J. McNulty and their marriage is recorded in Volume 1, page 147.

The *1850 Census for Cincinnati Ward 10, Hamilton, Ohio* lists Benjamin F. Van Amringe, age 4, born *circa* 1846, in Ohio. Also listed are his parents: John, age 53, born *circa* 1797; and Eliza, age 43, born *circa* 1807; both are natives of Pennsylvania. Additionally Benjamin's nine siblings are listed: Susan R., age 23, born *circa* 1827; James L., age 21, born *circa* 1829; William A., age 20, born *circa* 1830; and Eliza Jane, age 18, born *circa* 1832; all are natives of Pennsylvania. Other siblings were: Emma S., age 15, born *circa* 1835; Ellen, age 13, born *circa* 1837; John, age 11, born *circa* 1839; and Edwin A., age 8, born *circa* 1842; all are natives of New York; and, Mary U., age 1, born *circa* 1849, a native of Ohio.

In the *1870 Census for Township Three, Contra Costa County, California*, Ellen Van Amringe, age 21, a native of England, is listed as keeping house. Her husband, Frank Van Amringe, age 24, is listed as a native of Ohio and a farmer.

The obituary in the *Contra Costa Gazette* newspaper, April 3, 1872, states that Ellen's husband was Benjamin F. Van Amringe and that her age at death was 22 years, 7 months, and 20 days. Perhaps the "F" in Benjamin's middle name was the initial for Frank.

The *1900 Census for Alhambra, Contra Costa County, California* lists B. F. Van Amringe, age 60, as a native of Ohio.

See Davied R. Jones, Elizabeth Jones (died March 10, 1876), Ellen Jones, and Hugh R. Jones.

**ADDITIONAL GRAVESITE INFORMATION:**
Cemetery lists compiled in 1935 and 1936 (reference lists 2 and 3 on page 1004) by the Daughters of the American Revolution, are the only sources that record Ellen's burial in Rose Hill Cemetery. Her gravestone was missing prior to East Bay Regional Park District acquisition. Her burial location is unknown.

**REFERENCES:** 2, 3, 8 (April 13, 1872), 12, see newpaper appendix page 766

## PERSONAL INFORMATION:

| | |
|---|---|
| SEX: | Male |
| DATE OF BIRTH: | 1840 |
| DATE OF DEATH: | April 11, 1901 |
| PLACE OF DEATH: | San Francisco, San Francisco County, California |
| AGE AT DEATH: | 61 years |
| CAUSE OF DEATH: | Paralysis/stroke |
| BIRTHPLACE: | Wales |
| SPOUSE: | Hannah (Pugh) Vaughn |
| PARENTS: | |

## GRAVESITE INFORMATION:

| | |
|---|---|
| LOCATION OF GRAVESITE: | Section N-D, Plot #33 |
| GRAVESTONE: | Exists |
| TYPE OF GRAVESTONE: | Marble |
| SHAPE OF GRAVESTONE: | Obelisk |
| INSCRIPTION: | *Vaughn/Children of A. & H. Vaughn/Wife of* |
| EPITAPH: | |
| MOTIF: | Flower and anchor |
| CARVER: | Plymire Sons, Vallejo, California |
| BASE: | Exists |
| TYPE OF BASE: | Granite base with a middle marble base |
| ENCLOSURE: | Exists |
| TYPE OF ENCLOSURE: | Brick faced with mortar coating and scored to simulate masonry blocks |
| FENCE: | Exists |
| TYPE OF FENCE: | Iron |
| FENCE MOTIF: | |

# VAUGHN, Abel Sr.

**ADDITIONAL PERSONAL INFORMATION:**
In July 1869, Abel Vaughn was listed as a miner and resident of Nortonville, Contra Costa County, California.

The *1870 Census for Township Three, Contra Costa County, California* lists Abel Vann [sic], age 30, as a miner and native of Wales. Also recorded are his wife, Anna [sic - Hannah], age 27, a native of Wales, and their children: Anna [sic - Hannah], age 2; and John, age 7 months; both natives of California.

The *Contra Costa County Directory, 1871-2*, also lists Abel Vaughn as a miner in Nortonville.

The *1880 Census for Nortonville, Contra Costa County, California* lists Amnie [sic - Hannah] Vaughn, age 37, as a housekeeper and native of Wales. Also recorded are her children: Hannah, age 12; John, age 10; Elizabeth [sic], age 6; Abel, age 3; and Mary, age 1. All are natives of California. Abel Vaughn Sr. was not listed in the census with them.

*The Great Register of Contra Costa County, California, 1894*, page 51, lists Abel Vaughn, age 52, as 5' 6" tall with a light complexion, gray eyes and hair. He was a miner and native of Great Britain living in Nortonville. He was naturalized July 18, 1891 in Contra Costa County District Court. The *Great Register of the County of Contra Costa in the State of California, 1898* lists Abel's occupation as a farmer.

The *1900 Census for Somersville, Contra Costa County, California* lists Abel Vaughn as a native of Wales, age 59, a farmer and widower. His year of immigration is recorded as 1865. Also listed are his children: John, age 30, a native of California and day laborer; Abel, age 24, a native of California and a farm laborer; and Nellie Vaughn, age 29, a native of California.

**ADDITIONAL GRAVESITE INFORMATION:**
Zelma Myrick, who recorded information in a notebook in the 1930s during a visit to Rose Hill Cemetery, reported "Monument top shot off by high powered gun."

Abel Vaughn Sr. shares a gravestone with wife, Hannah, daughters Hannah, and Mary, and son Abel. The inscription for Abel Vaughn Sr. is on the north side, bottom portion of the stone.

The lettering on the stone was painted black sometime after 1939 (based on Zelma Myrick photographs; see page 605). The ornament (finial) that once sat on top of the gravestone is missing.

See Mrs. Hannah Vaughn and children Abel, Hannah, and Mary.

**REFERENCES:** 1, 2, 3, 4, 5, 6, 8 (Feb. 13, 1897), 9 (April 13, 1901-two articles, July 6, 1901, Oct. 16, 1909, March 16, 1942, and Nov. 30, 1954), 11 (P610.31.124, P610.31.215, P610.146.2, P610.153.11, P610.168.18, P610.168.19, P610.168.26, P610.178.1, P610.285.6, P610.317.17, P610.317.18, and P610.362.7), 12, 14; *Contra Costa Times* newspaper (May 13, 1969, page 8A); *Pittsburg Post Dispatch* newspaper (March 16, 1942, March 17, 1942, Feb. 25, 1946, Dec. 27, 1946, Dec. 30, 1946, Nov. 29, 1954, Dec. 2, 1954, June 15, 1955, Aug. 21, 1957, and Aug. 23, 1957); *Contra Costa Standard* newspaper (March 20, 1942); *California Death Index 1940-1997 Record*; Oak View Memorial Park Cemetery, Antioch, California; see newspaper appendix page 767

The north side of Vaughn family gravestone, January 1968.
A photograph taken by Zelma Myrick *circa* 1939 (see page 605) shows the
gravestone without the black paint used to highlight the lettering and motifs.

### Law.

As we go to press a case is being tried in the Justice's Court—W. Nooks and E. Griffith vs. Abel Vaughan. This is an action for damages under the stock law. The evidence adduced is of vital importance to the farming community. We propose next week to give the evidence in full.

From the *Antioch Ledger* newspaper, May 21, 1870.

The above photograph was taken in the 1920s on the road beside Rose Hill Cemetery (now called Nortonville Trail). Left to right are: Tom (Thomas) Davis and his sister, Sarah (Davis) Schmutzler. Most likely they are the siblings of Margaret Davis (died 1878, approximately 17 years) and Catherine (Davis) Stine (died 1882, approximately 17 years) who are buried in Rose Hill Cemetery.

Also pictured is Dave Watkins and his son Charlie, standing behind him. Watkins visited the area every year from his home in Black Diamond, King County, Washington. As a child he lived in Nortonville.

Meeting them with the horse and buggy, as she heads toward Somersville town site, is Lizzie (Vaughn) Wallis, a widow. Lizzie kept house for her two brothers, John and Abel Vaughn of the Vaughn Ranch on Nortonville Road near Nortonville town site. Every week she drove from the ranch into Pittsburg for groceries. Five members of the Vaughn family are buried in Rose Hill Cemetery. Lizzie (Vaughn) Wallis, the daughter of Abel and Hannah Vaughn, died in 1946, and was interred in Oak View Cemetery in Antioch, Contra Costa County, California.

## PERSONAL INFORMATION:

| | |
|---|---|
| SEX: | Male |
| DATE OF BIRTH: | *Circa* September 1876 |
| DATE OF DEATH: | December 30, 1876 |
| PLACE OF DEATH: | |
| AGE AT DEATH: | 3 months |
| CAUSE OF DEATH: | |
| BIRTHPLACE: | |
| SPOUSE: | None |
| PARENTS: | Abel and Hannah (Pugh) Vaughn |

## GRAVESITE INFORMATION:

| | |
|---|---|
| LOCATION OF GRAVESITE: | Section N-D, Plot #33 |
| GRAVESTONE: | Exists |
| TYPE OF GRAVESTONE: | Marble |
| SHAPE OF GRAVESTONE: | Obelisk |
| INSCRIPTION: | *Vaughn/Children of A. & H. Vaughn/Wife of* |
| EPITAPH: | |
| MOTIF: | Flower and anchor |
| CARVER: | Plymire Sons, Vallejo, California |
| BASE: | Exists |
| TYPE OF BASE: | Granite base with a middle marble base |
| ENCLOSURE: | Exists |
| TYPE OF ENCLOSURE: | Brick faced with mortar coating and scored to simulate masonry blocks |
| FENCE: | Exists |
| TYPE OF FENCE: | Iron |
| FENCE MOTIF: | |

# VAUGHN, Abel Jr.

**ADDITIONAL PERSONAL INFORMATION:**
Including Abel Jr., five members of this family are buried in Rose Hill Cemetery and share one gravesite. See Abel Vaughn Sr., Mrs. Hannah Vaughn, and sisters, Hannah and Mary.

According to records and the gravestone at Oak View Memorial Park Cemetery, East 18th Street, Antioch, Contra Costa County, California, another son, also called Abel, was born January 1, 1876 and died November 27, 1954 at age 78 years, 10 months, and 26 days. It is unclear why there were two children, both named Abel, born in 1876. According to the *1901 census*, the Abel interred in Oak View Cemetery would have been born in 1877.

**ADDITIONAL GRAVESITE INFORMATION:**
The inscription for Abel Vaughn Jr. appears on the south side, bottom section of the gravestone. His sister, Mary, is listed above him. Abel also shares a gravestone with his father, Abel Sr., mother, Hannah, and sister, Hannah. The ornament (finial) that once sat on top of the gravestone is missing.

**REFERENCES:** 1, 2, 3, 4, 6, 11 (P610.31.124, P610.31.215, P610.146.2, P610.153.11, P610.168.18, P610.168.19, P610.168.26, and P610.362.4), 12, 14

Reference 31.131

The vandalized Vaughn family gravestone without the obelisk top, July 1977.
Photograph by Traci (Gibbons) Parent.

Reference 317.18                                    Reference 362.4

The Vaughn family gravestone, left, before black highlight painting. This photograph was taken *circa* 1939 by Zelma Myrick. Notice the footstone (marker placed at the foot of a grave) for a Vaughn family member in the lower right portion of the photograph. The photograph on the right shows the stone with black highlight painting *circa* 1967. At the time this photograph was taken, the top portion of the obelisk had been placed back on bottom piece in a different direction so that Mary Vaughn's name (shown in the left photograph) no longer faces south as it did in 1939.

Reference 336.1

Vandalized Vaughn gravestone. The dates of these photographs are unknown.

# VAUGHN,
## (Mrs.) Hannah

## PERSONAL INFORMATION:

| | |
|---|---|
| SEX: | Female |
| DATE OF BIRTH: | 1842 |
| DATE OF DEATH: | July 18, 1881 |
| PLACE OF DEATH: | Nortonville, Contra Costa County, California |
| AGE AT DEATH: | 39 years |
| CAUSE OF DEATH: | |
| BIRTHPLACE: | Wales |
| SPOUSE: | Abel Vaughn Sr. |
| PARENTS: | Mr. and Mrs. Pugh |

## GRAVESITE INFORMATION:

| | |
|---|---|
| LOCATION OF GRAVESITE: | Section N-D, Plot #33 |
| GRAVESTONE: | Exists |
| TYPE OF GRAVESTONE: | Marble |
| SHAPE OF GRAVESTONE: | Obelisk |
| INSCRIPTION: | *Vaughn/Children of A. & H. Vaughn/Wife of* |
| EPITAPH: | |
| MOTIF: | Flower and anchor |
| CARVER: | Plymire Sons, Vallejo, California |
| BASE: | Exists |
| TYPE OF BASE: | Granite base with a middle marble base |
| ENCLOSURE: | Exists |
| TYPE OF ENCLOSURE: | Brick faced with mortar coating and scored to simulate masonry blocks |
| FENCE: | Exists |
| TYPE OF FENCE: | Iron |
| FENCE MOTIF: | |

# VAUGHN, (Mrs.) Hannah

**ADDITIONAL PERSONAL INFORMATION:**
Hannah's birthplace was obtained from the *1870 Census for Township Three, Contra Costa County, California*. Hannah's maiden name was Pugh. The *Contra Costa Gazette* newspaper, July 23, 1881, lists her date of death as July 17 and not July 18 as stated on the gravestone.

There were at least eight children in the Vaughn family. Including Mrs. Hannah Vaughn, five members of this family are buried in Rose Hill Cemetery and share one gravestone.

A small piece of marble gravestone with the name Vaughn was found at this plot in the early 1980s. The stone indicates that the first name of the individual ended with an "H" and the death year was 1875.

Other members of the Vaughn family are buried in Oak View Memorial Park Cemetery, East 18th Street, Antioch, Contra Costa County, California. The birth and death dates of the family members interred at Oak View Cemetery come from the grave markers found and/or cemetery interment records.

The children included:

- Hannah, interred in Rose Hill Cemetery (born April 19, 1868; died April 18, 1888)
- John, interred in Oak View Cemetery (born Dec. 23, 1869; died Feb. 23, 1946)
- Mary, interred in Rose Hill Cemetery (born 1872; died Sept. 20, 1880)
- Elizabeth, interred in Oak View Cemetery (born Jan. 1, 1874; died Dec. 26, 1946)
- Abel, interred in Oak View Cemetery (born Jan. 1, 1876 [Note: Both the 1900 Census and World War I Draft Registration Card 1917-1918, state that he was born in May 1876.]; died Nov. 27, 1954)

- Abel, interred in Rose Hill Cemetery (born *circa* Sept. 1876; died Dec. 30, 1876)
- Mary, interred in Oak View Cemetery (born Oct. 15, 1879 [based on cemetery records] or 1876 [based on gravestone]; died Aug. 20, 1957)
- Nellie, interred in Oak View Cemetery (born Nov. 7, 1880; died March 15, 1942)

It is unclear why two children, both named Abel, were born in 1876. The Abel interred in Rose Hill Cemetery died at age three months. The Abel interred in Oak View Cemetery died at age 78 years, 10 months, and 26 days. See Abel Vaughn Sr., Abel Vaughn Jr., Hannah Vaughn, and Mary Vaughn.

**ADDITIONAL GRAVESITE INFORMATION:**
The inscription for Mrs. Hannah Vaughn appears on the top portion of the gravestone and faces east. She shares the gravestone with her husband, Abel, and children Abel Jr., Hannah, and Mary. The ornament (finial) that once sat on top of the gravestone is missing.

The photograph on page 606 shows the vandalized gravestone lying on the ground. It is not certain if the gravestone was uprighted in its original position.

**REFERENCES:** 1, 2, 3, 4, 6, 8 (July 23, 1881), 11 (P610.31.124, P610.31.131, P610.146.2, P610.31.215, P610.153.11, P610.168.18, P610.168.19, P610.168.26, and P610.312.6), 12, 14, *California Death Index 1940-1997 Record*, see newpaper appendix page 768

# VAUGHN,
## Hannah

## PERSONAL INFORMATION:

|                    |                                                   |
|--------------------|---------------------------------------------------|
| SEX:               | Female                                            |
| DATE OF BIRTH:     | April 19, 1868                                    |
| DATE OF DEATH:     | April 18, 1888                                    |
| PLACE OF DEATH:    | San Francisco, San Francisco County, California   |
| AGE AT DEATH:      | 19 years, 11 months, 29 days                      |
| CAUSE OF DEATH:    |                                                   |
| BIRTHPLACE:        | California                                         |
| SPOUSE:            | None                                              |
| PARENTS:           | Abel and Hannah (Pugh) Vaughn                     |

## GRAVESITE INFORMATION:

|                     |                                                                        |
|---------------------|------------------------------------------------------------------------|
| LOCATION OF GRAVESITE: | Section N-D, Plot #33                                               |
| GRAVESTONE:         | Exists                                                                 |
| TYPE OF GRAVESTONE: | Marble                                                                 |
| SHAPE OF GRAVESTONE: | Obelisk                                                               |
| INSCRIPTION:        | *Vaughn/Children of A. & H. Vaughn/Wife of*                            |
| EPITAPH:            |                                                                        |
| MOTIF:              | Flower and anchor                                                      |
| CARVER:             | Plymire Sons, Vallejo, California                                      |
| BASE:               | Exists                                                                 |
| TYPE OF BASE:       | Granite base with a middle marble base                                 |
| ENCLOSURE:          | Exists                                                                 |
| TYPE OF ENCLOSURE:  | Brick faced with mortar coating and scored to simulate masonry blocks  |
| FENCE:              | Exists                                                                 |
| TYPE OF FENCE:      | Iron                                                                   |
| FENCE MOTIF:        |                                                                        |

# VAUGHN, Hannah

**ADDITIONAL PERSONAL INFORMATION:**
Hannah's birthplace was obtained from the *1870 Census for Township Three, Contra Costa County, California.*

The *Contra Costa Gazette* newspaper, May 2, 1888, lists her date of death as April 19 and not April 18 as stated on her gravestone. Her age at death was listed as 20 years and not 19 years, 11 months, and 29 days as stated on her gravestone.

See Abel Vaughn Sr., Mrs. Hannah Vaughn, Abel Vaughn, Jr., and Mary Vaughn.

**ADDITIONAL GRAVESITE INFORMATION:**
The inscription for Hannah is listed on the east side of the gravestone. Hannah shares the gravestone with her father Abel Sr., mother Hannah, sister Mary, and brother Abel Jr. The ornament (finial) that once sat on top of gravestone is missing.

**REFERENCES:** 1, 2, 3, 4, 6, 8 (May 2, 1888), 11 (P610.31.124, P610.31.215, P610.146.2, P610.153.11, P610.168.18, P610.168.19, P610.168.26, P610.285.6, and P610.362.7), 12, 14, *Contra Costa Times* newspaper (May 14, 1969, page 8A), see newspaper appendix page 768

Courtesy of CCCHS

Carbondale school class, Nortonville, *circa* 1893. From left to right are (first row seated): Louis Ginochio and Will Abrams; (second row, standing) John Ginochio (standing at far left with arms crossed), Lizzie Ginochio, Alice Lougher, Sarah Banchero, and John (Jack) Buffo; (third row, standing) George Cooper, Miss Brown (teacher), May Edwards, Nellie Vaughn, and Warren Abrams.

Nellie Vaughn was born November 7, 1880, and was the daughter of Abel and Hannah (Pugh) Vaughn. Nellie died March 15, 1942, and was interred in Oak View Cemetery, Antioch, Contra Costa County, California. Nellie's mother, Hannah Vaughn, and siblings Abel, Hannah, and Mary were already deceased at the time this photograph was taken.

# VAUGHN,
## Mary

## PERSONAL INFORMATION:

| | |
|---|---|
| SEX: | Female |
| DATE OF BIRTH: | 1872 |
| DATE OF DEATH: | September 20, 1880 |
| PLACE OF DEATH: | |
| AGE AT DEATH: | 8 years |
| CAUSE OF DEATH: | |
| BIRTHPLACE: | |
| SPOUSE: | None |
| PARENTS: | Abel and Hannah (Pugh) Vaughn |

## GRAVESITE INFORMATION:

| | |
|---|---|
| LOCATION OF GRAVESITE: | Section N-D, Plot #33 |
| GRAVESTONE: | Exists |
| TYPE OF GRAVESTONE: | Marble |
| SHAPE OF GRAVESTONE: | Obelisk |
| INSCRIPTION: | Vaughn/*Children of A. & H. Vaughn/Wife of* |
| EPITAPH: | |
| MOTIF: | Flower and anchor |
| CARVER: | Plymire Sons, Vallejo, California |
| BASE: | Exists |
| TYPE OF BASE: | Granite base with a middle marble base |
| ENCLOSURE: | Exists |
| TYPE OF ENCLOSURE: | Brick faced with mortar coating and scored to simulate masonry blocks |
| FENCE: | Exists |
| TYPE OF FENCE: | Iron |
| FENCE MOTIF: | |

# VAUGHN, Mary

**ADDITIONAL PERSONAL INFORMATION:**
Mary is one of at least eight children of Abel Sr. and Hannah Vaughn. Her birth date was calculated by www.timeanddate.com, based on her date of death and age at death listed on her gravestone. Abel and Hannah Vaughn named another daughter Mary. The second Mary was born on October 15 1876 (based on records at Oak View Memorial Park Cemetery, Antioch, California) or 1879 (based on her gravestone); and died August 20, 1957. Since the first Mary died September 20, 1880, it is more likely that the second Mary was born sometime after the death of the first Mary, and not 1879 as indicated on her gravestone. Additionally, the two obituary notices from the *Pittsburg Post Dispatch* newspaper (Aug. 12, 1957 and Aug. 23, 1957) state that second Mary was age 77 at the time of her death, making her birth year *circa* 1880. Perhaps the gravestone at Rose Hill Cemetery for the first Mary or the gravestone at Oakview Cemetery for the second Mary has an incorrect date. It is unlikely that this family would have two daughters, both named Mary, living at the same time. See Abel Vaughn Sr., Mrs. Hannah Vaughn, Abel Vaughn Jr., and Hannah Vaughn.

**ADDITIONAL GRAVESITE INFORMATION:**
The inscription for Mary is listed on the south side of the gravestone. Mary shares the gravestone with her father Abel Sr., mother Hannah, sister Hannah, and brother Abel Jr. The ornament (finial) that once sat on top of gravestone is missing.

**REFERENCES:** 1, 2, 3, 4, 6, 11 (P610.31.124, P610.31.215, P610.117.11, P610.146.2, P610.153.11, P610.168.18, P610.168.19, and P610.168.26), 12, 14

Courtesy of CCCHS

Carbondale School, Nortonville, Contra Costa County, California, *circa* 1894. Nellie Vaughn, daughter of Abel, is standing on the far right. May Edwards can be seen in the window. From left to right are (first row seated): George Cooper, Willie Abrams, Louis Ginochio, Willie Edwards, Albert Edwards, Jack Buffo, Warren Abrams; (second row, standing) an unidentified teacher (possibly Grace Williams), Edna Hanlon, Maggie Hanlon, John Ginochio Jr., Annie Edwards, Sarah Banchero, and possibly Alice Lougher.

# VESTNYS,
## Lorenda A.

**PERSONAL INFORMATION:**

| | |
|---|---|
| SEX: | Female |
| DATE OF BIRTH: | 1869 |
| DATE OF DEATH: | April 1, 1870 |
| PLACE OF DEATH: | Nortonville, Contra Costa County, California |
| AGE AT DEATH: | 1 year |
| CAUSE OF DEATH: | |
| BIRTHPLACE: | Nortonville, Contra Costa County, California |
| SPOUSE: | None |
| PARENTS: | Peter Lassesen and Mary Frances (Saddler) Vestnys |

**GRAVESITE INFORMATION:**

| | |
|---|---|
| LOCATION OF GRAVESITE: | Unknown |
| GRAVESTONE: | Missing or never placed |
| TYPE OF GRAVESTONE: | |
| SHAPE OF GRAVESTONE: | |
| INSCRIPTION: | |
| EPITAPH: | |
| MOTIF: | |
| CARVER: | |
| BASE: | |
| TYPE OF BASE: | |
| ENCLOSURE: | |
| TYPE OF ENCLOSURE: | |
| FENCE: | |
| TYPE OF FENCE: | |
| FENCE MOTIF: | |

# VESTNYS, Lorenda A.

**ADDITIONAL PERSONAL INFORMATION:**
A family tree provided by descendants states that Lorenda's mother, Mary Frances Saddler, was born May 7, 1847, in Virginia and died October 10, 1894, in Black Diamond, King County, Washington. Lorenda's father, Peter Lassesen Vestnys, was born July 2, 1835, in Vestnys (Vestnes), More og Romsdal, Norway. Information obtained from www.ancestry.com, states that Peter Vestnys died August 23, 1917, in Sand, Nord-Odal, Norway.

The *1876 Contra Costa County Voting Register*, lists Peter Vestnys, age 32, of Nortonville as a miner and native of Norway. He registered to vote on June 21, 1866.

*Washington State and Territorial Censuses, 1857-1892 for Black Diamond, King County, Territory of Washington*, taken June 10, 1887, lists P. L. Vestenys [sic], age 50, a native of Norway and occupation carpenter. Also listed are his wife, Mary, age 40, and their children: Peter, age 20, a miner; H. (Harriet), age 15; W. (Walter), age 13; Della, age 12; B. (Bertha), age 9; Lena, age 7; and an unnamed child (probably Lillie), age 3. All are natives of the United States.

*The Washington State and Territorial Censuses, 1857-1892 for Black Diamond, King County, Territory of Washington*, taken June 15, 1889, lists Peter Vestings [sic], a native of Norway, age 52. Also recorded are his wife, Mary, age 42, and children: Harriet, age 17; Walter, age 14; Delia, age 13; Bertha, age 11; Lena, age 10; all are natives of California. Also Lillie, age 5, a native of Washington; Violet, age 1, a native of California; Peter, age 21, a native of California; and Carrie, age 17, a native of Oregon. Both Peter and Carrie are listed as married (most likely to each other).

According to descendants, Lorenda's mother, Mary Vestrys, died in October 1894.

The *1900 Census for Black Diamond, King County, Washington* lists Peter Vesteny [sic], age 64, born May 1836, as a native of Sweden. His spouse of four years is Jula, a native of Norway (Sweden). The census states that they married in 1896. (A descendant states that Peter L. Vestnys married his second wife, Julie Nos, on Jan. 7, 1896.) Also listed are Peter Vestnys' children from his first marriage: Wilburt [sic], age 22; Lillie, age 16; and Voilet [sic], age 13. Arthur Aruvos, age 19, a mine laborer from Norway, is living with them.

The *Contra Costa Gazette* newspaper, November 4, 1876, records the birth of a daughter to Mr. and Mrs. Peter Vestness [sic] in Nortonville, Contra Costa County, on October 9, 1876. Perhaps the paper recorded the birth of Delphine, although family members state she was born in September 1876.

The *Contra Costa Gazette* newspaper, March 15, 1884, states that Harriet A. Saddler, Lorenda's grandmother, died March 6, 1884, in Nortonville. Descendants believe that Harriet A. Saddler is buried in Rose Hill. This family is also related to the Bussey, Saddler, and Parsons families. See Joseph Bussey, Jeanette Parsons, Harriet A. Saddler, and Saddler (male child).

**ADDITIONAL GRAVESITE INFORMATION:**
According to descendants, Lorenda is most likely buried in Rose Hill Cemetery. However there is no document recording her burial there.

**REFERENCES:** 9 (April 16, 1870), 12

## DIED.

In Antioch, April 13th, 1870, Albert, son of Charles and Augusta Wenig, aged 3 years and 7 months.

In Nortonville, April 1st, 1870, Lorenda A., daughter of Mary and Peter Vestrys, aged 1 year.

In Nortonville, April 8th, 1870, Jennie Gertrude, daughter of W. M. and Mary E. Cantrill, aged 3 years, 2 months and 9 days.

This newspaper article from the *Antioch Ledger*, April 16, 1870, announces the death of Lorenda A. Vestnys. Her last name was incorrectly spelled as Vestrys. Lorenda's parents, Mary (Saddler) and Peter Vestnys, were married on July 3, 1862. Lorenda was one of twelve children in the family. The children of Mary (Saddler) and Peter Vestnys were:

- Mary Louisa, born May 7, 1863, Benicia, Solano County, California
- Patrina, born April 26, 1866, Nortonville, Contra Costa County, California
- Peter Francis, born June 12, 1867, Nortonville, Contra Costa County, California
- Lorenda A., born 1869 and died in Nortonville, Contra Costa County, California
- Harriet (Hattie) Ann, born December 1872, Nortonville, Contra Costa County, California
- Walter Norman, born June 30, 1874, Nortonville, Contra Costa County, California
- Delphine, born September 1876, Nortonville, Contra Costa County, California
- Wilbert M., born January 24, 1879, Nortonville, Contra Costa County, California
- Bertha, born 1880/1881, Nortonville, Contra Costa County, California
- Lena, born June 1882, Nortonville, Contra Costa County, California
- Lillie, born October 5, 1883, Nortonville, Contra Costa County, California
- Violet Mary, born August 5, 1886, Black Diamond, King County, Washington

## FROM NORTONVILLE.

NORTONVILLE, April 14.

EDS. LEDGER: Each number of your valuable paper has been received and read by most of the people in our little village. I notice that it has also found its way into the villages on either side of us, as each of them has made contributions to its columns.

Now, we do not propose to remain mute or have you infer that we do not appreciate anything that benefits our State and its inhabitants, but prove that we are as cognizant of any and everything that adds to our well-being as our neighbor. Until within the last few weeks business has been very dull. This has arisen from two causes—the demand for coal has not been equal to the amount that can be supplied by the number of men employed. The second cause is the stagnation of business in other parts of the State, thereby deluging the few places that are in active operation with men. Now, however, it promises fairly, and we anticipate better times.

The health of our community is below par at present. The scarlet fever has been and is still preying upon our youth. A number have already died, and more are still suffering from its pangs.

I have very little in the matrimonial line to communicate, though there are a goodly number of each sex who claim eligibility to that state. The fair ones are in the minority, and, as a matter of course, they have any quantity of admirers. There is a lively competition between the young and old bachelors. I stand aloof, and watch with eager eye the contest, but predict a success on the side of the old bachelors, as they seem more determined than do the others for when once discarded they do not give it up, but try a fresh bait; while the others, when similarly treated, "throw up the sponge," thereby acknowledging a jilt.

Mr. Scammon is making preparations to build a brick store. It will add to the appearance and interests of our town. We also need a new hotel, and will probably have one before the year ends.

We have one establishment run in our midst which will not be conducive to the welfare of our village, and I hope to see steps taken to have its inmates ousted. I will withhold any further comment on it at present, but will probably allude to it in future.

Our base ball club has reorganized, and propose going into practice immediately. No doubt they will be waited upon by some of our county clubs, who, according to reports, are making great proficiency in the game. OBSERVER.

Lorenda Vestnys died in April 1870, the same month that this article appeared in the *Antioch Ledger* newspaper. This article from April 16, 1870, discusses the "little village" of Nortonville, the community that the Vestnys' family lived in at the time of Lorenda's death. The article states:

> The scarlet fever has been and is still preying upon our youth. A number have already died, and more are still suffering from its pangs.

# WATERS,
## Edna Isabella (Bella)

**PERSONAL INFORMATION:**

| | |
|---|---|
| SEX: | Female |
| DATE OF BIRTH: | September 1, 1889 |
| DATE OF DEATH: | November 18, 1892 |
| PLACE OF DEATH: | West Hartley, Contra Costa County, California |
| AGE AT DEATH: | 3 years, 2 months, 18 days |
| CAUSE OF DEATH: | Diphtheria |
| BIRTHPLACE: | Probably Somersville, Contra Costa County, California |
| SPOUSE: | None |
| PARENTS: | Robert and Isabella (Reid) Waters |

**GRAVESITE INFORMATION:**

| | |
|---|---|
| LOCATION OF GRAVESITE: | Section S-B, Plot #116 |
| GRAVESTONE: | None |
| TYPE OF GRAVESTONE: | |
| SHAPE OF GRAVESTONE: | |
| INSCRIPTION: | |
| EPITAPH: | |
| MOTIF: | |
| CARVER: | |
| BASE: | |
| TYPE OF BASE: | |
| ENCLOSURE: | |
| TYPE OF ENCLOSURE: | |
| FENCE: | Missing |
| TYPE OF FENCE: | Wood and wire |
| FENCE MOTIF: | |

# WATERS, Edna Isabella (Bella)

**ADDITIONAL PERSONAL INFORMATION:**
According to descendants, Edna's father, Robert Waters, was born in 1846 and arrived in California from Pictou County, Nova Scotia, Canada, in 1878 or 1879. His wife, Isabella (known as Bella or Belle), joined him in 1880. Bella was the first postmistress of Somersville and held the position for many years. She also taught Sunday school for many years at West Hartley, Contra Costa County, California.

*The Great Register of the County of Contra Costa in the State of California, 1898*, lists Robert Waters, as a miner, age 51, 5' 8" tall with a fair complexion, gray eyes, brown hair, and a scar on the back of his right hand. He was a native of Nova Scotia, Canada, and a resident of Somersville. He was naturalized May 9, 1888 in the Superior Court of Contra Costa County.

The *Index of Voters Somersville Precinct, Contra Costa County*, for 1902 and 1904, lists Robert Waters as residing in Somersville.

The *Index to the Great Register of Contra Costa County, 1906*, lists Robert, age 60, as a teamster in Somersville. The *Index to the Great Register of Contra Costa County, 1908*, lists Robert Waters, age 61, as a miner in Somersville. Robert Waters is listed as a teamster in the *Contra Costa County Directory, 1908*, page 286.

Information obtained on www.ancestry.com, states that Belle Johnson Waters was born in June 1851 and that her children were: Irene Johnson Waters, born 1878; Mary A. Waters, born in 1883; and Clyde Waters, born in 1892.

According to *Trip of Louis Stein and D. F. Myrick to Stewartsville* [sic], *June 24, 1967, accompanied by Mrs. James Parsons and her daughter, Mrs. Gibbel*, page 1: The Waters family (originally spelled Watters) lived in Nortonville, Empire, Stewartville, West Hartley, and Somersville. Edna Bella's brother, John Robert, died on December 2, 1892, shortly after she died.

See John Robert Waters and William Waters for additional information.

**ADDITIONAL GRAVESITE INFORMATION:**
Edna shares the gravesite with her brothers John Robert Waters and William (Willie) Waters.

According to Edna (Parsons) Gibbel, daughter of Wilbert and Irene (Waters) Parsons, a wood and wire fence was erected around the burial sites, but a marker was never placed there. Edna Gibbel visited Rose Hill Cemetery in the early 1980s and showed park staff the location of the Waters gravesite.

**REFERENCES:** 9 (Dec. 17, 1892), 11 (P610.2.18, P610.43.4, P610.56.16, P610.267.1, P610.312.5, and P610.352.4), 12, see newspaper appendix page 769

Robert and Isabella "Bella" Janet (Reid) Waters, parents of Edna Isabella Waters.
Robert and Isabella married on December 22, 1870.

Members of the Waters family are pictured with this West Hartley school group in 1890. Although not known for certain, this may possibly be a Sunday school group since Mrs. Waters is pictured in this photograph. It was reported by descendants that she taught Sunday school for many years at West Hartley, Contra Costa County, California.

Pictured here are, from left to right (first row) Bert Waters [This might possibly be John Robert Waters who died Dec. 1892 at almost 6 years and was buried in Rose Hill; no Bert is listed on the Waters family tree and this is the only Waters boy to be this young in 1890.], Alice [perhaps this is Mary Alice born in 1883] Waters, Grace Riddock, Edna Waters [this might possibly be Edna Isabella who died in Nov. 1892 and was buried in Rose Hill Cemetery], Clara Williams, ? Woods, and Mamie Williams; (second row) Frank Irwin, John Courtney, Joe Rodda, Joe McAvoy, Charles Irwin, and Martin Golden; (third row) Charles Sorgenfrey, Joe Lilley, Ben Williams, Harry Sorgenfrey, unidentified, Frank Thomas, George Stone, Peter McDermott, Irene Waters [born 1878], ? Woods, and Joe Woods (right of post); (fourth row) Louis Stone, Mrs. A. Riddock (teacher), John Daley (teacher), Mrs. Belle Waters [wife of Robert Waters], Alice Sorgenfrey, Maggie Harroway, Lizzie Courtney, ? Lilley, George Riddock, and Frank Stone; (fifth row) William (Bill) Lilley, and Al Riddock.

# WATERS,
## John Robert

## PERSONAL INFORMATION:

| | |
|---|---|
| SEX: | Male |
| DATE OF BIRTH: | May 10, 1887 |
| DATE OF DEATH: | December 2, 1892 |
| PLACE OF DEATH: | West Hartley, Contra Costa County, California |
| AGE AT DEATH: | 5 years, 6 months, 22 days |
| CAUSE OF DEATH: | Diphtheria |
| BIRTHPLACE: | Probably Somersville, Contra Costa County, California |
| SPOUSE: | None |
| PARENTS: | Robert and Isabella (Reid) Waters |

## GRAVESITE INFORMATION:

| | |
|---|---|
| LOCATION OF GRAVESITE: | Section S-B, Plot #116 |
| GRAVESTONE: | None |
| TYPE OF GRAVESTONE: | |
| SHAPE OF GRAVESTONE: | |
| INSCRIPTION: | |
| EPITAPH: | |
| MOTIF: | |
| CARVER: | |
| BASE: | |
| TYPE OF BASE: | |
| ENCLOSURE: | |
| TYPE OF ENCLOSURE: | |
| FENCE: | Missing |
| TYPE OF FENCE: | Wood and wire |
| FENCE MOTIF: | |

# WATERS, John Robert

**ADDITIONAL PERSONAL INFORMATION:**
John's birth date was provided by descendants. According to the *Antioch Ledger* newspaper, December 17, 1892, John Robert Waters died at age 5 years, 7 months.

Information obtained from descendants and www.ancestry.com, state that John's father, Robert Waters (Watters), was born September 15, 1849, in Green Hill, Pictou, Nova Scotia, Canada. He died February 24, 1926, in San Francisco, San Francisco County, California.

John's mother, Isabella, was born June 10, 1852, in Prob. Mount Thom, Pictou, Nova Scotia, Canada. She died less than a month after her husband on March 11, 1926, in San Francisco.

Robert Waters married Isabella J. Reid on December 22, 1870, in Durham, West River, Pictou, Nova Scotia, Canada. They had nine children:

- George Thomas, born February 24, 1873, Westville, Pictou, Nova Scotia, Canada

- Alexander Cameron, born April 22, 1874, Westville, Pictou, Nova Scotia, Canada

- James Thomas, born May 15, 1876, Westville, Pictou, Nova Scotia, Canada

- Irene Johnson, born June 15, 1878, Westville, Pictou, Nova Scotia, Canada

- William W., born March 28, 1882, Somersville, Contra Costa County, California; and died April 6, 1882, Somersville at age 9 days old

- Mary Alice, born September 15, 1883, Stewartville, Contra Costa County, California

- John Robert, born May 10, 1887, probably in Somersville, Contra Costa County, California; and died Dec. 2, 1892, at age 5 yrs., 6 months, and 22 days, West Hartley, Contra Costa County, California

- Edna Isabella, born September 1, 1889, probably in Somersville, Contra Costa County, California; and died Nov. 18, 1892, at age 3 years, 2 months, and 18 days, West Hartley, Contra Costa County, California

- Lester Clyde, born April 2, 1892 in San Francisco, California

John's sister, Edna Bella, died on November 18, 1892, less than a month before he did.

See Edna Isabella (Bella) Waters and William Waters.

**ADDITIONAL GRAVESITE INFORMATION:**
The Waters family never placed a marker at the gravesite. John shares the burial site with his siblings, Edna Isabella (Bella) Waters and William (Willie) Waters.

**REFERENCES:** 9 (Dec. 17, 1892), 11 (P610.2.18, P610.2.53, P610.43.4, P610.267.1, and P610.312.5), 12; *Trip of Louis Stein and D. F. Myrick to Stewartsville [sic] June 24, 1967, accompanied by Mrs. James Parsons and her daughter, Mrs. Gibbel,* page 1; see newspaper appendix page 769

The photograph above shows the wood and wire fence at the Waters family gravesite prior to 1938. Pictured below is the wood and wire fence (foreground) surrounding the gravesite of the Waters children (Edna Isabella, John Robert, and William) in 1938. Note that the photograph below shows fewer trees than the photograph above.

Reference 43.4

Wilbert "Bert" Augustus and Irene Johnson (Waters) Parsons, date unknown. Irene was the daughter of Robert and Isabella "Bella" Waters. Her three siblings (Edna, John, and William Waters) are buried in Rose Hill Cemetery. Wilbert was the son of Walter and Emma H. Parsons. His sister, Jeanette Parsons, and grandmother, Harriet A. Saddler, are also buried in Rose HIll Cemetery.

# WATERS,
## William (Willie)

## PERSONAL INFORMATION:

| | |
|---|---|
| SEX: | Male |
| DATE OF BIRTH: | March 28, 1882 |
| DATE OF DEATH: | April 6, 1882 |
| PLACE OF DEATH: | Somersville, Contra Costa County, California |
| AGE AT DEATH: | 9 days |
| CAUSE OF DEATH: | Diphtheria |
| BIRTHPLACE: | Somersville, Contra Costa County, California |
| SPOUSE: | None |
| PARENTS: | Robert and Isabella (Reid) Waters |

## GRAVESITE INFORMATION:

| | |
|---|---|
| LOCATION OF GRAVESITE: | Section S-B, Plot #116 |
| GRAVESTONE: | None |
| TYPE OF GRAVESTONE: | |
| SHAPE OF GRAVESTONE: | |
| INSCRIPTION: | |
| EPITAPH: | |
| MOTIF: | |
| CARVER: | |
| BASE: | |
| TYPE OF BASE: | |
| ENCLOSURE: | |
| TYPE OF ENCLOSURE: | |
| FENCE: | Missing |
| TYPE OF FENCE: | Wood and wire |
| FENCE MOTIF: | |

# WATERS, William (Willie)

**ADDITIONAL PERSONAL INFORMATION:**
The place of birth and death was obtained from family history documents provided by Waters (Watters) family descendants.

The *1880 Census for Reveille, Nye County, Nevada* lists William's father, Robert Waters, age 32, as single, a miner, and native of Nova Scotia, Canada. His father's birthplace is listed as Scotland.

The *1900 Census* for Somersville Precinct lists Robert Waters, age 53, born in September 1846, a native of "Canada (Eng)," and a coal miner. He immigrated to the United States in 1878. Also listed is his wife Belle J., age 48, born June 1851, a native of "Canada (Eng)." She immigrated to the United States in 1880. Their children, both natives of California, are also listed: Clyde, age 8, born April 1892; and Mary A., age 16, born September 1883. Their married daughter and her family are listed as living with them: Irene J. (Waters) Parsons, age 21, born June 1878; and Irene's husband, Wilbert A., age 25, born March 1875, a coal miner; and their son, Walter C., age 1, born December 1898.

The *1910 Census for San Francisco Assembly District 36, San Francisco, California* lists Robert Waters, age 63, as a native of Canada and year of immigration as 1878. Also listed are his wife, Isabel J. [sic], age 58, a native of Canada and year of immigration as 1886, and their children: Alice M., age 26; and L. Clyde Waters, age 18; both natives of California.

The *1920 Census for San Francisco Assembly District 27, San Francisco, California* lists Robert Waters as a native of Nova Scotia, age 73, and year of immigration as 1879. Also listed is his wife, Isabel J. [sic], a native of Nova Scotia, age 68, and year of immigration as 1880. They are recorded as living with their son-in-law, Wilbert A. Parsons, age 43, a native of California and Wilbert's wife (their daughter), Irene J., age 41, a native of Nova Scotia and year of immigration as 1880. Also listed are the children of Wilbert and Irene: Walter C., age 21, and Edna I., age 19; both natives of California.

See Edna Isabella (Bella) Waters and John Robert Waters for additional information.

**ADDITIONAL GRAVESITE INFORMATION:**
The Waters family never placed a marker at the gravesite. William shares the burial site with siblings Edna Isabella (Bella) Waters and John Robert Waters.

**REFERENCES:** 11 (P610.2.18, P610.2.53, P610.43.4, P610.267.1, P610.312.5, and P610.352.7), 12, *Trip of Louis Stein and D. F. Myrick to Stewartsville* [sic] *June 24, 1967, accompanied by Mrs. James Parsons and her daughter, Mrs. Gibbel,* page 1

Isabella Waters and husband Robert Waters, *circa* late 1890s, with two of their children: Mary Alice Waters (sitting on chair, front right), born September 15, 1883 in Stewartville, Contra Costa County, California; and Lester Clyde Waters (standing in back between his mother and father), born April 2, 1892 in San Francisco, San Francisco County, California.

Their other children: George, born 1873; Alexander, born 1874; James, born 1876; and Irene, born June 15, 1878; were most likely adults and living away from home at the time this photograph was taken. Three of the Waters children: William W., born 1882 and died 1882; John Robert, born 1887 and died 1892; and Edna Isabella, born 1889 and died 1892; were already deceased and buried in Rose Hill Cemetery at the time this photograph was taken.

Reference 352.6

Reference 352.3

Irene Johnson (Waters) Parsons and her husband, Wilbert "Bert" Augustus Parsons, date unknown. Irene was born in Nova Scotia, Canada in 1878. She was the daughter of Robert and Isabella "Bella" Waters and sibling to the three Waters children buried in Rose Hill Cemetery. Wilbert was born in 1875 in Nortonville, Contra Costa County, California and was the son of Emma Henrietta (Saddler) and Walter Parsons. He was also the brother of Jeanette Parsons who is buried in Rose Hill Cemetery. Irene married Wilbert Parsons on January 31, 1898. The *Contra Costa Gazette* newspaper, February 12, 1898 reported: "Bert Parson [sic] and Miss Irene Waters of Somersville eloped and got married a short time ago."

Reference 41.7

Picnic group at Stewart's Grove located southeast and across Sand Creek from the Central Mine in Stewartville, Contra Costa County, California, date unknown. Standing left to right are: Elizabeth Singlewood, Wilbert (Bert) Parsons, Watkins Evans, and Hannah Griffith. Seated left to right are: Sarah Griffith, George Parsons, and Sarah Evans.

## PERSONAL INFORMATION:

| | |
|---|---|
| SEX: | Male |
| DATE OF BIRTH: | |
| DATE OF DEATH: | July 25, 1876 |
| PLACE OF DEATH: | Nortonville, Contra Costa County, California |
| AGE AT DEATH: | Adult |
| CAUSE OF DEATH: | Mine explosion |
| BIRTHPLACE: | |
| SPOUSE: | |
| PARENTS: | |

## GRAVESITE INFORMATION:

| | |
|---|---|
| LOCATION OF GRAVESITE: | Section S-D, Plot #50 |
| GRAVESTONE: | Missing |
| TYPE OF GRAVESTONE: | White bronze (zinc) with moveable tablets |
| SHAPE OF GRAVESTONE: | Obelisk |
| INSCRIPTION: | *In Memory of/Erected by the Citizens of Nortonville* |
| EPITAPH: | |
| MOTIF: | Clasped hands/leaves |
| CARVER: | |
| BASE: | Exists |
| TYPE OF BASE: | Concrete |
| ENCLOSURE: | Exists |
| TYPE OF ENCLOSURE: | Brick |
| FENCE: | Exists |
| TYPE OF FENCE: | Iron (replica) |
| FENCE MOTIF: | Urns and vases (missing) |

# WATTS, David

**ADDITIONAL PERSONAL INFORMATION:**
David Watts, his brother, Theophilus Watts, and Thomas D. James are buried in the same plot. These men were killed by a powder explosion which occurred at the Black Diamond Mine in Nortonville, Contra Costa County, California on July 24, 1876.

Two years after the death of these men, the citizens of Nortonville erected a large monument in their memory. According to former resident Ellis Griffiths, who recorded his memories of Nortonville:

> The three best singers of the village [Nortonville] were two brothers, David Watts, Theophilus Watts and their companion, Thomas James. These boys lead all the entertainments and also the choir of the church. Other men who died in the same accident are buried nearby.

See Theophile Dumas, William Gething, David W. Griffiths, Thomas D. James, Meredith Lewis, George M. Reynolds, Evan Smith, and Theophilus Watts.

**ADDITIONAL GRAVESITE INFORMATION:**
The galvanized iron two bar fence that once existed at this site was replicated based on the last existing piece located at the site. The new replicated fence was placed at the gravesite in September 2007. The original piece was placed in storage.

**REFERENCES:** 2, 8 (July 29, 1876, Aug. 12, 1876, and Nov. 23, 1878), 9 (July 29, 1876), 10 (page 474), 11 (P610.5.2, P610.31.128, P610.31.204, P610.43.4, P610.84.2, P610.139.2, P610.207.1, P610.247.1, P610.248.1, P610.294.6, P610.312.3, P610.312.4, P610.317.3, P610.363.1, and P610.363.2), 12; *Pittsburg Daily Independent* newspaper (April 30, 1941, page 8); *Nortonville Memories* by Ellis Griffiths, no date; see newspaper appendix (William Gething) pages 706 and 707, and (Thomas D. James) page 720

Reference 31.204

All that remains of the "white bronze" miners' monument and fence, August 1977.
Photograph by Traci (Gibbons) Parent. See also photographs on pages 138, 289, 631, and 634.

The white bronze miners' obelisk monument (left of center) erected in 1878 by the citizens of Nortonville in memory of David Watts, Theophilus Watts, and Thomas D. James. Date unknown. The *Contra Costa Gazette* newspaper, November 23, 1878 described the "new monument" and the gravesite:

> The lot is sixteen feet long by ten feet wide. A substantial brick wall has been constructed, four feet high in the lower corner and about one foot high in the upper corner, above ground. The fence is of galvanized iron, two bars, with chain and neat urns and vases. It is by far the neatest and most substantial fence in the Cemetery, and is the admiration of all. In the centre of this enclosure the monument stands. The base is a solid sandstone, twenty-four inches square by twenty inches high. The bronze monument is placed on this foundation and strongly anchored to it. The monument is sixty inches high; base eighteen inches square, ten and a half inches thick.

Reference 247.1

Reference 248.1

The leaves and clasped hands motifs from the base of the
"white bronze" miners' monument, *circa* 1980s.

## PERSONAL INFORMATION:

|  |  |
|---|---|
| SEX: | Male |
| DATE OF BIRTH: | *Circa* 1849 |
| DATE OF DEATH: | July 24, 1876 |
| PLACE OF DEATH: | Nortonville, Contra Costa County, California |
| AGE AT DEATH: | 27 years |
| CAUSE OF DEATH: | Suffocation from mine explosion |
| BIRTHPLACE: | Glamorganshire, South Wales |
| SPOUSE: | None |
| PARENTS: | |

## GRAVESITE INFORMATION:

|  |  |
|---|---|
| LOCATION OF GRAVESITE: | Section S-D, Plot #50 |
| GRAVESTONE: | Missing |
| TYPE OF GRAVESTONE: | White bronze (zinc) with moveable tablets |
| SHAPE OF GRAVESTONE: | Obelisk |
| INSCRIPTION: | *In Memory of/Erected by the Citizens of Nortonville* |
| EPITAPH: | |
| MOTIF: | Clasped hands/leaves |
| CARVER: | |
| BASE: | Exists |
| TYPE OF BASE: | Concrete |
| ENCLOSURE: | Exists |
| TYPE OF ENCLOSURE: | Brick |
| FENCE: | Exists |
| TYPE OF FENCE: | Iron (replica) |
| FENCE MOTIF: | Urns and vases (missing) |

# WATTS, Theophilus

**ADDITIONAL PERSONAL INFORMATION:**
Theophilus Watts, his brother, David Watts, and Thomas D. James are buried in the same plot. Watts was interred by the Independent Order of Odd Fellows (I.O.O.F.).

These men were killed by a powder explosion which occurred in the Black Diamond Mine in Nortonville, Contra Costa County, California, on July 24, 1876. The citizens of Nortonville erected a large monument in their memory. According to the *Antioch Ledger* newspaper, July 29, 1876, Theophilus Watts was single at the time of his death.

See Theophile Dumas, William Gething, David W. Griffiths, Thomas D. James, Meredith Lewis, George M. Reynolds, Evan Smith, and David Watts.

**ADDITIONAL GRAVESITE INFORMATION:**
See Thomas D. James and David Watts.

**REFERENCES:** 2, 4, 5, 8 (July 29, 1876, Aug. 12, 1876, and Nov. 23, 1878), 9 (July 29, 1876), 10 (page 474), 11 (P610.5.2, P610.31.128, P610.31.204, P610.43.2, P610.84.2, P610.139.2, P610.207.1, P610.247.1, P610.248.1, P610.294.6, P610.312.3, P610.312.4, P610.317.3, P610.363.1, and P610.363.2), 12; *Pittsburg Daily Independent* newspaper (April 30, 1941, page 8); *Nortonville Memories* by Ellis Griffiths, no date; see newspaper appendix (William Gething) pages 706 and 707, and (Thomas D. James) page 720

Reference 139.2

Pictured on the left is all that remains of the miners' monument in Rose Hill Cemetery in 1953. Although much of the galvanized two bar iron fence and brick enclosure was still present when this photograph was taken, most of the the white bronze obelisk is missing from the site. See also photographs on pages 138, 289, and 631.

# WILLIAMS,
## Annie

## PERSONAL INFORMATION:

| | |
|---|---|
| SEX: | Female |
| DATE OF BIRTH: | May 13, 1875 |
| DATE OF DEATH: | December 4, 1876 |
| PLACE OF DEATH: | |
| AGE AT DEATH: | 1 year, 6 months, 21 days |
| CAUSE OF DEATH: | |
| BIRTHPLACE: | |
| SPOUSE: | None |
| PARENTS: | J. H. and M. Williams |

## GRAVESITE INFORMATION:

| | |
|---|---|
| LOCATION OF GRAVESITE: | Section S-E, Plot #83 |
| | (gravestone located at Section S-D, Plot #55) |
| GRAVESTONE: | Exists |
| TYPE OF GRAVESTONE: | Marble |
| SHAPE OF GRAVESTONE: | Tablet |
| INSCRIPTION: | *Daughter of* |
| EPITAPH: | *Our Annie has gone to Heaven to rest* |
| | *To sing happy greetings* |
| | *To God among the blessed.* |
| MOTIF: | Hand plucking rosebud/rope with tassels |
| CARVER: | |
| BASE: | Exists |
| TYPE OF BASE: | Sandstone with middle marble base |
| ENCLOSURE: | Exists |
| TYPE OF ENCLOSURE: | Brick with granite cornerstones |
| FENCE: | Missing |
| TYPE OF FENCE: | Iron |
| FENCE MOTIF: | Stars |

# WILLIAMS, Annie

**ADDITIONAL PERSONAL INFORMATION:**
Annie Williams' date of birth was calculated by www.timeanddate.com, based on her age at death and date of death.

**ADDITIONAL GRAVESITE INFORMATION:**
The gravestone is most likely not at the original gravesite. The Annie Williams gravestone sits at the burial site of Rebecca Abraham (see photograph on page 43).

A photograph of Annie's gravesite appears in the *California Monthly* magazine, "Back Yard Ghost Towns," May 1949, page 22, and shows Annie's gravestone at what is believed to be the Elizabeth Jones gravesite, Section S-E, Plot # 83.

The Annie Williams gravestone was broken into three pieces and concreted flat to the ground prior to East Bay Regional Park District acquisition.

The brick wall enclosure surrounding the Annie Williams gravestone was rebuilt in 1988 by the East Bay Regional Park District. A seashell and shell fragments were found at this site in 1988.

**REFERENCES:** 1, 2, 3, 4, 6, 11 (P610.113.6, P610.168.24, P610.168.29, P610.285.7, and P610.326.1), 12, 14, *Pittsburg Post Dispatch* newspaper (Wed., June 15, 1955, pages 9 and 12)

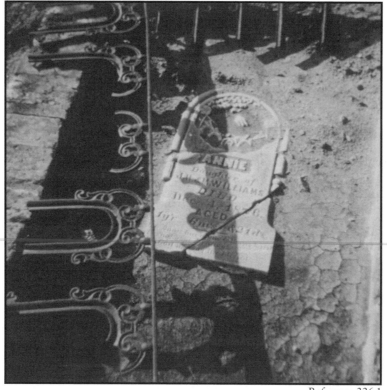

Reference 326.1

Annie Williams' gravestone sits at the gravesite of Rebecca Abraham, January 1973.

## PERSONAL INFORMATION:

| | |
|---|---|
| SEX: | Male |
| DATE OF BIRTH: | 1850 |
| DATE OF DEATH: | July 8, 1873 |
| PLACE OF DEATH: | Nortonville, Contra Costa County, California |
| AGE AT DEATH: | 23 years |
| CAUSE OF DEATH: | Crushed by coal car |
| BIRTHPLACE: | Wales |
| SPOUSE: | |
| PARENTS: | |

## GRAVESITE INFORMATION:

| | |
|---|---|
| LOCATION OF GRAVESITE: | Section S-D, Plot # 58 |
| GRAVESTONE: | Exists |
| TYPE OF GRAVESTONE: | Marble |
| SHAPE OF GRAVESTONE: | Tablet |
| INSCRIPTION: | *Sacred to the Memory of/Erected by the Cambrian Mutual Aid Society* |
| EPITAPH: | |
| MOTIF: | |
| CARVER: | Pioneer Steam Marble Works, San Francisco, California |
| BASE: | Exists |
| TYPE OF BASE: | Sandstone |
| ENCLOSURE: | |
| TYPE OF ENCLOSURE: | |
| FENCE: | |
| TYPE OF FENCE: | |
| FENCE MOTIF: | |

# WILLIAMS, David R.

**ADDITIONAL PERSONAL INFORMATION:**
In November 1868, David R. Williams was listed as a resident and miner in Nortonville, Contra Costa County, California.

The *1870 Census for Township Three, Contra Costa County, California* lists David Williams, age 20, as a coal miner and a native of England.

David Williams was working at the bottom of the Mount Hope Slope coal mine in Nortonville at the time of his death. His job was to attach and detach the rope to and from the coal cars as they ascended and descended the slope. One of the cables pulling a loaded car broke, causing the car to descend to the bottom of the slope, crushing Williams.

The *Antioch Ledger* newspaper, July 12, 1873, recorded his age at death as 25, and not 23 years as stated on his gravestone.

**ADDITIONAL GRAVESITE INFORMATION:**
The gravestone was broken into four pieces and concreted flat to the ground prior to East Bay Regional Park District acquisition. A small portion of the gravestone is missing. A sandstone base was found buried at the site by Black Diamond Rangers in 1996.

**REFERENCES:** 1, 2, 3, 4, 5, 6, 9 (July 12, 1873), 11 (P610.31.137 and P610.317.21), 12, 14; *Contra Costa Coal Mines* by Paul L. Henchey, June 1951, 33 pages; see newspaper appendix page 770

Reference 31.137

The David R. Williams vandalized gravestone.
Photograph taken by Traci (Gibbons) Parent, July 1977.

## PERSONAL INFORMATION:

| | |
|---|---|
| SEX: | Male |
| DATE OF BIRTH: | September 1821 |
| DATE OF DEATH: | May 12, 1874 |
| PLACE OF DEATH: | |
| AGE AT DEATH: | 52 years, 8 months |
| CAUSE OF DEATH: | Black lung disease |
| BIRTHPLACE: | Llanelly [sic], Carmarthenshire, South Wales |
| SPOUSE: | Ann (Morgan) Williams |
| PARENTS: | |

## GRAVESITE INFORMATION:

| | |
|---|---|
| LOCATION OF GRAVESITE: | Section N-E, Plot #74 |
| GRAVESTONE: | Missing |
| TYPE OF GRAVESTONE: | Marble |
| SHAPE OF GRAVESTONE: | Tablet |
| INSCRIPTION: | *In Memory of* |
| EPITAPH: | *Edward a wyt yn adwaen- rhyw filoedd* |
| | *O fodau uwch haulwen?* |
| | *Ai siriol yw dy seren* |
| | *Yn llonni'r llu tu draw ir llen?* |
| | *Adwaen ydwyf wrth edrych - ar dy fedd* |
| | *Fodolant. Llwyr eurwych* |
| | *Uwch haul di-draul yw i'm drych,* |
| | *Heb wrthol ar un gwrthych.* |
| MOTIF: | Lily and rope with tassels |
| CARVER: | Pioneer Steam Marble Works, 422 & 424 Jackson St., San Francisco, California |
| BASE: | Exists |
| TYPE OF BASE: | Concrete |
| ENCLOSURE: | |
| TYPE OF ENCLOSURE: | |
| FENCE: | |
| TYPE OF FENCE: | |
| FENCE MOTIF: | |

# WILLIAMS, Edward F.

**ADDITIONAL PERSONAL INFORMATION:**
Edward's middle name may have been Francis.

The *1870 Census for Empire, Ormsby County, Nevada* lists E. F. Williams, age 49, born *circa* 1821, in Wales. Also recorded are his wife, A. M. Williams, born *circa* 1827, in Wales; son, John, age 9, born *circa* 1861, in California; and daughter, M. A. Williams, age 10, born *circa* 1860, in California.

In October 1872, Edward was listed as a miner and resident of Nortonville, Contra Costa County, California.

According to information obtained from descendants and www.ancestry.com, Edward married Ann Morgan and they had three children:

- William Morgan, born January 29, 1856, in Ogden, Weber County, Utah
- Mary Ann, born December 31, 1858 (?), in Coloma, El Dorado County, California
- John, born 1860 or 1861, in California

The *1876 Contra Costa County Voting Register*, lists Edward, age 51, as a native of Wales and a miner living in Nortonville. His date of registration was October 24, 1872.

According to descendants, Edward died of black lung disease. After his death, his wife, Ann, age 50, a resident of Nortonville, married John D. Bowen, age 52, of Nortonville in October 1876.

According to family records and *Ancestry.com*, Ann was born January 10, 1827, in Swansea, South Wales. Ann and her new husband, John Bowen, moved to Washington state, where John worked in the coal mines. Ann died at 90+ years of age in October 1917, in Cumberland, King County, Washington.

**ADDITIONAL GRAVESITE INFORMATION:**
Edward's place of birth is incorrectly spelled on the gravestone as Llanelly. The correct spelling is Llanelli.

Zelma Myrick, who recorded information in a notebook in the 1930s during a visit to Rose Hill Cemetery, reported "Stone on ground." The stone was present in 1963 because it is listed on a student term paper by Jim Rotelli.

Photographs show that the gravestone was once repaired by backing the stone with a concrete and granite aggregate mix. A small piece of this backing sits in the base today. The repair was made to stand the gravestone back upright. A bronze plaque was purchased by descendants and placed at the site to mark the burial location. Although the plaque indicates it was placed in 1999, it was actually placed in 2000. The brass plaque says:

*EDWARD F. WILLIAMS*
*1821 – 1874*
*PLACED IN 1999*

**REFERENCES:** 1, 2, 3, 5, 6, 11 (P610.13.10, P610.146.1, P610.211.5, P610.211.8, P610.237.1, P610.268.13, and P610.294.4), 12, *Ledger Dispatch* newspaper (June 9, 2000), *Contra Costa Times* newspaper (June 7, 2000), *San Ramon Valley Times* newspaper (June 7, 2000), and the *San Francisco Chronicle* newspaper (June 8, 2000)

Reference 237.1

Reference 13.10

Pictured above is Nortonville resident, Edward F. Williams. The photograph, right, shows his vandalized gravestone, *circa* 1951. Edward's gravestone contained a Welsh epitaph. The translation of the epitaph was provided by Idris Evans of the Welsh American Society of Northern California and Tegwyn Jones, a bardic adjudicator in the annual Welsh National Eisteddfod. The translation of the epitaph is:

*Edward, do you recognize some thousands of heavenly bodies above the sun?*
*Is your star cheerful and a source of delight to the host on the other side of the grave?*

*I know as I look on your grave that they exist. Entirely glorious above an*
*undiminishing sun they seem to me, without a blemish on any object.*

Reference 268.13

Reference 146.1

Above, Edward F. Williams' gravestone (left, no date and right, *circa* 1958), after repairs were made by backing the stone with a concrete and granite aggregate mix. Note that the lettering on the gravestone has been highlighted with black paint. Below, Edward F. Williams' gravestone (seen on the right), broken a second time, sits beside the vandalized Bowman family gravestone in Rose Hill Cemetery, *circa* late 1960s to early 1970s.

Courtesy of CCCHS

## PERSONAL INFORMATION:

| | |
|---|---|
| SEX: | Male |
| DATE OF BIRTH: | July 1869 |
| DATE OF DEATH: | July 6, 1871 |
| PLACE OF DEATH: | |
| AGE AT DEATH: | 2 years, 23 days |
| CAUSE OF DEATH: | |
| BIRTHPLACE: | |
| SPOUSE: | None |
| PARENTS: | William M. and Elizabeth Williams |

## GRAVESITE INFORMATION:

| | |
|---|---|
| LOCATION OF GRAVESITE: | Unknown |
| GRAVESTONE: | Missing |
| TYPE OF GRAVESTONE: | |
| SHAPE OF GRAVESTONE: | |
| INSCRIPTION: | *Son of* |
| EPITAPH: | |
| MOTIF: | |
| CARVER: | |
| BASE: | |
| TYPE OF BASE: | |
| ENCLOSURE: | |
| TYPE OF ENCLOSURE: | |
| FENCE: | |
| TYPE OF FENCE: | |
| FENCE MOTIF: | |

# WILLIAMS, Howell M.

**ADDITIONAL PERSONAL INFORMATION:**
The *Assessment List, Contra Costa County, for 1872-73*, lists Howell's father, William M. Williams, as owning a house in the town of Somersville valued at $50.

See Mary M. Williams.

**ADDITIONAL GRAVESITE INFORMATION:**
Zelma Myrick, who recorded information in a notebook in the 1930s during a visit to Rose Hill Cemetery, reported "Next to this plot is an Odd Fellow plot but no stone. The Odd Fellow flag was there."

Howell shares the gravesite with his sister, Mary M. Williams. The gravestone was present in 1963 when it was listed in a student term paper by Jim Rotelli.

**REFERENCES:** 1, 2, 3, 5, 6, 12

---

## New Buildings.

The carpenters are busily engaged, in Somersville, on various buildings. The new hotel is nearly completed, and the painters have commenced operations. Red Men's Hall will be completed in a week, and small dwelling houses are springing up in all directions—a sure sign of prosperity.

---

The above article regarding Somersville, is from the *Antioch Ledger* newspaper, July 2, 1870. The Williams family was documented as living in Somersville in the early 1870s.

## PERSONAL INFORMATION:

| | |
|---|---|
| Sex: | Female |
| Date of Birth: | May 22, 1872 |
| Date of Death: | April 22, 1875 |
| Place of Death: | |
| Age at Death: | 2 years, 11 months |
| Cause of Death: | |
| Birthplace: | |
| Spouse: | None |
| Parents: | William M. and Elizabeth Williams |

## GRAVESITE INFORMATION:

| | |
|---|---|
| Location of Gravesite: | Unknown |
| Gravestone: | Missing |
| Type of Gravestone: | |
| Shape of Gravestone: | |
| Inscription: | |
| Epitaph: | |
| Motif: | |
| Carver: | |
| Base: | |
| Type of Base: | |
| Enclosure: | |
| Type of Enclosure: | |
| Fence: | |
| Type of Fence: | |
| Fence Motif: | |

# WILLIAMS, Mary M.

**ADDITIONAL PERSONAL INFORMATION:**
See Howell M. Williams.

**ADDITIONAL GRAVESITE INFORMATION:**
Mary shares the gravesite with her brother,

Howell M. Williams. The gravestone was present in 1963 when it was listed in a student term paper by Jim Rotelli.

**REFERENCES:** 1, 2, 3, 5, 6, 12

Reference 147.19

Rose Hill Cemetery, *circa* 1969, looking east toward Somersville town site. At the time this photograph was taken, a cyclone fence surrounded the cemetery. This type of fence was installed to help reduce vandalism. The lack of vegetation in the cemetery caused erosion gullies to form during winter rains.

## PERSONAL INFORMATION:

|  |  |
|---|---|
| SEX: | Female |
| DATE OF BIRTH: | 1870s |
| DATE OF DEATH: | |
| PLACE OF DEATH: | Nortonville, Contra Costa County, California |
| AGE AT DEATH: | Approximately 2 years |
| CAUSE OF DEATH: | Epidemic |
| BIRTHPLACE: | Nortonville or Black Diamond, Contra Costa County, California |
| SPOUSE: | None |
| PARENTS: | Mr. and Mrs. Williams |

## GRAVESITE INFORMATION:

|  |  |
|---|---|
| LOCATION OF GRAVESITE: | Unknown |
| GRAVESTONE: | Missing or never placed |
| TYPE OF GRAVESTONE: | |
| SHAPE OF GRAVESTONE: | |
| INSCRIPTION: | |
| EPITAPH: | |
| MOTIF: | |
| CARVER: | |
| BASE: | |
| TYPE OF BASE: | |
| ENCLOSURE: | |
| TYPE OF ENCLOSURE: | |
| FENCE: | |
| TYPE OF FENCE: | |
| FENCE MOTIF: | |

# WILLIAMS, Sara Elizabeth

**ADDITIONAL PERSONAL INFORMATION:**
Sara Elizabeth had fifteen brothers and sisters. David John Williams, born April 5, 1882, was one of Sara's brothers.

The Williams family lived in Nortonville, Contra Costa County, California and eventually moved to Tacoma, Pierce County, Washington in 1890.

The *1910 Census for Tacoma Ward 2, Pierce County, Washington* lists Sara's brother; David J. Williams, age 29, as a native of California. Also listed are his wife, Vera (Eshelman) Williams, age 22, a native of Washington, born *circa* 1888, and their son, Paul E. Williams, age 6 months, born *circa* 1909, in Washington. They are all listed as living with Vera's parents.

**ADDITIONAL GRAVESITE INFORMATION:**
According to descendants, Sara Elizabeth died during an epidemic and is buried in Rose Hill Cemetery. No other source documents her burial there.

**REFERENCES:** 12

# WILLIAMS,
## Watkin

**PERSONAL INFORMATION:**

| | |
|---|---|
| SEX: | Male |
| DATE OF BIRTH: | March 25, 1828 |
| DATE OF DEATH: | October 22, 1881 |
| PLACE OF DEATH: | San Francisco, San Francisco County, California |
| AGE AT DEATH: | 53 years, 6 months, 27 days |
| CAUSE OF DEATH: | |
| BIRTHPLACE: | Aberdar, Glamorganshire, South Wales |
| SPOUSE: | Jane Williams |
| PARENTS: | |

**GRAVESITE INFORMATION:**

| | |
|---|---|
| LOCATION OF GRAVESITE: | Section S-D, Plot #51 |
| GRAVESTONE: | Exists |
| TYPE OF GRAVESTONE: | Marble |
| SHAPE OF GRAVESTONE: | Tablet |
| INSCRIPTION: | *Farewell* |
| EPITAPH: | |
| MOTIF: | Clasped hands/Odd Fellows Emblem with F. L. T. |
| CARVER: | F. Field, San Jose, California |
| BASE: | Exists |
| TYPE OF BASE: | Granite base with middle marble base |
| ENCLOSURE: | Exists |
| TYPE OF ENCLOSURE: | Brick |
| FENCE: | Missing |
| TYPE OF FENCE: | Iron |
| FENCE MOTIF: | |

# WILLIAMS, Watkin

**ADDITIONAL PERSONAL INFORMATION:**
Watkin Williams is buried next to his son, William L. Williams. Watkin Williams was proprietor of the Black Diamond Exchange Hotel in Nortonville.

The *1870 Census for Mauch Chunk, Carbon County, Pennsylvania* lists Watkin Williams, age 48, as a coal miner, and native of Wales. Also listed are his wife, Jane, age 54, a native of Wales, and William, age 45, a coal miner and native of Wales. The William Williams listed could be their son with an incorrect age recorded or possibly Watkin's brother. Their son William Williams would have been approximately 12 years old in 1870 and not 45 years as indicated on the census.

Watkin Williams was injured in the July 24, 1876 explosion in the Black Diamond Mine in Nortonville, but survived. His son, William L. Williams, and many other men were killed in the accident. (See pages 706 and 707.)

The *1880 Census for Nortonville Precinct, Contra Costa County, California* lists Watkin Williams, age 52, as a Hotel Keeper and a native of Wales. Also listed are his wife, Jane, age 49, a native of Wales and their son, David, age 16, a native of California. Hotel boarders listed are: Owens Evans, age 54, a miner; Thomas Oliver, age 40, a store clerk; and John Long, age 51, a miner. All are natives of Wales. See William L. Williams.

**ADDITIONAL GRAVESITE INFORMATION:**
The three rings with the initials that appear on the stone are the symbol for the Independent Order of Odd Fellows (I.O.O.F.). The initials F. L. T., found within the three rings, stand for Friendship, Love, and Truth. Social Encampment, No. 50, Independent Order of Odd Fellows was instituted in Nortonville in December 1874.

The lower left corner of the gravestone is broken. The stone was vandalized prior to East Bay Regional Park District acquisition. The gravestone has been placed in storage until repairs can be made.

The brick wall enclosure was rebuilt in 2004 by contractors for the East Bay Regional Park District. The bottom and middle bases were removed from the cemetery for safekeeping prior to the brick wall reconstruction. In March 2004, the carver's signature (F. Field) was discovered when the base was removed and re-leveled. A new middle marble base was purchased to hold the gravestone upright. A clay pipe bowl, dating to the coal mining days, was found by the Black Diamond Rangers in the dirt pile while excavating to do repair work at the site.

Watkin Williams' stone appears in a Sunset book titled *Beautiful California*, Lane Book Company, Menlo Park, California, 1963, Page 83.

**REFERENCES:** 1, 2, 3, 4, 5, 6, 8 (Oct. 29, 1881), 9 (July 29, 1876), 11 (P610.5.2, P610.117.1, P610.139.2, P610.207.1, P610.294.6, P610.317.3, P610.317.5, and P610.363.2), 12, 14, see newspaper appendix page 771

Reference 317.5

The gravesites of Watkin Williams (left) and William L. Williams (right).
Photograph taken *circa* 1939 by Zelma Myrick.

William L. Williams' gravestone, 1962. Photograph by Madison Devlin.

# WILLIAMS,
## William L.

## PERSONAL INFORMATION:

| | |
|---|---|
| SEX: | Male |
| DATE OF BIRTH: | March 1858 |
| DATE OF DEATH: | July 24, 1876 |
| PLACE OF DEATH: | Nortonville, Contra Costa County, California |
| AGE AT DEATH: | 18 years, 4 months |
| CAUSE OF DEATH: | Suffocation from mine explosion |
| BIRTHPLACE: | Wales |
| SPOUSE: | None |
| PARENTS: | Watkin and Jane Williams |

## GRAVESITE INFORMATION:

| | |
|---|---|
| LOCATION OF GRAVESITE: | Section S-D, Plot #52 |
| GRAVESTONE: | Missing |
| TYPE OF GRAVESTONE: | Marble |
| SHAPE OF GRAVESTONE: | Tablet |
| INSCRIPTION: | *Son of/WILLIAMS* (on middle marble base) |
| EPITAPH: | *The storm that rocks the wintery sky* |
| | *No more disturbs his deep repose,* |
| | *Than summer-evening's latest sigh* |
| | *That shuts the rose.* |
| MOTIF: | Hand plucking rosebud/rope with tassels |
| CARVER: | |
| BASE: | Exists |
| TYPE OF BASE: | Sandstone with middle marble base |
| ENCLOSURE: | Exists |
| TYPE OF ENCLOSURE: | Brick |
| FENCE: | Missing |
| TYPE OF FENCE: | Iron |
| FENCE MOTIF: | |

# WILLIAMS, William L.

**ADDITIONAL PERSONAL INFORMATION:**
The *History of Contra Costa County*, published by W. A. Slocum and Company, 1882, states that William Williams and five others were killed by a powder explosion which occurred in the Black Diamond Mine in Nortonville, Contra Costa County, California, on July 24, 1876. The newspaper article from the *Antioch Ledger*, July 29, 1876, indicates Williams was single at the time of his death.

Zelma Myrick, who recorded information in a notebook in the 1930s during a visit to Rose Hill Cemetery, documented William's epitaph. The epitaph is from a poem called *The Grave*, verse 2, by James Montgomery, Scotland, 1771-1854.

See Theophile Dumas, William Gething, David W. Griffiths, Thomas D. James, Meredith Lewis, George M. Reynolds, Evan Smith, David Watts, Theophilus Watts, and Watkin Williams.

**ADDITIONAL GRAVESITE INFORMATION:**
William L. Williams shares the burial plot with his father, Watkin Williams.

A bronze plaque marking the burial location was placed at this gravesite in 1999. The plaque says:

> *WILLIAM L. WILLIAMS*
> *DIED JULY 24, 1876*
> *AGE 18 YRS. 4 MOS.*
> *PLACED IN 1999*

It is unusual for an adult to have a rosebud motif. More commonly this type of motif is found on gravestones of young children.

**REFERENCES:** 1, 2, 3, 4, 6, 8 (July 29, 1876 and Aug. 12, 1876), 9 (July 29, 1876), 10 (page 474), 11 (P610.5.2, P610.31.214, P610.98.18, P610.139.1, P610.207.1, P610.294.6, P610.317.3, P610.317.5, and P610.363.2), 12, *San Francisco Chronicle* newspaper (May 1, 1949, page 3L), see newspaper appendix (William Gething) pages 706 and 707

Reference 31.214

A bottom sandstone base with a middle marble base containing the name "Williams" is all that remained of the William L. Williams gravesite when the cemetery became part of the East Bay Regional Park District. Photograph taken in 1977 by Traci (Gibbons) Parent.

## PERSONAL INFORMATION:

|  |  |
|---|---|
| SEX: | Female |
| DATE OF BIRTH: | September 3, 1864 |
| DATE OF DEATH: | April 9, 1877 |
| PLACE OF DEATH: |  |
| AGE AT DEATH: | 12 years, 7 months, 6 days |
| CAUSE OF DEATH: |  |
| BIRTHPLACE: | California |
| SPOUSE: | None |
| PARENTS: | Joseph and Annie M. Willis |

## GRAVESITE INFORMATION:

|  |  |
|---|---|
| LOCATION OF GRAVESITE: | Unknown |
| GRAVESTONE: | Missing |
| TYPE OF GRAVESTONE: |  |
| SHAPE OF GRAVESTONE: |  |
| INSCRIPTION: | *Daughter of* |
| EPITAPH: |  |
| MOTIF: |  |
| CARVER: |  |
| BASE: |  |
| TYPE OF BASE: |  |
| ENCLOSURE: |  |
| TYPE OF ENCLOSURE: |  |
| FENCE: |  |
| TYPE OF FENCE: |  |
| FENCE MOTIF: |  |

# WILLIS, Mary Blanche

**ADDITIONAL PERSONAL INFORMATION:**
The *1870 Census for Township Three, Contra Costa County, California* lists Joseph Wells [sic], age 43, as a miner and a native of England. Also listed are his wife, Ann Wells [sic], age 43, a native of England, and their children: Mary, age 5, and Blanch [sic], age 4; both natives of California.

The *1880 Census for Somersville Precinct, Contra Costa County, California* lists Joseph Willis, age 54, as a miner and native of England. Also recorded is his wife, Annie, age 53, a native of England, and their daughter, Margaret, age 13, a native of California.

The *Washington State and Territorial Census, 1857-1892*, lists Joseph Willis as a resident of Tacoma, Pierce County, Washington in 1885. He is listed again in the 1889 census as a resident of Pierce County, Washington.

**ADDITIONAL GRAVESITE INFORMATION:**
Zelma Myrick, who recorded information in a notebook in the 1930s during a visit to Rose Hill Cemetery, reported the gravestone in "Good condition."

Nothing remains in the cemetery to indicate where Mary Blanche might be buried.

**REFERENCES:** 1, 2, 3, 4, 6, 12

Reference 317.8

Rose Hill Cemetery looking southeast, *circa* 1939. Photograph by Zelma Myrick.

# WINGATE,
## Robert

## PERSONAL INFORMATION:

| | |
|---|---|
| SEX: | Male |
| DATE OF BIRTH: | January 14, 1874 |
| DATE OF DEATH: | February 22, 1875 |
| PLACE OF DEATH: | Somersville, Contra Costa County, California |
| AGE AT DEATH: | 13 months, 8 days |
| CAUSE OF DEATH: | |
| BIRTHPLACE: | Coos Bay, Coos County, Oregon |
| SPOUSE: | None |
| PARENTS: | Robert and Sarah Mary Jane (Davis) Wingate |

## GRAVESITE INFORMATION:

| | |
|---|---|
| LOCATION OF GRAVESITE: | Section N-D, Plot #37 |
| GRAVESTONE: | Exists |
| TYPE OF GRAVESTONE: | Marble |
| SHAPE OF GRAVESTONE: | Tablet |
| INSCRIPTION: | *To the Memory of/Son of/Died at Somersville* |
| EPITAPH: | *Not lost but gone before.* |
| MOTIF: | Weeping willow tree and lamb/rope with tassels |
| CARVER: | |
| BASE: | Exists |
| TYPE OF BASE: | Sandstone |
| ENCLOSURE: | |
| TYPE OF ENCLOSURE: | |
| FENCE: | |
| TYPE OF FENCE: | |
| FENCE MOTIF: | |

# WINGATE, Robert

## ADDITIONAL PERSONAL INFORMATION:

The *1870 Census for Coos* [sic]*, Oregon*, lists Robert's parents, Robert Wingate, age 30, a native of Scotland and Sarah J., age 22, a native of Pennsylvania. Also listed is his sister, Agnes J., age 1, a native of California. In 1876, one year after Robert's death, Robert and Sarah Wingate had another son and named him Robert as well.

The *1880 Census for Pierce, New Tacoma, Washington* lists Robert's family. Recorded are his father, Robert, age 40, proprietor of a coal mine and native of Scotland; and his wife, Sarah, age 33, a native of Pennsylvania; and their children, Agnes, age 10, a native of California; Bella, age 7, a native of Oregon; Robert, age 4, a native of California; and Sarah, age 2, a native of Oregon.

The *Tacoma, Washington Directories 1889-1891*, lists Robert Wingate as an officer for the Tacoma National Bank in 1890. The same directory lists him as a mining engineer in 1889 and 1890.

According to the *History of the Pacific Northwest: Oregon and Washington, Volume II - 1889*, North Pacific History Company of Portland, Oregon: Robert Wingate, was born near Glasgow, Scotland on March 17, 1840. At age 18, he served as underground foreman in the Craig End Colliery. At age 20, he was promoted to Superintendent and served in that position until 1864, when he arrived in California. He worked in quartz mining in Grass Valley, Nevada County, California. In September 1864, when he was 24, he managed the Eureka and Independent Coal Mines in Somersville until August 1869. From there he went to the Eastport Mine at Coos Bay, Oregon. In early 1875 he was in San Francisco, California where he continued to serve as a mining expert, visiting and prospecting for coal in Vancouver Island, British Columbia, Canada.

In 1878, he opened the South Wellington Mine, Vancouver Island. At the close of 1878, Wingate went to Tacoma, Washington. In November 1879, he prospected the coal fields near Carbon River, Pierce County, Washington. There he developed coal mines at Carbonado for two years for the Carbon Hill Coal Company. After the mines were sold he settled in Tacoma County, Washington to practice his profession of mining engineer. He also served as vice president of the Olympia and Chehalis Valley Railroad Company and as a director in Tacoma National Bank. He was a large stockholder in both of these companies.

## ADDITIONAL GRAVESITE INFORMATION:

Zelma Myrick, who recorded information in a notebook in the 1930s during a visit to Rose Hill Cemetery, reported "Stone over." The gravestone was broken into two pieces prior to East Bay Regional Park District acquisition. The gravestone was repaired and placed upright in Rose Hill Cemetery by Black Diamond Rangers and volunteers in June 1995. No base was used. The original base for the stone sits nearby. The marble tablet stone was repaired by backing the stone with white cement mortar and then resetting it into concrete below ground level.

REFERENCES: 1, 2, 3, 6, 11 (P610.31.125, P610.117.14, P610.204.2 to P610.204.9, P610.263.6, and P610.284.1 to P610.284.5), 12, 14, *Carbon River Coal County*, Nancy Irene Hall, 1980, The Courier Herald Publishing Company, Enumclaw, WA, page 68; *History of the Pacific Northwest: Oregon and Washington, Volume II - 1889*, North Pacific History Company of Portland, Oregon; *MacPhee Family History*, prepared by Chester Riddoch MacPhee and Marjorie Young Otton MacPhee, June 5, 1983; *Robert Wingate (1840-1905) – American Coal Mining Entrepreneur*, 9 pages, prepared by Dr. Guy Wingate, no date

Reference 284.1

Reference 284.4

Pictured are former Somersville residents, Robert and Sarah Mary Jane (Davis) Wingate, in Tacoma, Pierce County, Washington, date unknown. An early photograph of Sarah Mary Jane is pictured on the right. Robert and Sarah were the parents of Robert Wingate. Sarah was born March 12, 1848, at Tamaqua, Schuylkill County, Pennsylvania. She was the daughter of William Oliver Davis, Superintendent of the Black Diamond Coal Mining Company of Nortonville. Sarah married Robert Wingate in Somersville, Contra Costa County, California, on May 28, 1868. Robert Wingate was employed as Superintendent of the Independent Coal Mining Company in Somersville in 1867-1869. He worked in the mines for four years after his marriage and before he and his family moved to Coos Bay, Coos County, Oregon. The family eventually settled in Tacoma, Pierce County, Washington where Robert died on March 2, 1905 and his wife died on November 5, 1921. Robert and Sarah Wingate had at eight children. They were:

- Agnes, born April 1870, California
- Isabella (Bella), born June 1872, Oregon
- Robert , born January 14, 1874, Oregon
- Robert Lennox, born May 1876, California
- Sarah M. (Sadie), born June 1878, Washington Territory
- Grace E., born August 1882, Washington Territory
- Ralph, born April 1884, Washington Territory
- James G., born April 1891, Washington

Pictured are the children of Robert and Sarah (Davis) Wingate and siblings of Robert Wingate.
Above Agnes Wingate (born 1870) and Isabella Wingate (born 1872).
Below, brother Robert Lennox Wingate (born 1876).

## PERSONAL INFORMATION:

| | |
|---|---|
| SEX: | Female |
| DATE OF BIRTH: | May 27, 1858 |
| DATE OF DEATH: | August 7, 1876 |
| PLACE OF DEATH: | |
| AGE AT DEATH: | 18 years, 2 months, 10 days |
| CAUSE OF DEATH: | |
| BIRTHPLACE: | Pennsylvania |
| SPOUSE: | William B. Witherow |
| PARENTS: | Mr. and Mrs. Morgan |

## GRAVESITE INFORMATION:

| | |
|---|---|
| LOCATION OF GRAVESITE: | Section N-D, Plot #32 |
| GRAVESTONE: | Exists |
| TYPE OF GRAVESTONE: | Marble |
| SHAPE OF GRAVESTONE: | Tablet |
| INSCRIPTION: | *Farewell/Wife of* |
| EPITAPH: | |
| MOTIF: | Clasped hands with "farewell"/rope with tassels |
| CARVER: | Excelsior Marble Works, San Jose, California |
| BASE: | Exists |
| TYPE OF BASE: | Sandstone with new middle marble base |
| ENCLOSURE: | Exists |
| TYPE OF ENCLOSURE: | Brick |
| FENCE: | |
| TYPE OF FENCE: | |
| FENCE MOTIF: | |

# WITHEROW, Barbara L.

**ADDITIONAL PERSONAL INFORMATION:**
Barbara L. Morgan, age 18, a resident of Nortonville, Contra Costa County, California, and William Witherow, age 26, also a resident of Nortonville, applied for a marriage license on October 3, 1874. The information was recorded in the *Applications for Marriage Licenses, Contra Costa County, 1873-1887*, page 29, located at the Contra Costa County Historical Society History Center in Martinez, California. The age recorded at the time of her application does not match her age listed on the gravestone.

According to the *Index to Marriage Certificates* located at the Contra Costa County Hall of Records, Martinez, California, William Withrow [sic] and Barbara L. Morgan were married by Thomas A. Brown; the information is recorded in Volume 2, page 61.

The *1876 Contra Costa County Voting Register* lists William R. Witherow, age 28, as a native of Pennsylvania and a shoemaker in Nortonville. His date of registration was October 7, 1872.

The *1880 Census for Nortonville Precinct* lists Barbara's husband, William, age 35, as a miner and native of Pennsylvania. He was residing in the boarding house of Margaret Davis.

**ADDITIONAL GRAVESITE INFORMATION:**
The gravestone was broken into two pieces and concreted flat to the ground prior to East Bay Regional Park District acquisition. The brick enclosure surrounding the gravesite was also placed at the site prior to Park District acquisition.

The gravestone was removed for repairs in August 2002. A marble middle base was purchased so that the stone could be placed upright. The marble base sits on top of the bottom sandstone base. The existing bottom base was re-leveled in August 2002. The gravestone was returned to the cemetery and attached to the middle marble base in November 2002.

**REFERENCES:** 1, 2, 3, 4, 6, 8 (Oct. 10, 1874), 11 (P610.31.176, P610.119.16, P610.119.17, P610.153.11, and P610.263.25), 12, 14

---

## MARRIED.

WITHEROW—MORGAN—In Martinez, Oct. 3d, by Hon. Thomas A. Bown, County Judge, Mr. William Witherow and Miss Barbara L. Morgan, both of Nortonville

From the *Contra Costa Gazette* newspaper, October 10, 1874.
Hon. Thomas A. Brown's name is incorrectly spelled as Bown in this article.

## PERSONAL INFORMATION:

| | |
|---|---|
| SEX: | Male |
| DATE OF BIRTH: | *Circa* 1867 |
| DATE OF DEATH: | June 26, 1870 |
| PLACE OF DEATH: | Somersville, Contra Costa County, California |
| AGE AT DEATH: | 3 years |
| CAUSE OF DEATH: | Scarlet fever |
| BIRTHPLACE: | Probably California |
| SPOUSE: | None |
| PARENTS: | John E. and Lucy A. Wright |

## GRAVESITE INFORMATION:

| | |
|---|---|
| LOCATION OF GRAVESITE: | Unknown |
| GRAVESTONE: | Missing or never placed |
| TYPE OF GRAVESTONE: | |
| SHAPE OF GRAVESTONE: | |
| INSCRIPTION: | |
| EPITAPH: | |
| MOTIF: | |
| CARVER: | |
| BASE: | |
| TYPE OF BASE: | |
| ENCLOSURE: | |
| TYPE OF ENCLOSURE: | |
| FENCE: | |
| TYPE OF FENCE: | |
| FENCE MOTIF: | |

# WRIGHT, Bertie

## ADDITIONAL PERSONAL INFORMATION:

The *Antioch Ledger* newspapers (Jan. 7, 1865 and July 2, 1870) and the *Contra Costa Gazette* newspaper (July 9, 1870), are the only sources that record the deaths of the Wright children in Somersville. It is likely that Bertie is buried in Rose Hill Cemetery although it is not stated in the July 2, 1870 article.

The *Contra Costa Gazette* newspaper, July 9, 1870, article "Somersville Correspondence" states that:

> Mr. John Wright buried his oldest daughter and youngest son in one grave last Sunday week, by the side of three children buried five years ago. Mr. Tolan, of Nortonville, has buried two, all of scarlet fever.

The *Antioch Ledger* newspaper, July 2, 1870, indicates that Bertie and his sister Minnie died of scarlet fever. Eighteen-month-old Violette I. Bowman of Somersville (also buried in Rose Hill Cemetery) died of scarlet fever on June 22, 1870, and is listed in the same obituary notice as Bertie and his sister, Minnie. The Wright family lived in Somersville.

According to the above sources, as well as the 1870 and 1880 Census records, John E. and Lucy A. Wright had at least ten children. They included:

- George, born *circa* 1852, Massachusetts
- Arthur, born *circa* 1854, Massachusetts
- John Edmund, born 1856, died Dec. 1865, presumed to be buried in Rose Hill Cemetery
- Isaac, born *circa* 1860, Massachusetts
- Newton, born *circa* 1860, California
- Minnie, born 1861, died June 1870, presumed to be buried in Rose Hill Cemetery
- Mary Elizabeth, born 1865, died Dec. 1865, presumed to be buried in Rose Hill Cemetery
- Martha, born *circa* 1866, California
- Bertie, born *circa* 1867, died June 1870, presumed to be buried in Rose Hill Cemetery
- Edith, born *circa* 1873, California

The *History of Contra Costa County, California* published by W. A. Slocum and Company in 1882, page 131 states: "The Central Mine, east of the Pittsburg [mine] was located by John E. Wright." The same publication (pages 493 and 494) states that John E. Wright was a charter member of Antioch Masonic Lodge, No. 175, F. and A. M. where he served as Treasurer in 1865. The Masonic lodge was organized October 12, 1865. John E. Wright died on April 22, 1894.

## ADDITIONAL GRAVESITE INFORMATION:

See John Edmund Wright, Mary Elizabeth Wright, Minnie Wright, and Wright (child).

REFERENCES: 8 (July 9, 1870), 9 (July 2, 1870 – two articles, Jan. 7, 1865 and April 28, 1894), 12, see newspaper appendix (Violette I. Bowman) page 683 and (the Wright family) page 772

**DIED.**

In Antioch, June 23, 1870, Charles Carman Israel, youngest son of George L. and Mary Israel, aged four months and twelve days.

> He took the cup of Life to drink,
>   But bitter 'twas to drain,
> He turned it meekly from his lips,
>   And went to sleep again.

In Somersville, June 22d, 1870, Violetta, daughter of Mr. and Mrs. Bowman, aged eighteen months.

In Somersville, June 26th, Minnie Wright, aged nine years, daughter of Mr. and Mrs. John Wright.

In Somersville, June 26th, Bertie Wright, youngest son of Mr. and Mrs. John Wright, aged three years.

The *Antioch Ledger* newspaper, July 2, 1870 printed this obituary for Minnie Wright and her brother Bertie Wright. Violetta Bowman is listed in the obituary with the Wright children and is also buried in Rose Hill Cemetery. Violetta (Violette I.), Minnie, and Bertie all died of scarlet fever. The article above states that the children died on June 26 (a Sunday). The article below, as well as the article on page 672, states the children died on a Saturday (June 25, 1870).

**Funeral Procession.**

A large number of people, on Sunday last, followed to the grave the mortal remains of the children who died of Scarlatina the day previous, thus showing their sympathy with the bereaved parents. This is truly an afflicted family, but, we are pleased to state that the other members of it are progressing favorably toward recovery.

The above article also appeared in the *Antioch Ledger* newspaper, on July 2, 1870. Although the article does not state where the grave was located and does not mention the names of the children who died of "Scarlatina" it is presumed that the children they are referring to may be the Wright children.

## Serious Accident.

Sunday last, as Mr. and Mrs. Wright, of this town, were on their way to Somersville, for the purpose of attending the funeral of their brother's children, (two of whom had died the night before of scarlet fever), the horse was seized with the blind staggers, and when near the outlet of the canyon fell so near the edge of the chasm that buggy, horse and driver were precipitated to the bottom of the gulch, twenty feet in depth. Mrs. Wright, seeing the danger and being on the side farthest from the gulch, managed to jump out of the buggy, but fell heavily on a rock, fracturing one of the bones in the thorasic region and being otherwise severely bruised. Mr. Wright's escape is miraculous. He fell under the horse, but beyond being rather stiff about the legs sustained no injury. Dr. Hamelln was summoned and attended the sufferers, and Mrs. Wright has so far recovered as to be moved to this place from Somersville. The buggy was a little shaken.

Mr. and Mrs. Wright, the uncle and aunt of the Wright children who died in Somersville, were coming from the nearby community of Antioch, Contra Costa County, California when the accident occurred. This newspaper article that appeared in the *Antioch Ledger*, July 2, 1870, indicates that the Wright children died of scarlet fever.

# WRIGHT,
## John Edmund

## PERSONAL INFORMATION:

| | |
|---|---|
| SEX: | Male |
| DATE OF BIRTH: | *Circa* February 28, 1855 |
| DATE OF DEATH: | December 28, 1864 |
| PLACE OF DEATH: | Somersville, Contra Costa County, California |
| AGE AT DEATH: | 9 years, 10 months |
| CAUSE OF DEATH: | Malignant Scarlatina (scarlet fever) |
| BIRTHPLACE: | |
| SPOUSE: | None |
| PARENTS: | John E. and Lucy A. Wright |

## GRAVESITE INFORMATION:

| | |
|---|---|
| LOCATION OF GRAVESITE: | Unknown |
| GRAVESTONE: | Missing or never placed |
| TYPE OF GRAVESTONE: | |
| SHAPE OF GRAVESTONE: | |
| INSCRIPTION: | |
| EPITAPH: | |
| MOTIF: | |
| CARVER: | |
| BASE: | |
| TYPE OF BASE: | |
| ENCLOSURE: | |
| TYPE OF ENCLOSURE: | |
| FENCE: | |
| TYPE OF FENCE: | |
| FENCE MOTIF: | |

# WRIGHT, John Edmund

**ADDITIONAL PERSONAL INFORMATION:**
The January 7, 1865 *Antioch Ledger* newspaper states that John Edmund is the second son of John and Lucy Wright.

The *Antioch Ledger* newspapers (Jan. 7, 1865 and July 2, 1870) and the *Contra Costa Gazette* newspaper (July 9, 1870), are the only sources that record the deaths of the Wright children in Somersville. It is likely that John Edmund is buried in Rose Hill Cemetery, although it is not stated in the articles.

John Edmund was one of many children who died in Somersville in 1864/1865 from scarlatina maligna (scarlet fever). The other children who died during this same period of time of this disease and who are buried in, or believed to be buried in, Rose Hill Cemetery include:

- Charles W. Blackburn, died February 20, 1865, age 9 years, 7 months
- Thomas Pratten Goulding, died January 31, 1865, age 7 years, 7 months, 17 days
- Jane Russel Muir, died January 4, 1865, age 4 years and 3 (?) months
- Elizabeth Richmond, died February 17, 1865, age 8 years, 5 months, 11 days
- John Tonkins, died December 29, 1864, age 16 years, 3 months
- Annie Tregellas, died February 19, 1865, age 7 years, 7 months
- James Tregellas, died December 28, 1864, age 2 years, 21 days
- Joseph Tregellas, died February 18, 1865, age 5 years, 1 month
- Mary Elizabeth Wright, died December 25, 1864, age 1 year, 6 months

John Edmund's date of birth was calculated by using www.timeanddate.com, based on his age at death and date of death reported in the *Antioch Ledger* newspaper, January 7, 1865 (see page 765).

**ADDITIONAL GRAVESITE INFORMATION:**
See Bertie Wright, Mary Elizabeth Wright, Minnie Wright, and Wright (child).

**REFERENCES:** 8 (July 9, 1870), 9 (Jan. 7, 1865 and July 2, 1870), 12, newspaper appendix (Violette I. Bowman) page 683, (John Tonkins) page 765, and (the Wright family) page 772

# WRIGHT,
## Mary Elizabeth

## PERSONAL INFORMATION:

SEX:                    Female

DATE OF BIRTH:          *Circa* June 25, 1863

DATE OF DEATH:          December 25, 1864

PLACE OF DEATH:         Somersville, Contra Costa County, California

AGE AT DEATH:           1 year, 6 months

CAUSE OF DEATH:         Malignant Scarlatina (scarlet fever)

BIRTHPLACE:

SPOUSE:                 None

PARENTS:                John E. and Lucy A. Wright

## GRAVESITE INFORMATION:

LOCATION OF GRAVESITE:  Unknown

GRAVESTONE:             Missing or never placed

TYPE OF GRAVESTONE:

SHAPE OF GRAVESTONE:

INSCRIPTION:

EPITAPH:

MOTIF:

CARVER:

BASE:

TYPE OF BASE:

ENCLOSURE:

TYPE OF ENCLOSURE:

FENCE:

TYPE OF FENCE:

FENCE MOTIF:

# WRIGHT, Mary Elizabeth

**ADDITIONAL PERSONAL INFORMATION:**
The *Antioch Ledger* newspapers (Jan. 7, 1865 and July 2, 1870) and the *Contra Costa Gazette* newspaper (July 9, 1870), are the only sources that record the deaths of the Wright children in Somersville.

It is likely that Mary Elizabeth is buried in Rose Hill Cemetery although it is not stated in the article. Mary Elizabeth was one of many children who died in Somersville in 1864/1865 from scarlatina maligna (scarlet fever). The other children who died during this same period of time of this disease and who are buried in, or believed to be buried in, Rose Hill Cemetery include:

- Charles W. Blackburn, died February 20, 1865, age 9 years, 7 months
- Thomas Pratten Goulding, died January 31, 1865, age 7 years, 7 months, 17 days
- Jane Russel Muir, died January 4, 1865, age 4 years, 3 (?) months
- Elizabeth Richmond, died February 17, 1865, age 8 years, 5 months, 11 days

- John Tonkins, died December 29, 1864, age 16 years, 3 months
- Annie Tregellas, died February 19, 1865, age 7 years, 7 months
- James Tregellas, died December 28, 1864, age 2 years, 21 days
- Joseph Tregellas, died February 18, 1865, age 5 years, 1 month
- John Edmund Wright, died December 28, 1864, age 9 years, 10 months

Mary Elizabeth's date of birth was calculated by using www.timeanddate.com, based on her age at death and date of death reported in the *Antioch Ledger* newspaper, January 7, 1865 (see page 765).

**ADDITIONAL GRAVESITE INFORMATION:**
See Bertie Wright, John Edmund Wright, Minnie Wright, and Wright (child).

**REFERENCES:** 8 (July 9, 1870), 9 (Jan. 7, 1865 and July 2, 1870), 12, see newspaper appendix (Violette I. Bowman) page 683, (John Tonkins) page 765, and (the Wright family) page 772

# WRIGHT,
## Minnie

**PERSONAL INFORMATION:**

| | |
|---|---|
| SEX: | Female |
| DATE OF BIRTH: | *Circa* 1861 |
| DATE OF DEATH: | June 26, 1870 |
| PLACE OF DEATH: | Somersville, Contra Costa County, California |
| AGE AT DEATH: | 9 years |
| CAUSE OF DEATH: | Scarlet fever |
| BIRTHPLACE: | |
| SPOUSE: | None |
| PARENTS: | John E. and Lucy A. Wright |

**GRAVESITE INFORMATION:**

| | |
|---|---|
| LOCATION OF GRAVESITE: | Unknown |
| GRAVESTONE: | Missing or never placed |
| TYPE OF GRAVESTONE: | |
| SHAPE OF GRAVESTONE: | |
| INSCRIPTION: | |
| EPITAPH: | |
| MOTIF: | |
| CARVER: | |
| BASE: | |
| TYPE OF BASE: | |
| ENCLOSURE: | |
| TYPE OF ENCLOSURE: | |
| FENCE: | |
| TYPE OF FENCE: | |
| FENCE MOTIF: | |

# WRIGHT, Minnie

**ADDITIONAL PERSONAL INFORMATION:**
The *Antioch Ledger* newspapers (Jan. 7, 1865 and July 2, 1870) and the *Contra Costa Gazette* newspaper (July 9, 1870), are the only sources that record the deaths of the Wright children in Somersville.

It is likely that Minnie is buried in Rose Hill Cemetery although it is not stated in the articles. Eighteen month old Violette I. Bowman of Somersville (also buried in Rose Hill Cemetery) died of scarlet fever on June 22, 1870 and is listed in the same obituary notice as Minnie and her brother Bertie.

The *1870 Census for Township 3, Contra Costa County, California* lists Bertie's father, John Wright, age 40, an engineer born *circa* 1830 in New York. Also listed are his mother, Lucy, age 39, born *circa* 1831 in Massachusetts and his siblings: George, age 18; Arthur, age 16; Isaac, age 10; all natives of Massachusetts; and Martha, age 5, a native of California.

The *1880 Census for Township 1, Contra Costa County, California* lists John E. Wright, age 51, an engineer born *circa* 1829, in New York. Also listed are his wife, Lucy, age 49, born *circa* 1831, in Massachusetts and their children: Newton, age 20, occupation "drives express"; Martha, age 14; and Edith, age 7. All are natives of California. Recorded as living with them is Joaõ Rosè, age 20, single, and a native of the Azores Islands. His occupation is listed as "H. man."

See page 665.

**ADDITIONAL GRAVESITE INFORMATION:**
See Bertie Wright, John Edmund Wright, Mary Elizabeth Wright, and Wright (child).

**REFERENCES:** 8 (July 9, 1870), 9 (Jan. 7, 1865 and July 2, 1870 – two articles), 12, see newspaper appendix (Violette I. Bowman) page 683, and (the Wright family) page 772

---

### Scarlet Fever.

This disease is now prevalent in the mines; a large number of children are suffering from it. On Saturday last Mr. Wright, of Somersville, lost a little boy, and some five hours afterward a daughter. Two other of the children were lying at the point of death. The physician of the district, Dr. Hamelin, is constantly occupied, and old residents inform us there is more sickness now in the mines than for years past.

---

This article, from the *Antioch Ledger* newspaper, July 2, 1870, refers to Mr. Wright's "little boy" and daughter who died as a result of the disease scarlet fever. Minnie Wright is the daughter, and the little boy who died five hours prior was her three year old brother, Bertie Wright.

## PERSONAL INFORMATION:

SEX: Unknown

DATE OF BIRTH:

DATE OF DEATH: *Circa* 1865

PLACE OF DEATH: Somersville, Contra Costa County, California

AGE AT DEATH: Child

CAUSE OF DEATH: Scarlet fever

BIRTHPLACE:

SPOUSE: None

PARENTS: John E. and Lucy A. Wright

## GRAVESITE INFORMATION:

LOCATION OF GRAVESITE: Unknown

GRAVESTONE: Missing or never placed

TYPE OF GRAVESTONE:

SHAPE OF GRAVESTONE:

INSCRIPTION:

EPITAPH:

MOTIF:

CARVER:

BASE:

TYPE OF BASE:

ENCLOSURE:

TYPE OF ENCLOSURE:

FENCE:

TYPE OF FENCE:

FENCE MOTIF:

# WRIGHT, (child)

**ADDITIONAL PERSONAL INFORMATION:**
The *Contra Costa Gazette* newspaper (July 9, 1870), is the only source that records the death of this Wright child in Somersville. The article states:

> Mr. John Wright buried his oldest daughter and youngest son in one grave last Sunday week, by the side of three children, buried five years ago.

The other Wright children believed to be buried in Rose Hill Cemetery are:

- Bertie, died June 26, 1870
- John Edmund, died Dec. 28, 1864
- Mary Elizabeth, died Dec. 25, 1864
- Minnie, died June 26, 1870

It is likely that this child is buried in Rose Hill Cemetery although it is not stated in the newspaper article.

**ADDITIONAL GRAVESITE INFORMATION:**
See Bertie Wright, John Edmund Wright, Mary Elizabeth Wright, and Minnie Wright.

**REFERENCES:** 8 (July 9, 1870), 9 (Jan. 7, 1865 and July 2, 1870 – two articles), 12, see newspaper appendix (Violette I. Bowman) page 683, and (the Wright family) page 772

# Chapter 5

# NEWSPAPER APPENDIX

# NEWSPAPER APPENDIX

## Articles Regarding
## the Deceased and Their Families

At least two newspapers, the *Antioch Ledger* and *Contra Costa Gazette*, were searched for death notices regarding the individuals buried in Rose Hill Cemetery. These local papers were active during the coal mining period and served the residents of the mining communities.

Often no article could be located regarding the death of the individual. For others, numerous articles were found. Occasionally one newspaper would impart information that was not provided in the other. As with all historic records, errors, such as dates and the spellings of names, were common. Occasionally the date of death and/or age of the individual recorded in the newspaper differed from the death date and age recorded on the gravestone. Regardless, if an article of interest was located pertaining to the deceased individual, or a family member of the deceased; it was included in this appendix to give the reader insight into the daily lives of coal field residents.

The articles included in this appendix were retyped to look as close to the original article as possible using the same spellings, grammar, punctuation, and formatting. For words that were incorrectly spelled or wrongly used, [sic] was placed next to the word in the article or a notation was made in the caption. These articles were retyped rather than scanned because the article was too lengthy and/or the quality of the microfilm image was too poor.

Other newspapers used to obtain information regarding those buried in Rose Hill Cemetery included:

- ☞ *Alameda Times Star*
- ☞ *Contra Costa Standard*
- ☞ *Contra Costa Times*
- ☞ *Daily Alta California*
- ☞ *Ledger Dispatch*
- ☞ *Livermore Echo*
- ☞ *Martinez Herald*
- ☞ *Oakland Tribune*
- ☞ *Pittsburg Daily Independent*
- ☞ *Pittsburg Post*
- ☞ *Pittsburg Post Dispatch*
- ☞ *Pittsburg Pride*
- ☞ *Sacramento Bee*
- ☞ *San Francisco Call*
- ☞ *San Francisco Chronicle*
- ☞ *The Livermore Herald*
- ☞ *The Placer Herald*
- ☞ *The Post Intelligencer*
- ☞ *Valley Pioneer*
- ☞ *Woodland Daily Democrat*

The above pieces come from the *Contra Costa Gazette* newspaper, October 20, 1900 and the *Weekly Antioch Ledger* May 19, 1877. According to the *History of Contra Costa County, California* by W. A. Slocum and Co., 1882, the *Contra Costa Gazette* was the first newspaper published in Contra Costa County. The newspaper office was originally located in Pacheco but later moved to the county seat in Martinez. The first issue appeared in September 1858. The *Weekly Antioch Ledger*, referred to as the *Antioch Ledger* in this document, was established in March 1869 by Messrs. Townsend and Wait. J. P. Abbott purchased a half interest in the paper in December 1869, and for eleven years he published the paper serving as editor and proprietor.

## DIED.

ABRAHAM—In Nortonville, November 1st, Rebecca, the beloved wife of Mr. Daniel Abraham.

The deceased met with her death in a most painful manner. About 7 P.M. on the 30th of October a small kerosene lamp fell off the table, breaking and upsetting the oil over her clothes. Fearing that the house would take fire the unfortunate woman endeavored to throw the burner out, and while in the act of doing so her own clothes became ignited and in a moment she was enveloped in flames. She ran out crying for help, and friends and neighbors came to her assistance, and in less than a minute she was wrapped in blankets and the fire put out, but alas not before she was terribly burnt, she lingered in great agony until 6 o'clock Friday morning Nov. 1st, when she died, aged, 18 years, 6 months. Her funeral took place on Sunday Nov. 3d, and it is said to have been the largest that has ever taken place in Nortonville. The cortege formed at the house at 2 P.M. Before starting the Rev. T. S. Griffiths gave out an appropriate hymn which was sung with much feeling. Then the long procession wended on its way to the church, the body being borne by 12 pallbearers. After religious service in the church, the procession re-formed and proceeded to the cemetary [sic]; and there to the grave was committed all that remained of the young, well, and happy wife of a few days previous.

The grass withereth and the flower fadeth; but the word of our God shall stand forever—Isaiah, XL: 6-8.

ELIZABETH GRIFFITHS.

NORTONVILLE, Nov. 5th, 1878.

*Contra Costa Gazette*
November 9, 1878

# ANDERSON, Robert

This article concerns Robert's father, Richard Anderson, who is mistakenly identified as Robert Anderson.

> **Bring on the Bronco.**
>
> Robert Anderson, the village black-smith of Somersville, while shoeing a horse last Monday, was badly cut by a horseshoe nail. The nail was driven partly in, when suddenly the horse gave a plunge and drawing his foot out cut a gash in the left thigh. On Friday, however, Dickey stood in the doorway waiting for the next bronco. Good for you!

*Antioch Ledger*
February 23, 1901

**Death of A. Banks.**

Our community was startled on Tuesday morning by announcement of the sudden death of Mr. A. Banks at Nortonville. It was reported that deceased was in the habit of taking laudanum and that he had overdosed himself, but this fact does not appear in the verdict of the Coroner's Jury, which reads as follows:

State of California, County of Contra Costa, Before D. Mayon, acting Coroner.

In the matter of the inquisition upon the body of A. Banks deceased. We the undersigned, the jurors summoned to appear before D. Mayon acting Coroner of the County of Contra Costa at Nortonville, the 22d day of August 1871 to inquire into the cause of the death of A. Banks, having been duly sworn according to law, and having made such inquiries after inspecting the body and having the testimony adduced upon our oaths each and all do say that we find the deceased was named A. Banks, was a native of Pennsylvania, aged about 38 years, that he came to his death on the 22d day of August, 1871, in the County of Contra Costa from causes to the jury unknown.        (Signed)

ASHER TYLER,            WILLIAM PROSSER,
WILLIAM ALLCOCK,            JOHN COLLINS,
JOHN STUART,            ALEX MULHERRIN,
        JOHN TIERNEN.

*Antioch Ledger*
August 26, 1871

**DIED.**

Banks—In Somersville, September 8, 1892, Ann
C. Banks, a native of Wales, aged 64 years.

*Antioch Ledger*
September 10, 1892

**DIED.**

Banks—In Somersville, September 8, 1892, Mrs.
Ann C. Banks, a native of Merthyr Tydvlle [sic],
South Wales, aged 67 years, 2 months and 28
days.

*Contra Costa Gazette*
September 14, 1892

**Somersville Correspondence.**

SOMERSVILLE, July 7th, 1870.

EDS. GAZETTE: After an absence of two weeks away from home I find, on my return, that death has been busy among the little ones. Mr. John Wright buried his oldest daughter and youngest son in one grave last Sunday week, by the side of three children, buried five years ago. Mr. Tolan, of Nortonville, has buried two, all of scarlet fever. Mr. David Bowman of this place, buried his only daughter this day week. The disease seems to have run its time, and all the sick are now convalascent.[sic] I hear there were very pleasant times on the Fourth at Nortonville. All say the celebration was a success; the horse racing "splendid," the ball magnificent; only one little drawback. One man named Jones, got severely stabbed in the breast and in the back; certainly cold water was not the cause of that. Times are dull here. Mr. Hawxhurst's new hotel is nearly finished. The Red Men's Hall, under the efficient supervision of C. W. Clark, is nearly completed.

PITTS.

This article, from the *Contra Costa Gazette* newspaper, July 9, 1870, states that "Mr. David Bowman of this place, buried his only daughter this day week." The "daughter" referred to in this article is Violette I. Bowman.

# BRADSHAW, John

---

**DIED.**

BRADSHAW—In Nortonville, October 25th, John Bradshaw, a native of Wales, aged 55 years, 4 months and 20 days.

---

*Contra Costa Gazette*
October 29, 1881

# BRYANT, Margaret

---

**DIED.**

BRYANT — In Nortonville, November 28, 1900.  Mrs. James Bryant, a native of Wales, aged 62 years.

---

*Antioch Ledger*
December 1, 1900

## The Stewartville Concert.

The entertainment and concert at Stewartville in aid of the Congregational Church Building Fund was a complete success. The entertainment, "An Only Daughter", was given by the Good Templars of Stewartville. Miss Annie Leam and Miss Nellie Riddock, with Messrs. Abe Leam, Thomas Shine, Rease Jones, John and Harry Leam, evinced more than ordinary talent and were loudly applauded. Mr. M. E. Richardson of Oakland and Mr. Thomas Tregalles (recently from Australia) are professional vocalists and gave evidence of this in the rendering of various songs. Miss Mattie Tubb of Martinez sang two songs. Mr. Thomas Buxton of Stewartville performed on the violincello, his children, Della and Garfield, sang a duet which pleased the people and added to the enjoyment of the evening. The writer sang a song. The financial success was due to the earnest indefatigable energy of Miss Annie Leam and Miss Nellie Riddock. The entertainment could not have been given at this time had it not been for the young ladies mentioned. The Good Templars of Stewartville deserve credit for their self-sacrificing exertions. Misses Leam and Riddock handed me $40.80, proceeds of the sale of tickets. Our success ensures that of another entertainment to be given in the future.

W. H. T.

*Contra Costa Gazette*
July 26, 1884

## DIED.

BUXTON—In Stewartville, October 22, 1890, Margaret, wife of Thomas Buxton, aged 42 years.

*Antioch Ledger*
October 25, 1890

## Death of Mrs. Buxton.

The wife of Mr. Thomas Buxton died in Somersville on Wednesday and was buried on Thursday last. She was the eldest daughter of John N. Jones, aged 40 years, and one of the old residents of that place. She leaves many warmly attached friends to mourn her sad death.

*Contra Costa Gazette*
October 29, 1890

## DIED.

BUXTON—In Stewartville, October 22, 1890, Mrs. Thomas Buxton, aged 40 years, 2 months and 27 days, a native of Pennsylvania.

*Contra Costa Gazette*
October 29, 1890

These newspaper articles from the *Antioch Ledger* and *Contra Costa Gazette* state that Margaret Buxton was the wife of Thomas Buxton. Marriage records state Margaret Cooper (a widow) married William Thomas Buxton in May 1886. Perhaps William Thomas Buxton was also known as Thomas Buxton.

The above article (on the left), is from the *Contra Costa Gazette*, July 26, 1884, and mentions Thomas Buxton and his children from a previous marriage, Della and Garfield.

# In Memoriam.

HALL OF MT. DIABLO LODGE, NO. 128, I.O.O.F.}
SOMERSVILLE, CAL., March 5, 1892. }

*To the officers and members of Mt. Diablo Lodge, No. 128, I.O.O.F.*

WHEREAS it has pleased an all-wise Providence to remove from our midst our late brother, William H. Clements [sic], and

WHEREAS in view of the loss we have sustained by the decease of our friend and brother, and of the still heavier loss sustained by those who were nearest and dearest to him, therefore be it

*Resolved* by Mt. Diablo Lodge, No. 128, I.O.O.F. of Somersville, Cal., that while we bow with humble submission to the will of the Most High we do not the less mourn for our brother who has been taken from us on the 29th day of February, 1892.

*Resolved*, that in the death of William H. Clements [sic] this Lodge laments the loss of a brother who was ever ready to proffer the hand of aid and the voice of sympathy to the needy and distressed of the Fraternity; an active member of this Order, whose utmost endeavors were extended for its welfare and prosperity; a friend and companion who was dear to us all; a citizen whose upright and noble life was a standard of emulation to his fellows.

*Resolved* that the heartfelt sympathy of this Lodge be extended to his family in their affliction.

*Resolved* that the charter of this Lodge be draped in mourning and the members wear the usual badge of mourning for a period of thirty days.

*Resolved* that these resolutions be spread upon the records of the Lodge and a copy thereof be transmitted to the family of the deceased brother, and to the *Contra Costa Gazette* and ANTIOCH LEDGER for publication.

Committee {
SAMUEL BROWN,
JOHN H. TRYTHALL,
J. C. McDERMOTT

*Antioch Ledger*
March 12, 1892

These articles concern Elizabeth's parents, William and Clarissa Crowhurst.

THE SOMERSVILLE SCHOOL—Says the Vallejo *Chronicle:* "Mr. Wm. Crowhurst has accepted the position of Principal of the Somersville, Contra Costa, school, and will enter on his duties next Monday. Miss Parker, late Matron at the Home, will be his first assistant and Mrs. Wm. Crowhurst, second assistant. The schools in that section are in a very flourishing financial condition and indicate a very generous public spirit on the part of the communities sustaining them. The Somersville school has now very nearly enough money on hand to run it for a year to come, and the Nortonville school has $6,000 in the bank placed to its credit. At the latter place the coal companies have an understanding with all their men that the latter are to give fifty cents out of every $100 they receive, to the school fund. The miners do this willingly, and it gives an income of over a hundred dollars a month ordinarily above and beyond the regular receipts from taxation."

Mr. Crowhurst is one of the best educators in the State and Somersville has been fortunate in securing the services of so excellent a man and teacher.

*Antioch Ledger*
July 21, 1877

TEMPERANCE LECTURE.—Wm. Crowhurst, of Somersville, State Deputy Grand Worthy Chief Templar, delivered a temperance lecture at the Congregational Church on Friday evening, Oct. 19. As a number of our citzens [sic] attended the Granger's ball at Point of Timber held on the same evening, the audience was not as large as the lecturer might have anticipated though a fair number listened attentively to the feeling and eloquent remarks of the speaker. Mr. Crowhurst is a ready and pleasing talker never wearies his audience and knows when to stop. He gave a condensed history of what has been accomplished in the temperance work by the Order of Good Templars and interspersed his lecture with pleasing anecdotes and illustrations apt and appropriate. Although a young man Mr. Crowhurst already ranks as a champion worker in the temperance cause in this State.

*Antioch Ledger*
October 27, 1877

# Somersville Memories

"I should like to add my story to the "Tale of Two Cities," the twin ghost towns, Somersville and Nortonville." Mrs. L. H. Harrington, of Berkeley, is speaking. "In 1877, my folks moved from Vallejo to Somersville, where my father and mother both taught school. There were three of us children, and later a sister was born, November 18, 1878, in Somersville. The only doctor was Granny Norton, general midwife and caretaker of both towns. I was 5 years old and Granny scared us with her big black bag, that brought the baby. Not long before that, there was a diphtheria epidemic. I came down with it but my sister and brother were sent to a ranch with many others to escape it. Doctors from Antioch and Walnut Creek came in to work. The hotel was the Scammon Hotel and George Scammon was our favorite playmate. There were quite a few hawks there, and the older children used to sing, "Chicken hawk, chicken hawk, carry me to Antioch." We younger ones believed and would run and hide, when we'd see a hawk. Mr. Hawxhurst was a leading man. My dad's name was Crowhurst and the youngsters would say the Hawk would eat the Crow. It was quite a climb over the hill to Nortonville and I remember my sister and I went around the long way, along a ravine. Sister slid down into the creek and I had to go home for help. Men came with lanterns to find her. I rode on the back of one of the men, to show where she had fallen. The Welsh miners were wonderful singers and had singfests quite often. My father had concerts and spelling bees as school entertainments. I have a lovely pair of vases that his pupils gave me on my fifth birthday, bought in Somersville. The only mode of travel was horse and buggy and there was a lively livery stable where you could hire horses for buggy or horseback. One time, riding down the hill, our horse slipped and slid all the way down, before he could get up. We were fortunate that the buggy didn't tip over. I have heard since, that Granny Norton met her death, in just that way. There was very poor sanitation, all the sewage and garbage emptying into big natural ditches. Both Somersville and Nortonville were very happy sociable towns. We had a neighborhood song that lived as long as the towns lasted. It went: From Somersville to Nortonville is just one mile; From Nortonville to Somersville is just one mile. —THE KNAVE.

*Oakland Tribune – Knave Section*
March 26, 1950

These articles spell the name of John Hay as "Hayes" and James Daley as "Daly."

---

## PACIFIC COAST TELEGRAMS

Fatal Boiler Explosion at Antioch.

ANTIOCH, December 17th. — One of the boilers in the Independent Mine at Somersville, exploded last night. John Hayes and James Daly were instantly killed and David Williams and one other man are in a very critical condition. Some pieces of iron, weighing several hundred pounds, were thrown a distance of over one hundred yards. Three other large boilers were moved by the explosion six to twelve feet.

*Daily Alta California*
December 18, 1873

---

THE DISASTER AT THE INDEPENDENT SHAFT.—A correspondent at Somersville, who stood within fifteen feet of the boiler at the Independent Coal Mine shaft on Tuesday last, and wonderfully escaped injury, writes us that the verdict of the inquest held on Wednesday, by Justice Abbott of Antioch, acting as Coroner, charges the disaster to the ignorance of the Foreman and the culpable negligence of the Superintendent. The engineer, John Hayes, and the fireman, James Daly, were instantly killed by the explosion, and David Williams and Henry Davis, so severely injured that the first named died on Wednesday, and Mr. Davis is still lingering in great distress; with very slight chance of life. All work was suspended at the mines on Wednesday, and the Brotherhood of the Working Mens' Association, to the number of about three hundred, attended the burial of the remains of the deceased engineer and fireman, both of whom were middle aged men without families, as we learn. The house and machinery of the hoisting works were completely wrecked by the explosion, and heavy pieces of the boiler and machinery were hurled with terrible force to a distance of a hundred yards or more, but, except the four persons named, no one is reported to have received any serious injury. Mr. Wm. T. Hendrick, who was standing within a few feet of the boiler when the explosion occurred, escaped with only a slight bruise upon one of his hands, and others, close about, escaped without injury of any kind.

*Contra Costa Gazette*
December 20, 1873

# DALEY, James

These articles spell the name of James Daley as "Daly."

---

MEMORIAM RESOLUTIONS. — The Resolutions of the Diablo Lodge of Odd Fellows, at Somersville, in memory of David Williams, and the Workingingmen's Accident and Relief Association, in memory of James Daly and John Hay, victims of the late boiler explosion at that place, came to hand on Friday at too late a moment for insertion in this issue, but will be published in our next.

*Contra Costa Gazette*
December 27, 1873

---

## IN MEMORIAM.

SOMERSVILLE, Dec. 17th, 1873.

To the PRESIDENT and members of the W. A. & R. A. No. 1, Somersville, Contra Costa County, California:

We the undersigned, your Committee appointed to draft Resolution in respect of the memory of our late Brother, JAMES DALY, who was accidentally killed by the explosion of the boiler at the INDEPENDENT Coal Mine, on the 16th day of December, 1873, respectfully submit the following:

WHEREAS:—It has pleased the Supreme Ruler of the Universe, in His infinite wisdom, to remove from among the members of this Association our well beloved Brother, JAMES DALY, therefore, be it—

*Resolved:—* That we humbly bow submission to the will of God in this dispensation of His divine providence, ever believing that He doeth all things well.

*Resolved:* — That in the death of our beloved Brother, JAMES DALY, our Association has lost a good and faithful Brother, his wife a most affectionate husband, and his relatives a kind kinsman.

*Resolved:—* That we tender our heart-felt sympathies to the wife and relatives of our deceased Brother.

*Resolved:—* That in token of respect to the memory of our late Brother, we will wear a badge of mourning and that the Charter of the Association be draped in mourning, for the period of thirty days.

*Resolved:—* That these resolutions be spread on the records in full, a copy sent the wife of the deceased, and that they be published in the ANTIOCH LEDGER and *Contra Costa Gazette*.

{ SEAL }    THOS. S. BROWN,
H. E. WARD,        } Com.
THOS. S. JONES,

JAMES RANKIN, Recording Secretary.

*Antioch Ledger*
December 27, 1873

THE BOILER EXPLOSION. — A correspondent whose article has place elsewhere, excepts to our remark of last week to the effect that, if the judgment of the experts, whose affidavits had been published, was correct, the jury of inquest was in error as to the cause of the late boiler explosion. We do not assume to be acquainted with the facts in the case; nor had we imagined anybody was suspected of a design to misrepresent them. If the judgment or honesty of the person who made the examinations and affidavits is distrusted, the authority should be invoked for such an investigation as will leave no doubt of the cause of the explosion, as it is only by a determination of such causes that the recurrence of such casualties can be avoided.

Contra Costa Gazette
January 10, 1874

THE SOMERSVILLE BOILER EXPLOSION. — An inspection of fragments of plate from the boiler that exploded at Somersville, which have been left with us by a friend, leaves us little ground of respect for the evidence of the "experts" in regard to the cause of the explosion, and the strength of the plates, to which we were inclined to defer, on reading their affidavits. We are still at loss for cause of the explosion, since its violence and force were so much greater than the resistance of a shell so weak, as it must have been, would account for. The pieces of plate on our table, which were chipped off at the request and in presence of the friend who left them with us, will hardly average the thickness of a twenty-five cent piece, and they have evidently been reduced by corrosion of the inner surface. We have no means of knowing to what extent the other plates of the boiler had been thus reduced; but can reasonably infer that all along the water line they were thin, except as they may have been repaired by patching.

The pieces left with us were taken from one of the ruptured plates, where Mr. Cole, in his affidavit, states that he found by actual measurement, the plates full "five-sixteenths of an inch" in thickness; and we are consequently constrained to believe that he must have made an intentional mis-statement, for we do not understand how plates of that thickness should have been ruptured by the explosion at any place, while it had only the resistance of less than a sixteenth of an inch to overcome at the point of rupture from which the pieces before us were taken, nor can we understand how, if he did find such a thickness of iron at any place of rupture, he could honestly have failed to notice that the plates were not much thicker than a piece of ticket card-board at other points of rupture. We are forced to conclude that the affidavits of the "experts" did not fairly and fully state the facts relating to the condition of the exploded boiler, and that the public, as well as those more immediately interested, are entitled to a more satisfactory solution of the causes of the fatal casualty.

Contra Costa Gazette
January 17, 1874

# DALEY, James

Although this newspaper printed the year as 1884, the article is from January 1874.

---

**Further Respecting the Boiler Explosion.**

SOMERSVILLE, Jan. 21st, 1884.
EDS. GAZETTE: In my previous letter to you I made a statement of facts which had directly come under my notice, without making a very strict examination. Since then I have made a kind of examination, and discovered some more facts which the "experts" in their careful examination did not happen to discover. I first found that new boilers had taken the place of the old ones, and that the old one had been condemned as unfit for further use; and I was informed by a former employe [sic] that they were to be used for water tanks. This certainly would not be done were the statement of the "experts" correct. I also found upon examination, that there were entire plates along the water line of the condemned boilers that varied from an eighth to a sixteenth of an inch in thickness. I also find places fully 5-16 of an inch, as the experts state. I also found that the steam gauges of the exploded boiler were and still are over two feet up from the bottom of the boiler. How the water could have been low enough for the boiler to have become red hot in less than ten minutes' time, and cause the explosion, I can not see, for Mr. Downey testified before the Coroner's Jury that ten minutes before the accident there was water in the two lower gauges, and steam and water in the upper one. I was also informed that a few days after the explosion, when the workmen were replacing the feed pump, which is a steam pump, it was found that the throttle valve wer [sic] perfectly closed, and in all probability was in taat [sic] condition when the explosion took place, and I was told the night of the explosion that not a particle of the machinery was in motion for at least twenty minutes before the explosion, thus making it utterly impossible for that being the cause of the accident. I also examined that parallel brace which the "experts" state would have required an expansive force of sixty thousand pounds to break it. Upon examination it will be seen that it is bent at almost right angles, and that there is a twist in it, indicating that it was twisted off; the twist being planly [sic] visible. It appears strange the "experts" did not notice it. These facts, in addition to my former statement, will no doubt convince any impartial mind that the experts made an intentional miss [sic]-statement to deceive the public, and nntil [sic] otherwise convinced, will be the candid opinion of your humble servant.

BONA FIDE.

*Contra Costa Gazette*
January 24, 1874

This article spells the name of Evan Davies as "Davis."

---

## IN MEMORIAM.

WHEREAS: - It has pleased the Supreme Chanceller of the universe to remove from our midst our late Brother, EVAN DAVIS, and

WHEREAS: - It is but just that a fitting acknowledgement of his many virtues and noble example should be made, therefore be it

*Resolved.-* By Black Diamond Lodge, No. 29, Knights of Pythias, that while we humbly bow to the will of the Supreme Ruler, we do not the less mourn for our Brother who has been taken from us.

*Resolved.-* That in the loss of Brother EVAN DAVIS this Lodge mourns the loss of one whose hand and heart was ever open to render assistance and give aid and sympathy whenever and wherever needed, a Brother to whom the prosperity and welfare of our Lodge and Order was the incentive to strong and unwearied exertion, a friend dear to us all and one in whom the feelings of friendship for those he loved was strong as life itself: one whose life was a fitting exemplification of the great principles of our Order, Friendship, Charity and Benevolence and whose many virtues are worthy of emulation by us all.

*Resolved.-* That as a slight testimonial to the worth and character of our deceased Brother, the Charter of this Lodge be draped in mourning for a period of thirty days. And be it further

*Resolved.-* That a copy of these resolutions, under the seal of the Lodge be forwarded to his relatives, a copy spread upon the minutes of the Lodge and a copy furnished the "Antioch Ledger" for publication.

{ A. A. PANE,
DAVID D. DAVIS, } Committee.
W. P. MORGANS, }

*Antioch Ledger*
January 27, 1877

# AN OLD TIMER DIES

## At Breneman's Hospital on Monday.

David Davis, Aged 79 Years, a
Miner at Nortonville and Farmer at Clayton.

At 9 o'clock on Monday morning, David Davis of Clayton passed away. He had been ailing for some time and had gone to Byron Hot Springs where for a time it seemed as if he might recover, but on Tuesday last he was brought to Martinez on his way home to the ranch at Clayton, where he desired to end his days. However, it was not so to be and the well known old timer died at the Breneman hospital where all that could be done for his comfort and assistance was done and every possibility of science made use of to save his life.

David Davis was 79 years of age at the time of his death, having been born in Wales in the year 1828. The cause of his death was Bright's disease.

It is difficult to give any details about his life; his friends, when it is a matter of strict fact, knowing very little of his life, except what passed before their eyes, while he lived among them.

The few details gathered amount to this that he was a Welchman [sic] that he came over to this country somewhere about the year 60, that he lived at Somersville for many years, working in the mines there and raising stock, and that some 25 years or more ago he came to Clayton and has lived there ever since.

Two children survive him, Mrs. George Schwartz who lives at Point Richmond and W. Davis, who was with the old man when he died. While at Somersville, his wife and two children had been buried there.

The bad condition of the roads will probably prevent the burial of David Davis alongside of his wife and children, but the place and time of his burial will be noted later.

David Davis, as one of his old friends says, was a good man, one you could trust and depend on, and if he had a fault; it was that he shared the obstinacy that is characteristic [sic] of his countrymen.

The old timer was respected and liked and his place will long remain empty for those who knew him.

*Contra Costa Gazette*
March 30, 1907

## Davis Services
## Set Saturday

Funeral services for William Thomas Davis, 79, who died last night at his home, 891 Mitchell Canyon road, Clayton, will be held at 2 p.m. Saturday at Brunscher and Connolly Chapel here. Cremation will follow at Mt. View Crematory.

He was the husband of the late Henrietta Davis, and survivors include two children, Melvin W. Davis and Mrs. Madeline Fragulia, and two grandchildren, Lloyd Davis and Jayne Fragulia, all of Clayton.

Born at Summersville [sic], an old coal mining town near Pittsburg, he had lived most of his life in Clayton at the ranch in Mitchell Canyon.

*Contra Costa Gazette*
May 27, 1954

## DOULTON, George

This article concerns George Doulton's son, Thomas.

### THOMAS DOULTON, ONCE SOMERVILLE MINER, DIES AT 62

Thomas Doulton, one of the two boys to enlist for service in the Spanish-American War from the little town of Somersville, died in San Francisco Monday at the age of 62 years.

Doulton was wounded in the war and had been in poor health ever since that time, spending his late years in government hospitals.

He was a native of Somersville and was a coal miner while residing there. He lived in Pittsburg for a short while but returned to San Francisco about two years ago. He was a member of Nelson A. Miles Camp No. 10, Spanish War Veterans.

Doulton leaves three sisters, Miss Margaret Doulton, Mrs. May Doulton Lee and Mrs. Rachel Doulton Burner and a niece, Georgia Martin Healy.

Funeral services will be held at 3:30 o'clock Wednesday afternoon at Ashley and McMullen's chapel, Sixth avenue and Geary boulevard.

*Contra Costa Gazette*
January 30, 1934

This article concerns Clyde and Lulu's father.

# LOREN DUNTON DIED MONDAY

----

## FUNERAL SERVICES AND INTERMENT ON WEDNESDAY

----

### Had Been Quite Seriously Ill About a Year and His Death Was Not Unexpected

A paralytic stroke, suffered about a year ago, followed by a general break-down of his nervous system, resulted in the death of Loren Dunton, who passed away at the family home, corner of Fourth and E streets, Monday afternoon.

Funeral services were held at the Preston Undertaking Chapel Wednesday afternoon, being conducted by Rev. T. Hector Dodd of the Congregational Church in an impressive manner. A choir composed of Mrs. T. Hector Dodd, Mrs. John Sheddrick, F. W. Breen and J. E. McElheney, rendered "Lead Kindly Light" and "We Are Going Down the River, One By One." Mr. Breen also sang a solo entitled "There'll Be Joy By and By." There was a good attendance of neighbors and friends and a profusion of flowers was banked around the casket, tokens of love from friends of the departed. The interment was in the Masons' and Odd Fellows' Cemetery.

The pall-bearers were George A. Knoll, M. D. Field, Sam Hobson, J. R. Glass, James P. Taylor and E. E. Thomas.

Although not one of the early pioneers of Eastern Contra Costa, nevertheless Loren Dunton had resided in this vicinity about thirty-five years and witnessed many changes. Born in Bath, Stuben county, New York, May 27, 1851, he grew to manhood at that place, working the greater part of the time on a farm during the earlier part of his life. From there he went to Illinois and spent several years in that state, being married to Miss Dora Laporte at Earlville, that state, in 1872. The same year they left for California, coming direct to this county, and located at Somersville, where Mr. Dunton was employed in the Black Diamond coal mine, then in active operation. About fifteen years were spent there, after which they took up their residence in Eureka, remaining three and a half years. Returning to Contra Costa, they located in Antioch, and remained here ever since. After coming to California from the East, Mr. Dunton took up the carpenter's trade which he followed up to a few years ago. He was a man of good habits, a loving husband and father and interested in the general welfare of the community, standing for honesty and integrity in public affairs.

Several years ago Mr. and Mrs. Dunton enjoyed an extended trip through the east and middle west states, visiting their former homes, it proving the last journey they were able to take together.

There survive besides the widow, a son, Adelbert and a daughter, Mrs. Frances Pettus, who have the sympathy of all in their sorrow.

*Antioch Ledger*
February 7, 1920

# EASTON, Mary

This article states that Mary Easton was buried in the "Stewartville cemetary" [sic].

## Obituary.

"In life, we are but in the midst of death"

All that was mortal of Mrs. Mary Easton was laid to rest in the Stewartville cemetary on the 19th of November. The death of our dear departed friend is but another instance to remind us that sooner or later we must all prepare ourselves for the same journey. Though we miss her from our midst none will miss her more sadly or feel her loss more deeply than her loved husband and three little children whom she has left sorrowing behind, for oh what is home without a mother? When she is gone home is no more, for none can guide our wandering footsteps like a mother, though the sunshine and joy and light of our home. Though she is gone far beyond their recall she is not dead, but only gone before — for we are taught by Holy religion that there is life eternal beyond this vale of tears, where freed from sin and sorrow the soul immortal expands into perfection where we will meet our loved ones across the dark river, there never to be separated. All will be united by him who died that we might live."

> When the last dim hours of death
> Had spread its vail [sic] of sadness o'er,
> The spirit of our love Mary,
> Left this dismal earthly shore.
> Mary we will miss thee sadly,
> And thy loss we'll deeply feel;
> But it's God who hath benefit us,
> He can all our sorrows heal.          J. W. B.

*Antioch Ledger*
November 27, 1886

**MARRIED.**

EDWARDS–EDWARDS–In Martinez, April 26th, by Wm. H. Ford, J. P., Hugh Edwards and Miss Catherine Edwards, both of Somersville.

*Contra Costa Gazette*
May 6, 1876

**DIED.**

EDWARDS–In Somersville, Nov. 25th, Mrs. Catharine [sic], wife of H. Edwards, aged 23 years, 5 months and 11 days.

*Contra Costa Gazette*
December 16, 1876

## EDWARDS, Emma

This article lists not only the death of Emma Edwards, but also of Robert and Mary Jane Riddock, who are buried in Rose Hill Cemetery. Their last name was spelled as "Reddock" in the article.

---

### DIED.

In Somersville, Feb. 24th, of phrenitis, or brain fever EMMA EDWARDS, aged 23 years, a native of New South Wales.

February 27th., ROBERT, only son of Alexander and Jesse Reddock [sic], aged 1 year and 10 months.

March 2d, MARY JANE, oldest daughter of Alexander and Jesse Reddock [sic], aged 7 years.

---

*Contra Costa Gazette*
March 11, 1865

## ANOTHER FATAL ACCIDENT.

Another of those accidents which have too frequently caused mourning in the community occurred in the Black Diamond Mine, at Nortonville, on Monday last, about noon, resulting in the almost instant death of John Edwards. He was at work, cutting under a "breast" of coal, and lying nearly on his side in order to reach under as far as possible, as is customary. When a certain extent of breast has been undermined, if the coal will not fall, a blast is put in. It frequently happens that the coal will crack slowly and come down of its own accord, giving the miner a chance to get safely out of the way; but in this instance, it appears that he cut into a seam or fissure which allowed a considerable quantity to fall before he could change his position, which he could have done had there not been a post behind to prevent. This obstruction was the cause of his death, as when found he was close up against it, showing that he had heard the coal cracking and endeavored to escape it.

As soon as the accident was known, all work in the mine was suspended, and everything was done to save the life of the unfortunate man, who was alive, but insensible, when extricated. Dr. McPhee was promptly on the spot, but Edwards was beyond the reach of surgical skill. A portion of skull was pressed in upon the brain without abrasing the skin. There were no contusions upon the body. Judge Mayon, acting coroner, was summoned, and held an inquest, which elicited the facts above stated, and that Edwards was a native of Wales, aged forty-one years old. He leaves a son about seven years old, in Tulare. As usual in such cases, the miners took charge of the remains, and on Wednesday they were interred at Somersville, beside those of his wife, who died a few years ago. The funeral was very large, and was attended by all his fellow workmen, the mines suspending operations during the day.

*Antioch Ledger*
September 24, 1870

### DIED.

EDWARDS—In Stewartsville [sic], Sept. 3, 1889, Joseph M. Williams [sic], a native of Wales, aged about 46 years.

*Contra Costa Gazette*
September 7, 1889

# ENGLER, Annie Henrietta, Charles, and John

## DIED.

ENGLER—In Nortonville, Oct. 20, Charles, son of John and Mary Engler, aged 1 year and 4 months.

*Contra Costa Gazette*
October 31, 1874

SUICIDE AT NORTONVILLE—John Engler, a German, age about forty five years committed suicide at Nortonville on Saturday last under the following circumstances. He was a shoemaker by occupation and had been to Black Diamond Landing to collect a bill, but succeeded in obtaining only one dollar. On retur- [sic] ing to Nortonville, he entered Sharp's saloon, called for a glass of beer, took from his pocket a bottle of strychnine, emptied the contents into the beer, said "good bye boys," swallowed the mixture and in two hours was a corpse. Medical aid was called and an effort made to save his life, but he refused to swallow an emetic and seemed desirous of ending his life. He leaves a wife and large family of children.

*Antioch Ledger*
September 11, 1875

SUICIDE.—John Engler, a shoemaker, with a large family living at Nortonville, died on Saturday evening last from the effects of strychnine. He survived in much agony some two hours after taking the poison, for the acknowledged purpose of destroying his life.

*Contra Costa Gazette*
September 11, 1875

DIED.

ENO — At Judsonville, February 3d. Susie, daughter of Mr. and Mrs. J. W. Eno, aged 7 years.

*Contra Costa Gazette*
February 14, 1880

# EVANS, John R. and William

---

**DIED.**

At Nortonville, February 2, 1877, John R.
Evans, aged about 35 years.

*Antioch Ledger*
February 10, 1877

---

**DIED.**

EVANS—In Nortonville, Feb. 3d., John R. Evans, aged
44 years, 11 months and 28 days.

*Contra Costa Gazette*
February 17, 1877

---

The article below refers to William Evans.

---

**DIED.**

At Nortonville, February 18, 1877, son of Mr.
and Mrs. John R. Evans, aged 2 years.

*Antioch Ledger*
March 3, 1877

---

DIED.

EVAN [sic] — In Concord, March 23, Mrs. John B. Evan [sic], aged about 35 years.

*Contra Costa Gazette*
March 27, 1886

# GETHING (GETHIN), William

## The Nortonville Disaster.

The terrible disaster at Nortonville Monday afternoon is the most fatal and distressing that has ever been experienced here in mining operations, always subject to great hazards. Up to this writing seven deaths have resulted from the disaster, and it is feared that one or two more may occur. Among those killed were several men of family, and who were among the most useful and highly respected members of the community in which they lived. A correspondent writing the morning after the sad occurrence indicates the anxiety and distress which the first rumors of the disaster occasioned among those who had fathers, husbands, brothers or friends in the mine. He writes:

"About 3 o'clock P. M. of Monday, July 24th, rumors of a terrible catastrophe spread through the village. Crowds began to gather around the mines, very anxious to know what the matter was. Women — wives and mothers — anxious for their loved ones, children trembling for the safety of their fathers, friends in fearful suspense for friends, thronged the approaches to the mines. The suspense was not long. It was broken by a terrible revelation. No less than six dead bodies were brought up from the mines in the course of an hour or two, together with eight persons more or less severely injured. The cause of the accident was a powder explosion, let off in the ordinary operation of mining, and that igniting sulphur gas and raising large volumes of what the miners call black damp or fine coal dust. Those who were brought up dead were smothered by the black damp-their death was almost instantaneous. Most of those who survived have been terribly scorched by the fire, and are understood as being in a very critical condition.

The deceased were: M. Lewis, aged 38; W. Gething, aged 35; D. Griffiths, aged 42; G. Reynolds, aged 29, T. Watts, aged 28; Wm. Williams, aged 18. The survivors are: Watkin Williams. Body Dumas, T. James, — Smith, T. Davies, D. Watts, H. Mannwaring, — Marengo"

A Coroner's inquest, held by Justice Woodruff on Tuesday, made the following report, viz:

NORTONVILLE, July 25, 1876.

We, the undersigned, called to investigate the causes of the death of the following mentioned persons, which occurred on the 24th day of July, 1876, between 3 and 4 o'clock P.M., viz: George M. Reynolds, Wm. Gething, David W. Griffiths, Theophilus Watts, Meredith Lewis and William Williams, believe that, according the evidence produced before the jury, G. M. Reynolds, W. Gething and D. W. Griffiths came to their death by burns or suffocation, or both, caused by the explosion of a blast which ignited coal dust, said coal dust igniting powder used by the deceased for mining purposes; secondly, that Theophilus Watts, Meredith Lewis and Wm. Williams came to their death by suffocation from said explosion.

| Thomas S. Griffiths, | David T. Jones, |
|---|---|
| Edward A. Dodge, | John N. Jones, |
| Robert Leam, | T. D. Howard, |
| Franklin Deemer, | Emanuel Grant, |
| Thomas Pritchard, | |

After the inquest, Mr. Dumas died, Tuesday night; and a dispatch received here Thursday forenoon reported two others — probably David Watts and — Smith — very low, and not expected to survive. Messrs. James and Davies, who suffered seriously, it is hoped will recover; and we understand the others, Watkins Williams, Harry Mannwaring and — Marengo are considered out of danger. There seems to be no difference of opinion as to the cause of the calamity, all the circumstances showing that it was occasioned by a blast which probably ignited the coal dust so that fire was communicated to a keg of blasting powder. Mr. Reynolds leaves a wife and three young children, and Lewis a wife and five children. Mr. Griffiths is also reported to have left a wife and several children to mourn his death. None of the other victims of the disaster, as we are informed, leave families. The six who were killed in the mine were interred at the Somersville cemetery on Tuesday. Mr. Reynolds by the Knights of Pythias, Messrs. Watts and Gething by the Odd Fellows, and Messrs. Griffiths and Lewis by the Cambrian Mutual Aid Society, the deceased having been respective members of the Societies named. Rev. Wm. Parry, of Nortonville, officiated in the religious services of the sad occasion.

*Contra Costa Gazette*
July 29, 1876

A Frightful Calamity. –On Monday evening a telegram from Nortonville requested the operator here to send immediately twenty gallons of linseed oil, as there had been a terrible explosion in the Black Diamond coal mine, killing six men and very severely burning nine others. The explosion occurred at three o'clock P. M. in the 400-foot level, the lowermost of the workings in what is denominated the new openings. The explosion is said to have been occasioned primarily by blasting in the mine, the coal dust igniting and thus communicating with the fire damp. There is also a supposition that a twenty-five pound keg of blasting powder in the mine also ignited from the fire. The names of the dead are William Gethen [sic], single; William L. Williams, single; Meredith Lewis, leaves a wife and seven children; George M. Reynolds, leaves a wife and three children; David W. Griffith [sic], leaves a wife; Theophilus Watts, single, and Theophile Dumas. Dangerously burned and recovery still doubtful, Thomas D. Davis, David Watts and Evan Smith. Slightly burned Thomas D. James, Harry Manvarring [sic] and Giacomo Larggo. Watkin Williams, asphyxiated, will recover. On four of the dead bodies there were no marks of violence, showing that they came to their death from asphyxia rather than from the immediate force of the explosion. The scene at the mine after the news of the explosion had spread through the town is described by those present as heart-rending. Women and children ran through the streets to the scene of disaster, each fearful lest a husband, brother or son might be numbered among the dead or burned. An inquest was held by Justice Woodruff, eliciting in substance the facts above related. Several of the dead men were members of the Masonic and Knights of Pythias fraternities and were buried in occordance [sic] with the rites of the Orders. All work was immediately suspended in the mine and everything possible done to alleviate the sufferings of the sick and distressed. During the past six years there has been a number of deaths from fire-damp in the Black Diamond, notwithstanding the great caution of the managers exercised in detecting its presence in the mine and removing the same by proper ventilation. Accidents of this kind are fearful to contemplate, and although perhaps no blame attaches to individuals in this instance the rules and regulations requiring thorough examination of the unworked passages daily should be rigidly enforced.

*Antioch Ledger*
July 29, 1876

# GRIFFITH, David E.

Although this newspaper article spells his name as "Griffiths," his gravestone says Griffith.

## A SAD AFFAIR.

### David E. Griffiths of Nortonville Meets with an Untimely Death.

David E. Griffiths an old and respected citizen of Nortonville, was almost instantly killed last Saturday evening about 7 o'clock in sight of his own home. Mr. Griffiths went to Somersville in the afternoon of that day to order coal and to get his mail. He rode horseback over to Somersville on as gentle a little pony as ever came to Antioch, and its former owner, C. W. Morse stands ready to vouch for its gentleness in the strongest terms. On the return trip home and when about one mile from the house the pony was observed galloping rapidly. Mr. Griffiths was in the habit of throwing his right leg around the horn of the saddle at times for relief, and on his left foot he wore a spur. It is supposed the sharp points of the spur irritated the horse and he broke into a gallop. When in front of the house Mr. Griffiths fell off the horse, probably from exhaustion after riding so hard and fell heavily against a barbed wire fence post, knocking it out of the ground and breaking three ribs on his right side near the arm pit. The force of the concussion must have been terrific. Hugh Medill and Rees Thomas, his stepson, who witnessed the accident, went to his assistance with a cart but he refused help and got into the cart alone. When they reached the house he got out alone crawled in on his hands [sic] and went to bed. Dr. George of Antioch was summoned and dressed his wounds. He was beyond medical aid, however, for he lingered until 8 o'clock the next evening, Sunday, when he expired. He retained consciousness up to the time of his death and was continually in conversation with a grandson by marriage. The Corner's jury on Tuesday evening returned a verdict of accidental death.

Mr. Griffiths came to Nortonville thirty-five years ago, and had resided there continuously until the accident. His estate consists of a 3/4 section of land and a number of cattle. The two grandchildren, by marriage, it is said, will receive the largest part of the estate. He leaves a widow two stepsons and four stepdaughters. Deceased was born in Wales seventy-six years ago and came to America when quite young. He was buried in the Somersville cemetery Tuesday afternoon.

*Antioch Ledger*
May 26, 1900

Although this newspaper article spells his name as Griffiths, his gravestone says Griffith.

## THE GRIFFITHS ESTATE.

————

### How a Large Fortune is Distributed Among Relatives.

————

### Will of a Pioneer of This County Filed for Probate in the Superior Court.

————

Last week David E. Griffiths of Nortonville, one of the best known residents in the county, while riding on a horse was thrown and received injuries that resulted in his death. This week in the Superior Court a petition for the probate of his will was filed by Attorney W. S. Tinning, acting for Samuel Brown and David Davis, who are named as executors in the document. The will is dated April 7, 1899, and bears the names of A. E. Dunkel and A. V. Ipswitch as subscribing witnesses. The matter will come up for hearing on the 16th of June.

The deceased left an estate worth $25,000, consisting of the Starr Hotel at Crockett, $8,000; 480 acres of land near Cornwall, $6,000; a lot in the town of Paso Robles, $1,000; live stock, $500; money in bank, $6,000, and claims against the estate of John E. Hughes, $2,000.

The only heir in this State is the widow. The others reside in the East and in Wales. This is where the great majority of them are. The following bequests are made: To his sister, Elizabeth Lewis, $2,000; to R. Griffiths, son of his brother, $2,000; to Mary and Ann Griffiths each $2,000; to his brother William Griffiths $2,000; to Warren and William Abrams, share and share alike, the S. ½ of Sec. 29 and the N. W. ¼ of Sec. 31, T. 2 N., R. 1 E; to Rees G. Thomas, the lot in Paso Robles; to Warren and William Abrams and Rees G. Thomas, share and share alike, all of the stock and farming implements; to Margaret Abrams, $1,000; to Elvira Thomas, $500; to his wife $100. He states that this is sufficient, as she has separate property of her own, and that during his life time he spent $5,000 of his own money in improving it. To David Griffiths of Pittsburg and David Griffiths of Macon county, Missouri, $500 each. All of the remainder of the property is left to Mary and Ann Griffiths, share and share alike.

He directs that his body be buried beside that of Joe E. [sic] Edwards in the Somersville cemetery, but if this is not possible, then his body is to be placed beside that of his old friend Thomas John in the cemetery at Clayton.

*Contra Costa Gazette*
May 26, 1900

# GRIFFITH, David E.

Although this newspaper article spells his name as Griffiths, his gravestone says Griffith.

## THE GRIFFITHS ESTATE.

--------

### Order Made Admitting First Will to Probate.

When the estate of the late David E. Griffiths came up in the Superior Court this week before Judge A. I. Buckles, it was ordered that the second will filed and bearing the earlier date be denied admission to probate. The will first filed and bearing the latest date was ordered admitted. Sam Brown and David Davis were appointed as executors to serve without bonds.

There are a number of heirs to the estate who reside in the east and in Wales. To represent these Attorney A. B. McKenzie was appointed. W. S. Tinning is the attorney for the estate.

*Contra Costa Gazette*
July 14, 1900

This article concerns Elias' father, Thomas Havard.

---

**DIED.**

HAVARD —In Martinez, October 30, 1893, Thomas
D. Havard, a native of Wales, aged 62 years,
7 months and 17 days.

---

*Contra Costa Gazette*
November 4, 1893

## IN MEMORIAM.

————

SOMERSVILLE, Dec. 17th, 1873.

To the PRESIDENT and members of the W. A. & R. A., No. 1.:

We the undersigned, your Committee appoint-[sic] to draft Resolutions in respect of the memory of our late Brother, JOHN HAY, who was accidentally killed by the explosion of the boiler at the INDEPENDENT Coal Mine, on the 16th day of December, 1873, respectfully submit the following:

WHEREAS: — It has pleased the Supreme Ruler of the Universe, in His infinite wisdom, to remove from among the members of this Association our well beloved Brother, JOHN HAY, therefore, be it—

*Resolved*: —That we humbly bow submission to the will of God in this dispensation of His di-divine [sic] providence, ever believing that He doeth all things well.

*Resolved*: —That in the death of our beloved Brother, JOHN HAY, our Association has lost a good and faithful Brother, his parents a most affectionate son, and his relatives a kind kinsman.

*Resolved:*— That we tender our heart-felt sympathies to the parents and relatives of our deceased Brother.

*Resolved:*— That in token of respect to the memory of our late Brother, we will wear a badge of mourning, and that the Charter of the Association be draped in mourning, for the period of thirty days.

*Resolved:* — That these Resolutions be spread on the records of the Association in full, a copy sent to the family of the deceased, and that they be printed in the ANTIOCH LEDGER and *Contra Costa Gazette.*

 {SEAL}

THOS. S. BROWN,
H. E. WARD,    } Com.
THOS. S. JONES

JAMES RANKIN, Recording Secretary.

*Antioch Ledger*
December 27, 1873

**DIED.**

At Nortonville, Nov. 14th, Richard Heycock, native of California, aged 9 years.

*Antioch Ledger*
November 17, 1877

**DIED.**

HEYCOCK–In Nortonville, Nov. 14th, Richard Heycock, aged 9 years.

*Contra Costa Gazette*
November 24, 1877

# HOWELLS, Isaac

This article concerns Isaac Howells' wife.

THE CAMBRIAN REUNION.—The exercises in celebration of St. David's day by the Cambrian Mutual Aid Society, at Platt's Hall in San Francisco last Monday evening, as reported by the *Bulletin,* were of highly interesting and pleasing character, and the Welsh population of our county had a representation in both those of a musical and literary character. Mrs. Howells of Nortonville, rendered a Welsh song, *Daffd y Gareg Wen,* with such pleasing effect that she was called out by the audience to repeat it, and a Welsh poem was read by Mr. Griffiths of Nortonville.

*Contra Costa Gazette*
March 7, 1874

This article concerns Isaac Howells' wife and daughter.

---

FESTIVAL OF THE CAMBRIAN SOCIETY.— The Welsh anniversary celebration at Platt's Hall last Monday evening was attended by representatives of the Welsh Societies and people of the entire state and coast to the number of six or seven hundred, including also many from the East, and the exercises were of a very pleasing character. The *Bulletin's* report thus mentions the performances of Mrs. Howells, of Nortonville, and her daughter:

The appearance of Mrs. Howells, who is better known to Welchmen [sic] everywhere as "Y Dryw Fach" — THE LITTLE WREN — was the signal for a most enthusiastic demonstration, and her exquisite warbling of the melody "Y Deryn Du" — the Blackbird — received an imperative *encore*. One of the features of the evening was the appearance for the first time before an audience of a juvenile vocal prodigy, Miss Howells, the daughter of the "Little Wren" who is now a pupil and the *protégé* of Professor Evans, and from whom great things, vocally, are expected hereafter. Her becoming modesty, naive appearance and sweetness of voice as she sang "The Bard," were irresistible and carried the audience by storm.

---

*Contra Costa Gazette*
March 6, 1875

# HOWELLS, Isaac

This article concerns Isaac Howells' wife.

## Old Nortonville

SONG BOOKS FOR shooting-irons. Community singing for gambling and dancing. A fine town chorus and band instead of jail and organized police force. Evidently not all ghost towns were "tough and rarin' to go" in the early days, for the above is a short, yet true, picture of Nortonville, once-thriving coal mining community of Contra Costa County. Delving into past history this is what is found by Mrs. Roy N. Wolfe of Pittsburg, chairman of the historical committee of the Contra Costa Federation of Women's Clubs. It seems Nortonville literally sang itself free of any possibility of a crime wave in the early days. Welsh people predominated, with a few Italian families scattered about, and at nights the surrounding hills resounded to the folk songs and anthems. The chorus reached its peak during the term of President Garfield, and when he was elected a holiday was declared, a member of the community dressed as the President was brought into town on the mine train, feted with a parade and reception, and honored by special songs from the chorus. Again, on Garfield's assassination, the chorus turned out and staged a funeral. A replica of the body of the deceased President was brought in on the train, was met by the chorus and band and a group of marchers and conducted to the local cemetery where a service was held. More dirge singing followed at night, when the ceremony was repeated with torch light. Probably the outstanding singer of the chorus was Mrs. Isaac Howell [sic], a washerwoman, who in her youth had been decorated by Queen Victoria. Said to have been born in Canada, Mrs. Howells moved to Wales when a child, and the excellence of her voice attracted the attention of the royal family. The Queen presented her with a silver replica of the Welsh national flower at a command performance and offered to educate her. She was engaged to be married at the time, and refused the offer in order to come to this country with her husband. Concerts in San Francisco won her wide acclaim.

*Oakland Tribune, Knave Section*
October 29, 1933

---

**MARRIED.**

HUGHES—HUGHES—At Hughes Ranch, near Nortonville, October 31st. By Rev. John J. Powell, David M. Hughes and Miss Maggie Hughes, both of Nortonville.

---

*Contra Costa Gazette*
November 16, 1878

# JAMES, Mary Ann

**MARRIED.**

JAMES—COOK— In Nortonville, June 30th, by Rev. W. Parry, Mr. Morgan C. [sic] James and Miss Mary Ann Cook, both of Nortonville.

*Contra Costa Gazette*
July 4, 1874

**DIED.**

At Nortonville, October 2d, Mrs. Morgan James, aged 20 years.

*Antioch Ledger*
October 13, 1877

**DIED.**

JAMES—In Nortonville, Oct. 2d, Mrs. Morgan James, aged 20 years.

*Contra Costa Gazette*
October 20, 1877

LOCAL AND PERSONAL.

...Mr. Morgan James, an old resident of the county died suddenly at Clayton on Wednesday. His remains were taken to Somersville for interment...

*Contra Costa Gazette*
September 6, 1890

DIED.

JAMES—In Clayton, Sept. 3, 1890, Morgan James, a native of Wales, aged 43 years.

*Contra Costa Gazette*
September 10, 1890

# JAMES, Thomas D.

This article identifies one of the three men killed in the July 1876 mine explosion as Thomas D. Jones, and not Thomas D. James. Additionally, five other sources list his name as Thomas D. James.

## Nortonville Correspondence.

————

### The New Monument.

NORTONVILLE, Nov. 19th, 1878. EDS. GAZETTE: Two years ago last July three young men were accidentally killed in the Black Diamond Coal Mines. These young men were far away from their homes and near relations when the sad accident occurred. Some of the leading citizens of the town suggested that a suitable monument should be erected to their memories. Last July a committee of five was appointed, consisting of the following gentlemen, viz: Watkin P. Morgans, John J. Powell, Wm. Griffiths, George Price and David Jones, to solicit funds for the erection of a monument. The Committee succeeded far beyond their expectations, considering the hard times and general depression of business. Near $300 was collected towards this worthy object. The committee sent forth proposals to some twenty of the leading marble and granite workers in the State, viz: Sacramento, Stockton, San Francisco, Vallejo, Oakland, etc. A large number of estimates were received. The Committee selected in preference to either marble or granite a white bronze monument, as being cheaper and more durable. They also ordered at the same time one of Kinney's patent tubular fences. Last week the monument and fence arrived, as ordered, and were set up immediately. The young men were buried in the same lot. The lot is sixteen feet long by ten feet wide. A substantial brick wall has been constructed, four feet high in the lower corner and about one foot high in the upper corner, above ground. The fence is of galvanized iron, two bars, with chain and neat urns and vases. It is by far the neatest and most substantial fence in the Cemetery, and is the admiration of all. In the centre of this enclosure the monument stands. The base is a solid sandstone, twenty-four inches square by twenty inches high. The bronze monument is placed on this foundation and strongly anchored to it. The monument is sixty inches high; base eighteen inches square, ten and a half inches thick; plinth fifteen inches square, die, eleven inches square, and fifteen inches long, with four moveable tablets. The spire is eight inches square at base. The inscriptions are made of raised work, or block letters, and are very attractive and neat. There are three inscriptions. The centre one is: "In Memory of David Watts," etc.; the south side; "In Memory of Theophilus Watts," etc.; and on the west side: "In Memory of Thomas D. Jones," etc. On the back the following: "Erected by the Citizens of Nortonville, August, 1878." The beauty of the fence and monument surpassed all expectations, the whole effect is one of harmony and beauty. The citizens of Nortonville deserve great credit for their liberality in erecting such a handsome and durable monument to the memory of deserving young men. Yours truly,                    J.J.P.

*Contra Costa Gazette*
November 23, 1878

---

**DIED.**

JENKINS- In Nortonville, June 23, Ebenezer Harris, oldest son of Thomas W. and Mary Jenkins, aged 7 years, 7 months and 19 days.

---

*Contra Costa Gazette*
July 4, 1874

---

**DIED.**

JENKINS- In Somersville, Sept. 14th, Thomas Joseph Jenkins, aged about 5 years.

---

*Contra Costa Gazette*
September 29, 1877

# JENKINS, Ebenezer Harris and Thomas Joseph

The article below concerns Thomas W. Jenkins, the father of Ebenezer, Elizabeth Ann, and two other boys, both named Thomas Joseph Jenkins.

CERTIFICATE OF COPARTNER-SHIP. Know all men by these presents, that we, AARON SENDERMAN and THOMAS W. JENKINS, residing at the town of Nortonville, Contra Costa County and State of Califor- [sic] do hereby certify and declare that we have organized and formed ourselves into a copartnership, and we covenant and agree each with the other, to be copartners for the purpose of carrying on and conducting a mercantile business for the buying and selling of general merchandise in the town of Nortonville, Contra Costa County and State of California, under the firm name and style of SENDERMAN & JENKINS. That the principal [sic] place of business of said copartnership is situated at the town of Nortonville, Contra Costa County, State aforesaid. That the names of all the persons interested as partners in such business are above stated and signed hereto, and that such partnership will continue and be in force until further notice by us. In witness whereof, we have hereunto set our hands and seals this eleventh day of June, A. D. 1874, in presence of J. P. Abbott.

Signed,      A. SENDERMAN,      [SEAL.]
             THOMAS W. JENKINS, [SEAL.]

*Antioch Ledger*
June 13, 1874

**DIED.**

JONES—In Nortonville, Nov. 20th, Austin Jones, a native of South Wales, aged 45 years.

*Contra Costa Gazette*
November 27, 1880

# DEATH FOLLOWED ARREST SUNDAY NIGHT

---

## FUNERAL WAS HELD THURSDAY FROM CHRISTIAN CHURCH IN CONCORD – REMAINS WERE BROUGHT TO THIS CITY.

---

Benjamin A. Jones for many years a resident of Clayton and well known in this county who has been living in Oakland, recently committed suicide by hanging himself with a bale rope in the Alden lockup at Telegraph Avenue and Forty-sixth street Sunday night. He had been drinking heavily during the evening and at last was arrested and held at the little lockup until the patrol wagon should arrive to take him to the county jail. When the officers opened the door to take out the prisoner they found him hanging from the wall dead.

Since the death of his wife recently Mr. Jones had sought to drown his troubles with drink and following his arrest of several weeks ago he told his sons that if he was ever arrested again he would kill himself rather than face the disgrace of going to jail. He was found with one end of the rope fastened around his neck and the other end tied to the knob of the iron door. The deceased was well known in Contra Costa county having resided for many years in Clayton and where he has numerous relatives residing at the present time.

He is survived by the following Children R. A., J. W., B. B., O. O., R. W., Earl and Miss Mary Jones. He was a native of Wales, aged 71 years.

---

The funeral of the late Benjamin A. Jones, formerly of Clayton, took place Thursday morning at 10:30 o'clock from the Christian Church in Concord Rev. B. A. Nesbit officiating. At the conclusion of the service the remains were carried to Clayton where the interment took place in Live Oak cemetery. The body was taken from Oakland to Concord this morning passing through Martinez on the San Ramon train.

*Contra Costa* Gazette
January 28, 1911

**DIED.**

JONES— In Somersville, Elizabeth, wife of Richard Jones, a native of Wales, aged 22 years.

*Contra Costa Gazette*
March 18, 1876

**AT REST.**

Died in Somersville on Friday, Aug. 15, Mrs. Ellen Jones.

All that is mortal of this dear old mother now lies by the side of her husband, who has bided her coming for twenty years. In patience and fortitude the dawning was awaited. Nursed by vigilant love, cheered by these twin blessings — devoted daughters and a Christian's hope, she passed from a quiet, happy, well-spent life on earth to the beginning of that other life, of which the Savior has said, "Enter thou in."

Mrs. Ellen Jones was a native of Pwllhelley, Wales, and for the last twenty-two years has been a resident of Somersville. She was the mother of five daughters, three of whom, Miss Jennie Jones, Mrs. John Trythall and Mrs. D. Williams, the last being a resident of The Pallsades, Nevada, are living.

A large concourse of friends, led by the Rev. Aaron Williams, gave to the departed the last attentions that may be given by loving ones, and in the sad, weird tones of that loved old Welsh hymn, commencing, "Yn y dyfroedd maurr ar tonau," wafted to the spirit land thoughts and hopes that this Christian mother learned long, long ago in her childhood's mountain home.

"E'en tho', it be a cross that raiseth me,
Still all my song shall be,
Nearer my God to Thee,
Nearer to Thee."

S.

*Contra Costa Gazette*
August 27, 1890

## JONES, John B.

> **DIED.**
>
> JONES—In Nortonville, February 9th, John B. Jones, a native of Tredegar, Monmouthshire, South Wales, aged 39 years.

*Contra Costa Gazette*
February 15, 1879

## JONES, Martha

> **DIED.**
>
> JONES—In Martinez, October 27th, Miss Martha Jones, aged 18 years and 9 months.

*Contra Costa Gazette*
October 30, 1886

## JONES, Thomas M.

> **DIED.**
>
> JONES—At Somersville, March 19, 1896, Thomas M. Jones, a native of Wales, aged 58 years, 1 month and 21 days.

*Contra Costa Gazette*
March 28, 1896

DEATH OF THOMAS S. JONES.—The funeral ceremonies of Thomas S. Jones, who died at Somersville on Monday last, were held on Wednesday. Deceased was an active member in good standing of the Masons, Odd Fellows and Workingmen's Association. The burial rites were under the auspices of the Masonic Order. The line of carriages extended over a mile — the largest funeral ever seen in Somersville. Work at the various mines was suspended, as is the usual custom on like occasions. He leaves a wife and three children. Deceased was about forty years of age. A just man, he dealt honorably with all men and his premature death will be sincerely regretted by a large circle of friends and acquaintances.

*Contra Costa Gazette*
January 9, 1875

## DIED.

At Somersville, January 4th, 1875, Thomas S. Jones, aged about 40 years.

*Antioch Ledger*
January 9, 1875

## DIED.

JONES—In Briones Valley, Contra Costa County, Jan. 5th, Thomas S. Jones, aged 44 years, 11 months and 5 days. The deceased was one of the oldest residents indentified with the coal mining interests of the county, and a man highly respected in all his social relations.

*Contra Costa Gazette*
January 19, 1875

# JONES, Thomas S.

## IN MEMORIAM.

WHEREAS:— God in his infinite wisdom has seen fit to remove from our midst, by the hand of Death, BRO. THOS. S. JONES P. G., the first V. G. of this Lodge, and a Charter Member: thereby severing the long unbroken chain of our fellowship: therefore be it

*Resolved:*— That while we bow with becoming humility to this stroke of God's providence, we cannot but deplore the loss of one who has long been a valued Brother, a true friend, and an honorable member of the order. His family has lost an affectionate father and husband.

*Resolved:*—That in the death of BRO. JONES P. G., our community has lost an industrious, useful and honest man: his friends a generous, warm hearted comrade, and our Lodge a zealous and worthy member.

*Resolved:*—That as a token of our esteem for our late brother, the Charter and furniture of our Lodge be draped in mourning and the members wear the usual badge of mourning for a period of thirty days.

*Resolved:*—That a copy of the foregoing resolutions be sent to the widow of the deceased and also a copy be forwarded to the ANTIOCH LEDGER, *New Age*, and *Contra Costa Gazette*, for publication, and the same to be spread on the minutes of the Lodge in full.

Committee, { THOMAS S. BROWN, P. G.;
HENRY E. WARD,
JOHN TRENGOVE.

The foregoing is a true copy of the resolutions unanimously adopted by this Lodge. Jan. 9th, 1875.          Attest, WM. M. SELLERS. R. S.
SEAL.

*Antioch Ledger*
January 16, 1875

---

**DIED.**

LEAM  In Stewartville, Oct. 3d, 1884, Margaret,
wife of Robt. Leam, a native of Pennsylvania, aged
48 years.
Funeral at 12 PM at Stewartville.

---

*Antioch Ledger*
October 4, 1884

---

**DIED.**

LEAM— In Stewartville, Sept, 3d, of pneumonia,
Mrs. Margaret Leam, beloved wife of of [sic] Robert
Leam.

> Sleep, gentle spirit, sleep.
>     Long vigils and in rest;
> Thy watch on earth no longer keep,
>     Awake in regions blest.
>
> We need not weep for thee —
>     Fond hearts their loss deplore;
> Fair Faith has set thy spirit free,
>     Upon a deathless shore.
>
> Adieu, until we meet
>     Beyond life's rapid stream,
> Released from pain, at Jesus feet,
>     Rest in a peace supreme.
>                                   W.  H.  T.

---

*Contra Costa Gazette*
October 18, 1884

## TESLA DOINGS.

————

### News Notes From the Corral Hollow Coal Mines.

————

...Robert Leam, who several years ago kept the Cosmopolitan hotel in Livermore, has been ill here for some months from an attack of pneumonia and is now very low. Little hopes are entertained of his recovery...

*The Livermore Herald*
February 24, 1900

## OBITUARY.

————

### ROBERT LEAM.

The death of Robert Leam at Tesla on Wednesday occasioned no surprise here as he was known to be in a critical condition. He had been a sufferer for many months from cancer of the stomach and death came as a relief. The deceased was for many years a resident of Livermore, having for a time managed the Cosmopolitan hotel. The remains were brought here and services were held at Feidler & Graham's undertaking parlors Wednesday at 11:30, which were attended by a number of local friends of the family. The remains were taken on the afternoon train to Summerville [sic] where the interment was made. Mr. Leam was a native of Manchester, England, aged 64 years. He leaves a wife and three children.

*The Livermore Herald*
March 3, 1900

# DEATH OF ROBERT LEAM.

————

Robert Leam, an old resident of Somersville, died in Tesla, Alameda county, last Tuesday. The direct cause of his death was cancer of the stomach, influenced by pneumonia. He was sick about four months, and until ravages of pneumonia commenced to assert itself no immediate danger was anticipated. His remains were brought to Antioch Wednesday and the funeral was held from the residence of his brother-in-law, Charles Baker, Thursday morning at 11 o'clock. Rev. A. E. Johnson conducted the services. The remains were interred in the Somersville cemetery. The funeral was largely attended.

Mr. Leam was born in England and came to the United States when but a boy. His early life was passed in the coal fields of Pennsylvania, where he soon became an expert at the business. The gold fever in California, however, attracted his attention and in 1858 he landed in Calaveras county and followed gold mining for four years, when he came to Somersville and entered the coal mines. He worked in all the coal mines in this vicinity, and in tern [sic] was superintendent of the Somersville and Stewartsville coal mines. For three years he followed the hotel business in Livermore, and about two years ago he went to Tesla and once more followed coal mining until his last sickness, just four months before his death.

Deceased was 61 years of age. His life was one of honesty and integrity; his feelings were kindly and charitable, and he was a good husband and kind father. Beside a widow he leaves six grown children — Harry, Robert and John and Mrs. Robert McClay [sic] of Somersville, Mrs. George Thomas of Sutter Creek, Mrs. Maggie Thomas of Sacramento, Miss Violet Leam of Amador City, Miss Ethel Leam of Tesla and a number of grandchildren — to mourn his loss. All were present at the funeral Thursday.

*Antioch Ledger*
March 3, 1900

## ANTIOCH SQUIBS.

...Robert Leam, an old pioneer in the mining districts, passed away in Tesla this week and was buried in Somersville Thursday. Mr. Leam has been in these coal mines for a good many years and was well known by all who were employed in the mine as a good Samaritan...

*Contra Costa Gazette*
March 3, 1900

## TESLA DOINGS.

————

### News Notes From the Corral Hollow Coal Mines.

————

...Robt. Leam, who had been sick the past four months, died at his residence in Jimtown Tuesday morning. The remains were taken to Livermore and the funeral took place Wednesday...

*The Livermore Herald*
March 3, 1900

## DIED.

LEAM —In Tesla, Alameda county, February 27, 1900, Robert Leam, a native of England, aged 64 years.

*Contra Costa Gazette*
March 10, 1900

HO FOR VOLUNTEERS.—Now is a chance for any that want to enlist in the service of Uncle Sam. Twenty-four men have already joined the company that is in process of formation in our county. Mr. M. S. Grover of San Pablo, and Mr. A. J. Markley of Somersville, are authorized to raise a Company in Contra Costa, to be Company D of the 8th Infantry Regiment. A bounty of $300 is paid to new recruits, of which $100 is paid upon being mustered in. This is paid by the United States. The State also pays $160 in addition, $40 of it as soon as mustered into service. If those enlisted are not needed for the full term of three years, they will yet receive the entire bounty when mustered out. Beside the above bounties, volunteers draw their regular monthly pay and their clothes and provisions, with medical attendance in case of sickness or wounds. Messrs. Grover and Markley are doing their best to fill up their company with 64 able-bodied men. As soon as they raise this number they will be mustered into service. The members of the Company elect their own non-commissioned officers. We hope to see the efforts to form a full Company in our county, crowned with complete success. Come forward, all ye who want to be soldiers. Now is your time.

*Contra Costa Gazette*
November 19, 1864

# MARKLEY, Andrew Jackson (A. J.)

POST MORTEM EXAMINATION.

Prior to its interment, the body of the late A. J. Markley was, by the consent of his relatives, subjected to an autopsy. The interesting character of the disease, scientifically considered, which so rapidly terminated his life, had induced his physician to ask such a concession in the interest of the profession. Accordingly the body was taken to the Somersville Dispensary, and with the joint assistance of Drs. McPhee, Holbrook, Carothers and Arnold, the necessary dissection was made. The entire thoaric viscera, with the exception of the heart, exhibited a normally healthy condition, but this latter organ showed even while *en siln*, marked hypertrophy of the left ventricle. Minuter dissection confirmed such fact. The heart itself weighed eighteen ounces, or, say eight ounces over the mean standard of that organ. The result of the autopsy went to confirm the diagnosis of the disease.

*Antioch Ledger*
May 7, 1870

THE FUNERAL PROCESSION

Of A. J. Markley, late County Clerk, was largely attended, there being present representatives from all the Lodges of Odd Fellows in the county, county officials, Sons of Temperance, and a numerous concourse of citizens, showing the respect and esteem in which the deceased was held. The funeral services were very impressive, although somewhat interrupted by the *post mortem* examination, which was deemed necessary at the last moment. Business in Somersville was suspended generally.

*Antioch Ledger*
May 7, 1870

## DIED.

At Martinez, on the 2d inst., ANDREW JACKSON MARKLEY, Esq., County Clerk, a native of Ohio, aged 41 years.

*Contra Costa Gazette*
May 7, 1870

## In Memoriam.

———————

Though we are comparatively a young community gathered within less than the term of a generation, from all sections of the conn-[sic] try, and all quarters of the world; and with few exceptions, are less intimate and less bound to each other, than those of older communities, those who have been longest together here, are brought to pause and consider the passage and claims of Time, as one after another is called away to be seen no more in the walks where we have been accustomed to meet them, through so many, and large a proportion of the most responsible and active years of life's labor. We are brought to realize then, perhaps, as at no other time, that we have been spending together, for good or ill, the best portion of our brief days on earth, and with better understanding and more unity of effort, how much better, possibly, we might have helped each other fill the measures and attain the ends of living in leaving the world the better for our lives in it.

Two of our oldest residents from the class of best known citizens within the week have been called to pay the inevitable mortal debt and have passed from the scenes of this life. Both have gone with the respects and regrets of those among whom they have been known so many of the years of our being as a community. John M. Jones after a long period of feeble health, died at his residence near Alamo in which vicinity he has lived for 16 or 18 years on Saturday morning last. His burial, under direction of the Masonic Order of which he was a member took place on Sunday, attended by a very large assemblage of people of the county desirous of paying this last token of respect to an esteemed citizen.

Andrew J. Markley, called by the suffrages of his fellow citizens to the duties of an important official position upon the discharge of which he entered only two months since, removing then from his former residence at Somersville, to the County Seat, died in Martinez, on Monday morning last, after a painful final struggle with a fatal disease that has occasioned the serious apprehensions of his friends and family during the past two or three months prior to which time his general health had been such as to create no suspicion of the lurking ailment. The final demise of Mr. Markley was so sudden that it caused a shock of surprise to his friends and the community of which he has long been a prominent and useful member. In accordance with one of his last uttered wishes that he might be laid with his children, his remains, followed by many mourning friends, were taken to Somersville for burial on Tuesday and outside the village, they were met by the members of the Odd Fellows Lodge and Sons of Temperance Division.

The funeral services at the church, conduc-[sic] ed by Rev. E. S. Todd and the services according to the prescribed ritual of the Odd Fellows, at the grave, were the impressive last tokens of respect to the mortal remains of our departed friend, the memory of whose generous and honorable sentiments as they have been revealed to us in the intercourse of the past five years. We hope to keep with respect while memory is preserved to us.

*Contra Costa Gazette*
May 7, 1870

# MARKLEY, David and Eliza Jane

---

**DIED.**

In Somersville, April 19th, DAVID, infant son of Andrew J. and Margaret Markley, aged 4 months and 11 days.

*Contra Costa Gazette*
April 24, 1869

---

**DIED.**

In Somersville, March 26th, ELIZA JANE, only daughter of Andrew J. and Margaret Markley, aged 13 years 3 months and 23 days.

Calm on the bosom of thy God,
Young spirit, rest thee now!
Even while with us thy footsteps trod,
His seal was on thy brow.

*Contra Costa Gazette*
April 10, 1869

---

---

DIED.

MILLS—In Black Diamond, Nov. 3d, Charles Walter, the only son of John X. and Elizabeth Mills, aged 2 years and 1 month.

---

*Contra Costa Gazette*
November 12, 1881

The article below lists the name of John Xerxes Mills (the father of Charles W. Mills) as "John S. Mills." John died in Black Diamond, King County, Washington.

---

## MINER IS CRUSHED UNDER COAL CARS AT BLACK DIAMOND

**John S. Mills, 69, Killed by Accident at Mine No. 11, Yesterday.**

John S. Mills, sixty-nine years old, one of the oldest residents of Black Diamond, was instantly killed while at work in Mine No. 11 at Black Diamond yesterday afternoon. He was struck by a motor train of coal cars.

Mills was working on the slope when the accident happened. He stepped out of the road of an approaching coal car into the path of the motor train.

He was a widower and is survived by three adult children, all residents of Seattle. They are Luther Mills, Mrs. Annie Davis and Mrs. John Lewis.

The body is at a Black Diamond undertaker's establishment. An investigation is being made by the coroner's office.

---

*The Post Intelligencer*
Seattle, Washington
September 19, 1920

# MILLS, Charles W.

The article below concerns John Mills, the father of Charles.

---

**I.O.O.F. AND U.M.W. OF A., ATTENTION!**

MILLS—At Black Diamond, Wash., Sept. 18, 1920, JOHN X. MILLS, beloved father of Luther Mills, Mrs. Annie Davis and Mrs. Edna Lewis, aged 70 years. A member of Wildey Lodge No. 54, I.O.O.F. and U.M. W. of A.

Funeral services will take place to-day from the Congregational Church, Black Diamond, at 1:30 p.m. All friends and members of above sociaties invited. Interment at Black Diamond by Butterworth & Sons, morticians.

---

*The Post Intelligencer*
Seattle, Washington
September 20, 1920

**DIED.**

MORTIMORE– At Somersville, September 4, 1894. Richard Mortimore, a native of England, aged fifty years.

*Contra Costa Gazette*
September 15, 1895

**DIED.**

In Somersville, Jan. 4th, of the same fatal disease, JANE RUSSEL, daughter of Thomas and Susan Muir, aged 4 years and 9 months.

*Contra Costa Gazette*
January 14, 1865

## NORTON, Sarah

**Death of an Aged Midwife.**

NORTONVILLE, October 5th.—Mrs. Sarah Norton, widow of one of the original locators of the Mount Diablo coal field, was killed near here to-day [sic], by a runaway horse. She was 68 years of age, and has practiced midwifery for the past eighteen years. During this time she has attended over 600 cases, and never lost one. It was while going on a professional visit that she met her death.

*Daily Alta California*
San Francisco, California
October 6, 1879

**DIED.**

NORTON— Near Clayton, October 5th, from runaway of horse and overturn of buggy, Mrs. Sarah Norton, of Nortonville, a native of Canada, aged 68 years.

*Contra Costa Gazette*
October 11, 1879

MRS. NORTON KILLED.—Mrs. Sarah Norton, of Nortonville, a lady sixty-eight years of age, was killed on Sunday last by being thrown from a buggy by a runaway team while on the road over the hill between Nortonville and Clayton. Morgan James of Clayton, rode a saddle horse to Nortonville to procure the services of Mrs. Norton as midwife. The saddle horse was hitched to a buggy and the old lady reluctantly consented to accompany Mr. James, her friends assuring her that the horse was not accustomed to being driven to a buggy. When descending the steep hill going toward Clayton the horse became unmanageable and ran down a steep embankment throwing both occupants to the ground. Mr. James was somewhat bruized [sic]. Mrs. Norton had both arms, both legs, and her neck broken dying instantly. She was the wife of Noah Norton who came to this county in 1860 and was one of the first locators of the Diablo coal mines. For several years past Mrs. Norton has quite successfully practiced medicine, giving especial attention, however, to midwifery. She had remarkable success and was highly esteemed by a large circle of relatives, friends and acquaintances.

*Antioch Ledger*
October 11, 1879

Correction.—In our account of the sudden death of Mrs. Norton last week it was stated that her friends advised her not to ride to Clayton with the horse brought over by Morgan James. We are informed by a son of Mrs. Norton that this was a mistake, and hence make this correction.

*Antioch Ledger*
October 18, 1879

# NORTON, Sarah

FATAL ACCIDENT. — Mrs. Sarah Norton, a lady 68 years of age, who resided at Nortonville, and was the widow of Noah Norton, from whom the town takes its name, was killed last Sunday afternoon by the runaway of a horse and the overturn of the buggy in descending the hill grade from Nortonville to Clayton. Mrs. Norton was a professional midwife and was on the way to answer a call for her services at Clayton, in company of Morgan E. James of that place, the messenger who had been sent to summon and bring her over. From the testimony given at the inquest held by Coroner Hiller the next day, it appears that James, on being requested to go for Mrs. Norton, went to James Curry's stable, in Clayton, for a team. Mr. Curry's son in charge at the time, told him the teams were all out at Mr. Gay's funeral, and there was nothing in but two saddle horses. James then said he would take one of the two saddle horses, naming as his preference, one known as the "race mare." When asked by the boy "How he would get Mrs. Norton over?" he said he would either get a team and buggy there or another horse to make a team with the mare. At Nortonville Mr. Green, the proprietor, was not at the livery stable, but was represented there by his son — a young man or boy — with whom James conferred about a team and conveyance for taking Mrs. Norton to Clayton. There being no carriage in that the boy thought fit to go out, or horse that he felt it safe to put in with the one James had ridden over, the latter concluded to borrow a harness and try the trip with the horse he had ridden over, in a single buggy, that the boy told him they were not in the habit of hiring out as it was old and not in good order.

Everything went well on the trip over until the first steep descent of grade towards Clayton had been passed and the comparatively level stretch along the spur ridge, before the last steep descent was reached. Here, upon her remarking that she was fond of driving, James gave the reins to Mrs. Norton, and had hardly done so when the horse began to kick and James was thrown out, striking the ground so violently that he was stunned for an instant, but recovered and regained his feet just as two boys on horseback, who were riding a few rods behind the buggy, rode up to his assistance. Finding him not seriously hurt, the boys pushed on after Mrs. Norton, who had gone out of sight where the road deflected behind an intervening ridge, with the horse in a furious run when last seen. They rode nearly in to Clayton without seeing anything of the horse, buggy, or Mrs. Norton, and just before reaching the village met two young men on horseback coming out, who reported that the horse had reached the stable with part of a harness and a part of a buggy shaft. This report left no room for doubt that the buggy and Mrs. Norton had been thrown down the steep declivity somewhere along the descending road grade over which the boys had just passed. And so it proved, as, on searching back, the buggy was found bottom up in the ravine at the foot of the 40° slope, some 300 feet below the road, and the mangled body of the poor old lady under it, with neck broken, left leg broken in three places, thigh dreadfully torn and a piece of the thigh bone entirely thrown out and lying apart from the limb; both arms broken, the right below the elbow, and the left, both above and below, and the body otherwise much lacerated and bruised.

The remains were carefully taken up and removed to the late residence of the deceased at Nortonville, where an inquest was held on Monday by Coroner Hiller, the following persons comprising the jury, viz: D. S. Woodruff, W. M. Reid, H. E. Ward, F. A. Saddler, John Tierney, Andrew Ferguson, John Burke, Frank Hollowwood, J. A. Barnard and J. W. Guy, who returned a verdict, in substance, to the effect that the deceased came to her death by being thrown from a buggy in which she was riding with one Morgan E. James, and that the accident resulting in the death of the deceased was due to the culpable negligence of the said James.

It is presumed the verdict is based upon evidence that James knew and had been warned that the horse could not be trusted to drive in single harness, and was not considered safe to go in harness, even with another horse that was accustomed to going in team.

*Contra Costa Gazette*
October 11, 1879

## 'Granny' Norton

ANOTHER FAMOUS character of the time was Sarah "Granny" Norton, a midwife, who was so accomplished in all forms of medicine and so well liked that no doctor ever managed to establish a practice in the mining district. One of the earliest settlers in the community, "Granny" was the wife of the manager of the Black Diamond Mine. She was constantly being called by sick persons in all parts of this section, and on many occasions traveled down to New York Landing, now Pittsburg and crossed the turbulent San Joaquin in a canoe to visit someone on the opposite shore who needed her help. After each birth at which she officiated, "Granny" planted a cottonwood tree, several of which are still standing in the yard of her home. Thrown from her buggy, when her horse ran away while she was going to visit a sick woman, Mrs. Norton died on October 5, 1879. The funeral is still remembered by many old-timers. "Granny" was never a devoutly religious woman. In fact she was somewhat of a scoffer. Just as her remains were brought into the church, a great storm broke that drove the people back to their homes and even caused animals to stampede for shelter. The next day friends returned to resume the service, and once again a storm broke, which drove them away from the church. Finally, the remains were taken to the grave and "Granny" was buried without a church service.

*Oakland Tribune, Knave Section*
October 29, 1933

---

**DIED.**

OLIVER—In Nortonville, March 17, Jane wife of Thomas J. Oliver, a native of Merthyr Tydfil, South Wales, aged 39 years and 6 months.

---

*Contra Costa Gazette*
March 27, 1880

## Thomas J. Oliver.

Thomas J. Oliver, a well known resident of this county, died suddenly in San Francisco on the 10th inst. He was going up the stairs of the Prescott House when he suddenly dropped and in a few minutes expired. Mr. Oliver was for sixteen or eighteen years a resident of Nortonville, where he was highly esteemed. For some time previous to his death he had been up the Coast. A few weeks ago he was in Martinez and was in apparent good health. His remains were interred in the Somersville cemetery last Saturday, under the auspices of the Masonic Order, many citizens not only from the mines but also from Concord, Antioch, Martinez and other portions of the county attending. There were also present from San Francisco Morgan Morgans, William A. Jones, Hugh Evens [sic], Ellis Roberts, William Griffith and others. Mr. Oliver's remains were laid by the side of his wife's body, who died several years ago and was buried in Somersville. One child, a daughter, is living, who returned to Wales some time ago. Mr. Oliver's death is deplored by many friends in this county and elsewhere.

Thanks are due Messrs. Rankin and Hawxhurst, who furnished free a train to convey the attendant mourners and friends from Los Medanos to Somersville, and returned them in the same manner in time to connect with the evening train on the overland.

*Contra Costa Gazette*
December 19, 1885

DIED.

At Nortonville, December 7th, JULIA ETTA, daughter of J. H. and Julia Piercey [sic], aged 2 years and 11 months. [(New York and Philadelphia papers please copy.)]

*Contra Costa Gazette*
December 17, 1870

The article below concerns John H. Piercy, father of Julia Etta Piercy.

**Nortonville Celebration.**

The citizens of Nortonville and vicinity held a grand picnic on the Fourth at the romantically located grounds near the Cumberland mine. The beauties of the spot selected were fully appreciated after suffering untold agonies in climbing mountain steeps, with sidling roads and clouds of dust. Some five hundred persons assembled early in the day, and the exercises were opened by a prayer by Rev. Wm. Parrey [sic]. The Sunday school children then sang several pieces, following which was the reading of the Declaration of Independence by John H. Piercy, and an oration by Rev. John Price. The speaker was listened to with marked attention and received frequent applause. Thirty-nine girls dressed in white, representing the several States of the Union with the goddess of Liberty were drawn in an open carriage to the grounds and accorded a position of honor in front of the speaker's platform. The Somersville brass band was in attendance and discoursed "music sweet music soft," while the lovers of the dance improved the opportunity afforded for this amusement. Notwithstanding the difficult approach to the grounds and constant passing of loaded teams on the narrow grade of the mountain, no accident occurred to mar the enjoyment of the occasion, and all took their departure homeward convinced that the generous people of Nortonville know how to get up a successful celebration.

*Antioch Ledger*
July 8, 1871

# PIERCY, Julia Etta

The article below concerns John H. Piercy, father of Julia Etta Piercy.

## Nortonville Correspondence.

NORTONVILLE, April 20th, 1875.

EDS. GAZETTE: Northeast from Nortonville nearly a mile, resides the patriarchal J. H. Piercy. His rural retreat is situated in a sequestered valley barricaded east and west by lofty chains of undulating hills, alive with the bleating of sheep and bellowing of cattle. A modern tourist, viewing the barrenness of the adjacent land, compared it to an Arabian desert. Partially true. But his ignorance was nursed in oversight and inexperience. He omitted the oasis skirting the bank of an inexhaustibly running brook on the Piercy ranch.

On Sunday a proposition to visit the desired locality was put into effect. After a brief chat with the proprietor, in one of his social moods we entreated a view at *Pet* (a model Devonshire and twin calves), also requested a survey at the poultry varieties. We were conveyed thence to the kitchen garden, containing trees of the plum, peach, apricot and gooseberry varieties, all with withered blossoms; but the blossomless trees were illuminated by fragrant rosebuds and variegated geraniums in bloom. A well of ice-cold water was enclosed within the garden fence, to which we paid a generous tribute. Indeed, at writing, like the amphibious otter absent from his watery element, our avaricious desire could only be satisfied by inward immersion of the exhilarating beverage. Facing northward from the porch of the dwelling the eye commands a view of natural scenery, worthy of artist's brush or poet's pen. By the aid of a telescope may be plainly discerned Collinsville, its whitened stores, residences, inhabitants and furrowed land on the background. Eastward may be observed Pittsburg Landing, with its railed thoroughfares reflecting the resplendent beams of a meridian sun. Nor is human anxiety yet satisfied with the sublimity of the grand panorama. Gazing still further, we behold two majestic rivers (the San Joaquin and Sacramento) pursuing their course, punctual to the influence of the queen of night, with solemn grandeur to their mother Pacific; the white-winged schooners gliding on their placid bosoms with almost instinctive accuracy to their ports of destination—unlike the Grecian Archipelago or Danube, neither infested with armed brigands nor bloodthirsty pirates. With the progress of civilization our waters as well as land has become the peaceful highway of commerce, from the dock at the metropolis to peasant's jetty at the interior.

Now, Mr. Editor, I wish to emphatically state, before concluding this epistle, that mine escort, including 'self, were amply compensated for our Sunday afternoon walk to Piercy Vale, the proprietor of which is better known by the familiar *sobriquet*, Honest John.          ALERT

*Contra Costa Gazette*
April 24, 1875

**DIED.**

PROSSER — In Somersville, Sept. 24th, Mrs. Mary
    Prosser, wife of W. Prosser, aged 52 years.

The deceased was a native of Wales, and emigrated to
America in 1848. In 1861 she came to California.
She was one of the oldest settlers in Somersville,
having lived there, and in the adjoining village of
Nortonville, almost from the first discovery of the
mines there.

Mrs. Prosser was a woman of deep religious convic-
tions, was a member of the Welsh church at Nortonville, and took a great interest in its welfare. Preach-
ing was often held in her house before any church
was organized in either of the villages. Her remains
were interred Sept. 26th, in Somersville cemetery in
the presence of a large number of friends and mourners. May she rest in peace.— [COM.

*Contra Costa Gazette*
October 7, 1876

# RICHARDS, Daniel

## DEATH OF DANIEL RICHARDS.

Daniel Richards, an old and esteemed resident of Somersville, died at his home at that place, on Thursday last, after a long and lingering illness. Mr. Richards had lived in the vicinity of the coal mines for the last thirty years, and had many warm friends throughout that district. His funeral took place on Sunday, and his remains were interred in the cemetery at Somersville.

*Contra Costa Gazette*
September 17, 1890

## DIED.

RICHARDS—At his residence in Somersville, September 11, 1890, Daniel Richards, a native of Wales, aged 69 years, 1 month and 21 days.

Mr. Daniel Richards was born in Wales July 20, 1821, and came to this county soon after the discovery of coal in Somersville, where he has spent the ripening years of his manhood. In December, 1888, Mr. Richards was called to part with his beloved wife, and the writer was then, as now, called to solemnize the departure of Mary, his wife, to a better and brighter country. Since the departure of his wife Mr. Richards had felt that all his earthly ties were severed, having no children to care for and no relatives, except a cousin of Mary, his wife. He had gathered some of this world's goods in cash, and also his home in Somersville. What disposition he has made of his wealth the writer did not inquire. His remains were laid to rest by the side of his wife in the Somersville burying grounds on Sunday, September 14, 1890, when the writer preached a sermon from John 3:16 to a crowded house. Mr. and Mrs. Tousey were also present and were invited by us to take part in the funeral exercises. Mrs. Tousey read to us the 23rd Psalm and Mr. Tousey made the opening prayer for the living.

WM. W. SMITH
Antioch, Sept. 15, 1890.

*Antioch Ledger*
September 20, 1890

## DIED.

In Somersville, Contra Costa county, January 31, of that dreadful disease, scarlatina maligna, Thomas Goulding, aged 7 years 7 months and 17 days.

At the same place, February 17, of the same disease, Elizabeth Richmond, aged 8 years and 5 months.

At the same place, February 19, of the same disease, Annie Tregellas, aged 7 years and 7 months.

At the same place, February 18, of the same disease, Joseph Tregellas, (brother to Annie,) aged 5 years and 1 month.

At the same place, February 20, of the same disease, Charles W. Blackburn, aged 9 years and 7 months.

These young creatures were taken away, with the exception of one, in about twelve hours. This new disease is making affecting breaches in our family circles. It seems that nothing can prevent it doing its work. Ten little ones have been swept away in a few weeks. The malady has proved fatal in almost every case. It is one of the most deceitful diseases in existence. The symptoms of death were upon one of the little sufferers in less than four minutes after his being taken ill. The pulse runs up to 154 or 160 in a few minutes.                J. J. P.

*Contra Costa Gazette*
February 25, 1865

Thomas Richmond will run as the Tax-Payers ticket for County Recorder in the election to be held 3 September. Mr. Richmond is a resident of Somersville.

*Antioch Ledger*
August 23, 1873

### DEATH OF THOMAS RICHMOND.

Mr. Thomas Richmond, an old and highly respected resident, was killed in the Hawxhurst mine at Somersville, on the 7th instant. Mr. Richmond was Foreman of the mine and was giving his attention to some matter at the foot of the slope up which a loaded car was being drawn, when the rope broke, and in swift descent the car caught and crushed him to a shap- [sic] less mass against the side-wall of the gangway. The death of Mr. Richmond deprives the community of a considerate and useful citizen.

*Contra Costa Gazette*
April 15, 1882

### In Memoriam.

To the N.G.V.G. officers and members of Mt. Diablo Lodge 128, I.O.O.F. We, your committee appointed to draft resolutions of respect to the memory of our late brother Thomas Richmond, respectfully submit the following

WHEREAS, It has pleased the Supreme Ruler of the Universe to remove from our midst our late Brother Thomas Richmond, and we cannot forget that there are others outside of our Fraternity who will mourn his loss as deeply as we; it is but just then that a fitting recognition of his many virtues should be had; therefore be it

*Resolved*, By Mt. Diablo Lodge No. 128 I.O. O.F. that while we bow with humble submission to the will of the Most High, we do not the less mourn for our Brother who has been taken from us.

*Resolved*, That in the death of Brother Thomas Richmond this Lodge laments the loss of a Brother who was ever ready to proffer the hand of aid and the voice of sympathy to the needy and distressed of the Fraternity, an active member of this Society whose utmost endeavors were exerted for its welfare and prosperity, a friend and companion who was dear to us all, and a citizen whose upright and noble life was a standard of emulation to his Fellows.

*Resolved*, That the wife and children of the deceased have our heartfelt sympathies in this their hour of trial and distress.

*Resolved*, That the Charter of this Lodge be draped in mourning for a period of thirty days and the members of the Lodge wear the usual badge of mourning for thirty days.

*Resolved*, That the foregoing preamble and resolutions be spread upon the minutes of our Lodge in full, and copies of the same be sent to the family of the deceased and to the CONTRA COSTA GAZETTE and *New Age* for publication.

All of which is respectfully submitted.

SAMUEL BROWN  
ED. MCLEOD     } Committee.  
H.E.WARD

*Contra Costa Gazette*
April 29, 1882

# RITCHARDS (RICHARDS), Mary

## DIED.

RICHARDS- In Somersville, Dec. 13th, Mrs. Mary, wife of Daniel Richards, aged 62 years and 5 months.

*Contra Costa Gazette*
December 19, 1888

## MRS. MARY RICHARDS.

Mrs. Mary Richards who died in Somersville on the 13th Inst, was the wife of Daniel Richards. They were among the earliest Welch [sic] families in Somersville, the deceased coming to her new home as a bride. She early become [sic] a convert and united with the Baptist Church. Her funeral took place on Saturday, and the large numbers who came from Empire, Stewartvill [sic], Nortonville and Antioch, testified to the high estimation in which she was held. The services were conducted by Rev. W. W. Smith, and at the grave a Welch [sic] poet sang a stanza of a Welch [sic] hymn. The mound that marks her last resting place was covered with the finest flowers, placed there by the loving hands of sorrowing friends.

*Contra Costa Gazette*
December 19, 1888

**DIED.**

SADDLER- In Nortonville, March 6, Harriet A., beloved wife of F. A. Saddler, aged 60 years, 5 months and 4 days.

After having been confined to her bed 18 months, during most of the time suffering the most intense pain, this Christian woman has successfully crossed that mysterious river to that bourne where suffering is unknown and joy is indescribable; as were our friend's suffering so will be her reward. Mrs. Saddler was a native of Yorktown, Va., and came to California in 1849, residing for some time at Benicia, where her husband, a Mexican war veteran and then a Sergeant in the regular army, was stationed. For 19 years they have lived in Nortonville, Mrs. Saddler, I believe, being the second women [sic] to make her home here.

> While the last dim hour of midnight
>     Spread its veil of silence o'er,
> The pure soul of our dear mother,
>     Left this dismal earthly shore.
>
> Mother, we have loved thee fondly,
>     But we will not ask thee here;
> You have suffered long and patient;
>     But you have gone to one who loved you dear.
>                         E.

*Contra Costa Gazette*
March 15, 1884

## Small Pox at Somersville.

We are credibly informed that there is one case of small-pox at Somersville. Persons are prohibited from entering the house and all possible precautions have been taken to prevent the further spread of this loathsome disease. By our exchanges we learn that in Solano County and in several other portions of the State this scourge has made itself manifest. The fearful ravages of this disease in San Francisco a few years since are still fresh in the minds of the people, and every sanitary means possible should be adopted to guard against its further spread. This remedy is going the rounds of the press, which we publish for the benefit of any one who may be so unfortunate as to become victim of this contagion. It originally appeared as a communication to the Stockton *Herald,* and is as follows: "I herewith append a receipe [sic] which has been used, to my own knowledge in hundreds of cases. It will prevent or cure small-pox though the pittings are filling. When Jenner discovered cow-pox in England, the world of science hurled an avalanche of fame upon his head; but when the most scientific school of medicine in the world — that of Paris — published this recipe as a panacea for small-pox it passed unheeded. It is as unfailing as fate, and conquers in every instance. It is harmless when taken by a well person. It will also cure scarlet fever. Here is the recipe as I have used it, and cured my children of the scarlet fever; here it is as I have used it to cure the small-pox; when learned physicians said the patient must die, it cured: Sulphate of zinc, one grain; fox-glove (digitalis), one grain; half a teaspoonful of sugar; mix with two table-spoonfuls of water. When thoroughly mixed add four ounces of water. Take a spoonful every hour. Either disease will disappear in twelve hours. For a child, smaller doses, according to age. If counties would compel their physicians to use this there would be no need of pest-houses."

Since putting the above in type, we learn that the young lady at Somersville, Annie Spowart, has died.

*Antioch Ledger*
June 8, 1872

## DIED.

In Somersville, June 7th, ANNIE SPOWART, aged 13 years.

*Contra Costa Gazette*
June 15, 1872

This article concerns David Spowart, father of Annie and Eliza Spowart.

## LETTER FROM NORTONVILLE.

———

NORTONVILLE, Sept. 15th, 1874.
ED. LEDGER:— The Workingmen's Accident and Relief Association, No. 2, of Mt. Diablo District, celebrated their first anniversary on Friday of last week by a picnic and grand ball. Owing to the early hour the procession was announced to start those who were at work during the previous night were unable to join the ranks. Nevertheless, about two hundred assembled at the hall and the procession was formed about ten o'clock, headed by the Contra Costa Brass Band, and Alexander Mulhern, mounted on a prancing charger, as Grand Marshal.

Passing in front of the Black Diamond store, the procession was brought to a halt, ordered to open ranks, and the Grand Marshal rode through until facing the balcony of the store, where the procession was reviewed by the *bon ton* of the town. The procession proceeded thence to the picnic grounds, where preparations were supposed to have been made to spend the day in merry-making, but lo! to behold, every available space around the platform was occupied by alcoholic vendors, and it would not take a Green Mountain boy to guess the result. Dancing was commenced at one o'clock and kept up until about three (save only when a sortie would be made on the platform by those who partook of the sediments compounded for the occasion, by those who want the last cent from the working man's pocket). The Committee who had charge of the affair are wholly to blame and should be brought to account for allowing intoxicating liquors to be taken to the grounds.

A deputation from Somersville Lodge, No. 1, attended the picnic. David Spowarts [sic], one of its early organizers, was called to the stand, and spoke for about half an hour upon the benefits to be derived from their organizations and unity of action. He also rendered a song on "Unity," composed by himself, for the occasion. He was loudly cheered at the conclusion of his remarks.

*Antioch Ledger*
September 19, 1874

## SOMERSVILLE NOTES.

—

ED. GAZETTE:— All mining work at the new Pittsburg shaft has been suspended for the time being for the purpose of clearing the shaft of the surplus water. The shaft is about six hundred feet deep to the landing station, with a sump of about 24 feet. A tunnel has been driven north a distance of 140 feet and the little vein struck, the coal being 2 ½ feet thick. An air shute has been driven up on the bogus vein about 380 feet and the old bogus gangway struck, and the water from the old works is now being drained off. The water is hoisted up in a tank holding 385 gallons; 260 tanks are hoisted up in the 24 hours, making an average of about 100,000 gallons a day.

Mr. and Mrs. Thos. Spratt suffered a sad loss in the death of their infant child on Sunday, Jan. 18th, after a severe illness lasting five days. On Tuesday the remains of the little one were deposited in their final resting place in the Somersville cemetery. They were encased in a handsome white casket tastefully decorated and covered with floral tributes, four young girls, Misses Lottie Thomas, Bertha Clifford, Rachael Doulton and Amanda Anderson, acting as pall bearers. Divine services were conducted by the Rev. Dr. Van Anda of Antioch. The funeral was largely attended by friends of the family, the mines closing at noon to give the men an opportunity of attending. Mr. Spratt's remaining child is also very sick with the scarlatina, but with strong hopes of recovery. The family has the heartfelt sympathy of the entire community in this their hour of affliction.

Mr. and Mrs. Spratt desire to return their sincere thanks to their friends and acquaintances for their kindness and assistance in their late bereavement.

Mrs. Robert Tait, whose life was for a long time despaired of, has under the careful treatment of Dr. W. S. George recovered, and is able to be around again.

The weather for the last week has been pleasant and warm, but all are looking anxiously for rain as the feed on the hills for stock is getting scarce. CLIMAX.

Somersville, Jan. 22, 1891.

*Contra Costa Gazette*
January 24, 1891

This article concerns Handel's mother, Mary Thomas.

## BURNS ARE FATAL TO MRS. THOMAS ON MONDAY AFTERNOON

Burns suffered by Mrs. Mary Thomas, 86, of Nortonville, whose body was seriously scorched last week when she rescued her son, Handel Thomas, from their burning home, proved fatal Monday at the hospital here.

Immediately after the fire Mrs. Thomas was removed to the hospital and little hope was held for her recovery because of her advanced age. She rallied remarkably, however, and the belief was later expressed that she might recover.

Monday she began to sink and death came at five o'clock in the afternoon.

Mrs. Thomas was 85 years of age and a native of Wales. In 1864 she came to California with her husband and they settled in the old coal mining town of Nortonville where she has made her home for sixty years.

She was the mother of Mrs. Sarah Davies of Pittsburg, formerly a resident of Martinez, and one son, Handel Thomas.

Funeral services will be held from the H. J. Curry parlors here on Wednesday afternoon at 1:30 following which interment will be made in Alhambra cemetery.

*Contra Costa Gazette*
January 29, 1924

# THOMAS, Handel

The article below, from the *Pittsburg Post* newspaper, spells his first name as "Handell," and the community of Somersville as "Sommerville."

## HANDELL THOMAS PASSES AWAY

Handell Thomas of Sommerville passed away Tuesday morning at the home of his sister, Mrs. E. G. Davies, Eleventh and York streets, this city. The deceased was 49 years old and had been in declining health for several years. His mother died several months ago as the result of burns she received while rescuing the son from their burning home.

The Thomas family located at Sommerville when times were flourishing there on account of coal mining, and it was there that the husband and father, Howell Thomas, died and was buried. When mining activities ceased there was a general exodus of the people, excepting Mrs. Thomas and her son, who clung affectionately to the old home and remained there until fire destroyed their shelter and they were compelled to leave.

Funeral services were held Thursday afternoon from the Nuttman funeral parlors where the Rev. Jas. Muir delivered the funeral sermon. Interment took place in the family burial plot at Sommerville.

*Pittsburg Post*
April 12, 1924

## LAST NORTONVILLE RESIDENT BURIED

Pittsburg, April 10. — Handel Thomas, last resident of the mining town of Nortonville today was buried at the place where he had resided for the 42 years of his life. Following services at the Nuttman parlors at Pittsburg the body was conveyed to the Nortonville cemetery for burial. Thomas died Tuesday, a few months after the death of his mother, Mrs. Mary Thomas, who sacrificed her life in rescuing her son when fire destroyed their home, the last building in Nortonville.

*Antioch Ledger*
April 17, 1924

## THE COAL MINES.

————

BLACK DIAMOND, Oct. 3, 1894. EDITORS GAZETTE:—This little hamlet which has for a long time lain still, is assuming the appearance of its old time prosperity. The coal mines at Nortonville, which has been developing for some time past under the able management of Howell Thomas, has fully shown its merits against all coal used on the river and now stands next to none in the market as a steam producer. This has demonstrated fully the report of W. B. Jones that the surface coal at Nortonville would hold its own against any deep coal produced in the county. It was on this report that the cars and dump at this place, which have lain idle for nine years, have again been put in use as a trial run on the coal, and now it is sincerely hoped by all the friends of "Little Howell" that prosperity awaits him now and for ever more. P. B. Cornwall, the well-known coal king, visited our town Thursday, after an absence of over ten years, and in company with W. B. Jones visited the various interests he controls. What it means no one knows, but it is evident a move of some kind is on foot. Strangers have been dropping in every few days and taking a trip to Nortonville. They are said by good authority to be capitalists looking up the situation. At the present time a number of teams are hauling coal from the mines. The daily Stockton boats are coaling here, and it is understood that they are to make this a regular landing for freight and passengers, when we can compete with our neighboring towns. A new wharf is about to be built by the steamer line known as the California Transportation Co. The cannery which was recently burned down is about to be rebuilt. The coal dumps and wharf are being repaired, and there is talk that a track will be relaid to the mines before the wet weather sets it. They have already started to open the Clark vein of coal at Nortonville, and in less than a month will be able to furnish a coal that is known and has a demand all over the State. Mr. Jones, who has charge of the coal business here, being not only a mining expert, has successfully developed and worked mines before and thoroughly understands his business. Mr. Thomas has been over thirty years in Nortonville and is thoroughly posted as to where the coal lies and the amount. All one has to do to be convinced is to take a trip with Mr. Thomas and take a look at the works he has opened. They will then wonder why it is that so much coal easy of access has been allowed to remain unworked so long. Taking everything into consideration our town is about to experiance [sic] a boom. Property has advanced 25 per cent [sic] in the last few weeks, and old timers who a month or two ago wanted to sell out and get away, no matter where, now shake their heads and say nothing. There is no doubt but what Black Diamond has a bright future and will soon assume its old time prosperity.

*Contra Costa Gazette*
October 6, 1894

# PIONEER COAL MINER AT REST

Howell Thomas Laid To His
Last Rest Sunday In
Somersville

Another of the pioneers of Contra Costa county and one of the oldest of the early day miners in California was laid to his final rest Sunday afternoon when the funeral of the late Howell Thomas of Nortonville was held from his home. Rev. E. G. Davies of Martinez, whose wife is a daughter of the deceased conducted the service and interment was in the Somersville burying ground. The pall bearers were W. N. Jones, John Ginochio, John Vaughn, William Thomas, William Latimer, and Warren Abrams.

Howell Thomas was a native of Wales emmigrating [sic] to the United States in 1856 and taking up his abode in Johnstone, Pa., for several years prior to coming to California by way of Nicaragua. Mr. Thomas followed prospecting for a year or two in Mariposa county before finally settling in Nortonville in 1861.

Ever since that date he followed the coal mining business in the above locality, customers coming from all ends of the county to prosure [sic] their yearly sales of coal from him, some of whom he retained for 30 years. His life long motto was: "The good to others I can do, I will do."

"His princely hand, his kingly heart was not bought or sold in 'cities mart'."

*Contra Costa Gazette*
May 22, 1915

# DEATH OF PIONEER

Old time residents of Contra Costa County will be pained at learning of the death of an old comrade in the person of Howell M. Thomas, whose demise occurred last Friday, May 14, at his home in Nortonville.

Mr. Thomas enjoyed remarkable good health throughout life, save for the past 18 months, when hemorrhage of the lungs set in, causing his death at the age of 78 years.

The deceased was a native of Wales, immigrating to the United States in 1856, taking up his abode in Johnstone, Pa., where he married his now widowed wife. He came to California via the Nicauraguan [sic] route in an early day and followed prospecting in Mariposa county prior to 1861, when he arrived in Nortonville.

Ever since that date the aged resident had followed the coal mining business, customers coming from all parts of the county to procure their yearly supply of fuel, some of whom he served for over thirty years. His life-long motto was "The good to others I can do I will do."

The deceased is survived by his aged widow, a daughter, Mrs. E. Glandon Davies of Martinez, and a son, Handel Thomas of Nortonville. "His princely hand, his kingly heart, Were not bought or sold in cities' mart."

Funeral services were held Sunday afternoon in Nortonville where the remains were interred under the direction of Undertaker George Higgins of Pittsburg.

*Pittsburg Post*
May 22, 1915

# THOMAS, Charles Morgan and Peter Benjamin

> Several cases of diphtheria among
> children are reported at Nortonville.

*Antioch Ledger*
August 18, 1877

> **DIED.**
>
> At Nortonville, August 12, of diphtheria, Peter
> Benjamin Thomas, aged 8 months.
> At Nortonville, August 12, of diphtheria, Charles
> Morgan, aged 6 years.

*Antioch Ledger*
August 18, 1877

This newspaper article from the *Antioch Ledger*, August 18, 1877, records the death of Peter Benjamin Thomas, and his brother, Charles Morgan Thomas, from diphtheria. The last name for Charles was not printed in the article.

# THOMAS, Charles Morgan, John H., and Peter Benjamin

## Nortonville Correspondence.

ED. LEDGER: — Since your espousal of our cause in the Berry matter your paper has been very popular with our citizens. You have not had any communication from here for several weeks, I might say months, and so I think it about time the mines were heard from. Work is quite steady now and the men are consequently in much better spirits and gradually working out of debt. We have shipped six trains of coal to-day [sic]. The Company has recently "placed" a new pair of boilers, which gives them five pair, four pair being constantly in use and one under repair. They are preparing to sink the Mount Hope slope for another "lift" of three hundred and fifty or four hundred feet, and will commence operations thereon this week. Also, they are about to construct a mammoth exhausting or drawing fan of 25 feet diameter, to be located at the main perpendicular shaft and rotated by a 24-horse-power engine. It is thought that this arrangement, although reversing the natural course of the air, will greatly improve the ventilation of the mine, though it is now very good. The Root blower now in use is showing signs of an early dissolution, hence this improvement.

Under the leadership of Professor Meredith an interesting musical entertainment was given at the Good Templar's Hall last Tuesday evening, which was well attended and greatly enjoyed by all present. The rendition of many of the pieces showed that clear conception of the true principles of instrumental and vocal music which is a sure indication of thorough, practical and theoretical training, and reflected much credit upon the Professor. We all hope he will favor us soon again.

Our primary election passed off in a very quiet manner, although there was much feeling manifested and great interest taken in its progress and the result. There were two sets of delegates in the field, one decidedly in favor of Mr. Barnard for Sheriff and backed by his particular friends, and the other in favor of the re-elections or nomination of Mr. Tyler for County Treasurer. It was generally accepted as a fact that this town could not have more than one representative on the Republican county ticket and that if Mr. Barnard was nominated for Sheriff Mr. Tyler would not receive the nomination for Treasurer, and vice versa. Mr. Barnard had unfortunately selected delegates favorable to himself but not popular with the mine management and of course they were beaten. There was no ill feeling against Joe Barnard, but against some of his delegates, he being one of the most popular men in the town and I believe in this end of the county. He went to the Convention a crippled man, so to speak, not knowing how they (the delegates) stood toward him he could say but little for himself, and was, unfortunately for everybody interested in the Republican ticket, defeated. There is great disatisfaction here at the result, but I suppose that the "powers that be" will see that a large vote is cast here for the

(continued on next page)

# THOMAS, Charles Morgan, John H., and Peter Benjamin

**(con't)**

straight Republican ticket. The claim that this place was only entitled to one representative on the ticket is all nonsense. We are as clearly entitled to two as Martinez is to six or seven.

There has been considerable sickness here among the children, while your citizens have been suffering from typhoid and other malarial fevers. Mr. Wm. M. Thomas lost three children within the past two weeks from diphtheria. No physician was called to any of them, though a man who has *lived* with a physician did prescribe for them. I wonder what has become of the "Quackery Law?"

Quite a number of our young people have been, are being, or are about to be, married. Mr. Geo. S. Miller has taken unto himself Mrs. Lena Thomas; Mr. Wm. W. Davis is about to take Miss Annie Jones, and several other couple [sic] are spoken of as about to jump over a broom-stick, but as there is nothing positive I won't give their names.

I can think of nothing more of interest; I am not sure this will be, so I'll close. Yours truly,    JNO BROWN.
August 21, 1877.

## A COSTLY ACCIDENT.

News of a costly accident on the Clayton hill last Saturday afternoon reached Antioch early in the week. A number of Somersville people engaged three double-seated carriages and a single buggy at the Concord livery stable for the purpose of attending the funeral of the late Mrs. Thomas, held on that day. The teams were driven over from Concord by men furnished by the owner to Somersville and then turned over to the parties renting them. Owing to a mistake at the Antioch cemetery, the mourners from Somersville were late in returning home. The first mishap encountered was on the hill just before Somersville is reached. The horses of one of the teams became balky and the ladies and gentlemen were compelled to alight from the buggy, in the heavy rain and mud. They all finally reached home in safety, but not until the rain had thoroughly drenched them. The teams were then turned over to the Concord men and they started on the return trip home. It was about 5 o'clock when they left. By this time the storm in the hills had increased in fury. While driving over the Clayton hills a terrific gale was encountered, which turned the four vehicles completely over, threw the occupants out and wrecked the buggies. It is said the men were not injured. They had a narrow escape, however. The damage done is estimated at over $500.

The article on the left, from the *Antioch Ledger* newspaper, August 25, 1877, states that "Mr. Wm. M. Thomas lost three children within the past two weeks from diptheria." The three children the article is referring to are Mr. Thomas' sons, Peter B. (died Aug. 12, 1877), Charles M. (died August 12, 1877), and John H. (died Aug. 16, 1877).

The article on the right, from the *Antioch Ledger* newspaper, March 8, 1902, describes an accident that occurred following the funeral of Mrs. Catherine Thomas. Catherine was the mother of Charles M., John H., and Peter B. Thomas. Mrs. Thomas was interred at Holy Cross Cemetery in Antioch, Contra Costa County, California on March 1, 1902.

## DIED.

In Somersville, December 29th of Scarlatina Maligna, JOHN TONKINS, son of John and Nancy Tonkins, aged 16 years and 3 months.

At Somersville, December 28th of malignant scarlatina, JAMES, youngest son of Samuel and Sarah Tergelais [sic], aged 2 years and 21 days.

At Somersville, Dec. 25th, of malignant scarlatina, MARY ELIZABETH, only daughter of J. E. and Lucy A. Wright, aged 1 year and 6 months. December 28th, of same disease, JOHN EDMUND, second son of J. E. and Lucy A. Wright, aged 9 years and 10 months.

There are scenes through which we pass in our journey through time to eternity, which are clad with the bitterest trophies of the power of death. All things earthly are frail and unstable. "Man cometh forth like a flower and is cut down, he fleeth also as a shadow." How suddenly? How unexpectedly were they called away? "In the midst of life we are in death." Bereaved parents, look across the flood of Jordan and see them happy, planting their feet on the heavenly shore, the land of ceaseless joy and deathless love. They are blessed. "Absent from the body present with the Lord."

We think as their happy souls were nearing the mystic Jordan and passing though the swelling floods, that a host of redeemed children were waiting at the portals of glory, singing welcome, welcome, welcome home, then led them through the golden streets of the new Jerusalem, and introduced them to the innumerable company of angels to the general assembly, the church of the first born whose names are written in heaven. Last Sabbath they were with us singing that beautiful song.

"I want to be an angel,
And with the angels stand.
A crown upon my forehead,
A harp within my hand."

Their sweet voices shall be heard no more in our Sabbath school. They have been removed from this vale of tears to the calm regions above. From the Sabbath school to join the shining throng who stand before the throne of God and the lamb. They have joined the white vested elders and angels to chant Hosannah to the son of David. One of them, a short time before he closed his eyes in death, was asked, are you afraid to die? He said, No, No, I am not afraid to die. Then he commenced to sing in the sweetest strains.

"Come sing to me of heaven,
When I'm about to die.
Sing songs of holy ecstacy [sic]
To waft my soul on high."

Then he said I am singing alone, girls why don't you sing with me. His sister joined him, that dying chamber was ringing with the sweetest music. About one o'clock a shining angel was sent to bear his soul to the skies, to receive the crown of glory, the palms of victory, the snowy robes of light. Let the bereaved parents take comfort, because they have reasons to believe that those from whom they are severed rested in Jesus. Follow those who have fallen asleep in Jesus. Darkness has been around the eternal throne, but we believe that a wise purpose moves behind the cloud.— "Therefore be ye also ready." Yours truly,

J. J. P.

*Antioch Ledger*
January 7, 1865

# VAN AMRINGE, Ellen

DIED.

Near Antioch, April 3d, ELLEN, wife of Benjamin F. Van Amringe, age 22 years, 7 months and 20 days.

*Contra Costa Gazette*
April 13, 1872

LOST.

BETWEEN ANTIOCH AND VAN-AMRINGE'S ranch, a Ladies Gold Watch and Chain. The finder will be liberally rewarded by leaving the same at this office.

*Antioch Ledger*
April 6, 1872

## CATTLE STOLEN.

Abel Vaughn of Nortonville was sick at Byron Springs for some weeks, and during his absence from home, thieves ran off fifteen head of his stock, there being no one on the ranch to care for the animals. The cattle were branded AV on left hip. They have been traced to the head of Marsh Creek canyon, where all trace of the animals was lost. It is supposed they were driven to Oakland or Livermore and sold to butchers. The cattle are short horns and mullys and black and white in color. Twenty dollars reward is offered for the recovery of the cattle and conviction of the thief or thieves.

*Contra Costa Gazette*
*February 13, 1897*

## Death of Abel Vaughn.

Abel Vaughn, an old resident of Somersville, was stricken with paralysis last Saturday and was immediately removed to St. Luke's hospital, San Francisco, for treatment. It is supposed he received another stroke Thursday which ended his life. Deceased was about sixty-one years of age and had been a resident of Somersville for about thirty years.

*Antioch Ledger*
*April 13, 1901*

## DIED.

VAUGHN—In San Francisco, April 11, 1901, Abel Vaughn, a native of Wales, aged 61 years.

*Antioch Ledger*
*April 13, 1901*

VAUGHN — In San Francisco, June 23, 1901 [sic], Abel Vaughn, a native of Wales, aged 60 years, 11 months and 28 days.

*Antioch Ledger*
*July 6, 1901*

## Value of an Estate.

The value of the estate of the late Abel Vaughn is given at $7000, and the heirs named are John Vaughn of Byron Springs, Abel Vaughn Jr., Mary and Nellie Vaughn of Nortonville, and Mrs. Elizabeth Walls [sic] of San Francisco.

*Antioch Ledger*
*July 6, 1901*

# VAUGHN, Hannah and Mrs. Hannah

> **DIED.**
>
> VAUGHN— In San Francisco, April 19, 1888, Hannah Vaughn, of Nortonville aged 20 years.

*Contra Costa Gazette*
May 2, 1888

> **DIED.**
>
> VAUGHN—In Nortonville, July 17th, Mrs. Abel Vaughn.

*Contra Costa Gazette*
July 23, 1881

**DIED.**

WATERS—In West Hartley, December 2, 1892, John Robert, son of Robert and Belle Jane Waters, aged 5 years and 7 months.

WATERS—In West Hartley, November 18, 1892, Edna Belle, daughter of Robert and Belle Jane Waters, aged 3 years, 2 months and 18 days.

*Antioch Ledger*
December 17, 1892

# WILLIAMS, David R.

MAN KILLED. — A shocking and fatal accident occurred at the Black Diamond coal mine, Nortonville, on Tuesday morning last. David Williams was engaged in work at the bottom of the Mount Hope Slope, his duty being to attach and detach the rope to and from the loaded and empty cars as they ascend and descend the incline of the slope. Having attached the rope, which is made of steel wire five-eights [sic] of an inch in thickness, to the loaded car, it was taken up as usual. Having risen four hundred feet, and when within thirty feet of the top, the rope parted, and the loaded car with terrible momentum went to the bottom again, crushing the man Williams to atoms. His limbs were broken in several places, and his head completely mashed. The body was immediately taken out, being at the time seven hundred feet underground. Coroner McNulty was summoned and an inquest held. Following is the verdict of the Coroner's Jury:

State of California, County of Contra Costa:

We the undersigned, the jurors summoned to appear before J. J. McNulty, acting Coroner for the county of Contra Costa, at Nortonville, in the said county, on the eighth day of July, A. D. 1873, to inquire into the cause of death of David R. Williams, lying at the residence of Wm. Prosser, in the town of Nortonville, in said Contra Costa county, having been duly sworn according to law, and having made such inquisitions after inspecting the body, and hearing the testimony adduced upon our oaths, each and all do say, that we find the deceased was named David R. Williams, was a native of Wales, aged about twenty-five years, that he came to his death, in this county, on the 8th day of July, A. D. 1873, by the collision of coal cars, and at that time he was hooking or unhooking said cars at the bottom of slope in the Mountain Hope Mine.          (Signed.)

Wm. M. Thomas,          W. C. Crall,
Thomas McLoughlin,     O. Clasby,
George Cowper,           R. A. Davis,
James T. Evans,           J. Cushine,
Robert Morgan,           J. Higgins,
                               David W. Rees.

*Antioch Ledger*
July 12, 1873

DIED.

WILLIAMS— In San Francisco, October 22, Watkin Williams, proprietor Black Diamond Hotel, Nortonville, a native of Wales, aged 54 years.

*Contra Costa Gazette*
October 29, 1881

### Obituary.

Another death has made it obligatory upon us to give another obituary notice, for there died in Oakland, April 22d, John E. Wright, a gentleman well known in this community, one of California's pioneers. Mr. Wright was born in the State of New York in the month of September, A. D. 1829, being therefore 64 years, 7 months and 22 days old at the time of his death. In the year 1851 he left the Empire State for the Pacific Coast, sailing around the Horn, and soon gravitated to this section, opening the first coal mine in Somersville somewhere in the early sixties, the exact year has not been ascertained. Here he continued in business till 1872, when he engaged in the vocation of erecting plants for the Giant powder works — which he followed till the time of his last sickness, which seized him some six months since while engaged in his business in British Columbia. Hoping that a change of climate and rest from all cares would again restore him to his wonted health, he came to Oakland, but he never rallied, and he finally passed peacefully away to that "bourne from which no traveler has ever yet returned."

Mr. Wright was a consistent member of the Masonic fraternity and well beloved by his brethren. He is the father of Newton, Arthur and Mattie Wright, and is uncle of George C. and Edwin Wright and Mrs. R. Metcalf and of Mrs. L. Dahnken, the last four being residents of Antioch. The death of Mr. Wright forcibly recalls the fact that the angel of death with his remorseless scythe has been cutting lately a great swath in the ranks of the pioneers of this State and soon they will all have passed across the silent river. It will be well indeed if succeeding generations will only engrave the history of their heroic deeds and indomitable energy on the tablets of enduring memory. Certainly the children of those who braved the horrors of a six months' journey over a then pathless desert, or successfully encountered the fearful tempests which greeted them as they doubled Cape Horn for the purpose of settling an almost unknown country, to make it the paradise it is to-day [sic], ought to remember the virtues of their fathers and put them late practice, too, so that by the exercise of the same patience, industry, perseverance, the future of California will be still more glorious than the past.

We extend to the bereaved relatives of the deceased our heartfelt sympathies. Death must come to all; may our lives be such that we will not fear him when he comes.

*Antioch Ledger*
April 28, 1894

# Chapter 6

# NATIVE SONS
# AND
# NATIVE DAUGHTERS
# OF THE
# GOLDEN WEST MONUMENT

# NATIVE SONS AND NATIVE DAUGHTERS OF THE GOLDEN WEST MONUMENT

In October 1934, Stirling Parlor No. 146, Native Daughters of the Golden West, and Diamond Parlor, No. 246, Native Sons of the Golden West, erected a 10-foot high monument in Rose Hill Cemetery "in memory of the pioneers of Nortonville and Somersville." The following newspaper articles discuss the monument planning and subsequent dedication on October 7, 1934.

Reference 98.16

Native Sons and Native Daughters monument, 1962. Photograph by Madison Devlin.

East Bay Regional Park District

## PIONEER MARKER TO BE ERECTED AT SOMERSVILLE

Pittsburg Parlor, Native Daughters of the Golden West, is arranging to place a suitable marker at the entrance of the old Somersville cemetery, where many pioneers of Contra Costa County are at rest.

A committee consisting of Mrs. Amy McAvoy, past grand president; Mrs. Estelle Evans, past grand president, and Mrs. Margaret Delph has been selected to investigate the plan.

*Antioch Ledger*
*June 29, 1934*

## Nortonville Shaft Plans Given Boost

PITTSBURG, July 21. – Plans for the erection of a monument at the old Nortonville Cemetery, situated in the ghost mining area south of here, in honor of the many pioneers buried there, were being furthered today by special committee workers of the Sterling [sic] Parlor of Native Daughters.

Mrs. Estelle Evans and Mrs. Amy McAvoy were named as joint chairmen when the project was approved, and the following persons have been named to assist them: Mrs. Vera Laederich, Mrs. Rose Noia, Mrs. Ethel Schmalholtz, Miss Mary Felix, Mrs. Leslie Clement, Mrs. Margaret Delp and Mrs. Marie Antrobus.

*Oakland Tribune*
*July 22, 1934*

We hear that Bill Cohn has donated to the Native Daughters in behalf of Columbia Steel Co., the plaque which is to be placed on the monument to the pioneer miners at the old cemetery, saving the Daughters about $2,000.

*Pittsburg Post Dispatch*
*August 16, 1934*

## Memorial Will Be Dedicated at Somersville Oct. 7

The Native Daughters of the Golden West are making preparations for dedicating the monument in honor of the pioneers of Nortonville and Somersville on Sunday, October 7, at 1:30 p.m.

The monument is a ten-foot concrete shaft, which has been placed in the old Somersville cemetery where many pioneers of the county and relatives of many Antioch and Pittsburg residents are buried.

The ceremony will be under the auspices of the Pittsburg Parlor of Native Daughters, and many members of the order from all over the State, as well as those interested in the historical shrines of pioneer days will be present.

In the monument will be placed a memorial plaque, which was donated by the Columbia Steel Company through Superintendent William Cohn. It is inscribed:

"Erected by Stirling Parlor, No. 146 N. D. G. W. and Diamond Parlor, N. S. G. W. in memory of the pioneers of Nortonville and Somersville."

Mrs. Amy McAvoy of Pittsburg, former grand president of the Native Daughters, is chairman of the program which she will announce in detail next week.

*Antioch Ledger*
*September 24, 1934*

# Native Daughters Plan for Memorial Shaft Dedication

## Monument Already Half Completed; Ceremony To Be Attended by Many

With the monument in memory of the Nortonville and Somersville pioneers half completed, Stirling Parlor No. 146 Native Daughters of the Golden West was making final plans today for dedication ceremonies.

The ten-foot concrete shaft, situated in the old Somersville cemetery, will be dedicated October 7th at one-thirty p.m. with all Native Daughters and Native Sons of Contra Costa county taking part.

Many pioneers of the region have signified their intentions to be present and city, county, and state officials have been invited to attend.

### Plaque Donated

A $200 plaque, donated by the Columbia Steel company through Superintendent William Cohn, will be placed in the monument.

It is inscribed: "Erected by Stirling Parlor No. 146, N. D. G. W. and Diamond Parlor No. 246, N. S. G. W. in memory of the pioneers of Nortonville and Somersville."

A sketch of the history of the two Contra Costa "ghost towns" follows: The discovery of the famous Mount Diablo coal fields was the immediate cause of the existence of the town of Nortonville.

Francis Somers and James T. Cruikshank were the discovers of the Black Diamond vein, and Noah Norton, after whom Nortonville was named, soon afterward located the Black Diamond mine.

### Norton Early Builder

In the basin where were located the principle mine lands, the town soon grew up, the first house being built in 1851 by Norton. A cosmopolitan community of English, Welsh and Americans from all states soon developed.

In 1874 part of the town was wiped out by fire, and in 1876 six miners were killed by an explosion in the depths of the mine.

Nortonville was connected with New York Landing by the Black Diamond railroad and with Pittsburg Landing by a private rail line.

Somersville, also built in the basin of coal lands and also connected with Pittsburg Landing by rail, began as a city about 1860 with the opening of the Pittsburg mine. The town was named for Francis Somers.

This *Pittsburg Post Dispatch* newspaper article from September 20, 1934 states that a $200 plaque was donated for the monument. However the *Pittsburg Post Dispatch* newspaper August 16, 1934, states that the price of the plaque is about $2,000.

## Monument Honors Cities' Pioneers

State, county and city officials have been invited to attend dedication of a monument at Somersville erected in honor of the pioneer residents of Nortonville and Somersville, "ghost" towns of the county, on Sunday, October 7. The dedication will be in the Somersville cemetery.

Ceremonies are being arranged by the Native Sons and Native Daughters of Pittsburg and Sheriff R. R. Veale, one of the oldest, from the point of membership, in the Native Sons, will be one of the honored guests.

*Martinez Herald*
*September 28, 1934*

## Dedication of Pioneer Tablet At Somersville

Ceremony Honoring Settlers of Ghost Towns Will Be Held Sunday at 1:30 O'clock.

Pioneers of the Antioch and Pittsburg district who formerly resided in Nortonville or Somersville, and also members of the Native Sons and Native Daughters of this district are planning to attend the dedication Sunday of the memorial tablet, erected in memory of the pioneers of Contra Costa County's ghost towns.

Mrs. Amy McAvoy of Pittsburg is in charge of the program, which will be held at the Nortonville cemetery and she is being assisted by members of Stirling Parlor, Native Daughters of the Golden West.

Invitations have been issued to city and county officials and to all civic and fraternal organizations to be present at the dedication. Relatives of many people from this section found their last resting place in the historic cemetery and it is anticipated there will be a large crowd.

Among the notables to attend and who will speak a few words are Dr. Mariana Bertola, past president of the California Federation of Woman's Clubs and past president of the Native Daughters; Senator Will R. Sharkey, Sheriff R. R. Veale, Joseph Mulhare and Richard Uren of Antioch.

The three latter are charter members of general Winn Parlor, Native Sons of the Golden West, and have been members of the order for fifty years. Master of Ceremonies will be William Buchanan, chairman of the Contra Costa County Board of Supervisors.

Rev. C. C. Champlin, pastor of the Pittsburg Community church will pronounce the invocation and Mayor Hugh Donovan of Pittsburg will give a short address. After the benediction the Pittsburg Band, under the direction of Jack King will play "Taps" and a wreath will be laid at the foot of the monument in memory of the pioneers.

The program will open at one-thirty o'clock.

*Antioch Ledger*
*October 5, 1934*

## Somersville Rites Mark Dedication Of Pioneer Shaft

More than 200 members of the Native Sons and Native Daughters of the Golden West, pioneers of Nortonville and Somersville and county and city officials were present at the dedication of the marker at Somersville cemetery yesterday.

J. W. [sic] Buchanan, chairman of the board of supervisors, was master of ceremonies. Rev. C. C. Champlin of Pittsburg Community church gave the invocation and benediction.

Mayor Hugh H. Donovan made the address of welcome, congratulating Stirling Parlor for its fine work in preparing the monmument.

### Dr. Bertola Talks

Dr. Mariana Bertola, past "flag" grand president, spoke in memory of the pioneers and of the American flag, telling its meaning to the early settlers here.

District attorney James F. Hoey addressed the gathering on the pioneer days and the history of the "ghost towns." He was followed by Sheriff R. R. Veale, in-
(Continued on Page Three.)

## Somersville
(Continued from Page One.)
troduced by Chairman Buchanan as one of three oldest members of the Native Sons in Contra Costa county.

Sheriff Veale, Joseph Mulhare and Richard Uren, the latter two of Antioch, have belonged to the Antioch General Winn Parlor for the past fifty years.

Other speakers included Charles Dodge, past grand president of the N. S. G. W., Mrs. Estelle Evans, past grand president of the Native Daughters, and Mrs. Amy V. McAvoy, past grand president.

Mrs. McAvoy, also chairman of arranging for the monument, thanked General Superintendent William Cohn of Columbia Steel for the plaque dedicated by the plant.

Mrs. Alpha Barnes, president of Stirling Parlor, and Salvatore Carusa of Diamond Parlor were introduced.

The monument was unveiled by Adrian Clement, and Mrs. Lavina Nicholls of San Francisco, mother of Mrs. McAvoy and pioneer of the district, laid a wreathe [sic] at the foot of the shaft.

*Pittsburg Post Dispatch*
October 8, 1934

# Dedication of Monument to Pioneers Sunday

Somersville Cemetery Scene of Unique Ceremony Yesterday Afternoon Under Organizations' Auspices.

With the unveiling of the monument and memorial marker yesterday afternoon at the Somersville Cemetery, time was rolled back two or three decades for many Antioch and Pittsburg people. There was a large gathering to witness the dedication ceremony which was held under the auspices of Stirling Parlor, Native daughters of the Golden West and Diamond Parlor, Native Sons.

The monument was inscribed to the memory of the pioneers of Somersville and Nortonville of which little remains but the cemetery and the entrance to the mine.

Mrs. Amy McAvoy was chairman and William Buchanan, chairman of the Board of Supervisors was master of ceremonies. The speakers all made references to the past, and to some of the older people present it was hard to realize that the hills were no longer covered with houses and that the bustling, thriving communities were gone.

Mayor Hugh Donovan of Pittsburg as the first speaker. He said:

"This place will always be regarded as a shrine because it contains the remains of the pioneers of this community. We'll always remember the men who went down to the mines for their daily bread, and the women who stood by to encourage them. It was a hard life but it was not without its joys. What one had shared with the others and everyone stood ready to help in any emergency.

"Those pioneers worked hard so that their children might enjoy a fuller life than they had known."

Dr. Mariana Bertola, past grand president of the Native Daughters and past president of the California State Federation of Women's Clubs was the next speaker. She said:

"This is a thrilling occasion. We should not be somber about it but jubilant. When we think of what these mighty hills meant to the pioneers, it is symbolic of the future.

"These pioneers didn't have what we have today. They didn't come here in automobiles as we do today and things were not easy for them, but they had one thing we do not have, contentment.

"In California we are going through crucial times. You who are descendants of these pioneers know the Bear Flag stands for something. Those who brought it here stood for a safe and sane government. It is our duty and the duty of the young to come to this hallowed spot and reflect upon the heritage they have given us. There is so much breaking down of old ideals. We are beginning to forget what these who we are honoring today worked for. We are getting lost in Utopian dreams. It is all right to look at the clouds but we must have our feet on terra firma.

"The names on these monuments all stood for honesty. I am told you had a fine school system here. Are we going to forget what they taught? No voter should shirk his duty. Any voter who does not use his right to vote should not have the privilege of voting."

District Attorney James F. Hoey, past grand president of the Native Sons, gave some of the history of Nortonville and Somersville. He told many incidents he had gathered in compiling historical notes of the county. He also said that people of Contra Costa County should appreciate the present resources and assets of the county.

Mr. Buchanan then introduced three men who were charter members of General Winn Parlor, Native Sons. They have all been (Continued on Page Four.)

*Antioch Ledger*
October 8, 1934

## Dedication of Monu-
##    ment to Pioneers Sunday

(Continued from Page One)
members of the order for fifty
years or over. Joe Mulhare, who
has been at the county hospital for
several years, sat in an automo-
bile and smiled his thanks at the
ovation given him. He lived for
many years in Somersville.

Richard U'Ren, who now lives
on a ranch near Antioch, said the
occasion took him back fifty-eight
years. He had ridden over the
hills around Somersville as a cow-
boy. On many of these ridges William Hornback, now of Antioch,
was his companion. He said he still
has in his possession a shoe worn
by one of the mules which hauled
coal from the mine. Later this
shoe was placed over the entrance
of the home Mr. Hornback built
at Somersville. It was in this home
where Charles Hornback, Antioch
merchant and former president of
the Chamber of Commerce was
born.

"Horses belonging to William
Stewart roamed the hills in those
days," said Mr. U'Ren.

Sheriff R. R. Veale said there
was nothing more fitting than to
honor the people who had helped
to make Contra Costa County the
place it is today. He said we had
many things in which to take
pride, and he called attention to

the fact the Contra Costa County has four past presidents of the
Native Daughters and three past
presidents of the Native Sons.

Sheriff Veale, as he concluded
his address, pointed to one of the
marble monuments which had fall-
en to the ground and broken into
several pieces. Then he pointed to
another one, which though lying
flat on the ground, had been pieced
together.

"Here is something we should
look after, " he said. "We should
rehabilitate these monuments. We
should find some way to raise the
money, either take up a collection
or get all interested in making
this cemetery a beautiful place to
contribute so the work can be
done."

Past Grand President of the
Native Sons Charles G. Dodge
was next presented, then past
grand president of the Native
Daughters, Mrs. Estelle Evans.
Mrs. Evans was born not far from
the cemetery where the exercises
were being held.

She said that Mrs. McAvoy had
worked for months to get the
monument and she must be given
credit for the time and effort she
spent on the project.

Mrs. McAvoy was then called on
to say a few words. She explained

the purpose of the gathering, then
introduced Mrs. Alta Barnes, president of Stirling Parlor and Salvatore Caruso, president of Diamond Parlor.

Then the monument was un-
veiled. It is a tall, concrete shaft,
with the bronze placque[sic] set within it. It will be visible from the
highway for a great distance.

Mrs. McAvoy said that in getting
such a monument, the financial
side is one that is the most important one. In this William Cohn,
head of the Columbia Steel Company came to the rescue and she
introduced Irving Skeoch, of the
Steel Company, who superintend-
ed the building of the monument.

Completing the suggestion made
by Sheriff Veal, Mrs. McAvoy
said that preparations were being
made to ask the board of supervisors for an appropriation to put
a steel or rock fence around the
cemetery.

Mrs. McAvoy's mother, Mrs. Lavina Nicholas of San Francisco,
placed a wreath at the foot of the
monument in memory of the pioneers, after which Rev. C. C.
Champlin, pastor of the Pittsburg
Community Church pronounced
the benediction. The singing of
"America" concluded the dedication.

*Antioch Ledger* (con't)
October 8, 1934

Reference 31.199

Reference 379.15

Pictured on the left is the Native Sons and Native Daughters of the Golden West monument in Rose Hill Cemetery in July 1977. When the cemetery was acquired by the East Bay Regional Park District in 1973, the memorial plaque was already missing from the monument. The plaque had been taken years prior (sometime after 1971) by thieves.

In 1974, an Oakland Police officer discovered the plaque while checking wrecking and junk yards for stolen property. The plaque was returned to the Park District and placed in storage for safe-keeping. In *circa* 1977, vandals broke into the storage area and once again took the plaque. The plaque was retrieved for the second time when a Concord, Contra Costa County, California salvage yard operator recognized the historical significance of the plaque and contacted staff at Black Diamond Mines Regional Preserve. The plaque was once again retrieved and now stands on the monument in the cemetery.

A wreath was placed at the monument (picture right) during the 75th anniversary commemorative event in Rose Hill Cemetery on Saturday, October 10, 2009. The celebration was organized by Black Diamond Mines Regional Preserve staff and was attended by approximately 100 people, many of whom were coal field descendants. Photographs by Traci (Gibbons) Parent.

The plaque says:
1934
ERECTED BY
STIRLING PARLOR
NO. 146   N. D. G. W.
AND
DIMAOND PARLOR
NO. 246   N. S. G. W.
IN MEMORY OF
THE PIONEERS OF
NORTONIVLLE
AND
SOMERSVILLE

# Chapter 7

# EPITAPHS

East Bay Regional Park District

# EPITAPHS

*Webster's Ninth New College Dictionary* defines an epitaph as "an inscription on or at a tomb or grave in memory of the one buried there; a brief statement commemorating or epitomizing a deceased person or something past."

Epitaphs convey a message and/or information to the reader about the departed. Epitaphs may provide the following information:

- Cause of death
- The goodness of the deceased
- Something about the person's life
- Beliefs and attitudes toward death

- Expressions of grief
- Faith and religious beliefs of the deceased
- Feelings and expressions of the surviving family and friends

Epitaphs come from a variety of sources including the *Bible*, church hymns, and poems. Although many were standard epitaphs provided by the carver, some were written by the deceased, or by family members and friends after the death.

Regardless of their origin, epitaphs give us a glimpse into the past, reflecting the beliefs of the individuals who lived before us.

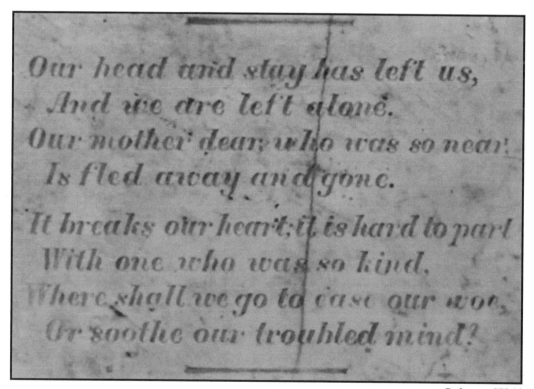

Reference 379.16

Epitaph from Sarah Norton's gravestone, Section N-B, Plot #6. Sarah died October 5, 1879, age 68 years.

East Bay Regional Park District

This poem was published in the *Contra Costa Gazette* newspaper, date unknown. It was written by Rutliven Jerhyns, about 1700. *Though Lost to Sight, To Memory Dear*, was a popular epitaph that appeared on many gravestones of the time.

---

## Though Lost To Sight, To Memory Dear

Sweetheart, good-by!  The fluttering sail
   Is spread to waft me far from thee;
And soon before the favoring gale
   My ship shall bound across the sea.

Perchance, all desolate and forlorn,
   These eyes shall miss thee many a year;
But unforgotten every charm-
   Though lost to sight, to memory dear.

Sweetheart, good-by!  One last embrace!
   O cruel fate, two souls to sever!
Yet in this heart's most sacred place
   Thou, thou alone shall dwell forever.

And still shall recollection trace,
   In Fancy's mirror ever near,
Each smile, each tear upon that face
   Though lost to sight, to memory dear.

---

# Epitaph List

The following is a list of people for whom an epitaph has been obtained. The epitaphs were found on the gravestone and/or obtained through a newspaper obituary. Also indicated are those epitaphs written in Welsh and those that come from the *Bible*. The translation of Welsh epitaphs was provided by Idris Evans of the Welsh American Society of Northern California.

| NAME | NEWSPAPER | GRAVESTONE | WELSH EPITAPH | BIBLICAL EPITAPH |
|---|---|---|---|---|
| ABRAHAM, Rebecca | X | X | | |
| AITKEN, Katie | | X | | |
| BANKS, Joseph | | X | | |
| BOWMAN, Charles H. | | X | | |
| BOWMAN, David G. | | X | | |
| BOWMAN, Violette I. | | X | | |
| BRADSHAW, John | | X | | |
| BRYANT, Elizabeth Ann | | X | | |
| BUXTON, Alfred W. | | X | | |
| BUXTON, Lulu | | X | | |
| BUXTON, Maggie | | X | | |
| CAIN, Elizabeth O. | | X | | |
| CLARE, Walter E. | | X | | |
| CLEMENT, Ann | | X | | |
| CLEMENT, William H. | | X | | |
| COOPER, George | | X | | |
| DAVIS, Anna | | X | | X |
| DAVIS, Ellen | | X | X | |
| DAVIS, Peter | | X | | |
| DAVIS, Thomas. J. | | X | | |
| DAWSON, Mary A. | | X | | |
| EDWARDS, Catherine | | X | | X |
| ENO, Susan J. | | X | | |
| EVANS, Rebecca | | X | | |

| NAME | NEWSPAPER | GRAVESTONE | WELSH EPITAPH | BIBLICAL EPITAPH |
|---|---|---|---|---|
| EVANS, William Rodirick | | X | | X |
| GREEN, Martha J. | | X | | |
| GRIFFITHS, David W. | | X | | X |
| HABENICHT, Wilhelm C. | | X | | |
| HAVARD, Elias | | X | | |
| HEYCOCK, Richard | | X | X | X |
| HOOK, Alice J. | | X | | |
| HOWELL, Sarah | | X | | |
| HOWELL, Thomas M. | | X | | |
| HUGHES, David M. | | X | | |
| HUGHES, Margaret | | X | | X |
| JAMES, Mary Ann | | X | | |
| JENKINS, Ebenezer H. | | X | | |
| JENKINS, Elizabeth Ann | | X | | |
| JENKINS, Infant | | X | | |
| JENKINS, Thomas H. | | X | | |
| JEWETT, Walter S. | X | | | |
| JENKINS, Thomas J. (died 1870) | | X | | |
| JONES, Austin | | X | | |
| JONES, Catherine | | X | | |
| JONES, Davied R. | | X | X | X |
| JONES, Elizabeth (died 1876) | | X | X | X |
| JONES, Ellen | | X | | |
| JONES, Hugh R. | | X | | |
| JONES, Isabella | | X | | |
| JONES, John B. | | X | | |
| JONES, Mary E. & "Infant Babe" | | X | | |
| JONES, Thomas (died 1878) | | X | | |
| JONES, Thomas S. & 2 Infants | | X | | |
| LEAM, Margaret | | X | | |

| NAME | NEWSPAPER | GRAVESTONE | WELSH EPITAPH | BIBLICAL EPITAPH |
|---|---|---|---|---|
| LEAM, May | | X | | |
| LOVE, John | | X | | |
| MARKLEY, Eliza Jane | X | | | |
| MINETT, William C. | | X | | |
| MORGAN, Ann | | X | X | |
| MORRIS, Alexander | | X | | |
| NORTON, Sarah | | X | | |
| OLIVER, Jane | | X | | X |
| OTT, Georg Adam | | X | | |
| PIERCY, Julia Etta | | X | | |
| POWELL, Mary | | X | | |
| PROSSER, Mary | | X | | |
| REES, Elizabeth Ann | | X | | |
| RICHARDS, Daniel | | X | | |
| RICHARDS, John | | X | X | |
| RICHARDS, William Timothy | | X | X | |
| RICHMOND, Anne | | X | | |
| RICHMOND, Elizabeth | | X | | |
| RICHMOND, Thomas | | X | | |
| RITCHARDS, Mary | | X | | |
| SADDLER, Harriet A. | X | | | |
| SPOWART, Annie | | X | | |
| THOMAS, Elvira | | X | | |
| THOMAS, Rees G. | | X | | |
| TULLY, Mary | | X | | |
| UNKNOWN, Adult | | X | | |
| WILLIAMS, Annie | | X | | |
| WILLIAMS, Edward F. | | X | X | |
| WILLIAMS, William L. | | X | | |
| WINGATE, Robert | | X | | |

# Epitaphs of Rose Hill

| EPITAPH | NAME OF DECEASED | SECTION/ PLOT |
|---|---|---|
| *Gone but not forgotten.*<br><br>*The grass withereth and the flower fadeth; but the word of our God shall stand forever-Isaiah, XL: 6-8.*<br><br>*(From the Contra Costa Gazette newspaper, Nov. 9, 1878)* | REBECCA ABRAHAM<br>DIED NOVEMBER 1, 1878<br>AGE 18 YRS., 4 MOS. | S-D, 55 |
| *Weep not Father and Mother for me*<br>*For I am waiting in glory for thee.* | KATIE AITKEN<br>DIED DECEMBER 24, 1879<br>AGE 8 YRS., 4 MOS., 12 DYS. | S-C, 17 |
| *Green be the turf above thee,*<br>*Companion of my happier days,*<br>*None knew thee but to love thee,*<br>*Nor named thee but to praise.*<br><br>*Tears fell when thou wert dying,*<br>*From eyes unused to weep,*<br>*And long where thou art lying,*<br>*Will tears the cold turf steep.* | JOSEPH BANKS<br>DIED AUGUST 29, 1883<br>AGE 65 YRS., 2 MOS., 24 DYS. | N-A, 3 |
| *Tis hard to part with those we love,*<br>*To God thy meek smiles are gone;*<br>*Assured a brighter home than ours,*<br>*In Heaven is now thine own.* | CHARLES H. BOWMAN<br>DIED APRIL 5, 1874<br>AGE 1 YR., 11 MOS.<br><br>DAVID G. BOWMAN, JR.<br>DIED FEBRUARY 3, 1871<br>AGE 1 MO., 14 DYS.<br><br>VIOLETTE I. BOWMAN<br>DIED JUNE 29, 1870<br>AGE 1 YR., 3 MOS. | N-E, 75 |
| *Weep not for me as you stand by*<br>*As I was once as you are now*<br>*Prepare for death and follow me.* | JOHN BRADSHAW<br>DIED OCTOBER 25, 1881<br>AGE 55 YRS., 4 MOS., 20 DYS. | S-C, 16 |
| *Though lost to sight, to memory dear.* | ELIZABETH ANN BRYANT<br>DIED MAY 21, 1877<br>AGE 10 YRS., 7 MOS., 21 DYS. | S-D, 57 |

| EPITAPH | NAME OF DECEASED | SECTION/ PLOT |
|---|---|---|
| Our sweet little children have gone<br>To mansions above yonder sky,<br>To gaze on the beautiful throne,<br>Of Him who is seated on high. | ALFRED W. BUXTON<br>DIED SEPTEMBER 25, 1878<br>AGE 8 YRS., 8 MOS., 8 DYS.<br><br>LULU BUXTON<br>DIED DECEMBER 15, 1874<br>AGE 1 YR., 2 MOS., 18 DYS. | N-D, 60 |
| Two precious ones from us<br>has [sic] gone,<br>Two voices we loved are<br>stilled;<br>A place is vacant in our<br>home,<br>Which never can be<br>filled. | MAGGIE BUXTON<br>DIED OCTOBER 22, 1890<br>AGE 40 YRS., 2 MOS., 27 DYS.<br><br>GEORGE COOPER<br>DIED NOVEMBER 9, 1884<br>AGE 40 YEARS | S-B, 25 |
| Dear Mother we miss thee. | ELIZABETH O. CAIN<br>DIED OCTOBER 27, 1881<br>AGE 47 YRS., 7 MOS., 23 DYS. | N-A, 2 |
| Open wide are the pearly gates<br>That lead to the shining shore<br>Our Walter suffered in passing through<br>But his sufferings now are o'er. | WALTER E. CLARE<br>DIED MAY 4, 1883<br>AGE 8 YRS., 2 MOS., 27 DYS. | N-B, 112 |
| Where immortal spirits<br>reign we shall meet again. | ANN CLEMENT<br>DIED FEBRUARY 13, 1875<br>AGE 40 YRS., 10 MOS., 17 DYS.<br><br>WILLIAM H. CLEMENT<br>DIED FEBRUARY 29, 1892<br>AGE 66 YRS., 7 MOS., 5 DYS. | S-F, 100 |
| Therefore be ye also ready for<br>in such an hour as ye think not<br>the Son of man cometh.<br>S. Math XXIV 44V<br><br>(From the *Bible*, St. Matthew 24:44) | ANNA DAVIS<br>DIED AUGUST 9, 1869<br>AGE 25 YRS. | S-E, 90 |
| The grave is the cold dwelling place<br>Which we have, not our happiness.<br>One must be under the sward<br>Why must we love the world.<br><br>(Transcribed from Welsh epitaph) | ELLEN DAVIS<br>DIED JULY 16, 1878<br>AGE 33 YRS., 28 DYS. | N-F, 101 |

| EPITAPH | NAME OF DECEASED | SECTION/PLOT |
|---------|------------------|--------------|
| *Judge not that ye be not judged.* | PETER DAVIS<br>DIED MARCH 14, 1872<br>AGE 52 YRS. | S-F, 111 |
| *Lost to sight but to memory dear.* | THOMAS J. DAVIS<br>DIED APRIL 9, 1883<br>AGE 39 YRS. | S-D, 59 |
| *Gone but not forgotten.* | MARY A. DAWSON<br>DIED OCTOBER 7, 1879<br>AGE 4 MOS., 7 DYS. | S-F, 106 |
| *To me to live is Christ*<br>*and to died gine.* [sic]<br><br>(From the *Bible*, Philippians 1:21) | CATHERINE EDWARDS<br>DIED NOVEMBER 25, 1876<br>AGE 24 YRS., 5 MOS., 13 DYS. | N-C, 31 |
| *Alas how changed that lovely flower,*<br>*Which bloomed and cheered our heart,*<br>*Fair fleeting comforts of an hour,*<br>*How soon we er [we're] called to part.* | SUSAN J. ENO<br>DIED FEBRUARY 3, 1880<br>AGE 6 YRS., 7 MOS., 28 DYS. | N-F, 71 |
| *Lost to sight but to*<br>*memory dear.* | REBECCA EVANS<br>DIED MARCH 24, 1886<br>AGE 33 YRS., 1 MO., 23 DYS. | S-B, 27 |
| *Let not the foot of pride*<br>*come against me, and*<br>*let not the hand of the*<br>*wicked remove me.*<br><br>(From the *Bible*, Psalms 36:11) | WILLIAM RODRICK EVANS<br>DIED FEBRUARY 8, 1870<br>AGE 8 YRS., 17 DYS. | S-E, 93 |
| *Gone but not forgotten.* | MARTHA J. GREEN<br>DIED DECEMBER 8, 1879<br>AGE 7 MOS., 19 DYS. | S-F, 107 |
| *In the morning it flourisheth, and groweth up.*<br>*In the evening it is cut down and witherd.*<br><br>(From the *Bible*, Psalms 90:6) | DAVID W. GRIFFITHS<br>DIED JULY 25, 1876<br>AGE 42 YRS. | S-D, 49 |
| *Tis hard to part*<br>*With the one so dear as thee*<br>*Our loved and gentle boy*<br>*No more on earth thy smiles to see*<br>*Thy smiles that gave us joy.* | WILHELM C. HABENICHT<br>DIED FEBRUARY 25, 1882<br>AGE 18 YRS., 10 MOS., 27 DYS. | N-A, 4 |

| EPITAPH | NAME OF DECEASED | SECTION/ PLOT |
|---|---|---|
| *He left this earth to bloom in heaven.* | ELIAS HAVARD<br>DIED AUGUST 27, 1875<br>AGE 4 YRS., 10 MOS., 17 DYS. | N-D, 39 |
| *In the morning it flourisheth, and groweth up; in the evening it is cut down and withereth."*<br><br>(From the *Bible*, Psalms 90:6; transcribed from Welsh epitaph) | RICHARD HEYCOCK<br>DIED NOVEMBER 14, 1877<br>AGE 8 YRS., 11 MOS., 10 DYS. | N-D, 35 |
| *God took thee from a world*<br>*of care.* | ALICE J. HOOK<br>DIED FEBRUARY 20, 1875<br>AGE 3 MOS., 4 DYS. | S-F, 108 |
| *May their souls rest in Peace.* | SARAH HOWELL<br>DIED OCTOBER 9, 1870<br>AGE 4 YRS., 9 MOS.<br><br>THOMAS M. HOWELL<br>DIED SEPTEMBER 2, 1870<br>AGE 10 YRS., 1 MO., 12 DYS. | N-C, 8 |
| *Absent, But Not Forgotten* | DAVID M. HUGHES<br>DIED MARCH 12, 1888<br>AGE 37 YRS. | S-B, 12 |
| *For me to live is Christ*<br>*and to die is gain.*<br><br>(From the *Bible*, Philippians 1:21) | MARGARET HUGHES<br>DIED MAY 11, 1876<br>AGE 37 YRS., 11 MOS., 5 DYS. | S-D, 54 |
| *We miss thee at home.* | MARY ANN JAMES<br>DIED OCTOBER 1, 1877<br>AGE 20 YRS., 6 MOS. | N-C, 28 |
| *Gone but not forgotten.* | THOMAS H. JENKINS<br>DIED MARCH 24, 1882<br>AGE 52 YRS., 1 MO., 19 DYS.<br><br>INFANT DAUGHTER<br>DIED APRIL 15, 1880<br>AGE 1 DY. | N-B, 9 |

| EPITAPH | NAME OF DECEASED | SECTION/ PLOT |
|---|---|---|
| *Gone but not forgotten.* | EBENEZER H. JENKINS DIED JUNE 23, 1874 7 YRS., 6 MOS., 19 DYS.<br><br>ELIZABETH ANN JENKINS DIED SEPTEMBER 22, 1870 AGE 1 MO., 20 DYS.<br><br>THOMAS JOSEPH JENKINS DIED AUGUST 5, 1870 AGE 1 YR., 5 MOS., 3 DYS.<br><br>THOMAS JOSEPH JENKINS DIED SEPTEMBER 5, 1877 AGE 5 YRS., 1 MO., 6 DYS. | S-D, 88 |
| *Ye have gone in manhood's earliest hour,*<br>*Ye have passed away with the spring's sweet flowers,*<br>*When wild birds were trilling notes that ye loved,*<br>*And all things were bright where thy footsteps had*<br>*    roved.*<br><br>*Ye have gone from the scenes of pleasure and mirth.*<br>*Ye have passed away from the beautiful earth,*<br>*And places ye loved shall know you no more,*<br>*Thy bark is afloat on the other shore.*<br><br>*Ye died in life's morn, when thy spirit was free.*<br>*Ere dark pages in life were unfolded to thee,*<br>*When flower's of affection seemed everywhere found,*<br>*And Hope's rose tinted hues clothed all things around.* | WALTER S. JEWETT DIED APRIL 21, 1869 AGE 19 YRS. | N-F, 105 |
| *Death passed unto life, aye, with a sweet trust!*<br>*Thy soul to its Heaven-dust unto dust,*<br>*With such glory around-with thy parting breath,*<br>*We could not but whisper, can this be death?*<br><br>*Ye have gone-and a pall is over our hearts,*<br>*We mourn that the noble of earth should depart;*<br>*But 'round thy remembrance a halo is set,*<br>*And words ye have uttered we cannot forget.*<br><br>*R.P.B.*<br><br>(From the *Contra Costa Gazette* newspaper, June 19, 1869) | | |

| EPITAPH | NAME OF DECEASED | SECTION/ PLOT |
|---|---|---|
| *I Fear Not Death.* | AUSTIN JONES DIED NOVEMBER 20, 1880 AGE 46 YRS. | S-C, 23 |
| *My wife how fondly shall thy memory* *Be shrined within the chambers of my heart.* *Thy virtuous worth was only known to me* *And I can feel how sad it is to part.* | CATHERINE JONES DIED MAY 27, 1867 AGE 34 YRS. | S-E, 82 |
| *The memory of the righteous is blessed.* (From the *Bible*, Proverbs 10:7, transcribed from Welsh epitaph) | DAVIED R. JONES DIED OCTOBER 29, 1875 AGE 6 MOS., 28 DYS. ELIZABETH JONES DIED MARCH 10, 1876 AGE 25 YRS. | S-E, 83 |
| *Gone but not forgotten.* | ELLEN JONES DIED AUGUST 15, 1890 AGE 69 YRS. HUGH R. JONES DIED NOVEMBER 1869 AGE 44 YRS. | S-E, 89 |
| *Weep not for me my parents dear.* *I am not dead but sleeping here.* *I am not your's but Jesus alone.* *He thought it best to take me home.* | ISABELLA JONES DIED FEBRUARY 5, 1872 AGE 3 YRS., 10 MOS. | S-E, 84 |
| *Gone But Not Forgotten* | JOHN B. JONES DIED FEBRUARY 9, 1879 AGE 38 YRS., 9 MOS. | S-D, 59 |
| *Two pilgrims for the holy land* *Have left our lonely door,* *Two sinless angels, hand in hand* *Have reached promised shore.* | MARY E. JONES DIED AUGUST 21, 1865 AGE 3 MOS. INFANT BABE AGE 3 DYS. | S-E, 79 |
| *To us for sixteen an-xious months* *His infant smile was given:* *And then he bade farewell to earth and went to live in Heaven.* | THOMAS JONES DIED NOVEMBER 10, 1878 AGE 16 MOS. | S-C, 113 |

| EPITAPH | NAME OF DECEASED | SECTION/PLOT |
|---|---|---|
| *Though lost to sight to memory dear.* | THOMAS S. JONES<br>DIED JANUARY 5, 1875<br>AGE 45 YRS.<br><br>TWO UNNAMED INFANTS | N-E, 69 |
| *We will not mourn,*<br>*For her tasks are done,*<br>*Her trials are ended,*<br>*And Glory won.* | MARGARET LEAM<br>DIED OCTOBER 3, 1884<br>AGE 47 YRS., 9 MOS., 8 DYS.<br><br>MAY LEAM<br>DIED SEPTEMBER 7, 1870<br>AGE 10 YRS., 4 MOS., 4 DYS. | S-E, 91 |
| *Farewell my wife and my children all.*<br>*From you a Father Christ doth call.*<br>*Mourn not for me it is in vain.*<br>*To call me to your sight again.* | JOHN LOVE<br>DIED MARCH 3, 1877<br>AGE 41 YRS., 6 MOS., 17 DYS. | N-C, 30 |
| *Calm on the bosom of thy God,*<br>*Young spirit, rest thee now!*<br>*Even while with us thy footsteps trod,*<br>*His seal was on thy brow.*<br><br>(From the *Contra Costa Gazette* newspaper, April 10, 1869) | ELIZA JANE MARKLEY<br>DIED MARCH 26, 1869<br>AGE 13 YRS., 3 MOS., 23 DYS. | N-E, 67 |
| *Write the errors of your Brother*<br>*in sand, but engrave his Virtues*<br>*on the tablets of enduring memory.* | WILLIAM C. MINETT<br>DIED MAY 27, 1866<br>AGE 25 YRS. | N-E, 66 |
| *My days have gone by*<br>*My aspirations have been taken away*<br>*That is, the meditations*<br>*of my heart.*<br><br>(Transcribed from Welsh epitaph) | ANN MORGAN<br>DIED SEPTEMBER 19, 1873<br>AGE 26 YRS. | Unknown |
| *Farewell my Father and Mother dear*<br>*My love for you is very near*<br>*Dry up your tears & do not weep*<br>*I hope in heaven we shall meet.* | ALEXANDER MORRIS<br>DIED APRIL 19, 1875<br>AGE 8 YRS., 20 DYS. | N-D, 38 |

| EPITAPH | NAME OF DECEASED | SECTION/ PLOT |
|---|---|---|
| *Our head and stay has left us,*<br>*And we are left alone.*<br>*Our mother dear, who was so near,*<br>*Is fled away and gone.*<br>*It breaks our heart; it is hard to part.*<br>*With one who was so kind,*<br>*Where shall we go to ease our woe,*<br>*Or soothe our troubled mind?* | SARAH NORTON<br>DIED OCTOBER 5, 1879<br>AGE 68 YRS. | N-B, 6 |
| *Blessed are the dead*<br>*who die in the Lord.*<br><br>(From the *Bible*, Revelation: 14:13) | JANE OLIVER<br>DIED MARCH 17, 1880<br>AGE 39 YRS., 6 MOS. | S-D, 95 |
| *To [sic] Sweet a flower to*<br>*bloom on earth, he is gone*<br>*to bloom in Heaven.* | GEORG ADAM OTT<br>DIED NOVEMBER 7, 1873<br>AGE 3 MOS. | S-E, 76 |
| *Too sweet a flower to bloom on Earth*<br>*she is gone to bloom in Heaven.* | JULIA ETTA PIERCY<br>DIED DECEMBER 7, 1870<br>AGE 2 YRS., 11 MOS., 8 DYS. | S-F, 85 |
| *Gone but not forgotten.* | MARY POWELL<br>DIED APRIL 7, 1878<br>AGE 60 YRS. | S-C, 42 |
| *"Take ye heed, watch and pray,*<br>*for ye know not when the time is."* | MARY PROSSER<br>DIED SEPTEMBER 24, 1876<br>AGE 52 YRS. | S-E, 78 |
| *Forever with Christ* | ELIZABETH ANN REES<br>DIED APRIL 6, 1877<br>AGE 6 YRS., 8 MOS., 15 DYS. | S-C, 19 |
| *Gone by sight but not by memory.* | DANIEL RICHARDS<br>DIED SEPTEMBER 11, 1890<br>AGE 69 YRS., 1 MO., 22 DYS. | S-C, 15 |
| *Hidden in a grave,*<br>*In a wooden coffin.*<br>*Not perceived from the outside*<br>*Nor recognized by anyone*<br>*After closing my grave I am but a memory.*<br><br>(Transcribed from Welsh epitaph) | JOHN RICHARDS<br>DIED AUGUST 4, 1874<br>AGE 30 YRS.<br><br>WILLIAM TIMOTHY RICHARDS<br>DIED JUNE 2, 1874<br>AGE 17 MOS. | N-E, 64 |

| EPITAPH | NAME OF DECEASED | SECTION/ PLOT |
|---|---|---|
| *WE HOPE TO MEET AGAIN.* | ANNE RICHMOND DIED MAY 31, 1882 AGE 56 YRS., 4 MOS., 21 DYS. THOMAS RICHMOND DIED APRIL 7, 1882 AGE 57 YRS., 8 MOS., 22 DYS. | S-E, 80 |
| *Farewell dear Lizzie, she is gone the way we all must go, And may we be at peace with God. Before it happens so.* | ELIZABETH RICHMOND DIED FEBRUARY 17, 1865 AGE 8 YRS., 5 MOS., 11 DYS. | S-E, 81 |
| *Asleep in Jesus.* | MARY RITCHARDS DIED DECEMBER 13, 1888 AGE 63 YRS. | S-C, 14 |
| *While the last dim hour of midnight Spread its veil of silence o'er, The pure soul of our dear mother, Left this dismal earthly shore.* *Mother, we have loved thee fondly, But we will not ask thee here; You have suffered long and patient, But you have gone to one who loved you dear.* (From the *Contra Costa Gazette* newspaper, March 15, 1884) | HARRIET A. SADDLER DIED MARCH 6, 1884 AGE 60 YRS., 5 MOS., 4 DYS. | unknown |
| *Here lies the darling of my heart, It was hard oh yes, it was hard to part, But I hope to meet at mansion's door, My Annie dear and part no more.* | ANNIE SPOWART DIED JUNE 7, 1872 AGE 11 YRS., 6 MOS. | N-D, 68 |
| *We miss thee at home.* | ELVIRA THOMAS DIED JULY 18, 1870 AGE 1 YR., 5 MOS., 11 DYS. REES G. THOMAS DIED DECEMBER 6, 1875 AGE 48 YRS., 3 MOS., 6 DYS. | S-D, 56 |
| *Rest Mother, rest in quiet sleep While friends in sorrow o'er the [sic] weep.* | MARY TULLY DIED NOVEMBER 10, 1879 AGE 52 YRS., 10 MOS., 15 DYS. | S-C, 18 |
| *Tis God lifts our comforts high Or sinks them in the grave, He gives and when he takes away, He takes but what he gave.* | UNKNOWN ADULT DIED FEBRUARY 13, 1875 AGE 42 YRS. | S-F, 99 |

| EPITAPH | NAME OF DECEASED | SECTION/ PLOT |
|---|---|---|
| *Our Annie has gone to Heaven to rest*<br>*To sing happy greetings*<br>*To God among the blessed.* | ANNIE WILLIAMS<br>DIED DECEMBER 4, 1876<br>AGE 1 YR., 6 MOS., 21 DYS. | S-E, 83;<br>now at<br>S-D, 55 |
| *Edward, do you recognize some thousands of heavenly bodies above the sun?*<br>*Is your star cheerful and a source of delight to the host on the other side of the grave?*<br><br>*I know as I look on your grave that they exist. Entirely glorious above an*<br>*undiminishing sun they seem to me, without a blemish on any object.*<br><br>(Transcribed from Welsh epitaph) | EDWARD F. WILLIAMS<br>DIED MAY 12, 1874<br>AGE 52 YRS., 8 MOS. | N-E, 74 |
| *The storm that rocks the wintery sky*<br>*No more disturbs his deep repose,*<br>*Than summer-evening's latest sigh*<br>*That shuts the rose.* | WILLIAM L. WILLIAMS<br>DIED JULY 24, 1876<br>AGE 18 YRS., 4 MOS. | S-D, 52 |
| *Not lost but gone before.* | ROBERT WINGATE<br>DIED FEBRUARY 22, 1875<br>AGE 13 MOS., 8 DYS. | N-D, 37 |

Rose Hill Cemetery looking east toward Somersville town site, *circa* 1950s. On the far right, the two-bar galvanized iron fence surrounds the miners' monument (plot 50). In the foreground stands the gravestone for Watkin Williams (plot 51) and on the far left is the stone for Margaret Hughes (plot 54). The iron fence in the center of the photograph sits at the gravesite of Rebecca Abraham (plot 55) and the iron fence on the far right, near the tree, encloses the gravesite of Rees G. Thomas and his daughter, Elvira Thomas (plot 56). Partially visible and sitting next to the Italian cypress tree is the newer grave marker (concrete tile aggregate covering) for the Jenkins family (plot 88). In the distance sits the granite obelisk gravestone for Ellen Jones and Hugh R. Jones (plot 89), and the iron fence marking the Peter Davis gravesite (plot 111).

# Chapter 8

# SICKNESS IN THE
# MOUNT DIABLO COAL FIELD

# SICKNESS IN THE MOUNT DIABLO COAL FIELD

The majority of individuals interred in Rose Hill Cemetery are children who died from disease when epidemics swept through the Mount Diablo Coal Field. Scarlet fever was reported to be "prevalent in the mines" in July 1870. Several cases of smallpox and diphtheria were reported in Nortonville and Somersville in 1877. However individuals living in the Mount Diablo Coal Field died from a variety of illnesses which included:

Black lung

Brain and spinal disease

Bright's disease

Cancer

Consumption

Diphtheria

Dropsy

Heart disease

Kidney disease

Measles

Phrenitis

Pneumonia

Scarlet fever

Smallpox

Typhoid fever

The following newspaper articles from the *Contra Costa Gazette* and *Antioch Ledger*, discuss some of the more prevalent diseases encountered by coal town residents including consumption, diphtheria, scarlet fever, and smallpox.

*Antioch Ledger*
September 3, 1892

CURE FOR THE TYPHUS FEVER.—A correspondent of the London *Times* says: "I think it desirable to make generally known a very cheap and simple remedy for typhus or other low fever. The remedy is yeast. A table-spoonful of this administered in a case where life was all but extinct, repeated every ten minutes, till the cure was effected, restored the patient to such perfect health that he was at his work in a few days' time. A small quantity infused in the common drink of those who cannot obtain a sufficiency of nourishing food, might infuse such an amount of vitality in the constitution as to enable it to resist the depressing tendencies of the disease. I trust to your paper to make this simple remedy generally known—with the suggestion of its use as a preventive as well as a cure."

*Contra Costa Gazette*
April 18, 1863

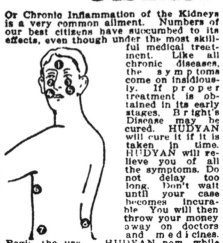
*Contra Costa Gazette*
January 20, 1900

# THE LOCOMOTIVE

## CHOLERA CURE

Is guaranteed to cure any case of Cholera, Cholera Morbus, Bloody-Flux Dysentery in any form, Cramps and Pain in Stomach or Bowels, and never fails. Sent to any address on receipt of price, or can be found in the principal drug stores and groceries. Price, $1.00 per bottle. Ask for it. Try it once and you will never be without it. If not satisfied return the medicine and your money will be refunded.

## S. H. McKELLIPS,

### ANTIOCH, CALIFORNIA.

---

S. H. McKellips is pushing his Locomotive Cholera Cure with considerable vim. He is busy establishing an agency in San Francisco, and in fact, all over the State, and the remedy is rapidly growing in popular favor. The remedy certainly has great merit in all bowel complaints, such as dysentery, cholera morbus, etc.

---

The above articles come from the *Antioch Ledger* newspaper, Saturday, October 22, 1892. Stephen Horace McKellips (S. H. McKellips) served as an engineer on the Empire Railroad that transported the coal from the mining towns of Stewartville, Judsonville, and West Hartley six miles north to Antioch, Contra Costa County, California. His product is appropriately named "The Locomotive Cholera Cure."

*Antioch Ledger*
February 5, 1876

*Antioch Ledger*
June 17, 1876

# CONSUMPTION

This disease is now known as tuberculosis. Although it may occur in any part of the body, the tubercular deposits usually affect the lungs. It is characterized by emaciation and loss of strength, followed by a cough, expectoration, difficulty breathing, fever, night sweats, hemorrhage, and death.

*Antioch Ledger,*
September 17, 1892

# CONSUMPTION :
## CAN BE CURED

### The Doctor Slocum System Has Proven Beyond Any Doubt Its Positive Power Over the Dread Disease.

### EXTERMINATING THE CURSE OF AGES

By Special Arrangement with the Doctor, Three Free Bottles Will be Sent to All Readers of This Paper.

The Doctor Slocum System, as the name implies, is a comprehensive and complete system of treatment, which attacks every vulnerable point of the disease and completely vanquishes it. It leaves no point unguarded; it leaves no phase of the trouble neglected; it cures, and cures forever, Weak Lungs, Coughs, Bronchitis, Catarrh, Consumption and all other throat and lung diseases by absolutely obliterating the cause.

FREE

EDITORIAL NOTE.—The Doctor Slocum System is Medicine reduced to an Exact Science by the World's most Famous Physician. All readers of this paper, anxious regarding the health of themselves, children, relatives or friends, may have three free bottles as represented in the above illustration, with complete directions, pamphlets, testimonials, advice, etc., by sending their full address to Dr. T. A. Slocum, the Slocum Building, New York City. This is a plain, honest, straightforward offer, and is made to introduce the merits of The New System of Treatment that Cures, and we advise all sufferers to accept this philanthropic offer at once. When writing the Doctor please mention this paper. All letters receive immediate and careful attention.

*Antioch Ledger*
October 1, 1898

## The Beginning of Consumption.

We find the following views on the manner in which consumption begins, in the *Specialist*. It will be seen that Dr. Hunter regards consumption as the consequence of neglecting certain affections of the throat and bronchial tubes, and places more reliance on the removal of these than on the cure of deeper seated disease:

"There is one more point to which I shall refer before I close, and that is the unwillingness of those suffering to acknowledge themselves in any danger until their disease has reached an advanced stage. This has, no doubt, arisen, in a great degree, from the presumed hopelessness of such cases. Still, it is suicidal — for all who have a frequent desire to 'clear the throat,' and who become fatigued and 'out of breath' on every slight occasion, are on the high road to pulmonary consumption. This disease begins, in the majority of cases, as a 'cold,' ending in a 'sore throat;' gradually it extends down the windpipe, rendering the voice slightly hoarse and indistinct, first observed on reading aloud; and finally, it involves the 'bronchial tubes' and 'air cells.' The seat of the primary disease is the mucus membrane of the throat, windpipe, and bronchial tubes. The expectoration comes from the membrane, and the tubercular matter is deposited on its surface. If, therefore, you would avoid the dangers which attend consumption in an advanced stage, you will not disregard these signs of impending evil; but by prompt and judicious means, seek to restore the offending organ to its former tone and health. You may think I give undue importance to these affections, from which most persons suffer in some degree; but go to those among your own immediate relations and friends, who are now in the last stage of consumption, and ask them how *their* disease began. They will, in most every instance, tell you of a slight cold, a hacking cough, or a little soreness in the throat which were treated as scarcely worthy of notice a few weeks ago, and will say that their cough grew worse, their expectorations increased, that hectio fever set in, and they began to loose flesh. Still they regarded it as a 'light bronchial affection,' and utterly unconscious of their true state, have journeyed onward to the brink of the grave. I cannot too strongly impress upon the minds of those suffering from catarrhal or bronchial affection the importance of this connection. If catarrh and sore throat were successfully treated we should have few causes of bronchitis. If bronchitis was generally cured, we should have few cases of consumption. All are but links in the same chain, and hang upon each other as cause and effect."

*Contra Costa Gazette*
December 1, 1860

*Hayward Review*
February 2, 1899

THE FROG REMEDY FOR CONSUMPTION.
A Toledo, (Ohio) paper says: "Some question has arisen among our exchanges, as to the truth of the statement, that a female in this city is in the habit of swallowing six live frogs daily as a remedy for consumption. We will simply state that there are at the present time more than six ladies of this city swallowing live frogs daily in hopes of permanent eradication of that disease, and if we may credit the statements of our practicing physicians—they are of the upper ten, too."

*Contra Costa Gazette*
December 8, 1860

A FROG STORY.— The Hartford *Press* prints the story about six ladies of Toledo swallowing live frogs daily, to cure them of consumption, and following it up with another, e.g.: "A couple of gentlemen from a neighboring town, who were called to watch with a sick person, who had been given over by his physicians and apparently had but a short time to live, after some conversation relative to the improbability of stories of recovery by frogs inhaling a sick person's breath, resolved to test it. The first frog placed at the dying man's mouth was as dead as Julius Caesar after only three or four breaths had been drawn; the second lived some time longer and died; the third lived about half an hour, and though others were applied, none of them died. The sick person immediately began to mend, and finally recovered. The parties to the transaction, who tell the story themselves, are highly respectable."

*Contra Costa Gazette*
January 12, 1861

# DIPHTHERIA

Diphtheria is an acute bacterial infection of the throat. The first symptoms include fever, sore throat, and swollen neck glands. Diphtheria bacteria toxins destroy the mucous membranes lining the throat causing a grey, veil-like appearance resulting in the swelling of underlying tissues. Breathing may be obstructed as the tissues swell and the membranes slough off. The nervous system and heart may also be damaged by these toxins. Later signs of this disease may include irregular pulse, obstructed breathing, vomiting, and difficulty focusing or swallowing. The spelling of diphtheria in the following articles was often spelled "diptheria."

**Hearse Wanted.**

All civilized communities are careful to pay due respect to the remains of the dead. A decent burial should be given, and in order to do this, it is necessary to have a suitable Hearse. The advertising job wagons generally used for this purpose, in this place, are not at all appropriate, and we hope to see in their stead a respectable hearse.

*Antioch Ledger*
June 22, 1872

**H. B. REED,**

**UNDERTAKER**

Cor. Marsh and Kimball streets,

ANTIOCH, CAL.

Am prepared to furnish Hearse, Robes, Coffins, etc., for funerals. Will take charge of Funerals.

☞ Coffins and Caskets constantly on hand and made to order. Tombstones furnished at city prices.
H. B. REED.

*Antioch Ledger*
April 11, 1885

DIPTHERIA AND ITS REMEDY.— Late intelligence from the East assures us that the disease known as "Diptheria," is quite prevelent at present in our Western cities. St. Louis and certain portions of Illinois have suffered greatly. It is also prevalent in many portions of California, and is what is known here as "putrid sore throat." The distinguishing mark of this malady from other diseases of the throat, is the formation of a membrane which increases gradually until the patient is strangled to death. It is sometimes accompanied with ulceration and great bodily prostration. To prevent the formation of this membrane is to arrest and cure the disease. A cotemporary [sic] gives the following simple remedy:

"In the early stages of the complaint, which is always accompanied by a soreness and swelling of the throat, let the patient use a simple solution of salt and water, as a gargle, every fifteen minutes. At the same time moisten a piece of flannel with a solution of the same kind made warm as the patient can bear it, and bind it around the throat, renewing it as often as the gargle is administered, and in the meanwhile sprinkling fine salt between the flannel and the neck. Use inwardly some tonic or stimulant either separately, or if the prostration be great, use both together. The treatment as may be seen, is extremely simple, and, if used in the earlier stages of the disease, will effect a complete cure."

A better plan, in our opinion, is to send for a physician on the appearance of the first symptoms, as it is too dangerous a disease to trust to unskillful hands.

*Contra Costa Gazette*
November 17, 1860

Diptheria.—This unaccountable epidemic is now prevailing to a limited extent in Martinnz [sic] and vicinity, as well as in other portions of the State. Dr. Logan says there have been several fatal cases in Sacramento. He pronounces its causes beyond the knowledge of man, and its progress in a community beyond human control; but gives this counsel: "To eschew all drugging, and place no dependence on the certain cures to be found in the newspapers, etc. They are all deceptive, and most of them inconsistant [sic] and ridiculous. The difference between life and death in this disease often depends upon early and enlightened medical advice."

*Contra Costa Gazette*
December 15, 1860

To Cure Diptheria. — A gentleman who has administered the following remedy for diptheria, informs us that it has always proved effectual in affording speedy relief: Take a common tobacco pipe, place a live coal within the bowl, drop a little tar upon the coal, and let the patient draw smoke into the mouth and discharge it through the nostrils. The remedy is safe and simple, and should be tried whenever occasion may require. Many valuable lives may be saved, our informant confidently believes, by prompt treatment as above.

*Contra Costa Gazette*
July 5, 1862

CURE FOR DIPTHERIA. — There is high medical authority for the statement that ice is a specific for diptheria. The patient must be in a half-reclining position, and must take the ice in small pieces, allowing it to melt in the back part of his mouth before swallowing. The treatment is equally efficacious in ordinary sore throat and croup and the ice should be administered for half an hour at a time two or three times a day.

*Contra Costa Gazette*
November 7, 1863

DIPTHERIA. —This disease has been raging to an alarming extent in Suisun, Solano county. It has been quite prevalent in this county also, but has abated very much recently.

*Contra Costa Gazette*
December 19, 1863

DIPTHERIA. — The following extract from a treatise upon diseases of the Throat and Lungs by R. T. Trall, M. D., is published by request of a medical gentleman. It indicates what he regards as the correct practice in those cases, so many of which have lately proved fatal in and about Somersville. Those interested will do well to give it a careful perusal:

During the last year or two this disease has appeared in various parts of the United States. In some places nearly all the cases have been fatal. Medical men are not agreed as to its nature. Some regard it as a form of croup; others as a variety of malignant scarlet fever, and others as a new and distinct disease. I am of opinion it is nothing more nor less than a modification of *scarlatina maligna*, in which the febrile effort is determined imperfectly to the skin, and partially also to the mucous membrane of the mouth and throat, often involving to some extent the upper part of the windpipe. In this latter case the symptoms will somewhat resemble those of croup. Though children are most commonly the subjects of it — as is the case with croup and scarlet fever — it sometimes affects adults. It is certain that many cases of well developed scarlet-fever are attended with what is called the *"diptheritic throat,"* which goes to prove that diphtheria is really a form of this disease, the peculiarity of which consists in a deposit of layers of lymph in the early stage, concreting into a membranous covering, analogous to that of true croup, and which runs into gangrene. It is attended, of course, with low fever and extreme depression of the vital powers. In many cases the patient died in one or two days.

In some cases a diptheritic affection of the throat succeeds an ordinary attack of scarlet-fever, from which circumstances some authors infer that the diseases are necessarily distinct. I do not think the conclusion follows from the premises. I should rather infer that, for some reason — probably injudicious or mal-treatment the scarlet-fever did not succeed in eliminating from the system all the offending impurities— all the *maleries morbi* — through the cutaneous emunctory, and so nature makes an effort to expel the remainder through the mucous membrane of the throat.

Medical authors are not at all agreed as to the best or proper mode of treating this affection. The measures and the remedies which some practitioners recommend as useful and even essential, others of equal experience condemn as useless, and even pernicious, and *vice versa*; from which the conclusion is legitimate and undoubtedly correct, that recoveries, when they do occur, take place in spite of the drug-medicines employed, rather than with their assistance.

So far as Hygienic medication has been tried in this disease, its incomparable superiority over all the drug systems has been fully sustained. Of several cases subjected to the water-treatment, to the exclusion of all drugs, which have come under the cognizance of Hydropathic physicians, all have recovered. This result seems to confirm the opinion I have often had occasion to express, viz: that there is scarcely any form of acute febrile or inflammatory disease known to physicians which is not curable, provided the efforts of nature are judiciously aided by water, air, temperature, and general regimen, and not interfered with by the administration of poisonous drugs.

Among the drug-remedies which are most frequently prescribed by Allopathic physicians are calomel, chlorate of potash, chlorate of lime or soda, common salt, sesqui-chloride of iron, sulphate of zinc, antimony, caustic applications of nitrate of silver, with various tonics and stimulants as quinine, wine, porter, beef tea, etc.

The proper and the only rational plan of medication consists in local and general bathing, regulated precisely and at all times by the local distress and superficial temperature of the patient, and a due regard to a pure air and proper ventilation. The patient is not inclined to take, and does not require food of any kind until the severity of the local inflammation and the violence of the fever have materially abated. The practice of continually stuffing the patient on stimulating slop-food, or on food of any kind, because he is weak and prostrated, is a most pernicious one, and is enough of itself to cause a fatal termination in many cases. In these low diatheses and malignant forms of disease all the powers of the constitution are struggling with all their energies to throw out the morbid matter. If they succeed, the patient will recover, but if this effort is unsuccessful, the patient must die. He has no ability, until this struggle is decided, to digest food; and to cram his stomach with it, or to irritate the di-

(con't)

(con't)

gestive organs with tonics an stimulants, is merely adding fuel to the fire; it is adding another to the great burden the vital powers are obliged to sustain, and thus lessening the chances for nature to effect a cure.

Cold wet cloths, well covered with dry ones, should be applied to the throat, as in cases of quinsy and croup: frequent sips of cool water may be taken, sufficiently to allay the painful sensation of thirst; the bowels should be freed by copious enemas; the feet, if inclined to be cold, must be kept warm and comfortable by warm flannels or bottles of hot water; when the head is hot, painful, or the brain inclined to delirium, a cold cloth should be applied to the forehead and crown of the head, and the whole surface should be sponged with tepid or moderately cold water so often as the surface becomes very warm. When the whole surface is very dry and hot, the wet-sheet pack is the most appropriate. In the later stage of the disease, when the heat on the surface inclines to be irregular and the extremities to become cold, the warm bath, if practicable, is the best appliance. Under this management the patient will, in most cases, be fairly convalescent within one week from the attack. Occasionally, however, the disease will continue till nearly or quite the end of the second week. In a very severe case which was treated at our Hygienic Institute, 15 Laight Street, New York (reported in the *Water-Cure Journal* for May, 1860) the patient remained in a critical state from the sixth to the ninth day (and much of this time was thought by his friends to be dying;) but on the ninth day the breathing became easier, the frequency of the pulse abated, and the patient was fairly convalescent. I have no manner of doubt that, in this case, had the patient taken any one of the many drug-poisons which are administered for this disease by the drug-doctors, it would have turned the scale in favor of death.

*Contra Costa Gazette*
March 11, 1865

## Cure For Diphtheria.

Mrs. G. C. Carman sends us the following recipe for the cure of diphtheria, which she received from Mr. B. Pilkington of Santa Cruz, State Grange Lecturer. It is said to be a certain remedy:

Put not to exceed two (2) drops of Tincture of Cantharis in a half tumbler of pure water and stir with a spoon for not less than three minutes (five minutes are better). Of this medicated water give two (2) teaspoonfuls every 80 minutes until three or four doses are given. If given in the evening and sleep ensues, the disease ought to be arrested, especially if taken as soon as the first symptoms appear. Prostration, greater or less, will appear for several days thereafter, so that complete quiet and rest, with simple and nourishing diet, will be necessary; but the disease ought to be not only arrested, but cured the first night; if not, repeat the first dose as at first. Be sure that the Tincture is a homeopathic preparation obtained from a pharmacy or physician.

*Antioch Ledger*
March 24, 1877

THE fatal disease, diphtheria still stalks through the land cutting down scores and hundreds of children and youths. The Health officer reports that not less than one hundred deaths occur monthly in San Francisco from this cause. Many of the interior towns and cities of the coast are afflicted similarly. It is reported that there are a number of cases at the coal mining towns in this county. In San Francisco the chief cause is attributed to filthy sewers and general disregard of sanitary precautions.

*Antioch Ledger*
April 14, 1877

...Disease and death is the great scourge of our town. Children are dying all the time from some sort of throat affecttion which we suppose to be Diphtheria. Mrs. Jno. T. Davis has lost three between the ages of eight months and five years in the last three weeks. Joseph Jones, Joseph Harris and Jno. Irwin, each lost a small child of the same disease. Others are very sick. Typhoid fever is also raging and death from this disease is expected every day. It has been a rich harvest for our druggist and undertaker, D. S. Woodruff; we wish him no harm but do hope his business in that line will be dull for some time at least...

*Antioch Ledger*
May 12, 1877

DIPHTHERIA.—There are a number of cases of diphtheria reported by physicians in all parts of the County. At no time during the past twelve months have the towns of Somersville and Nortonville been wholly free from this painful and dangerous malady. There have been many deaths among the children. The disease has proved especially fatal at Martinez. The families of Geo. A. Sherman and K. W. Taylor lost each their youngest child recently and on Sunday last the death of little Percy, the youngest son of Under-Sheriff Girvan is reported — three grand-children of Mr. Chas Sherman the well known proprietor of the Morgan House, at Martinez.

*Antioch Ledger*
December 1, 1877

DIPHTHERIA.—Deaths from this seeminly contageous [sic] and fatal malady continue to be reported. The family of N. A. Tyler, residing at the Empire Coal Mine, has been severely afflicted. Two promising yound [sic] daughters have died within a few weeks, and others of the family are still suffering from the same disease. Dr. Fletcher, of San Francisco, came up Sunday night and hopes are entertained of the recovery of those at present afflicted.

*Antioch Ledger*
December 22, 1877

# DIPHTHERIA'S HAVOC.

### Report of New York's Board of Health.
FACTS REGARDING THE DREADED SCOURGE

### Suggestions of Vital Interest to Everybody.

The annual report of the state board of health presents some important fact regarding the prevalence of diphtheria—the most important of the zymotic diseases. Probably few persons are aware of the extent of the havoc worked by this scourge. For three years past almost exactly one-third of all the mortality from contagious diseases has been due to it, and during the past year the percentage showed a slight increase. During the winter months it sometimes reaches nearly one-half the mortality under this head. The total number of deaths from diphtheria has been increasing during the past three years, being 4,500 out of 80,400 in 1885, 5,600 out of 86,800 in 1883, and during the twelve months ending Dec. 1, 1887, 6,271 out of 96,500.

### ITS DESTRUCTIVENESS.

It is more destructive than diarrheal diseases, which, in summer, cause two-thirds of the deaths from zymotic diseases. It was especially prevalent during last autumn, causing 42.2 per cent of the deaths from zymotic diseases, but did not reach the grim average of the preceding winter, when it caused no less than 47.6 per cent of such deaths. Practically the same state of things exists in northern states generally, and in the northern countries of Europe.

Investigations are steadily in progress in all countries so afflicted, as to the causes of the disease and the possibility of restricting it. These all point to the general fact that the persistence of the disease is due to the presence of filth in some form. Epidemics in villages and small towns, where the sanitary conditions are more easily determined than in the large cities, have demonstrated this so often that it hardly needs to be proved. Anything which poisons air or water may be set down as a cause of diphtheria, and recent cases have even brought milk within the category of the agents of contagion. Lack of drainage, and the contamination of wells and cellars by leaking cesspools, are among the most obvious causes of contagion. But there are others quite as dangerous, which are commonly supposed to be harmless. The board reports that there is too great an indifference to the danger from kitchen wastes, which is quite as great as from more offensive accumulations. The New Jersey board of health has also directed attention strongly to neglected cellars as a cause of diphtheria. This is a point of great importance, for the air in the cellar will surely find its way up into the house. A vigilant cleanliness is the best preventive of diphtheria.

### NECESSITY OF ISOLATION.

The board reports that the experience of the past year has made the necessity of isolation in the treatment of the disease more apparent than ever. All the evidence tends increasingly to show that the germs of the disease may be carried by persons in good health who have been in contact with the sick, that they find place in clothing, bedclothes and all other fabrics, adhere to the walls, and wherever they settle retain their power for mischief for a considerable time. If the patient is properly isolated, these germs will die in time, or can be destroyed by fumigation after the patient's recovery and removal. The board recommends that the isolation should be for a long time, at least until entire recovery from sore throat.

A special evil is the too early return of children to school after an attack. In these two measures — cleanliness and isolation — the sole hope seems to lie against the spread of diphtheria. A notable instance of the effective use of isolation and disinfection on a large scale has been afforded in Michigan. The state board of health enforced this policy in 116 outbreaks in 1886, in which there were 332 cases and 75 deaths, but in 102 outbreaks, where no restrictive measures were taken, there were 1,650 cases and 829 deaths. This is sufficient to show that when diphtheria has actually broken out, its ravages can be much diminished by a stern quarantine. — New York Tribune.

*Antioch Ledger*
January 31, 1891

## SYNOPSIS OF DISEASES, WITH SYMPTOMS, AND THE LIKE.

| Disease. | Mode of onset. | Latent period. | Day on which rash appears. | First situation of rash. | Appearance of rash. | Eruption fades. | Chief symptoms. | Length of infection. Remarks. |
|---|---|---|---|---|---|---|---|---|
| CHICKEN-POX | Slight fever | 13 to 16 days | 1st day | All over body. | Red pimples and small blisters in crops | 3rd or 4th day | Rash | Until scabs are all gone. |
| MEASLES | Feverish cold | 10 to 14 days | 4th day | Forehead | Red pimples in crescents. | 7th day | Cold in the head | Until peeling and cough have ceased. |
| GERMAN MEASLES | Slight symptoms or none | 2 to 3 weeks | 1st day | Face | Rose-red patches, not in crescents or general redness | 3rd-4th day | Rash | 2 to 3 weeks from appearance of rash. |
| SCARLET FEVER | Sudden, with vomiting, shivering, and fever | 2 to 5 days | 2nd day | Neck | General redness with red points. | 5th day | Sore throat and peeling | 6 weeks, until all peeling and discharges are gone. |
| SMALLPOX | 2 or 3 days' fever, severe premonitory symptoms | 12 days | 4th day | Face | Red spots which form matter | Scabs form 9th-10th; fall 14th day | Backache. | Until scabs have dropped off. |
| TYPHOID FEVER | Gradual | 6 to 24 days | 7th-11th day | Abdomen | Rosy red spots in crops | 3rd-4th day | Fever, diarrhea | Stools contagious. |
| TYPHUS FEVER | Gradual | 7 days | 4th-7th day | Abdomen | Dusky brown spots, mottling | 14th day | Brain symptoms and exhaustion | 10 days after entire absence of fever. |

| Disease. | Onset. | First symptoms. | Incubation. | Chief symptoms. | Length of illness. | Quarantine. | Means of infection. |
|---|---|---|---|---|---|---|---|
| WHOOPING-COUGH | Gradual | Feverish cold | 7 to 14 days | "Whoop" | Indefinite | 6 weeks, until "whoop" has gone | Breath. |
| MUMPS | Gradual | Stiffness of jaw | 14 to 21 days | Swelling at side of face | 1 to 2 weeks | 3 to 4 weeks, until swelling has gone | Breath. |
| DIPHTHERIA | Gradual | Fever and sore throat | 1 to 8 days | Membrane on affected part | 1 to 2 weeks | 3 to 4 weeks, until membrane has gone | Breath and discharges. |
| INFLUENZA | Sudden | Shivering, fever and general aching | A few hours | Vary with attack | 3 to 10 days or longer | Until fever has abated | In atmosphere. |
| CHOLERA | Suddenly or with premonitory diarrhea | Diarrhea | A few hours to 3 days | Rice-water stools, cramps, exhaustion | Varies | 7 days after cessation of diarrhea | Discharges from bowels and stomach. |

Taken from: *Nature's Secrets Revealed, Scientific Knowledge of the Laws of Sex Life and Heredity or EUGENICS*. The S. A. Mullikin Company. Marietta, Ohio. 1917. Page 416.

# SCARLET FEVER

Also known as "Scarlatina," this acute contagious disease was characterized by: inflammation of the nose, mouth, and throat; a red rash with a scarlet colored eruption on the skin; and watery, red eyes. Symptoms of this disease included sore throat, vomiting, and shivering. Kidney disease was a frequent complication associated with this illness. Scarlet Fever was often confused with measles.

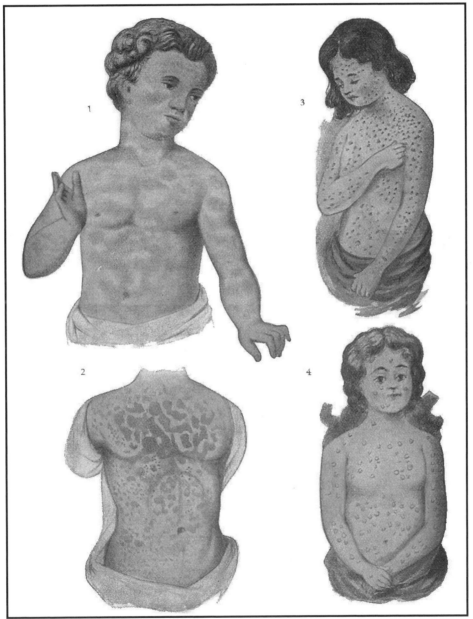

Fig. 1 Scarlet Fever   Fig. 2 Measles   Fig. 3 Smallpox   Fig. 4 Chickenpox

Illustration taken from:
*Nature's Secrets Revealed, Scientific Knowledge of the Laws of Sex Life and Heredity or EUGENICS.* The S. A. Mullikin Company. Marietta, Ohio. 1917.

FATAL DISEASE.—We learn that there are many and sudden deaths occurring lately in the neighborhood of Somersville in our county. In spite of the skill of the doctors the cases seem uniformly fatal. Some call this disease malignant scarlet fever. The symptoms are thus described by Rev. J. J. Powell who lives in the vicinity: Cold chills, with a stiffness about the neck, and pain in the back of the head. Then a violent fever which lasts from one to three hours. During the fever there is no pain. After the fever the patient seems to be drowsy and sleepy; then the collapse comes on, the lips turn pale, the eye glistens. After death the corpse becomes spotted with brown and red spots, and the general appearance of the body is bluish. We trust there will be no general epidemic, but that the evil will yield to a more thorough examination and the application of appropriate remedies.

*Contra Costa Gazette*
January 7, 1865

THE HARVEST OF DEATH.—The singularly fatal disease to which we alluded some weeks since as prevailing in Somersville and Antioch, has not yet disappeared, but keeps adding fresh victims to its already fearfully long list. We again call attention to the symptoms as described by Rev. J. J. Powell in the hope that physicians may devise some means to stay this appaling [sic] fatality among the children:

"Cold chills, with a stiffness about the neck and pain in the back of the head. Then a violent fever which lasts from one to three hours. During the fever there is no pain. After the fever the patient seems to be drowsy and sleepy; then the collapse comes on, the lips turn pale, the eye glistens. After death the corpse becomes spotted with brown and red spots, and the general appearance of the body is bluish."

*Contra Costa Gazette*
March 4, 1865

*Contra Costa Gazette*
September 29, 1877

# The Sickness in Somersville.

San Francisco, March 7th, 1865.
Eds. Gazette. I noticed in the "*Call*" a few days since an article headed "The Harvest of Death," giving a description of a disease, or rather the symptoms prevailing in your section of the county and for which no remedy seems to have been found. From the character of the symptoms given, I infer the disease to be one common enough in flat marshy districts liable to sudden changes in the atmosphere, congestive fever.

I will briefly give you the symptoms of the true congestive fever, and you will be able to judge how nearly they compare with the diease in your District. The disease commences with obscure headache, slight orbital pain and a well marked chill, which lasts from half an hour to two hours; pain in the back of the head, with stiffness in the muscles of the neck, as if one had taken a severe cold. The pain extends to the small of the back. Fever followed by drowsiness, and sometime delirium. Purplish brown spots on the forehead, neck or chest and finally death from coma. These spots may be present early in the disease, or may not occur till the moment of dissolution.

I had occasion to treat many cases of this form of disease among our troops at New Orleans, and have met it frequently in warm countries, after some sudden though slight change in temperature.

The treatment is simple and will prove successful in *all* cases if attended to before the period of Fever or of excessive stiffness in the muscles of the neck.

For a child of six years the feet should be placed in a bath of hot mustard water, and a dose of five grains of calomel and three grains of quinine administered every four hours until two doses are taken. The patient should be placed in bed, covered warmly that he may perspire and not be allowed to rise for *any purpose*. And on the observance of this, I believe depends the success of the treatment, for I have found that upon an attempt to rise from bed a faintness occurs and relapse is sure to follow which almost always proves fatal. The patient must thus be confined in bed for three days.— Gruel is the only admissible article of diet. No other medicine will be necessary unless that taken fails to operate upon the bowels in six hours; when an injection of warm water with a little salt will hasten its operation. For older patients the dose of course will be larger.

If this disease proves to be what I have described, and is of interest to you, I will write you more fully its pathology, and the method of its action on the human body. If the Rev. gentleman who gave you the symptoms will kindly furnish me with the symptoms of each stage or those of *one fatal case*, I shall be very much obliged to him, and will write him in return, such information as may enable him to relieve much suffering. Very respectfully yours

C. W. Moore, M.D.

No. 641 Commercial St.

*Contra Costa Gazette*
March 11, 1865

SCARLET FEVER CURED.

As this dreaded and dreadful disease is unusually prevalent, it may not be inopportune to state that an eminent physician claims to rob it of many of its terrors by prescribing for the patient warm lemonnade [sic], with a little mucilage, as often as is desired, and the application of warmth to the stomach. He directs that a cloth be wrung out of hot water, and laid on the stomach, renewing it as often as it cools. With this treatmet [sic] he guarantees that not one in a hundred cases will prove fatal.

*Antioch Ledger*
September 24, 1870

...The health of our community is below par at present. The scarlet fever has been and is still preying upon our youth. A number have already died, and more are still suffering from its pangs...

*Antioch Ledger*
April 16, 1870

**Be Cautious.**

There have been two cases of scarlet fever in Antioch within the past two weeks, and both have been fatal. It is admitted that this malignant disease is contagious, and great care should be exercised to prevent its spread. All known sanitary regulations should be attended to, and especially should the cases be isolated as much as possible. There should be no public funerals, and every precaution should be taken to prevent contact with the disease.

*Antioch Ledger*
July 26, 1890

# Scarlet Fever.

The Scourge of the Nursery and How to Treat It.

[From the New York Times.]

Beside the character common to the group known as exanthemata, scarlatina is almost always attended by sore throat, and the scarlet rash or eruption, which gives the name to the disease, breaks out as early as the second day after the appearance of the fever, and ends on the sixth or seventh day in the separation of the cuticle. Nearly all medical writers mention three varieties of the disease — scarlatina simplex, in which scarcely any throat trouble attends the fever and the rash; scarletina [sic] anginosa, in which throat trouble is more prominent than in either of the other affections, and scarlatina maligna, in which the system is immediately overborne by the violence of the disorder, and the patient exhibits great weakness and loss of vitality. The disease begins with chilliness, lassitude, headache, rapid pulse, dry, hot skin, flushed face, loss of appetite and furred tongue. Presently the throat feels irritated, grows red, and is often swollen. The small points of the rash so increase that the skin soon seems almost uniformly red, extending from the face, neck and breast to the trunk and extremities. The separation of the cuticle in the scales usually ends in a fortnight or more from the declaration of the distemper. The fever continues with the rash; is sometimes accompanied with delirium, even coma. In the malignant, or third form, the rash comes out late and partially, being at times barely perceptible. At other times it may abruptly recede, or be mingled with livid spots. The skin is cold, with feeble pulse and extreme prostration, and death may occur —frequently from blood-poisoning—in a few hours. In such cases the tongue is dry, brown, tremulous; the throat is livid, swollen, ulcerated, gangrenous; breathing is impeded by viscid mucus that collects about the fauces, and medicine avails little. Even in scarlatina anginosa there is considerable danger. It may prove fatal from the inflammation or effusion within the head, or from disorganization of the throat and sloughing off of adjacent parts. Teeming women are in imminent peril from the mildest phase of the fever. When it seems to be cured its consequences are hazardous. Children, to whom it is mainly confined, of course, are subject after a severe attack to permanent ill-health, and to some of the many forms of chronic scrofula, as shown by boils, sores behind the ears, inflammation of the eyes, glandular swellings, and strumous ulcers. Scarlatina is often followed by a peculiar dropsy, affecting the subcutaneous cellular tissues and larger serous cavities. It occurs, like all the exanthemata, as an epidemic — sometimes in very virulent type. In the simple variety, remaining within doors, non-stimulating diet and regulation of the bowels are generally found sufficient. In the second variety, leeches are often employed, especially where delirium supervenes. The two principal sources of danger in the malignant variety are from the primary effect of the contagious poison upon the body and from gangrenous ulceration of the throat. The final result is always uncertain. Whether it is contagious throughout its course, or at one period alone, has never been ascertained; but that the power of contagion remains in clothing, furniture, etc., is unquestioned and unquestionable.

*Contra Costa Gazette*
May 13, 1882

## A Method of Embalming.

J. Hamell, of Vallejo, is perfecting a process for embalming, from which he expects important results. It is the result of fifteen years of study and experiment, and is different from any yet conceived. It differs from most methods in that no incision in the body is required. No removal of the intestines or any organs are required. The operation consists of the injection of a prepared liquid with a hypodermic syringe into the *vena cava*, and an external application of certain drugs. The effect of the process is to indurate the flesh of the corpse; making it almost as hard as marble. The features are preserved as natural as in life. In a recent case under Mr. Hamell's treatment the face turned perfectly black; but he restored the complexion to its former color. By his method of embalming the disagreeable oder of the corpse is entirely removed. One of the bodies subjected to the conserving treatment of Mr. Hamell, remained in a perfectly natural condition for three or four months. When he has further perfected his invention, he is satisfied that he can extend the period of preservation much longer.

*Antioch Ledger*
February 6, 1875

Also known as "variola," this acute contagious disease is caused by a pox virus. It is characterized by a sudden onset of high fever and diarrhea followed by skin eruptions with pustules, sloughing, and often permanent scarring. It can be transmitted by air droplet (sneezing, coughing, etc.) or direct contact (exchange of bodily fluids). Although spelled as one word, smallpox was often spelled as two words or hyphenated in the following articles.

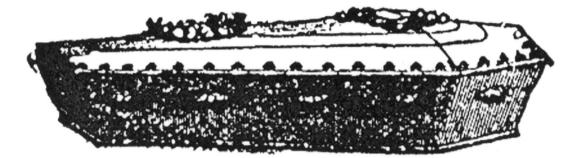

H. B. REED,

UNDERTAKER.

MARSH AND KIMBALL STS.,         ANTIOCH, CAL.

Coffins and Caskets constantly on hand and made to order. Tombstones furnished at city prices. I am prepared to furnish Hearse, Robes, Coffins, etc., for funerals. Will take charge of Funerals.

**All Orders Promptly Attended to**
aug8.

*Antioch Ledger*
May 27, 1893

A SMALL POX PANIC. — The reported arrival of a covered wagon in Martinez last Monday evening, with a small pox patient for the County Hospital, created something like a panic for a while in that easy going village; and the demand for chloride of lime, carbolic acid and other disinfectants, speedily exhausted the stock of the drug store. The patient, an infant of 12 or 15 months accompanied by its parents, in care of a driver, had been dispatched from Nortonville and consigned to the County Physician, for hospital treatment. Dr. Holbrook was out of town and did not return for some hours. Mr. Briare the purveyor, and de-facto superintendent of county hospital, as a matter of course and duty, declined admitting the patient to the hospital; and the considerate driver employed his time until the Doctor's arrival riding his passengers about the village. During the evening, after much difficulty in finding any place at all Dr. Holbrook got the family into an unoccupied house about half a mile from town and made the best provisions in his power for their comfort and care. The family had but recently arrived at Nortonville from Salt Lake and the disease, which the physician pronounces a mild type of small pox, was probably taken on the route. It was certainly a very unwarrantable and imprudent measure to send a suffering infant abroad on such a journey, with a liability of scattering contagion all the way, to a place where there was no provision for its reception and care. People should realize that such a course is not only improper but is a breach of law, subject to penalties for the exposure to contagion which attends it. Moreover, the county physician has no authority to put a small pox patient into the county hospital, but is subject to penalty of a thousand dollars if he does so, and thereby exposes the inmates to contagion.

Until some other public regulation in the premises is, or can be, made, every case of contagious disease should be cared for where it occurs if possible, and all necessary expense incurred is properly a county charge, when the subjects are unable to defray it themselves; and it is the duty of the county physician to attend such cases when summoned.

*Contra Costa Gazette*
December 7, 1872

Fortunately, we have no case of small pox in town as yet, and if our citizens will observe the ordinary sanitary rules by proper diet, bathing and temperance, we may avoid altogether this loathesome [sic] disease now prevailing in most of the large cities of the State. But no one should fail or delay to be vaccinated. Dr. Wemple has some excellent virus, and it is a duty each one owes to himself or herself to take all possible precautions against this disease.

*Antioch Ledger*
August 12, 1876

Small Pox At Nortonville. - Nearly all the interior towns of the State have reported one or more cases of small-pox, yet the contagion has not spread, and in most cases has been confined to isolated cases first afflicted. Antioch escaped with one case, and now we learn that a case exists at Nortonville. Several days elapsed before the attendants were aware of the nature of the disease, and it is presumed several have been exposed, though we learn every precaution has been taken and there is hope that no other cases will be reported.

*Antioch Ledger*
September 23, 1876

## E. L. WEMPLE, M. D.,
(Late Resident Physician of U. S. Marine Hospital San Francisco.)
### Practicing Physician,
NORTONVILLE.          nov 29

*Contra Costa Gazette*
March 7, 1874

Small Pox Cure. — "I am willing to risk my reputation," said Edward Hine in a letter not long since published in the Liverpool *Mercury*, "if the worst case of smallpox cannot be cured in three days simply by the use of cream tartar. One ounce of cream tartar dissolved in a pint of water, drank at intervals when cold, is a certain, never failing remedy. It has cured thousands, never leaves a mark, never causes blindness, and avoids tedious lingering." This may or may not be true, but the remedy is a simple one, and if efficacious what a blessing would be conferred upon the world! Will some or many of the California physicians try it and let the public know whether there is such, or any virtue in the use of cream tartar as a smallpox cure? — *Sac. Bee.*

*Contra Costa Gazette*
November 20, 1880

## History of the Small-Pox.

How small-pox arose among men it is difficult to conjecture. It has been supposed that it may have been originally derived from some disease in the camel. Its history leads to the settled belief that, while few persons are not readily susceptible of it, it never occurs now except from contagion. It does not appear to have been known in Europe till the beginning of the eighth century. No mention of any such disease is to be found in the Greek or Roman authors of antiquity. Now, whatever may have been the deficiencies of ancient physicians, they were excellent observers and capital describers of disease; and it seems to me scarcely possible that a disease so diffusive, and marked by characters so definite and conspicuous should have escaped there [sic] notice, or, if known, should have been obscurely portrayed in their writings. On the other hand, Mr. Moor, in his learned and interesting "History of Small-Pox," has shown that it prevailed in China and Hindostand [sic] from a very early period—even more than one thousand years before the advent of our Savior. That it did not sooner make its way westward into Persia and thence into Greece, may be attributed partly to the horror which the complaint everywhere inspired, and the attempts which were consequently made to check its progress by prohibiting all communication with the sick, partly to limited intercourse which took place among Eastern nations, but principally to the peculiar position of the regions through which the infection was distributed, separated as they were from the rest of the world by immense deserts and by the ocean. The disease is said to have broken out in Arabia, at the siege of Mecca, in the year in which Mohammed was born, *i. e.*, in the latter half of the sixth century. It was widely propagated by his wars, and by those of the Arabs afterward; and it is generally believed to have first found enterance [sic] into Europe at the time of the overthrow of the Gothic monarchy in Spain by the Moors, when to avenge the outrage upon his daughter, "Count Julian called the Invaders." Whensoever and wheresoever it came, it spread with fearful rapidity and havoc. What is worthy of special remark is this, that while almost all men are prone to take the disorder, large portions of the world have remained for centuries entirely free from it, until at length it was imported, and that it then infallibly diffused and established itself in those parts. Of the modern disease our knowledge is more precise and sure. It tends uniformly to the same conclusion. There was no small-pox in the New Wold [sic] before the discovery of Columbus in 1492. In 1517 the disease was imported into Santo Domingo. Three years later, in one of the Spanish expeditions from Cuba to Mexico, a negro covered with the pustules of small-pox was landed on the Mexican coast. From him the disease spread with such desolation that within a very short time, according to Robertson, 3,500,000 people were destroyed within that Kingdom alone. Small-pox was introduced into Ireland in 1707, when 16,000 people were carried off by its ravages — more than a fourth part of the whole population of the island. It reached Greenland still later, appearing there for the first time in 1733, and spreading so fatally as to almost depopulate the country. Evidence of the same effect is furnished by results of vaccination in some countries. To take one instance: Vaccination was adopted in Denmark in 1801, and made compulsory. From that time small-pox disappeared altogether for fifteen years, whereas during the twelve years preceeding [sic] the introduction of the preventive disorder upward of three thousand persons died of the small-pox in Copenhagen alone.—*Nineteenth Century.*

*Antioch Ledger*
August 4, 1877

# Chapter 9

# GRAVESTONE MOTIFS

# GRAVESTONE MOTIFS

Over twenty different motifs are found on gravestones in Rose Hill Cemetery. Motifs symbolize many things including: fraternal organizations, feelings about grief, religious beliefs, hope, and life after death. While they often have a general meaning, some may have a meaning known only to the deceased or to the family. Sometimes more than one motif adorns the gravestone. Listed below are motifs found on the gravestones in Rose Hill Cemetery and the generally accepted interpretation of their meaning.

| MOTIF | MEANING |
|---|---|
| Acorn | Eternity; strength; seed that starts growth again. |
| Anchor | The early Christian symbol of hope. |
| Basket with lilies | Purity, resurrection. |
| Bible | The scripture and resurrection. |
| Clasped hands/handshake | Saying goodbye to a loved one or friend. |
| Compass and square | See Masonic. |
| Cross | Salvation. |
| Dove with olive branch | Peace. Typically this appeared on the gravestones of adults. |
| Dove with rosebud | The soul being carried to Heaven. Typically this appeared on the gravestones of children. |
| Drapery | Mourning; sorrow. |
| Fleur-de-lis | Virgin; Trinity. |
| Flower (broken) | Premature death. |

East Bay Regional Park District

| MOTIF | MEANING |
|---|---|
| Flowers/floral | Brevity of existence; sorrow. |
| Hand with finger pointing to Heaven | Implies the direction the soul was taken. The hope of going to Heaven. Sometimes associated with the expression "Gone Home" or "Gone to Heaven." |
| Hand plucking rosebud | The hand of God taking the life of a young one. |
| IOOF | Independent Order of Odd Fellows, a Fraternal organization founded in 1819. The motif includes three inter-locking rings sometimes with the initials FLT standing for Friendship, Love, and Truth. |
| Ivy | Friendship; abiding memory. |
| Knights of Pythias | A Fraternal organization founded in 1864 in Washington, D.C. The motif includes a knight's helmet and shield with the initials FCB standing for Friendship, Charity, and Benevolence. |
| Lamb | Innocence; the death of an infant or young child. |
| Leaves | Oak tree leaves may symbolize many things including eternity, strength, and faith. |
| Lily | Purity. |

| MOTIF | MEANING |
|---|---|
| Masonic | A Fraternal organization of the Free and Accepted Masons. The motif includes a compass and square, sometimes with the initial "G" in the center.<br><br>[Note: the illustration (left) depicts two fraternal organizations; the Masonic emblem with the compass, square and initial "G" and the three rings and initials FLT for the Odd Fellows organization.] |
| Nipped flower bud | "Nipped in the bud" symbolizing life ended at a young age. |
| Rope with tassels | Drawing of the curtain; life has ended. |
| Sheaf of wheat | Time; the harvesting of life; "the divine harvest." |
| Shells (scallop) | Resurrection; a journey or pilgrimage; Baptism of Christ. |
| Shield with knight's helmet and initials FCB | See Knights of Pythias. |
| Three rings with the initials FLT | See IOOF |
| Weeping Willow tree | Mourning over the death of a family member or friend; grief. |

Primary sources for the information about motifs comes from "Symbols on Gravestones and Their Interpretations," a publication of the Association for Gravestone Studies, from the collection of Barbara Rotundo, Laurel Gabel, and Francis Duval, no date. Motif drawings were made by Lew Crutcher, former Chief of Planning and Design, East Bay Regional Park District.

# Motifs Of Rose Hill

| MOTIF | NAME ON GRAVESTONE |
|---|---|
| ACORN | |
| | HUGHES, Margaret |
| ANCHOR | |
| | VAUGHN, family |
| BASKET WITH LILIES | |
| | BUXTON, Maggie |
| | CLEMENT, William H. & Ann |
| | COOPER, George |
| BIBLE | |
| | HUGHES, Margaret |
| CLASPED HANDS | |
| | DAVIS, Thomas J. |
| | FRENCH, Ruth |
| | GOULDING, Joseph & Thomas John |
| | JAMES, Thomas D. |
| | JENKINS, Thomas H. & infant |
| | JEWETT, Walter S. & Milton |
| | JONES, Catherine |
| | JONES, John B. |
| | LOVE, John |
| | PROSSER, Mary |
| | RICHMOND, Elizabeth |
| | SMITH, Evan |
| | THOMAS, Elvira & Rees G. |
| | TULLY, Mary |
| | WATTS, David & Theophilus |
| | WILLIAMS, Watkin |
| | WITHEROW, Barbara L. |
| CROSS | |
| | POHL, Dora & Millie |
| DOVE WITH OLIVE BRANCH | |
| | BRADSHAW, John |
| | RICHARDS, John & William Timothy |

| MOTIF | NAME ON GRAVESTONE |
|---|---|
| **DOVE WITH ROSEBUD** | |
| | MORRIS, Alexander |
| | REES, Elizabeth Ann |
| **DRAPERY** | |
| | CLARE, Walter E. |
| **FINGER POINTING TO HEAVEN** | |
| | HUGHES, Margaret |
| | JONES, Mary E. & "Infant babe" |
| | POWELL, Mary |
| **FLEUR-DE-LIS** | |
| | EVANS, John |
| | EVANS, John R. |
| | EVANS, William |
| **FLORAL** | |
| | CAIN, Elizabeth O. |
| | DAVIS, William T. |
| | EDWARDS, Catherine |
| | HUGHES, Margaret |
| | JAMES, Mary Ann |
| | JEWETT, Emeline F. |
| | JONES, Davied R. & Elizabeth |
| | RICHMOND, Anne & Thomas |
| | THOMAS, Frederick Elias & John |
| | VAUGHN, family |
| | WILLIAMS, Edward F. |
| **HAND PLUCKING ROSEBUD** | |
| | BRYANT, Elizabeth Ann |
| | WILLIAMS, Annie |
| | WILLIAMS, William L. |
| **INDEPENDENT ORDER OF ODD FELLOWS (IOOF)** | |
| | BANKS, Joseph |
| | BRADSHAW, John |
| | CLEMENT, William H. |
| | GETHING, William |
| | JONES, Thomas S. |
| | WILLIAMS, Watkin |

| MOTIF | NAME ON GRAVESTONE |
|---|---|
| IVY | |
| | BUXTON, Alfred W. & Lulu |
| | BUXTON, Maggie |
| | COOPER, George |
| | EVANS, Rebecca |
| | HUGHES, David M. |
| | JONES, Ellen & Hugh R. |
| KNIGHTS OF PYTHIAS | |
| | DAVIES, Evan |
| | GETHING, William |
| LAMB | |
| | BUSSEY, Joseph |
| | BUXTON, Alfred W. & Lulu |
| | MILLS, Charles W. |
| LEAVES | |
| | JAMES, Thomas D. |
| | WATTS, David & Theophilus |
| MASONIC | |
| | DUMAS, Theophile |
| | JONES, Thomas S. |
| | MORTIMORE, Richard |
| NIPPED ROSEBUD | |
| | AITKEN, Katie |
| | ENO, Susan J. |
| ROPE WITH TASSELS | |
| | BRYANT, Elizabeth Ann |
| | DAVIS, Anna |
| | DAVIS, Thomas J. |
| | EDWARDS, Catherine |
| | EDWARDS, Joseph M. |
| | FRENCH, Ruth |
| | GETHING, William |
| | HOWELL, Sarah & Thomas M. |
| | JEWETT, Walter S. & Milton |
| | JONES, Austin |
| | JONES, Davied R. & Elizabeth |
| | JONES, Isabella |
| | JONES, John B. |

| MOTIF | NAME ON GRAVESTONE |
|---|---|
| ROPE WITH TASSELS (con't) | |
| | JONES, Thomas S. & two infants |
| | MORGAN, David |
| | NORTON, Sarah |
| | PIERCY, Julia Etta |
| | RICHARDS, John & William Timothy |
| | SMITH, Evan |
| | THOMAS, Elizabeth Ann, John D. & Joseph |
| | UNKNOWN, adult |
| | WILLIAMS, Annie |
| | WILLIAMS, Edward F. |
| | WILLIAMS, William L. |
| | WINGATE, Robert |
| | WITHEROW, Barbara L. |
| SHEAF OF WHEAT | |
| | JONES, Ellen & Hugh R. |
| SHELLS | |
| | HUGHES, David M. |
| | JEWETT, Emeline F. |
| | RICHMOND, Anne & Thomas |
| WEEPING WILLOW TREE | |
| | LEAM, Margaret & May |
| | MARKLEY, A. J., David, & Eliza Jane |
| WEEPING WILLOW TREE AND LAMB | |
| | OTT, Georg Adam |
| | PIERCY, Julia Etta |
| | WINGATE, Robert |
| WEEPING WILLOW TREE AND OBELISK | |
| | JONES, Isabella |

Catherine Jones, died May 27, 1867,
age 34 yrs.

Barbara L. Witherow, died Aug. 7, 1876,
age 18 yrs., 2 mos., 10 dys.

Walter S. Jewett, died April 21, 1869, age 19 yrs.
& Milton Jewett, died Aug. 20, 1874, age 16 yrs.

Mary Tully, died Nov. 10, 1879,
age 52 yrs., 10 mos., 15 dys.

Miners' monument for three men who died in
the Nortonville mine accident in July 1876:
David Watts, died July 25, 1876, age unknown;
Theophilus Watts, died July 24, 1876, age 27 –
28 yrs. & Thomas D. James, died
July 24, 1876, age 29 yrs.

Watkin Williams, died Oct. 22, 1881,
age 53 yrs., 6 mos., 27 dys.

William Timothy Richards, died June 2, 1874, age 17 mos. & John Richards, died Aug. 4, 1874, age 30 yrs.

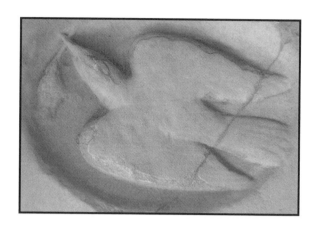

Elizabeth Ann Rees, died April 6, 1877, age 6 yrs., 8 mos., 15 dys.

Alexander Morris, died April 19, 1875, age 8 yrs., 20 dys.

John Bradshaw, died Oct. 25, 1881, age 55 yrs., 4 mos., 20 dys.

# FINGER POINTING TO HEAVEN

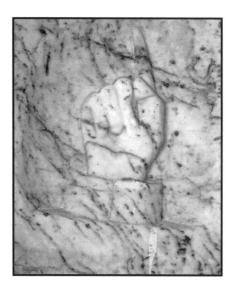

Mary E. Jones, died Aug. 21, 1865,
age 3 mos.

Margaret Hughes, died May 11, 1876,
age 37 yrs., 11 mos., 5 dys.

Mary Powell, died April 7, 1878,
age 60 yrs.

Elizabeth Jones, died March 10, 1876,
age 25 yrs. & Davied R. Jones,
died Oct. 29, 1875, age 6 mos., 28 dys.

Annie Williams, died Dec. 4, 1876,
age 1 yr., 6 mos., 21 dys.

Margaret Hughes, died May 11, 1876,
age 37 yrs., 11 mos., 5 dys.

Katie Aitken, died Dec. 24, 1879,
age 8 yrs., 4 mos., 12 dys.

Catherine Edwards, died Nov. 25, 1876,
age 24 yrs., 5 mos., 13 dys.

Susan Eno, died Feb. 3, 1880,
age 6 yrs., 7 mos., 28 dys.

Thomas Richmond, died April 7, 1882, age 57
yrs., 8 mos., 22 dys. & Anne Richmond, died
May 31, 1882, age 56 yrs., 4 mos., 21 dys.

Vaughn family, died 1876-1901

# FRATERNAL ORGANIZATIONS
## (Masonic, Knights of Pythias and Odd Fellows)

Masonic and Odd Fellows emblems,
Thomas S. Jones, died Jan. 5, 1875,
age 45 yrs.

Odd Fellows emblem with clasped hands
Watkin Williams, died Oct. 22, 1881,
age 53 yrs., 6 mos., 27 dys.

Masonic emblem,
Richard Mortimore, died Sept. 4, 1895,
age 52 yrs., 5 mos., 29 dys.

Odd Fellows emblem with dove
John Bradshaw, died Oct. 25, 1881,
age 55 yrs., 4 mos., 20 dys.

Knights of Pythias emblem,
Evan Davies, died Dec. 23, 1876,
age 30 yrs., 4 mos., 29 dys.

Odd Fellows emblem
Joseph Banks, died Aug. 29, 1883,
age 65 yrs., 2 mos., 24 dys.

Odd Fellows and Knights of Pythias emblems,
William Gething, died July 24, 1876,
age 36 yrs.

Odd Fellows emblem with basket of lilies
William H. Clement, died Feb. 29, 1892,
age 66 yrs., 7 mos., 5 dys.

Rebecca Evans, died March 24, 1886,
age 33 yrs., 1 mo., 23 dys.

Vine on Buxton/Cooper marble middle base
Maggie Buxton, died Oct. 22, 1890,
age 40 yrs., 2 mos., 27 dys. &
George Cooper, died Nov. 9, 1884,
age 40 yrs.

David M. Hughes, died March 12, 1888,
age 37 yrs.

Leaves on white bronze miners'
monument for three men who died in the
Nortonville mine accident in July 1876:
David Watts, died July 25, 1876, age unknown;
Theophilus Watts, died July 24, 1876, age 27–28 yrs.
& Thomas D. James, died
July 24, 1876, age 29 yrs.

Oak leaves on Clement gravestone base,
Ann Clement, died Feb. 13, 1875,
age 40 yrs., 10 mos., 17dys. &
William H. Clement, died Feb. 29, 1892,
age 66 yrs., 7 mos., 5 dys.

Catherine Edwards, died Nov. 25, 1876,
age 25 yrs., 5 mos., 13 dys.

William Gething, died July 24, 1876,
age 36 yrs.

Barbara L. Witherow, died Aug. 7, 1876,
age 18 yrs., 2 mos., 10 dys.

John Richards, died Aug. 4, 1874, age 30 yrs. &
William T. Richards, died June 2, 1874, age 17 mos.

Robert Wingate, died Feb. 22, 1875,
age 13 mos., 8 dys.

Thomas S. Jones, died Jan. 5, 1875, age 45 yrs.
& two infant children

Julia Etta Piercy, died Dec. 7, 1870,
age 2 yrs., 11 mos., 8 dys.

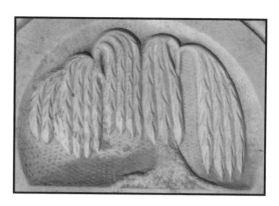

A. J. Markley, died May 2, 1870, age 40 yrs.,
David Markley, died April 19, 1869, age 4 mos.,
11 dys. & Eliza Jane Markley, died March 26, 1869,
age 13 yrs., 3 mos., 23 dys.

Georg Adam Ott, died Nov. 7, 1873,
age 3 mos.

Margaret Leam, died Oct. 3, 1884, age 47 yrs.,
9 mos., 8 dys. & May Leam, died Sept. 7, 1870,
age 10 yrs., 4 mos., 4 dys.

Robert Wingate, died Feb. 22, 1875,
age 13 mos., 8 dys.

Lulu Buxton, died Dec. 15, 1874, age 1 yr.,
2 mos., 27 dys. & Alfred W. Buxton, died
Sept. 25, 1878, age 8 yrs., 8 mos., 8 dys

# FRATERNAL ORGANIZATIONS REPRESENTED

| ORGANIZATION | INDIVIDUAL | LOCATION OF ORGANIZATION | ON GRAVESTONE |
|---|---|---|---|
| **CAMBRIAN MUTUAL AID SOCIETY** | | | |
| | David W. Griffiths | Nortonville | |
| | Meredith Lewis | Nortonville | |
| | David R. Williams | Nortonville | ✓ |
| **GRAND ARMY OF THE REPUBLIC** Post 28, Somersville | | | |
| | Albert Banks | Somersville | |
| **INDEPENDENT ORDER OF ODD FELLOWS** Social Encampment #50, Nortonville | | | ✓ |
| | Joseph Banks | Nortonville | |
| | Thomas J. Davis | Nortonville | |
| | William Gething | Nortonville | ✓ |
| | Theophilus Watts | Nortonville | |
| | John Bradshaw | Nortonville | ✓ |
| | Watkin Williams | Nortonville | ✓ |
| **INDEPENDENT ORDER OF ODD FELLOWS** Mt. Diablo Lodge #128, Somersville | | | |
| | William H. Clement | Somersville | ✓ |
| | Thomas S. Jones | Somersville | ✓ |
| | Thomas Richmond | Somersville | |
| | Andrew J. Markley | Somersville | |
| **KNIGHTS OF PYTHIAS** Black Diamond Lodge #29, Nortonville | | | |
| | Evan Davies | Nortonville | ✓ |
| | William Gething | Nortonville | ✓ |
| | Thomas J. Oliver | Nortonville | |
| | George M. Reynolds | Nortonville | |
| **MASONIC LODGE** Contra Costa Lodge #227, Somersville | | | |
| | Thomas S. Jones | Somersville | ✓ |
| | Richard Mortimore | Somersville | ✓ |
| | Thomas J. Oliver | Nortonville | |
| | Theophile Dumas | Nortonville | ✓ |
| **SONS OF TEMPERANCE** #43, Somersville | | | |
| | Andrew J. Markley | Somersville | ✓ |
| | William C. Minett | Somersville | ✓ |

# Chapter 10

# GRAVESTONE CARVERS
# & COMPANIES

# GRAVESTONE CARVERS & COMPANIES

Although at least nine gravestone companies are represented in Rose Hill Cemetery, only a small percentage of the remaining stones have the carvers mark. To locate the carver's mark, look at the bottom of the gravestone. It is usually on the lower corner of the stone. Sometimes the carver's mark was placed on the gravestone base.

Carvers traditionally used marble from Italy, Vermont, and the California gold country. Gravestone carvers and companies represented in Rose Hill Cemetery include:

☞ **Aitken and Fish of Sacramento**

Andrew M. Aitken and Frank N. Fish, Proprietors

☞ **Aitken and Luce of Sacramento**

Andrew M. Aitken and Israel Luce, Proprietors

☞ **Excelsior Marble Works of San Jose**

John W. Combs and Alexander De Long, Proprietors

☞ **F. Field, Excelsior Marble Works of San Jose**

Frederick Field, Proprietor

☞ **J. Daniel of San Francisco**

John Daniel, Proprietor

☞ **Pioneer Steam Marble Works of San Francisco**

Michael Heverin, Proprietor

☞ **A. Paltenghi (Metropolitan Marble Works) of San Francisco**

Andrew Paltenghi, Proprietor

☞ **Plymire and Sons of Vallejo**

James Plymire and sons Frederick A. and D. B. Plymire, Proprietors

☞ **W. H. McCormick of San Francisco**

William H. McCormick, Proprietor

| STONE CARVER | NAME OF INDIVIDUAL | DATE OF DEATH | SECTION/ PLOT |
|---|---|---|---|
| AITKEN AND FISH MARBLE WORKS SACRAMENTO, CALIFORNIA | | | |
| | HEYCOCK, Richard | 1877, Nov. 14 | N-D, 35 |
| AITKEN AND LUCE PIONEER MARBLE WORKS SACRAMENTO, CALIFORNIA | | | |
| | POHL, Dora* | 1874, July 14 | S-F, 110 |
| | POHL, Millie* | 1875, Jan. 16 | S-F, 110 |
| | RICHMOND, Elizabeth | 1865, Feb. 17 | S-E, 81 |
| EXCELSIOR MARBLE WORKS SAN JOSE, CALIFORNIA | | | |
| | BRYANT, Elizabeth Ann | 1877, May 21 | S-D, 57 |
| | GRIFFITHS, David W. | 1876, July 25 | S-D, 49 |
| | HUGHES, Margaret | 1876, May 11 | S-D, 54 |
| | JAMES, Mary Ann | 1877, Oct. 1 | N-C, 28 |
| | JEWETT, Milton* | 1874, Aug. 20 | N-F, 105 |
| | JEWETT, Walter S.* | 1869, April 21 | N-F, 105 |
| | JONES, Thomas S.* | 1875, Jan. 5 | N-E, 69 |
| | PROSSER, Mary | 1876, Sept. 24 | S-E, 78 |
| | SMITH, Evan | 1876, July 30 | S-C, 48 |
| | THOMAS, Elvira* | 1870, July 18 | S-D, 56 |
| | THOMAS, Rees G.* | 1875, Dec. 6 | S-D, 56 |
| | WITHEROW, Barbara L. | 1876, Aug. 7 | N-D, 32 |
| | TWO INFANTS* | unknown | N-E, 69 |
| F. FIELD SAN JOSE, CALIFORNIA | | | |
| | DAVIS, Ellen | 1878, July 16 | N-F, 101 |
| | WILLIAMS, Watkin | 1881, Oct. 22 | S-D, 51 |

\* Refers to individuals who share gravestones

| STONE CARVER | NAME OF INDIVIDUAL | DATE OF DEATH | SECTION/ PLOT |
|---|---|---|---|
| **JOHN DANIEL MARBLE WORKS** **SAN FRANCISCO, CALIFORNIA** | | | |
| | MINETT, William C. | 1866, May 27 | N-E, 66 |
| **M. HEVERIN** **PIONEER STEAM MARBLE WORKS** **SAN FRANCISCO, CALIFORNIA** | | | |
| | HOWELL, Sarah* | 1870, Oct. 9 | N-C, 8 |
| | HOWELL, Thomas M.* | 1870, Sept. 2 | N-C, 8 |
| | DAVIS, Peter | 1872, Mar. 14 | S-F, 111 |
| | RICHARDS, John* | 1874, Aug. 4 | N-E, 64 |
| | RICHARDS, William T.* | 1874, June 2 | N-E, 64 |
| | WILLIAMS, David R. | 1873, July 8 | S-D, 58 |
| | WILLIAMS, Edward F. | 1874, May 12 | N-E, 74 |
| **ANDREW PALTENGHI** **METROPOLITAN MARBLE WORKS** **SAN FRANCISCO, CALIFORNIA** | PIERCY, Julia Etta | 1870, Dec. 7 | S-F, 85 |
| **PLYMIRE AND SONS** **VALLEJO, CALIFORNIA** | | | |
| | VAUGHN, Abel Sr.* | 1901, April 11 | N-D, 33 |
| | VAUGHN, Abel* | 1876, Dec. 30 | N-D, 33 |
| | VAUGHN, Hannah* | 1888, April 18 | N-D, 33 |
| | VAUGHN, Hannah (Mrs.)* | 1881, July 18 | N-D, 33 |
| | VAUGHN, Mary* | 1880, Sept. 20 | N-D, 33 |
| **W. H. MCCORMICK** **SAN FRANCISCO, CALIFORNIA** | | | |
| | DOULTON, George | 1884 | unknown |
| | HAVARD, Elias | 1875, Aug. 27 | N-D, 39 |
| | LEAM, Margaret* | 1884, Oct. 3 | S-E, 91 |
| | LEAM, May* | 1870, Sept. 7 | S-E, 91 |

* Refers to individuals who share gravestones

East Bay Regional Park District

Advertisement from the *Sacramento City Directory 1856-1857*, page 3.

# Andrew M. Aitken

According to *History of Sacramento County, California*, published by Thompson and West, Oakland, California, 1880, page 279, Andrew Aitken was born in 1824 in Fifeshire, Scotland. He arrived in California in 1849 and by 1852 was engaged in the stone and marble business.

Aitken erected a mill and opened a marble quarry at Indian Springs, El Dorado County. He once operated the leading marble establishment outside of San Francisco. The marble works, known as Aitken & Luce, lasted for 27 years.

Aitken married Jessie Davidson, a native of Scotland, in 1860. After his wife's death in 1868, Aitken married Hattie C. Marsh in 1869. He had two sons and two daughters. One son died in 1869.

*Colville's Sacramento Directory for 1856* lists Andrew Aitken, "Marble and Stone Cutter, yard L, next cor Third, s, Scot'ld." It also states "Established as Luce & Aitken, Sept. 1852; changed to present style Nov., 1854." In the 1850s, Aitken formed a co-partnership with Israel Luce that existed for twenty-five years. Their partnership was dissolved in 1878. (For more information on Luce, see Israel Luce on pages 911-916.)

The *1870 Census for Consumnes, El Dorado County, California* lists Andrew Aitken, age 46, born *circa* 1824, in Scotland and his wife, Hattie W. [sic] Aitken, age 36, born *circa* 1834, in New Jersey.

The *Sacramento Directory for 1873*, page 136, advertises Aitken & Luce (Andrew Aitken and Israel Luce), as proprietors of "Pioneer Marble Works, wholesale and retail, 177 K bet 6th and 7th."

The *Business Directory of San Francisco 1877*, page 198, lists Aitken & Luce of Sacramento under the heading *marble works*.

In 1878, Aitken joined with Frank N. Fish and his business was known as Aitken & Fish Marble Works. This partnership lasted until 1885. (For more information on Fish, see Frank N. Fish on pages 897-902.) *McKenney's District Directory 1879-80, Sacramento City and County*, page 59, lists Aitken & Fish Premium Pioneer Marble Works, at 177 K.

Recorded in the *1880 Census for Sacramento, Sacramento County, California* are Aitken, age 56, and his wife, Hattie, age 45, and their children: Jessie, age 9; Annie, age 7; and Andrew, age 5; all natives of California. Aitken's occupation was listed as "marble works."

In the *Sacramento City Directory 1883-1884*, page 570, under "Marble Works," the location of Aitken & Fish is listed as 617 K [street] in Sacramento.

The *1900 Census, Sacramento Ward 8, California*, records Andrew Aitken's age as 77 years, and his spouse as Hattie N. [sic], age 65. Also listed are his children: Jessie Aitken, age 29; Annie Aitken, age 27; and Andrew M. Aitken, age 25.

According to the *Great Register for 1892*, Aitken stood 5' 8" tall and had a light complexion and blue eyes. He was also listed as having an extra thumb on his right hand.

Andrew Aitken died in Sacramento on September 20, 1904 at age 84 years, and was interred in the Sacramento City Cemetery. Cause of death was pulmonary consumption.

*Advertisement from the Sacramento City Directory 1857-1858, page 5.*

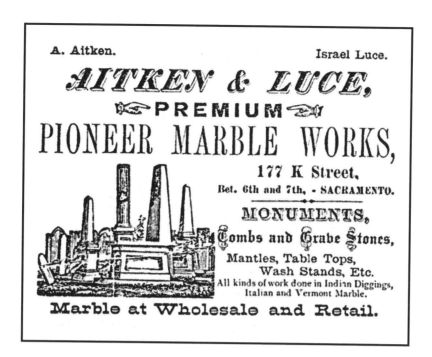

Advertisement from the *1873 Sacramento Business Directory*, page XXXV.

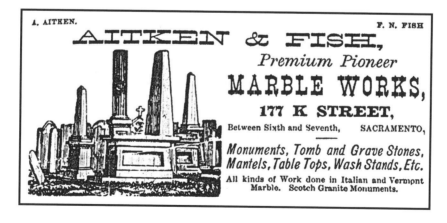

Advertisement from the *Sacramento Daily Union* newspaper, April 14, 1873.

Advertisement from *McKenney's District Directory, 1879-80, Sacramento City and County*, page 309.

## MARBLE CUTTING.

One of the finest pieces of marble cutting we have seen exhibited in this State is a specimen of mantel work at one of the yards in this city. It was designed and executed by a young man accustomed to employ his chisel on the ordinary plain work of building stones and grave monuments; but the merit of this performance will award him, in the eyes of judges, a more enviable place in his profession. It is to be sent to the Mechanics' Fair, and it is only to be regretted that its value as a California work was not enhanced by being done in native marble. The two yards in Sacramento are now introducing our native stone in all branches of their work. The quarry of Aiken & Co., at Indian Diggings, has begun to furnish marble for the trade. Twelve tons were sent down a couple of weeks since, and the supply will hereafter be regular, we are advised. The first work from this marble was turned out a couple of months ago It has since been carved into tombstones and monuments, with great success. It has been pronounced, in fineness and closeness of grain; equal to the best Italian marble. It is freer from flint and iron than any ever imported; and when the arrangements for its cutting are fully completed the proprietors will be able to sell from the saw at less than one-half the price per foot that Eastern marble brings. The best Vermont marble is worth in that State from eighty cents to one dollar and sells in San Francisco at two dollars per foot Aiken & Co. think they will be able to furnish their marble at the quarry at seventy-five cents, and one dollar. About $10,000 worth of material is consumed yearly by both yards in this city. This is used chiefly for buildings and tombstones. Fine mantels are worth from $300 to $700. Labor in marble cutting is paid $5 per day. The two yards are owned by Devine & Brother and Aiken & Co.

This newspaper article from the *Sacramento Daily Union*, July 1, 1858, discusses the marble yard and quarry of Aiken [sic] & Co.

This advertisement for Aitken & Luce appeared
in the *Antioch Ledger* newspaper, May 20, 1876.

*The Daily Bee* (Sacramento) newspaper printed
this advertisement on December 24, 1880.

**DIED.**

AITKEN—In this city, September 20, 1904, Andrew, husband of Harriet M. Aitken, father of Jessie, Anna and Andrew M. Aitken, a native of Fifeshire, Scotland, aged 84 years and 7 months.

Funeral private.      11389

*The Evening Bee* (Sacramento)
September 20, 1904

# ANOTHER PIONEER PASSES AWAY

Andrew Aitken died in this city this morning. He was a native of Scotland and in his eighty-fourth year. Deceased was a marble cutter by trade and hundreds of monuments in the City Cemetery at their base have his name chiseled thereon. He was a pioneer resident of Sacramento and always one of its most respected citizens. For a number of years he was in partnership with Israel Luce. The latter died some years ago. Deceased leaves a wife, two daughters, Jessie and Annie, and one son Andrew M. Aitken.

*The Evening Bee* (Sacramento)
September 20, 1904

# A Pioneer Citizen Was Laid at Rest

The funeral of Andrew Aitken, a well known and respected citizen of this city, took place from the family residence, 1818 F Street, yesterday afternoon. The funeral, being private, was attended by members of the family and a few intimate friends. The services were conducted by Rev. Wills, of the Presbyterian Church, assisted by Rev. Mayhew.

The pall-bearers were F. B. Jackson, J. H. Johnson, W. H. Gibson, W. T. Phipps, W. Dosoh and A. B. Cheeney, members of the Session of the Presbyterian Church, of which Mr. Aitken was a member during his life. Many beautiful floral tokens adorned the newly made grave in the City Cemetery, where interment was made.

*The Evening Bee* (Sacramento)
Thursday, September 22, 1904, page 10

Reference 379.17

A wooden headboard originally marked Andrew Aitken's gravesite at Old City Cemetery in Sacramento, Sacramento County, California. After the wooden headboard was stolen, a polished granite gravestone was created and placed at Aitken's grave by Ruhkala Monument Company in 1992. Photograph by Traci (Gibbons) Parent, 2007.

# Gravestone Manufactured by
# Aitken & Luce

Gravestone for Elizabeth Richmond, Section S-E, Plot 81,
manufactured by Aitken & Luce of Sacramento, California.

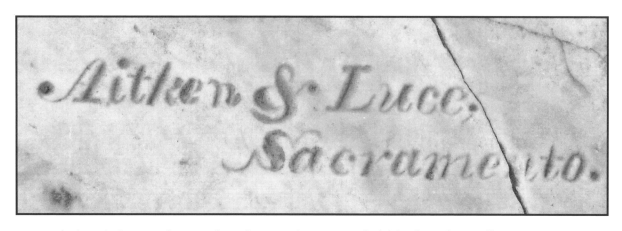

Aitken & Luce makers mark on lower right corner of Elizabeth Richmond's gravestone.

# John W. Combs

Reference 355.1

John W. Combs, no date.

According to *Pen Pictures from the Garden of the World or Santa Clara County, California*, The Lewis Publishing Company, Chicago, 1888, pages 199 and 200, John W. Combs was born in New York on October 17, 1836. His father died when Combs was a child and since he had his blind mother, Prudence (Bogart) Combs, to support, he attended school for only fourteen months. (According to documents obtained through www.ancestry.com, John's father, Lewis Combs, died May 10, 1893 in Ogdensburg, Saint Lawrence County, New York. If this statement is true, John would have been 57 years old at the time of his father's death.) Early in life Combs worked as a butcher boy, leading him to study animal forms and structures. He acquired a block of marble from a marble cutter and chiseled a lamb out of it while sitting with his sick mother. At age seventeen he started to learn the marble cutting trade and soon became an expert at figure carving. He made many pieces, including busts and faces from photographs, even though he had never taken an art lesson. His figure work won first prizes at exhibitions and fairs.

This same source states that Combs married in Ogdensburg, New York. His wife, Catherine McDonald, died in 1865, leaving him with two sons and a daughter. On January 19, 1867, he married Frances M. Rutherford, also in Ogdensburg, New York. Combs arrived in San Jose, Santa Clara County, California in 1870, where he worked in the marble business as proprietor or joint partner. His two sons also worked in the marble business. According to a descendant of John W. Combs, John and Frances had four children. All were born in Ogdensburg, New York:

- John William Jr., born June 5, 1856; died January 22, 1858

- Fannie, born January 11, 1858; died February 11, 1922

- Angus W., born June 12, 1861; died December 25, 1927

- John Albert, born March 22, 1863; died February 20, 1914 in San Diego, California of Stonecutters dust

Information obtained from *Ancestry.com* states that John William Combs was born October 18, 1836 in Alexander, Jefferson County, New York. He married his first wife, Catherine McDonald, on January 2, 1856. Catherine was born *circa* 1840 in Alexander, Jefferson County, New York.

The *1860 Census for Ogdensburg, Saint Lawrence, New York* lists John Combs, born *circa* 1835 in New York, age 25, and his occupation as stone cutter. Also listed is his wife, Catharine [sic] Combs, age 22, born *circa* 1838 in Scotland; Fanny Combs, age 20, born *circa* 1840 in New York (most likely a sister to John Combs); and James Clark an apprentice.

Information obtained from *Ancestry.com* states that Combs married his second wife, Frances M. Rutherford, on January 9, 1866, in Edwardsburg, Grenville, Ontario, Canada. [Note the difference in day, year and place of marriage as stated in *Pen Pictures From the "Garden of the World"* source on previous page.]

The *1870 Census for San Jose, Santa Clara County, California* lists John W. Combs, born *circa* 1837 in New York, age 33, and his occupation as marble worker. Also recorded is his wife, Frances Combs, born *circa* 1841 in Canada, age 29. Their children listed are: Fannie E.; age 12; Angus, age 9; and John A., age 7. All are natives of New York.

In the *Santa Clara County Directory, for 1871-72*, page 105, Combs is listed as a partner with De Long and their company was known as Excelsior Marble Works, located at 287 Second, San Jose. An advertisement is listed on page 106 of the Directory.

In the *San Jose Directory for 1882-83*, published by the Southern California Publishing Company, Combs is listed in an advertisement as the proprietor of the Alameda Marble and Granite Works, on the Alameda, near Stockton Ave. He apparently is no longer in partnership with De Long. See Alexander De Long (pages 877-880) for additional information.

*Pen Pictures from the "Garden of the World"* states that Combs served as the president of the Western Granite and Marble Company of San Jose, Santa Clara County, California, which was organized in May 1888. The company owned its own granite quarries at Yuba Pass and used marble predominantly from Vermont. Forty to fifty skilled workmen were employed by the company, including a designing artist. In 1883, a partnership was formed between Combs, W. W. Blanchard, and Timothy O'Neil. The latter two had opened the first granite manufactory in San Jose.

On March 27, 1893, Combs married for a third time, this time to Oreta T. Calhoun in Salinas, Monterey County, California. Oreta was born July 11, 1862 in Paducah, McCracken County, Kentucky. Oreta and John had five children:

- Son - Wesley Irvine, born Dec. 31, 1893, San Jose, Santa Clara County, CA

- Daughter – Frankie Oreta, born Sept. 19, 1895, Placerville, El Dorado County, CA

- Son – Calhoun Morey, born Oct. 8, 1897, Missouri Flat, El Dorado County, CA

- Son – Kenfield Nelson, born March 9, 1899, San Jose, Santa Clara, County, CA

- Son – Nephi Pratt, born April 28, 1903, Spokane, Spokane County, WA

The *1900 Census for San Jose Ward 4, Santa Clara County, California* lists John W. Combs, age 60, born *circa* 1840 in New York. Also listed are his wife Oreta, age 37, a native of Kentucky, born *circa* 1863 and their children: son Calhoun, age 2, a native of California born *circa* 1898; daughter Francis [sic], age 4, a native of California born *circa* 1896; and son Kanfield [sic], age 1, a native of California born *circa* 1899.

John William Combs died April 2, 1909 in Walla Walla, Walla Walla County, Washington at the age of 72 years, 5 months, and 15 days. He was buried in Walla Walla on April 5, 1909.

The *1910 Census for Union, Union County, Oregon* lists John's widow, Oreta C. Combs, age 47, born *circa* 1863, as a native of Kentucky and their children: daughter Frankie O., age 14, born *circa* 1896 in California; son Calhoun N., age 12, born *circa* 1898 in California; Kenfield N., age 11, born *circa* 1899 in California; and son Nephi P., age 6, born *circa* 1904 in Washington.

The *1920 Census for Hot Lake, Union County, Oregon* lists Oreta C. Combs, age 57, marital status widow, born *circa* 1863 in Kentucky, and son Nephy [sic] P. Combs, age 16, born *circa* 1904 in Washington.

Oreta C. Combs died July 28, 1925 in La Grande, Union County, Oregon at age 63 years and 17 days.

Reference 360.1

John William Combs gravestone, Walla Walla, Washington.
Photograph by Cheryl Heller, 2010.

From the *San Jose Directory, 1882-83,*
Southern California Publishing Company, page 114.

Workmen excavating for a cesspool in the yard of J. W. Coombs, at the corner of Julian and Center streets yesterday afternoon unearthed a human skeleton, at the depth of some four feet. The skull and arm bones were in good condition, and the teeth were bright and sound.

*San Jose Daily Mercury*
November 15, 1887

Reference 355.2

John W. Combs, no date.

East Bay Regional Park District

# Gravestones Manufactured by
## Excelsior Marble Works
### (J. W. Combs and A. De Long, Proprietors)

Reference 98.19

Margaret Hughes' gravestone, Section S-D, Plot 54.
The carver's mark is located in the lower left corner of gravestone.
Photograph by Madison Devlin, 1962.

Excelsior Marble Works mark on the gravestone of Margaret Hughes.

# Gravestones Manufactured by
# Excelsior Marble Works
### (J. W. Combs and A. De Long, Proprietors)

Barbara L. Witherow,
Section N-D, Plot 32

Walter S. Jewett & Milton Jewett,
Section N-F, Plot 105

David W. Griffiths,
Section S-D, Plot 49

Thomas S. Jones & Two Infant Children,
Section N-E, Plot 69

East Bay Regional Park District

# Gravestones Manufactured by
# Excelsior Marble Works
### (J. W. Combs and A. De Long, Proprietors)

Evan Smith,
Section S-C, Plot 48

Mary Prosser,
Section S-E, Plot 78

Rees G. Thomas & Elvira Thomas,
Section S-D, Plot 56

# John Daniel

John Daniel was born March 19, 1834 in Penetanguishene, Ontario, Canada. His parents were John and Mary (Brown) Daniel. On October 17, 1865, John Daniel married Emma Fielding, in San Francisco, San Francisco County, California. Emma, a native of Rochdale, Lanchashire, England, was born May 15, 1843. Her parents were Abraham and Mary (Whitehead) Fielding. Family group sheets on www.ancestry.com list seven children for John and Emma Daniel:

- John, born Jan 1, 1871, San Francisco, California

- Ella Ross, born May 14, 1873, San Francisco, California

- Susie Melrose, born November 18, 1881, California

- Laura, born August 23, 1887

- Josefina, born December 15, 1888

- Emma, born July 28, 1889

- Ella, born January 10, 1891

*Records of the Families of California Pioneers, Volume XVI*, compiled under the direction of The Genealogical Records Committee, California State Society, Daughters of the American Revolution, 1952, page 108, states that John and Emma Daniel had four children: Mary Warren, born September 23, 1866; John, born January 1, 1871; Ella Ross, born May 14, 1873; and Susie Melrose, born November 20, 1887. This same record also states that Daniel died June 1, 1895.

*The Bay of San Francisco – the Metropolis of the Pacific Coast*, Vol. 1, 1892, page 560, states that John Daniel started learning the marble cutting trade in Albany County, New York, in 1855. He arrived in California from New York in November 1859, seeking a better climate. Daniel opened a shop on Pine Street after working at his trade for some time in San Francisco. He eventually moved his marble business to the opposite side of the street at 421 Pine and employed forty to fifty men. Previously he operated a large business in marble mantels, but later gave his attention to monumental and other cemetery work and marble stairways. Daniel primarily used the Colton (San Bernardino County) and Inyo (Inyo County) California marbles. His work was distributed all over the Pacific slope as well as in Central and South America. He ranked among the leaders in the marble trade on this side of the continent. He was a member of the Mechanics' Institute, the Masonic and Odd Fellows organizations and a Knight of Honor. This same source states: "He married his English wife in San Francisco and they had one son, Charles."

According to *The Buyers' Manual and Business Guide*, by J. Price and C. S. Haley, Francis and Valentine, Steam Book and Job Printing Establishment, San Francisco, 1872, page 60, the principal marble quarries of the State were located at Colfax (Placer County), Drytown (Amador County), Columbia (Tuolumne County), and Indian Diggings (El Dorado County). Daniel commenced his business on Pine Street in San Francisco in 1862, and by 1872 had about thirty hands working for him manufacturing items including monuments, headstones, plumbers' slabs, mantels, and furniture slabs. Daniel's company had about ten thousand dollars worth of manufactured goods, having the largest stock in marble on the Pacific Coast.

The *San Francisco 1863 City Directory*, page 117, lists John Daniel Marble Works on Pine Street.

The *San Francisco 1864 City Directory*, page 126, documents his marble works at 421 Pine Street. A business advertisement which appears on page 624 of the same directory lists his marble works at 406 Pine Street.

*Langley's San Francisco Directory for December 1869* lists John Daniel as having a marble yard. His marble works is listed as 421 Pine and his dwelling as 1110 Market.

Business directories for 1872, 1877-1885, 1888, and 1890 record his marble works at 421 Pine in San Francisco.

The *1900 Census, San Francisco, California* lists John Daniel's widow, Emma age 56, born May 1844, a native of England, and her six children living with her: Laura Daniel, age 30, born September 1869, school teacher; John Daniel, age 29, born January 1871, marble dealer; Ella Daniel, age 27, born May 1873, school teacher; Emma Daniel, age 23, born August 1876; Hosapher Daniel, age 21, born November 1878; and Susie Daniel, age 18, born November 1881. All are natives of California.

The *1910 Census* records their home as San Rafael, Marin County, California. In 1910 only Mrs. Daniel's three daughters, Laura, Emma, and Hosapha [sic] are listed as living with her.

The *1920 Census* lists their home as San Anselmo, Marin County, California.

The *1930 Census* for San Anselmo, Marin County, California lists Emma and her three daughters, Laura, Emma, and Josefa [sic] living with her daughter Susie and husband Ralph Roy and family. Laura Daniel, age 58; Emma Daniel, age 51; and Josefa Daniel, age 48; are listed as single.

No census information was found for John Daniel in San Francisco even though he was very active in the marble business there from the 1860s to 1890s.

Information obtained from *Ancestry.com* states that John Daniel died on June 3, 1895 in San Francisco. According to *San Francisco Deaths, May 21 1895 – July 8, 1895, San Francisco County Pre-1905 California Death Index*, Daniel died on June 4, 1895. He died at age 61 years, and 2 months. His wife, Emma, died January 18, 1932 in San Anselmo, Marin County, California.

Advertisement from the *San Francisco 1864 City Directory*, page 624.

JOHN DANIEL,

(SUCCESSOR TO O. GORI)

MARBLE WORKS,

No. 408 Pine st. bet. Montgomery and Kearny, San Francisco.

Mantels, Monuments, Tombs, Plumbers' Slabs
Etc., On hand and Manufactured to order.

☞ Goods shipped to all parts of the State. Orders respectfully solicited.
5v8-3m

Advertisement from *Mining and Scientific Press*, April 28, 1866, page 263.

# JOHN DANIEL,

## MARBLE WORKS,

### 421 Pine Street,

Between Montgomery and Kearny,     SAN FRANCISCO.

## MANTLES, MONUMENTS, TOMBS,

### Plumbers' Slabs, Etc., Etc.

On hand and Manufactured to Order.

## Orders Respectfully Solicited.

Advertisement from the *San Francisco Directory for 1867*, page 50.

# JOHN DANIEL,

(SUCCESSOR TO O. GORI,)

## MARBLE WORKS,

### 421 Pine Street,

Between Montgomery and Kearny,     SAN FRANCISCO.

Advertisement from the *1869 San Francisco Directory*, page 48.

Advertisement from the *Pacific Coast Business Directory for 1871-3*, page 27.

Advertisement from *Langley's San Francisco Directory for 1877*, page 592.

# Gravestone Manufactured by John Daniel

William C. Minett,
Section N-E, Plot 66

J. Daniel mark on the lower left corner of the William C. Minett gravestone.

Courtesy of the Merced County Historical Society Archives

The De Long family left to right: Carrie (Caroline), age 54;
Alexander, age 59; and Chester, age 14. Photograph taken by
the Loryea Bros., 26 S. First St., San Jose, California.

The *1870 Census for San Jose, Santa Clara County, California*, lists Alexander De Long, age 36, born in New York, *circa* 1834. His occupation is listed as a marble worker. Also listed is his wife, Carrie A. De Long, age 30, born *circa* 1840 in Massachusetts.

In the *Santa Clara County Directory for 1871-72*, De Long is listed as a partner with John W. Combs, with their company, Excelsior Marble Works, 287 Second, San Jose. An advertisement is listed on page 106 of the directory. They are also recorded under "Marble Work" on page 389, in the same directory.

See John W. Combs (pages 863-870) for more information.

The *1880 Census for San Jose, Santa Clara County, California*, lists Alexander De Long, age 45, a native of New York, born *circa* 1835. His occupation is listed as "Marble Cutter." Also recorded is his wife Caroline, age 39, a native of Maine, born *circa* 1841; and their son Chester age 1, born *circa* 1879, in California.

The *1900 Census for Township 2, Merced County, California*, lists Alexander De Long, and his relationship to the head of the household is "lodger." Combs was also listed as age 64, born *circa* 1836 in New York. His occupation was recorded as a stone cutter. His wife Caroline De Long, age 60, is listed as a native of Massachusetts, born *circa* 1840. Also listed is their son, Chesler [sic] De Long, age 21, a native of California, born *circa* 1879 and occupation stone cutter.

The *1910 Census, North West Merced, Merced County, California* records Alexander De Long, age 66, born *circa* 1844 in New York. His occupation is listed as "engraver marble." Also listed is Caroline De Long, age 72, a native of Massachusetts.

De Long's wife, Caroline, died Sunday evening, October 16, 1910, at age 73 years. The obituary for Caroline A. De Long appeared in the *Merced Express* newspaper on October 22, 1910. The obituary stated that Alexander and Caroline De Long arrived in Merced in the early 1880s. De Long established a marble factory there and several years afterwards, the family moved to San Jose to reside, but continued the marble business in Merced. About 1900, they again took up residence in Merced and for some time the aged couple made their home at the Wolfsen sanitarium. Caroline De Long died at the sanitarium and her remains were taken to San Jose for interment. De Long, his son, Chester De Long, and daughter-in-law (Lula De Long) accompanied the remains to San Jose.

The *Merced City Directory 1914*, page 29, lists De Long's son, C. A. De Long and H. E. Westervelt, as proprietors of Merced Granite & Marble Works.

The *1920 Census for San Luis Obispo, San Luis Obispo County, California* lists Alex De Long, age 83 years, born *circa* 1837 in New York. De Long is a patient at the county hospital on Johnson Street. Although he was widowed in 1910, his martial status is indicated as divorced on the census record.

According to the *1920 Census for San Jose, Santa Clara County, California* his son, Chester De Long, age 39, and wife Lula D., age 40, along with step-daughters Margaret C. Crist, age 15, and Marion V. Crist, age 10, are living in San Jose.

In the *1930 San Luis Obispo, San Luis Obispo County, California Census*, Chester C. De Long, age 52, is listed with his wife Lula, age 52. Chester's occupation is recorded as "manager, stone cutter" for monuments.

According to the *California Death Index 1905-1929, Volume II, C-E*, Alexander L. De Long was born June 2, 1836, and died October 28, 1922. Arroyo Grande District Cemetery records indicate he died on September 28, 1922 and was buried at the Arroyo District Cemetery, 895 El Camino Real, Arroyo Grande, San Luis Obispo County, California. He was 86 years old at the time of his death.

Courtesy of the Merced County Historical Society Archives

Caroline and Alexander De Long.

Advertisement from the *Santa Clara County Directory for 1871-72*, page 106.

Reference 379.18

Reference 379.19

Alex De Long and A. L. De Long gravestone, Section A, Lot S ½, Block 5, Plot 14, Arroyo Grande Cemetery, San Luis Obispo County, California, November 29, 2007. Only the date of birth (June 2, 1836) is listed on the gravestone for Alexander De Long. On the other side of the gravestone is the inscription for A. L. De Long. The inscription lists the birth date as Dec. 24, 1847 and the death date as Nov. 29, 1890. The age at death for this individual was recorded as 42 y'rs., 11 mo's., and 5 dys. Photographs by Traci (Gibbons) Parent.

# FREDERICK FIELD

Courtesy of California History Section, California State Library, Sacramento.

Pictured above are Elders of the First Presbyterian Church, San Jose, Santa Clara County, California, 1875. Standing in back row, left to right are: Frederick Field, Dr. China Smith, Dr. C. W. Breyfogle, and Henry H. Reynolds. Sitting in front row, left to right: Dr. Berryman Bryant, Rev. Betts, and Thomas Drughlas.

Family tree documents obtained through www. ancestry.com indicate Frederick Field was born October 12, 1821 in Dorset, Bennington County, Vermont. His parents were Alfred Field, born March 15, 1787 in Dorset, Bennington, Vermont and Sophronia (Gilbert) Field, born October 26, 1799 in Cavendish, Windsor County, Vermont. Frederick Field married Mary Hannah Bacon on October 16, 1856 and they had seven children:

- Son – Alfred Bacon, born Oct. 21, 1857 in Dorset , Bennington, Vermont

- Son – Edward Sweetman, born May 17, 1862 in Dorset, Bennington, Vermont

- Son – Arthur Gilbert, born May 17, 1862 in Dorset, Bennington, Vermont

- Daughter – Mabel Jeanette, born June 30, 1866 in Dorset, Bennington, Vermont

- Daughter – Amy Gertrude, born Nov. 7, 1869 in Dorset, Bennington, Vermont

- Son – Wilfred Bacon, born Feb. 6, 1873 in Dorset, Bennington, Vermont

- Son – Charles Hubert, born Nov. 26, 1875 in San Jose, Santa Clara County, California

East Bay Regional Park District

Additional information obtained from www.santaclararesearch.net states that Field owned a great deal of property, including the Italian marble quarries in Bennington County, near Rutland, Vermont. Field, realizing that Chicago would be a good distribution point, had marble transported to the site by ship. He established the first brick kiln in Chicago, built a brick factory and the first brick house in Chicago. He operated between Vermont and Chicago and other points in the country for ten years. It was during this time that he met Mary H. Bacon, daughter of Honorable Nathaniel Bacon of Niles, Michigan. Nathaniel Bacon served as one of the Justices of the Supreme Court for the state of Michigan. This same source states that their marriage date was in 1858, not 1856 as indicated in www.ancestry.com. Mary (Bacon) Field was a well-known author.

The *1860 Census for Dorset, Bennington, Vermont* lists Frederick Field, age 39, born *circa* 1821 in Vermont. Also listed are his wife Mary H., age 26, born *circa* 1834 in Michigan, and their son, Alfred B. age 2, born *circa* 1858 in Vermont, and Ellen Field, age 32, born *circa* 1828 in Vermont. Ellen is listed as a school teacher and presumed to be the sister of Frederick Field. Olevia Topping, age 20, born *circa* 1840, a native of Ireland, is listed as living at this household as well.

The *1880 Census for San Jose, Santa Clara County, California*, lists Fredrick [sic] Field, age 60, as a native of Vermont, born *circa* 1820. His occupation is recorded as "Marble Works Owner." Also listed are his wife Mary H., age 40, a native of Michigan, born *circa* 1840; and their children: Arthur Field, age 18, a native of Vermont, born *circa* 1862, occupation is listed as "marble cutter;" daughter Mabel, age 11, born *circa* 1869; and sons Wilfred, age 6, born *circa*

1874, a native of Vermont, and Hubert, age 3, born *circa* 1877, a native of California.

F. Field was listed in the *San Jose City Directory for 1882-83*, page 174, as "proprietor of Excelsior marble and granite work, res 5 Clinton place." His place of business was listed as 275, 277 and 279 Second Street, San Jose, California.

Frederick Field died November 17, 1887, in San Jose, Santa Clara County, California at age 66. He died as a result of an accident (fractured skull) at the Southern Pacific Railroad Depot. According to the *San Jose Daily Mercury* newspaper, November 9, 1887, Field served as a deacon of the First Presbyterian Church and was a member of the Executive Committee of the State Board of Trade at the time of his death. No burial site was located for Frederick Field in San Jose or Santa Clara County. According to the *Amos O. Williams Funeral Book*, Field's body was removed in June 1907. Where it was removed from and where it was sent to is unknown.

The *1900 Census for Manhattan, New York, New York* lists Mary H. Field (no age or date of birth listed) as a boarder with the George and Catherine Metzer family. Also listed as a boarder in the same household is her daughter, Mabel Field. Both Mary and Mabel are recorded as widows. Mabel's occupation was listed as artist.

The *1910 Census for Greenburgh, Westchester, New York* lists Mary H. Field, age 76, a native of Michigan and widowed. Also recorded is her daughter Mabel (Field) Hastings, age 43, born *circa* 1867 and a native of Vermont. Although no husband is listed as living in the household, the census record indicates Mabel is married. Thomas Daly, age 46, a native of Ireland, is listed as a lodger.

**FIELD'S**

**MARBLE and GRANITE**

**WORKS,**

**42 TO 48 NORTH SECOND ST.,**

**SAN JOSE.**

**SCOTCH AND EASTERN GRANITE MONUMENTS.**

Advertisement from the *San Jose Directory, 1882-83,* page 86,
published by the Southern California Publishing Company.

**F. FIELD,**

# Manufacturer of Monuments

And all other kinds of

# CEMETERY WORK

In the Most Approved Modern Styles

IMPORTER OF

## Scotch Granite and Italian Marbles,

**275, 277 and 279 SECOND STREET, SAN JOSE.**

Advertisement from the *San Jose City Directory 1887-8,*
Uhlhorn and McKenney Publishers, page 6.

East Bay Regional Park District

The First Presbyterian Church of San Jose stands next to the marble works of Field, Combs and Gregory, *circa* 1875 - 1885. The location for Field, Combs & Gregory, Marble Works, was listed at 227 Second, San Jose, Santa Clara County, California according to the *Hand-Book Directory of Santa Clara, San Benito, Santa Cruz, Monterey and San Mateo Counties, 1875*, Compiled and Published by L. L. Paulson, Francis & Valentine, San Francisco, page 69.

Excelsior Marble Works yard and office for business partners Frederick Field, John W. Combs, and J. M. Gregory, *circa* 1880, San Jose, Santa Clara County, California. For more information on Combs, see the section regarding John W. Combs on pages 863-870.

# A SEVERE FALL.

## Frederick Field Sustains a Fracture of the Skull.

### HIS CRITICAL CONDITION.

#### In Endeavoring to Board a Moving Train He Loses His Balance and Falls—His Condition This Morning.

A most shocking accident occurred at the Southern Pacific Railroad depot at 7:15 o'clock yesterday morning, in which Frederick Field was the victim.

At the hour named Mr. Field arrived at the depot with the intention of taking the first train for San Francisco, where he wished to be present at the meeting of the State Board of Trade.

He was a little late for the train, and it was just in the act of pulling out from the station when he came up. The train was not moving fast, however, and Mr. Field thought that he would be able to board it. With this intention he rushed forward, caught the railing and sprang on to the step and endeavored to reach the platform. He lost his balance, however, and fell backward, striking the back of his head on the asphaltum pavement.

The unfortunate gentleman lay motionless and a number of people who were at the depot rushed to his assistance. It was seen at once that he was dangerously injured and Drs. Breyfogle and Pierce were sent for immediately and arrived in a short time.

A superficial examination showed a large swelling on the back of the head where it had come in contact with the pavement and it was not supposed that he was dangerously injured. Mr. Field was then conveyed to his home on Clinton place off Stockton avenue, where a further examination revealed the startling fact that the skull was fractured and other alarming facts were disclosed, from which it was judged that the condition of the patient was very critical and escape from death almost impossible.

A short time after his arrival at home blood began to trickle from Mr. Field's ears, which was considered a very alarming symptom. The patient was unconscious when removed home and remained in a semi-comatose condition all day. He was unable to speak, but when spoken to would sometimes understand and make reply.

Mr. Field is one of the most prominent and substantial business men of San Jose. He was very energetic. He was very methodical in his habits and prompt in his engagements, and in taking the train for San Francisco had frequently jumped on the train after it had started. Whether engaged in a private or public enterprise he always attended to it faithfully and with exactness. He was very anxious to catch the train yesterday morning, the primary object of the trip being the meeting of the Board of Trade, in which he is the representative of the local board here.

Mr. Field is the proprietor of the San Jose Marble and Granite Works located on Second street. He is well and favorably known throughout the county. He is a deacon of the First Presbyterian Church, of which he is an active and influential member. He is a native of Vermont, 66 years of age and has resided in this city for many years. His estimable wife, Mrs. M. H. Field, is a prominent member of the Chautauqua Circle and W. C. T. U.

As the day wore on Mr. Field gradually improved and the hope for his recovery began to grow stronger.

Dr. Keith was also summoned and the three physicians used every endeavor to aid the patient. Their efforts were rewarded by favorable symptoms appearing and the evening passed without any change for the worse. At 10 o'clock Mr. Field was resting quietly and the physicians left for home. At that hour they considered the chances favorable for his recovery. Mr. Field and family have many friends here and the news of the sad accident will be received with great sorrow, and numerous will be the earnest wishes for his recovery.

At 1:30 o'clock this morning a representative of the MERCURY called at the residence of Mr. Field and was informed that no unfavorable change had occurred and he was still resting quietly.

*San Jose Daily Mercury*
November 9, 1887

## F. FIELD'S CONDITION.

### Symptoms Have a Slight Tendency for the Worse.

The condition of Frederick Field yesterday exhibited no particular change except in the afternoon when he was slightly worse. During the evening Drs. Breyfogle, Pierce and Keith visited him, and at their departure, about 8 o'clock, he was resting quietly. As the night wore on he became more restless, and at 1:45 this morning was very restless and delirious, but the symptoms were not considered necessarily unfavorable.

*San Jose Daily Mercury*
November 10, 1887

## Mr. Field's Condition.

At 1:30 o'clock this morning Mr. Field's condition was considered more hopeful than heretofore. He had been lying in a stupor since Thursday noon until yesterday afternoon, when he appeared, at several times, to have approached a certain degree of consciousness. The attending physicians thought that if he should experience no reaction before morning they would have fair hopes of his recovery.

*San Jose Daily Mercury*
November 12, 1887

## Mr. Field's Condition.

At 1:30 o'clock this morning F. Field's condition had not materially changed. He was still unconscious, but was resting quietly. Drs. Pierce and Keith were in almost constant attendance yesterday, and Dr. Breyfogle called last evening.

*San Jose Daily Mercury*
November 11, 1887

## F. FIELD'S CONDITION.

### A Slight Improvement Noticed—Conscious Moments.

F. Field's condition was considerably improved yesterday. He rested easily throughout the day, sleeping most of the time and exhibiting conscious moments immediately after awaking. At such times, he would recognize members of the family and would make coherent utterances, though not forming sentences. Throughout the evening and night he slept quietly, occasionally waking and becoming conscious. Up to midnight no change was noticed, and at 12:30 he was resting easily. The symptoms are considered entirely favorable and there is some hope of recovery.

*San Jose Daily Mercury*
November 14, 1887

East Bay Regional Park District

The condition of Mr. Field remains favorable, and from present indications the physicians have hope of his recovery.

*San Jose Daily Mercury*
November 15, 1887

## Mr. Field's Condition.

At half-past 1 o'clock this morning the condition of Mr. F. Field was not as hopeful as for several days past. At times during the last twenty-four hours his body would become cold and his pulse low. Again his pulse was as high as 140 and his temperature unnatural. At intervals he would arouse from his stupor and would be rational, recognizing those who gathered around him and endeavoring to talk to them, but his words were unintelligible.

*San Jose Daily Mercury*
November 16, 1887

## F. Field Dying.

As announced in last evening's HER-ALD, Mr. Field's condition yesterday was far from hopeful. He grew worse last night. Extreme variations of the pulse were characteristic features of his condition during the night, and this morning it began to become apparent that the end could not be far away. Mr. Field has been sinking during the day and it is believed this afternoon that he is dying.

*San Jose Daily Herald*
November 16, 1887

## Mr. Field's Condition.

About half-past 1 o'clock this morning the condition of Mr. Field was, if anything, less favorable. He has been gradually sinking for some time. The intermittent attacks of chill and fever have ceased, leaving him very weak.

*San Jose Daily Mercury*
November 17, 1887

# STATE BOARD OF TRADE.

## Death of a Prominent Member—Many Visitors Call.

The State Board of Trade rooms on Second street since the various county exhibits have been arranged in order presents a very neat and attractive appearance, and even to old Californians the exhibition of the products of the State is one of interest and gratifying to the pride.

The number of visitors at the rooms yesterday was large, and among them was a party of business men from St. Louis who are looking about the State for a suitable business location. After traveling through the southern part of the State they are now taking in the northern portion, and they express a preference for the latter.

Another party was from Chicago and their object was to find a suitable locality for a colony of about one hundred families. So far seventy-three families have affiliated in the movement.

D. Blake, of the Gilroy *Advocate*, and a member of the Gilroy Board of Trade, was also among the visitors, he being there in behalf of his Board of Trade. He was much impressed with what he saw, and promised to recommend the Gilroy Board to join in the movement.

During the day a dispatch from San Jose was received at the rooms announcing the death of Frederick Field, who was a very active member of the Executive Committee. Mr. Field last Tuesday was about to board the train at San Jose, his purpose being to attend the meeting of the Board here, when his foot slipped causing him to fall with such force as to cause his skull to be fractured, resulting in his death. He was a prominent wholesale merchant of San Jose.

*The Morning Call* (San Francisco)
November 18, 1887

## FREDERICK FIELD.

The death of Frederick Field is a mournful loss, not only to his family and to the inner social circle of which he was a loved and honored member, but to the community as well wherein he has spent fourteen years of his useful life. It is not every section that is blessed with citizens who serve the public so unselfishly and manifest so constant and earnest a desire to do something for the common weal.

The manner of his taking off seems all unsuited to the quiet, careful method of his days. We think of such men as he going down the shady vale of life in gentleness, gradually withdrawing from the dusty highways of business to the retired and love-strewn foot paths of a good old age. It seems almost unkind in Providence to permit the grim destroyer to exercise so harsh and cruel a method upon so kind and just a man.

And yet, after all, there is a fitness behind it, for he fell in the direct path of duty and in the very midst of his endeavor for the general good. Few men can know or guess or choose the time and manner of their death, but to die in the harness of duty is better than this knowledge or choice. Macaulay puts thought in the lips of the brave old Roman, Horatius, when he makes him say, beside the Tiber bridge:

> "To every man upon this earth,
> Death cometh soon or late;
> But how can man die better
> Than facing fearful odds
> For the ashes of his fathers,
> And the temples of his Gods."

*San Jose Daily Mercury*
November 18, 1887

The San Jose Granite and Marble Works will close their place of business to-day at 12 o'clock, in order to attend the funeral of F. Field. COOMBS, BLANCHARD & O'NEIL.

*San Jose Daily Mercury*
November 19, 1887

# THE LAST RITES.

## The Funeral of the Late Frederick Field.

### AN IMPRESSIVE DISCOURSE.

#### A Vast Assemblage of the Friends of the Deceased do Honor to His Memory —Floral Offerings.

The Presbyterian Church early began to fill yesterday afternoon with the friends and acquaintances of the late Frederick Field, who were in attendance to participate in the services at the church in honor of his memory. The Board of Trade had announced its intention of attending in a body, and several members of the Executive Committee of the State Board, of which Mr. Field was a member, were present. The San Jose Women's Christian Temperance Union also resolved to attend.

The fore part of the church had been very tastefully decorated with the floral offerings of friends and members of the Presbyterian Church. The front of the altar was draped with sprays of smilax and ivy, while relieving the dark coloring were baskets profuse with snowy flowers and prepared floral pieces of rare exotics. The pulpit railing was wound with smilax, while on the sides were stands bearing large bouquets on baskets of roses and chrysanthemums. Ivy and smilax clung to every projecting part of the large pipe organ, while the forward part of the gallery railing was banked with roses and chrysanthemums intertwined with green leaves and vines. Some of the individual offerings were very appropriate and beautiful. An anchor and cross with an encircling wreath, the whole of Marechal Neil roses and maiden's hair ferns, bore the draped card of the San Jose W. C. T. U. An elegant basket of rare rosebuds, chrysanthemums and smilax was from the Alexander Duff Missionary Society of the church. A lyre from Prof. Pomeroy was to the left of the pulpit. An an anchor and heart of heliotrope bore the card of Misses Jennie Kent and Mary Mabury, former Sunday School pupils. Other beautiful offerings were:

A bouquet by Mrs. Everett Pomeroy; a bouquet by Mrs. Calhoun; a cross and anchor, Mrs. Loryea; bouquet, Mrs. D. R. Wagner.

At 2:15 o'clock the cortege arrived, the casket being borne by pall-bearers Messrs. Dr. C. W. Breyfogle, D. G. Kent, Judge Reynolds, N. Cadwallader, D. B. Moody, A. S. Evans, F. H. Babb and Mr. Oliver. As the pall bearers entered the Church bearing the casket and preceded by Mr. Field's pastor during life, Rev. H. C. Minton, and followed by the relatives, a quiet as of the peaceful memory of the deceased reigned over the assemblage which was fitly accompanied by the opening hymn, "Jesus, Lover of My Soul." The services were conducted according to the ritual of the Presbyterian Church, the appropriate texts of which referred to the immortal nature of life. Miss Carrie Foster McLellan sang Mrs. Browning's beautiful verses, "He Giveth His Beloved Sleep," the soft cadences of which were followed by a few remarks by the Rev. Minton. The tenor of his remarks was such as could not but find echo in the minds of all present. He referred to the shadow of mourning which brooded over the day, a melancholy one, for California has lost a faithful citizen; the community an able resident; the Church a consistant and genuine Christian man; the home, a kind and sympathetic father. No eulogy was necessary for such a life for the plainest truth is the highest eulogy while the quick verdict of all who knew the humility of his Christian life is that the city mourns a public loss. God's best gift is a good man but it takes a lifetime to develop such a strong, well-formed character. As experience is the mother of wisdom so it takes the conflicts of a long life to deepen and strengthen the tissues of a virtuous man. Men develop; time is an equal factor with growth; many seasons are needed to strengthen the braces of our moral nature. Therefore in this age of shams, genuine manhood commands the premium. A man who has lived sixty-seven years in this unparalleled country and century of money-making ambition and is loved more and more to the last is the man we adore.

The best way to convince men you are good is to be good. Blessed is the man whom God has endowed with a generous nature and a noble soul but thrice blessed is he who has gone forward day after day doing his simple duty and commanding the respect and admiration of his fellow men. There are times when the word Christian is best not spoken or with muffled tones and bated breath but there are other times, as the present, when in highest accents should be told what it signifies and what it dignifies. Do men call him good? Such faith linked with such truth is a living argument which silences the voice of skepticism. Talk bout the logic of infidelity, such a life outweighs it and destroys the fond images of the skeptic's dream. This genial fraternal spirit, the sharer of our joys, the bearer of our griefs, as a character is of more value than the bloated capitalist, stuffed with government bonds or millions of filthy coin. He was the man to love; ever faithful and gentle; even his faults leaned toward virtue's side. The speaker said it was a common loss, for all hearts are sad to-day for we mourn with a common sympathy. Another link has been forged that binds us to the unseen shore; another tie is made that draws us to Jesus Christ. It is fitting, he said, that these words should be spoken here where his voice had been often heard in prayer; where he had sang in praise of the land he loved and partaken of the tokens of Christ's dying love. He has merely gone before, closed his eyes to open them in another world. God grant that through our tears we may perceive the blessing of the hour and understand the blessed legacy of a life which stimulates those left behind to follow in the footsteps of the Lord as he did.

Mr. Minton's remarks were very appropriate and such as to heal the sting of a wounded heart with the salve of contentment. He referred truthfully to Mr. Field's public spirited character for he had been an energetic worker for all that would be of general benefit.

At the services at the church the solemn cortege of over one hundred carriages formed and followed the remains to the cemetery where they were deposited in their last resting place according to the ritual of the church.

*San Jose Daily Mercury* (con't)
November 20, 1887

---

## PROBATE OF WILL.

### The Estate and Heirs of the Late Frederick Field.

The will of the late Frederick Field has been filed for probate with the County Clerk. It is dated March 10, 1879, and is witnessed by Gouveneur M. Bruce and Starr M. Bruce. The testator bequeaths to his wife, Mary H. Field, all of his estate, both real, personal and mixed and wheresoever situated. He does not devise anything to his children, for the stated reason that he deems it to their best interest to leave them to the care of their mother, whom he herewith nominates and appoints as their guardian. He also nominates her as the sole executrix without any requirements as to bonds and empowers her to sell and dispose of any and all of his estate without any order of the court.

Accompanying the will is a petition by Mrs. M. H. Field for the probating of the same and the issuance to her of letters testamentary. The heirs are Mabel I., Arthur G., Wilfred E. and Herbert C. Field. The estate consists of the following properties: Lot on northwest corner of Sainsevain and Northrup streets, $3,000; one hundred feet frontage on Sunol street, $1,000; one-fourth interest in lot on southeast corner of Sunol and South streets, $1,000; lot on University grounds, $800; 100 feet front on lot 4, block 18, University tract, $1,000; lot 10, block 22, in East San Jose Homestead tract, $300; one-half interest in Excelsior Marble Works, $4,000; horse and buggy, $150; gold watch, $50 Total, $11,300.

---

*San Jose Daily Herald*
November 22, 1887

## IN MEMORIAM.

### Resolutions Adopted by the W. C. T. U. on the Death of Mr. Field.

The annexed resolutions were adopted by San Jose W. C. T. U. at its regular meeting on the 24th:

WHEREAS, In the providence of God our friend and brother, one of our honorary members, also a member of our Advisory Committee, Frederick Field, has been removed by death, and

WHEREAS, We realize in his death we have lost one who was always true to the cause we represent, and who had its interest near his heart; therefore

*Resolved*, That we hereby express our appreciation of the great loss we sustain in his death. We feel that we have lost one of our most faithful advisers and constant friends, and we trust his earnest and faithful example will stimulate our zeal and incite us to more earnest efforts in the cause which was so dear to his heart.

*Resolved*, That we hereby tender to our beloved sister, Mrs. M. H. Field, the wife, and to the sons and daughters of Mr. Field, our heartfelt sympathy in their sad bereavement, and assure them that our earnest prayers are offered that God will comfort and sustain them and enable them to follow in the path to which his earnest and devoted life would lead.

*Resolved*, That these resolutions be sent to the bereaved family, be spread on our minutes and published in the San Jose daily papers.

S. J. CHURCHILL,
M. S. CAREY,
MRS. C. E. BABB,
Committee.

This article from the *San Jose Daily Herald*, November 26, 1887, states that the W. C. T. U. (Woman's Christian Temperance Union) adopted resolutions regarding the death of Frederick Field.

# Gravestones Manufactured by Frederick Field

Watkin Williams,
Section S-D, Plot 51

Ellen Davis,
Section N-F, Plot 101

# FRANK N. FISH

Courtesy of California History Section, California State Library, Sacramento.

Frank N. Fish, no date.

According to *Headstones of the Gold Rush Era: Sculpting Masterpieces in Marble*, Fall 1997, page 8, published by Sacramento County Historical Society, Frank N. Fish established his marble works, known as Frank N. Fish Marble Works, in 1873 in Sacramento, California. He worked with his two brothers, Anthony and Morris Fish. In 1878 he joined with Andrew Aitken and established Aitken & Fish Pioneer Marble Works. This partnership lasted until 1885, when he became a traveling agent for Aitken. In 1893, Fish worked as a traveling agent and marble cutter for W. H. McCormick in San Francisco (for more information on McCormick, see the section on William H. McCormick pages 917-922).

The *Sacramento Directory, 1873*, page 239, lists "John N. Fish, marble cutter with F. N. Fish, 252 K, bet 8th and 9th, res same."

The *McKenney's District Directory for 1879-80, Sacramento County*, page 59, lists Aitken and Fish, Premium Pioneer Marble Works, 177 K in Sacramento. (For more information on Aitken, see Andrew M. Aitken pages 854-862.)

The *Sacramento Directory for the Year 1880*, page 172, records F. N. Fish (Aitken & Fish), residence at 1416 12th in Sacramento and as a "marblecutter" with Aitkin [sic] & Fish, on K between 6th and 7th in Sacramento.

The *Sacramento City Directory 1883-1884*, page 215, lists Frank N. Fish with Aitken & Fish, res 1416 12th. Also listed are Anthony N. Fish and Morris N. Fish, marble cutters with Aitken & Fish.

The *1900 Census for Oakland Ward 4, Alameda County, California*, records Frank Fish, age 52, born *circa* 1848 in the Azore Islands. His year of immigration is 1860. Also listed are his wife Anna, age 45, a native of Portugal, and children: Sybil, age 18; Lauren, age 16; and Roy, age 13; all natives of California.

The *1900 Census for Woodland, Yolo County, California* also lists Frank W. [sic] Fish, age 54, born *circa* 1846 in the Azore Islands as a lodger with James R. Mitchell and his family. Fish's occupation is listed as marble cutter. James R. Mitchell's occupation is listed as granite cutter.

According to the *1910 Census, Oakland Ward 1, Alameda County, California*, Frank N. Fish, age 61, was born *circa* 1849 in Portugal. His date of immigration is listed as 1855, his occupation is listed as stone cutter, monuments, and his relation to the head of the household is father-in-law. Also listed are his wife Anna M. Fish, age 56, year of immigration 1868, and other family members: George W. White, age 37; Anna M. White (Fish's daughter), age 36; Merrill G. White, age 8; and Miriam B. White, age 4.

The *1910 Census for Woodland Ward 2, Yolo County, California* also lists Frank Fish, age 64, born *circa* 1846 in Portugal. He is listed as a lodger with James Mitchell and family. Fish's occupation is recorded as stone cutter, monuments. James Mitchell's occupation is also listed as stone cutter, monuments.

The *1920 Census, Woodland, Yolo County, California* lists Frank N. Fish, age 73, as a lodger and widower, born *circa* 1847 or 1848 in the Azores. His occupation is listed as marble dealer, granite works. He is a lodger with the James Mitchell family.

The *1930 Census, Sacramento, California*, lists Frank N. Fish, age 82. His relation to the head of the household is father-in-law. Also listed are William H. Roberts, age 55, his son-in-law; Sybil E. Roberts, age 47, his daughter; and grandchildren, Edith Roberts, age 25; Edward L. Roberts, age 19; Delbert M. Roberts, age 18; and Jack M. Brown, age 8. Fish's occupation is listed as "none."

According to the *California Death Index, 1930-1939, Vol. III, F-H*, Frank N. Fish died in Sacramento County on September 29, 1936, at age 89. *The Sacramento Union*, Wednesday, September 30, 1936 states that private funeral and interment services for Frank N. Fish will be held in Sunset View cemetery, Berkeley, Alameda County, California. Sunset View Cemetery is actually located at 101 Colusa Ave., El Cerrito, Contra Costa County, California.

Advertisement from the *Sacramento Directory, 1874*, page lii.

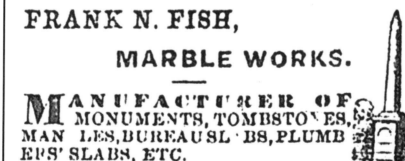

Advertisement from the *Sacramento Daily Union* newspaper, April 14, 1873.

FRANK N. FISH,

MARBLE WORKS.

MANUFACTURER OF
MONUMENTS, TOMBSTONES,
MANTLES, BUREAU SLABS, PLUMB
ERS' SLABS, ETC.
73 J street.
Between Third and Fourth.   j15-1m

Advertisement from *The Daily Bee* (Sacramento) newspaper, January 24, 1877.

# Frank N. Fish

Private funeral and interment services for Frank N. Fish, 89, a resident of California for 70 years, will be held tomorrow in Sunset View cemetery, Berkeley.

Fish, a native of the Azores Islands, died yesterday at his home, 2840 Santa Cruz way, after a long illness. He had worked as a marble cutter.

Six children, Mrs. George White, Oakland; Mrs. Dora Morris, Reno; Frank N. Fish, San Anselmo; Roy H. Fish and Lauren S. Fish, San Francisco, and Clarence T. Fish, Los Angeles.

The body is at Andrews & Greilich mortuary, 28th and W streets.

*The Sacramento Union*
September 30, 1936

Reference 379.20

Top photograph: front side of Fish gravestone, Sunset View Cemetery, El Cerrito, Contra Costa County, California, 2007. Bottom photograph: back side of Frank Fish gravestone. Buried at the same site with Frank Fish are his wife, daughter and son-in-law. Photographs by Traci (Gibbons) Parent, 2007.

The gravestone inscription left to right says:

JOSEPH DANIEL MORRIS
January 29, 1868 – May 13, 1921

FRANK NICHOLAS FISH
May 4, 1848 – September 29, 1936

DORA MABEL FISH MORRIS
January 7, 1876 – February 23, 1962

ANNA MARIA GOETHE FISH
September 25, 1855 – January 22, 1917

"LOOKING UNTO JESUS, THE AUTHOR AND FINISHER OF OUR FAITH."

Reference 379.21

# Gravestone Manufactured by Frank N. Fish
## (and Andrew M. Aitken)

Richard Heycock gravestone, Section N-D, Plot 35.
The carver's mark, located on the lower right corner of this stone, is Aitken and Fish, Sacramento.

# MICHAEL HEVERIN

The *1850 Census for Davidson, Tennessee* lists Michael Hevrin [sic] age 25, born *circa* 1825, in England. His occupation is noted as stone cutter.

Heverin is listed as operating a marble yard and/or marble works in various business directories between 1864 and 1879.

The *San Francisco Directory, 1869*, page 306, lists Michael Heverin as proprietor of Pioneer Steam Marble Works located at 422 and 424 Jackson, and stone yard foot of Third. His dwelling is recorded as 1817 Stockton. An advertisement is printed on page 11 of the directory.

The *1870 Census for San Francisco Ward 2, San Francisco County, California*, records Michael Heverin, age 44, born *circa* 1826, as a native of England. Also listed are his wife, Elizabeth Heverin, age 40, born *circa* 1830 in Ireland; and their children: Edward, age 15; Margaret, age 13; Anna, age 11; Charles, age 7; and Angelo, age 6. All are natives of California.

The *1880 Census for San Francisco, San Francisco County, California*, records Michael Hevrin [sic], age 55, born *circa* 1825, a native of England, and his occupation Marble Works. Also listed are his wife Elizabeth, age 50, born *circa* 1830 in Ireland, and their children: Edward, age 31, occupation Marble Cutter; Margaret Hevrin [sic], age 23, occupation Dressmaker; Annie Hevrin [sic], age 21, occupation Dressmaker; Charles, age 17, occupation "Works in Foundry"; and Angelo, age 15, "at School." All are natives of California.

The *San Francisco Directory 1880* lists Heverin's son, Edward J. Heverin, 17 Larkin in San Francisco, under the heading "Marble Works."

The *San Francisco, California Directories, 1889-91* lists Michael Heverin, 1605 Jones, as a marble dealer in 1889.

According to *The San Francisco Call* newspaper, July 10, 1895, Heverin died at age 70 years and had been dying for three months with dropsy.

The *San Francisco Chronicle* newspaper, July 10, 1895, states Heverin died in Tiburon, Marin County, California on July 8, 1895. Funeral services were held on Wednesday, July 10, 1895. Interment was at Laurel Hill Cemetery in San Francisco.

Heverin's burial and gravestone inscription was documented in *Records from Tombstones in Laurel Hill Cemetery, 1853-1937*, San Francisco, California, compiled by the Daughters of the American Revolution (D.A.R.), 1935, page 54. This document is located at the Sutro Library in San Francisco. The document states that M. Heverin was born in Liverpool, England, and that he died July 6, 1896, aged 70 years.

According to obituaries that appeared in the *San Francisco Call* and *San Francisco Chronicle* newspapers, Heverin died July 8, 1895. Heverin's body was disinterred from Laurel Hill Cemetery and re-interred at the Laurel Hill Memorial, Cypress Lawn Cemetery, Colma, San Mateo County, California. A large obelisk marks the burial location for Heverin and the other 35,000 individuals moved from Laurel Hill.

Reference 379.22

Obelisk Monument at Laurel Hill Memorial, Cypress Lawn Cemetery, Colma, California.
Photograph by Traci (Gibbons) Parent, 2007.

A memorial plaque located at Laurel Hill Garden at the Cypress Lawn site states:

*In 1902, by order of the San Francisco Board of Supervisors, Laurel Hill was closed to further burials.*

*Formal attempts to force abandonment of the cemetery came in 1913 and again in 1924. Both attempts failed.*

*In April, 1937, the San Francisco Board of Supervisors, for the third time, passed an ordinance demanding evacuation of Laurel Hill, so its land could be converted to housing and street development.*

*In May, 1937, the Board was presented referendum petitions bearing the signatures of 21,000 protesting San Franciscans. It refused to repeal the ordinance, and at the election of the following November, the citizens of San Francisco upheld the ordinance and ratified the actions of the Board of Supervisors by a vote of 82,983 to 65,920. [...]*

*Removal from Laurel Hill began February 26, 1940. Some remains were placed by descendants in other cemeteries; most of them were brought here, to Cypress Lawn. And now 35,000 of San Francisco's pioneer dead lie in underground vaults, a few paces north of this tablet.*

**M. HEVERIN,**

Importer and Manufacturer of

## Italian and American Marbles, Mantels

GRATES, MONUMENTS, HEADSTONES,

**TOMBS, WASHSTANDS,**

Bureau and Counter Tops,

783 Cor. Market and Fourth Sts.

All kinds of Cemetery Work promptly attended to, and done on reasonable terms.

Advertisement from the *San Francisco City Directory, 1864,* page 629.

**M. HEVERIN,**

*Importer and Manufacturer of*

## Italian & American Marbles, Mantels,

GRATES, MONUMENTS, HEADSTONES, TOMBS,

**WASHSTANDS,**

BUREAU AND COUNTER TOPS,

783 Market, Cor. Fourth Street.

All kinds of Cemetery Work promptly attended to, and done on Reasonable Terms.

Advertisement from the *San Francisco Directory, 1866,* page 659.

Advertisement from the *San Francisco Directory, 1867*, page 60.

Advertisement from the *San Francisco Directory, 1869*, page 11.

Advertisement from the *Pacific Coast Business Directory for 1871-3*, page 46.

Advertisement from the *San Francisco Directory for the Year Commencing April, 1876*, page 31.

# ANOTHER VETERAN GONE.

## Michael Heverin Died Last Monday at the Home of His Daughter in Belvedere.

Another of the pioneers has gone. M. Heverin, who was for thirty-five years at the head of the marble-cutting business in California, breathed his last at the residence of his daughter, Mrs. T. F. Harley, Belvedere, last Monday night. He was 70 years of age and an old-time member of the Exempt Firemen. He leaves three sons and two daughters. One of the sons, Charles R. Heverin, is freight clerk on the San Francisco and North Pacific Company's steamer Tiburon.

When Mr. Heverin went into the marble-cutting business in San Francisco he determined to make this one of the principal States in the Union in that line. He opened up quarries at Suisun, Haywards, Tehachapi, Penryn and Rutland, Vt., and also went into partnership with Tomasso Gogliadi of Carrara, Italy. He established the steam marble works on Jackson street, and there a great deal of the marble work used in the big buildings in this City was turned out. His workmanship can now be seen in the Palace Hotel and Lick House, and City Hall.

For many years Mr. Heverin was treasurer of the Exempt Firemen, and the old boys are going to turn out en masse at his funeral. He was 70 years old, and had been dying for three months with dropsy.

San Francisco Call
July 10, 1895

HEVERIN—In Tiburon, July 8, Michael Heverin, father of Edward J., Charles R. and Angelo M. Heverin and Mrs. George E. Luther and Mrs. T. F. Harley, and grandfather of James Emmett, Mary E. and Amelia S. Hayden, a native of England, aged 70 years.

San Francisco Bulletin
July 10, 1895

M. Heverin mark on lower right corner of the gravestone.
Sarah Howell and Thomas M. Howell,
Section N-C, Plot 8

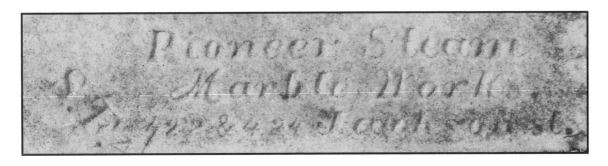

Pioneer Steam Marble Works mark on the lower right corner of the gravestone.
Michael Heverin was the proprietor of this company.
William Timothy Richards and John Richards,
Section N-E, Plot 64

Pioneer Steam Marble Works mark on the lower right corner of the gravestone.
Peter Davis,
Section S-F, Plot 111

Pioneer Steam Marble Works mark on the lower left corner of the gravestone.
David R. Williams,
Section S-D, Plot 58

# Gravestones Manufactured by Pioneer Steam Marble Works
### (Michael Heverin, Proprietor)

Sarah Howell & Thomas M. Howell,
Section N-C, Plot 8

John Richards & William Timothy Richards,
Section N-E, Plot 64

Peter Davis,
Section S-F, Plot 111

David R. Williams,
Section S-D, Plot 58

# ISRAEL LUCE

Israel Luce, no date.

According to *An Illustrated History of Sacramento County, California*, 1890, The Lewis Publishing Company, pages 470 and 471, Israel Luce was born in Tompkins County, New York, in the village of Newfield near Ithaca. He was the son of New Jersey natives, James and Mary (Barber) Luce. Luce learned the marble-cutter's trade at the age of twenty at West Troy, Rensselaer County, New York. The monument work he learned at Pittsfield, Berkshire County, Massachusetts. Luce carried on the marble business for three years while he was employed at Woonsocket, Providence County, Rhode Island.

On January 29, 1849 he left New York on the sailing vessel *John Castner*, and arrived in San Francisco on May 25, 1849. Upon arrival, he traveled to Sacramento on his way to the Coloma gold mining camps in El Dorado County,

California. In September 1849 he returned to Sacramento and worked as a clerk in a store. In March 1850 he left Sacramento again and this time traveled nine miles up the American River where he built and served as the proprietor of the Nine-Mile House, an establishment that sold rum. This business was not agreeable to him and he sold it and moved back to Sacramento.

According to *Golden Notes, Headstones of the Gold Rush Era: Sculpturing Masterpieces in Marble*, Vol. 43, Number 3, Fall 1997, page 2, in December 1850 Luce purchased marble from Charles Minturn of San Francisco and brought it to Sacramento, establishing the first marble yards in February 1851 located on 7th Street, between J and K Streets. It was known as Luce and Loveland's Marble Works. He formed a co-partnership with Andrew

East Bay Regional Park District

Aitken in 1853 and carried on this business for twenty-five years, dissolving the business in 1878. Luce and Aitken worked the quarry at Indians' Diggings, El Dorado County for eighteen years. (For more information on Aitken, see Andrew M. Aitken pages 854-862.) In September 1885 Luce served as the superintendent of the Inyo marble quarries. Luce discovered at least four quarries between Inyo and Placer Counties.

Israel Luce was married twice, first to Mary Adeline Nichols of Worcester, Worcester County, Massachusetts whom he married in 1848. Mary died in 1861, leaving him two sons, John C. and G. W., and one daughter, Mary. In 1863 he married Mrs. Eliza Elliott. They had two children, Fannie and Charles S.

Luce was one of the oldest Odd Fellow members in the State, having been initiated into the Berkshire Lodge, No. 57, Independent Order of Odd Fellows, in Massachusetts in May 1848 and eventually joining Eureka No. 4. In his early years he was also devoted to politics.

The *1870 Census, Sacramento Ward 5, Sacramento County, California* lists Israel Luce, age 45, born *circa* 1825 in New York. Also listed are his wife Eliza, age 33, born *circa* 1837, a native of Wisconsin, and their children: John C., age 16 born *circa* 1854; Willie, age 13, born *circa* 1857; Mary R., age 13, born *circa* 1857; and Fannie, age 5, born *circa* 1865. All are natives of California.

Luce was recorded in the *Business Directory of San Francisco and Principal Towns of California and Nevada, 1877*, page 198, under "Marble Works" with Aitken & Luce, Sacramento.

The *1880 Census, Sacramento , Sacramento County, California* lists Israel Luce, age 55, born *circa* 1825 in New York, occupation marble cutter. Also listed are his wife Eliza, age 42, born *circa* 1838 in Illinois, and their children: John, age 26, born *circa* 1854, a marble cutter; Fannie, age 15, born *circa* 1865; and Charles, age 9, born *circa* 1871. All are natives of California.

The *Sacramento City Directory 1883-1884*, page 570, lists Israel Luce & Co., 611 K.

According to the obituary for his granddaughter, Mrs. Ethel U. Lee, that appeared in the *Sacramento Bee* newspaper, October 25, 1955, Israel Luce settled in Sacramento about 1850. He founded the Luce & Luce Granite and Monumental Works at 10th Street and Broadway. Luce's son, John C. Luce, operated the monument works until his retirement. According to the obituary for another granddaughter, Myrtle Everett, which appeared in the *Sacramento Bee*, February 9, 1965, Luce helped with the building of Sutter's lumber mill at Coloma, El Dorado County, California.

Luce died on October 11, 1898 in Sacramento from heart disease and was interred at Sacramento City Cemetery. According to his obituary in the *Evening Sacramento Bee*, October 12, 1898, he was 74 years, 1 month, and 27 days old.

The following poems were written by Israel Luce (presumably the carver Luce) in 1894.

[For the RECORD-UNION.]

## THE VACANT CHAIRS.

How many chairs are vacant, around the once
    bright hearth
Where once, from joyous laughter, broke
    forth the songs of mirth?
Where young and old together, joined voice
    in songs of glee:
But now, alas! all that is left is the sad
    memory.

My father and my mother joined in the cheer-
    ful song,
Whose voices now are hushed in death; have
    lain there long—so long!
And since I have to manhood grown, how
    often I have longed
For mother's hand my steps to guide—the
    streets have been so thronged.

If, mother, dear, in heaven, you still can
    watch your child,
Oh! let me not be led astray from mother's
    loving smile;
But let me hear thy angel wings, and thy dear
    loving voice
Whisper, "Come back to me, my child; and
    evermore rejoice."

And, mother, often in my dreams, I've seen
    thy loving face
Lean over me, as though you would catch me
    in your embrace;
And, mother, dear, when I awoke, all I'd so
    plainly seen
Had vanished with the morning sun—'twas
    only in my dream.

But, mother, dear, I love to think you still
    watch over me,
And lead my footsteps in a way, the end I
    cannot see;
I trusted thee in childhood days, I now will
    trust thee more,
For thou wilt lead me where thou art upon
    the other shore.

And, mother, when that time shall come, and
    I am called away,
Meet me on the other side, to lead me on my
    way;
Where there will be no parting, in sorrow or
    in pain,
For Christ shall be our all in all, and over all
    shall reign.            —ISRAEL LUCE.
Sacramento, February 24th.

*The Daily Record – Union* (Sacramento)
February 10, 1894

East Bay Regional Park District

[For the RECORD-UNION.]

## IS THERE NO GOD?

There is no God, the fool hath said,
Nor do we know from what we're bred,
Nor where we go to when we're dead,
    And leave this great formation.
If may be tree, it may be shrub,
It may be monkey, or it may be grub.
Then what am I?  Ah! there's the rub—
    Small part of this formation.

There is no God, thus saith the fool,
Who would measure eternity with a rule,
And try his inner self to school
    That there is no creation.
There is no law with beams of light
To pierce the darkness of the night.
Can Chance alone reveal the sight,
    The cause of this formation?

If there's no law, then why not I
Eat, drink, be merry, to-morrow die.
If no law's broken, why fear and fly
    Since there's no retribution?
Yet guilt I feel.  Some broken law
Must needs exhibit.  But where or how?
That question makes the savants bow
    To that which caused creation.

As I feel guilt, then there must be
A power above and over me,
A power whose source I cannot see,
    A Power of Retribution.
Wrong I have done?  Who ever saw
Wrong only from some broken law?
Convinced of guilt I humbly bow
    To that which caused creation.

There is no Future?  Oh! there must be
A Future somewhere, or why have we
A sense of guilt from which we flee
    In fear of Retribution.
There is a Power by us unseen
From which we strive our lives to screen,
Whose broken law leaves guilt within
    That speaks of Retribution.
            —ISRAEL LUCE.

*The Daily Record – Union* (Sacramento)
March 3, 1894

[For the RECORD-UNION.]

# THE DESPISED AND FORSAKEN.

"I'm alone, all alone, though in crowded
  street,
Of the thousands of faces there are none that
  I greet.
While many seem happy and have little care,
I—I am so lonely, almost in despair."

Thus cried the poor outcast as she paced the
  street,
Asking for pennies, for something to eat:
"Alone! All alone! Oh, I shall go wild!
Oh, God, send me someone to care for Thy
  child!

"Yes, I am Thy child, for my dear mother
  said
That You would care for me and give me daily
  bread.
'Twas the prayer of the Savior she taught me
  to say,
  'Our Father in Heaven'—'Give us bread day
  by day.' "

She looked in the faces of those that she met,
As she struggled along, with her feet cold and
  wet.
In some she saw sorrow and grief in their face,
While others bore marks of sin and disgrace.

Then the thought came to her: "They have
  not always been so;
They were somebody's darlings, though now
  brought so low.
Oh, God! in Thy mercy, oh, save from sin!
And help me my dear mother's Heaven to
  win."

I looked on and listened to her mournful cry,
When the question came to me, Why was it
  not I?
'Twas not by my wisdom or goodness I know;
Then why should I spurn those in suffering
  and woe?

They're our brothers and sisters, were darlings
  in truth,
As pure and as good as we in their youth.
They have stumbled and fallen, and have led
  lives of sin,
So nobody cared for them, nor their love tried
  to win.

Before you condemn put yourself in their
  place;
Would not we be the same but for God's
  mercy and grace?
If those without sin would alone cast the
  stone,
As in days of our Savior, she'd be standing
  alone.                          ISRAEL LUCK.

*The Daily Record – Union* (Sacramento)
April 21, 1894

Reference 379.23

Israel Luce's polished granite gravestone,
Sacramento City Cemetery, 2003.
Photograph by Traci (Gibbons) Parent.

The gravestone inscription says:
ISRAEL LUCE
1824 – 1898
MARY A. LUCE
1828 – 1861

## DIED.

LUCE—In this city, October 11, 1898, Israel
Luce, husband of Eliza Luce, father of
G. W. and C. S. Luce of San Fran-
cisco, Mrs. Mary Marsh, Mrs. Fanny
Clary and J. C. Luce of this city, a
native of New York, aged 74 years, 1
month and 27 days.
  Friends and acquaintances are re-
spectfully invited to attend the funeral
Thursday, at 1:30 o'clock, from the
Sixth-Street M. E. Church. Interment
City Cemetery.                    10886

*The Evening Bee* (Sacramento)
October 12, 1898

### Stricken by Heart Disease.

SACRAMENTO, Oct. 11.—Israel Luce,
a pioneer Californian, who was for nearly twenty-five years engaged in the
marble-cutting business in this city,
dropped dead this morning from heart
disease. He was a native of Ithaca, N.
Y., aged 73 years. Luce arrived in California in May, 1849.

*The San Francisco Call*
October 12, 1898

### Death of a Pioneer.

Israel Luce, a pioneer of Sacramento,
died very suddenly in the latter city yesterday morning. He was a brother-in-
law of J. C. Stubbs, third vice president
of the Southern Pacific Railroad Company, and has two sons in the employ of
the same company—G. W. Luce, assistant general freight and passenger agent
at Los Angeles, and Charles S. Luce, in
the freight department of this city. Both
of his sons leave for Sacramento to-day
to attend the funeral.

*The San Francisco Call*
October 15, 1898

# WILLIAM H. McCORMICK

The *1870 Census for San Francisco Ward 8, San Francisco County, California*, lists William McCormack [sic], age 30, born *circa* 1840 as a native of Ireland. His occupation is recorded as marble dealer. Also documented are his wife, Sarah, age 29, born *circa* 1841, a native of Missouri, and their children: Emanuel, age 8, born *circa* 1862; and Elizabeth, age 4, born *circa* 1866. Both are natives of California.

According to *San Francisco Business Directories* from 1872 to 1878, William H. McCormick was in business with Leon R. Myers & Company marble works at 861 Market. By 1879, William H. McCormick marble works is listed, indicating that he is no longer in business with Myers.

McCormick's marble works remains at 861 Market in San Francisco. In the same directory, Leon Myers marble yard is located at 30 Main. From 1882-1885 the address of McCormick's marble works is listed as 827 Market and by 1889 it is 1422 Market.

The *San Francisco, California Directories, 1889-91*, for the year 1889 lists his business as 1422 Market and residence as 1715 Larkin and his occupation as marble works.

The *San Francisco, California Directories, 1889-91*, for the year 1890 lists his business as 1522 Market and residence as 1715 Larkin and his occupation as marble works.

According to the *San Francisco Call* newspaper, in 1896, McCormick submitted a bid for the marble and tile work in the City Hall dome. See article on page 928.

The *1900 Census for San Francisco, San Francisco County, California*, records Wm. H. McCormick, age 62, born *circa* 1838, as a native of Ireland. His occupation is listed as marble dealer. Also listed is his wife Sarah J., age 54, born *circa* 1846, a native of Missouri; and their son, Ernest L., age 23, born *circa* 1877 in California.

The *1910 Census for San Francisco Assembly District 41, San Francisco County, California*, lists Wm. H. McCormick, age 73, born *circa* 1837 in Ireland and his occupation as retired contractor. Also listed are: his wife, Sarah J., age 70, born *circa* 1840 in Missouri; their son, E.B. McCormick, age 46, born *circa* 1864 a native of California; and their daughter and her family, Elizabeth W. Mathieu, age 41, born *circa* 1869 in California; husband Frank L. Mathieu, and daughters Marianne, age 16, and Frances, age 7.

The *San Francisco Examiner* newspaper, May 8, 1914, page 4, stated that William Henry McCormick died in San Francisco on May 7, 1914. He was in his seventies when he died and was interred in Woodlawn Memorial Park, Section E, lot 277, Colma, San Mateo County, California.

McCormick William H., *(Leon R. Myers & Co.)*
   dwl 108 Taylor

*The San Francisco General Directory, 1872*, page 439.

Myers Leon R. *(Leon R. Myers & Co.)*, dwl 1511 Mission
**MYERS LEON R. & CO.** *(Leon R. Myers and William
   H. McCormick)*, marbleworks, office and warerooms
   861 Market, yard and works 28 and 30 Main

*The San Francisco Directory, 1877*, page 646.

Myers Leon R. *(Leon R. Myers & Co.)*, dwl 1511 Mission
**MYERS LEON R. & CO.** *(W. H. McCormick)*, marble
   works, office and warerooms 861 Market, yard 28 and
   30 Main

*The San Francisco Directory, 1878*, page 633.

McCormick William H., marble and granite works,
   861 Market, r. 208 Jones

*The San Francisco Directory, 1880*, page 605.

## MARBLE WORKS.

*MANTELS and GRATES, MONUMENTS and HEADSTONES,*
   *In Marble and Scotch Granite,*
827 Market street...................bet. Fourth and Fifth.
   ☞ Send for Designs and Prices.   **W. H. McCORMICK.**

*San Francisco News Letter California Advertiser*, May 16, 1885, page 16.

Advertisement from the *San Francisco General Directory of Residents*
*and a Business Directory, Commencing March 1872*, page 768.
During this time, McCormick was in business with Leon R. Myers.

McCORMICK—In this city, May 7, William Henry, beloved husband of Sarah J. McCormick and loving father of E. B., E. L. and W. H. McCormick and Mrs. Frank L. Mathieu, a native of Ireland.
* * Services and interment private.

*San Francisco Examiner*
May 8, 1914

Reference 379.24

William H. McCormick gravesite, Section E, Lot 277, Woodlawn Memorial Park, Colma, San Mateo County, California, 2007. Names listed on the gravestone include William Henry McCormick, died May 7, 1914; his wife, Sarah Juliet McCormick, died October 11, 1918; and son, Emanuel B. McCormick, born 1863 and died 1928. Photograph by Traci (Gibbons) Parent.

Elias Havard,
Section N-D, Plot 39

# Gravestones Manufactured By W. H. McCormick

Margaret Leam & May Leam,
Section S-E, Plot 91

W. H. McCormick mark on the Margaret Leam and May Leam gravestone.

Andrew Paltenghi was born in Lugano, Canton Ticino, Switzerland *circa* 1824. According to the *San Francisco Directory for the Year Commencing October, 1864*, page 615, Andrew Paltenghi was in business with P. (Peter) Larseneur at 422 and 424 Jackson Street, San Francisco.

Larseneur was later with the firm of Pioneer Steam Marble Works in San Francisco and died April 2, 1867 in Geyser Springs, Sonoma County, California. Michael Heverin, of Pioneer Steam Marble Works, was appointed one of the executors of Larseneur's estate. (For more information on Heverin, see Michael Heverin on page 903-910.)

The *Contra Costa Gazette* newspaper, August 4, 1866, published an advertisement for Paltenghi listing his place of business as 812 Montgomery Street (between Jackson and Pacific Streets) in San Francisco. Additionally, the *Pacific Coast Directory, 1867* lists A. Paltenghi as a proprietor, marble yard at this same address.

The *1870 Census for San Francisco, San Francisco County, California*, records Andrw [sic] Paltanghi [sic], age 46, as a native of Switzerland, born *circa* 1824. Also listed are his wife Fanny, age 42, a native of Switzerland, and children: Minnie, age 10; Louis, age 9; Andrew, age 7; Antoinette, age 5; and Cecelia, age 5 months. All are natives of California.

The *San Francisco Directory for the Year Commencing March, 1875*, page 580, lists Andrea [sic] Paltenghi marble works at 1029 Market. His marble yard is listed at this same address in *the San Francisco Directory for the Year Commencing April, 1876*.

The *Business Directory of San Francisco and Principal Towns of California and Nevada, 1877*, page 540, records Paltenghi in partnership with Campodonico at 25-27 Turk, in San Francisco.

The *1880 Census for San Francisco, San Francisco County, California*, lists Andeo [sic] Paltenghi, age 54, as a native of Switzerland, born *circa* 1826. Also recorded are his wife Fannie, age 52, and their children: Minnie, age 20; Louis, age 18; Nettie, age 15; and Cecelia, age 11.

Paltenghi is listed at the "cor [corner] Ellis and Devisadero" under "Marble Works" in the *1880-1881 McKenney's Pacific Coast Business Directory*, page 1403. He is also listed on page 1230 of the same directory.

*Langley's San Francisco Directory for the Year Commencing April, 1882*, page 1122, records Andrew Paltenghi as operating a marble works at 1235 Market in San Francisco.

*Langley's San Francisco Directory for the Year Commencing April, 1884*, page 1234, lists Paltenghi at this same address. An ad for Metropolitan Marble Works also appears on this page. The same directory for the year 1885, page 1327, lists Paltenghi and contains an advertisement for his company.

The *San Francisco, California Directories, 1889-91*, page 26, lists Andrew Paltenghi as proprietor of the Metropolitan Marble Works at 1241 Market in San Francisco in 1889. The 1890 directory recorded him as proprietor of Metropolitan Marble Works at 1219 Market.

The *1890 Great Register of Voters*, San Francisco, California records Paltenghi, as age 66, a native of Switzerland and his occupation "marble." He lived at 100 6th Street and was naturalized on August 21, 1869 in San Francisco. He registered to vote on September 30, 1890.

The *San Francisco Directory 1891-1892*, page 1089, records Paltenghi as the proprietor of Metropolitan Marble Works at 1219 Market and his residence at 26 Page. His advertisement is also listed on page 974 of the same directory.

Recorded at this same address is The Chatain-Giletti Ornamental Stone Company. Their ad states that they provide architectural work on buildings and in cemeteries.

*Langley's San Francisco Directory for the Year Commencing May, 1892*, page 1599, lists Paltenghi's marble works at 1219 Market. On page 977 of the same directory it records Metropolitan Marble Works, A. Paltenghi proprietor, manufacturer foreign and domestic marble mantels, tombstones, monuments, tiling, etc., 1219 Market. On page 1090 it lists his residence at 928 ½ Pacific.

The *Crocker-Langley San Francisco Directory for 1899*, page 1210, lists the Metropolitan Marble and Granite Works. A. Paltenghi & Co. proprietors manufacturers foreign and domestic marble mantels, tombstones, monuments, tiling,

etc. at 1219 market. This same directory, on page 1357, lists Andrew Paltenghi and Thomas Maino as proprietors of Metropolitan Marble and Granite Works, 1219 Market. Paltenghi's residence is recorded at 928 Pacific.

The *San Francisco Directory for 1901-1902*, page 2095, lists A. Paltenghi & Co. at 1219 Market under the heading "Marble Dealers."

The *San Francisco Directory for 1902* lists the estate A. Paltenghi and Co. (estate of Andrew Paltenghi and Thomas Maino) proprietors Metropolitan Marble and Granite Works at 1219 Market.

Andrew's wife, Fanny Paltenghi, died in 1897 at the age of 69. Andrew died in San Francisco on April 21, 1901, at the age of 77 years and 2 months.

*Advertisement from the San Francisco Directory for the Year Commencing October, 1864, page 615.*

## A. PALTENGHI,

No. 812 Montgomery street,

Between Jackson and Pacific streets, just above Pioneer Hall.

## San Francisco.

DEALER IN MARBLE OF ALL KINDS. ALSO MAN-
tle-Pieces, Monuments. Gravestones, Marble
Slabs, etc. Sculpture and Ornaments made to order;
also Marble Fountains, Statues, etc.        aug 4 1y

*Contra Costa Gazette*
August 4, 1866

## Metropolitan Marble Works.

## A. PALTENGHI,

Manufacturer of

## Foreign and Domestic Marble Mantels,

Tombstones, Monuments, Tiling,
Plumbers' Slabs, Vases, Statu-
ary, Fountains, etc.

## 1235 MARKET ST., SAN FRANCISCO

Estimates furnished for Granite Work.

Advertisement from *Langley's San Francisco Directory for the Year Commencing April, 1884,* page 1234.

Advertisement from *Langley's San Francisco Directory for the Year Commencing April, 1885*, page 1327.

Advertisement from the *San Francisco Directory 1890 - 1891*, page 1532.

# BIDS FOR THE ROOF.

## City Hall Commissioners Open Tenders for Work on the Municipal Building.

The City Hall Commissioners opened bids for the construction of a new roof for the municipal building, for completing the dome and for the construction of an electric elevator in one of the wings yesterday.

The first bids opened were those on contract 83 for the construction of the roof. They were as follows: Thomas Butler, $224,450; James J. O'Brien, $197,079; San Francisco Bridge Company, $187,900; Rea Building and Construction Company, $200,960; M. McGowan, $299,000; J. H. McKay, $198,220.

The bids on contract 84 for the steel, iron, concrete, electric wiring and plastering work in the dome were as follows: Laney & Co., $98,200; J. H. McKay, $113,240; Western Iron Works, $91,302; San Francisco Novelty and Plating Works, $89,601 46; M. C. Lynch, $91,900.

The following bids were received on contract 85, for the marble and tile work in the dome: Inyo Company, $3268 67; California Travertine Company, $16,584; W. H. McCormick, $23,862 15; A. Paltenghi, $13,683.

The bids on contract No. 86, for work in the northeast wing, including the electric elevator, were as follows: Cahill & Hall Elevator Company, $3675; W. H. Hofman, $4350.

The bids on contract No. 87, for work in the attic, rotunda and dome, including all plumbing and gasfitting, were: J. J. McGowan, $1895; S. Rischelheimer, $2500; John P. Culley, $1950; R. Rice, $3385; P. F. Ward, $2800, and H. Williamson, $2224.

The bidders for the art glass work in the dome were: Pacific American Decorating Company, Thomas F. Butterworth, California Art Glass Bending Works and F. N. Woods & Co.

They submitted various designs, with bids for each, and the entire matter was sent to print, and will be acted on at the next meeting.

This newspaper article from *The San Francisco Call*, May 27, 1896, states that the San Francisco City Hall commissioners opened bids for work on City Hall. A. Paltenghi submitted a bid for the marble and the tile work in the dome.

PALTENGHI—In this city, April 21, 1901, Andrew Paltenghi, beloved husband of the late Fannie Paltenghi, and father of Mrs. A. C. Juillerat, Mrs. J. E. Carter, Mrs. A. E. Ulrich and Louis Paltenghi, a native of Lugano, Canton Ticino, Switzerland, aged 77 years and 2 months.

☞ Notice of funeral hereafter. Remains at the funeral parlors of Charles H. Jacob & Co., 318 Mason street, between O'Farrell and Geary

*The San Francisco Call*
April 22, 1901

PALTENGHI—In this city, April 21, 1901, Andrew Paltenghi, beloved husband of the late Fannie Paltenghi, and father of Mrs. A. E. Juillerat, Mrs. J. E. Carter, Mrs. A. E. Ulrich and Louis Paltenghi, a native of Lugano, Canton Ticino, Switzerland, aged 77 years and 2 months.

☞ Friends and acquaintances are respectfully invited to attend the funeral this day (Wednesday), at 12:15 o'clock, from the funeral parlors of Charles H. Jacob & Co., 318 Mason street, between O'Farrell and Geary, thence to Masonic Temple, corner Post and Montgomery streets, where services will be held under the auspices of Speranza Lodge No. 219, F. and A. M., commencing at 1 o'clock. Interment Masonic Cemetery.

*The San Francisco Call*
April 24, 1901

# Gravestone Manufactured by Andrew Paltenghi

Julia Etta Piercy, Section S-F, Plot #85, with new middle marble base.
The original middle base with the Paltenghi makers mark could not be used
when this gravestone was repaired. The original base was broken.
See photograph on page 445.

A. Paltenghi mark on the original marble middle base of Julia Etta Piercy,
Section S-F, Plot #85.

# James A. Plymire

The *1850 Census for W. Bethlehem, Washington County, Pennsylvania* lists James Plymire, age 10, born *circa* 1840, and a native of Pennsylvania. Also listed are his father, Wm. Plymire, age 32 a native of Pennsylvania; his mother, Eliza, age 30, a native of Ireland; and his siblings Mary I., age 8; Isabella, age 6; Sarah C., age 5; and Eliza A., age 1. All are natives of Pennsylvania. Recorded at the same household is Sarah Plymire, age 23, and Daniel Stern, age 29, a laborer from Pennsylvania.

The *1860 Census for South Strabane, Washington County, Pennsylvania* lists James as age 20, born *circa* 1840 in Pennsylvania. Also recorded are his father William, age 44, a native of Pennsylvania; his mother Eliza, age 43, a native of Ireland; and siblings Jane, age 18; Isabell, age 16; Sarah, age 14; William, age 10; John, age 5; and Martha, age 3. All are natives of Pennsylvania.

The *1870 Census for Clark, Harrison County, West Virginia* lists James A. Plymire, age 31, born *circa* 1839 in Pennsylvania. His occupation is recorded as marble cutter. Also listed are his wife, Elizabeth, age 26, a native of Ohio, born *circa* 1844; and their children: Fred A., age 2, born *circa* 1868 in West Virginia; and David B., age 1, born *circa* 1869 in West Virginia.

The *Yuba Sutter, Colusa, Butte and Tehama Counties California Directory 1885* lists J. A. Plymire, Frederick A. Plymire, and D. B. Plymire. Location "Odd Fellows Bldg. cor Wash and Oak," Red Bluff, Tehama County, California as proprietors of Red Bluff Marble Works. The business name is J. A. Plymire and Sons.

The *1900 Census for San Francisco, San Francisco County, California* lists James Plymire, age 61, born *circa* 1839 in Pennsylvania. His occupation is listed as "marble, granite." Also listed is his wife Susan E., age 55, born *circa* 1845 in Ohio.

The *1910 Census for San Francisco Assembly District 35, California*, lists James A. Plymire, age 71, born *circa* 1839 in Pennsylvania. His occupation is recorded as marble and granite cutter. Also listed is his wife Susan E., born *circa* 1845 in Ohio.

The *Antioch Ledger* newspaper, June 15, 1901 lists an advertisement for James' son, Charles, as "Plymire & Elsworth, dealers in Marble, Granite and all kinds of Cement Work" on Mission Street in San Francisco.

According to the *Who's Who on the Pacific Coast*, Harper Publishing Company, Los Angeles, California, 1913, page 457, Plymire's son, D. (David) Brandley Plymire was once the director of Nevada Marble Company. He later became a physician and surgeon.

The *San Francisco Chronicle* newspaper, March 23, 1917, page 4, states that James A. Plymire had five sons: Dr. Fred A. Plymire, Dr. D. (David) Brandley Plymire, Charles J. Plymire, William Plymire, and Dr. Harry G. Plymire. At the time of his death in 1917, his wife, Susan E., and sons, Harry G. and William H., were already deceased.

James Adam Plymire died March 20, 1917 in San Francisco, California at the age of 78 years, 7 months, and 1 day. On March 24, 1917, he was interred in Section G, lot 282 of Woodlawn Memorial Park in Colma, San Mateo County, California. Although not indicated on the gravestone, cemetery records show that Plymire shares the burial plot with his wife, Susan Elizabeth Plymire, and sons, Dr. D. Brandley Plymire and William H. Plymire. Plymire's stone denotes that he was a member of the Masonic Lodge and the Grand Army of the Republic (GAR). Other members of the Plymire family are buried in Section E of Woodlawn Memorial Park.

*Antioch Ledger*
January 16, 1892

*Antioch Ledger*
March 31, 1894

*Antioch Ledger*
June 15, 1901

This article, from the *Antioch Ledger* newspaper, June 15, 1901, advertises Charles Plymire in partnership with Desmond Elsworth in San Francisco, California. Charles Plymire was the son of James Plymire of Plymire and Sons of Vallejo, California. Plymire and Sons provided the gravestone for Abel Vaughn and his family who are buried in Rose Hill Cemetery. Able died in April 11, 1901, just two months before this advertisement appeared in the newspaper.

*San Francisco Chronicle*
March 22, 1917

*San Francisco Chronicle*
March 23, 1917

Reference 379.25

Plymire gravesite, Section G, Lot 282, Woodlawn Memorial Park,
Colma, San Mateo County, California.
Photograph by Traci (Gibbons) Parent, 2007.

# Gravestone Manufactured by Plymire & Sons

Vaughn family gravestone,
Section N-D, Plot 33

# Chapter 11

# ANALYSIS OF
# INDIVIDUALS INTERRED

East Bay Regional Park District

# BURIALS LISTED ACCORDING TO OCCUPATION OF THE DECEASED

| OCCUPATION | NAME | TOWN OF RESIDENCE |
|---|---|---|
| Butcher | GRIFFITH, David E. | Township 3 |
| | HOOK, George B. | Nortonville |
| Clerk | BANKS, Albert | Township 3 |
| | OLIVER, Thomas J. | Nortonville |
| Constable | JONES, John B. | Nortonville |
| County Clerk | MARKLEY, Andrew Jackson | Somersville/Martinez |
| Hotel Proprietor | WILLIAMS, Watkin | Nortonville |
| Housewife | BANKS, Ann | Somersville |
| Keeping House/House keeper | DAVIS, Ellen | Township 3 |
| | JONES, Ellen | Somersville |
| Laborer | HABENICHT, Wilhelm C. | Somersville |
| | HOOK, George B. | Nortonville |
| Midwife | NORTON, Sarah | Nortonville |
| Miner | COOPER, George | Nortonville |
| | DAVIES, Evan | Nortonville |
| | DOULTON, George | Nortonville |
| | DUMAS, Theophile | Nortonville |
| | EDWARDS, John | Township 3 |
| | EDWARDS, Joseph M. | Stewartville |
| | EVANS, John R. | Township 3 |
| | GETHING, William | Nortonville |
| | GRIFFITHS, David W. | Nortonville |
| | HOOK, George B. | Nortonville |
| | HUGHES, David M. | Nortonville |

| OCCUPATION | NAME | TOWN OF RESIDENCE |
|---|---|---|
| Miner | JAMES, Morgan E. | Nortonville |
| | JAMES, Thomas D. | Nortonville |
| | JENKINS, Thomas H. | Nortonville |
| | JONES, Austin | Nortonville |
| | JONES, Hugh R. | Somersville |
| | JONES, Thomas M. | Somersville/West Hartley |
| | JONES, Thomas S. | Somersville |
| | LEAM, Robert | Judsonville |
| | LEWIS, Meredith | Nortonville |
| | MORTIMORE, Richard | Somersville |
| | REYNOLDS, George M. | Nortonville |
| | RICHARDS, Daniel | Somersville |
| | RICHARDS, John | Township 3 |
| | RICHMOND, Thomas | Somersville |
| | SMITH, Evan | Nortonville |
| | THOMAS, Handel | Nortonville |
| | THOMAS, Howell | Nortonville |
| | THOMAS, Rees G. | Nortonville |
| | VAUGHN, Abel Sr. | Nortonville |
| | WATTS, David | Nortonville |
| | WATTS, Theophilus | Nortonville |
| | WILLIAMS, David R. | Nortonville |
| | WILLIAMS, Edward F. | Nortonville |
| | WILLIAMS, William L. | Nortonville |
| Saloon Keeper | LEAM, Robert | Nortonville |
| Shoe Maker | ENGLER, John | Nortonville |
| Stagecoach Driver | LOVE, John | Somersville |
| Stock Raiser | GRIFFITH, David E. | Nortonville |
| | MARKLEY, Andrew Jackson | Somersville |

# Births in the United States

## CALIFORNIA

Bryant, Elizabeth Ann
Bryant, Ida Mary
Buxton, Lulu
Clare, Walter E.
Davis, Morgan
Heycock, Richard
Howell, Sarah
Howell, Thomas M.
Jewett, Milton
Jones, Martha
Mills, Charles W.
Morris, Alexander
Rees, Elizabeth Ann
Thomas, Joseph (born 1867)
Thomas, Peter Benjamin
Vaughn, Hannah
Willis, Mary Blanche

*Contra Costa County, Near Antioch*
Markley, Eliza Jane

*Contra Costa County, Nortonville*
Bryant, Eva Sitera
Dawson, Mary A.
Evans, John
Evans, William
Green, Martha J.
Hook, Alice J.
Jones, Lewis James
Jones, Thomas
Mortimore, Harriet

Rees, Margaret
Thomas, Handel
Vestnys, Lorenda A.
Williams, Sara Elizabeth (or Black Diamond, CA)

*Contra Costa County, Somersville*
Anderson, Robert
Bussey, Joseph
Davis, William T.
Jones, Davied R.
Jones, George T.
Jones, Henry
Jones, John
MacLeod, John
Markley, David
Mortimore, Alvin
Richmond, Elizabeth
Riddock, Robert (born 1867)
Schwartz, infant #1
Schwartz, infant #2
Waters, William

*Placer County, Foresthill*
Evans, William Rodrick
Stine, Catherine

*Sierra County, Port Wine*
Havard, Elias

*Solano County, Vallejo*
Crowhurst, Elizabeth

East Bay Regional Park District

# BIRTHS IN THE UNITED STATES (CON'T)

**ILLINOIS**
Habenicht, Wilhelm C.

**MISSOURI**
Lewis, Seth John

**NEW YORK**
*Oneida County, Steuben*
Jones, Elizabeth (born 1851)

**OHIO**
Hook, George B.
Jewett, Emeline F.

*Champaign County, Near West Field*
Markley, Andrew Jackson

*Trumbull County, Weathersfield*
Guilding, Thomas John

**OREGON**
Maddin, Ella

*Coos County, Coos Bay*
Wingate, Robert

**PENNSYLVANIA**
Banks, Albert
Buxton, Maggie
Cooper, George (or England)
Davis, Margaret
Easton, Mary
Edwards, John
Evans, Rebecca
James, Mary Ann
Leam, Margaret
Leam, May
Witherow, Barbara

*Schuylkill County, Pottsville*
Rogers, Elizabeth

**VIRGINIA**
Daley, James

*York County, Yorktown*
Saddler, Harriet A.

**WISCONSIN**
Edwards, Catherine

# Births In Other Countries

**AT SEA**
>Edwards, Clara

**AUSTRALIA**
*New South Wales, Castle Hills*
>Edwards, Emma
>Spowart, Annie
>Spowart, Eliza

*New South Wales, Newcastle*
>Goulding, Fanny Sarah
>Goulding, Thomas John
>Goulding, Thomas Pratten

**CANADA**
>Dumas, Theophile
>Norton, Sarah

*British Columbia, Nanaimo*
>Malpass, Sidney Percival

**ENGLAND**
>Banks, Joseph
>Bryant, Margaret (or Wales)
>Cooper, George (or Pennsylvania)
>Jones, Austin
>Reynolds, George M.

*Devonshire, Tavistock*
>Mortimore, Richard

*Lancashire, Manchester*
>Leam, Robert

*Warwickshire*
>Minett, William C.

**GERMANY**
>Engler, John

**SCOTLAND**
>Cain, Elizabeth O.
>Love, John
>Hay, John

**WALES**
>Dodsworth, George Washington
>Doulton, George
>Hughes, David M.
>Hughes, Margaret
>James, Morgan E.
>Jenkins, Thomas H.
>Jones, Benjamin A.
>Jones, Thomas M.
>Lewis, Meredith
>Thomas, Howell
>Thomas, John
>Thomas, Rees G.
>Vaughn, Abel (Sr.)
>Vaughn, Hannah (Mrs.)
>Williams, David R.
>Williams, William L.

*Cardiganshire*
>Griffith, David E.

**NORTH WALES**
*Caernarvonshire*
>Van Amringe, Ellen
>Jones, Hugh R.

*Caernarvon, Pwlllheli*
>Jones, Ellen

## SOUTH WALES

Clement, Ann
Clement, William H.
Richards, John
Ritchards, Mary

*Carmarthenshire*

Davis, Peter
James, Thomas D.
Oliver, Thomas J.

*Carmarthenshire, Llanelli*

Williams, Edward F.

*Carmarthenshire, Llanybri*

Evans, John R.

*Carmarthenshire, Troedyrhiw, Cayo.* [sic]

Edwards, Joseph M.

*Glamorganshire*

Davis, David B.
Gething, William
Jones, Elizabeth (born *circa* 1838)
Watts, Theophilus

*Glamorganshire, Aberdare*

Williams, Watkin
Jones, Thomas S.

*Glamorganshire, Cwm-Bach*

Davies, Evan

*Glamorganshire, Dyffryn Near Merthyr Tydfil*

Morgan, David

*Glamorganshire, Merthyr Tydfil*

Banks, Ann C.
Richards, Daniel
Oliver, Jane
Morgan, Ann

*Glamorganshire, Troedyrhiw, Merthyr*

Prosser, Mary

*Monmouthshire*

Bradshaw, John
Griffiths, David W.

*Monmouthshire, Aberystruth*

Richmond, Anne
Richmond, Thomas

*Monmouthshire, Risca*

Goulding, Joseph

*Monmouthshire, Tredegar*

Jones, John B.

*Pembrokeshire*

Davis, Ellen

**Nortonville**

Abraham, Rebecca
Banks, Albert
Bradshaw, John
Bryant, Eva Sitera
Bryant, Margaret
Davis, Margaret
Dawson, Mary A.
Dumas, Theophile
Edwards, John
Engler, Annie Henrietta
Engler, Charles
Engler, John
Evans, John
Evans, John R.
Evans, Rebecca (or Concord, CA)
Evans, William
Evans, William Rodrick
Gething, William
Goulding, Thomas John
Green, Martha J.
Griffiths, David W.
Havard, Elias
Heycock, Richard
Hook, Alice J.
Hook, George B.
Howell, Sarah
Howell, Thomas M.
James, Mary Ann
James, Thomas D.
Jenkins, Ebenezer H.
Jones, Austin
Jones, George T.
Jones, John B.
Jones, Thomas
Lewis, Meredith
Maddin, Ella
Morgan, David
Mortimore, Harriet
Muir, Jane Russel
Oliver, Jane
Piercy, Julia Etta
Pritchard, Lupyester

Rees, Margaret
Reynolds, George M.
Saddler, Harriet A.
Smith, Evan
Stine, Catherine
Thomas, Howell
Thomas, John
Thomas, Charles Morgan
Thomas, John H.
Thomas, Peter Benjamin
Vaughn, Hannah (Mrs.)
Vestnys, Lorenda A.
Watts, David
Watts, Theophilus
Williams, David R.
Williams, Sara Elizabeth
Williams, William L.

**Somersville**

Anderson, Robert
Banks, Ann C.
Blackburn, Charles W.
Bowman, Violette I.
Bussey, Joseph
Clement, Ann
Clement, William H.
Crowhurst, Elizabeth (or Nortonville)
Daley, James
Davis, Ellen
Davis, Morgan
Edwards, Catherine
Edwards, Clara
Edwards, Emma
Goulding, Fanny Sarah
Goulding, Thomas Pratten
Hay, John
Jenkins, Thomas Joseph (died 1877)
Jewett, Emeline F.
Jewett, Walter S.
Jones, Davied R.
Jones, Elizabeth (died 1876)
Jones, Ellen
Jones, Hugh R.
Jones, John
Jones, Thomas M.

**Somersville (Con't)**
Jones, Thomas S. (or Briones Valley, CA)
Malpass, Percival Sidney
Markley, David
Markley, Eliza Jane
Minett, William C.
Mortimore, Alvin
Mortimore, Richard
Parsons, Jeanette
Prosser, Mary
Richards, Daniel
Richmond, Elizabeth
Richmond, Thomas
Ritchards, Mary
Schwartz, infant #1
Schwartz, infant #2
Shaw, Hazel Beatrice
Spowart, Annie
Spowart, Eliza
Spratt, William Gladstone
Tolan, child #1
Tolan, child #2
Tonkins, John
Tregellas, Annie
Tregellas, James
Tregellas, Joseph
Waters, William
Wingate, Robert
Wright, Bertie
Wright, (child)
Wright, John Edmund
Wright, Mary Elizabeth
Wright, Minnie

**Stewartville**
Buxton, Maggie
Edwards, Joseph M.
Leam, Margaret
Leam, May

**Judsonville**
Eno, Susan J.

**West Hartley**
Waters, Edna Isabella
Waters, John Robert

# Known Places Of Death
## Other Than The Mount Diablo Coal Field

**Contra Costa County, California**

Goulding, Joseph

*Near Antioch*
Van Amringe, Ellen

*Black Diamond* (now *Pittsburg*)
Mills, Charles W.

*Clayton*
Davis, David B.
Davis, William T.
James, Morgan E.
Rogers, Elizabeth

*Near Clayton*
Norton, Sarah

*Concord*
Hughes, David M.

*Near Cornwall* (now *Pittsburg*)
Griffith, David E.

*Martinez*
Jones, Martha
Markley, Andrew Jackson

*New York Landing* (now *Pittsburg*)
Clare, Walter E.

*Pittsburg*
Thomas, Handel

**Alameda County, California**

*Oakland*
Jones, Benjamin A.

*Tesla*
Leam, Robert

**San Francisco County, California**

*San Francisco*
Oliver, Thomas J.
Thomas, Rees G.
Vaughn, Able (Sr.)
Vaughn, Hannah
Williams, Watkin

# Deaths Listed In Order Of Age

## Infants Less than One Month (16)

| | |
|---|---|
| Jenkins, (infant) | 1 day |
| Jones, John | 1 day |
| Unknown, "infant babe" | 3 days |
| Waters, William (Willie) | 9 days |
| Riddock, Robert | 3 weeks |
| Bussey, Joseph | infant |
| Dunton, Clyde C. | infant |
| Dunton, Lulu B. | infant |
| Griffith, infant | infant |
| Jones, Jennie | infant |
| Lewis, Seth John | infant |
| Parsons, Jeanette | infant |
| Schwartz, #1 | infant |
| Schwartz, #2 | infant |
| Unknown #1 (plot #69) | infant |
| Unknown #2 (plot #69) | infant |

## One Month to One Year (19)

| | |
|---|---|
| Bowman, David G. (Jr.) | 1 mo., 14 dys. |
| Jenkins, Elizabeth Ann | 1 mo., 20 dys. |
| Thomas, Frederick Elias | 2 mos. |
| Jones, Henry | 2 mos., 20 dys. |
| Jones, Mary E. | 3 mos. |
| Ott, Georg Adam | 3 mos. |
| Pritchard, Lupyester | 3 mos. (approx.) |
| Vaughn, Abel | 3 mos. |
| Hook, Alice J. | 3 mos., 4 dys. |
| Jones, Lewis James | 3 mos., 11 dys. |
| Dawson, Mary A. | 4 mos., 7 dys. |
| Markley, David | 4 mos., 11 dys. |
| Shaw, Hazel Beatrice | 4 mos., 24 dys. |
| Spratt, William G. | 6 mos. |
| MacLeod, John | 6 mos. |
| Pohl, Dora | 6 mos. |
| Jones, Davied R. | 6 mos., 28 dys. |
| Green, Martha J. | 7 mos., 19 dys. |
| Conner, John T. | 9 mos., 3 dys. |

## One to Two Years (18)

| | |
|---|---|
| Vestnys, Lorenda A. | 1 yr. |
| Thomas, Elizabeth Ann | 1 yr., 10 dys. |
| Mortimore, Alvin | 1 yr., 1 mo. |
| Wingate, Robert | 1 yr., 1 mo., 8 dys. |
| Buxton, Lulu | 1 yr., 2 mos., 18 dys. |
| Bowman, Violette I. | 1 yr., 3 mos. |
| Edwards, Clara | 1 yr., 3 mos. |
| Rees, Margaret | 1 yr., 3 mos., 15 dys. |
| Engler, Charles | 1 yr., 4 mos. |
| Jones, Thomas | 1 yr., 4 mos. |
| Richards, William Timothy | 1 yr., 5 mos. |
| Jenkins, Thomas Joseph | 1 yr., 5 mos., 3 dys. |
| Thomas, Elvira | 1 yr., 5 mos., 11 dys. |
| Wright, Mary Elizabeth | 1 yr., 6 mos. |
| Williams, Annie | 1 yr., 6 mos., 21 dys. |
| Malpass, Percival Sidney | 1 yr., 8 mos. |
| Riddock, Robert | 1 yr., 10 mos. |
| Bowman, Charles H. | 1 yr., 11 mos. |

## Two to Three Years (12)

| | |
|---|---|
| Williams, Sara Elizabeth | 2 yrs. (approximately) |
| Tregellas, James | 2 yrs., 21 dys. |
| Williams, Howell M. | 2 yrs., 23 dys. |
| Mills, Charles W. | 2 yrs., 1 mo. |
| Engler, Annie Henrietta | 2 yrs., 4 mos. |
| Evans, William | 2 yrs., 4 mos., 6 dys. |
| Jones, David Thomas | 2 yrs., 5 mos., 21 dys. |
| Maddin, Ella | 2 yrs., 6 mos., 10 dys. |
| Williams, Mary M. | 2 yrs., 11 mos. |
| Thomas, Joseph | 2 yrs., 11 mos., 6 dys. |
| Piercy, Julia Etta | 2 yrs., 11 mos., 8 dys. |
| Saddler, (male) | 2 - 3 yrs. |

## Three to Four Years (7)

| | |
|---|---|
| Crowhurst, Elizabeth | 3 yrs. |
| Thomas, John D. | 3 yrs. |
| Wright, Bertie | 3 yrs. |
| Pohl, Millie | 3 yrs., 4 dys. |
| Waters, Edna Isabella | 3 yrs., 2 mos., 18 dys. |
| Thomas, John H. | 3 yrs., 2 mos., 20 dys. |
| Jones, Isabella | 3 yrs., 10 mos. |

## Four to Five Years (8)

| | |
|---|---|
| Tierney, John | 4 yrs. (approximately) |
| Lewis, David John | 4 yrs. |
| Riddock, William | 4 yrs. |
| Jones, George T. | 4 yrs., 7 mos., 9 dys. |
| Howell, Sarah | 4 yrs., 9 mos. |
| Muir, Jane Russel | 4 yrs., 9 mos. |
| Anderson, Robert | 4 yrs., 10 mos., 7 dys. |
| Havard, Elias | 4 yrs., 10 mos., 17 dys. |

## Five to Six Years (6)

| | |
|---|---|
| Bassett, child | 5 yrs. |
| Tregellas, Joseph | 5 yrs., 1 mo. |
| Jenkins, Thomas Joseph | 5 yrs., 1 mo., 6 dys. |
| Waters, John Robert | 5 yrs., 6 mos., 22 dys. |
| Goulding, Fanny Sarah | 5 yrs., 9 mos., 28 dys. |
| Thomas, Charles M. | 5 yrs., 10 mos., 25 dys. |

## Six to Seven Years (4)

| | |
|---|---|
| Evans, Elizabeth | 6 yrs. |
| Humphreys, Gwelym | 6 yrs. |
| Eno, Susan J. | 6 yrs., 7 mos., 28 dys. |
| Rees, Elizabeth Ann | 6 yrs., 8 mos., 15 dys. |

## Seven to Eight Years (5)

| | |
|---|---|
| Riddock, Mary Jane | 7 yrs. |
| Jenkins, Ebenezer H. | 7 yrs., 6 mos., 19 dys. |
| Tregellas, Annie | 7 yrs., 7 mos. |
| Goulding, Thomas P. | 7 yrs., 7 mos., 17 dys. |
| Davis, David | 7 yrs., 8 mos., 29 dys. |

## Eight to Nine Years (12)

| | |
|---|---|
| Evans, John | 8 yrs. |
| Vaughn, Mary | 8 yrs. |
| Evans, William Rodrick | 8 yrs., 17 dys. |
| Morris, Alexander | 8 yrs., 20 dys. |
| Mortimore, Harriet | 8 yrs., 1 mo., 7 dys. |
| Clare, Walter E. | 8 yrs., 2 mos., 27 dys. |
| Aitken, Katie | 8 yrs., 4 mos., 12 dys. |
| Richmond, Elizabeth | 8 yrs., 5 mos., 11 dys. |
| Buxton, Alfred W. | 8 yrs., 8 mos., 8 dys. |
| Holt, Walter L. | 8 yrs., 9 mos. |
| Thomas, Peter B. | 8 yrs., 11 mos., 4 dys. |
| Heycock, Richard | 8 yrs., 11 mos., 10 dys. |

## Nine to Ten Years (5)

| | |
|---|---|
| Spowart, Eliza | 9 yrs. (approximately) |
| Wright, Minnie | 9 yrs. |
| Blackburn, Charles W. | 9 yrs., 7 mos. |
| Wright, John Edmund | 9 yrs., 10 mos. |
| Davis, Morgan | 9 yrs., 11 mos., 26 dys. |

## Ten to Eleven Years (5)

| | |
|---|---|
| Dennis, John | 10 yrs. (approximately) |
| Thomas, Joseph | 10 yrs. |
| Howell, Thomas M. | 10 yrs., 1 mo., 12 dys. |
| Leam, May | 10 yrs., 4 mos., 4 dys. |
| Bryant, Elizabeth Ann | 10 yrs., 7 mos., 21 dys. |

## Eleven to Twelve Years (1)

| | |
|---|---|
| Spowart, Annie | 11 yrs., 6 mos. |

## Twelve to Thirteen Years (1)

| | |
|---|---|
| Willis, Mary Blanche | 12 yrs., 7 mos., 6 dys. |

## Thirteen to Fourteen Years (2)

| | |
|---|---|
| Goulding, Thomas J. | 13 yrs. |
| Markley, Eliza Jane | 13 yrs., 3 mos., 23 dys. |

## Fourteen to Fifteen Years (0)

0

## Fifteen to Sixteen Years (0)

0

## Sixteen to Seventeen Years (2)

| | |
|---|---|
| Jewett, Milton | 16 yrs. |
| Tonkins, John | 16 yrs., 3 mos. |

## Seventeen to Eighteen Years (2)

| | |
|---|---|
| Davis, Margaret | 17 yrs. (approximately) |
| Stine, Catherine | 17 yrs. (approximately) |

## Eighteen to Nineteen Years (5)

| | |
|---|---|
| Witherow, Barbara L. | 18 yrs., 2 mos., 10 dys. |
| Abraham, Rebecca | 18 yrs., 4 mos. |
| Williams, William L. | 18 yrs., 4 mos. |
| Jones, Martha | 18 yrs., 7 mos., 13 dys. |
| Habenicht, Wilhelm C. | 18 yrs., 10 mos., 27 dys. |

## Nineteen to Twenty Years (3)

| | |
|---|---|
| Goulding, Joseph | 19 yrs. |
| Jewett, Walter S. | 19 yrs. |
| Vaughn, Hannah | 19 yrs., 11 mos., 29 dys. |

## Twenty to Thirty Years (16)

| | |
|---|---|
| James, Mary Ann | 20 yrs., 6 mos. |
| Bryant, Eva Sitera | 21 yrs., 11 mos., 21 dys. |
| Van Amringe, Ellen | 22 yrs., 7 mos., 20 dys. |
| Edwards, Emma | 23 yrs. |
| Thomas, John | 23 yrs. |
| Williams, David R. | 23 yrs. |
| Davis, Anna | 25 yrs. |
| Jones, Elizabeth | 25 yrs. |
| Minett, William C. | 25 yrs. |
| Edwards, Catherine | 25 yrs., 5 mos., 13 dys. |
| Morgan, Ann | 26 yrs. |
| Smith, Evan | 27 yrs. |
| Watts, Theophilus | 27-28 yrs. |
| Rogers, Elizabeth | 28 yrs. |
| James, Thomas D. | 29 yrs. |
| Reynolds, George M. | 29 yrs. |

## Thirty to Forty Years (18)

| | |
|---|---|
| Richards, John | 30 yrs. |
| Davies, Evan | 30 yrs., 4 mos., 29 dys. |
| Hook, George B. | 31 yrs. |
| Easton, Mary | 32 yrs. (approximately) |
| Daley, James | 33 yrs. (approximately) |
| Davis, Ellen | 33 yrs., 28 dys. |
| Evans, Rebecca | 33 yrs., 1 mo., 23 dys., |
| Jones, Catherine | 34 yrs. |
| Morgan, David | 35 yrs., 7 mos., 19 dys. |
| Banks, Albert | 35 yrs. - 38 yrs. |
| Gething, William | 36 yrs. |

## Thirty to Forty Years (18) con't

| | |
|---|---|
| Hughes, David M. | 37 yrs. |
| Hughes, Margaret | 37 yrs., 11 mos., 5 dys. |
| Lewis, Meredith | 38 yrs. |
| Jones, John B. | 38 yrs., 9 mos. |
| Davis, Thomas J. | 39 yrs. |
| Vaughn, Hannah (Mrs.) | 39 yrs. |
| Oliver, Jane | 39 yrs., 6 mos. |

## Forty to Fifty Years (22)

| | |
|---|---|
| Hay, John | 40 yrs. (approximately) |
| Cooper, George | 40 yrs. |
| Markley, Andrew Jackson | 40 yrs. |
| Buxton, Maggie | 40 yrs., 2 mos., 27 dys. |
| Clement, Ann | 40 yrs., 10 mos., 17 dys. |
| Edwards, John | 41 yrs. |
| Love, John | 41 yrs., 6 mos., 17 dys. |
| Griffiths, David W. | 42 yrs. |
| Unknown (plot #99) | 42 yrs. |
| Engler, John | 42 yrs., 9 mos., 9 dys. |
| James, Morgan E. | 43 yrs. (approximately) |
| Jones, Elizabeth | 43 yrs. |
| Jones, Hugh R. | 44 yrs. |
| Evans, John R. | 45 yrs. |
| Jones, Thomas S. | 45 yrs. |
| Oliver, Thomas J. | 45 yrs. (approximately) |
| Edwards, Joseph M. | 46 yrs. |
| Jones, Austin | 46 yrs. |
| Cain, Elizabeth O. | 47 yrs., 7 mos., 23 dys. |
| Leam, Margaret | 47 yrs., 9 mos., 8 dys. |
| Thomas, Rees G. | 48 yrs., 3 mos., 6 dys. |
| Thomas, Handel | 49 yrs., 29 dys. |

## Fifty to Sixty Years (14)

| | |
|---|---|
| Davis, Peter | 52 yrs. |
| Prosser, Mary | 52 yrs. |
| Jenkins, Thomas H. | 52 yrs., 1 mo., 19 dys. |
| Mortimore, Richard | 52 yrs., 5 mos., 29 dys. |
| Williams, Edward F. | 52 yrs., 8 mos. |
| Tully, Mary | 52 yrs., 10 mos., 15 dys. |
| Howells, Isaac | 53 yrs. |
| Williams, Watkin | 53 yrs., 6 mos., 27 dys. |
| Doulton, George | 54 yrs. |
| Bradshaw, John | 55 yrs., 4 mos., 20 dys. |
| Richmond, Anne | 56 yrs., 4 mos., 21 dys. |
| Jewett, Emeline F. | 57 yrs., 4 mos., 3 dys. |
| Richmond, Thomas | 57 yrs., 8 mos., 22 dys. |
| Jones, Thomas M. | 58 yrs., 1 mo., 2 dys. |

## Sixty to Seventy Years (12)

| | |
|---|---|
| Powell, Mary | 60 yrs. |
| Saddler, Harriet A. | 60 yrs., 5 mos., 4 dys. |
| Vaughn, Abel (Sr.) | 61 yrs. |
| Bryant, Margaret | 62 yrs. |
| Ritchards, Mary | 63 yrs. |
| Leam, Robert | 63 yrs., 9 mos., 26 dys. |
| Banks, Ann C. | 64 yrs., 3 mos |
| Banks, Joseph | 65 yrs., 2 mos., 24 dys. |
| Clement, William H. | 66 yrs., 7 mos., 5 dys. |
| Norton, Sarah | 68 yrs. |
| Jones, Ellen | 69 yrs. |
| Richards, Daniel | 69 yrs., 1 mo., 22 dys. |

## Seventy to Eighty Years (5)

| | |
|---|---|
| Jones, Benjamin A. | 71 yrs. |
| Griffith, David E. | 76 yrs. |
| Thomas, Howell | 78 yrs. |
| Davis, David B. | 79 yrs. |
| Davis, William T. | 79 yrs., 4 mos., 24 dys. |

## Eighty to Ninety Years (1)

| | |
|---|---|
| French, Ruth | 81 yrs. |

## Ages Unknown (14)

Buxton, Thomas
Bryant, Ida Mary
Cooper, John L.
Dodsworth, George W. (adult)
Dumas, Theophile (adult)
Griffith, Emma (adult)
Griffith, Jack (adult)
Price, Hazel
Ramsay, (child)
Tolan, (child #1)
Tolan, (child #2)
Unknown (plot #87)
Watts, David (adult)
Wright, (child)

# DEATHS LISTED BY ORDER OF INTERMENT

*Note: Adults recorded here are individuals 18 years of age and older.*

| Death Year | Death Date | Name | Child or Adult |
|---|---|---|---|
| 1863 | Jan. 16 | BRYANT, Ida Mary | unknown |
| 1864 | Dec. 25 | WRIGHT, Mary Elizabeth | C |
| | Dec. 28 | WRIGHT, John Edmund | C |
| | Dec. 28 | TREGELLAS, James | C |
| | Dec. 29 | TONKINS, John | C |
| 1865 | Jan. 4 | MUIR, Jane Russel | C |
| | Jan. 27 or 31 | GOULDING, Thomas Pratten | C |
| | Feb. 17 | RICHMOND, Elizabeth | C |
| | Feb. 18 | TREGELLAS, Joseph | C |
| | Feb. 19 | TREGELLAS, Annie | C |
| | Feb. 20 | BLACKBURN, Charles W. | C |
| | Feb. 24 | EDWARDS, Emma | A |
| | Feb. 27 | RIDDOCK, Robert | C |
| | March 2 | RIDDOCK, Mary Jane | C |
| | April 30 | GOULDING, Fanny Sarah | C |
| | Aug. 21 | JONES, Mary E. | C |
| | August | EDWARDS, Clara | C |
| | unknown | RIDDOCK, William | C |
| | unknown | WRIGHT, child | C |
| 1866 | May 27 | MINNETT, William C. | A |
| 1867 | May 27 | JONES, Catherine | A |
| | unknown | RIDDOCK, Robert | C |
| 1869 | Mar. 26 | MARKLEY, Eliza Jane | C |
| | April 19 | MARKLEY, David | C |
| | April 21 | JEWETT, Walter S. | A |
| | July 14 | JONES, John | C |
| | Aug. 9 | DAVIS, Anna | A |
| | Nov. | JONES, Hugh R. | A |
| 1870 | Feb. 8 | EVANS, William Rodrick | C |
| | April 1 | VESTNYS, Lorenda A. | C |
| | May 2 | MARKLEY, A. J. | A |
| | June 26 | WRIGHT, Bertie | C |
| | June 26 | WRIGHT, Minnie | C |
| | June 29 | BOWMAN, Violette I. | C |
| | July 18 | THOMAS, Elvira | C |

| Death Year | Death Date | Name | Child or Adult |
|---|---|---|---|
| 1870 con't | Aug. 2 | THOMAS, Joseph | C |
| | Aug. 5 | JENKINS, Thomas Joseph | C |
| | Aug. 27 | JONES, Henry | C |
| | Sept. | EDWARDS, John | A |
| | Sept. 2 | HOWELL, Thomas M. | C |
| | Sept. 7 | LEAM, May | C |
| | Sept. 22 | JENKINS, Elizabeth Ann | C |
| | Oct. 9 | HOWELL, Sarah | C |
| | Dec. 7 | PIERCY, Julia Etta | C |
| | unknown | TOLAN, child #1 | C |
| | unknown | TOLAN, child #2 | C |
| 1871 | Feb. 3 | BOWMAN, David G. (Jr.) | C |
| | July 6 | WILLIAMS, Howell M. | C |
| | Aug. 21 or 22 | BANKS, Albert | A |
| | Oct. 6 | GOULDING, Joseph | A |
| | Oct. 6 | THOMAS, Joseph | C |
| 1872 | Feb. 5 | JONES, Isabella | C |
| | Mar. 14 | DAVIS, Peter | A |
| | April 2 | VAN AMRINGE, Ellen | A |
| | June 7 | SPOWART, Annie | C |
| | *Circa* June 11 | SPOWART, Eliza | C |
| 1873 | July 8 | WILLIAMS, David R. | A |
| | Sept. 19 | MORGAN, Ann | A |
| | Nov. 7 | OTT, Georg Adam | C |
| | Dec. 16 | DALEY, James | A |
| | Dec. 16 | HAY, John | A |
| 1874 | April 5 | BOWMAN, Charles H. | C |
| | May 12 | WILLIAMS, Edward F. | A |
| | June 2 | RICHARDS, William Timothy | C |
| | June 23 | JENKINS, Ebenezer H. | C |
| | July 10 | JONES, David Thomas | C |
| | July 14 | POHL, Dora | C |
| | Aug. 4 | RICHARDS, John | A |
| | Aug. 20 | JEWETT, Milton | C |
| | Aug. 30 | DAVIS, Morgan | C |
| | Sept. 11 | FRENCH, Ruth | A |
| | Oct. 6 | ENGLER, Charles | C |
| | Dec. 15 | BUXTON, Lulu | C |
| *Circa* 1874 | unknown | MACLEOD, John | C |

| Death Year | Death Date | Name | Child or Adult |
|---|---|---|---|
| 1875 | Jan. 5 | JONES, Thomas S. | A |
| | Jan. 16 | POHL, Millie | C |
| | Feb. 6 | JONES, Lewis James | C |
| | Feb. 13 | CLEMENT, Ann | A |
| | Feb. 13 | UNKNOWN (Plot #99) | A |
| | Feb. 20 | HOOK, Alice J. | C |
| | Feb. 22 | WINGATE, Robert | C |
| | April 19 | MORRIS, Alexander | C |
| | April 22 | WILLIAMS, Mary M. | C |
| | Aug. 15 | GOULDING, Thomas J. | C |
| | Aug. 27 | HAVARD, Elias | C |
| | Sept. 4 | ENGLER, John | A |
| | Oct. 22 | REES, Margaret | C |
| | Oct. 29 | JONES, Davied R. | C |
| | Dec. 6 | THOMAS, Rees G. | A |
| 1876 | Mar. 10 | JONES, Elizabeth | A |
| | Mar. 21 | JONES, George T. | C |
| | May 11 | HUGHES, Margaret | A |
| | June 27 | THOMAS, Elizabeth Ann | C |
| | July 24 | GETHING (GETHIN), William | A |
| | July 24 | JAMES, Thomas D. | A |
| | July 24 | LEWIS, Meredith | A |
| | July 24 | REYNOLDS, George M. | A |
| | July 24 | WATTS, Theophilus | A |
| | July 24 | WILLIAMS, William L. | A |
| | July 25 | DUMAS, Theophile | A |
| | July 25 | GRIFFITHS, David W. | A |
| | July 25 | WATTS, David | A |
| | July 30 | SMITH, Evan | A |
| | Aug. 3 | THOMAS, John D. | C |
| | Aug. 7 | WITHEROW, Barbara L. | A |
| | Sept. 24 | PROSSER, Mary | A |
| | Sept. 29 | THOMAS, John | A |
| | Nov. 25 | EDWARDS, Catherine | A |
| | Dec. 4 | WILLIAMS, Annie | C |
| | Dec. 23 | DAVIES, Evan | A |
| | Dec. 30 | VAUGHN, Abel | C |
| 1877 | Jan. 22 | EVANS, John | C |
| | Feb. 3 | EVANS, John R. | A |

| Death Year | Death Date | Name | Child or Adult |
|---|---|---|---|
| 1877 con't | Feb. 18 | EVANS, William | C |
| | Mar. 3 | LOVE, John | A |
| | April 6 | REES, Elizabeth Ann | C |
| | April 9 | WILLIS, Mary Blanche | C |
| | May 21 | BRYANT, Elizabeth Ann | C |
| | Aug. 12 | THOMAS, Charles Morgan | C |
| | Aug. 12 | THOMAS, Peter Benjamin | C |
| | Aug. 16 | THOMAS, John H. | C |
| | Sept. 5 | JENKINS, Thomas Joseph | C |
| | Sept. 15 | ENGLER, Annie Henrietta | C |
| | Oct. 1 | JAMES, Mary Ann | A |
| | Nov. 4 | CONNER, John T. | C |
| | Nov. 14 | HEYCOCK, Richard | C |
| | unknown | HUMPHREYS, Gwelym | C |
| 1878 | April 7 | POWELL, Mary | A |
| | July 3 | DAVIS, David | C |
| | July 16 | DAVIS, Ellen | A |
| | Sept. 25 | BUXTON, Alfred W. | C |
| | Nov. 1 | ABRAHAM, Rebecca | A |
| | Nov. 10 | JONES, Thomas | C |
| | unknown | DAVIS, Margaret | C |
| | unknown | PARSONS, Jeanette (infant) | C |
| 1879 | Feb. 9 | JONES, John B. | A |
| | Oct. 5 | NORTON, Sarah | A |
| | Oct. 7 | DAWSON, Mary A. | C |
| | Nov. 10 | TULLY, Mary | A |
| | Dec. 8 | GREEN, Martha J. | C |
| | Dec. 24 | AITKEN, Katie | C |
| 1870s | unknown | HOWELLS, Isaac | A |
| | unknown | SCHWARTZ, infant # 1 | C |
| | unknown | SCHWARTZ, infant # 2 | C |
| | unknown | WILLIAMS, Sara Elizabeth | C |
| 1880 | Feb. 3 | ENO, Susan J. | C |
| | Mar. 17 | OLIVER, Jane | A |
| | April 15 | JENKINS, (infant) | C |
| | July 28 | MADDIN, Ella | C |
| | Sept. 20 | VAUGHN, Mary | C |
| | Nov. 20 | JONES, Austin | A |
| | Dec. 16 | HOOK, George B. | A |

| Death Year | Death Date | Name | Child or Adult |
|---|---|---|---|
| *Circa* 1880 | unknown | PRITCHARD, Lupyester (infant) | C |
| 1881 | July 18 | VAUGHN, Hannah (Mrs.) | A |
| | Sept. 17 | JONES, Elizabeth | A |
| | Oct. 22 | WILLIAMS, Watkin | A |
| | Oct. 25 | BRADSHAW, John | A |
| | Oct. 27 | CAIN, Elizabeth O. | A |
| | Nov. 3 | MILLS, Charles W. | C |
| *Circa* 1881 | unknown | LEWIS, David John | C |
| 1882 | Jan. 1 | HOLT, Walter L. | C |
| | Feb. 25 | HABENICHT, Wilhelm C. | A |
| | Mar. 24 | JENKINS, Thomas H. | A |
| | April 6 | WATERS, William (Willie) | C |
| | April 7 | RICHMOND, Thomas | A |
| | May 16 | MORGAN, David | A |
| | May 31 | RICHMOND, Anne | A |
| | unknown | STINE, Catherine | C |
| | unknown | CROWHURST, Elizabeth | C |
| 1883 | Jan. 14 | JEWETT, Emeline F. | A |
| | April 9 | DAVIS, Thomas J. | A |
| | May 4 | CLARE, Walter E. | C |
| | Aug. 29 | BANKS, Joseph | A |
| 1884 | Oct. 3 | LEAM, Margaret | A |
| | Oct. 6 | SADDLER, Harriet A. | A |
| | Nov. 9 | COOPER, George | A |
| | unknown | DOULTON, George | A |
| | unknown | ROGERS, Elizabeth | A |
| 1885 | Jan. 15 | MORTIMORE, Harriet | C |
| | Dec. 10 | OLIVER, Thomas J. | A |
| 1886 | Mar. 24 | EVANS, Rebecca | A |
| | Oct. 27 | JONES, Martha | A |
| | Nov. | EASTON, Mary | A |
| 1888 | Mar. 12 | HUGHES, David M. | A |
| | April 18 | VAUGHN, Hannah | A |
| | Dec. 13 | RITCHARDS, Mary | A |
| 1889 | Sept. 4 | EDWARDS, Joseph M. | A |
| 1890 | Aug. 15 | JONES, Ellen | A |
| | Sept. 3 | JAMES, Morgan E. | A |
| | Sept. 11 | RICHARDS, Daniel | A |
| | Oct. 22 | BUXTON, Maggie | A |

| Death Year | Death Date | Name | Child or Adult |
|---|---|---|---|
| 1891 | Jan. 18 | SPRATT, William Gladstone | C |
| 1892 | Feb. 29 | CLEMENT, William H. | A |
| | Mar. 17 | SHAW, Hazel Beatrice | C |
| | Sept. 8 | BANKS, Ann C. | A |
| | Nov. 18 | WATERS, Edna Isabella | C |
| | Dec. 2 | WATERS, John Robert | C |
| 1893 | Aug. 3 | MORTIMORE, Alvin | C |
| | Dec.13 | GRIFFITH, infant | C |
| | unknown | BUSSEY, Joseph | C |
| 1895 | Sept. 4 | MORTIMORE, Richard | A |
| | Oct. 18 | BRYANT, Eva Sitera | A |
| 1896 | Mar. 19 | JONES, Thomas M. | A |
| 1897 | *Circa* June | MALPASS, Percival Sidney | C |
| 1890s | unknown | DODSWORTH, George W. | A |
| 1900 | Feb. 27 | LEAM, Robert | A |
| | May 20 | GRIFFITH, David E. | A |
| | Oct. 17 | ANDERSON, Robert | C |
| | Nov. 28 | BRYANT, Margaret | A |
| 1901 | April 11 | VAUGHN, Abel | A |
| 1907 | March 25 | DAVIS, David B. | A |
| 1911 | Jan. 22 | JONES, Benjamin A. | A |
| 1915 | May 14 | THOMAS, Howell | A |
| 1924 | April 10 | THOMAS, Handel | A |
| 1954 | May 26 | DAVIS, William T. | A |

# Unknown Death Dates

| Name | Child or Adult |
| --- | --- |
| BASSETT, _____ | C |
| BUXTON, Thomas | unknown |
| COOPER, John L. | unknown |
| DENNIS, John | C |
| DUNTON, Clyde C. | C |
| DUNTON, Lulu B. | C |
| EVANS, Elizabeth | C |
| GRIFFITH, Emma | A |
| GRIFFITH, Jack | A |
| JONES, Jennie | C |
| LEWIS, Seth John | C |
| PRICE, Hazel | unknown |
| RAMSAY, _____ | C |
| SADDLER, (male) | C |
| THOMAS, Frederick Elias | C |
| TIERNEY, John | C |
| UNKNOWN (infant #1), plot #69 | C |
| UNKNOWN (infant #2), plot #69 | C |
| UNKNOWN ("Infant babe"), plot #79 | C |
| UNKNOWN, plot #87 | unknown |

## Registration of Births, Deaths, and Marriages.

On the first of January next, the law requiring a registration of all births, deaths, and marriages goes into effect ; and as any person on whom the law imposes a duty in relation to the matter incurs a penalty of $50 by failure to perform such duty, it will be well for clergymen, midwives, sextons, justices and others, to be getting posted up in the requirements. Every person performing the marriage ceremony is to keep a record of the time, place of the ceremony, the names, in full of the parties joined in marriage, the age, condition, and place of birth each, whether either or both were ever before married, and if so, whether the party to whom formerly married is.living or dead. All professional attendants in cases of birth must make a record of the time, place, sex, and color of the child, and the names and residence of the parents. Physicians, or clergymen, attending or officiating in a case of death, coroners who hold inquests. and sextons who bury deceased persons, must keep a register of the name, age, and residence of the deceased person in each case, and certify to a copy of their register every quarter to the County Recorder, whose duty it will be to keep separate registers of births, deaths and marriages, and certify an abstract from them quarterly to the Secretary of the State Board of Health, at Sacramento. The penalty for neglect of the duties prescribed by the law is recoverable by the District Attorney for the use of the county general fund.

This article from the *Contra Costa Gazette* newspaper, December 7, 1872, states that the law requiring registration of all births, deaths and marriages goes into effect on January 1, 1873. Failure to perform the duty of registering the individuals will result in a penalty of $50

# DEATHS LISTED BY YEAR

| YEAR | ADULT MALE | ADULT FEMALE | CHILD | TOTAL |
|------|------------|--------------|-------|-------|
| 1864 | 0 | 0 | 4 | 4 |
| 1865 | 0 | 1 | 11 | 12 |
| 1866 | 1 | 0 | 1 | 2 |
| 1867 | 0 | 1 | 1 | 2 |
| 1868 | 0 | 0 | 0 | 0 |
| 1869 | 2 | 1 | 3 | 6 |
| 1870 | 2 | 0 | 16 | 18 |
| 1871 | 2 | 0 | 3 | 5 |
| 1872 | 1 | 1 | 3 | 5 |
| 1873 | 3 | 1 | 1 | 5 |
| 1874 | 2 | 1 | 9 | 12 |
| 1875 | 3 | 1 | 10 | 14 |
| 1876 | 12 | 5 | 5 | 22 |
| 1877 | 2 | 1 | 13 | 16 |
| 1878 | 0 | 3 | 5 | 8 |
| 1879 | 1 | 2 | 3 | 6 |
| 1880 | 2 | 1 | 4 | 7 |
| 1881 | 2 | 3 | 1 | 6 |
| 1882 | 4 | 1 | 4 | 9 |
| 1883 | 2 | 1 | 1 | 4 |
| 1884 | 2 | 3 | 0 | 5 |
| 1885 | 1 | 0 | 1 | 2 |
| 1886 | 0 | 3 | 0 | 3 |
| 1887 | 0 | 0 | 0 | 0 |
| 1888 | 1 | 2 | 0 | 3 |
| 1889 | 1 | 0 | 0 | 1 |
| 1890 | 2 | 2 | 0 | 4 |
| 1891 | 0 | 0 | 1 | 1 |
| 1892 | 1 | 1 | 3 | 5 |
| 1893 | 0 | 0 | 3 | 3 |
| 1894 | 0 | 0 | 0 | 0 |
| 1895 | 1 | 1 | 0 | 2 |
| 1896 | 1 | 0 | 0 | 1 |
| 1897 | 0 | 0 | 1 | 1 |
| 1898 | 0 | 0 | 0 | 0 |
| 1899 | 0 | 0 | 0 | 0 |
| 1900 | 2 | 1 | 1 | 4 |
| 1901 | 1 | 0 | 0 | 1 |
| 1907 | 1 | 0 | 0 | 1 |
| 1911 | 1 | 0 | 0 | 1 |
| 1915 | 1 | 0 | 0 | 1 |
| 1924 | 1 | 0 | 0 | 1 |
| 1954 | 1 | 0 | 0 | 1 |
| TOTAL | 59 | 37 | 108 | 204 |

The following 31 individuals, out of the 235 interred, are not included in the above total:
- 20 children with unconfirmed death dates; total 129 children
- 3 adult males (G.W. Dodsworth, J. Griffith, and I. Howells) with unknown death years; total 62 men
- 1 adult female, (Emma Griffith) with unknown death year; total 38 women
- 6 individuals, unknown if adult or child

# DEATHS LISTED BY YEAR AND MONTH

| YEAR | JAN | FEB | MAR | APR | MAY | JUN | JUL | AUG | SEP | OCT | NOV | DEC | TOTAL |
|---|---|---|---|---|---|---|---|---|---|---|---|---|---|
| 1863 | 1 | | | | | | | | | | | | 1 |
| 1864 | | | | | | | | | | | | 4 | 4 |
| 1865 | 2 | 6 | 1 | 1 | | | | 2 | | | | | 12 |
| 1866 | | | | | 1 | | | | | | | | 1 |
| 1867 | | | | | 1 | | | | | | | | 1 |
| 1868 | | | | | | | | | | | | | 0 |
| 1869 | | | 1 | 2 | | | 1 | 1 | | | 1 | | 6 |
| 1870 | | 1 | | 1 | 1 | 3 | 1 | 3 | 4 | 1 | | 1 | 16 |
| 1871 | | 1 | | | | | 1 | 1 | | 2 | | | 5 |
| 1872 | | 1 | 1 | 1 | | 2 | | | | | | | 5 |
| 1873 | | | | | | | 1 | | 1 | | 1 | 2 | 5 |
| 1874 | | | | 1 | 1 | 2 | 2 | 3 | 1 | 1 | | 1 | 12 |
| 1875 | 2 | 5 | | 2 | | | | 2 | 1 | 2 | | 1 | 15 |
| 1876 | | | 2 | | 1 | 1 | 10 | 2 | 2 | | 1 | 3 | 22 |
| 1877 | 1 | 2 | 1 | 2 | 1 | | | 3 | 2 | 1 | 2 | | 15 |
| 1878 | | | | 1 | | | 2 | | 1 | | 2 | | 6 |
| 1879 | | 1 | | | | | | | | 2 | 1 | 2 | 6 |
| 1880 | | 1 | 1 | 1 | | | 1 | | 1 | | 1 | 1 | 7 |
| 1881 | | | | | | | 1 | | 1 | 3 | 1 | | 6 |
| 1882 | 1 | 1 | 1 | 2 | 2 | | | | | | | | 7 |
| 1883 | 1 | | | 1 | 1 | | | 1 | | | | | 4 |
| 1884 | | | | | | | | | | 1 | 1 | | 2 |
| 1885 | 1 | | | | | | | | | | | 1 | 2 |
| 1886 | | | 1 | | | | | | | 1 | 1 | | 3 |
| 1887 | | | | | | | | | | | | | 0 |
| 1888 | | | 1 | 1 | | | | | | | | 1 | 3 |
| 1889 | | | | | | | | | 1 | | | | 1 |
| 1890 | | | | | | | | 1 | 2 | 1 | | | 4 |
| 1891 | 1 | | | | | | | | | | | | 1 |
| 1892 | | 1 | 1 | | | | | | 1 | | 1 | 1 | 5 |
| 1893 | | | | | | | | 1 | | | | 1 | 2 |
| 1894 | | | | | | | | | | | | | 0 |
| 1895 | | | | | | | | | 1 | 1 | | | 2 |
| 1896 | | | 1 | | | | | | | | | | 1 |
| 1897 | | | | | | | | | | | | | 0 |
| 1898 | | | | | | | | | | | | | 0 |
| 1899 | | | | | | | | | | | | | 0 |
| 1900 | | 1 | | | 1 | | | | | 1 | 1 | | 4 |
| 1901 | | | 1 | | | | | | | | | | 1 |
| 1907 | | | 1 | | | | | | | | | | 1 |
| 1911 | 1 | | | | | | | | | | | | 1 |
| 1915 | | | | | 1 | | | | | | | | 1 |
| 1924 | | | 1 | | | | | | | | | | 1 |
| 1954 | | | | | 1 | | | | | | | | 1 |
| TOTAL | 11 | 21 | 13 | 18 | 12 | 8 | 20 | 20 | 19 | 17 | 14 | 19 | 192 |

# Summary of Recorded Deaths

In addition to the 192 deaths documented on page 958, an additional 43 interments were reported and recorded with either a *circa* date or an unknown date of death. The sum of these totals indicates that there are 235 burials in Rose Hill Cemetery.

The highest death toll month was February, followed by July. The worst month and year for deaths was July 1876. This was due to the accident that occurred at the Black Diamond Mine in Nortonville on July 24, 1876, resulting in the death of many miners.

Other years with high death tolls were 1865, 1870, and 1875. *The Contra Costa Gazette* newspaper, January 7, 1865, reported that "many and sudden deaths" were occurring in Somersville from malignant scarlet fever. Scarlet fever was also listed as "prevalent in the mines" in the *Antioch Ledger* newspaper, July 2, 1870. Diphtheria was another cause of death in 1870. It is presumed an epidemic also existed in the area in 1875.

# A HUNDRED YEARS TO COME.

Who'll press for gold this crowded street,
 A hundred years to come ?
Who'll tread yon church with willing feet,
 A hundred years to come ?
Pale, trembling age, and fiery youth,
And childhood, with its brow of truth,
The rich and poor, on land, on sea,
Where will the mighty millions be,
 A hundred years to come ?

We all within our graves shall sleep,
 A hundred years to come ;
No living soul for us will weep,
 A hundred years to come ;
But other men our land will till,
And others then our streets will fill;
And other birds will sing as gay,
And bright the sun shines as to-day,
 A hundred years to come.

*Contra Costa Gazette*
September 22, 1866

# Adult Male Deaths
## Listed By Year And Month

| YEAR | MONTH/DAY | NAME | SECTION/PLOT | TOTAL |
|------|-----------|------|--------------|-------|
| 1865 | | | | 0 |
| 1866 | May 27 | MINETT, William C. | N-E, 66 | 1 |
| 1867 | | | | 0 |
| 1868 | | | | 0 |
| 1869 | April 21 | JEWETT, Walter S. | N-F, 105 | 2 |
| | November | JONES, Hugh R. | S-E, 89 | |
| 1870 | May 2 | MARKLEY, Andrew Jackson | N-E, 67 | 2 |
| | September | EDWARDS, John | unknown | |
| 1871 | August 21 or 22 | BANKS, Albert | unknown | 2 |
| | October 6 | GOULDING, Joseph | N-F, 72 | |
| 1872 | March 14 | DAVIS, Peter | S-F, 111 | 1 |
| 1873 | July 8 | WILLIAMS, David R. | S-D, 58 | 3 |
| | December 16 | DALEY, James | unknown | |
| | December 16 | HAY, John | unknown | |
| 1874 | May 12 | WILLIAMS, Edward F. | N-E, 74 | 2 |
| | August 4 | RICHARDS, John | N-E, 64 | |
| 1875 | January 5 | JONES, Thomas S. | N-E, 69 | 3 |
| | September 4 | ENGLER, John | unknown | |
| | December 6 | THOMAS, Rees G. | S-D, 56 | |
| 1876 | July 24 | GETHING, William | S-C, 46 | 12 |
| | July 24 | JAMES, Thomas D. | S-D, 50 | |
| | July 24 | LEWIS, Meredith | unknown | |
| | July 24 | REYNOLDS, George M. | unknown | |
| | July 24 | WATTS, Theophilus | S-D, 50 | |
| | July 24 | WILLIAMS, William L. | S-D, 52 | |
| | July 25 | DUMAS, Theophile | S-D, 47 | |
| | July 25 | GRIFFITHS, David W. | S-D, 49 | |
| | July 25 | WATTS, David | S-D, 50 | |
| | July 30 | SMITH, Evan | S-C, 48 | |
| | September 29 | THOMAS, John | N-B, 5 | |
| | December 23 | DAVIES, Evan | S-D, 53 | |
| 1877 | February 3 | EVANS, John R. | S-E, 94 | 2 |
| | March 3 | LOVE, John | N-C, 30 | |
| 1878 | | | | 0 |
| 1879 | February 9 | JONES, John B. | S-D, 59 | 1 |
| 1880 | November 20 | JONES, Austin | S-C, 23 | 2 |
| | December 16 | HOOK, George B. | S-F, 109 | |
| 1881 | October 22 | WILLIAMS, Watkin | S-D, 51 | 2 |
| | October 25 | BRADSHAW, John | S-C, 16 | |
| 1882 | February 25 | HABENICHT, Wilhelm C. | N-A, 4 | 4 |
| | March 24 | JENKINS, Thomas H. | N-B, 9 | |
| | April 7 | RICHMOND, Thomas | S-E, 80 | |
| | May16 | MORGAN, David | S-E, 92 | |
| 1883 | April 9 | DAVIS, Thomas J. | S-D, 59 | 2 |
| | August 29 | BANKS, Joseph | N-A, 3 | |

| YEAR | MONTH/DAY | NAME | SECTION/PLOT | TOTAL |
|------|-----------|------|--------------|-------|
| 1884 | November 9 | COOPER, George | S-B, 25 | 2 |
|      | Unknown | DOULTON, George | unknown | |
| 1885 | December 10 | OLIVER, Thomas J. | beside S-D, 95 | 1 |
| 1886 | | | | 0 |
| 1887 | | | | 0 |
| 1888 | March 12 | HUGHES, David M. | S-B, 12 | 1 |
| 1889 | September 4 | EDWARDS, Joseph M. | N-B, 7a | 1 |
| 1890 | September 3 | JAMES, Morgan E. | unknown | 2 |
|      | September 11 | RICHARDS, Daniel | S-C, 15 | |
| 1891 | | | | 0 |
| 1892 | February 29 | CLEMENT, William H. | S-F, 100 | 1 |
| 1893 | | | | 0 |
| 1894 | | | | 0 |
| 1895 | September 4 | MORTIMORE, Richard | S-C, 21 | 1 |
| 1896 | March 19 | JONES, Thomas M. | N-E, 70 | 1 |
| 1897 | | | | 0 |
| 1898 | | | | 0 |
| 1899 | | | | 0 |
| 1900 | February 27 | LEAM, Robert | near S-E, 91 | 2 |
|      | May 20 | GRIFFITH, David E. | N-B, 7b | |
| 1901 | April 11 | VAUGHN, Abel (Sr.) | N-D, 33 | 1 |
| 1902-1906 | | | | 0 |
| 1907 | March 25 | DAVIS, David B. | unknown | 1 |
| 1908-1910 | | | | 0 |
| 1911 | January 22 | JONES, Benjamin A. | unknown | 1 |
| 1912-1914 | | | | 0 |
| 1915 | May 14 | THOMAS, Howell | unknown | 1 |
| 1916-1923 | | | | 0 |
| 1924 | April 10 | THOMAS, Handel | unknown | 1 |
| 1925-1953 | | | | 0 |
| 1954 | May 26 | DAVIS, William T. | N-F, 104 | 1 |
| 1955-Present | | | | 0 |
| TOTAL | | | | 59 |

## ADULT MALE DEATHS
### Year, Month and Day of Death Unknown

| YEAR | NAME | SECTION/PLOT | TOTAL |
|------|------|--------------|-------|
| Unknown | GRIFFITH, Jack | unknown | 1 |
| 1870s | HOWELLS, Isaac | N-F, 73 | 1 |
| 1890s | DODSWORTH, George W. | unknown | 1 |
| TOTAL | | | 3 |

## TOTAL ADULT MALE DEATHS = 62

# MALE DEATHS LISTED BY YEAR AND MONTH

| YEAR | JAN | FEB | MAR | APR | MAY | JUN | JUL | AUG | SEP | OCT | NOV | DEC | TOTAL |
|---|---|---|---|---|---|---|---|---|---|---|---|---|---|
| 1865 | | | | | | | | | | | | | 0 |
| 1866 | | | | | 1 | | | | | | | | 1 |
| 1867 | | | | | | | | | | | | | 0 |
| 1868 | | | | | | | | | | | | | 0 |
| 1869 | | | | 1 | | | | | | | 1 | | 2 |
| 1870 | | | | | 1 | | | | 1 | | | | 2 |
| 1871 | | | | | | | | 1 | | | 1 | | 2 |
| 1872 | | | 1 | | | | | | | | | | 1 |
| 1873 | | | | | | | 1 | | | | | 2 | 3 |
| 1874 | | | | | 1 | | | 1 | | | | | 2 |
| 1875 | 1 | | | | | | | | 1 | | | 1 | 3 |
| 1876 | | | | | | | 10 | | 1 | | | 1 | 12 |
| 1877 | | 1 | 1 | | | | | | | | | | 2 |
| 1878 | | | | | | | | | | | | | 0 |
| 1879 | | 1 | | | | | | | | | | | 1 |
| 1880 | | | | | | | | | | | 1 | 1 | 2 |
| 1881 | | | | | | | | | | 2 | | | 2 |
| 1882 | | 1 | 1 | 1 | 1 | | | | | | | | 4 |
| 1883 | | | | | 1 | | | 1 | | | | | 2 |
| 1884 | | | | | | | | | | | 1 | | 1 |
| 1885 | | | | | | | | | | | | 1 | 1 |
| 1886 | | | | | | | | | | | | | 0 |
| 1887 | | | | | | | | | | | | | 0 |
| 1888 | | | 1 | | | | | | | | | | 1 |
| 1889 | | | | | | | | | 1 | | | | 1 |
| 1890 | | | | | | | | | | | 2 | | 2 |
| 1891 | | | | | | | | | | | | | 0 |
| 1892 | | 1 | | | | | | | | | | | 1 |
| 1893 | | | | | | | | | | | | | 0 |
| 1894 | | | | | | | | | | | | | 0 |
| 1895 | | | | | | | | | | 1 | | | 1 |
| 1896 | | | 1 | | | | | | | | | | 1 |
| 1897 | | | | | | | | | | | | | 0 |
| 1898 | | | | | | | | | | | | | 0 |
| 1899 | | | | | | | | | | | | | 0 |
| 1900 | | 1 | | | 1 | | | | | | | | 2 |
| 1901 | | | | 1 | | | | | | | | | 1 |
| 1907 | | | | 1 | | | | | | | | | 1 |
| 1911 | 1 | | | | | | | | | | | | 1 |
| 1915 | | | | | 1 | | | | | | | | 1 |
| 1924 | | | | 1 | | | | | | | | | 1 |
| 1954 | | | | | 1 | | | | | | | | 1 |
| TOTAL | 2 | 5 | 6 | 5 | 7 | 0 | 11 | 3 | 5 | 5 | 3 | 6 | 58 |

In addition to the above total, one male death occurred in each of the following years with no month and day of death listed: in the 1870s, 1884, and in the 1890s. No year or date of death was listed for one male. The sum of these deaths is 4, resulting in the recording of 62 total male burials in Rose Hill Cemetery.

# PASSING AWAY.

## BY ANNIE R. HOWE.

Passing away; passing away;
The sweet Summer roses are passing away;
Their beauty is wasted, their fragrance has fled,
And with'ring they lie in their damp, lowly bed,
The fair, dewy morns in their splendor will rise,
The pale stars grow soft in evenings' clear skies:
But these roses will brighten, ah, never again!

Passing away; passing away;
Bright hopes of my youth—how they're passing
    away,
With the beautiful visions that gladden my eyes
By daytime and nighttime, as sunlight the skies!
Oh, hope may come back to my sorrowful heart;
Bright dreams from their long-silent chambers may
    start,
But those of my youth I may woo all in vain,
For they ne'er will return in their beauty again!

Passing away; passing away;
Friends I have loved—how they're passing away!
I have watched them go down to that cold, solemn
    tide,
While the pale, silent boatman kept close to their
    side;
I've caught the dull dip of their deep, muffled oar,
As he bore them away to that echoless shore!
And my heart cryeth out in its desolate pain,
But they ne'er will return to bless me again!

Passing away; passing away;
Yet I know of a land where there is no decay,
Where the balmy air's filled with the richest per-
    fume
From sweet, fragrant flowers, and fadeless their
    bloom;
Where the soul never grieves as it doth here below,
O'er fair, vanished dreams, o'er hope's fitful glow,
Where linked and forever is love's golden chain,
And parting words chill us, Oh, never again!

*Antioch Ledger*
September 29, 1877

# ADULT FEMALE DEATHS
## LISTED BY YEAR AND MONTH

| YEAR | MONTH/DAY | NAME | SECTION/PLOT | TOTAL |
|------|-----------|------|--------------|-------|
| 1865 | February 24 | EDWARDS, Emma | unknown | 1 |
| 1866 | | | | 0 |
| 1867 | May 27 | JONES, Catherine | S-E, 82 | 1 |
| 1868 | | | | 0 |
| 1869 | August 9 | DAVIS, Anna | S-E, 90 | 1 |
| 1870 | | | | 0 |
| 1871 | | | | 0 |
| 1872 | April 2 | VAN AMRINGE, Ellen | unknown | 1 |
| 1873 | September 19 | MORGAN, Ann | unknown | 1 |
| 1874 | September 11 | FRENCH, Ruth | N-F, 115 | 1 |
| 1875 | February 13 | CLEMENT, Ann | S-F, 100 | 1 |
| 1876 | March 10 | JONES, Elizabeth | S-E, 83 | 5 |
| | May 11 | HUGHES, Margaret | S-D, 54 | |
| | August 7 | WITHEROW, Barbara L. | N-D, 32 | |
| | September 24 | PROSSER, Mary | S-E, 78 | |
| | November 25 | EDWARDS, Catherine | N-C, 31 | |
| 1877 | October 1 | JAMES, Mary Ann | N-C, 28 | 1 |
| 1878 | April 7 | POWELL, Mary | S-C, 42 | |
| | July 16 | DAVIS, Ellen | N-F, 101 | 3 |
| | November 1 | ABRAHAM, Rebecca | S-E, 55 | |
| 1879 | October 5 | NORTON, Sarah | N-B, 6 | 2 |
| | November 10 | TULLY, Mary | S-C, 18 | |
| 1880 | March 17 | OLIVER, Jane | S-D, 95 | 1 |
| 1881 | July 18 | VAUGHN, Hannah (Mrs.) | N-D, 33 | 3 |
| | September 17 | JONES, Elizabeth | Unknown | |
| | October 27 | CAIN, Elizabeth O. | N-A, 2 | |
| 1882 | May 31 | RICHMOND, Anne | S-E, 80 | 1 |
| 1883 | January 14 | JEWETT, Emeline F. | unknown | 1 |
| 1884 | March 6 | SADDLER, Harriet A. | unknown | 3 |
| | October 3 | LEAM, Margaret | S-E, 91 | |
| | unknown | ROGERS, Elizabeth | unknown | |
| 1885 | | | | 0 |
| 1886 | March 24 | EVANS, Rebecca | S-B, 27 | 3 |
| | October 27 | JONES, Martha | S-C, 22 | |
| | November | EASTON, Mary | unknown | |
| 1887 | | | | 0 |
| 1888 | April 18 | VAUGHN, Hannah | N-D, 33 | 2 |
| | December 13 | RITCHARDS, Mary | S-C, 14 | |
| 1889 | | | | 0 |
| 1890 | August 15 | JONES, Ellen | S-E, 89 | 2 |
| | October 22 | BUXTON, Maggie | S-B, 25 | |
| 1891 | | | | 0 |

| YEAR | MONTH/DAY | NAME | SECTION/PLOT | TOTAL |
|------|-----------|------|--------------|-------|
| 1892 | September 8 | BANKS, Ann C. | unknown | 1 |
| 1893 | | | | 0 |
| 1894 | | | | 0 |
| 1895 | October 18 | BRYANT, Eva Sitera | unknown | 1 |
| 1896 | | | | 0 |
| 1897 | | | | 0 |
| 1898 | | | | 0 |
| 1899 | | | | 0 |
| 1900 | November 28 | BRYANT, Margaret | unknown | 1 |
| TOTAL | | | | 37 |

## ADULT FEMALE DEATHS
### Year, Month, and Day of Death Unknown

| YEAR | NAME | SECTION/PLOT | TOTAL |
|------|------|--------------|-------|
| unknown | GRIFFITH, Emma | unknown | 1 |
| TOTAL | | | 1 |

## TOTAL ADULT FEMALE DEATHS = 38

# ADULT FEMALE DEATHS
## LISTED BY YEAR & MONTH

| YEAR | JAN | FEB | MAR | APR | MAY | JUN | JUL | AUG | SEP | OCT | NOV | DEC | TOTAL |
|---|---|---|---|---|---|---|---|---|---|---|---|---|---|
| 1865 | | 1 | | | | | | | | | | | 1 |
| 1866 | | | | | | | | | | | | | 0 |
| 1867 | | | | 1 | | | | | | | | | 1 |
| 1868 | | | | | | | | | | | | | 0 |
| 1869 | | | | | | | | 1 | | | | | 1 |
| 1870 | | | | | | | | | | | | | 0 |
| 1871 | | | | | | | | | | | | | 0 |
| 1872 | | | | | 1 | | | | | | | | 1 |
| 1873 | | | | | | | | | 1 | | | | 1 |
| 1874 | | | | | | | | | 1 | | | | 1 |
| 1875 | | 1 | | | | | | | | | | | 1 |
| 1876 | | | 1 | | 1 | | | 1 | 1 | | 1 | | 5 |
| 1877 | | | | | | | | | | 1 | | | 1 |
| 1878 | | | | | 1 | | 1 | | | | 1 | | 3 |
| 1879 | | | | | | | | | | 1 | 1 | | 2 |
| 1880 | | | 1 | | | | | | | | | | 1 |
| 1881 | | | | | | | 1 | | 1 | 1 | | | 3 |
| 1882 | | | | | 1 | | | | | | | | 1 |
| 1883 | 1 | | | | | | | | | | | | 1 |
| 1884 | | | | | | | | | | 2 | | | 2 |
| 1885 | | | | | | | | | | | | | 0 |
| 1886 | | | 1 | | | | | | | 1 | 1 | | 3 |
| 1887 | | | | | | | | | | | | | 0 |
| 1888 | | | | | 1 | | | | | | | 1 | 2 |
| 1889 | | | | | | | | | | | | | 0 |
| 1890 | | | | | | | | 1 | | 1 | | | 2 |
| 1891 | | | | | | | | | | | | | 0 |
| 1892 | | | | | | | | | | 1 | | | 1 |
| 1893 | | | | | | | | | | | | | 0 |
| 1894 | | | | | | | | | | | | | 0 |
| 1895 | | | | | | | | | | 1 | | | 1 |
| 1900 | | | | | | | | | | | 1 | | 1 |
| TOTAL | 1 | 3 | 4 | 3 | 3 | 0 | 2 | 3 | 5 | 7 | 4 | 1 | 36 |

In addition to the above total, one female death (Elizabeth Rogers) occurred in 1884 and another (Emma Griffith) occurred with no month and day of death listed, making 38 total female burials in Rose Hill Cemetery.

# THE BABY THAT'S GONE.

Silent we stood by the window,
  Watching the twilight fall,
Till the cool gray shadows of evening
  Had gathered over all.

And now the lamp has been lighted,
  And the fire burns warmly and bright,
How sadly our thoughts still wander
  Without to the cold dark night.

There are children playing around us,
  As in many a bygone year,
But one little voice is missing,
  Which we never more shall hear.

The parlor is warm and lightsome,
  But without how the night-winds rave!
And we think of the darkness falling
  Round a little lonely grave.

*Antioch Ledger*
January 14, 1871

# CHILDREN DEATHS
## LISTED BY YEAR AND MONTH

| YEAR | MONTH/DAY | NAME | SECTION/PLOT | TOTAL |
|---|---|---|---|---|
| 1864 | December 25 | WRIGHT, Mary Elizabeth | unknown | |
| | December 28 | TREGELLAS, James | unknown | |
| | December 28 | WRIGHT, John Edmund | unknown | |
| | December 29 | TONKINS, John | unknown | |
| 1865 | January 4 | MUIR, Jane Russel | unknown | 16 |
| | January 27 or 31 | GOULDING, Thomas Pratten | unknown | |
| | February 17 | RICHMOND, Elizabeth | S-E, 81 | |
| | February 18 | TREGELLAS, Joseph | unknown | |
| | February 19 | TREGELLAS, Annie | unknown | |
| | February 20 | BLACKBURN, Charles W. | unknown | |
| | February 27 | RIDDOCK, Robert | unknown | |
| | March 2 | RIDDOCK, Mary Jane | unknown | |
| | April 30 | GOULDING, Fanny Sarah | unknown | |
| | August 21 | JONES, Mary E. | S-E, 79 | |
| | August | EDWARDS, Clara | unknown | 1 |
| | unknown | RIDDOCK, William | unknown | |
| Circa 1865 | unknown | WRIGHT, child | unknown | |
| 1867 | unknown | RIDDOCK, Robert | unknown | 1 |
| 1868 | | | | 0 |
| 1869 | March 26 | MARKLEY, Eliza Jane | N-E, 67 | 3 |
| | April 19 | MARKLEY, David | N-E, 67 | |
| | July 14 | JONES, John | Near N-E, 70 | |
| 1870 | February 8 | EVANS, William Rodrick | S-E, 93 | 16 |
| | April 1 | VESTNYS, Lorenda A. | unknown | |
| | June 26 | WRIGHT, Bertie | unknown | |
| | June 26 | WRIGHT, Minnie | unknown | |
| | June 29 | BOWMAN, Violette I. | N-E, 75 | |
| | July 18 | THOMAS, Elvira | S-D, 56 | |
| | August 2 | THOMAS, Joseph | unknown | |
| | August 5 | JENKINS, Thomas Joseph | S-D, 88 | |
| | August 27 | JONES, Henry | near N-E, 70 | |
| | September 2 | HOWELL, Thomas M. | N-C, 8 | |
| | September 7 | LEAM, May | S-E, 91 | |
| | September 22 | JENKINS, Elizabeth Ann | S-D, 88 | |
| | October 9 | HOWELL, Sarah | N-C, 8 | |
| | December 7 | PIERCY, Julia Etta | S-F, 85 | |
| | unknown | TOLAN, child #1 | unknown | |
| | unknown | TOLAN, child #2 | unknown | |
| 1871 | February 3 | BOWMAN, David G. | N-E, 75 | 3 |
| | July 6 | WILLIAMS, Howell M. | unknown | |
| | October 6 | THOMAS, Joseph | unknown | |
| 1872 | February 5 | JONES, Isabella | S-E, 84 | 3 |

| YEAR | MONTH/DAY | NAME | SECTION/PLOT | TOTAL |
|---|---|---|---|---|
| 1872 (con't) | June 7 | SPOWART, Annie | N-D, 68 | |
| | *Circa* June, 11 | SPOWART, Eliza | unknown | |
| 1873 | November 7 | OTT, Georg Adam | S-E, 76 | 1 |
| 1874 | April 5 | BOWMAN, Charles H. | N-E, 75 | 10 |
| | June 2 | RICHARDS, William Timothy | N-E, 64 | |
| | June 23 | JENKINS, Ebenezer H. | S-D, 88 | |
| | July 10 | JONES, David Thomas | unknown | |
| | July 14 | POHL, Dora | S-F, 110 | |
| | August 20 | JEWETT, Milton | N-F, 105 | |
| | August 30 | DAVIS, Morgan | N-F, 102 or 103 | |
| | October 6 | ENGLER, Charles | unknown | |
| | December 15 | BUXTON, Lulu | N-D, 60 | |
| *Circa* 1874 | unknown | MACLEOD, John | unknown | |
| 1875 | January 16 | POHL, Millie | S-F, 110 | 10 |
| | February 6 | JONES, Lewis James | near S-C, 23 | |
| | February 20 | HOOK, Alice J. | S-F, 108 | |
| | February 22 | WINGATE, Robert | N-D, 37 | |
| | April 19 | MORRIS, Alexander | N-D, 38 | |
| | April 22 | WILLIAMS, Mary M. | unknown | |
| | August 15 | GOULDING, Thomas J. | N-F, 72 | |
| | August 27 | HAVARD, Elias | N-D, 39 | |
| | October 22 | REES, Margaret | unknown | |
| | October 29 | JONES, Davied R. | S-E, 83 | |
| 1876 | March 21 | JONES, George T. | Near N-E, 70 | 5 |
| | June 27 | THOMAS, Elizabeth Ann | unknown | |
| | August 3 | THOMAS, John D. | unknown | |
| | December 4 | WILLIAMS, Annie | S-E, 83 & S-D, 55 | |
| | December 30 | VAUGHN, Abel (Jr.) | N-D, 33 | |
| 1877 | January 22 | EVANS, John | S-E, 93 | 13 |
| | February 18 | EVANS, William | S-E, 93 | |
| | April 6 | REES, Elizabeth Ann | S-C, 19 | |
| | April 9 | WILLIS, Mary Blanche | unknown | |
| | May 21 | BRYANT, Elizabeth Ann | S-D, 57 | |
| | August 12 | THOMAS, Charles Morgan | unknown | |
| | August 12 | THOMAS, Peter Benjamin | unknown | |
| | August 16 | THOMAS, John H. | unknown | |
| | September 5 | JENKINS, Thomas Joseph | S-D, 88 | |
| | September 15 | ENGLER, Annie Henrietta | unknown | |
| | November 4 | CONNER, John T. | unknown | |
| | November 14 | HEYCOCK, Richard | N-D, 35 | |
| | unknown | HUMPHREYS, Gwelym | S-C, 43 | |
| 1878 | July 3 | DAVIS, David | N-F, 102 or 103 | 5 |
| | September 25 | BUXTON, Alfred W. | N-D, 60 | |
| | November 10 | JONES, Thomas | S-C, 113 | |

| YEAR | MONTH/ DAY | NAME | SECTION/PLOT | TOTAL |
|---|---|---|---|---|
| 1878 (con't) | unknown | DAVIS, Margaret | unknown | |
| | unknown | PARSONS, Jeanette | unknown | |
| 1879 | October 7 | DAWSON, Mary A. | S-F, 106 | 3 |
| | December 8 | GREEN, Martha J. | S-F, 107 | |
| | December 24 | AITKEN, Katie | S-C, 17 | |
| *Circa* 1870s | unknown | SCHWARTZ, child #1 | unknown | 3 |
| | unknown | SCHWARTZ, child #2 | unknown | |
| | unknown | WILLIAMS, Sara Elizabeth | unknown | |
| 1880 | February 3 | ENO, Susan J. | N-F, 71 | 5 |
| | April 15 | JENKINS, infant | N-B, 9 | |
| | July 28 | MADDIN, Ella | unknown | |
| | September 20 | VAUGHN, Mary | N-D, 33 | |
| *Circa* 1880 | unknown | PRITCHARD, Lupyester | unknown | |
| 1881 | November 3 | MILLS, Charles W. | N-B, 11 | 2 |
| *Circa* 1881 | unknown | LEWIS, David John | unknown | |
| 1882 | January | HOLT, Walter L. | N-B, 10 | 4 |
| | April 6 | WATERS, William (Willie) | S-B, 117 | |
| | unknown | CROWHURST, Elizabeth | unknown | |
| | unknown | STINE, Catherine | unknown | |
| 1883 | May 4 | CLARE, Walter E. | N-B, 112 | 1 |
| 1884 | | | | 0 |
| 1885 | January 15 | MORTIMORE, Harriet | S-C, 21 | 1 |
| 1886 | | | | 0 |
| 1891 | January 18 | SPRATT, William Gladstone | unknown | 1 |
| 1892 | March 17 | SHAW, Hazel Beatrice | unknown | 3 |
| | November 18 | WATERS, Edna Bella | S-B, 116 | |
| | December 2 | WATERS, John Robert | S-B, 116 | |
| 1893 | August 3 | MORTIMORE, Alvin | S-C, 21 | 3 |
| | December 13 | GRIFFITH, infant | unknown | |
| | unknown | BUSSEY, Joseph | unknown | |
| 1897 | *Circa* June | MALPASS, Percival Sidney | unknown | 1 |
| 1900 | October 17 | | S-B, 24 | 1 |
| TOTAL | | | | 115 |

In addition to the names listed above, 14 other children with unknown death dates are also buried in Rose Hill Cemetery.

**TOTAL CHILDREN DEATHS = 129**

# CHILDREN DEATHS LISTED BY YEAR & MONTH

| YEAR | JAN | FEB | MAR | APR | MAY | JUN | JUL | AUG | SEP | OCT | NOV | DEC | TOTAL |
|------|-----|-----|-----|-----|-----|-----|-----|-----|-----|-----|-----|-----|-------|
| 1865 | 2 | 5 | 1 | 1 | | | | 1 | | | | 4 | 14 |
| 1866 | | | | 1 | | | | | | | | | 1 |
| 1867 | | | | | | | | | | | | | 0 |
| 1868 | | | | | | | | | | | | | 0 |
| 1869 | | 1 | | 1 | | | 1 | | | | | | 3 |
| 1870 | | 1 | | 1 | | 3 | 1 | 3 | 3 | 1 | | 1 | 14 |
| 1871 | | 1 | | | | | 1 | | | 1 | | | 3 |
| 1872 | | 1 | | | | 2 | | | | | | | 3 |
| 1873 | | | | | | | | | | | 1 | | 1 |
| 1874 | | | 1 | | | 2 | 2 | 2 | | 1 | | 1 | 9 |
| 1875 | 1 | 3 | | 2 | | | | 2 | | 2 | | | 10 |
| 1876 | | | 1 | | | 1 | | 1 | | | | 2 | 5 |
| 1877 | 1 | 1 | | 2 | 1 | | | 3 | 2 | | 2 | | 12 |
| 1878 | | | | | | | 1 | | 1 | | 1 | | 3 |
| 1879 | | | | | | | | | | 1 | | 2 | 3 |
| 1880 | | 1 | | 1 | | | 1 | | 1 | | | | 4 |
| 1881 | | | | | | | | | | | 1 | | 1 |
| 1882 | 1 | | | 1 | | | | | | | | | 2 |
| 1883 | | | | 1 | | | | | | | | | 1 |
| 1884 | | | | | | | | | | | | | 0 |
| 1885 | 1 | | | | | | | | | | | | 1 |
| 1886 | | | | | | | | | | | | | 0 |
| 1887 | | | | | | | | | | | | | 0 |
| 1888 | | | | | | | | | | | | | 0 |
| 1889 | | | | | | | | | | | | | 0 |
| 1890 | | | | | | | | | | | | | 0 |
| 1891 | 1 | | | | | | | | | | | | 1 |
| 1892 | | | 1 | | | | | | | | 1 | 1 | 3 |
| 1893 | | | | | | | | | 1 | | | 1 | 2 |
| 1894 | | | | | | | | | | | | | 0 |
| 1895 | | | | | | | | | | | | | 0 |
| 1896 | | | | | | | | | | | | | 0 |
| 1897 | | | | | | | | | | | | | 0 |
| 1898 | | | | | | | | | | | | | 0 |
| 1899 | | | | | | | | | | | | | 0 |
| 1900 | | | | | | | | | | 1 | | | 1 |
| 1901 | | | | | | | | | | | | | 0 |
| TOTAL | 7 | 13 | 4 | 10 | 3 | 8 | 7 | 11 | 7 | 7 | 6 | 12 | 97 |

In addition to the above total, no month and day of death and/or year of death is known for 32 children (listed on the following page). A total of 129 children are believed to be buried in Rose Hill Cemetery.

The following is a list of children believed to be buried in Rose Hill Cemetery with *circa* death dates or unknown death dates.

- BASSETT child, no date - burial location unknown
- BUSSEY, Joseph, died 1893 - burial location unknown
- CROWHURST, Elizabeth, died 1882 - burial location unknown
- DAVIS, Margaret, died 1878 - burial location unknown
- DENNIS, John, no date - burial location unknown
- DUNTON, Clyde C., no date - burial location unknown
- DUNTON, Lulu B., no date - burial location unknown
- EVANS, Elizabeth, no date - burial location unknown
- HUMPHREYS, Gwelym, died 1877 - Section S-C, plot 43
- JONES, Jennie, no date - buried near Section S-C, plot 23
- LEWIS, David John, died *circa* 1881 - burial location unknown
- LEWIS, Seth John, no date - burial location unknown
- MACLEOD, John, died *circa* 1874 - burial location unknown
- MALPASS, Percival Sidney, died *circa* 1897 - burial location unknown
- PARSONS, Jeanette, died 1878 - burial location unknown
- PRITCHARD, Lupyester, died *circa* 1880 - burial location unknown
- RAMSAY child, no date - burial location unknown
- RIDDOCK, Robert, died 1867 - burial location unknown
- RIDDOCK, William, died 1865 - burial location unknown
- SADDLER male child, no date - burial location unknown
- SCHWARTZ, infant #1, died *circa* 1870s - burial location unknown
- SCHWARTZ, infant #2, died *circa* 1870s - burial location unknown
- STINE, Catherine, died 1882 - burial location unknown
- THOMAS, Frederick Elias, no date - Section N-A, plot 5
- TIERNEY, John, no date - burial location unknown
- TOLAN child #1, died 1870 - burial location unknown
- TOLAN child #2, died 1870 - burial location unknown
- Unknown "Infant Babe," no date - Section S-E, plot 79
- Unknown infant #1, no date - buried near Section N-E, plot 69
- Unknown infant #2, no date - buried near Section N-E, plot 69
- WILLIAMS, Sara Elizabeth, died *circa* 1870s - burial location unknown
- WRIGHT child, died *circa* 1865 - burial location unknown

# KNOWN CAUSES OF DEATH

| DEATHS CAUSED BY ILLNESS | INDIVIDUAL INTERRED | DATE OF DEATH | AGE AT DEATH |
|---|---|---|---|
| Black lung disease | WILLIAMS, Edward F. | May 12, 1874 | 52 yrs., 8 mos. |
| Black measles | MARKLEY, Eliza Jane | March 26, 1869 | 13 yrs., 3 mos., 23 dys. |
| Brain & spinal disease | MORTIMORE, Alvin | Aug. 3, 1893 | 1 yr., 1 mo. |
| Brain fever | EDWARDS, Clara | Aug. 1865 | 15 mos. |
| Bright's disease | DAVIS, David B. | March 25, 1907 | 79 yrs. |
| Bright's disease | RICHARDS, Daniel | Sept. 11, 1890 | 69 yrs., 1 mo., 22 dys. |
| Cancer | JONES, Ellen | Aug. 15, 1890 | 69 yrs. |
| Cancer/complications from pneumonia | LEAM, Robert | Feb. 27, 1900 | 63 yrs., 9 mos., 26 dys. |
| Childbirth | BUXTON, Maggie | Oct. 22, 1890 | 40 yrs., 2 mos., 27 dys. |
| Childbirth | GRIFFITH, Emma | unknown | unknown |
| Childbirth (complications from) | BRYANT, Eva Sitera | Oct. 18, 1895 | 21 yrs., 11 mos., 21 dys. |
| Consumption | JEWETT, Walter S. | April 21, 1869 | 19 yrs. |
| Consumption | MORTIMORE, Richard | Sept. 4, 1895 | 52 yrs., 5 mos. 29 dys. |
| Consumption | RITCHARDS, Mary | Dec. 13, 1888 | 63 yrs. |
| Diphtheria | CROWHURST, Elizabeth | 1882 | 3 yrs. |
| Diphtheria | DAVIS, David | July 3, 1878 | 7 yrs., 8 mos., 29 dys. |
| Diphtheria | DAVIS, Morgan | Aug. 30, 1874 | 9 yrs., 11 mos., 26 dys. |
| Diphtheria | EVANS, John | Jan. 22, 1877 | 8 yrs. |
| Diphtheria | HOWELL, Sarah | Oct. 9, 1870 | 4 yrs., 9 mos. |
| Diphtheria | HOWELL, Thomas M. | Sept. 2, 1870 | 10 yrs., 1 mo., 12 dys. |
| Diphtheria | JONES, Martha | Oct. 27, 1886 | 18 yrs., 7 mos., 13 dys. |
| Diphtheria | LEWIS, David John | *circa* 1881 | 4 yrs. |
| Diphtheria | LEWIS, Seth John | unknown | infant |
| Diphtheria | THOMAS, Peter Benjamin | Aug. 12, 1877 | 8 yrs., 11 mos., 4 dys. |
| Diphtheria | THOMAS, Charles Morgan | Aug. 12, 1877 | 5 yrs., 10 mos., 25 dys. |
| Diphtheria | THOMAS, John H. | Aug. 16, 1877 | 3 yrs., 2 mos., 20 dys. |
| Diphtheria | WATERS, Edna Isabella | Nov. 18, 1892 | 3 yrs., 2 mos., 18 dys. |
| Diphtheria | WATERS, John Robert | Dec. 2, 1892 | 5 yrs., 6 mos., 22 dys. |
| Diphtheria | WATERS, William | April 6, 1882 | 9 dys. |
| Dropsy | HUGHES, Margaret | May 11, 1876 | 37 yrs., 11 mos., 5 dys. |
| Epidemic | WILLIAMS, Sara Elizabeth | 1870s | approximately 2 yrs. |
| Epidemic | REES, Margaret | Oct. 22, 1875 | 1 yr., 3 mos., 15 dys. |
| Heart attack | MORGAN, David | May 16, 1882 | 35 yrs., 7 mos., 19 dys. |
| Heart disease | MARKLEY, Andrew Jackson | May 2, 1870 | 40 yrs. |
| Hemorrhage of lungs | THOMAS, Howell | May 14, 1915 | 78 yrs. |

| DEATHS CAUSED BY ILLNESS | INDIVIDUAL INTERRED | DATE OF DEATH | AGE AT DEATH |
|---|---|---|---|
| Hernia or ruptured appendix | THOMAS, Rees G. | Dec. 6, 1875 | 48 yrs., 3 mos., 6 dys. |
| Kidney problems | BANKS, Ann C. | Sept. 8, 1892 | 64 yrs., 3 mos. |
| Paralysis/stroke | VAUGHN, Abel (Sr.) | April 11, 1901 | 61 yrs. |
| Phrenitis/brain fever | EDWARDS, Emma | Feb. 24, 1865 | 23 yrs. |
| Pneumonia | LEAM, Margaret | Oct. 3, 1884 | 47 yrs., 9 mos., 8 dys. |
| Pneumonia or black lung | JONES, Thomas M. | March 19, 1896 | 58 yrs., 1 mo., 2 dys. |
| Pulmonary Congestion | JAMES, Morgan E. | Sept. 3, 1890 | approximately 43 yrs. |
| Scarlet fever | BLACKBURN, Charles W. | Feb. 20, 1865 | 9 yrs., 7 mos. |
| Scarlet fever | BOWMAN, Violette I | June 29, 1870 | 1 yr., 3 mos. |
| Scarlet fever | GOULDING, Thomas P. | Jan. 27 or 31, 1865 | 7 yrs., 7 mos., 17 dys. |
| Scarlet fever | MACLEOD, John | circa 1874 | 6 mos. |
| Scarlet fever? | MUIR, Jane Russel | Jan. 4, 1865 | 4 yrs., 9 mos. |
| Scarlet fever/mountain fever | RICHMOND, Elizabeth | Feb. 17, 1865 | 8 yrs., 5 mos., 11 dys. |
| Scarlet fever/ congestion of brain | SPRATT, Wm. Gladstone | Jan. 18, 1891 | 6 mos. |
| Scarlet fever | TOLAN, (child #1) | 1870 | child |
| Scarlet fever | TOLAN, (child #2) | 1870 | child |
| Scarlet fever | TONKINS, John | Dec. 29, 1865 | 16 yrs., 3 mos. |
| Scarlet fever | TREGELLAS, Annie | Feb. 19, 1865 | 7 yrs., 7 mos. |
| Scarlet fever | TREGELLAS, James | Dec. 28, 1865 | 2 yrs., 21 dys. |
| Scarlet fever | TREGELLAS, Joseph | Feb. 18, 1865 | 5 yrs., 1 mo. |
| Scarlet fever | WRIGHT, Bertie | June 26, 1870 | 3 yrs. |
| Scarlet fever | WRIGHT, (child) | circa 1865 | child |
| Scarlet fever | WRIGHT, John Edmund | Dec. 28, 1865 | 9 yrs., 10 mos. |
| Scarlet fever | WRIGHT, Mary Elizabeth | Dec. 25, 1865 | 1 yr., 6 mos. |
| Scarlet fever | WRIGHT, Minnie | June 26, 1870 | 9 yrs. |
| Smallpox | SPOWART, Annie | June 7, 1872 | 11 yrs., 6 mos. |
| Smallpox | SPOWART, Eliza | circa June 11, 1872 | approximately 9 yrs. |
| Smallpox | THOMAS, Frederick Elias | Oct. 9 (yr. unknown) | 2 mos. |
| Smallpox | THOMAS, John | Sept. 29, 1876 | 23 yrs. |
| Tuberculosis | DAVIS, Ellen | July 16, 1878 | 33 yrs., 28 days |
| Typhoid or diphtheria | JONES, George T. | Mar. 21, 1876 | 4 yrs., 7 mos., 9 dys. |
| Typhoid or diphtheria | JONES, Henry | Aug. 27, 1870 | 2 mos., 20 dys. |
| Typhoid or diphtheria | JONES, Hugh R. | Nov. 1869 | 44 yrs. |
| Typhoid or diphtheria | JONES, John | July 14, 1869 | 1 dy. |
| Yellow jaundice | BASSETT, child | unknown | child |

| DEATHS CAUSED BY MINE ACCIDENTS | INDIVIDUAL INTERRED | DATE OF DEATH | AGE AT DEATH |
|---|---|---|---|
| Boiler explosion | Daley, James | Dec. 16, 1873 | approximately 33 yrs. |
| Boiler explosion | Hay, John | Dec. 16, 1873 | approximately 40 yrs. |
| Burns &/or suffocation from mine explosion | Gething, William | July 24, 1876 | 36 yrs. |
| Burns &/or suffocation from mine explosion | Griffiths, David W. | July 25, 1876 | 42 yrs. |
| Burns &/or suffocation from mine explosion | Reynolds, George M. | July 24, 1876 | 29 yrs. |
| Cave-in | Edwards, John | Sept. 1870 | 41 yrs. |
| Crushed by coal car | Williams, David R. | July 8, 1873 | 23 yrs. |
| Mine explosion | Dumas, Theophile | July 25, 1876 | 28 or 38 yrs. |
| Mine explosion | Smith, Evan | July 30, 1876 | 27 yrs. |
| Mine explosion | Watts, David | July 25, 1876 | adult |
| Mine explosion | Watts, Theophilus | July 24, 1876 | 27 yrs. - 28 yrs. |
| Run over by coal car | Richmond, Thomas | April 7, 1882 | 57 yrs., 8 mos., 22 dys. |
| Scorched by fire in mine explosion | James, Thomas D. | July 24, 1876 | 29 yrs. |
| Suffocation from mine explosion | Lewis, Meredith | July 24, 1876 | 38 yrs. |
| Suffocation from mine explosion | Williams, William L. | July 24, 1876 | 18 yrs., 4 mos. |

| DEATHS CAUSED BY ACCIDENTS/OTHER | INDIVIDUAL INTERRED | DATE OF DEATH | AGE AT DEATH |
|---|---|---|---|
| Burned in fire | Abraham, Rebecca | Nov. 1, 1878 | 18 yrs., 4 mos. |
| Effects of fire | Maddin, Ella | July 28, 1880 | 2 yrs., 6 mos., 10 dys. |
| Fell off horse | Griffith, David E. | May 20, 1900 | 76 yrs. |
| Kicked by horse | Anderson, Robert | Oct. 17, 1900 | 4 yrs., 10 mos., 7 dys. |
| Kicked by horse | Clare, Walter E. | May 4, 1883 | 8 yrs., 2 mos., 27 dys. |
| Killed by falling tree | Clement, William H. | Feb. 29, 1892 | 66 yrs., 7 mos., 5 dys. |
| Run away horse & thrown from buggy | Norton, Sarah | Oct. 5, 1879 | 68 yrs. |
| Suicide | Engler, John | Sept. 4, 1875 | 42 yrs., 9 mos., 9 dys. |
| Suicide | Jones, Benjamin A. | Jan. 22, 1911 | 71 yrs. |

# Known Burial Locations With
# Existing Markers Or Partial Markers

*= shared gravestone

| NAME | TYPE OF GRAVESTONE | SECTION/ PLOT NUMBER |
|---|---|---|
| AITKEN, Katie | marble | S-C, 17 |
| ANDERSON, Robert | bronze plaque embedded in concrete | S-B, 24 |
| BANKS, Joseph | marble | N-A, 3 |
| BOWMAN, Charles H.* | marble | N-E, 75 |
| BOWMAN, David G., (Jr.)* | marble | N-E, 75 |
| BOWMAN, Violette I.* | marble | N-E, 75 |
| BRADSHAW, John | marble | S-C, 16 |
| BRYANT, Elizabeth Ann | marble | S-D, 57 |
| BUXTON, Alfred W. | marble | N-D, 60 |
| BUXTON, Lulu* | marble | N-D, 60 |
| BUXTON, Maggie* | marble | S-B, 25 |
| CAIN, Elizabeth O. | marble | N-A, 2 |
| CLARE, Walter E. | marble | N-B, 112 |
| CLEMENT, Ann* | marble | S-F, 100 |
| CLEMENT, William H.* | marble | S-F, 100 |
| COOPER, George* | marble | S-B, 25 |
| DAVIES, Evan | marble | S-D, 53 |
| DAVIS, Anna | marble | S-E, 90 |
| DAVIS, Ellen | marble | N-F, 101 |
| DAVIS, Peter | marble | S-F, 111 |
| DAVIS, Thomas J.* | marble | S-D, 59 |
| DAVIS, William T. | granite | N-F, 104 |
| DAWSON, Mary A. | marble | S-F, 106 |
| DUMAS, Theophile | marble | S-D, 47 |
| EDWARDS, Catherine | marble | N-C, 31 |
| EDWARDS, Joseph M. | marble | N-B, 7A |
| ENO, Susan J. | marble | N-F, 71 |
| EVANS, Rebecca | marble | S-B, 27 |
| FRENCH, Ruth | marble | N-F, 115 |
| GETHING, William | marble | S-C, 46 |
| GREEN, Martha J. | marble | S-F, 107 |
| GRIFFITH, David E. | granite | N-B, 7b |
| GRIFFITHS, David W. | marble | S-D, 49 |
| HAVARD, Elias | marble | N-D, 39 |

| NAME | TYPE OF GRAVESTONE | SECTION/ PLOT NUMBER |
|---|---|---|
| HEYCOCK, Richard | marble | N-D, 35 |
| HOLT, Walter L. | marble | N-B, 10 |
| HOOK, Alice J. | marble | S-F, 108 |
| HOOK, George B. | marble | S-F, 109 |
| HOWELL, Sarah* | marble | N-C, 8 |
| HOWELL, Thomas M.* | marble | N-C, 8 |
| HOWELLS, Isaac | marble | N-F, 73 |
| HUGHES, David M. | marble | S-B, 12 |
| HUGHES, Margaret | marble | S-D, 54 |
| HUMPHREYS, Gwelym | concrete | S-C, 43 |
| JENKINS, Ebenezer H.* | marble, concrete, granite aggregate | S-D, 88 |
| JENKINS, Elizabeth Ann* | marble, concrete, granite aggregate | S-D, 88 |
| JENKINS, Infant Daughter* | marble | N-B, 9 |
| JENKINS, Thomas H.* | marble | N-B, 9 |
| JENKINS, Thomas Joseph* (died 1870) | marble, concrete, granite aggregate | S-D, 88 |
| JENKINS, Thomas Joseph* (died 1877) | marble, concrete, granite aggregate | S-D, 88 |
| JEWETT, Milton* | marble | N-F, 105 |
| JEWETT, Walter S.* | marble | N-F, 105 |
| JONES, Austin | marble | S-C, 23 |
| JONES, Catherine | marble | S-E, 82 |
| JONES, Davied R.* | marble | S-E, 83 |
| JONES, Elizabeth* | marble | S-E, 83 |
| JONES, Ellen* | granite | S-E, 89 |
| JONES, Hugh R.* | granite | S-E, 89 |
| JONES, Isabella | marble | S-E, 84 |
| JONES, John B.* | marble | S-D, 59 |
| JONES, Martha | marble | S-C, 22 |
| JONES, Mary E.* | marble | S-E, 79 |
| JONES, Thomas | marble | S-C, 113 |
| JONES, Thomas M. | granite | N-E, 70 |
| JONES, Thomas S. | marble | N-E, 69 |
| LEAM, Margaret* | marble | S-E, 91 |
| LEAM, May* | marble | S-E, 91 |
| LOVE, John | marble | N-C, 30 |
| MARKLEY, Andrew Jackson* | marble | N-E, 67 |
| MARKLEY, David* | marble | N-E, 67 |
| MARKLEY, Eliza Jane* | marble | N-E, 67 |
| MILLS, Charles W. | marble | N-B, 11 |
| MINETT, William C. | marble | N-E, 66 |

| NAME | TYPE OF GRAVESTONE | SECTION/PLOT NUMBER |
|---|---|---|
| MORGAN, David | marble | S-E, 92 |
| MORTIMORE, Alvin* | marble | S-C, 21 |
| MORTIMORE, Harriet* | marble | S-C, 21 |
| MORTIMORE, Richard* | marble | S-C, 21 |
| NORTON, Sarah | marble | N-B, 6 |
| OLIVER, Jane | marble | S-D, 95 |
| OTT, Georg Adam | marble | S-E, 76 |
| PIERCY, Julia Etta | marble | S-F, 85 |
| POHL, Dora* | marble | S-F, 110 |
| POHL, Millie* | marble | S-F, 110 |
| POWELL, Mary | marble | S-C, 42 |
| PROSSER, Mary | marble | S-E, 78 |
| REES, Elizabeth Ann | marble | S-C, 19 |
| RICHARDS, Daniel | marble | S-C, 15 |
| RICHARDS, John* | marble | N-E, 64 |
| RICHARDS, William T.* | marble | N-E, 64 |
| RICHMOND, Elizabeth | marble | S-E, 81 |
| RITCHARDS, Mary | marble | S-C, 14 |
| SMITH, Evan | marble | S-C, 48 |
| SPOWART, Annie | marble | N-D, 68 |
| THOMAS, Elvira* | marble | S-D, 56 |
| THOMAS, Rees G.* | marble | S-D, 56 |
| TULLY, Mary | marble | S-C, 18 |
| UNKNOWN adult | marble | S-F, 99 |
| UNKNOWN infant* | marble | N-E, 69 |
| UNKNOWN infant* | marble | N-E, 69 |
| UNKNOWN "infant babe"* | marble | S-E, 79 |
| VAUGHN, Abel (Sr.)* | marble | N-D, 33 |
| VAUGHN, Abel * | marble | N-D, 33 |
| VAUGHN, Hannah (Mrs.)* | marble | N-D, 33 |
| VAUGHN, Hannah* | marble | N-D, 33 |
| VAUGHN, Mary* | marble | N-D, 33 |
| WILLIAMS, Annie | marble | S-D, 55 |
| WILLIAMS, David R. | marble | S-D, 58 |
| WILLIAMS, Watkin | marble | S-D, 51 |
| WINGATE, Robert | marble | N-D, 37 |
| WITHEROW, Barbara L. | marble | N-D, 32 |

# KNOWN BURIAL LOCATIONS WITH
# MISSING OR NO GRAVE MARKERS

\* = shared gravestone

| NAME | TYPE OF MARKER | SECTION/ PLOT NUMBER |
|---|---|---|
| ABRAHAM, Rebecca | marble | S-E, 55 |
| DAVIS, David | marble | N-F, 102/103 |
| DAVIS, Morgan | marble | N-F, 102/103 |
| EVANS, John* | marble | S-E, 94 |
| EVANS, John R.* | marble | S-E, 94 |
| EVANS, William* | marble | S-E, 94 |
| EVANS, William Rodrick | marble | S-E, 93 |
| GOULDING, Joseph* H. | marble | N-F, 72 |
| GOULDING, Thomas* J. | marble | N-F, 72 |
| HABENICHT, Wilhelm C. | marble | N-A, 4 |
| JAMES, Mary Ann | marble | N-C, 28 |
| JAMES, Thomas D.* | white bronze | S-D, 50 |
| MORRIS, Alexander | marble | N-D, 38 |
| RICHMOND, Anne* | marble | S-E, 80 |
| RICHMOND, Thomas* | marble | S-E, 80 |
| THOMAS, Frederick Elias* | marble | N-B, 5 |
| THOMAS, John* | marble | N-B, 5 |
| UNKNOWN | marble | N-E, 87 |
| WATERS, Edna Isabella | none | S-B, 116 |
| WATERS, John Robert | none | S-B, 116 |
| WATERS, William | none | S-B, 116 |
| WATTS, David* | white bronze | S-D, 50 |
| WATTS, Theophilus* | white bronze | S-D, 50 |
| WILLIAMS, Edward F. | marble | N-E, 74 |
| WILLIAMS, William L. | marble | S-D, 52 |

# Known And Presumed Burials With
## Gravesite Locations Unknown

See the Reference List on page 1004 for a description of the sources used.

| NAME | TYPE OF MARKER | SOURCE/REFERENCE |
|------|------|------|
| BANKS, Albert | unknown | *Contra Costa Gazette*, Aug. 26, 1871 |
| BANKS, Ann C. | unknown | Contra Costa County Hall of Records, Martinez, CA |
| BASSETT, child | unknown | Former coal field resident |
| BLACKBURN, Charles W. | unknown | *Contra Costa Gazette*, Feb. 25, 1865 |
| BRYANT, Eva Sitera | unknown | Former coal field resident |
| BRYANT, Ida Mary | unknown | Former coal field resident |
| BRYANT, Margaret | unknown | Former coal field resident |
| BUSSEY, Joseph | unknown | Former coal field resident and descendants |
| BUXTON, Thomas | unknown | Cemetery list source 3 |
| CONNER, John T. | marble | Cemetery list sources 1-6; photograph P610-129-1 |
| COOPER, John L. | unknown | Cemetery list source 4 |
| CROWHURST, Elizabeth | unknown | Coal field descendant |
| DALEY, James | unknown | *Antioch Ledger*, Dec. 20, 1873 |
| DAVIS, David B. | unknown | Demographic records in Black Diamond archives |
| DAVIS, Margaret | unknown | Coal field descendants |
| DENNIS, John | unknown | Reported by park visitor |
| DODSWORTH, George W. | unknown | Coal field descendant |
| DOULTON, George | granite | Cemetery list compiled *circa* 1972; demographic records |
| DUNTON, Clyde C. | unknown | Cemetery list sources 1-3 |
| DUNTON, Lulu B. | unknown | Cemetery list sources 1-3 |
| EASTON, Mary | unknown | *Antioch Ledger*, Nov. 27, 1886 |
| EDWARDS, Clara | unknown | Coal field descendants |
| EDWARDS, Emma | unknown | Coal field descendants |
| EDWARDS, John | unknown | Coal field descendants; *Antioch Ledger*, Sept. 24, 1870 |
| ENGLER, Annie Henrietta | unknown | Cemetery list sources 1, 2, 4, 6 |
| ENGLER, Charles | unknown | Cemetery list sources 1-3 |
| ENGLER, John | unknown | Cemetery list sources 1-3 and 6 |
| EVANS, Elizabeth | unknown | Coal field descendant |
| GOULDING, Fanny Sarah | unknown | Coal field descendant |
| GOULDING, Thomas P. | unknown | Coal field descendant |
| GRIFFITH, Emma | unknown | Cemetery list source 3 |
| GRIFFITH, Infant | unknown | Cemetery list source 3 |
| GRIFFITH, Jack | unknown | Cemetery list source 3 |
| HAY, John | unknown | *Antioch Ledger*, Dec. 20, 1873 |
| JAMES, Morgan E. | unknown | *Contra Costa Gazette*, Sept. 6, 1890 |
| JEWETT, Emeline F. | marble | Cemetery list sources 1-3 and 6; gravestone |
| JONES, Benjamin A. | unknown | Coal field descendant |
| JONES, David Thomas | unknown | Cemetery list sources 1-3 |

| NAME | TYPE OF MARKER | SOURCE/REFERENCE |
|---|---|---|
| JONES, Davied R. | marble | Cemetery list sources 1-3, 5 and 6; gravestone |
| JONES, Elizabeth (d. 1876) | marble | Cemetery list sources 1-3, 5 and 6; gravestone |
| JONES, Elizabeth (d. 1881) | unknown | Cemetery list sources 2, 4 and 5 |
| JONES, George T. | unknown | Coal field descendant |
| JONES, Henry | unknown | Coal field descendant |
| JONES, Jennie | unknown | Coal field descendant |
| JONES, John | unknown | Coal field descendant |
| JONES, Lewis James | unknown | Coal field descendant |
| LEAM, Robert | unknown | *The Livermore Herald*, March 3, 1900 |
| LEWIS, David John | unknown | Coal field descendant |
| LEWIS, Meredith | unknown | *Contra Costa Gazette*, July 29, 1876 |
| LEWIS, Seth John | unknown | Coal field descendant |
| MACLEOD, John | unknown | Coal field descendant |
| MADDIN, Ella | unknown | Cemetery list sources 1-3, 6 and 8 |
| MALPASS, Percival Sidney | unknown | Coal field descendant |
| MORGAN, Ann | unknown | Cemetery list sources 1-4 and 6 |
| MUIR, Jane Russel | unknown | *Contra Costa Gazette*, Jan. 14, 1865 |
| OLIVER, Thomas J. | unknown | *Contra Costa Gazette*, Dec. 19, 1885 |
| PARSONS, Jeanette | unknown | Coal field descendants |
| PRICE, Hazel | unknown | Cemetery list source 2 |
| PRITCHARD, Lupyester | unknown | Coal field descendant |
| RAMSAY, child | unknown | Coal field descendant |
| REES, Margaret | unknown | Coal field descendant |
| REYNOLDS, George M. | unknown | *Contra Costa Gazette*, July 29, 1876 |
| RIDDOCK, Mary Jane | unknown | Coal field descendant |
| RIDDOCK, Robert (d. 1865) | unknown | Coal field descendant |
| RIDDOCK, Robert (d. 1867) | unknown | Coal field descendant |
| RIDDOCK, William | unknown | Coal field descendant |
| ROGERS, Elizabeth | unknown | Coal field descendant |
| SADDLER, Harriet A. | unknown | Coal field descendant |
| SADDLER, male child | unknown | Coal field descendant |
| SCHWARTZ, infant #1 | unknown | Coal field descendant |
| SCHWARTZ, infant #2 | unknown | Coal field descendant |
| SHAW, Hazel Beatrice | unknown | Cemetery list source 4 |
| SPOWART, Eliza | unknown | Coal field descendant |
| SPRATT, William Gladstone | unknown | *Contra Costa Gazette*, Jan. 24, 1891 |
| STINE, Catherine | unknown | Coal field descendant |
| THOMAS, Charles Morgan | unknown | *Pittsburg Post Dispatch*, March 11, 1938; *Antioch Ledger*, Aug. 25, 1877; and gravestone at Holy Cross Cemetery, Antioch, CA |
| THOMAS, Elizabeth Ann | marble | Cemetery list sources 1-4 and 6; photograph P610-98-15 |
| THOMAS, Handel | unknown | Cemetery list source 3 |

| NAME | TYPE OF MARKER | SOURCE/REFERENCE |
|---|---|---|
| THOMAS, Howell | unknown | Cemetery list source 3 |
| THOMAS, John D. | marble | Cemetery list sources 1-4 and 6; photograph P610-98-15 |
| THOMAS, John H. | unknown | *Pittsburg Post Dispatch*, March 11, 1938; and gravestone at Holy Cross Cemetery, Antioch, CA |
| THOMAS, Joseph (d. 1870) | marble | Cemetery list sources 1-4 and 6; photograph P610-98-15 |
| THOMAS, Joseph (d. 1871) | unknown | Cemetery list sources 3 and 4 |
| THOMAS, Peter Benjamin | unknown | *Pittsburg Post Dispatch*, March 11, 1938; *Antioch Ledger*, Aug. 25, 1877; and gravestone at Holy Cross Cemetery, Antioch, CA |
| TIERNEY, John | unknown | Coal field descendant |
| TOLAN, child #1 | unknown | *Antioch Ledger*, July 7, 1870 |
| TOLAN, child #2 | unknown | *Antioch Ledger*, July 7, 1870 |
| TONKINS, John | unknown | *Antioch Ledger*, January 7, 1865 |
| TREGELLAS, Annie | unknown | *Contra Costa Gazette*, Feb. 25, 1865 |
| TREGELLAS, James | unknown | *Antioch Ledger*, Jan. 7, 1865 |
| TREGELLAS, Joseph | unknown | *Contra Costa Gazette*, Feb. 25, 1865 |
| VAN AMRINGE, Ellen | unknown | Cemetery list sources 2 and 3 |
| VESTNYS, Lorenda A. | unknown | Coal field descendant |
| WILLIAMS, Howell M. | unknown | Cemetery list sources 1-3, 5 and 6 |
| WILLIAMS, Mary M. | unknown | Cemetery list sources 1-3, 5 and 6 |
| WILLIAMS, Sara Elizabeth | unknown | Coal field descendant |
| WILLIS, Mary Blanche | unknown | Cemetery list sources 1-4 and 6 |
| WRIGHT, Bertie | unknown | *Antioch Ledger*, July 2, 1870; *Contra Costa Gazette*, July 9, 1870 |
| WRIGHT, child | unknown | *Contra Costa Gazette*, July 9, 1870 |
| WRIGHT, John Edmund | unknown | *Antioch Ledger*, July 2, 1870; *Contra Costa Gazette*, July 9, 1870 |
| WRIGHT, Mary Elizabeth | unknown | *Antioch Ledger*, July 2, 1870; *Contra Costa Gazette*, July 9, 1870 |
| WRIGHT, Minnie | unknown | *Contra Costa Gazette*, July 9, 1870 |

Above, Black Diamond Ranger, Doug Fowler, prepares a marble slab to encase the broken pieces of the Joseph Banks gravestone in September 2009. To view a photograph of the repaired stone see page 1011. Below, Black Diamond Ranger, Monique Looney, cleans the gravestone of Barbara L. Witherow in May 2010 in preparation for its return to Rose Hill Cemetery. To view a photograph of the repaired stone see page 1021. To date, Black Diamond Rangers have stabilized, repaired, and/or uprighted nearly 40 gravestones in Rose Hill Cemetery since the area became an East Bay Regional Park. Photographs by Monique Looney and Doug Fowler.

# Chapter 12

# ROSE HILL CEMETERY TIMELINE

East Bay Regional Park District

# ROSE HILL CEMETERY TIMELINE

| DATE | FACT | SOURCE |
|---|---|---|
| 1859 | Early burial reported. | *Oakland Tribune*, June 3, 1941, page 20. |
| 1865, Jan. | There have been many and sudden deaths in Somersville of scarlet fever. | *Contra Costa Gazette*, Jan. 7, 1865. |
| 1865, Feb. 17 | First gravestone documented burial. Elizabeth Richmond was 8 years, 5 months, and 11 days old when she died of scarlatina maligna (scarlet fever) on February 17, 1865. | Elizabeth Richmond gravestone, Section S-E, plot 81, Rose Hill Cemetery.<br><br>*Contra Costa Gazette*, Feb. 25, 1865. |
| 1865, Feb. | Ten children died within two weeks time of scarlet fever. In the *Contra Costa Gazette* newspaper on this date, five children are listed as dead from the disease. | *Contra Costa Gazette*, Feb. 25, 1865. |
| 1865, March | Scarlet fever "keeps adding fresh victims to its already fearfully long list." | *Contra Costa Gazette*, March 4, 1865. |
| 1870, April | In Nortonville: "The scarlet fever has been and is still preying upon our youth. A number have already died, and more are still suffering from its pangs." | *Antioch Ledger*, April 16, 1870. |
| 1870, Sept. | Scarlet fever is prevalent in the mines; "a large number of children are suffering from it." | *Antioch Ledger*, July 2, 1870. |
| 1876, July 24 | An explosion occurs at the Black Diamond Mine in Nortonville "killing six men and very severely burning nine others. The explosion occurred at three o'clock P.M. in the 400-foot level, the lowermost of the workings in what is denominated the new openings." At least ten men who died in the accident are buried in Rose Hill Cemetery. | *Antioch Ledger*, July 29, 1876. |
| 1876, Sept. | A case of smallpox is reported at Nortonville. | *Antioch Ledger*, Sept. 30, 1876. |
| 1877, April | A number of cases of diphtheria are reported in the coal mining towns. | *Antioch Ledger*, April 14, 1877. |

East Bay Regional Park District

| DATE | FACT | SOURCE |
|---|---|---|
| 1877, Aug. | Several cases of diphtheria are reported among children in Nortonville. | *Antioch Ledger*, Aug. 18, 1877. |
| 1877, Dec. | There have been many deaths among children during the past twelve months in Nortonville and Somersville from diphtheria. | *Antioch Ledger*, Dec. 1, 1877. |
| 1878, Nov. | "The New Monument" is erected in Rose Hill Cemetery for the men who were killed in the July 1876 mine explosion. Three hundred dollars was collected and a "white bronze" monument was erected in memory of David and Theophilus Watts and Thomas D. James. A brick wall enclosure and Kinney's patent tubular fence were also placed at the site. | "Nortonville Correspondence – The New Monument." *Contra Costa Gazette*, Nov. 23, 1878. |
| 1881, Oct. | James Garfield, the 20th President of the United States, was shot by an assassin on July 2, 1881 and died eleven weeks later on September 19, 1881. After learning about his death: "The people of Nortonville …Somersville, Clayton, Judsonville and Stewartville, formed a pageant nearly half a mile in length. There were probably not less than 1,500 persons in the procession. The Knights of Pythias, Odd Fellows, Masons (with a life size portrait of the deceased President) and citizens marched to the cemetery and the choicest spot therein was dedicated as a plot sacred to the memory of President Garfield. | "Memorial Observances at Nortonville." *Contra Costa Gazette*, Oct. 1, 1881. |
|  | …on Garfield's assassination, the chorus [Nortonville Choir] turned out and staged a funeral. A replica of the body of the deceased President was brought in on the train, was met by the chorus and band and a group of marchers and conducted to the local cemetery where a service was held. More dirge singing followed at night, when the ceremony was repeated with torch light." | "Old Nortonville." *Oakland Tribune – Knave*, Oct. 29, 1933. |
| 1896, June | "Measles, imported from Oakland, are epidemic in Somersville." | *Antioch Ledger*, Sat. June 13, 1896. |

| DATE | FACT | SOURCE |
|---|---|---|
| 1916, July 25 | A... "fire originated in some unknown manner near Somersville. About 300 acres of land were swept by the flames, in which area were many fences and two uninhabited shacks which were consumed. The Somersville cemetery was also within the scope covered by fire." | "Fire Breaks Out Near Summerville [sic]." *Pittsburg Post*, Sat., July 29, 1916, page 1. |
| 1922, July 22 | John Sullenger created a list of 62 names of individuals interred in Rose Hill Cemetery. | John Sullenger list located in the Black Diamond archives; Source 4 for this document (see page 1004). |
| 1934, June | Pittsburg Parlor, Native Daughters of the Golden West, is arranging to place a suitable marker at the entrance of the old Somersville cemetery. A committee has been selected to investigate the plan. | "Pioneer Marker to be Erected at Somersville." *Antioch Ledger*, June 29, 1934. |
| 1934, July | Plans to erect a monument at the "old Nortonville Cemetery" were being furthered by a special committee of workers from Sterling [sic] Parlor of Native Daughters. Estelle Evans and Amy McAvoy were named as joint chairmen when the project was approved. | "Nortonville Shaft Plans Given Boost." *Oakland Tribune*, July 22, 1934. |
| 1934, Aug. | Bill Cohn, on behalf of Columbia Steel Company, donated $2,000 to the Native Daughters to purchase a plaque which will be placed on the pioneer monument in Rose Hill Cemetery. | *Pittsburg Post Dispatch*, Aug. 16, 1934, page 1. |
| 1934, Aug. 5 | An unknown person compiled a list of 35 names of individuals interred in Rose Hill Cemetery. | List located in the Black Diamond archives; Source 5 for this document (see page 1004). |
| 1934, Sept. | The Native Daughters of the Golden West are making preparations for dedicating the monument in the cemetery in honor of the pioneers of Nortonville and Somersville on Sunday, October 7, at 1:30pm.<br><br>The monument, a ten-foot concrete shaft in memory of the Nortonville and Somersville pioneers, is half completed. | "Memorial Will Be Dedicated at Somersville Oct. 7." *Antioch Ledger*, Sept. 24, 1934.<br><br>"Native Daughters Plan for Memorial Shaft Dedication." *Pittsburg Post Dispatch*, Sept. 20, 1934. |

| DATE | FACT | SOURCE |
|---|---|---|
| 1934, Oct. | Invitations to the dedication of the memorial tablet to be placed in the cemetery are "issued to city and county officials and to all civic and fraternal organizations." | "Dedication of Pioneer Tablet At Somersville." *Antioch Ledger*, Oct. 5, 1934. |
| 1934, Oct. 7 | The Native Sons and Native Daughters of the Golden West placed a monument in the cemetery in memory of the pioneers of Nortonville and Somersville. "More than 200 members of the Native Sons and Daughters of the Golden West, pioneers of Nortonville and Somersville and county and city officials were present at the dedication of the marker..."<br><br>The 10-foot high concrete monument contained a plaque donated by Columbia Steel Company.<br><br>Mrs. Amy McAvoy was chairman and William Buchanan, chairman of the Contra Costa County Board of Supervisors, was master of ceremonies for the event. | "Pioneer Marker To Be Erected At Somersville." *Antioch Ledger*, June 29, 1934.<br><br>"Memorial Will Be Dedicated at Somersville Oct. 7." *Antioch Ledger*, Sept. 24, 1934.<br><br>"Dedication of Pioneer Tablet At Somersville." *Antioch Ledger*, Oct. 5, 1934.<br><br>"Dedication of Monument to Pioneers Sunday." *Antioch Ledger*, Oct. 8, 1934.<br><br>"Somersville Rites Mark Dedication Of Pioneer Shaft." *Pittsburg Post-Dispatch*, Oct. 8, 1934. |
| 1935, spring | Eva Roath Olcott compiled *Vital Records from Cemeteries in California's Northern Counties* for the Daughters of the American Revolution. This document lists approximately 163 individuals interred in Rose Hill Cemetery. | Eva Roath Olcott list located in the Black Diamond archives; Source 3 for this document (see page 1004). |
| 1935, Aug. | "There is nothing growing on the hill [cemetery] but grass and a small clump of traditional cypress trees." | "A Ghost Town." *Oakland Tribune*, Aug. 18, 1935. |
| 1936 | Ann Louchs compiled *Vital Records from Cemeteries in California Northern Counties, Vol. III*, for the Daughters of the American Revolution. This document lists approximately 137 individuals interred in Rose Hill Cemetery. | Ann Louchs list located in the Black Diamond archives; Source 2 for this document (see page 1004). |

| DATE | FACT | SOURCE |
|---|---|---|
| 1938 | "Off and on, for the past few years, there have been efforts to preserve against the invasion of weeds and the menace of fire, the old cemetery at Nortonville." | "Nortonville." *Oakland Tribune Knave Section*, Aug. 21, 1938. |
| | A carbon pencil drawing of Rose Hill Cemetery is created and later appears in the book *Carbon Pencil Drawings*, by Gordena Parker Jackson in 1974. | *Carbon Pencil Drawings*, Gordena Parker Jackson, 1974. |
| | Prisoners from the County Jail work on a county improvement project at the cemetery. | "Fugitive Felon Faces Long Term." *Oakland Tribune*, June 7, 1938, page 8D. |
| 1939 | "...slowly becoming dilapidated by the ravages of time, is the little Somersville cemetery, which each week attracts scores of sightseers and visitors. Its fence is showing the marks of the years and in some sections nearly touches the ground. Grass covers most of the acreage, but in some places only bare rock and dirt remain. Many broken headstones have fallen over and are broken, and others are so obliterated it is impossible to read the inscriptions.<br><br>As the visitor enters the burying ground...he is forced to stoop and crawl through a makeshift entrance between two posts. The gate is near collapse and sagging awkwardly in the wind, which blows almost continually." | "Burial Ground." *Oakland Tribune – the Knave*, March 13, 1939, page 15. |
| 1940, Nov. | An organized move for the preservation of the "Somersville Cemetery" is expected soon with the support of the California Federation of Women's Clubs, Contra Costa group. | "Move to Preserve Somersville Cemetery of 80's Launched." *Oakland Tribune*, Nov. 6, 1940, page C 33. |
| 1941, *circa* | Supervisor W. J. Buchanan, a native of Nortonville, Contra Costa County, California, had thirty trees planted around the cemetery. | "Old Cemetery To Be Protected." *Oakland Tribune*, June 3, 1941, page 20. |
| 1941, spring | A detail of County jail trustees were sent to cemetery to "right" fallen headstones and clear the plot of debris and grass. | "Old Cemetery To Be Protected." *Oakland Tribune*, June 3, 1941, page 20. |

| DATE | FACT | SOURCE |
|------|------|--------|
| 1941, April | "About three blocks from the rest of the graves is one lonesome, unmarked little mound. It was a smallpox case, the first ever known there and the people were almost primitively superstitious about the disease."<br><br>Twenty Boy Scouts of Troop 7, sponsored by St. Peter's Catholic Church in Pittsburg, Contra Costa County, cleaned the cemetery and planted thirty trees. | "Nortonville Cemetery." *Pittsburg Daily Independent*, Wed., April 30, 1941, page 8.<br><br><br><br>"Boy Scouts Clean Old Nortonville Site." *Daily Pittsburg Independent*, April 23, 1941, page 4. |
| 1941, June | "Supervisor W. J. Buchanan said he would take steps at once to fortify fences and repair the gate to the hillside burial ground where...heifers have corralled, toppling headstones and trampling graves.<br><br>There have been only a few interments in the cemetery since 1916..."<br><br>The cemetery will "be permanently barred to invasion of cattle and preserved in the manner which sentiment and historic interest have demanded." | "Old Cemetery To Be Protected." *Oakland Tribune*, June 3, 1941, page 2D.<br><br><br><br><br><br>"Historic Cemetery." *Oakland Tribune – Knave*, June 15, 1941. |
| 1944, Jan. | The Federated Club Women of Contra Costa County are "vitally interested" in the "Somersville Cemetery" and "are anxious to have what is left of it preserved as quickly as possible. The club women have appealed to the Board of Supervisors to preserve what is left." | "Somersville Cemetery." *Oakland Tribune – Knave*, Jan. 16, 1944. |
| 1944, May | "...at the lower end of the cemetery was a small grave enclosed by an old iron fence, 3 x 6 feet; at one end a young cypress tree, while at the other end was an old 10-foot stump. Between them a little white marble cross with the names "Millie" and "Dora" [Pohl] engraved on the faces." | "Somersville, Nortonville." *Oakland Tribune – Knave*, May 28, 1944. |

| DATE | FACT | SOURCE |
|---|---|---|
| 1947 | Photographs of Rose Hill Cemetery appear in the DOW publication, *Bear Facts*.<br><br>"Unfortunately many of the stones are damaged due to the cattle, vandalism, and lack of care." | *The Bear Facts*, DOW Chemical, Vol. IV, No. 2, Feb. 1947, pages 2-8. |
| 1949, May | A story about Black Diamond and photographs of Rose Hill Cemetery appear in the University of California, Berkeley publication, *California Monthly*. | "Back Yard Ghost Towns." *California Monthly*, May 1949, pages 22 and 23. |
| 1952 | Photographs of Rose Hill Cemetery appear in *Sunset Magazine*. | "Mt. Diablo's ghost towns." *Sunset Magazine*, June 1952, pages 25-26. |
| 1953 | S. B. Vorenkamp compiled a list of approximately 125 individuals interred in Rose Hill Cemetery. | S. B. Vorenkamp list located in the Black Diamond archives; Source 6 for this document (see page 1004). |
| 1954 | Grace Clark compiled a cemetery list for the Daughters of the American Revolution titled *Nortonville and Somersville Cemetery Records*. This document lists approximately 138 individuals interred in Rose Hill Cemetery. | Grace Clark list located in the Black Diamond archives; Source 1 for this document (see page 1004). |
| 1954, May | Last known burial occurs in Rose Hill Cemetery. William T. Davis was buried next to his mother, Ellen Davis, and brothers Morgan and David Davis. | William T. Davis gravesite, Section N-F. plot 104. |
| 1955 | A barbed wire fence surrounds the cemetery. The 1934 Native Sons and Native Daughters of the Golden West Monument remains undisturbed. | "Old Nortonville Cemetery Recalls Historic Period." *Pittsburg Post Dispatch*, June 15, 1955, page 12. |
| 1957 | A photograph of Rose Hill Cemetery is taken by Ansel Adams and appears in his book, *Ansel Adams Singular Images – A Collection of Polaroid Land Photographs*. | *Ansel Adams Singular Images, A Collection of Polaroid Land Photographs*. New York Graphic Society, Boston, 1974. Cover and page 9. |
| 1958, Aug. | Two youths were arrested as they dug into a grave in the "Somersville Cemetery." Sheriff's deputies said about five or six feet of earth had been removed. "The youths told the deputies they were acting on a 'dare' by a third youth." | "Youths Dig into Grave on Dare." *Oakland Tribune*, Aug. 26, 1958, page 7. |

| DATE | FACT | SOURCE |
|---|---|---|
| 1961, April | A tombstone at Nortonville is stolen, three Concord youths are arrested. … "sheriff's deputies on patrol had found a 100-pound grave marker in the road leading to Nortonville Cemetery. While checking the area they discovered several grave markers were overturned or moved from their original locations and one tombstone was missing. When Concord police checked the auto; they found remmants [sic] of bricks used to break windows inside the car and the tombstone in the trunk." | "Tombstone At Nortonville Stolen, 3 Youths Arrested." *Antioch Daily Ledger*, April 20, 1961, page 1. |
| 1963 | A photograph of Rose Hill Cemetery appears on page 82 in the book by *Sunset* titled *Beautiful California*.<br><br>Jim Rotelli creates a list of individuals interred in Rose Hill Cemetery as a term report for Mr. Pope's California history class. | *Beautiful California*. Lane Book Company. Menlo Park, CA. pages 82 and 83, 1963.<br><br>Jim Rotelli list located in the Black Diamond archives. |
| 1963, Nov. | "Nortonville Cemetery is under an active rehabilitation program. …motorcycling hoodlums have attacked the cemetery, leaving only rubble. The repair jobs are constant. …At Nortonville, the county sends its prisoners to clean up the cemetery periodically. To thwart vandalism, they are now constructing a steel fence. The County Park Commission is considering keeping the cemetery as an historical monument in conjunction with a park." | "Forgotten Cemeteries-Eyesore for the County." *Contra Costa Times*, Nov. 10, 1963, page 1 and 16. |
| 1963, Nov. 7 | Contra Costa County Supervisor, Edmund A. Linscheid's office reported that a fence around the "Nortonville-Somersville cemetery" will be erected to eliminate further vandalism.<br><br>"Installation of the 6-foot chain link fence, topped with three strands of barbed wire, is to be completed before Dec. 13. Total length of the fence is 1,100 feet." | "New Fence To Surround Cemetery." *Pittsburg Post-Dispatch*, Thurs., Nov. 7, 1963, page 1. |

| DATE | FACT | SOURCE |
|---|---|---|
| 1963, Dec. | A proposal is made that funds, left over from a fencing project at the Nortonville-Somersville cemetery, be used to make the area a park...went before the board of Contra Costa County Supervisors. "Supervisor Edmund A. Linscheid of Pittsburg offered the plan at the board's Tuesday meeting. The fencing project, done to keep out vandals, cost $2600 for which $7700 has been appropriated." | "Fence Fund Surplus – Linscheid Offers Cemetery Park Plan." *Pittsburg Post-Dispatch*, Thurs., Dec. 26, 1963, page 1 and Tues., Dec. 31, 1963, page 5. |
| 1967-1969, *circa* | Simazine is applied to the soil in Rose Hill Cemetery in an effort to control grass and weed growth. As a result, winter rains wash soil downhill causing erosion problems and burying many gravestones and gravesites. | Conversation with John Waters, Black Diamond Park Supervisor in June 1984. |
| 1969, May | "There is no grass in the cemetery... and all that is left is cracked, dried mud. Only one or two of the graves have been maintained. The others are overgrown with what few weeds exist on the hillside – or else they are buried under the mud that has inched its way down the hill during the rains of many winters." | "Somersville Cemetery, All That's Left Of Early-Day Town." *Contra Costa Times*, May 13, 1969, page 8A. |
| 1971, April | An article, featuring photographs of six gravesites in Rose Hill Cemetery, appears in the *Contra Costa Sunday Times* newspaper. | "The past lingers on..." *Contra Costa Sunday Times – Contra Costa Living Section*, April 11, 1971 Supplement, pages 8-9. |
| 1971, Sept. | An article featuring Black Diamond Mines and Rose Hill Cemetery appears in *Peninsula Living*. | "Sun-Bleached Epitaph For a Black Dynasty." *Peninsula Living*, Sat., Sept. 18, 1971, pages 32-34. |
| 1971, *circa* | The top portion of Margaret Hughes gravestone is stolen from the cemetery and later returned to the East Bay Regional Park District in 1974. | "Give us back our tombstone." *Alameda Times Star*, May 18, 1974, page 10. |
| 1972, Oct. | A portion of the Vaughn family obelisk is taken from Rose Hill Cemetery and placed on the porch of an Antioch resident at midnight on Halloween. The gravestone remains in possession of the resident for two years until it is given to the Antioch Police Department. | "Missing tombstone returned to crypt." *Contra Costa Times*, April 10, 1974. |

| DATE | FACT | SOURCE |
|---|---|---|
| 1972, Dec. | The Contra Costa County Recreation and Natural Resources Commission, after hearing a plea to save the historic old Welsh coal miners burial ground, recommends that the remaining grave markers and fences be removed before more damage can be done by vandals and grave robbers. | "Gravestones' Removal Advised." *Contra Costa Times*, Dec. 6, 1972, page 31. |
| 1973 | Rose Hill Cemetery becomes part of Black Diamond Mines Regional Preserve when 2,443 acres of land are purchased by the East Bay Regional Park District. Although most of the land was acquired from the Ginochio family; the cemetery was purchased from Contra Costa County on Sept. 6, 1973. | East Bay Regional Park District Land Department Records. |
| 1973, Mar. - May | "Richmond-based 'psychic probers' under the tutelage of Frank R. ('Nick') Nocerino, San Pablo psychic consultant, 'ghost tamer,' para-psychologist and hypnotist made 43 trips to the pastoral little cemetery at all times of the day and night during March, April and May of last year. They are satisfied the spirits are now content. . . something is being done." "We have come to the conclusion that the situation at the Rose Hill cemetery was simply this: The spirits were disturbed by the intrusions into the peace and tranquility of the graveyard and the vandalism." "We feel strongly about this and earnestly appeal to those who have plundered the little cemetery and stolen tombstones, to return them, anonymously if they choose." | "Psychics probe cemetery to ease miner's souls." *Contra Costa Times*, Wed., March 20, 1974, page 34. "Something Is Stirring in an Old Graveyard." *Oakland Tribune*, Sat., March 23, 1974, page 17-E. |
| 1973, March | Contra Costa County ends its control of Nortonville Cemetery. Transfer of the 2.7 acre cemetery to the East Bay Regional Park District was approved by the Contra Costa County Board of Supervisors. | "County Ends Its Control Of Nortonville Cemetery." *Contra Costa Times*, March 28, 1973, page 2. |

| DATE | FACT | SOURCE |
|---|---|---|
| 1973, April | The East Bay Regional Park District assumes title to Rose Hill Cemetery. | "May they rest in peace...again." *Alameda Times Star,* Nov. 29, 1973, page 7. |
| 1973, Nov. | Jane Oliver's gravestone is found in the middle of a roadway near Concord by the California Highway Patrol. Jane is buried in Section S-D, plot 95 of Rose Hill Cemetery. Also returned to the East Bay Regional Park District is the gravestone of Catherine Edwards (Section N-C, plot 31). The stone was stored in the property room of the Walnut Creek Police Department for a decade before it was determined that it too belonged to Rose Hill Cemetery. | "Mystery Headstone-Where Does It Belong?" *Oakland Tribune,* Nov. 3, 1973.<br><br>"Errant Headstone Grave Found." *Oakland Tribune,* Nov. 6, 1973.<br><br>"May they rest in peace...again." *Alameda Times Star,* Nov. 29, 1973, page 7. |
| 1973, Dec. | East Bay Regional Park District Planner, Warren Gee, compiles a map of Nortonville [sic] Cemetery recording the names on gravestones and illustrating 111 gravesites. | *Rose Hill Cemetery Plot Plan,* EBRPD, Dec. 20, 1973, drawn by Warren Gee. |
| 1974, March | Clyde King, an Oakland Police Officer assigned to the "metals detail" of the auto theft division discovers the historic Native Sons and Native Daughters of the Golden West plaque after making his daily rounds of all wrecking and junk yards checking for possible stolen metals.<br><br>The plaque was placed and dedicated in the cemetery in 1934 in memory of the pioneers of Nortonville and Somersville. The 90 pound bronze plaque, which was stolen from the cemetery and sold, was turned over to the East Bay Regional Park District. | "Alert officer aids recovery of plaque." *Pittsburg Post-Dispatch,* Wed., March 27, 1974, page 20.<br><br>"Alert Cop Saves Memorial Plaque." *Oakland Tribune,* April 7, 1974, page 10-D.<br><br>"Alert officer aids recovery of plaque." *Antioch Ledger – East County Sentinel,* Wed., April 10, 1974, page 8.<br><br>"Alertness Saves Memorial Plate To Coal Miners." *News Gazette,* Martinez, March 26, 1974, page 3. |
| 1974, April | The gravestone for Mary and Hannah Vaughn is returned by an Antioch resident. "Park District officials are delighted that some of the graveyard tombstones are being returned... Anonymous returns are encouraged (con't next page) | "Missing tombstone returned to crypt." *Contra Costa Times,* Wed., April 10, 1974.<br><br>"Ghostly Return?" *Antioch Ledger,* Tues., April 9, 1974, page 3 and *Pittsburg Post-Dispatch,* Wed., April 10, 1974, page 2. |

| DATE | FACT | SOURCE |
|------|------|--------|
| 1974, April (con't) | and no prosecution is contemplated park district officials said." | "Local woman solves case of missing headstone." *Antioch Ledger*, Tues., April 9, 1974, page 2. |
| | The gravestone was returned by an Antioch resident who found it on her front porch on Halloween *circa* 1972 and didn't know where it came from. | "Ghostly Return?" *Pittsburg Post-Dispatch*, Wed., April 10, 1974, page 2.<br><br>"Returned by White Witch?" *Morning News Gazette*, Thurs., April 11, 1974, page 1. |
| 1974, May | The top portion of Margaret Hughes gravestone is returned to the East Bay Regional Park District. The rest of the Hughes stone is located at the gravesite, Section S-D, plot #54. | "Lost tombstone mystery has overtones from Poe." *Antioch Ledger*, Wed., April 24, 1974, page 2.<br><br>"Coal mine area saga of ghosts gets boost." *Pittsburg Post-Dispatch*, Thurs., April 25, 1974, page 5.<br><br>"Give us back our tombstone." *Alameda Times Star*, May 18, 1974, page 10. |
| 1976, May 8 | Black Diamond Mines Regional Preserve opens to the public. | *John Waters Progress Reports for the Week of May 3, 1976.* |
| 1977, Feb. | Members of the Mt. Diablo Regional Group of the Sierra Club constructed a new trail to Rose Hill Cemetery from Somersville town site. Workers, under the supervision of Jeff Wilson, East Bay Regional Park District Park Aide, "also worked at re-erecting tombstones that had been knocked over by vandals and performed other general restoration work at the cemetery." | "Sierra Club builds pathway to historic local cemetery." *Pittsburg Press*, Fri., Feb. 18, 1977, page 2. |
| 1977, June-Aug. | The East Bay Regional Park District hires summer intern, Traci Gibbons, to photograph and document gravestones and gravesites in Rose Hill Cemetery. | Traci (Gibbons) Parent, Supervising Naturalist, Black Diamond Mines Regional Preserve. |
| 1977, June | During a public hearing regarding future plans for Black Diamond, it was discussed that "Future plans for the park include restoring the cemetery to the condition it was in 1902 when the coal miners left." | "Concern over Black Diamond." *Pittsburg Post-Dispatch*, Fri., June 24, 1977, pages 1 and 2.<br><br>"Hearing on park draws big crowd." *Antioch Ledger – East County Sentinel*, Wed., June 29, 1977, page 1. |

| DATE | FACT | SOURCE |
|---|---|---|
| 1977, June (con't) | "...several headstones have been returned to the park district since the area became a preserve. But...vandalism in the area is posing an extraordinary problem." Five members of the Welsh American Society were concerned about vandalism at the cemetery. | "Concern over Black Diamond." *Pittsburg Post-Dispatch*, Fri., June 24, 1977, pages 1 and 2. |
| 1977, Aug. 11 | As part of developing a *Land Use Plan* for Black Diamond, a public hearing was held to hear comments. According to comments made by Peter Shields of Southport Land and Commercial Company, some gravestones may have been sold to antique buffs. Shields saw one such transaction several years ago in Port Costa, Contra Costa County.<br><br>Another article states that during a public hearing regarding development plans for Black Diamond Mines Regional Preserve, representatives from the Welsh American Society proposed the permanent removal of the headstones from Rose Hill Cemetery. The group "proposed putting the restored and retrieved headstones in a museum within the Preserve...Later, if no more vandalism occurs at the cemetery, they can be put back."<br><br>About 50 people attended the hearing. In addition to removing the headstones, the Welsh American Society proposed that the Park District "fill and grade the cemetery as necessary to fill eroded areas and return the surface to the original hill." | "Historic cemetery restoration asked." *Antioch Daily Ledger*, Fri., Aug. 12, 1977, page 14.<br><br>"Welsh-American plea for headstones." *Pittsburg Post-Dispatch*, Mon., Aug. 15, 1977, page 5.<br><br>"Group Fights to Save Historic Headstones." *Contra Costa Times*, Aug. 21, 1977. |
| 1981, April 21 | Vandalism was discovered at Rose Hill Cemetery. "At the vandalized cemetery, dozens of wooden pickets — carefully designed replicas of the original stakes that marked two gravesites — were (con't next page) | "Vandals spree defaces old Rose Hill Cemetery." *Daily Ledger*, Thurs., April 30, 1981, page 19. |

| DATE | FACT | SOURCE |
|------|------|--------|
| 1981, April 21 (con't) | broken and strewn across the cemetery." "Stacks of bricks also had been knocked over and scattered. And an old brick cornerstone was broken." "A sign explaining the cemetery and asking visitors to report vandals, also was torn apart." The granite obelisk gravestone for Hugh R. and Ellen Jones (Section S-E, plot 89) was knocked over. | "Black Diamond Mine Vandals Ruin Gravesites." *Contra Costa Times*, Thurs., April 30, 1981, page 12 A. |
| 1988, March | A $500 monetary gift from the Pittsburg Women's Community League was used to restore brick enclosures in the cemetery. In preparation of the work, volunteers cleaned old mortar off bricks that will be used to rebuild the brick wall enclosures. | "Sprucing up the mines." *Pittsburg Post Dispatch*, March 9, 1988, page 14. |
| 1995, Dec. | The gravestone for Rees G. Thomas and his daughter Elvira (Section S-D, plot 56) was repaired and placed upright in Rose Hill Cemetery. The stone had been knocked over by vandals over 30 years prior and was stored by Rees' grandson, Wayne Thomas, for safekeeping until repairs could be made by Park staff. | "Restoring history – Volunteers give mine's graveyard a facelift." *Ledger Dispatch*, Mon., Dec. 4, 1995, pages 1 and 8A. |
| 2001, Aug. 10 | Approximately 20 people from New York, Iowa, Oregon, Massachusetts, Washington, Maine, and Northern California participated in the Association for Gravestone Studies Conservation workshop, held in Rose Hill Cemetery. The three day conference was based in San Francisco. During the workshop a number of gravestones were cleaned and/or repaired. | "Graveyards offer history, mystery." *Contra Costa Times*, Aug. 11, 2001, page A3. "Black Diamond Mines Hosts Gravestone Repair Workshop." *Regional Parks News*, Vol. 15, Issue 2, July, Aug. Sept. 2001. |
| 2002, May 23 | Walter E. Clare's gravestone is returned to Black Diamond Mines Regional Preserve. *Evenflow Plumbing Company* of San Leandro, Alameda County, California discovered the gravestone while using a backhoe to dig (con't next page) | "Gravestone returned to Black Diamond." *Ledger Dispatch*, June 5, 2002, page 5. |

| DATE | FACT | SOURCE |
|---|---|---|
| 2002, May 23 (con't) | a trench at a home in Walnut Creek, Contra Costa County, California. The gravestone was probably dumped on the property between 1962 and 1969. | "Walter E. Clare Finally Comes Home." *Bulletin*. Contra Costa County Historical Society, June/July 2002, pages 1, 3, and 8. |
| 2004, Oct. 9 | An anniversary event is held in Rose Hill Cemetery to celebrate the Native Sons and Native Daughters Monument that was placed in the cemetery 70 years ago, as well as the 70th anniversary of the East Bay Regional Park District. Four new wayside panels, detailing the history of the cemetery and listing the people interred there, were unveiled. | 70th Anniversary Celebration, Black Diamond Mines Regional Preserve, East Bay Regional Park District. |
| 2007, April | Coal field descendant, Tony Dunleavy, donates to the Preserve a notebook and 22 black and white photographs, both from *circa* 1939. The photographs and inscriptions were recorded by Zelma Myrick. The notebook details numerous gravestone inscriptions and the photographs depict the condition of the cemetery *circa* 1939, showing many vandalized gravestones. | Items located in the Black Diamond archives. |
| 2008, Jan. | To date, Rangers at Black Diamond have stabilized, repaired, and/or up-righted 33 gravestones. Iron fences have been repaired or replicated and six brass plaques have been placed to mark gravesites with no gravestone. | Doug Fowler, Ranger, Black Diamond Mines Regional Preserve, February 2008. |
| 2009, April | After missing from Rose Hill Cemetery for approximately 37 years, the top piece of the John Bradshaw gravestone (Section S-C, plot 116), containing the motif, was returned to Black Diamond Mines Regional Preserve. The piece was left on rental property in Lafayette, Contra Costa County, California in the 1970s and was later retrieved by the property owner. | Black Diamond Supervising Naturalist, Traci Parent, and Rangers Doug Fowler and Monique Looney. |

| DATE | FACT | SOURCE |
|------|------|--------|
| 2009, Oct. 10 | An anniversary event was held in Rose Hill Cemetery to celebrate the Native Sons and Native Daughters of the Golden West Monument that was placed in the cemetery 75 years ago (October 7, 1934), as well as the 75th anniversary of the East Bay Regional Park District. The 1:30 pm event was attended by approximately 100 people with representatives from the Native Sons, local dignitaries, and coal field descendants participating in the celebration. The Pittsburg Community Band performed music. "Taps" was played as a wreath was placed at the foot of the monument by coal field descendants. | 75th Anniversary Celebration, Black Diamond Mines Regional Preserve, East Bay Regional Park District. |

# REFERENCE LIST

# REFERENCE LIST

## CEMETERY LISTS

1. Clark, Grace. *Nortonville and Somersville Cemetery Records.* Contra Costa County, CA. F 868 C76 Sutro Library. Daughters of the American Revolution. 1954.
2. Louchs, Ann. *Vital Records from Cemeteries in Northern Counties.* Vol. III. F 860 D31 Sutro Library. Daughters of the American Revolution. 1935/1936.
3. Olcott, Eva Roath. *Vital Records from Cemeteries in California's Northern Counties.* Vol. III. F 860 D31. Daughters of the American Revolution. 1935.
4. Sullenger, John. Rose Hill Cemetery list. 1922.
5. Anonymous. Rose Hill Cemetery list. 1934.
6. Vorenkamp, S. B. Rose Hill Cemetery list. 1953.

## DEATH RECORDS

7. Death Records. Hall of Records, Contra Costa County, Martinez, California.

## NEWSPAPERS

8. *Contra Costa Gazette.* Martinez, Contra Costa County, California.
9. *Antioch Ledger.* Antioch, Contra Costa County, California.

## BOOKS

10. Slocum, W. A. and Company. *History of Contra Costa County, California.* Originally published in 1882 by W. A. Slocum in San Francisco, California. Republished in 1974 by Brook-Sterling Company, Oakland, California.

## PHOTOGRAPHS

11. Photographs listed by catalog number and located in the Black Diamond Mines Regional Preserve archives.

## DEMOGRAPHIC RECORDS

12. Information and records obtained from Mount Diablo Coal Field descendants, Lowie Museum, University of California, Berkeley archaeological research records, historical societies and various other sources. The demographic records are stored in the Black Diamond Mines Regional Preserve archives.

## PROBATE OF WILL/COURT RECORDS

13. Most of these records were obtained from the Contra Costa County Historical Society, History Center, Pleasant Hill (now in Martinez), California.

## GRAVESTONE

14. Information recorded from gravestones that exist in Rose Hill Cemetery or in storage at Black Diamond Mines Regional Preserve. For some, only gravestone rubbings exist for a stone that was once present in the cemetery.

# GLOSSARY

# GLOSSARY

**Acute** – (i.e. acute contagious disease) – a disease of short duration; a sudden onset, sharp rise, and short course; very severe, but not chronic.

**Base** – the support or foundation for a gravestone commonly made of granite, marble, sandstone, or concrete.

**Block gravestone** – a rectangular piece, usually made of granite or marble, used to mark a burial site.

**Boss** – raised ornamentation.

**Box tomb** – a grave monument resembling a box that is constructed on top of the gravesite following burial.

**Bright's Disease** – A type of kidney disease; named after English physician, Richard Bright, in 1858.

**Burial ground** – a place where the deceased are interred; also called a burying ground, graveyard, or cemetery.

**Burial site** – a site, either in or above the ground, where the deceased are interred.

**Casket** – a decorative coffin.

**Cast iron fence** – a fence commonly found in a cemetery, made of iron that is cast in a mold and hardened.

**Cenotaph** – a gravestone or monument erected in honor of a person or group whose remains are elsewhere.

**Cemetery** – a burial ground.

**Coffin** – a chest or box in which a corpse is placed for burial.

**Confinement** – the process or time of a woman giving birth; beginning with labor and ending with the birth of a child.

**Consumption** – A disease now known as tuberculosis. Although it can occur in any part of the body, it usually affects the lungs.

**Die** – the gravestone without the base.

**Diphtheria** – an acute contagious disease recognized by inflammation and the formation of a thick covering on the mucus membranes of the nose and throat.

**Disease** – a sickness or illness.

**Dropsy** – an illness characterized by swelling due to the accumulation of excess fluids in the tissues and cavities of the body.

**Enclosure** – typically a wall made of brick or rock that surrounds a burial site(s).

**Epidemic** – a very fast spreading disease among many people.

**Epitaph** – an inscription on a gravestone or marker, often written in prose or verse, that commemorates the person buried there.

**Febrile** – feverish.

**Finial** – a crowning ornament or detail.

**Fleur-de-lis** – a conventional iris in artistic design which can sometimes be found as designs on gravestones and gravesite fences.

**Footstone** – a marker that is smaller than the headstone, and placed at the foot of a grave. Generally footstones are inscribed with only the initials, the word "mother," "father," "son," or "daughter" or first name and/or the date of birth and death of the deceased.

**Granite** – a very hard igneous rock used for gravestones. This rock was used for monuments after the invention of the pneumatic drill in the late 1800s.

**Granny Woman** – see midwife.

**Grave** – an excavation for burial of the dead.

**Gravestone** – a marker placed at a gravesite that is inscribed with information about the deceased and often decorated with a motif; used to commemorate the individual buried there. Also called a headstone or tombstone.

**Graveyard** – a cemetery that is small and private.

**Headstone** – an upright stone marker placed at the head of the grave; also called a tombstone or gravestone.

**Igneous rock** – rock formed by solidification of magma.

**Incised carving** – ornamentation made by cutting into or engraving the stone.

**Inscription** – the words found on a gravestone which generally may include the name, birth date, death date, place of birth, place of death, and names of parents or spouse.

**Interment** – the act of committing the dead to their grave.

**Kerbing** – (curbing) defining the burial site by physically creating boundaries using cement, marble, or granite. Kerbing can be found by itself or with a plot ledger.

**Marble** – limestone that is more or less characterized by metamorphism and that was commonly used for gravestones.

**Marble yard** – a site where blocks of marble were stored and carved into monuments.

**Midwife** – a person who assists women with childbirth.

**Motif** – a design or emblem. Motifs on gravestones may include clasped hands, doves, flowers, lambs, leaves, hands and fingers, the *Bible*, anchors, willow trees, etc.

**Plot ledger/ground ledger** – a flat, hard-surfaced or convex grave covering that marks entire area of the burial site and that may be associated with kerbing.

**Plinth** – the lowest base; sub base. A secondary or middle base sits on top of the plinth. The gravestone sits on top of the middle base.

**Relict** – a widow.

**Sandstone** – a sedimentary rock that is composed mainly of grains of sand.

**Sward** – a piece of ground covered by grass.

**Turrets** – raised structures found at the corners of kerbing that resemble corner posts.

**Undertaker** – a person who arranges funerals and prepares the dead for burial.

**White bronze** – monuments made of zinc.

**Wrought iron** – a commercial form of iron that is malleable and relatively soft and formed into decorative shapes.

**Zinc** – a grayish-white metal.

# PHOTOGRAPHS OF GRAVESTONES

## AND GRAVESITES

## LISTED BY PLOT NUMBER

# PHOTOGRAPHS OF GRAVESTONES AND GRAVESITES LISTED BY PLOT NUMBER

*No photographs exist for gravesites 40, 44, 61, and 62. Nothing is left at these locations to indicate a burial.*

Native Sons & Native Daughters of
the Golden West Monument,
Section N-A, Plot 1

Elizabeth O. Cain,
Section N-A, Plot 2

Elizabeth O. Cain,
Section N-A, Plot 2

Plaque on Native Sons & Native Daughters
of the Golden West Monument,
Section N-A, Plot 1

Joseph Banks,
Section N-A, Plot 3

Joseph Banks,
Section N-A, Plot 3

Wilhelm Habenicht,
Section N-A, Plot 4

Wilhelm Habenicht,
Section N-A, Plot 4

John Thomas & Frederick Elias Thomas,
Section N-A, Plot 5

East Bay Regional Park District

Joseph M. Edwards,
Section N-B, Plot 7a

Sarah Norton,
Section N-B, Plot 6

Sarah Norton,
Section N-B, Plot 6

David E. Griffith,
Section N-B, Plot 7b

Joseph M. Edwards & David E. Griffith,
Section N-B, Plots 7a & 7b

Thomas H. Jenkins & Infant Daughter,
Section N-B, Plot 9

Sarah Howell & Thomas M. Howell,
Section N-C, Plot 8

Thomas H. Jenkins & Infant Daughter,
Section N-B, Plot 9

Thomas H. Jenkins & Infant Daughter,
Section N-B, Plot 9

Sarah Howell & Thomas M. Howell,
Section N-C, Plot 8

Walter L. Holt,
Section N-B, Plot 10

Charles W. Mills,
Section N-B, Plot 11

Charles W. Mills,
Section N-B, Plot 11

David M. Hughes,
Section S-B, Plot 12

Unknown,
Section N-C, Plot 13

Left to Right:
Daniel Richards & Mary Ritchards [sic],
Section S-C, Plots 15 & 14

Mary Ritchards,
Section S-C, Plot 14

Daniel Richards,
Section S-C, Plot 15

John Bradshaw,
Section S-C, Plot 16

Katie Aitken,
Section S-C, Plot 17

John Bradshaw,
Section S-C, Plot 16

John Bradshaw,
Section S-C, Plot 16

Mary Tully,
Section S-C, Plot 18

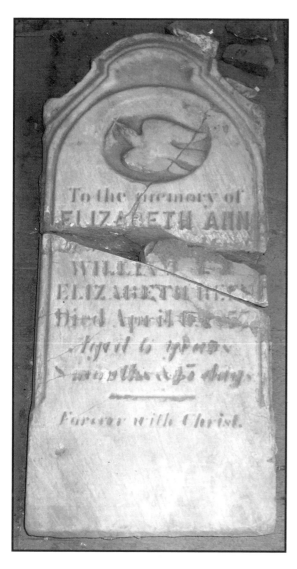

Elizabeth Ann Rees,
Section S-C, Plot 19

Richard, Alvin, & Harriet Mortimore (east side),
Section S-C, Plot 21

Unknown,
Section S-C, Plot 20

Richard, Alvin & Harriet Mortimore (south side),
Section S-C, Plot 21

East Bay Regional Park District

Martha Jones,
Section S-C, Plot 22

Robert Anderson,
Section S-B, Plot 24

Robert Anderson,
Section S-B, Plot 24

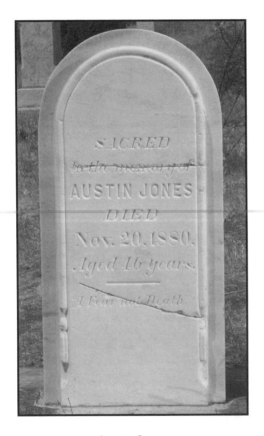

Austin Jones,
Section S-C, Plot 23

George Cooper & Maggie Buxton (east side),
Section S-B, Plot 25

George Cooper & Maggie Buxton (south side),
Section S-B, Plot 25

George Cooper & Maggie Buxton (west side),
Section S-B, Plot 25

George Cooper & Maggie Buxton footstones,
Section S-B, Plot 26

East Bay Regional Park District

Rebecca Evans,
Section S-B, Plot 27

Mary Ann James,
Section N-C, Plot 28

Mary Ann James,
Section N-C, Plot 28

Unknown,
Section N-C, Plot 29

John Love,
Section N-C, Plot 30

John Love,
Section N-C, Plot 30

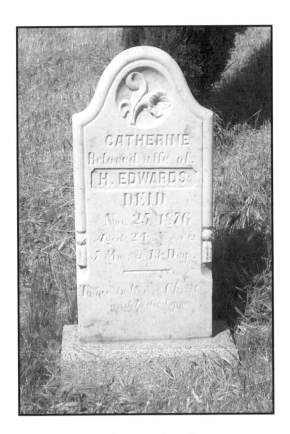

Catherine Edwards,
Section N-C, Plot 31

Vaughn Family,
Section N-D, Plot 33

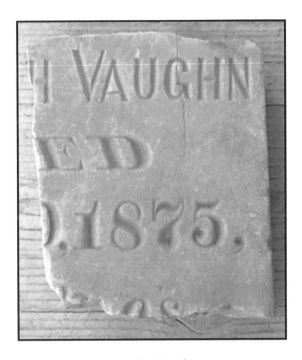

Vaughn Family,
Section N-D, Plot 33

Barbara L. Witherow,
Section N-D, Plot 32

East Bay Regional Park District

Hannah & Mrs. Hannah Vaughn (east side),
Section N-D, Plot 33

Mary & Abel Vaughn, Jr. (south side),
Section N-D, Plot 33

Abel Vaughn, Sr. (north side),
Section N-D, Plot 33

Unknown,
Section N-D, Plot 34

Richard Heycock,
Section N-D, Plot 35

Unknown,
Section N-D, Plot 36

Richard Heycock,
Section N-D, Plot 35

Robert Wingate,
Section N-D, Plot 37

Robert Wingate,
Section N-D, Plot 37

Alexander Morris,
Section N-D, Plot 38

Unknown,
Section S-C, Plot 41

Alexander Morris,
Section N-D, Plot 38

Mary Powell,
Section S-C, Plot 42

Elias Havard,
Section N-D, Plot 39

Gwelym Humphreys,
Section S-C, Plot 43

Gwelym Humphreys,
Section S-C, Plot 43

Unknown
Section S-C, Plot 45

William Gething,
Section S-C, Plot 46

William Gething,
Section S-C, Plot 46

Theophile Dumas,
Section S-C, Plot 47

Evan Smith,
Section S-C, Plot 48

Theophile Dumas,
Section S-C, Plot 47

Evan Smith, footstone,
Section S-C, Plot 48

David W. Griffiths,
Section S-D, Plot 49

Miners' Monument:
Theophilus & David Watts & Thomas D. James,
Section S-D, Plot 50

Miners' Monument:
Theophilus & David Watts & Thomas D. James,
Section S-D, Plot 50

Miners' Monument:
Theophilus & David Watts & Thomas D. James,
Section S-D, Plot 50

Miners' Monument:
Theophilus & David Watts & Thomas D. James,
Section S-D, Plot 50

Left to Right:
Watkin Williams & William L. Williams,
Section S-D, Plots 51 & 52

Left to Right:
Watkin Williams & William L. Williams,
Section S-D, Plots 51 & 52

Miners' Monument:
Theophilus & David Watts & Thomas D. James,
Section S-D, Plot 50

Watkin Williams,
Section S-D, Plot 51

Watkin Williams,
Section S-D, Plot 51

William L. Williams,
Section S-D, Plot 52

William L. Williams,
Section S-D, Plot 52

Evan Davies,
Section S-D, Plot 53

Margaret Hughes,
Section S-D, Plot 54

Rebecca Abraham's middle base,
Section S-D, Plot 55

Margaret Hughes,
Section S-D, Plot 54

Annie Williams' Gravestone sits at
Rebecca Abraham's Gravesite,
Section S-D, Plot 55

Margaret Hughes,
Section S-D, Plot 54

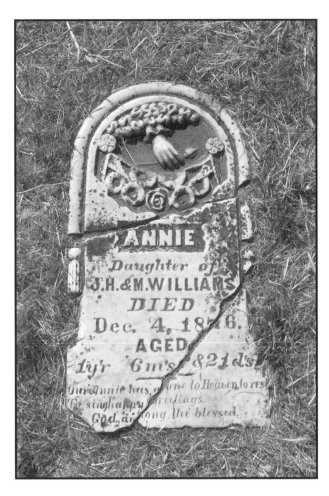

Annie Williams' Gravestone sits at
Rebecca Abraham's Gravesite,
Section S-D, Plot 55

Rees G. Thomas & Elvira Thomas,
Section S-D, Plot 56

Elizabeth Ann Bryant,
Section S-D, Plot 57

Rees G. Thomas & Elvira Thomas,
Section S-D, Plot 56

Elizabeth Ann Bryant,
Section S-D, Plot 57

David R. Williams,
Section S-D, Plot 58

John B. Jones & Thomas J. Davis,
Section S-D, Plot 59

Inside Enclosure, Left:
John B. Jones & Thomas J. Davis,
Section S-D, Plot 59

Right:  Lulu & Alfred W. Buxton,
Section N-D, Plot 60

Lulu Buxton & Alfred W. Buxton,
Section N-D, Plot 60

Unknown,
Section S-E, Plot 63

John Richards & William Timothy Richards,
Section N-E, Plot 64

Unknown,
Section N-E, Plot 65

William C. Minett,
Section N-E, Plot 66

Possibly the partial footstone for
William C. Minett,
Section N-E, Plot 66

A. J. Markley, Eliza Jane Markley,
& David Markley,
Section N-E, Plot 67

Thomas S. Jones & Two Infant Children,
Section N-E, Plot 69

Annie Spowart,
Section N-D, Plot 68

Thomas M. Jones,
Section N-E, Plot 70

Susan J. Eno,
Section N-F, Plot 71

Isaac Howells,
Section N-F, Plot 73

Isaac Howells,
Section N-F, Plot 73

Isaac Howells,
Section N-F, Plot 73

Thomas J. Goulding & Joseph H. Goulding,
Section N-F, Plot 72

Edward F. Williams,
Section N-E, Plot 74

Edward F. Williams,
Section N-E, Plot 74

Violette I. Bowman, David G. Bowman,
& Charles H. Bowman,
Section N-E, Plot 75

Georg Adam Ott,
Section S-E, Plot 76

Unknown,
Section S-E, Plot 77

Mary E. Jones & Infant Babe,
Section S-E, Plot 79

Mary Prosser,
Section S-E, Plot 78

Thomas Richmond & Anne Richmond,
Section S-E, Plot 80

Thomas Richmond & Anne Richmond,
Section S-E, Plot 80

East Bay Regional Park District

Thomas Richmond & Anne Richmond,
Section S-E, Plot 80

Catherine Jones,
Section S-E, Plot 82

Elizabeth Richmond,
Section S-E, Plot 81

Elizabeth Jones & Davied R. Jones,
Section S-E, Plot 83

Isabella Jones,
Section S-E, Plot 84

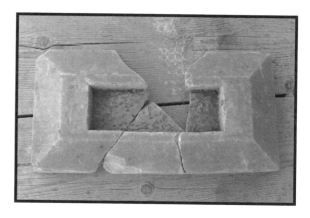

Julia Etta Piercy, middle base,
Section S-F, Plot 85

Unknown,
Section S-F, Plot 86

Julia Etta Piercy,
Section S-F, Plot 85

Unknown,
Section S-E, Plot 87

Jenkins Family (newer marker),
Section S-D, Plot 88

Thomas J. Jenkins, died 1870
(north side, original stone),
Section S-D, Plot 88

Jenkins Family (newer marker),
Section S-D, Plot 88

Elizabeth A. Jenkins (south side, original stone),
Section S-D, Plot 88

Ebenezer H. Jenkins (east side, original stone),
Section S-D, Plot 88

Hugh R. Jones & Ellen Jones,
Section S-E, Plot 89

Margaret Leam & May Leam,
Section S-E, Plot 91

Anna Davis,
Section S-E, Plot 90

David Morgan,
Section S-E, Plot 92

William Rodrick Evans,
Section S-E, Plot 93

Unknown,
Section S-F, Plot 96

John Evans, John R. Evans, & William Evans,
Section S-E, Plot 94

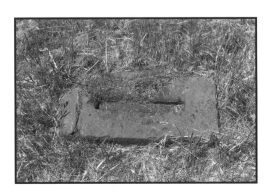

Unknown,
Section S-F, Plot 97

Jane Oliver,
Section S-D, Plot 95

Unknown,
Section S-F, Plot 98

Unknown Adult,
Section S-F, Plot 99

Unknown,
Section S-F, Plot 99

William H. Clement & Ann Clement (east side),
Section S-F, Plot 100

William H. Clement & Ann Clement (north side),
Section S-F, Plot 100

William H. Clement & Ann Clement (west side),
Section S-F, Plot 100

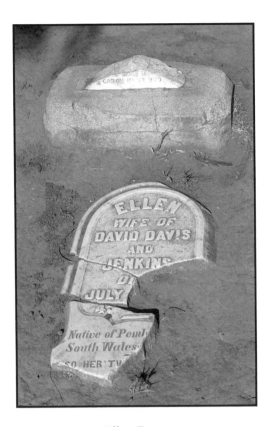

Ellen Davis,
Section N-F, Plot 101

Ellen Davis,
Section N-F, Plot 101

Davis Child,
Section N-F, Plot 102

Davis Child,
Section N-F, Plot 103

William T. Davis,
Section N-F, Plot 104

Walter S. Jewett & Milton Jewett,
Section N-F, Plot 105

Martha J. Green,
Section S-F, Plot 107

Mary A. Dawson,
Section S-F, Plot 106

Alice J. Hook,
Section S-F, Plot 108

George B. Hook,
Section S-F, Plot 109

Millie Pohl & Dora Pohl,
Section S-F, Plot 110

George B. Hook,
Section S-F, Plot 109

Millie Pohl & Dora Pohl,
Section S-F, Plot 110

Peter Davis,
Section S-F, Plot 111

Walter E. Clare,
Section N-B, Plot 112

Peter Davis,
Section S-F, Plot 111

Thomas Jones,
Section S-C, Plot 113

Unknown Base,
Section S-E, Plot 114

Edna Bella Waters, John R. Waters,
& William Waters,
Section S-B, Plot 116

[Note: The Waters' gravesite is located in the grassy area shown in foreground, east of the Robert Anderson gravesite, (plot 24), pictured in the middle of this photograph.]

Ruth French,
Section N-F, Plot 115

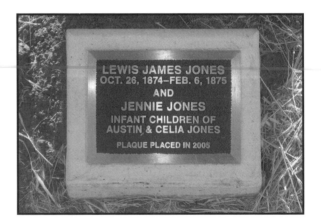

Lewis James Jones and Jennie Jones,
Section S-C, Plot 117

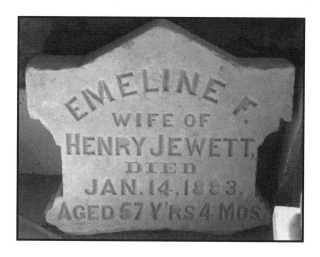

Emeline F. Jewett,
Plot location unknown

Emeline F. Jewett (backside),
Plot location unknown

All the photographs of the gravestones and gravesites were taken in 2005 – 2010 by Karen Terhune,
Black Diamond volunteer, and Traci (Gibbons) Parent.

Above, a rare snowfall blankets the gravesites of Alice J. Hook (left), Mary A. Dawson (middle), and Martha J. Green (right) in Rose Hill Cemetery on December 7, 2009. Below, the snow covered burial ground looking northwest. Photographs by Edward Willis, EBRPD.

# PLOT AND SECTION MAPS

# PLOT AND SECTION MAPS

The maps on the following pages record the name and burial location for the individuals interred in Rose Hill Cemetery. At some sites, only a base (the support or foundation for a gravestone) remains and the name of the individual buried there is not known.

The cemetery is divided into twelve sections. Each section is given a two letter designation based upon a location in the cemetery. The first letter indicates the north ("N") side of the cemetery, or south ("S") side of the cemetery. The second letter indicates the section where the person is buried. The sections are given a letter designation A – F. For example, William C. Minett is buried at plot 66 in section N-E. This indicates he is buried on the north side of the cemetery in section "E." Refer to the inside front or back cover of this publication to see a map of the entire cemetery with section and plot locations.

Reference 379.26

This aerial view of Rose Hill Cemetery, taken in October 2009, shows the west portion of the cemetery in the top of the photograph and the east portion in the lower section of the photograph. Photograph by Traci (Gibbons) Parent and pilot Randy Parent.

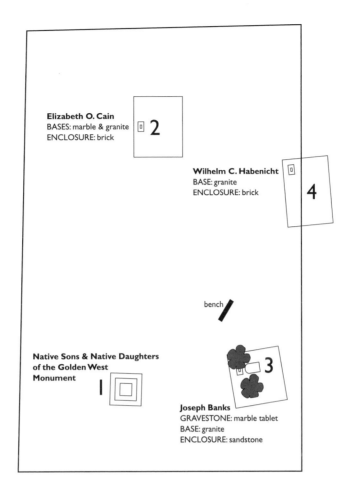

**Elizabeth O. Cain**
BASES: marble & granite
ENCLOSURE: brick

**Wilhelm C. Habenicht**
BASE: granite
ENCLOSURE: brick

bench

**Native Sons & Native Daughters
of the Golden West
Monument**

**Joseph Banks**
GRAVESTONE: marble tablet
BASE: granite
ENCLOSURE: sandstone

# Section N-A

1. Native Sons & Native Daughters of the Golden West Monument
2. CAIN, Elizabeth O.
3. BANKS, Joseph
4. HABENICHT, Wilhelm C.

North

**KEY**

 gravestone & base

base only

iron fence

pepper tree

gravestone only

no marker

brick or stone enclosure

cypress tree

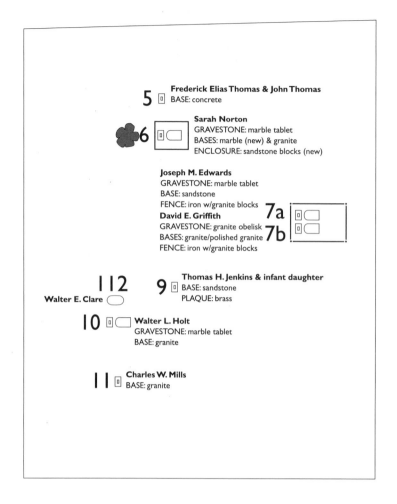

**Frederick Elias Thomas & John Thomas**
5   BASE: concrete

**Sarah Norton**
6   GRAVESTONE: marble tablet
BASES: marble (new) & granite
ENCLOSURE: sandstone blocks (new)

**Joseph M. Edwards**
GRAVESTONE: marble tablet
BASE: sandstone
FENCE: iron w/granite blocks
**David E. Griffith**   7a
GRAVESTONE: granite obelisk
BASES: granite/polished granite   7b
FENCE: iron w/granite blocks

**Thomas H. Jenkins & infant daughter**
112   9   BASE: sandstone
**Walter E. Clare**   PLAQUE: brass

10   **Walter L. Holt**
GRAVESTONE: marble tablet
BASE: granite

**Charles W. Mills**
11   BASE: granite

# Section N-B

5. THOMAS, Frederick Elias & John
6. NORTON, Sarah
7a. EDWARDS, Joseph M.
7b. GRIFFITH, David E.
9. JENKINS, Thomas H. & infant daughter
10. HOLT, Walter L.
11. MILLS, Charles W.
112. CLARE, Walter E.

North

**KEY**

gravestone & base    base only    iron fence    pepper tree

gravestone only    no marker    brick or stone enclosure    cypress tree

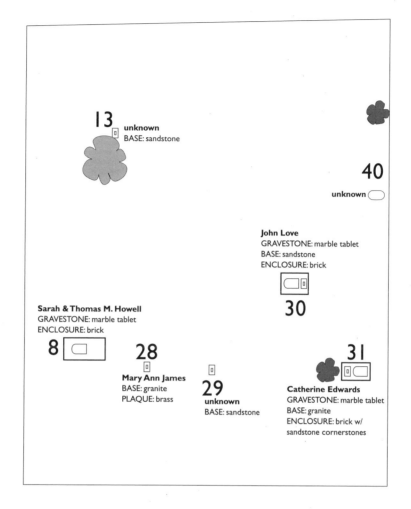

# Section N-C

North

**KEY**

| | |
|---|---|
| gravestone & base | base only |
| gravestone only | no marker |
| iron fence | pepper tree |
| brick or stone enclosure | cypress tree |

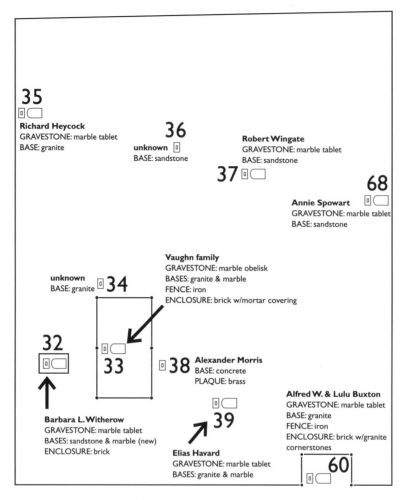

## Section N-D

| | | | |
|---|---|---|---|
| 32. | WITHEROW, Barbara L. | 37. | WINGATE, Robert |
| 33. | VAUGHN family | 38. | MORRIS, Alexander |
| 34. | unknown | 39. | HAVARD, Elias |
| 35. | HEYCOCK, Richard | 60. | BUXTON, Alfred W. & Lulu |
| 36. | unknown | 68. | SPOWART, Annie |

North
↑

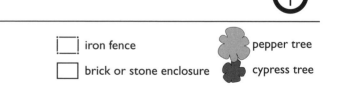

**KEY**

- ▯◻ gravestone & base
- ◻ gravestone only
- ▯ base only
- ◯ no marker
- ⬚ iron fence
- ◻ brick or stone enclosure
- 🌳 pepper tree
- 🌲 cypress tree

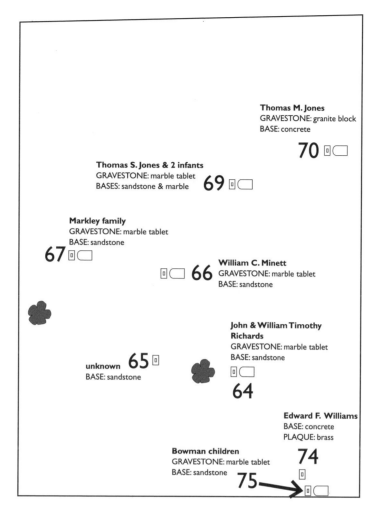

## Section N-E

| | | | |
|---|---|---|---|
| 64 | RICHARDS, John & William Timothy | 70. | JONES, Thomas M. |
| 65. | unknown | 74. | WILLIAMS, Edward F. |
| 66. | MINETT, William C. | 75. | BOWMAN, Charles H., David G., |
| 67. | MARKLEY, A. J., David, & Eliza Jane | | & Violette I. |
| 69. | JONES, Thomas S. & two infants | | |

North

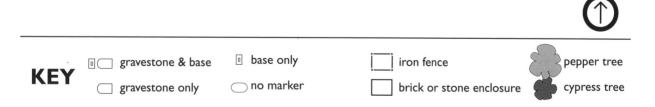

**KEY** — gravestone & base · gravestone only · base only · no marker · iron fence · brick or stone enclosure · pepper tree · cypress tree

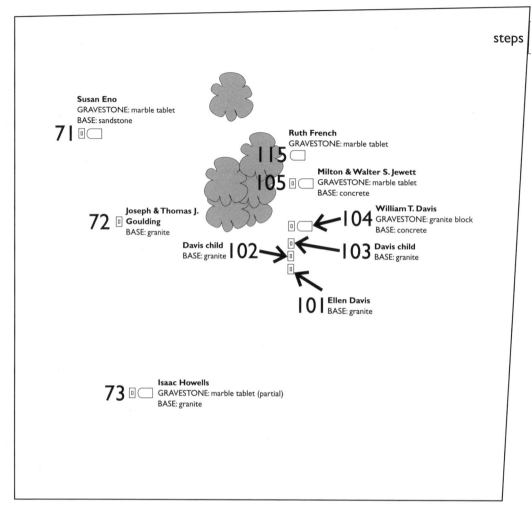

Susan Eno
GRAVESTONE: marble tablet
BASE: sandstone
**71**

Ruth French
GRAVESTONE: marble tablet
**115**

**105**

Milton & Walter S. Jewett
GRAVESTONE: marble tablet
BASE: concrete

**72** Joseph & Thomas J.
Goulding
BASE: granite

William T. Davis
**104** GRAVESTONE: granite block
BASE: concrete

Davis child
BASE: granite **102**

**103** Davis child
BASE: granite

**101** Ellen Davis
BASE: granite

Isaac Howells
**73** GRAVESTONE: marble tablet (partial)
BASE: granite

steps

# Section N-F

| | | | |
|---|---|---|---|
| 71. | ENO, Susan J. | 102. | DAVIS child |
| 72. | GOULDING, Joseph & | 103. | DAVIS child |
| | Thomas J. | 104. | DAVIS, William T. |
| 73. | HOWELLS, Isaac | 105. | JEWETT, Milton & Walter S. |
| 101. | DAVIS, Ellen | 115. | FRENCH, Ruth |

North
↑

**KEY**

 gravestone & base

🔲 base only

iron fence

pepper tree

🔲 gravestone only

◯ no marker

brick or stone enclosure

 cypress tree

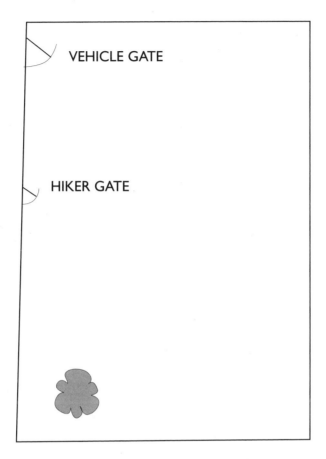

# Section S-A

no known gravesites

North

**KEY**

| | | | | |
|---|---|---|---|---|
| gravestone & base | base only | iron fence | pepper tree |
| gravestone only | no marker | brick or stone enclosure | cypress tree |

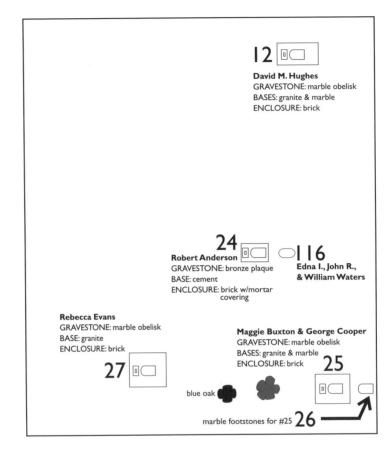

## Section S-B

12. HUGHES, David M.
24. ANDERSON, Robert
25. BUXTON, Maggie & COOPER, George
26. footstones for #25 Maggie Buxton & George Cooper
27. EVANS, Rebecca
116. WATERS, Edna I., John R., & William

North

**KEY**

🔲 gravestone & base   🔲 base only   ⬛ iron fence   ☁ pepper tree

◯ gravestone only   ◯ no marker   ⬜ brick or stone enclosure   🌲 cypress tree

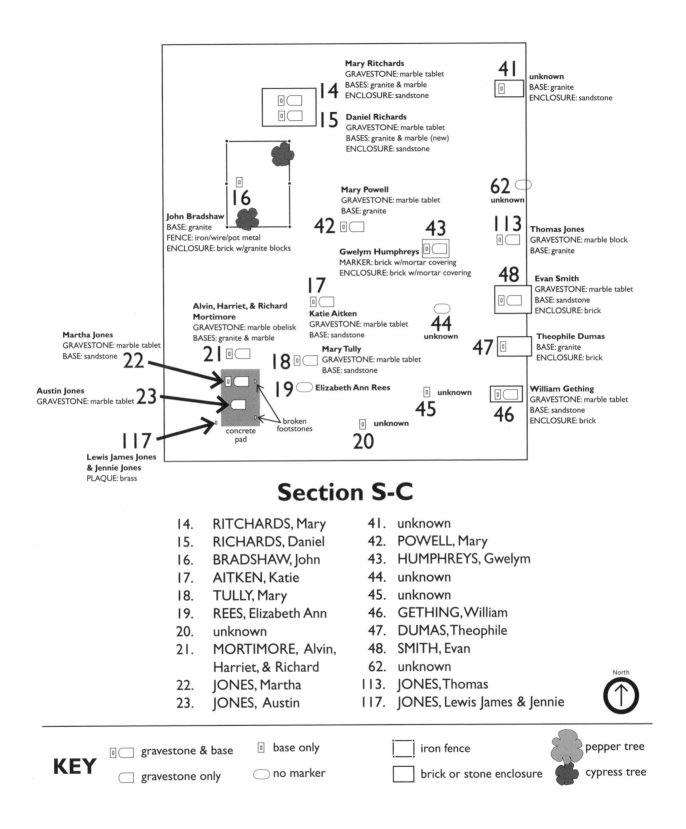

## Section S-C

| | |
|---|---|
| 14. RITCHARDS, Mary | 41. unknown |
| 15. RICHARDS, Daniel | 42. POWELL, Mary |
| 16. BRADSHAW, John | 43. HUMPHREYS, Gwelym |
| 17. AITKEN, Katie | 44. unknown |
| 18. TULLY, Mary | 45. unknown |
| 19. REES, Elizabeth Ann | 46. GETHING, William |
| 20. unknown | 47. DUMAS, Theophile |
| 21. MORTIMORE, Alvin, Harriet, & Richard | 48. SMITH, Evan |
| 22. JONES, Martha | 62. unknown |
| 23. JONES, Austin | 113. JONES, Thomas |
| | 117. JONES, Lewis James & Jennie |

North ↑

**KEY**

| | |
|---|---|
| ▯◻ gravestone & base | ▯ base only |
| ◻ gravestone only | ◯ no marker |
| ⬚ iron fence | |
| ▭ brick or stone enclosure | |
| 🌳 pepper tree | 🌳 cypress tree |

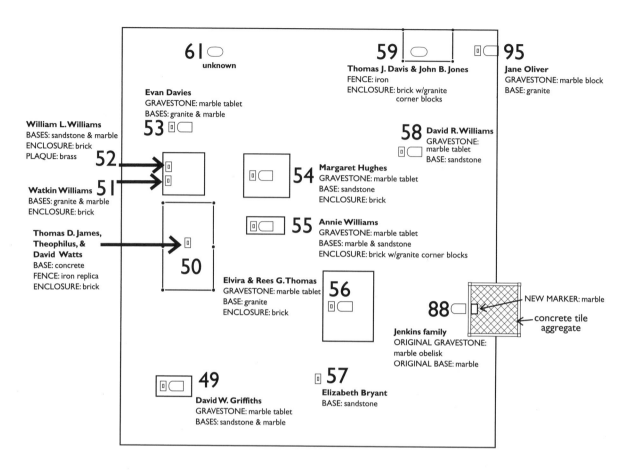

# Section S-D

| | | | |
|---|---|---|---|
| 49. | GRIFFITHS, David W. | 56. | THOMAS, Elvira & Rees G. |
| 50. | JAMES, Thomas D., WATTS, David & Theophilus | 57. | BRYANT, Elizabeth Ann |
| 51. | WILLIAMS, Watkin | 58. | WILLIAMS, David R. |
| 52. | WILLIAMS, William L. | 59. | DAVIS, Thomas J. & JONES, John B. |
| 53. | DAVIES, Evan | 61. | unknown |
| 54. | HUGHES, Margaret | 88. | JENKINS family (two markers) |
| 55. | WILLIAMS, Annie (Rebecca Abraham's stone originally sat at this site—the stone is missing today) | 95. | OLIVER, Jane |

North

↑

KEY

| | |
|---|---|
| ▯◻ gravestone & base | ▯ base only |
| ◻ gravestone only | ◯ no marker |

⬚ iron fence

▢ brick or stone enclosure

 pepper tree

🌳 cypress tree

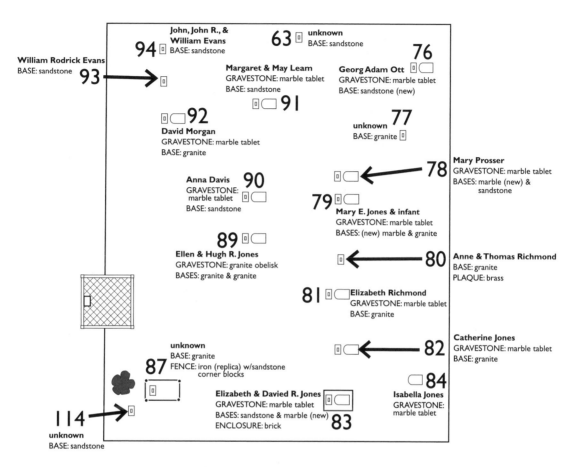

William Rodrick Evans
BASE: sandstone

**John, John R., &
William Evans**
94 BASE: sandstone

63 unknown
BASE: sandstone

76

93

**Margaret & May Leam**
GRAVESTONE: marble tablet
BASE: sandstone

**Georg Adam Ott**
GRAVESTONE: marble tablet
BASE: sandstone (new)

91

92

**David Morgan**
GRAVESTONE: marble tablet
BASE: granite

unknown 77
BASE: granite

**Anna Davis** 90
GRAVESTONE:
marble tablet
BASE: sandstone

78 **Mary Prosser**
GRAVESTONE: marble tablet
BASES: marble (new) &
sandstone

79
**Mary E. Jones & infant**
GRAVESTONE: marble tablet
BASES: (new) marble & granite

89

**Ellen & Hugh R. Jones**
GRAVESTONE: granite obelisk
BASES: granite & granite

80 **Anne & Thomas Richmond**
BASE: granite
PLAQUE: brass

81 **Elizabeth Richmond**
GRAVESTONE: marble tablet
BASE: granite

82 **Catherine Jones**
GRAVESTONE: marble tablet
BASE: granite

**unknown**
BASE: granite
87 FENCE: iron (replica) w/sandstone
corner blocks

84
**Isabella Jones**
GRAVESTONE:
marble tablet

114

**Elizabeth & Davied R. Jones**
GRAVESTONE: marble tablet
BASES: sandstone & marble (new)
ENCLOSURE: brick
83

**unknown**
BASE: sandstone

# Section S-E

| | | | |
|---|---|---|---|
| 63. | unknown | 84. | JONES, Isabella |
| 76. | OTT, Georg Adam | 87. | unknown |
| 77. | unknown | 89. | JONES, Ellen & Hugh R. |
| 78. | PROSSER, Mary | 90. | DAVIS, Anna |
| 79. | JONES, Mary E. & infant | 91. | LEAM, Margaret & May |
| 80. | RICHMOND, Anne & Thomas | 92. | MORGAN, David |
| 81. | RICHMOND, Elizabeth | 93. | EVANS, William Rodrick |
| 82. | JONES, Catherine | 94. | EVANS, John, John R., & William |
| 83. | JONES, Davied R. & Elizabeth | 114. | unknown |

North ↑

**KEY**

⬛▭ gravestone & base    ⬛ base only    ▭ iron fence    pepper tree

▭ gravestone only    ⬭ no marker    ▭ brick or stone enclosure    cypress tree

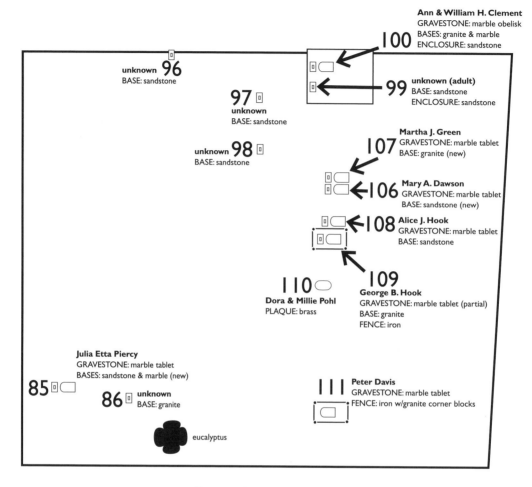

**Ann & William H. Clement**
GRAVESTONE: marble obelisk
BASES: granite & marble
ENCLOSURE: sandstone
**100**

**96** unknown
BASE: sandstone

**99** unknown (adult)
BASE: sandstone
ENCLOSURE: sandstone

**97**
unknown
BASE: sandstone

**Martha J. Green**
GRAVESTONE: marble tablet
BASE: granite (new)
**107**

**98** unknown
BASE: sandstone

**106** Mary A. Dawson
GRAVESTONE: marble tablet
BASE: sandstone (new)

**108** Alice J. Hook
GRAVESTONE: marble tablet
BASE: sandstone

**109**

**110**

**George B. Hook**
GRAVESTONE: marble tablet (partial)
BASE: granite
FENCE: iron

**Dora & Millie Pohl**
PLAQUE: brass

**Julia Etta Piercy**
GRAVESTONE: marble tablet
BASES: sandstone & marble (new)

**85**

**86** unknown
BASE: granite

**111** **Peter Davis**
GRAVESTONE: marble tablet
FENCE: iron w/granite corner blocks

eucalyptus

# Section S-F

| | | | |
|---|---|---|---|
| 85. | Piercy, Julia Etta | 106. | Dawson, Mary A. |
| 86. | unknown | 107. | Green, Martha J. |
| 96. | unknown | 108. | Hook, Alice J. |
| 97. | unknown | 109. | Hook, George B. |
| 98. | unknown | 110. | Pohl, Dora & Millie |
| 99. | unknown (adult) | 111. | Davis, Peter |
| 100. | Clement, Ann & William H. | | |

North

**KEY**

▢◻ gravestone & base ▢ base only ▭ iron fence  pepper tree

◻ gravestone only ⬭ no marker ▭ brick or stone enclosure cypress tree

# PEOPLE INDEX

*Bolded—italicized names* indicate individuals buried in Rose Hill Cemetery. For individuals with name variations, a.k.a. (also known as) was used. Women are indexed under maiden name as well as married name when both names are known.

*Bolded—italicized names indicate individuals buried in Rose Hill Cemetery.*

# PEOPLE INDEX

*Bolded—italicized names indicate individuals buried in Rose Hill Cemetery.*

*Bolded—italicized names indicate individuals buried in Rose Hill Cemetery.*

## C

# PEOPLE INDEX

*Bolded—italicized names indicate individuals buried in Rose Hill Cemetery.*

# PEOPLE INDEX

*Bolded—italicized names indicate individuals buried in Rose Hill Cemetery.*

# PEOPLE INDEX

*Bolded—italicized names indicate individuals buried in Rose Hill Cemetery.*

*Bolded—italicized names indicate individuals buried in Rose Hill Cemetery.*

*Bolded—italicized names indicate individuals buried in Rose Hill Cemetery.*

*Bolded—italicized names indicate individuals buried in Rose Hill Cemetery.*

# F

*Bolded—italicized names indicate individuals buried in Rose Hill Cemetery.*

# G

# PEOPLE INDEX

*Bolded—italicized names indicate individuals buried in Rose Hill Cemetery.*

*Bolded—italicized names indicate individuals buried in Rose Hill Cemetery.*

## H

# PEOPLE INDEX

*Bolded—italicized names indicate individuals buried in Rose Hill Cemetery.*

# PEOPLE INDEX

*Bolded—italicized names indicate individuals buried in Rose Hill Cemetery.*

*Bolded—italicized names indicate individuals buried in Rose Hill Cemetery.*

# PEOPLE INDEX

## *Bolded—italicized names indicate individuals buried in Rose Hill Cemetery.*

*Bolded—italicized names indicate individuals buried in Rose Hill Cemetery.*

*Bolded—italicized names indicate individuals buried in Rose Hill Cemetery.*

*Bolded—italicized names indicate individuals buried in Rose Hill Cemetery.*

# M

# PEOPLE INDEX

*Bolded—italicized names indicate individuals buried in Rose Hill Cemetery.*

# PEOPLE INDEX

## *Bolded—italicized names indicate individuals buried in Rose Hill Cemetery.*

# PEOPLE INDEX

### Bolded—italicized names indicate individuals buried in Rose Hill Cemetery.

*Bolded—italicized names indicate individuals buried in Rose Hill Cemetery.*

*Bolded—italicized names indicate individuals buried in Rose Hill Cemetery.*

## P

Page, S. P., 368

Paltenghi (*See* Ulrich, Mrs. A. E.)

Paltenghi, Andrew (Son of Andrew and Fanny Paltenghi), 923

Paltenghi, Andrew (*See also* General Index: Gravestone carvers and companies, A. Paltenghi and P. Larseneur, and A. Paltenghi), 443, 445, 851, 853, 923-930

Paltenghi, Antoinette, 923

Paltenghi, Cecelia, 923

Paltenghi, Fannie/Fanny, 923, 929

Paltenghi, Louis, 923, 929

Paltenghi, Minnie, 923

Parent, Randy, 6, 1053

Parent, Traci (*See also* Gibbons, Traci), vi, 1, 17, 18, 20, 46, 48, 70, 128, 130, 137, 161, 168, 195, 206, 262, 268, 270, 280, 352, 366, 370, 406, 424, 440, 452, 508, 520, 533, 558, 590, 596, 604, 630, 638, 654, 782, 861, 880, 901, 904, 916, 920, 933, 998, 1001, 1053

Parker, Miss, 687

Parker, (Professor), 513

Parkison, (Doctor), 308

Parry, Rev. William, 282, 286, 316, 317, 372, 392, 446, 706, 718, 745

Parsons, Edna I. (*See also* Gibbel, Edna), 618, 626

Parsons, Emma Harriett (*See also* Bussey, Emma Harriett), 87-90, 440, 441

Parsons, Emma Henrietta (*See also* Bussey, Emma Henrietta and Saddler, Emma Henrietta), 439-441, 624, 628

Parsons, George Walter, 90, 440, 441, 628

Parsons, Irene J. (*See also* Waters, Irene), 618, 624, 626, 628

Parsons, Mrs. James, 98, 102, 118, 618, 622, 626

***Parsons, Jeanette/Jeannette,*** *28, 182, 439-441, 506, 508, 614, 624, 628, 944, 946, 952, 971, 973, 982*

Parsons, Walter (Husband of Emma Henrietta (Saddler) Parsons), 88, 89, 440-442, 624, 628

Parsons, Walter C. (Son of Wilbert A. and Irene J. (Waters) Parsons), 626

Parsons, Wilbert (Bert) Augustus (Husband of Irene (Waters) Parsons), 90, 120, 440, 441, 618, 624, 626, 628

Payne, Dr. Clyde (Dentist), 56

Peel, Amelia (*See also* Ginochio, Amelia), 7, 76, 80, 547, 550

Perfecta Lopez, Maria (*See also* Pritchard, Maria), 457, 458

Peters, Peter, 256

Pettigrew, William, 152

Pettus, Frances E. (*See also* Dunton, Frances), 164, 166, 697

Phalin, (Professor), 468

Philips, William, 296

Phillips, John M., 146

Phipps, W. T., 861

Pierce (Doctor), 886, 887

Piercy, John Hay (J. H. Piercy), 443, 444, 446, 745, 746

Piercy, Julia (Wife of John Hay Piercy), 443, 444, 745

***Piercy, Julia Etta,*** *17, 28, 443-446, 745, 746, 789, 797, 839, 847, 853, 930, 943, 946, 950, 969, 979, 1039, 1066*

Pilkington, Mr. B., 817

Pinkerton, John W. (J. W. Pinkerton), 296, 461

Pitts, D. M., 56

Pitts, Frank, 84

Plymire, Charles J., 931-933

Plymire, Dr. David Brandley, 851, 931-933

Plymire, Eliza (Daughter of William and Eliza Plymire), 931

Plymire, Eliza (Wife of William Plymire), 931

Plymire, Dr. Frederick (Fred) A., 851, 931, 933

Plymire, Dr. Harry G., 931, 933

Plymire, Isabella/Isabell, 931

Plymire, James A. (*See also* General Index: Gravestone carvers and companies, Plymire and Sons), 851, 931-933

Plymire, Jane, 931

Plymire, John, 931

Plymire, Martha, 931

Plymire, Mary I., 931

Plymire, Sarah, 931

*Bolded—italicized names indicate individuals buried in Rose Hill Cemetery.*

# R

# PEOPLE INDEX

*Bolded—italicized names indicate individuals buried in Rose Hill Cemetery.*

*Bolded—italicized names indicate individuals buried in Rose Hill Cemetery.*

## S

# PEOPLE INDEX

*Bolded—italicized names indicate individuals buried in Rose Hill Cemetery.*

*Bolded—italicized names indicate individuals buried in Rose Hill Cemetery.*

*Bolded—italicized names indicate individuals buried in Rose Hill Cemetery.*

*Bolded—italicized names indicate individuals buried in Rose Hill Cemetery.*

# U

*Bolded—italicized names indicate individuals buried in Rose Hill Cemetery.*

# PEOPLE INDEX

*Bolded—italicized names indicate individuals buried in Rose Hill Cemetery.*

*Bolded—italicized names indicate individuals buried in Rose Hill Cemetery.*

*Bolded—italicized names indicate individuals buried in Rose Hill Cemetery.*

# GENERAL INDEX

# C

# D

Gravestone motifs (con't)

Ivy, 91, 95, 97, 98, 112, 117, 118, 203, 271, 272, 333, 341, 834, 838, 845

Knights of Pythias, 127, 128, 213, 834, 838, 844

Lamb(s), 87, 88, 91, 95, 403, 506, 834, 838, 847

Leaves, 112, 287, 629, 632, 633, 834, 838, 845

Lily, 98, 111–113, 639, 834

Masonic, 159, 160, 363, 417, 419, 421, 422, 591, 593, 835, 838, 844

Nipped rosebud/flower, 45, 189, 321, 325, 541, 551, 835, 838, 843

Rope with tassels, 75, 129, 145, 171, 179, 211, 213, 265, 267, 307, 309, 311, 321, 325, 345, 351, 363, 411, 429, 443, 475, 477, 519, 535, 553, 557, 589, 591, 593, 635, 639, 653, 657, 661, 835, 838, 839, 846

Rosette, 273, 281

Sheaf of wheat, 333, 341, 835, 839

Shells, 271, 272, 305, 479, 485, 835, 839

Vine, 845

Weeping willow tree, 365, 369, 397, 399, 401, 835, 839, 847

Weeping willow tree and lamb, 437, 443, 657, 839, 847

Weeping willow tree and obelisk, 345, 839

Gravestone repair, 14–18, 20, 58, 108, 128, 136, 146, 150, 180, 190, 214, 250, 262, 326, 356, 358, 370, 412, 430, 438, 444, 460, 466, 476, 478, 502, 564, 584, 596, 640, 642, 650, 658, 662

Drill and pin method, 15, 17, 128, 214, 242, 460

Encasement method, 15, 18, 262, 312, 356, 358, 366, 984

Lamination method, 15, 17, 584

Great Britain, 46, 86, 234, 550, 600

*Great Register of Contra Costa County, State of California* (1890), 86, 88, 92, 278, 362, 422, 504, 550

*Great Register of Contra Costa County, State of California* (1894), 46, 86, 88, 92, 98, 234, 362, 422, 508, 550, 600

*Great Register of Contra Costa County, State of California* (1898), 48, 86, 170, 234, 600, 618

Gwynn and Tyler (*See also* Tyler and Gwynn), 514

# H

Headstones (*See also* Tombstones), 859, 871, 875, 991, 992, 999

Health officer, 56, 817

Hearse, 811, 827

Holiday(s) (*See* Celebrations)

Hoodlums, 368, 994

Horse(s), 47, 49, 107, 109, 126, 233, 234, 236, 324, 330, 429, 514, 565, 602, 666, 680, 688, 740–742, 764, 976

mine, 416

race/racing, 514, 683

saddle, 286, 741, 742

team, 126, 742, 764

Horseback, 688, 708, 742

Hospital, 547, 565, 694, 696, 757, 767, 781, 828, 878

Hotel, 264, 296, 384, 385, 440, 547, 550, 616, 644, 731

Black Diamond Exchange (Nortonville), 284, 344, 468, 650, 771

Dickinson (Somersville), 154, 570

Fredrick Hunds (New York Landing), 440

Gwynn and Tyler (a.k.a. Tyler and Gwynn; Nortonville), 344, 514

Hawxhurst (Somersville), 683

H. M. Thomas (Nortonville), 514

Hollywood (Somersville), 154

Howell Thomas (Nortonville), 442, 550

J. E. Scammon (Somersville), 154, 296, 688

Mrs. W. E. D. Davis (Nortonville), 514

Nortonville, 466, 504

Pittsburg/Somersville (Somersville), 154

Riddock's (Somersville), 492

Singlewood (Stewartville), 100

Somersville, 36, 61, 66, 68, 154, 384

Union (Somersville), 296

Watkin Williams (Nortonville), 436

# I

Illnesses, 12, 13, 175, 475, 748, 756, 801, 803, 821, 974, 975, 1006, 1007

Independent Order of Odd Fellows (IOOF; *see* Organizations, Independent Order of Odd Fellows)

Indian Diggings, 857, 871

Instruments, 514

Ireland, 48, 104, 108, 444, 486, 562, 568, 572, 830, 882, 903, 917, 920, 931

Irish, 12, 344, 568

Irish Canyon, 317, 318

Isthmus of Panama, 134, 136, 202, 279, 565

Italy, 414, 518, 851

Italy, Carrara, 907

# J

Judsonville (*See* California, Contra Costa County, Judsonville)

Justice Court, 601

# K

Knights of Pythias (*See* Organizations, Knights of Pythias)

# L

La Perla Studio (Pittsburg, CA), 33

Languages, 124

Liquor(s) (*See also* Wines/liquor), 250, 251, 296, 458, 460, 462, 466, 504, 514, 516, 522, 755

Livestock/stock, 68, 235, 694, 709, 767

Livestock
    Chickens/poultry, 565, 746
    Cows/cattle, 14, 234, 364, 384, 431, 516, 565, 568, 708, 746, 767, 992, 993
    Horse(s), 47, 49, 107, 109, 233, 234, 236, 286, 330, 429, 565, 602, 680, 683, 688, 708, 709, 740–743, 764, 781, 976
    Pigs, 565

Local Option Law, 446

# M

Mail/mail service, 80, 84, 236, 708

Marble, 13–18, 34, 35, 977–983, 992, 1006–1008
    Billiard beds, 919
    Buildings, 858
    Bureau tops/bureau, 899, 905, 919
    Busts, 925
    Counter tops, 905, 919
    Cutting/cutter, 855, 858, 860, 863, 871, 877, 882, 897, 898, 900, 903, 908, 911, 912, 916, 931
    Fountains, 879, 925–927
    Grates, 905, 906, 918
    Gravestones, 906, 926
    Headstones, 879, 905, 918, 919, 932
    Imposing stones, 875
    Mantels, 857, 858, 871, 873–875, 879, 899, 905–907, 918, 919, 924–927, 932
    Monuments, 14, 781, 857, 858, 873, 874, 879, 899, 905, 907, 918, 919, 924–927, 932
    Mural, 906
    Ornamental/ornaments, 857, 926
    Plumbers' slabs, 873–875, 899, 906, 907, 926, 927
    Sculpture, 857, 926
    Slabs, 16, 926
    Statuary/statues, 907, 926, 927
    Table and counter tops, 857, 875, 905
    Tablets, 925, 932
    Tiling, 907, 924, 926, 927
    Tombs, 857, 873, 874, 905, 919
    Tombstones, 811, 827, 858, 899, 907, 924–927
    Warerooms, 916
    Washstands, 857, 905, 919

Marble and tile work, 917, 928

Marble/granite works, 878, 882, 903, 909, 910, 918, 924

Marble types
    American, 905, 907, 932
    California, 851, 857, 859
    Eastern, 858
    Foreign, 932
    Italian, 851, 857–859, 878, 882, 883, 902, 905
    Vein Italian, 907
    Vermont, 851, 857–859, 864

# Rose Hill Cemetery

**A**  **B**  **C**

**NORTH SECTIONS**

**SOUTH SECTIONS**

VEHICLE GATE

HIKER GATE